# FOUNDATIONS OF MACROECONOMICS

delivers a complete, hands-on learning system designed around active learning.

## A Learning-by-Doing Approach

The **Checklist** that begins each chapter highlights the key topics covered and the chapter is divided into sections that directly correlate to the Checklist.

The **Checkpoint** that ends each section provides a full page of practice problems to encourage students to review the material while it is fresh in their minds.

Each chapter opens with a question about a central issue that sets the stage for the material.

Why did the price of coffee rise in 2014?

# Demand and Supply

**4**

**CHAPTER CHECKLIST**

**When you have completed your study of this chapter, you will be able to**

1 Distinguish between quantity demanded and demand, and explain what determines demand.

2 Distinguish between quantity supplied and supply, and explain what determines supply.

3 Explain how demand and supply determine price and quantity in a market, and explain the effects of changes in demand and supply.

MyEconLab Big Picture Video

---

 **CHECKPOINT 4.1**

MyEconLab Study Plan 4.1
Key Terms Quiz
Solutions Video

**Distinguish between quantity demanded and demand, and explain what determines demand.**

### Practice Problems

The following events occur one at a time in the market for smartphones:
- The price of a smartphone falls.
- Producers announce that the price of a smartphone will fall next month.
- The price of a call made from a smartphone falls.
- The price of a call made from a land-line phone increases.
- An increase in memory makes smartphones more popular.

1. Explain the effect of each event on the demand for smartphones.
2. Use a graph to illustrate the effect of each event.
3. Does any event (or events) illustrate the law of demand?

### In the News

**Airline profits soar yet no relief for passengers**

**Eye On** boxes apply theory to important issues and problems that shape our global society and individual decisions.

## Confidence-Building Graphs

use color to show the direction of shifts and detailed, numbered captions guide students step-by-step through the action.

100% of the figures are animated in MyEconLab, with step-by-step audio narration.

### EYE on the PRICE OF COFFEE

MyEconLab Critical Thinking Exercise

#### Why Did the Price of Coffee Rise in 2014?

When a fungus called coffee rust swept through Brazil and other countries of South America in 2014, world coffee production decreased and the price of coffee beans increased.

The table below provides some data on the quantity and price of coffee in 2013 and 2014. What does the data table tell us?

It tells us that the quantity of coffee

You can answer this question from the information provided. You know that an increase in demand brings a rise in the price and an increase in the quantity bought, while a decrease in supply brings a rise in the price and a decrease in the quantity bought.

Because the quantity of coffee decreased and the price increased, there must have been a decrease in the sup-

The figure illustrates the global market for coffee in 2013 and 2014. The demand curve $D$ shows the demand for coffee, which we will assume was the same in both years.

In 2013, the supply curve was $S_{2013}$, the equilibrium price was $1.04 per pound and the equilibrium quantity traded was 19.4 billion pounds.

In 2014, decreased coffee produc-

---

**FIGURE 4.4**

Change in Quantity Demanded Versus Change in Demand

MyEconLab Animation

**1 A decrease in the quantity demanded**
The quantity demanded decreases and there is a movement up along the demand curve $D_0$ if the price of the good rises and other things remain the same.

**3 A decrease in demand**
Demand decreases and the demand curve shifts leftward (from $D_0$ to $D_1$) if
- The price of a substitute falls or the price of a complement rises.
- The price of the good is expected to fall.
- Income decreases.*
- Expected future income or credit decreases.
- The number of buyers decreases.

*Bottled water is a normal good.

**2 An increase in the quantity demanded**
The quantity demanded increases and there is a movement down along the demand curve $D_0$ if the price of the good falls and other things remain the same.

**4 An increase in demand**
Demand increases and the demand curve shifts rightward (from $D_0$ to $D_2$) if
- The price of a substitute rises or the price of a complement falls.
- The price of the good is expected to rise.
- Income increases.
- Expected future income or credit increases.
- The number of buyers increases.

# Practice, Engage, and Assess

- **Enhanced eText**—The Pearson eText gives students access to their textbook anytime, anywhere. In addition to note-taking, highlighting, and bookmarking, the Pearson eText offers interactive and sharing features. Students actively read and learn through auto-graded practice, real-time data-graphs, figure animations, author videos, and more. Instructors can share comments or highlights, and students can add their own, for a tight community of learners in any class.

- **Practice**—Algorithmically generated homework and study plan exercises with instant feedback ensure varied and productive practice, helping students improve their understanding and prepare for quizzes and tests. Draw-graph exercises encourage students to practice the language of economics.

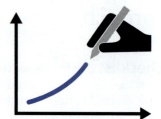

- **Learning Resources**—Personalized learning aids such as Help Me Solve This problem walkthroughs and Figure Animations provide on-demand help when students need it most.

- **Personalized Study Plan**—Assists students in monitoring their own progress by offering them a customized study plan based on Homework, Quiz, and Test results. Includes regenerated exercises with unlimited practice, as well as the opportunity to earn mastery points by completing quizzes on recommended learning objectives.

- **Dynamic Study Modules**—With a focus on key topics, these modules work by continuously assessing student performance and activity in real time and, using data and analytics, provide personalized content to reinforce concepts that target each student's particular strengths and weaknesses.

- **Digital Interactives**—Digital Interactives are engaging assessment activities that promote critical thinking and application of key economic principles. Each Digital Interactive has progressive levels where students can explore, apply, compare, and analyze economic principles. Many Digital Interactives include real time data from FRED® that displays, in graph and table form, up-to-the-minute data on key macro variables. Digital Interactives can be assigned and graded within MyEconLab, or used as a lecture tool to encourage engagement, classroom conversation, and group work.

# with MyEconLab®

- **NEW: Math Review Exercises in MyEconLab**—MyEconLab now offers an array of assignable and auto-graded exercises that cover fundamental math concepts. Geared specifically toward principles and intermediate economics students, these exercises aim to increase student confidence and success in these courses. Our new Math Review is accessible from the assignment manager and contains over 150 graphing, algebra, and calculus exercises for homework, quiz, and test use.

$$P = c + dQ_S$$

- **Real-Time Data Analysis Exercises**—Using current macro data to help students understand the impact of changes in economic variables, Real-Time Data Analysis Exercises communicate directly with the Federal Reserve Bank of St. Louis's FRED® site and update as new data are available.

- **Current News Exercises**—Every week, current microeconomic and macroeconomic news articles or videos, with accompanying exercises, are posted to MyEconLab. Assignable and auto-graded, these multi-part exercises ask students to recognize and apply economic concepts to real-world events.

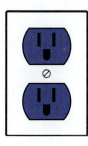

- **Experiments**—Flexible, easy-to-assign, auto-graded, and available in Single Player and Multiplayer versions, Experiments in MyEconLab make learning fun and engaging.

- **Reporting Dashboard**—View, analyze, and report learning outcomes clearly and easily. Available via the Gradebook and fully mobile-ready, the Reporting Dashboard presents student performance data at the class, section, and program levels in an accessible, visual manner.

- **LMS Integration**—Link from any LMS platform to access assignments, rosters, and resources, and synchronize MyLab grades with your LMS gradebook. For students, new direct, single sign-on provides access to all the personalized learning MyLab resources that make studying more efficient and effective.

- **Mobile Ready**—Students and instructors can access multimedia resources and complete assessments right at their fingertips, on any mobile device.

ALWAYS LEARNING

# Foundations of
# MACROECONOMICS

Robin Bade

Michael Parkin
*University of Western Ontario*

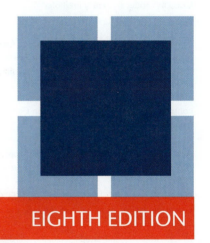

**EIGHTH EDITION**

330 Hudson Street, NY NY 10013

Vice President, Business Publishing: Donna Battista
Director of Portfolio Management: Adrienne
  D'Ambrosio
Portfolio Manager: Ashley Bryan
Editorial Assistant: Michelle Zeng
Vice President, Product Marketing: Roxanne McCarley
Director of Strategic Marketing: Brad Parkins
Strategic Marketing Manager: Deborah Strickland
Product Marketer: Tricia Murphy
Field Marketing Manager: Ramona Elmer
Field Marketing Assistant: Kristen Compton
Product Marketing Assistant: Jessica Quazza
Vice President, Production and Digital Studio, Arts
  and Business: Etain O'Dea
Director of Production, Business: Jeff Holcomb
Managing Producer, Business: Alison Kalil
Content Producer: Nancy Freihofer

Operations Specialist: Carol Melville
Creative Director: Blair Brown
Manager, Learning Tools: Brian Surette
Managing Producer, Digital Studio, Arts and
  Business: Diane Lombardo
Digital Studio Producer: Melissa Honig
Digital Studio Producer: Alana Coles
Digital Content Team Lead: Noel Lotz
Digital Content Project Lead: Noel Lotz
Full-Service Project Management and
  Composition: Integra Software Services
Interior Design: Integra Software Services
Cover Design: Jon Boylan
Cover Art: Panu Ruangjan/www.shutterstock.com
Technical Illustrator: Richard Parkin
Printer/Binder: LSC Communications
Cover Printer: Phoenix Color

To Erin, Tessa, Jack, Abby, and Sophie

# About the Authors

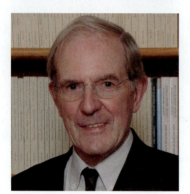

***Robin Bade*** was an undergraduate at the University of Queensland, Australia, where she earned degrees in mathematics and economics. After a spell teaching high school math and physics, she enrolled in the Ph.D. program at the Australian National University, from which she graduated in 1970. She has held faculty appointments at the University of Edinburgh in Scotland, at Bond University in Australia, and at the Universities of Manitoba, Toronto, and Western Ontario in Canada. Her research on international capital flows appears in the *International Economic Review* and the *Economic Record*.

Robin first taught the principles of economics course in 1970 and has taught it (alongside intermediate macroeconomics and international trade and finance) most years since then. She developed many of the ideas found in this text while conducting tutorials with her students at the University of Western Ontario.

***Michael Parkin*** studied economics in England and began his university teaching career immediately after graduating with a B.A. from the University of Leicester. He learned the subject on the job at the University of Essex, England's most exciting new university of the 1960s, and at the age of 30 became one of the youngest full professors. He is a past president of the Canadian Economics Association and has served on the editorial boards of the *American Economic Review* and the *Journal of Monetary Economics*. His research on macroeconomics, monetary economics, and international economics has resulted in more than 160 publications in journals and edited volumes, including the *American Economic Review*, the *Journal of Political Economy*, the *Review of Economic Studies*, the *Journal of Monetary Economics*, and the *Journal of Money, Credit, and Banking*. He is author of the best-selling textbook, *Economics* (Pearson), now in its Twelfth Edition.

Robin and Michael are a wife-and-husband team. Their most notable joint research created the Bade-Parkin Index of central bank independence and spawned a vast amount of research on that topic. They don't claim credit for the independence of the new European Central Bank, but its constitution and the movement toward greater independence of central banks around the world were aided by their pioneering work. Their joint textbooks include *Macroeconomics* (Prentice-Hall), *Modern Macroeconomics* (Pearson Education Canada), and *Economics: Canada in the Global Environment*, the Canadian adaptation of Parkin, *Economics* (Addison-Wesley). They are dedicated to the challenge of explaining economics ever more clearly to a growing body of students.

Music, the theater, art, walking on the beach, and five grandchildren provides their relaxation and fun.

# MACROECONOMICS     Brief Contents

# Contents

# PART 2   MONITORING THE MACROECONOMY

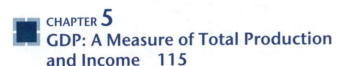

# PART 4  THE MONEY ECONOMY

# PART 5   ECONOMIC FLUCTUATIONS

# PART 6   MACROECONOMIC POLICY

**CHAPTER 18**
# International Trade Policy   455

**CHAPTER 19**
# International Finance   479

# Preface

Students know that throughout their lives they will make economic decisions and be influenced by economic forces. They want to understand the economic principles that can help them navigate these forces and guide their decisions. *Foundations of Macroeconomics* is our attempt to satisfy this want.

The response to our earlier editions from hundreds of colleagues across the United States and throughout the world tells us that most of you agree with our view that the principles course must do four things well. It must

- Motivate with compelling issues and questions
- Focus on core ideas
- Steer a path between an overload of detail and too much left unsaid
- Encourage and aid learning by doing

The Foundations icon with its four blocks (on the cover and throughout the book) symbolizes this four-point approach that has guided all our choices in writing this text and creating its comprehensive teaching and learning supplements.

## WHAT'S NEW IN THE EIGHTH EDITION

New in this Eighth Edition revision are: A further fine-tuning of the content; an enhanced focus on outcome-driven teaching and learning; and a further large investment in enhanced digital features to bring economics to life and provide an exciting interactive experience for the student on all platforms and devices.

### ■ Fine-Tuning the Content

The content of this revision is driven by the drama of the extraordinary period of economic history in which we are living and its rich display of events and forces through which students can be motivated to discover the economic way of thinking. Persistent slow economic growth; increasing concentration of wealth; headwinds from Europe's stagnant economy and the UK decision to leave the economic union (Brexit); ongoing tensions arising from the loss of American jobs to offshore outsourcing and the political popularity of trade protection; a slowing pace of China's expansion; enhanced concern about carbon emission and climate change; relentless pressure on the federal budget from the demands of an aging population and a sometimes dysfunctional Congress with its associated rising government debt; the dilemma posed by slow, almost decade-long recovery from the global financial crisis and recession and the related question of when and how fast to exit an era of extreme monetary stimulus. These are just a few of these interest-arousing events. All of them feature at the appropriate points in our new edition.

Every chapter contains many small changes, all designed to enhance clarity and currency, and the text and examples are all thoroughly updated to reflect the most recently available data and events.

Because the previous edition's revision was so extensive and well-received, we have limited our interventions and changes in this Eighth Edition to addressing the small number of issues raised by our reviewers and users, ensuring that we are thoroughly up-to-date, and focusing on the new digital tools that we've just described. Nonetheless, some changes that we now summarize are worth noting.

## ■ Notable Content Changes

In Chapter 1, Getting Started, we have added a new section, *Economics as a Life Skill*, which explains how economics is used as a decision tool, the scientific method the subject employs, and economics as an aid to critical thinking. A new *Eye on Your Life* looks at the BLS data on student time allocation (which contains some surprises).

In Chapter 3, The Economic Problem, we show explicitly how the outward-bowed production possibilities frontier arises from exploiting comparative advantage.

Chapter 6, Jobs and Unemployment, is motivated by the question of whether we are back at full employment. In seeking an answer, the chapter adds to the standard list of job market indicators the new Z-Pop measure of the percentage of the population that is fully occupied.

Chapter 7, The CPI and the Cost of Living, explains and presents data on the new "Sticky Price CPI" and its related "Flexible Price CPI" as an attempt to measure the underlying inflation rate.

In Chapter 9, Economic Growth, we have added an account of who gets the benefits of economic growth with a dramatic demonstration of the gains by the top one percent compared with the gains of the other 99 percent.

Chapter 16, Fiscal Policy, has a new and expanded explanation of the concepts of fiscal imbalance and generational imbalance and the magnitudes of these imbalances in the United States today.

Chapter 17, Monetary Policy, has a new discussion of the rules versus discretion dichotomy and a description of both the Taylor interest rate rule and the McCallum monetary base growth rate rule.

## ■ Outcome-Driven Teaching and Learning

An overarching revision message is that this text, its customized MyEconLab, and classroom resources are built to support an outcome-driven teaching and learning program in which the principles of economics course strengthens

* Problem solving
* Critical thinking
* Decision making
* Citizenship

Problem solving is central to the *Foundations* story. A Checkpoint at the end of each topic, typically three per chapter, provides a pause and opportunity to check understanding with problems, one of which is driven by a recent news clip, and worked solutions. A series of MyEconLab Solutions Videos then give the student an alternative way of reviewing the solutions to these problems.

Critical thinking is encouraged and supported through a series of interactive exercises in MyEconLab. In each chapter, there is one exercise that is based on the question or issue that opens and motivates the chapter, and a second that builds from an *Economics in Your Life* feature.

## ■ Enhanced eText

The new Enhanced Pearson eText gives students access to their textbook anytime, anywhere. In addition to note-taking, highlighting, and bookmarking, the Pearson eText offers interactive and sharing features. Students actively read and learn through embedded and auto-graded practice, real-time data-graphs, animations, author videos, and more. Instructors can share comments or highlights, and students can add their own, for a tight community of learners in any class.

The new eText includes:

- A Big Picture Video that motivates and summarizes each chapter and provides an outline answer to the chapter's motivating question.
- A series of Concept Videos that illustrate and explain the key ideas in each section of a chapter. These videos also contain animations and explanations of each figure, which can be played separately.
- A series of Solutions Videos that walk the student through the solutions to the Practice Problems and In the News exercises in each Checkpoint.
- Interactive data graphs that display real-time data from the St. Louis Federal Reserve data base, FRED.
- Study Plan links that provide opportunities for more practice with problems similar to those in the text, some with real-time FRED data, that give targeted feedback to guide the student in answering the exercises.
- Key Terms Quiz links that provide opportunities for students to check their knowledge of the definitions and uses of the key terms.

## THE FOUNDATIONS VISION

### ■ Focus on Core Concepts

Each chapter of *Foundations* concentrates on a manageable number of main ideas (most commonly three or four) and reinforces each idea several times throughout the chapter. This patient, confidence-building approach guides students through unfamiliar terrain and helps them to focus their efforts on the most important tools and concepts of our discipline.

### ■ Many Learning Tools for Many Learning Styles

*Foundations'* integrated print and electronic package builds on the basic fact that students have a variety of learning styles. Students have powerful tools at their fingertips: Within the eText, they can get an immediate sense of the content of a chapter by playing the Big Picture video; learn the key ideas by playing the Concept videos; and get a quick walkthrough of the Checkpoint Practice Problems and In the News exercises with the Solutions videos.

In MyEconLab, students can complete all Checkpoint problems and In the News exercises online and get instant feedback; work with interactive graphs and real-time data graphs; assess their skills by taking Practice Tests; receive a personalized Study Plan; and step-by-step help through the learning aid called "Help Me Solve This."

### ■ Diagrams That Tell the Whole Story

We developed the style of our diagrams with extensive feedback from faculty focus-group participants and student reviewers. All of our figures make consistent use of color to show the direction of shifts and contain detailed, numbered captions designed to direct students' attention step-by-step through the action.

Because beginning students of economics are often apprehensive about working with graphs, we have made a special effort to present material in as many as three ways—with graphs, words, and tables—in the same figure. In an innovation that seems necessary, but is to our knowledge unmatched, nearly all of the information supporting a figure appears on the same page as the figure itself. No more flipping pages back and forth!

### ■ Real-World Connections That Bring Theory to Life

Students learn best when they can see the purpose of what they are studying, apply it to illuminate the world around them, and use it in their lives.

*Eye On* boxes offer fresh new examples to help students see that economics is everywhere. Current and recent events appear in *Eye on the U.S. Economy* boxes; we place current U.S. economic events in global and historical perspectives in our *Eye on the Global Economy* and *Eye on the Past* boxes; and we show how students can use economics in day-to-day decisions in *Eye on Your Life* boxes.

Each chapter-opening question is answered in an Eye On box that helps students see the economics behind a key issue facing the world and highlights a major aspect of the chapter's story.

## ORGANIZATION

We have organized the sequence of material and chapters in what we think is the most natural order in which to cover the material. But we recognize that there are alternative views on the best order. We have kept this fact and the need for flexibility firmly in mind throughout the text. Many alternative sequences work, and the Flexibility Chart on p. xxiv explains the alternative pathways through the chapters. In using the flexibility information, keep in mind that the best sequence is the one in which we present the material. And even chapters that the flexibility charts identify as strictly optional are better covered than omitted.

## MYECONLAB                                        MyEconLab

MyEconLab has been designed and refined with a single purpose in mind: to create those moments of understanding that transform the difficult into the clear and obvious. With comprehensive homework, quiz, test, activity, and tutorial options, instructors can manage all their assessment needs in one program.

- All of the Checkpoint and Chapter Checkpoint Problems and Applications can be assigned and automatically graded in MyEconLab.
- Extra problems and applications, including algorithmic, draw-graph, and numerical exercises can be used for student practice or instructor assignment.
- Problems and applications that use real-time data continuously update directly from a feed to the Federal Reserve Bank of St. Louis.
- Test Item File questions can be assigned in quiz, test, or homework.
- The Custom Exercise Builder gives instructors the flexibility to create their own problems for assignment.
- The Gradebook records each student's performance and time spent on the Tests and Study Plan and generates reports by student or by chapter.

New for the Eighth Edition is an Enhanced Pearson eText, which includes embedded and auto-graded practice, real-time data graphs, animations, videos, and more. Instructors can share comments or highlights, and students can add their own, for a tight community of learners in any class.

With the Pearson eText 2.0 mobile app students can access the Enhanced eText and all its functionality from their computer, tablet, or cell phone. Because the student's progress is synced across all of their devices, they can stop what they're doing on one device and pick up again later on another one—without breaking their stride.

## ■ Features of the Enhanced eText

**Big Picture Videos**   Big Picture videos, tied to the Chapter Checklist, set the stage for the main concept that will be introduced throughout the chapter. Students can use these videos to prepare for today's lecture or to help them focus on main chapter ideas.

| DEMAND and SUPPLY: THE BIG PICTURE |
| --- |
| Buyers like a low price, and the lower the price, the greater is the quantity they plan to buy—the **law of demand**. |
| Sellers like a high price, and the higher the price, the greater is the quantity they plan to sell—the **law of supply**. |
| Too high a price brings a surplus, and too low a price brings a shortage. |
| When there is a surplus, the price falls; and when there is a shortage, the price rises—the **law of market forces**. |

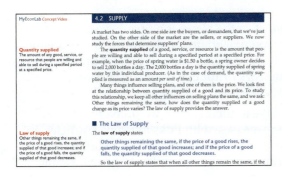

**Concept Videos**   Concept videos accompany every major section of each chapter and are designed to briefly present the major concepts and graphical tools covered within key sections. Using text, audio, and animation, Concept videos enable students with different learning styles to efficiently study and review key concepts of the chapter.

**Animations**   Every textbook figure includes a step-by-step animation, with audio, to help students learn the intuition behind reading and interpreting graphs. These animations may be used for review, or as an instructional aid in the classroom. Figures labeled *MyEconLab Real-Time Data* update using the most recent data available from the Federal Reserve Bank of St. Louis's FRED site.

**Embedded MyEconLab Assessment**   Every Checkpoint Practice Problem, every In the News problem, and every Study Plan Problem and Application in the enhanced eText can be worked by the student directly from the eText page on which it occurs. These problems are auto-graded and feed into the MyEconLab's Study Plan, where students receive recommendations based upon their performance.

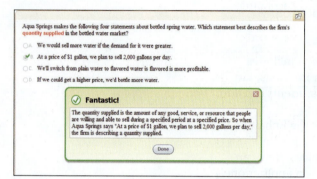

**Key Terms Quiz**   The Key Terms Quiz, accessible from each Checkpoint, allows students to check their understanding of key chapter concepts before moving onto the next section. The Interactive Glossary that supports the enhanced eText provides the key term definition, an example, and related terms.

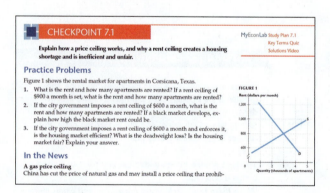

**Solutions Videos**   Every Checkpoint Practice problem and In the News problem is supported by a Solutions video that provides a step-by-step working of the problem, including graphical analysis. Text, audio, and animation ensure that a student understands how to set-up and solve each of the problems.

## ■ MyEconLab also includes:

**Economics in the News**   Economics in the News is a turn-key solution to bringing current news into the classroom. Updated daily during the academic year, we upload two relevant articles (one micro, one macro) and provide questions that may be assigned for homework or for classroom discussion.

**Current News**   Each week during the academic year, we upload multi-part microeconomic and macroeconomic exercises, with links to relevant articles, into the MyEconLab assignment manager. These enable instructors to bring current issues and events into the course with easy to assign and auto-graded exercises.

**Real-Time Data Analysis Exercises (FRED)**   Easy to assign and automatically graded, Real-Time Data Analysis exercises use up-to-the-minute, real-time macroeconomic data. These exercises communicate directly with the Federal Reserve Bank of St. Louis's FRED site, so every time FRED posts new data, students see new data. As a result, Real-Time Data Analysis exercises offer a no-fuss solution for instructors who want to make the most recent data a central part of their macro course. End-of-chapter exercises accompanied by the Real-Time Data Analysis icon (🔴) include Real-Time Data versions in MyEconLab. Select in-text figures, labeled Real-time data, update in the eText using FRED data.

**Digital Interactives:**   Economic principles are not static ideas, and learning them shouldn't be either! Digital Interactives are dynamic and engaging assessment activities that promote critical thinking and application of key economic principles.

Each Digital Interactive has 3 to 5 progressive levels and requires approximately 20 minutes to explore, apply, compare, and analyze each topic. Many Digital Interactives include real-time data from FRED™ allowing professors and students to display, in graph and table form, up-to-the-minute data on key macro variables.

Digital Interactives can be assigned and graded within MyEconLab, or used as a lecture tool to encourage engagement, classroom conversation, and group work.

Topics include:

Comparative Advantage
Opportunity Cost
Demand & Supply
GDP
Unemployment
Consumer Price Index/Inflation
Monetary Policy

**Math Review Exercises in MyEconLab**—MyEconLab now offers an array of assignable and auto-graded exercises that cover fundamental math concepts. Geared specifically toward principles economics students, these exercises aim to increase student confidence and success in these courses. Our new Math Review is accessible from the assignment manager and contains more than 150 exercises for homework, quiz, and test use.

**Learning Catalytics**   Learning Catalytics helps you generate class discussion, customize your lecture, and promote peer-to-peer learning with real-time analytics. As a student response tool, Learning Catalytics uses students' smartphones, tablets, or laptops to engage them in more interactive tasks and thinking.

- NEW! Upload a full PowerPoint® deck for easy creation of slide questions.
- Help your students develop critical thinking skills.
- Monitor responses to find out where your students are struggling.
- Rely on real-time data to adjust your teaching strategy.
- Automatically group students for discussion, teamwork, and peer-to-peer learning.

**Experiments in MyEconLab**  Experiments are a fun and engaging way to promote active learning and mastery of important economic concepts. Pearson's Experiments program is flexible and easy for instructors to assign and students to use.

- Single-player experiments, available to assign, allow your students to play against virtual players from anywhere at anytime so long as they have an internet connection.
- Multiplayer experiments allow you to assign and manage a real-time experiment with your class.
- Pre and post-questions for each experiment are available for assignment in MyEconLab.
- Experiments are auto-graded using algorithms that objectively evaluate a student's economic gain and performance during the experiment.

**AACSB and Learning Outcomes**  All end-of-chapter and Test Item File questions are tagged in two ways: to AACSB standards and to discipline-specific Learning Outcomes. These two separate tagging systems allow professors to build assessments around desired departmental and course outcomes and track results in MyEconLab's gradebook.

**Personalized Study Plan**  The Personalized Study Plan provides recommendations for each of your students based on his or her ability to master the learning objectives in your course. This allows students to focus their study time by pinpointing the precise areas they need to review and allowing them to use customized practice and learning aids—such as videos, eText, tutorials, and more—to get them back on track. The Study Plan also ensures that your students are mastering the concepts, not just guessing the answers.

Using the report available in the Gradebook, you can then tailor course lectures to prioritize the content where students need the most support—offering you better insight into classroom and individual performance.

**Dynamic Study Modules**  Dynamic Study Modules help students study effectively on their own by continuously assessing their activity and performance in real time. Here's how it works: students complete a set of questions with a unique answer format that also asks them to indicate their confidence level. Questions repeat until the student can answer them all correctly and confidently. Once completed, Dynamic Study Modules explain the concept using materials from the text. These are available as graded assignments prior to class, and accessible on smartphones, tablets, and computers.

NEW! Instructors can now remove questions from Dynamic Study Modules to better fit their course.

## SUPPORT MATERIALS FOR INSTRUCTORS AND STUDENTS

*Foundations of Macroeconomics* is accompanied by the most comprehensive set of teaching and learning tools ever assembled. Each component of our package is organized by Checkpoint topic for a tight, seamless integration with both the textbook and the other components. In addition to authoring the MyEconLab Study Plan and Assignment problems, PowerPoint resources, and Video scripts, we have helped in the reviewing and revising of the Solutions Manual, Instructor's Manual, and Test Item Files to ensure that every element of the package achieves the consistency that students and teachers need.

## ■ PowerPoint Resources

We have created the PowerPoint resources based on our 24 years of experience using this tool in our own classrooms. We have created four sets of PowerPoint presentations for instructors. They are:

- Lecture notes with full-color, animated figures, and tables from the textbook
- Figures and tables from the textbook, animated with step-by-step walk-through for instructors to use in their own personal slides
- *Eye On* features
- Alternative micro lecture notes with full-color, animated figures and tables that use examples different from those in the textbook

A student version of the lecture notes is also available on MyEconLab.

## ■ Instructor's Manual

The Instructor's Manual, written by Luke Armstrong and reviewed by Mark Rush, contains chapter outlines and road maps, additional exercises with solutions, a comprehensive Chapter Lecture resource, and a virtual encyclopedia of suggestions on how to enrich class presentation and use class time efficiently. The Instructor's Manual has been updated to reflect changes in the main text as well as infused with a fresh and intuitive approach to teaching this course. The Instructor's Manual is available for download in Word and PDF formats.

## ■ Solutions Manual

The Solutions Manual, written by Mark Rush and checked for accuracy by Jeannie Gillmore, contains the solutions to all Chapter Checkpoint Study Plan Problems and Applications, Instructor Assignable Problems and Applications, and the Multiple Choice Quiz. The Solutions Manual is available for download in Word and PDF formats.

## ■ Three Test Item Files and TestGen

More than 6,000 multiple-choice, numerical, fill-in-the-blank, short answer, essay, and integrative questions make up the three Test Item Files that support *Foundations of Macroeconomics*. Mark Rush reviewed and edited the updated and new questions from three dedicated principles instructors to form one of the most comprehensive testing systems on the market. Our questions were written by Svitlana. Maksymenko (University of Pittsburgh) and David Black (University of Toledo). The entire set of questions is available for download in Word, PDF, and TestGen formats.

All three Test Item Files are available in test generator software (TestGen with QuizMaster). TestGen's graphical interface enables instructors to view, edit, and add questions; transfer questions to tests; and print different forms of tests. Instructors also have the option to reformat tests with varying fonts and styles, margins, and headers and footers, as in any word-processing document. Search and sort features let the instructor quickly locate questions and arrange them in a preferred order. QuizMaster, working with your school's computer network, automatically grades the exams, stores the results on disk, and allows the instructor to view and print a variety of reports.

## ■ Instructor's Resource Center

This page on the Pearson Higher Education website (www.pearsonhighered.com/IRC) contains the Instructor's Manual, Solutions Manual, and Test Item Files in Word and PDF formats. It also contains the Computerized Test Item Files (with a TestGen program installer) and PowerPoint resources. It is compatible with both Windows and Macintosh operating systems.

For access or more information, contact your local Pearson representative or request access online at the Instructor Resource Center.

# ACKNOWLEDGMENTS

Working on a project such as this one generates many debts that can never be repaid. But they can be acknowledged, and it is a special pleasure to be able to do so here and to express our heartfelt thanks to each and every one of the following long list, without whose contributions we could not have produced *Foundations*.

Mark Rush again coordinated, managed, and contributed to our Solutions Manual, Instructor's Manual, and Test Item Files. He assembled, polished, wrote, and rewrote these materials to ensure their close consistency with the text. He and we were in constant contact as all the elements of our text and package came together. Mark also made many valuable suggestions for improving the text and the Checkpoint Problems. His contribution went well beyond that of a reviewer, and his effervescent sense of humor kept us all in good spirits along the way.

Working closely with Mark, Luke Armstrong wrote content for the Instructor's Manual. Svitlana Maksymenko and David Black authored new questions for the Test Item Files.

Luke Armstrong and Carol Dole recorded the narrations that accompany the Big Picture, Concept, and Solutions Videos in the eText. The engaging style and clarity of these outstanding teachers makes these videos a powerful learning tool.

Fred Bounds (Georgia Perimeter College) and Carol Dole provided outstanding reviews of the Study Plan and Assessment problems in MyEconLab that helped to make our exercises as effective as possible.

The ideas from which *Foundations* grew began to form over dinner at the Andover Inn in Andover, Massachusetts, with Denise Clinton and Sylvia Mallory. We gratefully acknowledge Sylvia's role not only at the birth of this project but also in managing its initial development team. Denise was an ongoing inspiration for 15 years, and we are privileged to have had the benefit of her enormous experience.

The success of *Foundations* owes much to its outstanding editors: Director of Portfolio Management, Adrienne D'Ambrosio, and Portfolio Manager, Ashley Bryan. Adrienne's acute intelligence and sensitive understanding of the market have helped sharpen our vision of this text and package over several editions, and Ashley has brought a fresh perspective to this Eight edition revision. The value-added of Adrienne and Ashley is huge. It has been, and we hope it will for many future editions remain, a joy to work with them.

Jonathan Boylan created the new impressive cover design and converted the raw ideas of our brainstorms into an outstandingly designed text.

Melissa Honig, Digital Studio Producer, and Noel Lotz, Digital Content Team Lead have set a new standard for online learning and teaching resources. They have been sources of high energy, good sense, and level-headed advice and quickly found creative solutions to all our technology problems.

Nancy Freihofer, our outstanding, ever calm, Content Producer, worked with a talented team at Integra, Project Editor, Heather Johnson, and designer, art coordinator, and typesetter. Our copy editor, Catherine Baum, gave our work a thorough review and helpful polish, and our proofreader ensured the most error-free text we have yet produced.

Our marketing team, comprised of Ramona Elmer, Tricia Murphy, and Brad Parkins, has been an integral part of this revision process. They have provided great knowledge and strategies to help continuously improve our suite of materials and keep them relevant and valuable in these ever-changing times.

Richard Parkin, our technical illustrator, created the figures in the text, the dynamic figures in the eText, the animated figures in the PowerPoint presentations, created the animations for and assembled the enhanced eText videos, and contributed many ideas to improving the clarity of our illustrations in all media.

Jeannie Gillmore, our long-standing personal assistant, worked closely with us to create MyEconLab Study Plan and Assignment problems and to ensure the highest standards for our feedbacks and "help me solve this" question help.

Finally, our reviewers, whose names appear on the following pages, have made an enormous contribution to this text and MyEconLab resources. Once again we find ourselves using superlatives, but they are called for. In the many texts that we've written, we've not seen reviewing of the quality that we enjoyed on this revision. It has been a pleasure (if at times a challenge) to respond constructively to their many excellent suggestions.

Robin Bade
Michael Parkin
London, Ontario, Canada
robin@econ100.com
mparkin@uwo.ca

# FOUNDATIONS OF MACROECONOMICS: FLEXIBILITY CHART

## Flexibility

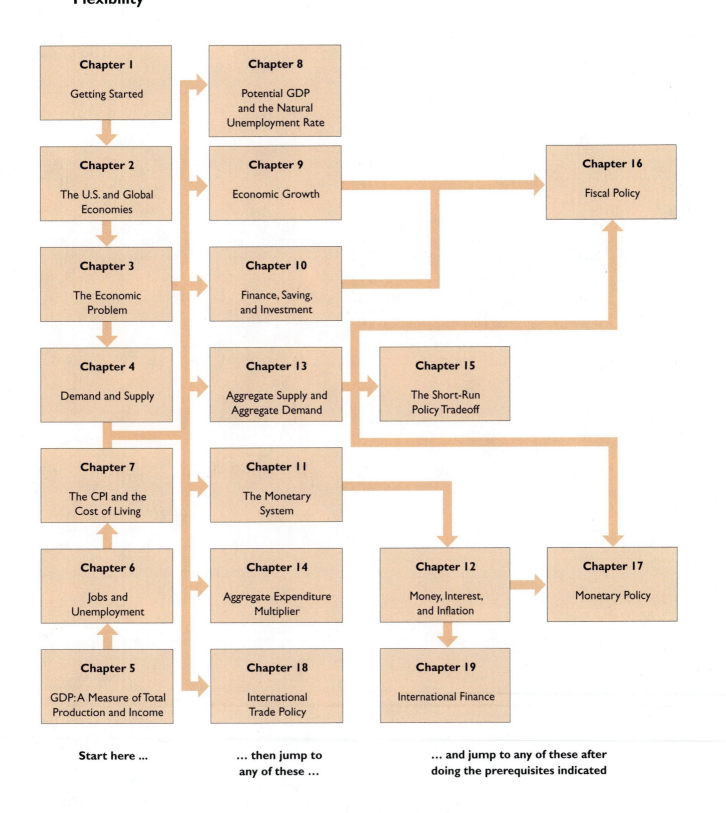

**Start here ...**          **... then jump to
any of these ...**          **... and jump to any of these after
doing the prerequisites indicated**

# Reviewers

Eunice Akoto, Henderson State University

Mehdi Arman, Columbia State Community College

Luke Armstrong, Lee College

Michael Aubry, Cuyamaca College

Bizuayehu Bedane, Southern Illinois University at Carbondale

Victor Claar, Henderson State University

Earl Davis, Nicholls State University

Carol Dole, Jacksonville University

Byron Gangnes, University of Hawaii at Manoa

Leon Hoke, University of Tampa

Christopher Jeffords, Indiana University of Pennsylvania; University of Connecticut

Stephen Jerbic, San Jose State University

Vicki King-Skinner, Coastal Carolina University

David Manifold, Caldwell Community College & Technical Center

Michael Nuwer, State University of New York at Potsdam

Abdulhamid Sukar, Cameron University

Lisa Takeyama, San Francisco State University

Benjamin Zamzow, Campbell University

Ting Zhang, University of Baltimore

Alfredo A. Romero Aguirre, North Carolina A&T State University

Seemi Ahmad, Dutchess Community College

William Aldridge, Shelton State Community College

Rashid B. Al-Hmoud, Texas Tech University

Neil Alper, Northeastern University

Nejat Anbarci, Deakin University

J.J. Arias, Georgia College & State University

Luke A. Armstrong, Lee College

Leland Ash, Skagit Valley College

Ali Ataiifar, Delaware County Community College

John Baffoe-Bonnie, Pennsylvania State University, Delaware County Campus

A. Paul Ballantyne, University of Colorado

Tyra D. Barrett, Pellissippi State Community College

Sue Bartlett, University of South Florida

Gerald Baumgardner, Penn College

Klaus Becker, Texas Tech University

Clive Belfield, Queen's College, City University of New York

William K. Bellinger, Dickinson College

John Bethune, Barton College

Prasun Bhattacharjee, East Tennessee State University

Gautam Bhattacharya, University of Kansas

Gerald W. Bialka, University of North Florida

David Bivin, Indiana University–Purdue University at Indianapolis

Geoffrey Black, Boise State University

Carey Anne Borkoski, Arundel Community College

Jurgen Brauer, Augusta State University

Greg Brock, Georgia Southern University

Barbara Brogan, Northern Virginia Community College

Bruce C. Brown, California State Polytechnic University, Pomona

Christopher Brown, Arkansas State University

James O. Brown, Delta State University

Brian Buckley, Clemson University

Donald Bumpass, Sam Houston State University

Seewoonundun Bunjun, East Stroudsburg University

Nancy Burnett, University of Wisconsin at Oshkosh

James L. Butkiewicz, University of Delaware

Barbara Caldwell, Saint Leo University

Bruce Caldwell, University of North Carolina, Greensboro

Joseph Calhoun, Florida State University

Robert Carlsson, University of South Carolina

Shawn Carter, Jacksonville State University

Regina Cassady, Valencia Community College

Jack Chambless, Valencia Community College

Joni Charles, Southwest Texas State University

Anoshua Chaudhuri, San Francisco State University

Robert Cherry, Brooklyn College

Chi-Young Choi, University of New Hampshire

Paul Cichello, Xavier University

Quentin Ciolfi, Brevard Community College

Victor V. Claar, Henderson State University

Jane L. Cline, Forsyth Technical Community College

Jim Cobbe, Florida State University

John Cochran, University of Chicago

Mike Cohick, Collin County Community College

Ludovic Comeau, De Paul University

Carol Conrad, Cerro Coso Community College

Christopher Cornell, Vassar College

Richard Cornwall, University of California, Davis

Kevin Cotter, Wayne State University

Erik Craft, University of Richmond

Tom Creahan, Morehead State University

Elizabeth Crowell, University of Michigan at Dearborn

Susan Dadres, Southern Methodist University

David Davenport, McLennan Community College

Troy Davig, College of William and Mary

Jeffrey Davis, ITT Technical Institute (Utah)

Lewis Davis, Union College

Dennis Debrecht, Carroll College

Al DeCooke, Broward Community College

Jason J. Delaney, Georgia Gwinnett College

Vince DiMartino, University of Texas at San Antonio

Vernon J. Dobis, Minnesota State University–Moorhead

Carol Dole, Jacksonville University

Kathleen Dorsainvil, American University

John Dorsey, University of Maryland, College Park

Amrik Singh Dua, Mt. San Antonio College

Marie Duggan, Keene State College

Allen Dupont, North Carolina State University

David Eaton, Murray State University

Kevin J. Egan, University of Toledo

Harold W. Elder, University of Alabama

Harry Ellis, University of North Texas

Stephen Ellis, North Central Texas College

Carl Enomoto, New Mexico State University

Chuen-mei Fan, Colorado State University

Chris Fant, Spartanburg Community College

Elena Ermolenko Fein, Oakton Community College

Gary Ferrier, University of Arkansas

Rudy Fichtenbaum, Wright State University

Donna K. Fisher, Georgia Southern University

Kaya Ford, Northern Virginia Community College

Robert Francis, Shoreline Community College

Roger Frantz, San Diego State University

Amanda S. Freeman, Kansas State University

Marc Fusaro, East Carolina University

Arthur Friedberg, Mohawk Valley Community College

Julie Gallaway, Southwest Missouri State University

Byron Gangnes, University of Hawaii

Gay GareschÈ, Glendale Community College

Neil Garston, California State University, Los Angeles

Lisa Geib-Gunderson, University of Maryland

Lisa M. George, City University of New York

Linda Ghent, Eastern Illinois University

Soma Ghosh, Bridgewater State College

Kirk Gifford, Ricks College

Scott Gilbert, Southern Illinois University

Maria Giuili, Diablo Valley Community College

Mark Gius, Quinnipiac College

Gregory E. Givens, University of Alabama

Randall Glover, Brevard Community College

Stephan Gohmann, University of Louisville

Richard Gosselin, Houston Community College

John Graham, Rutgers University

Patricia E. Graham, University of Northern Colorado

Warren Graham, Tulsa Community College

Homer Guevara, Jr., Northwest Vista College

Osman Gulseven, North Carolina State University

Jang-Ting Guo, University of California, Riverside

Dennis Hammett, University of Texas at El Paso

Leo Hardwick, Macomb Community College

Mehdi Haririan, Bloomsburg University

Paul Harris, Camden County Community College

Mark Healy, William Rainey Harper College

Rey Hernandez-Julian, Metropolitan State College of Denver

Gus Herring, Brookhaven College

Michael Heslop, Northern Virginia Community College

Steven Hickerson, Mankato State University

Frederick Steb Hipple, East Tennessee State University

Lee Hoke, University of Tampa

Andy Howard, Rio Hondo College

Yu Hsing, Southeastern Louisiana University

Greg Hunter, California State Polytechnic University, Pomona

Matthew Hyle, Winona State University

Todd Idson, Boston University

Harvey James, University of Hartford

Russell Janis, University of Massachusetts at Amherst

Ricot Jean, Valencia College

Jay A. Johnson, Southeastern Louisiana University

Ted Joyce, City University of New York, Baruch College

Ahmad A. Kader, University of Nevada, Las Vegas

Jonathan D. Kaplan, California State University, Sacramento

Arthur Kartman, San Diego State University

Chris Kauffman, University of Tennessee

Diane Keenan, Cerritos College

Brian Kench, University of Tampa

John Keith, Utah State University

Kristen Keith, University of Toledo

Joe Kerkvliet, Oregon State University

Randall Kesselring, Arkansas State University

Gary Kikuchi, University of Hawaii at Manoa

Douglas Kinnear, Colorado State University

Morris Knapp, Miami Dade Community College

Steven Koch, Georgia Southern University

Kate Krause, University of New Mexico

Stephan Kroll, California State University, Sacramento

Joyce Lapping, University of Southern Maine

Tom Larson, California State University, Los Angeles

Robert Lemke, Florida International University

J. Mark Leonard, University of Nebraska at Omaha

Tony Lima, California State University, Hayward

Joshua Long, Ivy Tech Community College

Kenneth Long, New River Community College

Noel Lotz, Middle Tennessee State University

Marty Ludlum, Oklahoma City Community College

Brian Lynch, Lake Land College

Michael Machiorlatti, Oklahoma City Community College

Roger Mack, De Anza College

Michael Magura, University of Toledo

Mark Maier, Glendale College

Svitlana Maksymenko, University of Pittsburgh

Paula Manns, Atlantic Cape Community College

Dan Marburger, Arkansas State University

Kathryn Marshall, Ohio State University

John V. Martin, Boise State University

Drew E. Mattson, Anoka-Ramsey Community College

Stephen McCafferty, Ohio State University

Thomas S. McCaleb, Florida State University

Katherine S. McCann, University of Delaware

William McLean, Oklahoma State University

Diego Mendez-Carbajo, Illinois Wesleyan University

Evelina Mengova, California State University, Fullerton

Thomas Meyer, Patrick Henry Community College

Meghan Millea, Mississippi State University

Michael Milligan, Front Range Community College

Jenny Minier, University of Miami

David Mitchell, Valdosta State University

Dr. Carl B. Montano, Lamar University

Christine Moser, Western Michigan University

William Mosher, Clark University

Mike Munoz, Northwest Vista College

John R. Mundy, St. Johns River State College

Kevin Murphy, Oakland University

Ronald Nate, Brigham Young University, Idaho

Nasrin Nazemzadeh, Rowan Cabarrus Community College

Michael Nelson, Texas A&M University

Rebecca Neumann, University of Wisconsin—Milwaukee

Charles Newton, Houston Community College Southwest

Melinda Nish, Salt Lake Community College

Lee Nordgren, Indiana University at Bloomington

Norman P. Obst, Michigan State University

Inge O'Connor, Syracuse University

William C. O'Connor, Western Montana College–University of Montana

Fola Odebunmi, Cypress College

Victor I. Oguledo, Florida A&M University

Charles Okeke, College of Southern Nevada

Lydia M. Ortega, St. Philip's College

P. Marcelo Oviedo, Iowa State University

Jennifer Pate, Ph.D., Loyola Marymount University

Sanjay Paul, Elizabethtown College

Ken Peterson, Furman University

Tim Petry, North Dakota State University

Charles Pflanz, Scottsdale Community College

Jonathon Phillips, North Carolina State University

Basharat Pitafi, Southern Illinois University

Anthony Plunkett, Harrison College

Paul Poast, Ohio State University

Greg Pratt, Mesa Community College

Fernando Quijano, Dickinson State University

Andy Radler, Butte Community College

Ratha Ramoo, Diablo Valley College

Karen Reid, University of Wisconsin, Parkside

Mary Rigdon, University of Texas, Austin

Helen Roberts, University of Illinois at Chicago

Greg Rose, Sacramento City College

Barbara Ross, Kapi'olani Community College

Elham Rouhani, Gwinnett Technical College

Jeffrey Rous, University of North Texas

June Roux, Salem Community College

Udayan Roy, Long Island University

Nancy C. Rumore, University of Louisiana–Lafayette

Mark Rush, University of Florida

Rolando Sanchez, Northwest Vista College

Joseph Santos, South Dakota State University

Roland Santos, Lakeland Community College

Mark Scanlan, Stephen F. Austin State University

Ted Scheinman, Mount Hood Community College

Buffie Schmidt, Augusta State University

Jerry Schwartz, Broward Community College

Gautam Sethi, Bard College

Margaret Anne Shannon, Georgia Southern University

Mushtaq Sheikh, Union County College

Michelle Sheran-Andrews, University of North Carolina at Greensboro

Virginia Shingleton, Valparaiso University

Steven S. Shwiff, Texas A & M University—Commerce

Charles Sicotte, Rock Valley College

Issoufou Soumaila, Texas Tech University

Martin Spechler, Indiana University

Leticia Starkov, Elgin Community College

Stela Stefanova, University of Delaware

John Stiver, University of Connecticut

Richard W. Stratton, The University of Akron

Abdulhamid Sukar, Cameron University

Terry Sutton, Southeast Missouri State University

Janet M. Thomas, Bentley College

Donna Thompson, Brookdale Community College

Deborah Thorsen, Palm Beach State College

James Thorson, Southern Connecticut State University

Marc Tomljanovich, Colgate University

Cynthia Royal Tori, Valdosta State University

Ngoc-Bich Tran, San Jacinto College South

Nora Underwood, University of California, Davis

Jogindar S. Uppal, State University of New York

Va Nee L. Van Vleck, California State University, Fresno

Victoria Vernon, Empire State College / SUNY

Christian Weber, Seattle University

Ethel Weeks, Nassau Community College

Jack Wegman, Santa Rosa Junior College

Jason White, Northwest Missouri State University

Benjamin Widner, Colorado State University

Barbara Wiens-Tuers, Pennsylvania State University, Altoona

Katherine Wolfe, University of Pittsburgh

Kristen Wolfe, St. Johns River State College

You're in school!
Did you make the right decision?

# Getting Started

**When you have completed your study of this chapter, you will be able to**

**1** Define economics and explain the kinds of questions that economists try to answer.

**2** Explain the ideas that define the economic way of thinking.

**3** Explain how economics is useful as a life skill.

MyEconLab Big Picture Video

## 1.1    DEFINITION AND QUESTIONS

Well, did you make the right decision? Is being in school the best use of your time? You'll soon know how an economist answers this question—for it is an economic question. It arises from the fact that you want more than you can get. You want to be in school. But you also want the time to enjoy your favorite sports and movies, to travel, and to hang out with friends—time that right now you don't have because you've got classes to attend and assignments due. Your time is scarce.

### ■ Scarcity

**Scarcity**
The condition that arises because wants exceed the ability of resources to satisfy them.

Our inability to satisfy all our wants is called **scarcity**. The ability of each of us to satisfy our wants is limited by the time we have, the incomes we earn, and the prices we pay for the things we buy. These limits mean that everyone has unsatisfied wants. The ability of all of us as a society to satisfy our wants is limited by the productive resources that exist. These resources include the gifts of nature, our labor and ingenuity, and the tools and equipment that we have made.

Everyone, poor and rich alike, faces scarcity. A student wants Taylor Swift's latest album and a paperback but has only $10.00 in his pocket. He faces scarcity. Gwen Stefani wants to spend a week on the set of *The Voice* in L.A., but she also wants to devote time and energy to her successful clothing line. She faces scarcity. The U.S. government wants to increase spending on homeland security and cut taxes. It faces scarcity. An entire society wants improved healthcare, an Internet connection in every classroom, clean lakes and rivers, and so on. Society faces scarcity. Scarcity is everywhere: Even parrots face scarcity!

Faced with scarcity, we must make choices. We must choose among the available alternatives. The student must choose the download or the paperback. Gwen Stefani must choose shooting episodes of *The Voice* or designing her next clothing collection. The government must choose greater security or tax cuts. And society must choose among healthcare, computers, the environment, and so on.

Not only do I want a cracker—we all want a cracker!

© The New Yorker Collection 1985 Frank Modell from cartoonbank.com. All Rights Reserved.

### ■ Economics Defined

**Economics**
The social science that studies the choices that individuals, businesses, governments, and entire societies make as they cope with *scarcity*, all the things that influence those choices, and the arrangements that coordinate them.

**Economics** is the social science that studies the choices that individuals, businesses, governments, and entire societies make as they cope with *scarcity*, all the things that influence those choices, and the arrangements that coordinate them.

The subject has two broad parts:

- Microeconomics, and
- Macroeconomics

### Microeconomics

**Microeconomics**
The study of the choices that individuals and businesses make and the way these choices interact and are influenced by governments.

**Microeconomics** is the study of the choices that individuals and businesses make and the way these choices interact and are influenced by governments. Some examples of microeconomic questions are: Will you buy a 3-D TV or a standard one? Will Nintendo sell more units of Wii if it cuts the price? Will a cut in the income tax rate encourage people to work longer hours? Will a hike in the gas tax encourage more people to drive hybrid or smaller automobiles? Is music streaming killing song downloads?

## Macroeconomics

**Macroeconomics** is the study of the aggregate (or total) effects on the national economy and the global economy of the choices that individuals, businesses, and governments make. Some examples of macroeconomic questions are: Why did production and jobs expand slowly in the United States during 2014 and 2015? Why are incomes growing much faster in China and India than in the United States? Why is unemployment in Europe so high? Why are Americans borrowing more than $1 billion a day from the rest of the world?

Two big questions define the scope of economics:

- How do choices end up determining *what, how,* and *for whom* goods and services get produced?
- When do choices made in the pursuit of *self-interest* also promote the *social interest*?

**Macroeconomics**
The study of the aggregate (or total) effects on the national economy and the global economy of the choices that individuals, businesses, and governments make.

## ■ What, How, and For Whom?

**Goods and services** are the objects and actions that people value and produce to satisfy human wants. Goods are *objects* that satisfy wants. Sports shoes and ketchup are examples. Services are *actions* that satisfy wants. Haircuts and rock concerts are examples. We produce a dazzling array of goods and services that range from necessities such as food, houses, and healthcare to leisure items such as Blu-ray players and roller coaster rides.

**Goods and services**
The objects (goods) and the actions (services) that people value and produce to satisfy human wants.

### What?

*What* determines the quantities of corn we grow, homes we build, and healthcare services we produce? Sixty years ago, farm output was 5 percent of total U.S. production. Today, it is 1 percent. Over the same period, the output of mines, construction, and utilities slipped from 9 percent to 7 percent of total production and manufacturing fell from 28 percent to 12 percent. These decreases in output are matched by increases in the production of a wide range of services, up from 58 percent of total production 60 years ago to 80 percent today. How will these quantities change in the future as ongoing changes in technology make an ever-wider array of goods and services available to us?

### How?

*How* are goods and services produced? In a vineyard in France, a hundred basket-carrying workers pick the annual grape crop by hand. In a vineyard in California, a huge machine and a few workers do the same job. Look around and you will see many examples of this phenomenon—the same job being done in different ways. In some stores, checkout clerks key in prices. In others, they use a laser scanner. One farmer keeps track of his livestock feeding schedules and inventories by using paper-and-pencil records, while another uses a computer. In some plants, GM hires workers to weld auto bodies and in others it uses robots to do the job.

Why do we use machines in some cases and people in others? Do mechanization and technological change destroy more jobs than they create? Do they make us better off or worse off?

*In a California vineyard a machine and a few workers do the same job as a hundred grape pickers in France.*

*A doctor gets more of the goods and services produced than a nurse or a medical assistant gets.*

### For Whom?

*For whom* are goods and services produced? The answer depends on the incomes that people earn and the prices they pay for the goods and services they buy. At given prices, a person who has a high income is able to buy more goods and services than a person who has a low income. Doctors earn much higher incomes than do nurses and medical assistants, so doctors get more of the goods and services produced than nurses and medical assistants get.

You probably know about many other persistent differences in incomes. Men, on average, earn more than women. Whites, on average, earn more than minorities. College graduates, on average, earn more than high school graduates. Americans, on average, earn more than Europeans, who in turn earn more, on average, than Asians and Africans. But there are some significant exceptions. The people of Japan and Hong Kong now earn an average income similar to that of Americans. And there is a lot of income inequality throughout the world.

What determines the incomes we earn? Why do doctors earn larger incomes than nurses? Why do men earn more, on average, than women? Why do college graduates earn more, on average, than high school graduates? Why do Americans earn more, on average, than Africans?

Economics explains how the choices that individuals, businesses, and governments make and the interactions of those choices end up determining *what*, *how*, and *for whom* goods and services are produced. In answering these questions, we have a deeper agenda in mind. We're not interested in just knowing how many Blu-ray players are produced, how they are produced, and who gets to enjoy them. We ultimately want to know the answer to the second big economic question that we'll now explore.

## ■ Can the Pursuit of Self-Interest Be in the Social Interest?

Every day, you and 321 million other Americans, along with 7.2 billion people in the rest of the world, make economic choices that result in *"what," "how,"* and *"for whom"* goods and services are produced.

Are the goods and services produced, and the quantities in which they are produced, the right ones? Are the scarce resources used in the best possible way? Do the goods and services we produce go to those who benefit most from them?

### Self-Interest and the Social Interest

**Self-interest**
The choices that are best for the individual who makes them.

**Social interest**
The choices that are best for society as a whole.

Choices that are the best for the individual who makes them are choices made in the pursuit of **self-interest**. Choices that are the best for society as a whole are said to be in the **social interest**. The social interest has two dimensions: *efficiency* and *equity*. We'll explore these concepts in later chapters. For now, think of efficiency as being achieved by baking the biggest possible pie, and think of equity as being achieved by sharing the pie in the fairest possible way.

You know that your own choices are the best ones for you—or at least you *think* they're the best at the time that you make them. You use your time and other resources in the way that you think is best. You might consider how your choices affect other people, but you order a home delivery pizza because you're hungry and want to eat, not because you're concerned that the delivery person or the cook needs an income. You make choices that are in your self-interest—choices that you think are best for you.

When you act on your economic decisions, you come into contact with thousands of other people who produce and deliver the goods and services that you decide to buy or who buy the things that you sell. These people have made their own decisions—what to produce and how to produce it, whom to hire or whom to work for, and so on. Like you, all these people make choices that they think are best for them. When the pizza delivery person shows up at your home, he's not doing you a favor. He's earning his income and hoping for a good tip.

Can it be possible that when each one of us makes choices that are in our own best interest—in our self-interest—it turns out that these choices are also the best choices for society as a whole—in the social interest?

Adam Smith, regarded as the founder of economic science, (see *Eye on the Past* on p. 18) said the answer is *yes*. He believed that when we pursue our self-interest, we are led by an *invisible hand* to promote the social interest.

Is Adam Smith correct? Can it really be possible that the pursuit of self-interest promotes the social interest? Much of the rest of this book helps you to learn what economists know about this question and its answer. To help you start thinking about the question, we're going to illustrate it with four topics that generate heated discussion in today's world. You're already at least a little bit familiar with each one of them. They are

- Globalization
- The information revolution
- Climate change
- Government budget deficit and debt

## Globalization

Globalization—the expansion of international trade and the production of components and services by firms in other countries—has been going on for centuries. But in recent years, its pace has accelerated. Microchips, satellites, and fiber-optic cables have lowered the cost of communication and globalized production decisions. When Nike produces more sports shoes, people in Malaysia get more work. When Steven Spielberg makes a new movie, programmers in New Zealand write the code that makes magical animations. And when China Airlines wants a new airplane, Americans who work for Boeing build it.

*Workers in Asia make our shoes.*

Globalization is bringing rapid income growth, especially in Asia. But globalization is leaving some people behind. Jobs in manufacturing and routine services are shrinking in the United States, and some nations of Africa and South America are not sharing in the prosperity enjoyed in other parts of the world.

The owners of multinational firms benefit from lower production costs and consumers benefit from low-cost imported goods. But don't displaced American workers lose? And doesn't even the worker in Malaysia, who sews your new shoes for a few cents an hour, also lose? Is globalization in the social interest, or does globalization benefit just some at the expense of others?

## The Information Revolution

We are living at a time of extraordinary economic change that has been called the *Information Revolution*. This name suggests a parallel with the *Industrial Revolution* of the 1800s and the *Agricultural Revolution* of 12,000 years ago.

The changes that have occurred during the last 35 years are based on one major technology: the microprocessor or computer chip. The spin-offs from faster and cheaper computing have been widespread in telecommunications, music, and the automation of millions of tasks that previously required human decisions. You encounter some of these tasks when you check out at the grocery store or use an ATM. Less visible, but larger in scope, are the robots that assemble cars and move goods around warehouses. Over the next 20 years, more than one third of today's jobs will be done by a new generation of robots.

*Robots fill orders at Amazon.*

The computing and robot revolution resulted from people pursuing their self-interest. Gordon Moore, the chip maker who set up Intel, and Bill Gates, who quit Harvard to set up Microsoft, weren't thinking how much easier it would be for you to turn in your essay on time if you had a computer. Moore and Gates and thousands of other entrepreneurs were in pursuit of big rewards. Yet their actions made many other people better off. They advanced the social interest.

But are resources used in the best possible way? Or do Intel and Microsoft set their prices too high and put their products out of reach for too many people? And is it in the social interest for robots to take people's jobs?

## Climate Change

The Earth is getting hotter and the ice at the two poles is melting. Since the late nineteenth century, the Earth's surface temperature has increased about 1 degree Fahrenheit, and close to a half of that increase occurred over the past 25 years.

*Human activity is raising the Earth's surface temperature.*

Most climate scientists believe that the current warming has come at least in part from human economic activity—from self-interested choices—and that, if left unchecked, the warming will bring large future economic costs.

Are the individual energy choices that each of us makes damaging the social interest? What needs to be done to make our choices serve the social interest? Would the United States joining with other nations to limit carbon emissions serve the social interest? What other measures might be introduced?

## Government Budget Deficit and Debt

Every year since 2000, the U.S. government has run a budget deficit. On average, the government has spent $2.3 billion a day more than it has received in taxes. The government's debt has increased each day by that amount. Over the 15 year period from 2000 to 2015, government debt increased by $12.5 trillion. Your personal share of this debt is $56,000.

*A government budget time bomb is ticking as spending grows faster than tax revenues.*

This large deficit and debt is just the beginning of an even bigger problem. From about 2020 onwards, the retirement and healthcare benefits to which older Americans are entitled are going to cost increasingly more than current taxes can cover. With no changes in tax or benefit rates, the budget deficit will increase and the debt will swell ever higher.

Deficits and the debts they create cannot persist indefinitely, and debts must somehow be repaid. They will most likely be repaid by you, not by your parents. When we make our voter choices, we pursue our self-interest. Do our choices serve the social interest? Do the choices made by politicians and bureaucrats in Washington and the state capitals promote the social interest, or do they only serve their own self-interests?

The four issues we've just reviewed raise questions that are hard to answer. We'll return to each of them at various points throughout this text and explain when the social interest is served and when there remain problems to be solved.

# CHECKPOINT 1.1

MyEconLab Study Plan 1.1
Key Terms Quiz
Solutions Video

**Define economics and explain the kinds of questions that economists try to answer.**

## Practice Problems

1.  Economics studies choices that arise from one fact. What is that fact?
2.  Provide three examples of wants in the United States today that are especially pressing but not satisfied.
3.  In the following three news items, find examples of the *what, how,* and *for whom* questions: "With more research, we will cure cancer"; "A good education is the right of every child"; "Congress raises taxes to curb the deficit."
4.  How does a new Starbucks in Beijing, China, influence self-interest and the social interest?
5.  How does Facebook influence self-interest and the social interest?

## In the News

1.  The Bureau of Labor Statistics (BLS) reports that high-paying jobs in healthcare and jobs in leisure, hospitality, and education will expand quickly over the next five years. How does the BLS expect *what* and *for whom* goods and services are produced to change in the next five years?
2.  Hewlett-Packard will cut 30,000 jobs and lower its cost by $2.7 billion a year.
                                            Source: *Fortune*, October 1, 2015

    Explain how Hewlett-Packard's decision made in its self-interest might also be in the social interest.

## Solutions to Practice Problems

1.  The fact is scarcity—human wants exceed the resources available.
2.  Examples would include security from terrorism, cleaner air in our cities, better public schools, and better public infrastructure. (Think of others.)
3.  More research is a *how* question, and a cure for cancer is a *what* question. Good education is a *what* question, and every child is a *for whom* question. Raising taxes is a *for whom* question.
4.  Decisions made by Starbucks are in Starbucks' self-interest but they also serve the self-interest of its customers and so contribute to the social interest.
5.  Facebook serves the self-interest of its investors, users, and advertisers. It also serves the social interest by enabling people to share information.

## Solutions to In the News

1.  The BLS expects the quantities of goods and services produced by workers in healthcare, leisure, hospitality, and education to increase. For whom they are produced depends on how people's incomes and the prices of goods and services will change in the next five years. The BLS expects workers in these high-paying jobs and expanding industries will get more of them.
2.  Hewlett-Packard's product prices might fall and benefit its customers. The laid-off workers will find new jobs, some of which might pay higher wages.

## 1.2    THE ECONOMIC WAY OF THINKING

The definition of economics and the kinds of questions that economists try to answer give you a flavor of the scope of economics. But they don't tell you how economists *think* about these questions and how they go about seeking answers to them. You're now going to see how economists approach their work.

We'll break this task into two parts. First, we'll explain the ideas that economists use to frame their view of the world. These ideas will soon have you thinking like an economist. Second, we'll look at economics both as a social science and as a policy tool that governments, businesses, and *you* can use.

Six ideas define the *economic way of thinking*:

- A choice is a *tradeoff*
- *Cost* is what you *must give up* to get something.
- *Benefit* is what you gain from something.
- People make *rational choices* by comparing benefits and costs.
- Most choices are "*how much*" choices made at the *margin*.
- Choices respond to *incentives*.

### ■ A Choice Is a Tradeoff

**Tradeoff**
An exchange—giving up one thing to get something else.

A **tradeoff** is an exchange—giving up one thing to get something else. Because we face scarcity, we must make choices. And when we make a choice, we select from the available alternatives. You can think about choices as tradeoffs. When you choose one thing, you give up something else that you could have chosen.

Think about what you will do on Saturday night. You can spend the night studying for your next economics test or having fun with your friends, but you can't do both of these activities at the same time. You must choose how much time to devote to each. Whatever choice you make, you could have chosen something else. When you choose how to spend your Saturday night, you face a tradeoff between studying and hanging out with your friends. To get more study time, you must give up some time with your friends.

### ■ Cost: What You *Must* Give Up

**Opportunity cost**
The opportunity cost of something is the best thing you must give up to get it.

The **opportunity cost** of something is the best thing you must give up to get it. You most likely think about the cost of something as the money you must spend to get it. But dig a bit deeper. If you spend $10 on a movie ticket, you can't spend it on a sandwich. The movie ticket really costs a sandwich. The *cost* of something is what must be given up to get it, not the money spent on it. Economists use the term *opportunity cost* to emphasize this view of cost.

The biggest opportunity cost you face is that of being in school. This opportunity cost has two components: things you can't afford to buy and things you can't do with your time.

Start with the things you can't afford to buy. You've spent all your income on tuition, residence fees, books, and a laptop. If you weren't in school, you would have spent this money on tickets to ball games and movies and all the other things that you enjoy. But that's only the start of the things you can't afford to buy because you're in school. You've also given up the opportunity to get a job and buy the things that you could afford with your higher income. Suppose that the

*The opportunity cost of being in school: things you can't buy and do.*

best job you could get if you weren't in school is working as a convenience store manager earning $24,000 a year. Another part of your opportunity cost of being in school is all the things that you would buy with that extra $24,000.

Now think about the time that being a student eats up. You spend many hours each week in class, doing homework assignments, preparing for tests, and so on. To do all these school activities, you must give up what would otherwise be time spent playing your favorite sport, time watching movies, and leisure time spent with your friends.

The opportunity cost of being in school is the best alternative things that you can't afford and that you don't have the time to enjoy. You might put a dollar value on this cost but the cost is the goods and services and time that you give up, not dollars.

*The opportunity cost of being in school includes forgone earnings.*

## ▇ Benefit: What You Gain

The **benefit** from something is the gain or pleasure that it brings, measured by what you are *willing to give up* to get it. Benefit is determined by personal *preferences*—by what a person likes and dislikes and the intensity of those feelings. If you get a huge kick out of Madden NFL, that video game brings you a large benefit. And if you have little interest in listening to Yo Yo Ma playing a Vivaldi cello concerto, that activity brings you a small benefit.

Some benefits are large and easy to identify, such as the benefit that you get from being in school. A big piece of that benefit is the goods and services that you will be able to enjoy with the boost to your earning power when you graduate. Some benefits are small, such as the benefit you receive from a slice of pizza.

Economists measure benefit as the most that a person is *willing to give up* to get something. You are willing to give up a lot for something that brings a large benefit. For example, because being in school brings a large benefit, you're *willing to give up* a lot of time and goods and services to get that benefit. But you're willing to give up very little for something that brings a small benefit. For example, you might be willing to give up one iTunes download to get a slice of pizza.

**Benefit**
The benefit from something is the gain or pleasure that it brings, measured by what you are *willing to give up* to get it.

## ▇ Rational Choice

A basic idea of economics is that in making choices, people act rationally. A **rational choice** is one that uses the available resources to best achieve the objective of the person making the choice.

But how do people choose rationally? The answer is by comparing the *benefits* and *costs* of the alternative choices and choosing the alternative that makes *net benefit*—benefit minus cost—as large as possible.

You have chosen to be a student. If that choice is rational, as economists assume, your benefit from being in school exceeds the cost, so your net benefit is maximized by being in school. For an outstanding baseball player, a high earning potential makes the opportunity cost of school higher than the benefit from school, so for that person, net benefit is maximized by choosing full-time sport. (*Eye on the Benefit and Cost of School* on p. 12 explores these examples more closely.)

The benefit from a choice is determined by the preferences of the person making the choice, so two people can make different rational choices even if they face the same cost. For example, you might like chocolate ice cream more than vanilla ice cream, but your friend prefers vanilla. So it is rational for you to choose chocolate and for your friend to choose vanilla.

**Rational choice**
A choice that uses the available resources to best achieve the objective of the person making the choice.

A rational choice might turn out not to have been the best choice after the fact. For example, a farmer might decide to plant wheat rather than soybeans. Then, when the crop comes to market, the price of soybeans might be much higher than the price of wheat. The farmer's choice was rational when it was made, but subsequent events made it less profitable than the alternative choice.

All the rational choices we've just considered (school or not, chocolate or vanilla ice cream, soybeans or wheat) involve choosing between two things. One or the other is chosen. We call such choices *all-or-nothing* choices. Many choices are of this type, but most choices involve *how much* of an activity to do.

### ■ How Much? Choosing at the Margin

You can allocate the next hour between studying and video chatting with your friends, but the choice is not all or nothing. You must decide how many minutes to allocate to each activity. To make this decision, you compare the benefit of a little bit more study time with its cost—you make your choice *at the margin*.

Other words for "margin" are "border" or "edge." You can think of a choice at the margin as one that adjusts the border or edge of a plan to determine the best course of action. Making a choice at the **margin** means comparing the relevant alternatives systematically and incrementally.

#### Marginal Cost

The opportunity cost of a one-unit increase in an activity is called **marginal cost**. The marginal cost of something is what you *must* give up to get *one additional* unit of it. Think about your marginal cost of going to the movies for a third time in a week. Your marginal cost of seeing the movie is what you must give up to see that one additional movie. It is *not* what you give up to see all three movies. The reason is that you've already given up something to see two movies, so you don't count that cost when making a decision to see the third movie.

The marginal cost of any activity increases as you do more of it. You know that going to the movies decreases your study time and lowers your grade. Suppose that seeing a second movie in a week lowers your grade by five percentage points. Seeing a third movie will lower your grade by more than five percentage points. Your marginal cost of moviegoing is increasing as you see more movies.

#### Marginal Benefit

The benefit of a one-unit increase in an activity is called **marginal benefit**. Marginal benefit is what you gain from having *one more* unit of something. But the marginal benefit from something is *measured* by what you *are willing* to give up to get that *one additional* unit of it.

A fundamental feature of marginal benefit is that it diminishes. Think about your marginal benefit from movies. If you've been studying hard and haven't seen a movie this week, your marginal benefit from seeing your next movie is large. But if you've been on a movie binge this week, you now want a break and your marginal benefit from seeing your next movie is small.

Because the marginal benefit from a movie decreases as you see more movies, you are willing to give up less to see one additional movie. For example, you know that going to the movies decreases your study time and lowers your grade. You pay for seeing a movie with a lower grade. You might be willing to give up ten percentage points to see your first movie in a week, but you won't be willing to take such a big hit on your grade to see a second movie in a week. Your willingness to pay to see a movie decreases as the number of movies increases.

---

**Margin**
A choice on the margin is a choice that is made by comparing *all* the relevant alternatives systematically and incrementally.

**Marginal cost**
The opportunity cost that arises from a one-unit increase in an activity. The marginal cost of something is what you *must* give up to get *one additional* unit of it.

**Marginal benefit**
The benefit that arises from a one-unit increase in an activity. The marginal benefit of something is *measured* by what you *are willing* to give up to get *one additional* unit of it.

### Making a Rational Choice

So, will you go to the movies for that third time in a week? The answer is found by comparing marginal benefit and marginal cost.

If the marginal cost of the movie is less than the marginal benefit from it, seeing the third movie adds more to benefit than to cost. Your net benefit increases, so your rational choice is to see the third movie.

If the marginal cost of the movie exceeds the marginal benefit from it, seeing the third movie adds more to cost than to benefit. Your net benefit decreases, so your rational choice is to spend the evening studying.

When the marginal benefit from something equals its marginal cost, the choice is rational and it is not possible to make a better choice. Scarce resources are being used in the best possible way.

## ■ Choices Respond to Incentives

The choices we make depend on the incentives we face. An **incentive** is a reward or a penalty—a "carrot" or a "stick"—that encourages or discourages an action. We respond positively to "carrots" and negatively to "sticks." The carrots are marginal benefits; the sticks are marginal costs. A change in marginal benefit or a change in marginal cost changes the incentives that we face and leads us to change our actions.

Most students believe that the payoff from studying just before a test is greater than the payoff from studying a month before a test. In other words, as a test date approaches, the marginal benefit from studying increases and the incentive to study becomes stronger. For this reason, we observe an increase in study time and a decrease in leisure pursuits during the last few days before a test. And the more important the test, the greater is this effect.

A change in marginal cost also changes incentives. For example, suppose that last week, you found your course work easy and you scored 100 percent on your practice quizzes. You figured that the marginal cost of taking an evening off to enjoy a movie was low and that your grade on the next test would not suffer, so you headed to the Cineplex. But this week the going has gotten tough. You're just not getting it, and your practice test scores are low. If you take off even one evening this week, your grade on the next test will suffer. The marginal cost of seeing a movie is now high, so you decide to give the movies a miss.

A central idea of economics is that by observing *changes in incentives*, we can predict how *choices change*.

**Incentive**
A reward or a penalty—a "carrot" or a "stick"—that encourages or discourages an action.

*Changes in marginal benefit and marginal cost change the incentive to study or to enjoy a movie.*

# EYE on the BENEFIT AND COST OF SCHOOL

## Did You Make the Right Decision?

Your decision to be in school is an economic decision. You faced a tradeoff between school, a job, and leisure time. You compared benefits and costs, and you responded to incentives.

Did you make the right decision when you chose school over a full-time job? Or, if you have a full-time job and you're studying in what would be your leisure time, did you make the right choice? Does school provide a big enough benefit to justify its cost?

### The Benefits of School

Being in school has many benefits for which people are willing to pay. They fall into two broad categories: present enjoyment and a higher future income.

You can easily make a list of all the fun things you do with your friends in school that would be harder to do if you didn't have these friends and opportunities for social interaction that school provides.

Putting a dollar value on the items in your list would be hard, but it is possible to put a dollar value, or rather an expected dollar value, on the other benefit—a higher future income.

A high-school graduate earns, on average, an annual income of $40,000 a year. A graduate with a bachelor's degree earns, on average, $76,000 a year.

So by being in school, you can expect (on average) to increase your annual earnings by $36,000 a year.

This number is likely to grow as the economy becomes more productive and prices and earnings rise.

### The Costs of School

The opportunity cost of being in school is your best forgone alternative. It is all the things you would have been able to enjoy if you were not in school. An opportunity cost is goods and services and time that must be forgone. Putting a dollar value on opportunity cost for a full-time student includes

- Tuition
- Expenditure on books and other study aids
- Forgone earnings

For a student attending a state university in her or his home state, tuition is around $10,000 per year.

Books and other study aids cost around $1,000 per year.

Forgone earnings are the wage of a high-school graduate in a starter job, which is around $24,000 a year.

So the total cost of being in school is about $35,000 per year or $105,000 for a 3-year degree and $140,000 for a 4-year degree.

### Net Benefit

The benefit of extra earnings alone brings in $36,000 a year or $360,000 in 10 years and $1,440,000 in a working life of 40 years.

But you are incurring the costs now while you won't enjoy the benefits until some time in the future. We need to lower the benefits to compare them properly with the costs. You'll learn how to do that later in your economics course. But even allowing for the fact that the costs are incurred now while the benefits are received in the future, the net benefit is big!

### Is School Always Best?

At the age of 18, Clayton Kershaw was offered a baseball scholarship at Texas A & M. The scholarship wouldn't have covered all the costs of school, but it would have lowered them a long way below those that you face.

But Clayton had an alternative to school. He was considered the top high-schooler available entering the 2006 MLB Draft and he was offered a signing bonus by the Los Angeles Dodgers said to be $2.3 million.

Clayton turned down the baseball scholarship at Texas A & M and signed with the Dodgers.

As the starting pitcher, Clayton's value to the Dodgers is high and earned him a salary of $30 million in 2015.

Clayton Kershaw's opportunity cost of a college education vastly exceeded the benefit he could expect to get from it. So, like you, he made the right decision.

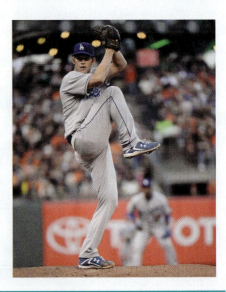

**CHECKPOINT 1.2**

**Explain the ideas that define the economic way of thinking.**

## Practice Problems

Every week, Kate plays tennis for two hours, and her grade on each math test is 70 percent. Last week, after playing for two hours, Kate considered playing for another hour. She decided to play for another hour and cut her study time by one hour. But last week, her math grade fell to 60 percent. Use this information to work Problems **1** to **4**.

1. What was Kate's opportunity cost of the third hour of tennis?
2. Given that Kate played the third hour, what can you conclude about her marginal benefit and marginal cost of the second hour of tennis?
3. Was Kate's decision to play the third hour of tennis rational?
4. Did Kate make her decision on the margin?

## In the News

The *New York Times* reports that cruise lines have been slashing prices and cruise sales are up. It says this surge of interest tells us that despite the uncertain economic climate, people clearly need more fun in their lives and view their vacations as valuable and necessary.

1. In deciding whether to take a cruise, would you face a tradeoff?
2. How would you make a rational choice about taking a cruise?
3. What would be the marginal benefit from a cruise? What would be the marginal cost of a cruise?
4. Why would you expect a lower price to increase the number of people who decide to take a cruise?

## Solutions to Practice Problems

1. Kate's opportunity cost of the third hour of tennis was the drop in her grade of ten percentage points.
2. The marginal benefit from the second hour of tennis must have exceeded the marginal cost of the second hour because Kate chose to play the third hour.
3. If marginal benefit exceeded marginal cost, Kate's decision was rational.
4. Kate made her decision on the margin because she compared the benefit and cost of one more hour (marginal benefit and marginal cost).

## Solutions to In the News

1. You would face a tradeoff because you would have to forgo something else that you might otherwise do with your resources (time and budget).
2. You would make a rational choice by comparing the marginal benefit from a cruise and the marginal cost of taking one.
3. The marginal benefit from a cruise is the most you are willing to pay for one. The marginal cost is what you would have to pay to take a cruise.
4. With a lower price, more people will have a marginal benefit that exceeds the price and they will choose to take a cruise.

## 1.3  ECONOMICS AS A LIFE SKILL

Economics is a life skill. It is a decision-making toolkit and, as a social science, it is a platform on which you will build critical thinking skills that prepare you for your career and life.

### ■ Economics as a Decision Tool

Economics is useful. The economic way of thinking provides you with tools for making decisions in all aspects of your lives:

- Personal
- Business
- Government

### Personal Decisions

Should you take a student loan? Should you get a weekend job? Should you rent an apartment or borrow and buy a condo? How should you allocate your time between study, working, volunteering, caring for others, and having fun?

Deciding the answers to these questions involves weighing a marginal benefit and a marginal cost. Although some of the numbers might be hard to pin down, you will make more solid decisions if you approach these questions with the tools of economics.

### Business Decisions

Should Sony compete with Apple in the smartphone market? Should Texaco get more oil from the Gulf of Mexico or from Alaska? Should Marvel Studios produce Spider-Man 4, a sequel to Spider-Man 3?

Like personal economic questions, these business questions involve the evaluation of a marginal benefit and a marginal cost. So again, by approaching these questions with the tools of economics and by hiring economists as advisers, businesses can make better decisions.

### Government Decisions

Should there be a special tax to penalize corporations that send jobs overseas? Should cheap foreign imports of furniture and textiles be limited? Should the farms that grow beets receive a subsidy?

These government policy questions call for decisions that involve the evaluation of a marginal benefit and a marginal cost and an investigation of the interactions of individuals and businesses. Yet again, by approaching these questions with the tools of economics, governments can make better decisions.

### ■ Economics as a Social Science

Economists try to understand and predict the effects of economic forces by using the *scientific method* first developed by physicists. The scientific method is a commonsense way of systematically checking what works and what doesn't work. It begins with a question about cause and effect arising from some observed facts. An economist might wonder why computers are getting cheaper and more computers are being used. Are computers getting cheaper because more people are buying them, or are more people buying computers because they are getting cheaper? Or is a third factor causing both the price fall and the quantity increase?

## Economic Models

A scientist's second step is to build a model that provides a possible answer to the question of interest. All sciences use models. An **economic model** is a description of the economy or a part of the economy that includes only those features assumed necessary to explain the observed facts.

A model is like a map. If you want to know about valleys and mountains, you use a physical map; if you're studying nations, you use a political map; if you want to drive from A to B in an unfamiliar city, you use a street map; and if you're a city engineer, you use a map of the cables and conduit under the streets.

In economics, we use mathematical and graph-based models. The questions posed above about the price and quantity of computers bought are answered by a graph-based model called "demand and supply" that you will study in Chapter 4.

## Check Predictions of Models Against Facts

A scientist's third step is to check the predictions of a proposed model against the facts. Physicists check whether their models correspond to the facts by doing experiments. For example, with a particle accelerator, a physicist can test a model of the structure of an atom.

Economists have a harder time than physicists, but they still approach the task in a scientific manner. To check predictions of a model against facts, economists use natural experiments, statistical investigations, and laboratory experiments.

A natural experiment is a situation that arises in the ordinary course of economic life in which the one factor of interest is different and other things are equal (or similar). For example, Canada has higher unemployment benefits than the United States, but the people in the two nations are similar. So to study the effect of unemployment benefits on the unemployment rate, economists might compare the United States with Canada.

A statistical investigation looks for a *correlation*—a tendency for the values of two variables to move together (either in the same direction or in opposite directions) in a predictable and related way. For example, cigarette smoking and lung cancer are correlated. Sometimes a correlation shows a causal influence of one variable on the other. Smoking causes lung cancer. But sometimes the direction of causation is hard to determine.

A laboratory experiment puts people (often students) in a decision-making situation and varies the influence of one factor at a time to discover how they respond to changed incentives. Some economists (neuroeconomists) are now studying what happens inside the brain of a decisionmaker.

## Disagreement: Normative versus Positive

Economists sometimes disagree. Some disagreements can be settled by checking facts, but others cannot.

Disagreements that can't be settled by facts are *normative*—disagreements about what *should be.* These disagreements turn on subjective values and cannot be tested. The statement "We *should* burn less coal" is normative. You may agree or disagree with it, but you can't test it. It doesn't assert a fact that can be checked. Economists as social scientists try to steer clear of normative statements.

Disagreements that *can* be settled by facts are *positive*—disagreements about *what is.* These disagreements can be settled by careful observation of facts. "Burning coal raises the temperature of the planet" is a positive statement. It can be tested. Sometimes the facts are hard to get and sometimes they are hard to interpret, so disagreement persists. It is an ongoing feature of a healthy science.

**Economic model**
A description of the economy or a part of the economy that includes only those features assumed necessary to explain the observed facts.

## ■ Economics as an Aid to Critical Thinking

Throughout your career you will need to engage in *critical thinking*. And throughout your life, if you strive to approach personal and social issues as a critical thinker, you will make better decisions and be a better friend, neighbor, and citizen.

### What is Critical Thinking?

Critical thinking is thinking that is logical and fact-based. It is thinking that

- begins with a question
- clarifies the question
- thinks with an open mind about how to answer the question
- identifies potential answers
- seeks the relevant facts to check the potential answers
- ends with a well-reasoned answer

Does this sequence of critical thinking activities seem familiar? It does if you have just read the previous page. You will recognize that critical thinking is just another name for approaching an issue like a scientist. Economic science begins with a question about some economic event or activity; uses the economic way of thinking to clarify the question, think about how to answer it, identify possible answers, and check them against the facts; and arrives at a well-reasoned answer.

As a student, you will have lots of opportunities to practice critical thinking. It will be a feature of almost all your courses, and it will be a major feature of your economics course. What you learn in this course and the critical thinking and economic thinking skills that you develop will enrich your career and your life.

### Learning-by-Doing

A central theme of this textbook is that the best way to learn economics is to do it—*learning-by-doing*. The mantra is "work the problem" and "draw the graph." This same message applies to critical thinking. The best way to become skilled at critical thinking is to do it.

To get you started, look at the example of a critical thinking question in *Eye on Your Life* on p. 17. The question is a simple one about facts. It doesn't have a cause-and-effect dimension, but it illustrates the central role that facts play. Facts always trump guesses and beliefs. The question also suggests another valuable activity: cooperating and working with others. Teamwork enables data to be shared and brainstorming a question often triggers better ideas about other possible answers that should be checked.

Throughout this textbook, we present you with a wide variety of critical thinking opportunities. Some arise from your life experiences in *Eye on Your Life* boxes like the one in this chapter. Others arise from economic events and issues in the news. News clips and the critical thinking questions that they raise appear in every chapter.

Also, every chapter starts with a question that is answered with a critical thinking box later in the chapter. The question on the opening page of this chapter and the *Eye on the Benefit and Cost of School* box on p. 12 are examples. Studying these examples and using what you learn to answer the economic questions that arise in your life and in the news will strengthen your critical thinking. You will emerge from your economics course with not only the ability to think like an economist but also more generally to be a critical thinker.

# EYE on YOUR LIFE
## Your Time Allocation

MyEconLab Critical Thinking Exercise

Your time is a scarce resource and how you allocate it impacts the quality of your life. Your physical fitness depends on how much time you allocate to sports and exercise, and your grade depends on the amount of time you allocate to studying.

Sleeping, personal care, eating and drinking, and traveling take a large chunk of your time, but you have choices about how much time to allocate to each of these activities. You also have choices about how much time to spend working for an income, enjoying sports and other leisure activities, and on educational activities (attending class, doing assignments, and studying).

Do you know the number of hours per day that you allocate to sleeping, personal care, eating and drinking, traveling, working, sports and leisure, and educational activities?

Here is a critical thinking question for you: Who works harder, you or the average student?

This question is one of fact, but answering requires agreement on what we mean by "works harder" and requires some data (the facts).

Let's agree that we will measure how hard a person works as the average number of hours per weekday spent working and on educational activities.

Next, we need the facts about time allocation—data about your time use and the time use of an average student.

The table above has eight activities and two columns for data. Complete the first column based on your current best guess about your time use.

Now keep a calendar for a normal week, and calculate your actual average hours for each activity. At the end of the week, complete the second column of the table.

How do your actual numbers compare with your guesses? Are there any surprises?

Now we need to compare your time use with that of the average student. The Bureau of Labor Statistics has conducted a survey to get the facts and the figure below shows what it found.

So, what is the answer? Are there any more surprises? Who works more hours, you or the average student?

Does the answer make you want to change your time allocation?

| **Your Time Use** | | |
| --- | --- | --- |
| **Activity** | **Guess** | **Actual average** |
| | **(hours per day)** | |
| Sleeping | | |
| Personal care | | |
| Eating and drinking | | |
| Traveling | | |
| Working and related activities | | |
| Leisure and sports | | |
| Educational activities | | |
| Other | | |
| **Total** | **24.0** | **24.0** |

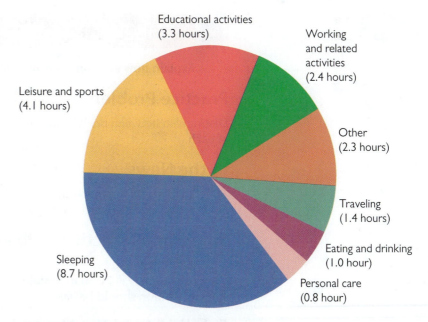

**Figure 1  Time Use for Full-Time Students**

SOURCE OF DATA: Bureau of Labor Statistics, American Time Use Survey, average on non-holiday weekdays for full-time university and college students 2010–2014.

# EYE on the PAST
## Adam Smith and the Birth of Economics as a Social Science

Many people had written about economics before Adam Smith did, but he made economics a social science.

Born in 1723 in Scotland, Smith became a full professor at 28 and published his masterpiece, *An Inquiry into the Nature and Causes of the Wealth of Nations,* in 1776.

Adam Smith asked: Why are some nations wealthy while others are poor? His answer: Through the division of labor and free markets, nations become wealthy. To illustrate his argument, he used the example of a pin factory. He guessed that one person, using the hand tools available in the 1770s, might make 20 pins a day. Yet,

he observed, by using the same hand tools but breaking the process into a number of individually small tasks in which people specialize—by the division of labor—ten people could make a staggering 48,000 pins a day.

But a large market is needed to support the division of labor: One factory employing ten workers would need to sell more than 15 million pins a year to stay in business!

Smith saw free competitive markets as a source of wealth. The self-interested pursuit of profit, led by an invisible hand, resulted in resources being used in ways that created the greatest possible value and wealth.

MyEconLab Study Plan 1.3
Key Terms Quiz
Solutions Video

# CHECKPOINT 1.3

**Explain how economics is useful as a life skill.**

## Practice Problem

Distinguish between positive and normative statements and provide an example of each.

## In the News

The *New York Times* reports that China will end its one-child policy. How would an economist study the effect of this policy change?

## Solution to Practice Problem

A positive statement is a statement of fact that can be checked, such as "grocery prices are rising." A normative statement is an opinion that cannot be checked, such as "tuition should be based on family income."

## Solution to In the News

As a social scientist, an economist would construct a population model. As a policy adviser, an economist would evaluate the benefits and costs of the change.

CHAPTER SUMMARY

## Key Points

1. **Define economics and explain the kinds of questions that economists try to answer.**

   - Economics is the social science that studies the choices that we make as we cope with scarcity and the incentives that influence and reconcile our choices.
   - Microeconomics is the study of individual choices and interactions, and macroeconomics is the study of the national economy and global economy.
   - The first big question of economics is: How do the choices that people make end up determining *what, how,* and *for whom* goods and services are produced?
   - The second big question is: When do choices made in the pursuit of *self-interest* also promote the *social interest*?

2. **Explain the ideas that define the economic way of thinking.**

   - Six ideas define the economic way of thinking:
     1. A choice is a *tradeoff*.
     2. *Cost* is what you *must* give up to get something.
     3. *Benefit* is what you gain when you get something (measured by what you *are willing to* give up to get it).
     4. People make *rational* choices by comparing benefits and costs.
     5. A "how much" choice is made on the *margin* by comparing *marginal benefit* and *marginal cost*.
     6. Choices respond to *incentives*.

3. **Explain how economics is useful as a life skill.**

   - Economics is a tool for personal, business, and government decisions.
   - Economists use the *scientific method* to try to understand how the economic world works. They create economic models and test them using natural experiments, statistical investigations, and laboratory experiments.
   - Economics and the economic way of thinking are foundations on which to build critical thinking skills.

## Key Terms

MyEconLab Key Terms Quiz

Benefit, 9
Economic model, 15
Economics, 2
Goods and services, 3
Incentive, 11
Macroeconomics, 3

Margin, 10
Marginal benefit, 10
Marginal cost, 10
Microeconomics, 2
Opportunity cost, 8
Rational choice, 9

Scarcity, 2
Self-interest, 4
Social interest, 4
Tradeoff, 8

CHAPTER CHECKPOINT

## Study Plan Problems and Applications

**LIST 1**

• Motor vehicle production in China is growing by 10 percent a year.
• Coffee prices skyrocket.
• Globalization has reduced African poverty.
• The government must cut its budget deficit.
• Apple sells 20 million iPhone 6 smartphones a month.

1. Provide three examples of scarcity that illustrate why even the 1,826 billionaires in the world face scarcity.

2. Label each entry in List 1 as dealing with a microeconomic topic or a macroeconomic topic. Explain your answer.

Use the following information to work Problems **3** to **6**.

*Jurassic World* had world-wide box office receipts of $1.66 billion. The movie's production budget was $150 million with additional marketing costs. A successful movie brings pleasure to millions, creates work for thousands, and makes a few people rich.

3. What contribution does a movie like *Jurassic World* make to coping with scarcity? When you buy a movie ticket, are you buying a good or a service?

4. Who decides whether a movie is going to be a blockbuster? How do you think the creation of a blockbuster movie influences *what*, *how*, and *for whom* goods and services are produced?

5. What are some of the components of marginal cost and marginal benefit that the producer of a movie faces?

6. Suppose that Chris Pratt had been offered a part in another movie and that to hire him for *Jurassic World*, the producer had to double Chris Pratt's pay. What incentives would have changed? How might the changed incentives have changed the choices that people made?

7. What is the social interest? Distinguish it from self-interest. In your answer give an example of self-interest and an example of social interest.

8. Pam, Pru, and Pat are deciding how they will celebrate the New Year. Pam prefers to take a cruise, is happy to go to Hawaii, but does not want to go skiing. Pru prefers to go skiing, is happy to go to Hawaii, but does not want to take a cruise. Pat prefers to go to Hawaii or to take a cruise but does not want to go skiing. Their decision is to go to Hawaii. Is this decision rational? What is the opportunity cost of the trip to Hawaii for each of them? What is the benefit that each gets?

9. Label each of the entries in List 2 as a positive or a normative statement.

**LIST 2**

• Low-income people pay too much for housing.
• The number of U.S. farms has decreased over the past 50 years.
• Toyota expands parts production in the United States.
• Imports from China are swamping U.S. department stores.
• The rural population in the United States is declining.

Use the following information to work Problems **10** to **12**.

**REI is paying its employees to take Black Friday, Thanksgiving off**

REI, the outdoor gear and apparel retailer, is paying employees to celebrate Thanksgiving 2015 by spending Black Friday outdoors with their families.

Source: *Sustainable Brands*, October 28, 2015

10. With Black Friday off with full pay, explain what is free and what is scarce.

11. What is REI's incentive to give its workers Black Friday off? Was REI's decision made in self-interest or in the social interest? Explain your answer.

12. Do you think that REI workers will shop or spend the day with family? Explain your answer.

 13. Read *Eye on the Benefit and Cost of School* on p. 12 and explain why both you and Clayton Kershaw made the right decision.

## Instructor Assignable Problems and Applications

MyEconLab Homework, Quiz, or Test if assigned by instructor

1. Which of the following items are components of the opportunity cost of being a full-time college student who lives at home? The things that the student would have bought with

   - A higher income
   - Expenditure on tuition
   - A subscription to the *Rolling Stone* magazine
   - The income the student will earn after graduating

2. Think about the following news items and label each as involving a *what*, *how*, or *for whom* question:

   - Today, most stores use computers to keep their inventory records, whereas 20 years ago most stores used paper records.
   - Healthcare professionals and drug companies recommend that Medicaid drug rebates be made available to everyone in need.
   - An increase in the gas tax pays for low-cost public transit.

3. The headlines in List 1 appeared in *The Wall Street Journal*. Classify each headline as a signal that the news article is about a microeconomic topic or a macroeconomic topic. Explain your answers.

4. Your school decides to increase the intake of new students next year. To make its decision, what economic concepts would it have considered? Would the school have used the "economic way of thinking" in reaching its decision? Would the school have made its decision on the margin?

5. Provide examples of (a) a monetary incentive and (b) a non-monetary incentive, a carrot and a stick of each, that governments use to influence behavior.

6. Think about each of the items in List 2 and explain how they affect incentives and might change the choices that people make.

7. Does the decision to make a blockbuster movie mean that some other more desirable activities get fewer resources than they deserve? Is your answer positive or normative? Explain your answer.

8. Provide two examples of economics being used as a tool by (a) a student, (b) a business, and (c) a government. Classify your examples as dealing with microeconomic topics and macroeconomic topics.

**LIST 1**

- Job Gains Calm Slump Worries
- Washington Post's Profit Falls
- Overcapacity, Fuel Costs Hit Shipping
- U.S. Budget Deficit Expands

**LIST 2**

- A hurricane hits Central Florida.
- The World Series begins tonight, but a storm warning is in effect for the area around the stadium.
- The price of a personal computer falls to $50.
- Unrest in the Middle East sends the price of gas to $5 a gallon.

Use the following news clip to work Problems **9** to **12**.

**Obama unveils major climate change policy**
Obama's Clean Power Plan, which will set federal limits on carbon emissions from coal-fired power plants, will cost $8.4 billion and reap benefits of more than $34 billion. Opponents of the plan say it will drive up the cost of electricity for millions of Americans.

Source: CNN, August 3, 2015

9. What are the more than $34 billion of benefits from using less coal to produce electricity? Who receives these benefits: the users of electricity or the owners of power plants, or both the users and the owners?

10. What are the $8.4 billion of costs arising from using less coal to produce electricity? Who bears these costs: the users of electricity or the owners of power plants, or both the users and the owners?

11. Explain why someone might oppose the Clean Power Plan when its benefits exceed its costs.

12. Explain whether the Clean Power Plan has an opportunity cost.

# Multiple Choice Quiz

**1.** Which of the following describes the reason why scarcity exists?

A. Governments make bad economic decisions.
B. The gap between the rich and the poor is too wide.
C. Wants exceed the resources available to satisfy them.
D. There is too much unemployment.

**2.** Which of the following defines economics?
Economics is the social science that studies _____.

A. the best way of eliminating scarcity
B. the choices made to cope with scarcity, how incentives influence those choices, and how the choices are coordinated
C. how money is created and used
D. the inevitable conflict between self-interest and the social interest

**3.** Of the three big questions, *what, how,* and *for whom,* which of the following is an example of a *how* question?

A. Why do doctors and lawyers earn high incomes?
B. Why don't we produce more small cars and fewer gas guzzlers?
C. Why do we use machines rather than migrant workers to pick grapes?
D. Why do college football coaches earn more than professors?

**4.** Which of the following is not a key idea in the economic way of thinking?

A. People make rational choices by comparing costs and benefits.
B. Poor people are discriminated against and should be treated more fairly.
C. A rational choice is made at the margin.
D. Choices respond to incentives.

**5.** A rational choice is _____.

A. the best thing you must forgo to get something
B. what you are willing to forgo to get something
C. made by comparing marginal benefit and marginal cost
D. the best for society

**6.** Which of the following best illustrates your marginal benefit from studying?

A. The knowledge you gain from studying two hours a night for a month
B. The best things forgone by studying two hours a night for a month
C. What you are willing to give up to study for one additional hour
D. What you must give up to be able to study for one additional hour

**7.** The scientific method uses models to _____.

A. clarify normative disagreements
B. avoid the need to study real questions
C. replicate all the features of the real world
D. focus on those features of reality assumed relevant for understanding a cause-and-effect relationship

**8.** Which of the following is a positive statement?

A. We should stop using corn to make ethanol because it is raising the cost of food.
B. You will get the most out of college life if you play a sport once a week.
C. Competition among wireless service providers across the borders of Canada, Mexico, and the United States has driven roaming rates down.
D. Bill Gates ought to spend more helping to eradicate malaria in Africa

# APPENDIX: MAKING AND USING GRAPHS

## When you have completed your study of this appendix, you will be able to

**1**  Interpret graphs that display data.

**2**  Interpret the graphs used in economic models.

**3**  Define and calculate slope.

**4**  Graph relationships among more than two variables.

## Basic Idea

A graph represents a quantity as a distance and enables us to visualize the relationship between two variables. To make a graph, we set two lines called *axes* perpendicular to each other, like those in Figure A1.1. The vertical line is called the *y*-axis, and the horizontal line is called the *x*-axis. The common zero point is called the *origin*. In Figure A1.1, the *x*-axis measures temperature in degrees Fahrenheit. A movement to the right shows an increase in temperature, and a movement to the left shows a decrease in temperature. The *y*-axis represents ice cream consumption, measured in gallons per day.

To make a graph, we need a value of the variable on the *x*-axis and a corresponding value of the variable on the *y*-axis. For example, if the temperature is 40°F, ice cream consumption is 5 gallons a day at point *A* in Figure A1.1. If the temperature is 80°F, ice cream consumption is 20 gallons a day at point *B* in Figure A1.1. Graphs like that in Figure A1.1 can be used to show any type of quantitative data on two variables.

### FIGURE A1.1

Making a Graph                                                          MyEconLab Animation

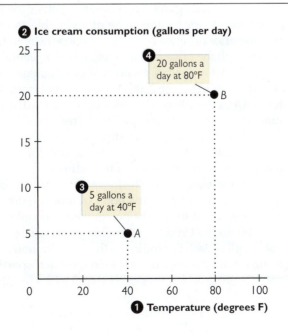

All graphs have axes that measure quantities as distances.

**❶**  The horizontal axis (*x*-axis) measures temperature in degrees Fahrenheit. A movement to the right shows an increase in temperature.

**❷**  The vertical axis (*y*-axis) measures ice cream consumption in gallons per day. A movement upward shows an increase in ice cream consumption.

**❸**  Point *A* shows that 5 gallons of ice cream are consumed on a day when the temperature is 40°F.

**❹**  Point *B* shows that 20 gallons of ice cream are consumed on a day when the temperature is 80°F.

## ■ Interpreting Data Graphs

A **scatter diagram** is a graph of the value of one variable against the value of another variable. It is used to reveal whether a relationship exists between two variables and to describe the relationship. Figure A1.2 shows two examples.

Figure A1.2(a) shows the relationship between expenditure and income. Each point shows expenditure per person and income per person in the United States in a given year from 2000 to 2015. The points are "scattered" within the graph. The label on each point shows its year. The point marked 10 shows that in 2010, income per person was $36,183 and expenditure per person was $32,758. This scatter diagram reveals that as income increases, expenditure also increases.

Figure A1.2(b) shows the relationship during the 1990s between the percentage of Americans who own a cell phone and the average monthly cell-phone bill. This scatter diagram reveals that as the cost of using a cell phone falls, the number of cell-phone subscribers increases.

A **time-series graph** measures time (for example, months or years) on the *x*-axis and the variable or variables in which we are interested on the *y*-axis. Figure A1.2(c) shows an example. In this graph, time (on the *x*-axis) is measured in years, which run from 1980 to 2016. The variable that we are interested in is the price of coffee, and it is measured on the *y*-axis.

A time-series graph conveys an enormous amount of information quickly and easily, as this example illustrates. It shows when the value is

1. High or low. When the line is a long way from the *x*-axis, the price is high, as it was in 1986. When the line is close to the *x*-axis, the price is low, as it was in 2001.
2. Rising or falling. When the line slopes upward, as in 2006, the price is rising. When the line slopes downward, as in 1997, the price is falling.
3. Rising or falling quickly or slowly. If the line is steep, then the price is rising or falling quickly. If the line is not steep, the price is rising or falling slowly. For example, the price rose quickly in 2006 and slowly in 2014. The price fell quickly in 1987 and slowly in 1996.

A time-series graph also reveals whether the variable has a trend. A **trend** is a general tendency for the value of a variable to rise or fall over time. You can see that the price of coffee had a general tendency to fall from 1980 to late in 2000. That is, although the price rose and fell, it had a general tendency to fall.

With a time-series graph, we can compare different periods quickly. Figure A1.2(c) shows that the 2000s were different from the 1990s, which in turn were different from the 1980s. The price of coffee started the 1980s high and then fell for a number of years. During the 1990s, the price was on a roller coaster. And during the 2000s, the price rose steadily through 2014. This graph conveys a wealth of information about the price of coffee, and it does so in much less space than we have used to describe only some of its features.

A **cross-section graph** shows the values of an economic variable for different groups in a population at a point in time. Figure A1.2(d) is an example of a cross-section graph. It shows the percentage of people who participate in selected sports activities in the United States. This graph uses bars rather than dots and lines, and the length of each bar indicates the participation rate. Figure A1.2(d) enables you to compare the participation rates in these ten sporting activities, and you can do so much more quickly and clearly than by looking at a list of numbers.

**Scatter diagram**
A graph of the value of one variable against the value of another variable.

**Time-series graph**
A graph that measures time on the *x*-axis and the variable or variables in which we are interested on the *y*-axis.

**Trend**
A general tendency for the value of a variable to rise or fall over time.

**Cross-section graph**
A graph that shows the values of an economic variable for different groups in a population at a point in time.

■ **FIGURE A1.2**

Data Graphs

**Expenditure (thousands of dollars per year)**

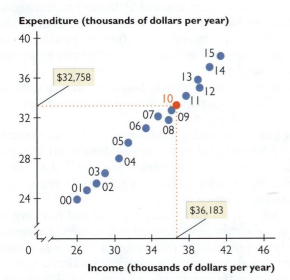

**(a) Scatter Diagram: Expenditure and income**

**Average monthly bill (dollars)**

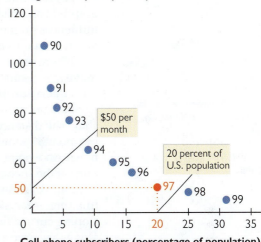

**(b) Scatter Diagram: Subscribers and cost**

**Price of coffee (dollars per pound)**

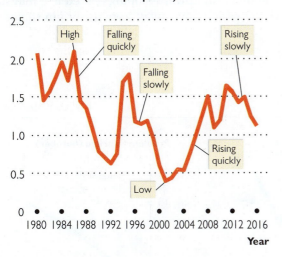

**(c) Time Series: The price of coffee**

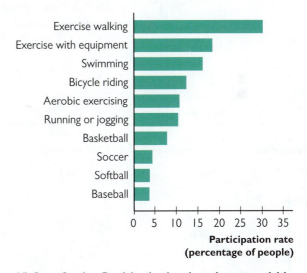

**(d) Cross Section: Participation in selected sports activities**

A scatter diagram reveals the relationship between two variables. In part (a), as income increases, expenditure almost always increases. In part (b), as the monthly cell-phone bill falls, the percentage of people who own a cell phone increases.

A time-series graph plots the value of a variable on the *y*-axis against time on the *x*-axis. Part (c) plots the price of coffee each

year from 1980 to 2016. The graph shows when the price of coffee was high and low, when it increased and decreased, and when it changed quickly and changed slowly.

A cross-section graph shows the value of a variable across the members of a population. Part (d) shows the participation rate in the United States in each of ten sporting activities.

## ■ Interpreting Graphs Used in Economic Models

We use graphs to show the relationships among the variables in an economic model. An *economic model* is a simplified description of the economy or of a component of the economy such as a business or a household. It consists of statements about economic behavior that can be expressed as equations or as curves in a graph. Economists use models to explore the effects of different policies or other influences on the economy in ways similar to those used to test model airplanes in wind tunnels and models of the climate.

**Positive relationship** or **direct relationship**
A relationship between two variables that move in the same direction.

Figure A1.3 shows graphs of the relationships between two variables that move in the same direction. Such a relationship is called a **positive relationship** or **direct relationship**.

Part (a) shows a straight-line relationship, which is called a **linear relationship**. The distance traveled in 5 hours increases as the speed increases. For example, point *A* shows that 200 miles are traveled in 5 hours at a speed of 40 miles an hour. And point *B* shows that the distance traveled in 5 hours increases to 300 miles if the speed increases to 60 miles an hour.

**Linear relationship**
A relationship that graphs as a straight line.

Part (b) shows the relationship between distance sprinted and recovery time (the time it takes the heart rate to return to its normal resting rate). An upward-sloping curved line that starts out quite flat but then becomes steeper as we move along the curve away from the origin describes this relationship. The curve slopes upward and becomes steeper because the extra recovery time needed from sprinting another 100 yards increases. It takes 5 minutes to recover from sprinting 100 yards but 15 minutes to recover from sprinting 200 yards.

Part (c) shows the relationship between the number of problems worked by a student and the amount of study time. An upward-sloping curved line that starts out quite steep and becomes flatter as we move away from the origin shows this

■ **FIGURE A1.3**

Positive (Direct) Relationships                    MyEconLab Animation

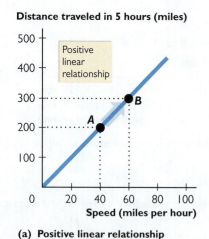

**(a) Positive linear relationship**

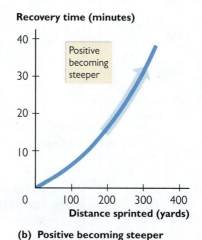

**(b) Positive becoming steeper**

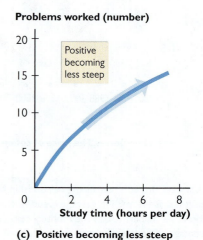

**(c) Positive becoming less steep**

Part (a) shows that as speed increases, the distance traveled in a given number of hours increases along a straight line.

Part (b) shows that as the distance sprinted increases, recovery time increases along a curve that becomes steeper.

Part (c) shows that as study time increases, the number of problems worked increases along a curve that becomes less steep.

relationship. Study time becomes less effective as you increase the hours worked and become more tired.

Figure A1.4 shows relationships between two variables that move in opposite directions. Such a relationship is called a **negative relationship** or **inverse relationship**.

Part (a) shows the relationship between the number of hours spent playing squash and the number of hours spent playing tennis when the total number of hours available is five. One extra hour spent playing tennis means one hour less playing squash and vice versa. This relationship is negative and linear.

Part (b) shows the relationship between the cost per mile traveled and the length of a journey. The longer the journey, the lower is the cost per mile. But as the journey length increases, the fall in the cost per mile becomes smaller. This feature of the relationship is shown by the fact that the curve slopes downward, starting out steep at a short journey length and then becoming flatter as the journey length increases. This relationship arises because some of the costs, such as auto insurance, are fixed, and as the journey length increases, the fixed costs are spread over more miles.

Part (c) shows the relationship between the amount of leisure time and the number of problems worked by a student. Increasing leisure time produces an increasingly large reduction in the number of problems worked. This relationship is a negative one that starts out with a gentle slope at a small number of leisure hours and becomes steeper as the number of leisure hours increases. This relationship is a different view of the idea shown in Figure A1.3(c).

Many relationships in economic models have a maximum or a minimum. For example, firms try to make the largest possible profit and to produce at the lowest possible cost. Figure A1.5 shows relationships that have a maximum or a minimum.

**Negative relationship or inverse relationship**
A relationship between two variables that move in opposite directions.

**FIGURE A1.4**

Negative (Inverse) Relationships

MyEconLab Animation

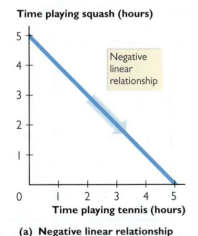

(a) **Negative linear relationship**

Part (a) shows that as the time playing tennis increases, the time playing squash decreases along a straight line.

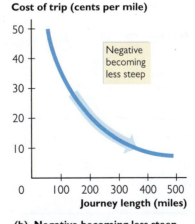

(b) **Negative becoming less steep**

Part (b) shows that as the journey length increases, the cost of the trip falls along a curve that becomes less steep.

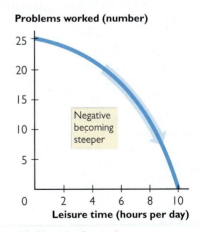

(c) **Negative becoming steeper**

Part (c) shows that as leisure time increases, the number of problems worked decreases along a curve that becomes steeper.

■ **FIGURE A1.5**

Maximum and Minimum Points

In part (a), as the rainfall increases, the curve ❶ slopes upward as the yield per acre rises, ❷ is flat at point A, the maximum yield, and then ❸ slopes downward as the yield per acre falls.

In part (b), as the speed increases, the curve ❶ slopes downward as the cost per mile falls, ❷ is flat at the minimum point B, and then ❸ slopes upward as the cost per mile rises.

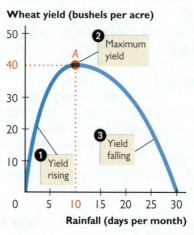

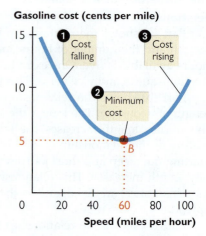

(a) Relationship with a maximum

(b) Relationship with a minimum

Part (a) shows a relationship that starts out sloping upward, reaches a maximum, and then slopes downward. Part (b) shows a relationship that begins sloping downward, falls to a minimum, and then slopes upward.

Finally, there are many situations in which, no matter what happens to the value of one variable, the other variable remains constant. Sometimes we want to show two variables that are unrelated in a graph. Figure A1.6 shows two graphs in which the variables are unrelated.

■ **FIGURE A1.6**

Variables That Are Unrelated

In part (a), as the price of bananas increases, the student's grade in economics remains at 75 percent. These variables are unrelated, and the curve is horizontal.

In part (b), the vineyards of France produce 3 billion gallons of wine no matter what the rainfall is in California. These variables are unrelated, and the curve is vertical.

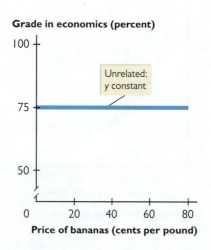

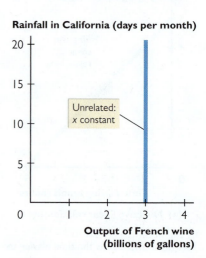

(a) Unrelated: y constant

(b) Unrelated: x constant

## ■ The Slope of a Relationship

We can measure the influence of one variable on another by the slope of the relationship. The **slope** of a relationship is the change in the value of the variable measured on the $y$-axis divided by the change in the value of the variable measured on the $x$-axis. We use the Greek letter $\Delta$ (delta) to represent "change in." So $\Delta y$ means the change in the value of $y$, and $\Delta x$ means the change in the value of $x$. The slope of the relationship is

$$\Delta y \div \Delta x.$$

If a large change in $y$ is associated with a small change in $x$, the slope is large and the curve is steep. If a small change in $y$ is associated with a large change in $x$, the slope is small and the curve is flat.

Figure A1.7 shows you how to calculate slope. The slope of a straight line is the same regardless of where on the line you calculate it—the slope is constant. In part (a), when $x$ increases from 2 to 6, $y$ increases from 3 to 6. The change in $x$ is 4—that is, $\Delta x$ is 4. The change in $y$ is 3—that is, $\Delta y$ is 3. The slope of that line is 3/4. In part (b), when $x$ increases from 2 to 6, $y$ *decreases* from 6 to 3. The change in $y$ is *minus* 3—that is, $\Delta y$ is $-3$ The change in $x$ is plus 4—that is, $\Delta x$ is 4. The slope of the curve is $-3/4$.

In part (c), we calculate the slope at a point on a curve. To do so, place a ruler on the graph so that it touches point $A$ and no other point on the curve, then draw a straight line along the edge of the ruler. The slope of this straight line is the slope of the curve at point $A$. This slope is 3/4.

**Slope**
The change in the value of the variable measured on the y-axis divided by the change in the value of the variable measured on the x-axis.

### ■ FIGURE A1.7

#### Calculating Slope

MyEconLab Animation

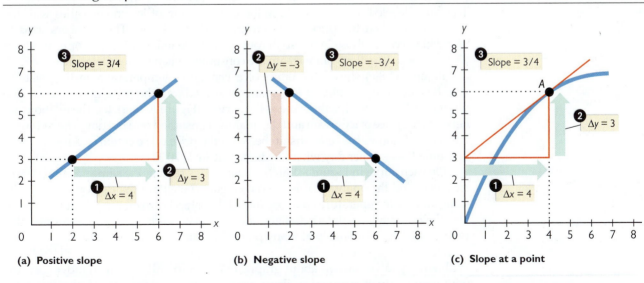

**(a) Positive slope**

**(b) Negative slope**

**(c) Slope at a point**

In part (a), ❶ when $\Delta x$ is 4, ❷ $\Delta y$ is 3, so ❸ the slope ($\Delta y \div \Delta x$) is 3/4.

In part (b), ❶ when $\Delta x$ is 4, ❷ $\Delta y$ is $-3$, so ❸ the slope ($\Delta y \div \Delta x$) is $-3/4$.

In part (c), the slope of the curve at point $A$ equals the slope of the red line. ❶ When $\Delta x$ is 4, ❷ $\Delta y$ is 3, so ❸ the slope ($\Delta y \div \Delta x$) is 3/4.

## ■ Relationships Among More Than Two Variables

All the graphs that you have studied so far plot the relationship between two variables as a point formed by the $x$ and $y$ values. But most of the relationships in economics involve relationships among many variables, not just two. For example, the amount of ice cream consumed depends on the price of ice cream and the temperature. If ice cream is expensive and the temperature is low, people eat much less ice cream than when ice cream is inexpensive and the temperature is high. For any given price of ice cream, the quantity consumed varies with the temperature; and for any given temperature, the quantity of ice cream consumed varies with its price.

Figure A1.8 shows a relationship among three variables. The table shows the number of gallons of ice cream consumed per day at various temperatures and ice cream prices. How can we graph these numbers?

To graph a relationship that involves more than two variables, we use the *ceteris paribus* assumption.

### Ceteris Paribus

The Latin phrase *ceteris paribus* means "other things remaining the same." Every laboratory experiment is an attempt to create *ceteris paribus* and isolate the relationship of interest. We use the same method to make a graph.

Figure A1.8(a) shows an example. This graph shows what happens to the quantity of ice cream consumed when the price of ice cream varies while the temperature remains constant. The curve labeled 90°F shows the relationship between ice cream consumption and the price of ice cream if the temperature is 90°F. The numbers used to plot that curve are those in the first and fifth columns of the table in Figure A1.8. For example, if the temperature is 90°F, 10 gallons of ice cream are consumed when the price is $3.25 a scoop.

We can also show the relationship between ice cream consumption and temperature while the price of ice cream remains constant, as shown in Figure A1.8(b). The curve labeled $3.25 shows how the consumption of ice cream varies with the temperature when the price of ice cream is $3.25 a scoop. The numbers used to plot that curve are those in the sixth row of the table in Figure A1.8. For example, at $3.25 a scoop, 10 gallons of ice cream are consumed when the temperature is 90°F.

Figure A1.8(c) shows the effect of a change in temperature on the relationship between the quantity of ice cream consumed and the price of ice cream. The blue curve labeled 90°F is the same as the curve in Figure A1.8(a). It is the relationship between the price of ice cream and the quantity consumed on a hot day. The red curve labeled 70°F shows the relationship between the price of ice cream and the quantity consumed on a cooler day when the temperature is 70°F.

On each curve in Figure A1.8(c), "other things remain the same" as the price of ice cream and the quantity consumed change. When other things don't remain the same and the termperature changes, the relationship between the price of ice cream and the quantity consumed changes and the curve shifts. You will encounter this type of shifting relationship at many points in your economics course.

With what you've learned about graphs in this Appendix, you can move forward with your study of economics. There are no graphs in this textbook that are more complicated than the ones you've studied here.

## ■ FIGURE A1.8

### Graphing a Relationship Among Three Variables

| Price (dollars per scoop) | Ice cream consumption (gallons per day) | | | |
|---|---|---|---|---|
| | 30°F | 50°F | 70°F | 90°F |
| 2.00 | 12 | 18 | 25 | 50 |
| 2.25 | 10 | 12 | 18 | 37 |
| 2.50 | 7 | 10 | 13 | 27 |
| 2.75 | 5 | 7 | 10 | 20 |
| 3.00 | 3 | 5 | 7 | 14 |
| **3.25** | 2 | 3 | 5 | **10** |
| 3.50 | 1 | 2 | 3 | 6 |

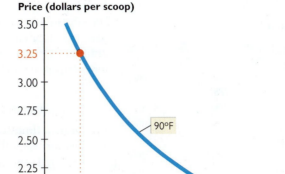

(a) Price and consumption at a given temperature

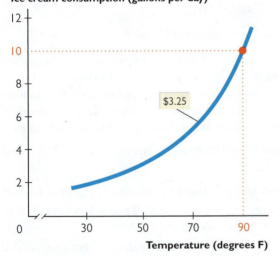

(b) Temperature and consumption of ice cream at a given price

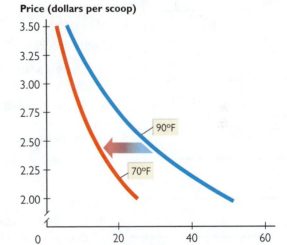

(c) A change in temperature shifts the curve

The table shows the quantity of ice cream consumed at different prices and different temperatures. For example, if the price is $3.25 a scoop and the temperature is 90°F, 10 gallons of ice cream are consumed. This set of values is highlighted in the table and in parts (a) and (b).

Part (a) shows the relationship between the price and consumption when the temperature is 90°F. The negative slope means that a higher price brings lower consumption.

Part (b) shows the relationship between the temperature and consumption when price is $3.25 a scoop. The positive slope means that a higher temperature brings greater consumption

Part (c) shows the change in the relationship between price and consumption when the temperature falls from 90°F to 70°F.

## APPENDIX CHECKPOINT

## Study Plan Problems

The spreadsheet in Table 1 provides data on the U.S. economy: Column A is the year; the other columns are quantities sold in millions per year of compact discs (column B), music videos (column C), and singles downloads (column D). Use this spreadsheet to work Problems **1** and **2**.

**TABLE 1**

|   | A | B | C | D |
|---|---|---|---|---|
| 1 | 2004 | 767 | 33 | 139 |
| 2 | 2006 | 620 | 23 | 586 |
| 3 | 2008 | 385 | 13 | 1,033 |
| 4 | 2010 | 226 | 9 | 1,162 |
| 5 | 2012 | 211 | 11 | 1,392 |
| 6 | 2014 | 144 | 4 | 1,200 |

1. Draw a scatter diagram to show the relationship between the quantities sold of compact discs and music videos. Describe the relationship.

2. Draw a time-series graph of the quantity of compact discs sold. Say in which year or years the quantity sold (a) was highest, (b) was lowest, (c) increased the most, and (d) decreased the most. If the data show a trend, describe it.

**TABLE 2**

| x | 0 | 1 | 2 | 3 | 4 | 5 |
|---|---|---|---|---|---|---|
| y | 32 | 31 | 28 | 23 | 16 | 7 |

3. Is the relationship between x and y in Table 2 positive or negative? Calculate the slope of the relationship when x equals 2 and when x equals 4. How does the slope change as the value of x increases?

4. Table 3 provides data on the price of a balloon ride, the temperature, and the number of rides a day. Draw graphs to show the relationship between
   - The price and the number of rides, when the temperature is 70°F.
   - The number of rides and the temperature, when the price is $15 a ride.

**TABLE 3**

| Price (dollars per ride) | Balloon rides (number per day) | | |
|---|---|---|---|
|  | 50°F | 70°F | 90°F |
| 5 | 32 | 50 | 40 |
| 10 | 27 | 40 | 32 |
| 15 | 18 | 32 | 27 |
| 20 | 10 | 27 | 18 |

## Instructor Assignable Problems

Use the information in Table 1 to work Problems **1** and **2**.

1. Draw a scatter diagram to show the relationship between quantities sold of music videos and singles downloads. Describe the relationship.

2. Draw a time-series graph of the quantity of music videos sold. Say in which year or years the quantity sold (a) was highest, (b) was lowest, (c) decreased the most, and (d) decreased the least. If the data show a trend, describe it.

**TABLE 4**

| x | 0 | 1 | 2 | 3 | 4 | 5 |
|---|---|---|---|---|---|---|
| y | 0 | 1 | 4 | 9 | 16 | 25 |

Use the information in Table 4 on the relationship between two variables x and y to work Problems **3** and **4**.

3. Is the relationship between x and y in Table 4 positive or negative? Explain.

4. Calculate the slope of the relationship when x equals 2 and when x equals 4. How does the slope change as the value of x increases?

5. Table 5 provides data on the price of hot chocolate, the temperature, and the cups of hot chocolate bought. Draw graphs to show the relationship between
   - The price and cups of hot chocolate bought, when the temperature is constant.
   - The temperature and cups of hot chocolate bought, when the price is constant.

**TABLE 5**

| Price (dollars per cup) | Hot chocolate (cups per week) | | |
|---|---|---|---|
|  | 50°F | 70°F | 90°F |
| 2.00 | 40 | 30 | 20 |
| 2.50 | 30 | 20 | 10 |
| 3.00 | 20 | 10 | 0 |
| 3.50 | 10 | 0 | 0 |

## Key Terms

Cross-section graph, 24
Direct relationship, 26
Inverse relationship, 27
Linear relationship, 26

Negative relationship, 27
Positive relationship, 26
Scatter diagram, 24
Slope, 29

Time-series graph, 24
Trend, 24

## Who makes the Dreamliner?

# The U.S. and Global Economies

**2**

**CHAPTER CHECKLIST**

**When you have completed your study of this chapter, you will be able to**

1 Describe what, how, and for whom goods and services are produced in the United States.

2 Describe what, how, and for whom goods and services are produced in the global economy.

3 Explain the circular flow model of the U.S. economy and of the global economy.

MyEconLab **Big Picture Video**

## 2.1    WHAT, HOW, AND FOR WHOM?

Who makes the Dreamliner? Boeing, right? Not exactly right. You'll see in this chapter that 400 firms around the world produce components of this airliner.

Airplanes are one of the many millions of different goods and services produced in the United States today. To see some more, walk around a shopping mall and go inside some of the shops and check the labels to see where things are made. Some are made in the United States but many, perhaps most, are made in other countries. We're going to look at what goods and services get produced and where; how they are produced, and who gets to enjoy them. We begin with *what* we produce in the United States..

### ■ What Do We Produce?

We place the goods and services produced into two large groups:

- Consumption goods and services
- Capital goods

### Consumption Goods and Services

**Consumption goods and services**
Goods and services that individuals and governments buy and use in the current period.

**Consumption goods and services** are items that individuals and governments buy and use up in the current period. Consumption goods and services bought by households include items such as housing, automobiles, bottled water, ramen noodles, chocolate bars, Po' boy sandwiches, movies, downhill skiing lessons, and doctor and dental services. Consumption goods and services bought by governments include items such as police and fire services, garbage collection, and education.

### Capital Goods

**Capital goods**
Goods bought by businesses and governments to increase productive resources and to use over future periods to produce other goods and services.

**Capital goods** are goods that businesses and governments buy to increase productive resources to use during future periods to produce other goods and services. Capital goods bought by businesses include items such as auto assembly lines, shopping malls, airplanes, and oil tankers. Capital goods bought by governments include missiles and weapons systems for national security, public schools and universities, and interstate highways.

Consumption goods and services represent 78.5 percent of U.S. production by value and that percentage doesn't fluctuate much. *Eye on the U.S. Economy* on p. 35 breaks the goods and services down into smaller categories.

Health services is the largest category, with 19.4 percent of the value of total production. Real estate services come next at 14.5 percent. The main components of this item are the services of rental and owner-occupied housing. Professional and business services, which include the services of accountants and lawyers, are 13.2 percent of total production. Other large components of services are education and retail and wholesale trades.

The manufacture of goods represents only 12.1 percent of total production and the largest category of goods produced, chemicals, accounts for less than 2 percent of total production.

Construction accounts for 3.7 percent of production, and utilities, mining, and agriculture together make up only 5.7 percent. The nation's farms produce only a bit more than 1 percent of total production.

# EYE on the U.S. ECONOMY
## What We Produce

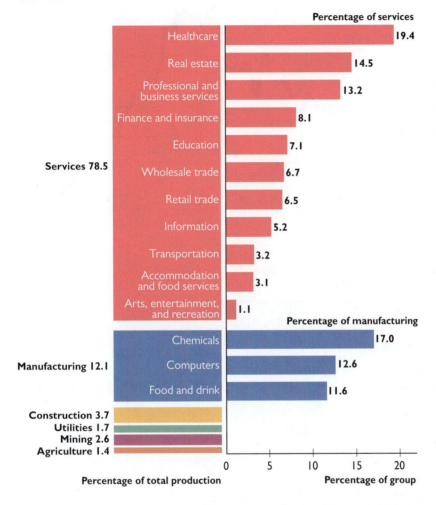

**Percentage of services**

| | |
|---|---|
| Healthcare | 19.4 |
| Real estate | 14.5 |
| Professional and business services | 13.2 |
| Finance and insurance | 8.1 |
| Education | 7.1 |
| Wholesale trade | 6.7 |
| Retail trade | 6.5 |
| Information | 5.2 |
| Transportation | 3.2 |
| Accommodation and food services | 3.1 |
| Arts, entertainment, and recreation | 1.1 |

Services 78.5

**Percentage of manufacturing**

| | |
|---|---|
| Chemicals | 17.0 |
| Computers | 12.6 |
| Food and drink | 11.6 |

Manufacturing 12.1

Construction 3.7
Utilities 1.7
Mining 2.6
Agriculture 1.4

Percentage of total production — Percentage of group

SOURCE OF DATA: Bureau of Economic Analysis.

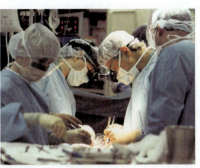

*Healthcare services, …*

*education services, …*

*and retail trades are among the largest categories of services produced.*

*Chemicals, ….*

*computer chips, …*

*and food are the largest categories of goods produced in the United States.*

# EYE on the PAST
## Changes in What We Produce

Freeport, Maine, became a shoemaking center in 1881 when the H.E. Davis Shoe Company opened its steam-powered factory in the town. Over the following years, many other shoemakers set up in Freeport and production steadily expanded. The town's shoe production peaked in 1968 after which it shrank rapidly. When the Freeport Shoe Company closed its factory in 1972, it became the fifteenth shoe factory to close in Freeport in four years. Today, the Freeport economy is based on shopping, not shoes.

Freeport's story of shoemaking was repeated across America and the figure tells this broader story. And as manufacturing has shrunk, retail and other services have expanded.

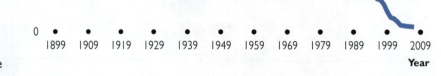

Sources of data: *Historical Statistics of the United States Millennial Edition Online* and *Statistical Abstract of the United States,* 2012.

---

## ◼ How Do We Produce?

**Factors of production**
The productive resources that are used to produce goods and services—land, labor, capital, and entrepreneurship.

Goods and services are produced by using productive resources. Economists call the productive resources **factors of production**. Factors of production are grouped into four categories:

- Land
- Labor
- Capital
- Entrepreneurship

### Land

**Land**
The "gifts of nature," or *natural resources*, that we use to produce goods and services.

In economics, **land** includes all the "gifts of nature" that we use to produce goods and services. Land is what, in everyday language, we call *natural resources*. It includes land in the everyday sense, minerals, energy, water, air, and wild plants, animals, birds, and fish. Some of these resources are renewable, and some are nonrenewable. The U.S. Geological Survey maintains a national inventory of the quantity and quality of natural resources and monitors changes to that inventory.

The United States covers almost 2 billion acres. About 45 percent of the land is forest, lakes, and national parks. In 2009, almost 50 percent of the land was used for agriculture and 5 percent was urban, but urban land use is growing and agricultural land use is shrinking.

Our land surface and water resources are renewable, and some of our mineral resources can be recycled. But many mineral resources can be used only once. They are nonrenewable resources. Of these, the United States has vast known reserves of coal, oil, and natural gas.

36

## Labor

**Labor** is the work time and work effort that people devote to producing goods and services. Labor includes the physical and mental efforts of all the people who work on farms and construction sites and in factories, shops, and offices. The Census Bureau and Bureau of Labor Statistics measure the quantity of labor at work every month.

In the United States in October 2015, 157 million people had jobs or were available for work. Some worked full time, some worked part time, and some were unemployed but looking for an acceptable vacant job. The total amount of time worked during 2015 was about 282 billion hours.

The quantity of labor increases as the adult population increases. The quantity of labor also increases if a larger percentage of the population takes jobs. During the past 50 years, a larger proportion of women have taken paid work and this trend has increased the quantity of labor. At the same time, a slightly smaller proportion of men have taken paid work and this trend has decreased the quantity of labor.

The *quality* of labor depends on how skilled people are. A laborer who can push a hand cart but can't drive a truck is much less productive than one who can drive. An office worker who can use a computer is much more productive than one who can't. Economists use a special name for human skill: human capital. **Human capital** is the knowledge and skill that people obtain from education, on-the-job training, and work experience.

You are building your own human capital right now as you work on your economics course and other subjects. Your human capital will continue to grow when you get a full-time job and become better at it. Human capital improves the *quality* of labor and increases the quantity of goods and services that labor can produce.

## Capital

**Capital** consists of the tools, instruments, machines, buildings, and other items that have been produced in the past and that businesses now use to produce goods and services. Capital includes hammers and screwdrivers, computers, auto assembly lines, office towers and warehouses, dams and power plants, airplanes, cookie factories, and shopping malls.

Capital also includes inventories of unsold goods or of partly finished goods on a production line. And capital includes what is sometimes called *infrastructure capital*, such as highways and airports.

Capital, like human capital, makes labor more productive. A truck driver can produce vastly more transportation services than someone pushing a hand cart; the Interstate highway system enables us to produce vastly more transportation services than was possible on the old highway system that preceded it.

The Bureau of Economic Analysis in the U.S. Department of Commerce keeps track of the total value of capital in the United States and how it grows over time. Today, the value of capital in the U.S. economy is around $50 trillion.

***Financial Capital Is Not Capital***   In everyday language, we talk about money, stocks, and bonds as being capital. These items are *financial capital*, and they are not productive resources. Stocks and bonds enable people to provide businesses with financial resources, but they are *not* used to produce goods and services. They are not capital.

**Labor**
The work time and work effort that people devote to producing goods and services.

**Human capital**
The knowledge and skill that people obtain from education, on-the-job training, and work experience.

**Capital**
Tools, instruments, machines, buildings, and other items that have been produced in the past and that businesses now use to produce goods and services.

# EYE on the U.S. ECONOMY

## Changes in How We Produce in the Information Economy

The information economy consists of the jobs and businesses that produce and use computers and equipment powered by computer chips. This information economy is highly visible in your daily life.

The pairs of images here illustrate two examples. In each pair, a new technology enables capital to replace labor.

The top pair of pictures illustrate the replacement of bank tellers (labor) with ATMs (capital). Although the ATM was invented almost 50 years ago, when it made its first appearance, it was located only inside banks and was not able to update customers' accounts. It is only in the last decade that ATMs have spread to corner stores and enable us to get cash and check our bank balance from almost anywhere in the world.

The bottom pair of pictures illustrate a more recent replacement of labor with capital: self-check-in. Air passengers today issue their own boarding pass, often at their own computer before leaving home. For international flights, some of these machines now

even check passport details.

The number of bank teller and airport check-in clerk jobs is shrinking, but these new technologies are

creating a whole range of new jobs for people who make, program, install, and repair the vast number of machines.

---

## Entrepreneurship

**Entrepreneurship** is the human resource that organizes land, labor, and capital to produce goods and services. Entrepreneurs are creative and imaginative. They come up with new ideas about what and how to produce, make business decisions, and bear the risks that arise from these decisions. If their ideas work out, they earn a profit. If their ideas turn out to be wrong, they bear the loss.

The quantity of entrepreneurship is hard to describe or measure. During some periods, there appears to be a great deal of imaginative entrepreneurship around. People such as Sam Walton, who created Wal-Mart, one of the world's largest retailers; Bill Gates, who founded the Microsoft empire; and Mark Zuckerberg, who founded Facebook, are examples of extraordinary entrepreneurial talent. But these highly visible entrepreneurs are just the tip of an iceberg that consists of hundreds of thousands of people who run businesses, large and small.

## ■ For Whom Do We Produce?

Who gets the goods and services depends on the incomes that people earn. A large income enables a person to buy large quantities of goods and services. A small income leaves a person with a small quantity of goods and services.

People earn their incomes by selling the services of the factors of production they own. **Rent** is paid for the use of land, **wages** are paid for the services of labor, **interest** is paid for the use of capital, and entrepreneurs receive a **profit** (or incur a **loss**) for running their businesses. What are the shares of these four factor incomes in the United States? Which factor receives the largest share?

Figure 2.1(a) answers these questions. It shows that wages were 63 percent of total income in 2014 and rent, interest, and profit were 37 percent of total income. These percentages remain remarkably constant over time. We call the distribution of income among the factors of production the *functional distribution of income*.

Figure 2.1(b) shows the *personal distribution of income*—the distribution of income among households—in 2014. Some households, like that of Clayton Kershaw, earn many millions of dollars a year. These households are in the richest 20 percent who earn 50 percent of total income. Households at the other end of the scale, like those of fast-food servers, are in the poorest 20 percent who earn only 3 percent of total income. The distribution of income has been changing and becoming more unequal. The rich have become richer. But it isn't the case, on the whole, that the poor have become poorer. They just haven't become richer as fast as the rich have.

**Rent**
Income paid for the use of land.

**Wages**
Income paid for the services of labor.

**Interest**
Income paid for the use of capital.

**Profit (or loss)**
Income earned by an entrepreneur for running a business.

■ **FIGURE 2.1**

*For Whom* in 2014                                        MyEconLab Animation

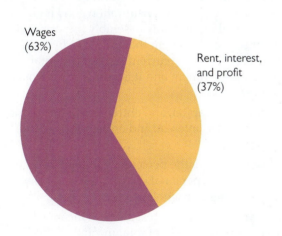

**(a) Functional distribution of income**

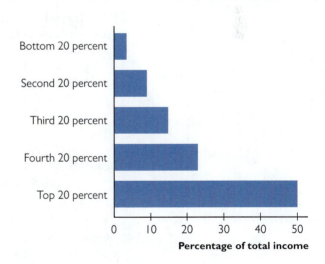

**(b) Personal distribution of income**

Sources of data: Bureau of Economic Analysis, *National Income and Product Accounts*, Table 1.10 and U.S. Census Bureau, *Income and Poverty in the United States*: 2014, Current Population Reports P60-252, 2015.

In 2014, wages (the income from labor) were **63** percent of total income. Rent, interest, and profit (the income from the services of land, capital, and entrepreneurship) totaled the remaining **37** percent.

In 2014, the 20 percent of the population with the highest incomes received **50** percent of total income. The 20 percent with the lowest incomes received only **3** percent of total income.

# CHECKPOINT 2.1

**Describe what, how, and for whom goods and services are produced in the United States.**

## Practice Problems

1. What are the types of goods and services produced? Give an example of each (different from those in the chapter) and distinguish between them.
2. Name the four factors of production and the incomes they earn.
3. Distinguish between the functional distribution of income and the personal distribution of income.
4. In the United States, which factor of production earned the largest share of income in 2014 and what percentage did it earn?

## In the News

**The frustration that drives people to become entrepreneurs**
A study by researchers at Stanford and the University of Chicago discovered that most of the people who quit their jobs and start their own business do so not because they have a billion-dollar idea but because they are frustrated in their jobs.
Source: Chad Brooks, *Business News Daily*, September 16, 2014

Why do people become entrepreneurs? What do we call the income earned by entrepreneurs? Are most people entrepreneurs? What is the factor of production supplied by people who are not entrepreneurs? What is their income called? What percentage of total income does their income represent?

## Solutions to Practice Problems

1. The goods and services produced fall into two types: consumption goods and services and capital goods. A hamburger is a consumption good and a haircut is a consumption service. An oil rig and auto assembly line are capital goods. A consumption good or service is an item that is bought by individuals or the government and is used up in the current period. A capital good is bought by businesses or the government and it is used over and over again to produce other goods and services.
2. The factors of production are land, labor, capital, and entrepreneurship. Land earns rent; labor earns wages; capital earns interest; and entrepreneurship earns profit or incurs a loss.
3. The functional distribution of income shows the percentage of total income received by each factor of production. The personal distribution of income shows how total income is shared among households.
4. Labor is the factor of production that earns the largest share of income. In 2014, labor in the United States earned 63 percent of total income.

## Solution to In the News

People become entrepreneurs because they are frustrated in their jobs. The income earned by entrepreneurs is called profit. Most people are suppliers of labor, for which they earn a wage. The data in Figure 2.1 show that wage income of labor represents 63 percent of total income.

## 2.2    THE GLOBAL ECONOMY

We're now going to look at *what, how,* and *for whom* goods and services get produced in the global economy. We'll begin with a brief overview of the people and countries that form the global economy.

### ■ The People

Visit the Web site of the U.S. Census Bureau and go to the population clocks to find out how many people there are today in both the United States and the entire world. On the day these words were written, November 8, 2015, the U.S. clock recorded a population of 322,115,000. The world clock recorded a global population of 7,284,290,000. The U.S. clock ticks along showing a population increase of one person every 15 seconds. The world clock spins faster, adding 30 people in the same 15 seconds.

### ■ The Economies

The world's 7.3 billion (and rising) population lives in 176 economies, which the International Monetary Fund classifies into two broad groups:

- Advanced economies
- Emerging market and developing economies

#### Advanced Economies

Advanced economies are the richest 29 countries (or areas). The United States, Japan, Italy, Germany, France, the United Kingdom, and Canada belong to this group. So do four new industrial Asian economies: Hong Kong, South Korea, Singapore, and Taiwan. The other advanced economies include Australia, New Zealand, and most of the rest of Western Europe. Almost 1 billion people (15 percent of the world's population) live in the advanced economies.

#### Emerging Market and Developing Economies

*Emerging market economies* are 28 countries in Central and Eastern Europe and Asia. Almost 500 million people live in these countries—about half of the number in the advanced economies. These countries are important because they are emerging (hence the name) from a system of state-owned production, central economic planning, and heavily regulated markets moving toward a system of free enterprise and unregulated markets.

*Developing economies* are the 119 countries in Africa, Asia, the Middle East, Europe, and Central and South America. More than 5.5 billion people—almost four out of every five people—live in the developing economies.

Developing economies vary enormously in size, the level of average income, and the rate of growth of production and incomes. But in all the developing economies, average incomes are much lower than those in the advanced economies, and in some cases, they are extremely low.

Five emerging market and developing economies, representing 3 billion people or 42 percent of the world's population and known as BRICS (Brazil, Russia, India, China, and South Africa), hold regular meetings to advance the interests of these nations and draw attention to their development problems.

### ■ *What* in the Global Economy

First, let's look at the big picture. Imagine that each year the global economy produces an enormous pie. In 2015, the pie was worth about $113 trillion! To give this number some meaning, if the pie were shared equally among the world's 7.3 billion people, each of us would get a slice worth a bit less than $15,500.

#### Where Is the Global Pie Baked?

Figure 2.2 shows us where in the world the pie is baked. The advanced economies produce 43 percent—16 percent in the United States, 17 percent in the European Union, and 10 percent in the other advanced economies. This 43 percent of global output (by value) is produced by 15 percent of the world's population.

The BRICS economies, highlighted in the figure, together produce 31 percent of the world's output. China, with 17 percent of world production, dominates this group and South Africa, the group's smallest member, produces barely 1 percent of global output. This 31 percent of the global pie is baked by 42 percent of the world's population.

The remaining 26 percent of the global pie comes from other emerging market and developing economies and is baked by 43 percent of the world's people.

Unlike the slices of an apple pie, those of the global pie have different fillings. Some slices have more oil, some more food, some more clothing, some more housing services, some more autos, and so on. Let's look at some of these different fillings and at some similarities too.

■ **FIGURE 2.2**

*What* in the Global Economy in 2015                                   MyEconLab Animation

If we show the value of production in the world economy as a pie, the United States produces a slice that is 16 percent of the total. The European Union produces 17 percent and other advanced economies 10 percent, so together, the advanced economies produce 43 percent of global output.

Another 31 percent of the global pie comes from the BRICS economies. China, which produces 17 percent of world output, dominates this group.

The remaining 26 percent of world output comes from other emerging market and developing economies in Africa, Asia, the Middle East, and the Western Hemisphere.

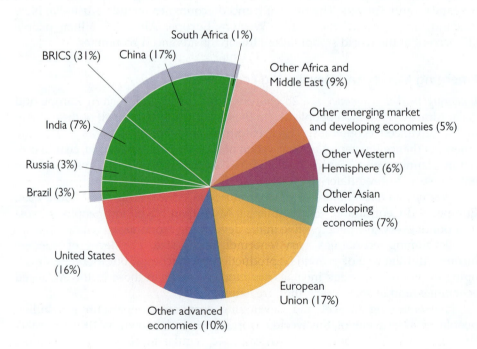

Source of data: International Monetary Fund, World Economic Outlook Database, April 2015.

# EYE on the DREAMLINER

MyEconLab Critical Thinking Exercise

## Who Makes the Dreamliner?

Boeing designed, assembles, and markets the Dreamliner, but the airplane is made by more than 400 firms on four continents that employ thousands of workers and millions of dollars' worth of specialized capital equipment. The graphic identifies some of the firms and the components they make.

Boeing and these firms make decisions and pay their workers, investors, and raw material suppliers to influence *what*, *how*, and *for whom* goods and services are produced. All these decisions are made in self-interest, and produce an airplane at the lowest possible cost.

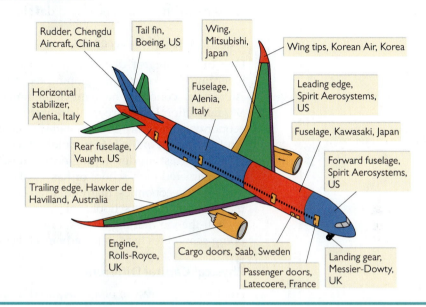

Rudder, Chengdu Aircraft, China

Tail fin, Boeing, US

Wing, Mitsubishi, Japan

Wing tips, Korean Air, Korea

Horizontal stabilizer, Alenia, Italy

Fuselage, Alenia, Italy

Leading edge, Spirit Aerosystems, US

Fuselage, Kawasaki, Japan

Rear fuselage, Vaught, US

Forward fuselage, Spirit Aerosystems, US

Trailing edge, Hawker de Havilland, Australia

Engine, Rolls-Royce, UK

Cargo doors, Saab, Sweden

Landing gear, Messier-Dowty, UK

Passenger doors, Latecoere, France

## Some Differences in What Is Produced

What is produced in the developing economies contrasts sharply with that of the advanced economies. Manufacturing is the big story. Developing economies have large and growing industries, which produce textiles, footwear, sports gear, toys, electronic goods, furniture, steel, and even automobiles and airplanes.

Food production is a small part of the U.S. and other advanced economies and a large part of the developing economies such as Brazil, China, and India. But the advanced economies produce about one third of the world's food. How can this be? *Total* production is much larger in the advanced economies than in the developing economies, but a small percentage of a big number can be a *greater amount* than a large percentage of a small number!

## Some Similarities in What Is Produced

If you were to visit a shopping mall in Canada, England, Australia, Japan, or any of the other advanced economies, you would wonder whether you had left the United States. You would see Starbucks, Burger King, Pizza Hut, Domino's Pizza, KFC, Kmart, Wal-Mart, Target, Gap, Tommy Hilfiger, Lululemon, Banana Republic, the upscale Louis Vuitton and Burberry, and a host of other familiar names. And, of course, you would see McDonald's golden arches. You would see them in any of the 119 countries in which one or more of McDonald's 30,000 restaurants are located.

The similarities among the advanced economies go beyond the view from main street and the shopping mall. The structure of *what* is produced is similar in these economies. As percentages of the total economy, agriculture and manufacturing are small and shrinking whereas services are large and expanding.

*McDonald's in Shanghai.*

## ■ *How* in the Global Economy

Goods and services are produced using land, labor, capital, and entrepreneurial resources, and the combinations of these resources used are chosen to produce at the lowest possible cost. Each country or region has its own blend of factors of production, but there are some interesting common patterns and crucial differences between the advanced and developing economies that we'll now examine.

### Human Capital Differences

One of the biggest distinguishing features of an advanced economy from an emerging market or developing economy is its quantity of *human capital*. Advanced economies have much higher levels of human capital.

Education levels are the handiest measure of human capital. In an advanced economy such as the United States, almost everyone has completed high school. And 30 percent of the U.S. population has completed 4 years or more of college.

In contrast, in developing economies, the proportion of the population who has completed high school or has a college degree is small. In the poorest of the developing economies, many children even miss out on basic primary education—they just don't go to school at all.

On-the-job training and experience are also much less extensive in the developing economies than in the advanced economies.

### Physical Capital Differences

Another major feature of an advanced economy that differentiates it from a developing economy is the amount of capital available for producing goods and services. The differences begin with the basic transportation systems. In the advanced economies, a well-developed highway system connects all the major cities and points of production. Open a map app on your phone. Contrast the U.S. interstate highway system in Texas with the sparse highways of Mexico. You would see a similar contrast if you swiped across the Atlantic Ocean and checked out the highway structures in Western Europe and Africa.

But it isn't the case that the developing economies have no highways and no modern trucks and cars. In fact, some of them have the newest and the best. But the new and best are usually inside and around the major cities—see *Eye on the Global Economy* on p. 45.

The contrasts in the transportation system are matched by those on farms and in factories. In general, the more advanced the economy, the greater are the amount and sophistication of the capital equipment used in production. But again, the contrast is not all or nothing. Some factories in India, China, and other parts of Asia use the very latest technologies. Furniture manufacturing is an example. To make furniture of a quality that Americans are willing to buy, firms in Asia use machines like those in the furniture factories of North Carolina.

The differences in human capital and physical capital between advanced and developing economies have a big effect on *who* gets the goods and services, which we'll now examine.

## ■ *For Whom* in the Global Economy

Who gets the world's goods and services depends on the incomes that people earn. We're now going to see how incomes are distributed within economies and across the world.

# EYE on the GLOBAL ECONOMY
## Differences in How We Produce

Big differences exist in how goods and services are produced and the images here illustrate three examples.

Laundry services (top), transportation services (center), and highway systems (bottom) can use a large amount of capital and almost no labor (left) or use almost no capital and a large amount of labor (right).

Capital-intensive automatic laundry equipment, big trucks, and multi-lane paved freeways are common in advanced economies but rare in poorer developing economies.

Riverside clothes washing, human pedal power, and unsealed dirt tracks are seen only in developing economies.

But we also see huge differences even within a developing economy. The bottom pictures contrast Beijing's capital-intensive highway system with the unpaved and sometimes hazardous roads of rural China.

## Personal Distribution of Income

You saw earlier (on p. 39) that in the United States, the lowest-paid 20 percent of the population receives 3 percent of total income and the highest-paid 20 percent receives 50 percent of total income. The personal distribution of income in the world economy is much more unequal. According to World Bank data, the lowest-paid 20 percent of the world's population receives 2 percent of world income and the highest-paid 20 percent receives about 70 percent of world income.

## International Distribution

Much of the greater inequality at the global level arises from differences in average incomes among countries. Figure 2.3 shows some of these differences. It shows the dollar value of what people can afford each day on average. You can see that in the United States, that number is $153 a day—an average person in the United States can buy goods and services that cost $153. This amount is around five times the world average. The European Union has an average income of around two thirds that of the United States at $104 per day. Income levels fall off quickly as we move farther down the graph, with Russia at $65 a day, China $39 a day, India $17 a day, and Africa only $11 a day.

As people have lost well-paid manufacturing jobs and found lower-paid service jobs, inequality has increased in the United States and in most other advanced economies. Inequality is also increasing in the developing economies. People with skills enjoy rapidly rising incomes but the incomes of the unskilled are falling.

### A Happy Paradox and a Huge Challenge

Despite the increase in inequality inside most countries, inequality across the entire world has decreased during the past 20 years. And most important, according to Xavier Sala-i-Martin, an economics professor at Columbia University, extreme poverty has declined. Professor Sala-i-Martin estimates that between 1976 and 1998, the number of people who earn $1 a day or less fell by 235 million and the number who earn $2 a day or less fell by 450 million. This positive situation arises because in China, the largest nation, incomes have increased rapidly and lifted millions from extreme poverty. Incomes are growing quickly in India too.

Lifting Africa from poverty is today's big challenge. In 1960, 11 percent of the world's poor lived in Africa, but in 1998, 66 percent did. Between 1976 and 1998, the number of people in Africa who earn $1 a day or less rose by 175 million, and the number who earn $2 a day or less rose by 227 million.

■ **FIGURE 2.3**

*For Whom* in the Global Economy in 2015                    MyEconLab Animation

In 2015, the average income per person per day in the United States was $153. It was $104 in the European Union and $65 in Russia. The number falls to $39 in China, $17 in India, and $11 in Africa.

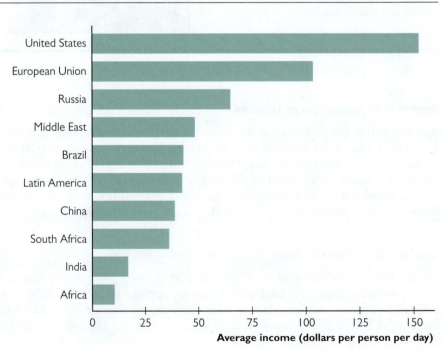

SOURCE OF DATA: International Monetary Fund, World Economic Outlook Database, October 2015.

# EYE on YOUR LIFE
## The U.S. and Global Economies in Your Life

MyEconLab Critical Thinking Exercise

You've encountered a lot of facts and trends about what, how, and for whom goods and services are produced in the U.S. economy and the global economy. How can you use this information? You can use it in two ways:

1. To inform your choice of career
2. To inform your stand on the politics of protecting U.S. jobs

### Career Choices

As you think about your future career, you are now better informed about some of the key trends. You know that manufacturing is shrinking.

The U.S. economy is what is sometimes called a *post-industrial economy*. Industries that provided the backbone of the economy in previous generations have fallen to barely a fifth of

the economy today, and the trend continues. It is possible that by the middle of the current century, manufacturing will be as small a source of jobs as agriculture is today.

So, a job in a manufacturing business is likely to lead to some tough situations and possibly the need for several job changes over a working life.

As manufacturing shrinks, so services expand, and this expansion will continue. The provision of healthcare, education, communication, wholesale and retail trades, and entertainment are all likely to expand in the future and be sources of increasing employment and rising wages. A job in a service-oriented business is more likely to lead to steady advances in income.

### Political Stand on Job Protection

As you think about the stand you will take on the political question of protecting U.S. jobs, you are better informed about the basic facts and trends.

When you hear that manufacturing jobs are disappearing to China, you will be able to place that news in historical perspective. You might reasonably be concerned, especially if you or a member of your family has lost a job. But you know that trying to reverse or even halt this process is flying in the face of stubborn historical trends.

In later chapters, you will learn that there are good economic reasons to be skeptical about any form of protection and placing limits on competition.

---

 ## CHECKPOINT 2.2

MyEconLab Study Plan 2.2
Solutions Video

Describe what, how, and for whom goods and services are produced in the global economy.

## Practice Problems

1. Describe what, how, and for whom goods and services are produced in developing economies.

2. A Clinton Foundation success story is that it loaned $23,000 to Rwandan coffee growers to support improvements to coffee washing stations and provided technical support. What was the source of the success?

## Solutions to Practice Problems

1. In developing countries, agriculture is the largest percentage, manufacturing is an increasing percentage, and services are a small percentage of total production. Most production does not use modern capital-intensive technologies, but some industries do. People who work in factories have rising incomes while those who work in rural industries are left behind.

2. The technical support allowed Rwandan coffee growers to improve their knowledge of coffee farming, which increased their human capital. The improvements to washing stations was a change in physical capital that allowed farmers to increase the quantity of washed coffee.

MyEconLab Concept Video

**Circular flow model**
A model of the economy that shows the circular flow of expenditures and incomes that result from decision makers' choices and the way those choices interact to determine what, how, and for whom goods and services are produced.

**Households**
Individuals or groups of people living together.

**Firms**
The institutions that organize the production of goods and services.

**Market**
Any arrangement that brings buyers and sellers together and enables them to get information and do business with each other.

**Goods markets**
Markets in which goods and services are bought and sold.

**Factor markets**
Markets in which the services of factors of production are bought and sold.

## 2.3 THE CIRCULAR FLOWS

We can organize the data you've just studied using the **circular flow model**—a model of the economy that shows the circular flow of expenditures and incomes that result from decision makers' choices and the way those choices interact to determine what, how, and for whom goods and services are produced. Figure 2.4 shows the circular flow model.

### ■ Households and Firms

**Households** are individuals or groups of people living together. The 124 million households in the United States own the factors of production—land, labor, capital, and entrepreneurship—and choose the quantities of these resources to provide to firms. Households also choose the quantities of goods and services to buy.

**Firms** are the institutions that organize the production of goods and services. The 28 million firms in the United States choose the quantities of the factors of production to hire and the quantities of goods and services to produce.

### ■ Markets

Households choose the quantities of the factors of production to provide to firms, and firms choose the quantities of the services of the factors of production to hire. Firms choose the quantities of goods and services to produce, and households choose the quantities of goods and services to buy. How are these choices coordinated and made compatible? The answer is: by markets.

A **market** is any arrangement that brings buyers and sellers together and enables them to get information and do business with each other. An example is the market in which oil is bought and sold—the world oil market. The world oil market is not a place. It is the network of oil producers, oil users, wholesalers, and brokers who buy and sell oil. In the world oil market, decision makers do not meet physically. They make deals by telephone, fax, and the Internet.

Figure 2.4 identifies two types of markets: goods markets and factor markets. Goods and services are bought and sold in **goods markets**; and the services of factors of production are bought and sold in **factor markets**.

### ■ Real Flows and Money Flows

When households choose the quantities of services of land, labor, capital, and entrepreneurship to offer in factor markets, they respond to the incomes they receive—rent for land, wages for labor, interest for capital, and profit for entrepreneurship. When firms choose the quantities of factor services to hire, they respond to the rent, wages, interest, and profits they must pay to households.

Similarly, when firms choose the quantities of goods and services to produce and offer for sale in goods markets, they respond to the amounts that they receive from the expenditures that households make. And when households choose the quantities of goods and services to buy, they respond to the amounts they must pay to firms.

Figure 2.4 shows the flows that result from these choices made by households and firms. The flows shown in orange are *real flows:* the flows of the factors of production that go from households through factor markets to firms and of the goods and services that go from firms through goods markets to households. The flows in the opposite direction are *money flows:* the flows of payments made in exchange for the services of factors of production (shown in blue) and of expenditures on goods and services (shown in red).

Lying behind these real flows and money flows are millions of individual choices about what to consume and what and how to produce. These choices result in buying plans by households and selling plans by firms in goods markets. And the choices result in selling plans by households and buying plans by firms in factor markets that interact to determine the prices that people pay and the incomes they earn, and so determine for whom goods and services are produced. You'll learn in Chapter 4 how markets coordinate the buying plans and selling plans of households and firms and make them compatible.

Firms produce most of the goods and services that we consume, but governments provide some of the services that we enjoy. Governments also play a big role in modifying for whom goods and services are produced by changing the personal distribution of income. We're now going to look at the role of governments in the U.S. economy and add them to the circular flow model.

**FIGURE 2.4**

The Circular Flow Model

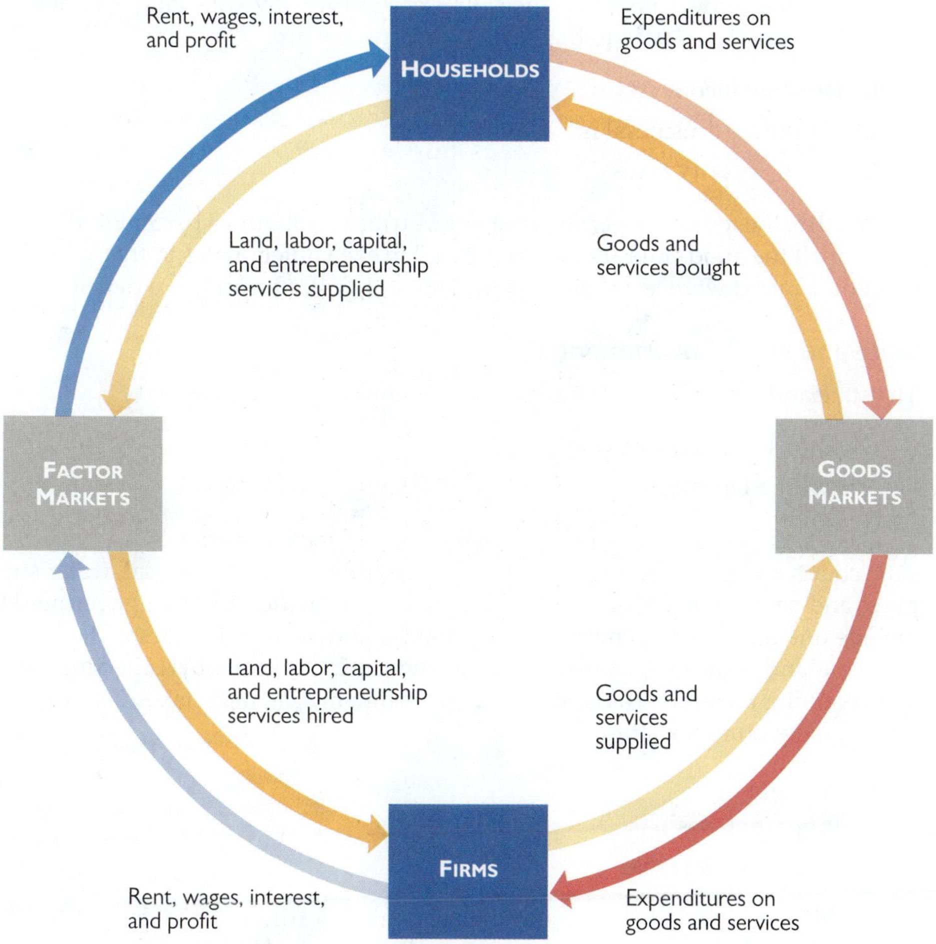

The orange flows are the services of factors of production that go from households through factor markets to firms and the goods and services that go from firms through goods markets to households. These flows are *real* flows.

The blue flow is the income earned by the factors of production, and the red flow is the expenditures on goods and services. These flows are *money* flows.

The choices that generate these real and money flows determine *what*, *how*, and *for whom* goods and services are produced.

## ■ Governments

More than 86,000 organizations operate as governments in the United States. Some are tiny like the Yuma, Arizona, school district and some are enormous like the U.S. federal government. We divide governments into two levels:

- Federal government
- State and local government

### Federal Government

The federal government's major expenditures provide

1. Goods and services
2. Social Security and welfare payments
3. Transfers to state and local governments

The goods and services provided by the federal government include the legal system, which protects property and enforces contracts, and national defense. Social Security and welfare benefits, which include income for retired people and programs such as Medicare and Medicaid, are transfers from the federal government to households. Federal government transfers to state and local governments are payments designed to provide more equality across the states and regions.

The federal government finances its expenditures by collecting a variety of taxes. The main taxes paid to the federal government are

1. Personal income taxes
2. Corporate (business) income taxes
3. Social Security taxes

In 2015, the federal government spent $4 trillion—about 23 percent of the total value of all the goods and services produced in the United States in that year. The taxes they raised were less than this amount—the government had a deficit.

### State and Local Government

The state and local governments' major expenditures are to provide

1. Goods and services
2. Welfare benefits

The goods and services provided by state and local governments include the state courts and police, schools, roads, garbage collection and disposal, water supplies, and sewage management. Welfare benefits provided by state governments include unemployment benefits and other aid to low-income families.

State and local governments finance these expenditures by collecting taxes and receiving transfers from the federal government. The main taxes paid to state and local governments are

1. Sales taxes
2. Property taxes
3. State income taxes

In 2015, state and local governments spent $2.5 trillion or 14 percent of the total value of all the goods and services produced in the United States.

## ■ Governments in the Circular Flow

Figure 2.5 adds governments to the circular flow model. As you study this figure, first notice that the outer circle is the same as in Figure 2.4. In addition to these flows, governments buy goods and services from firms. The red arrows that run from governments through the goods markets to firms show this expenditure.

Households and firms pay taxes to governments. The green arrows running directly from households and firms to governments show these flows. Also, governments make money payments to households and firms. The green arrows running directly from governments to households and firms show these flows. Taxes and transfers are direct transactions with governments and do not go through the goods markets and factor markets.

Not part of the circular flow and not visible in Figure 2.5, governments provide the legal framework within which all transactions occur. For example, governments operate the courts and legal system that enable contracts to be written and enforced.

■ **FIGURE 2.5**

Governments in the Circular Flow

MyEconLab Animation

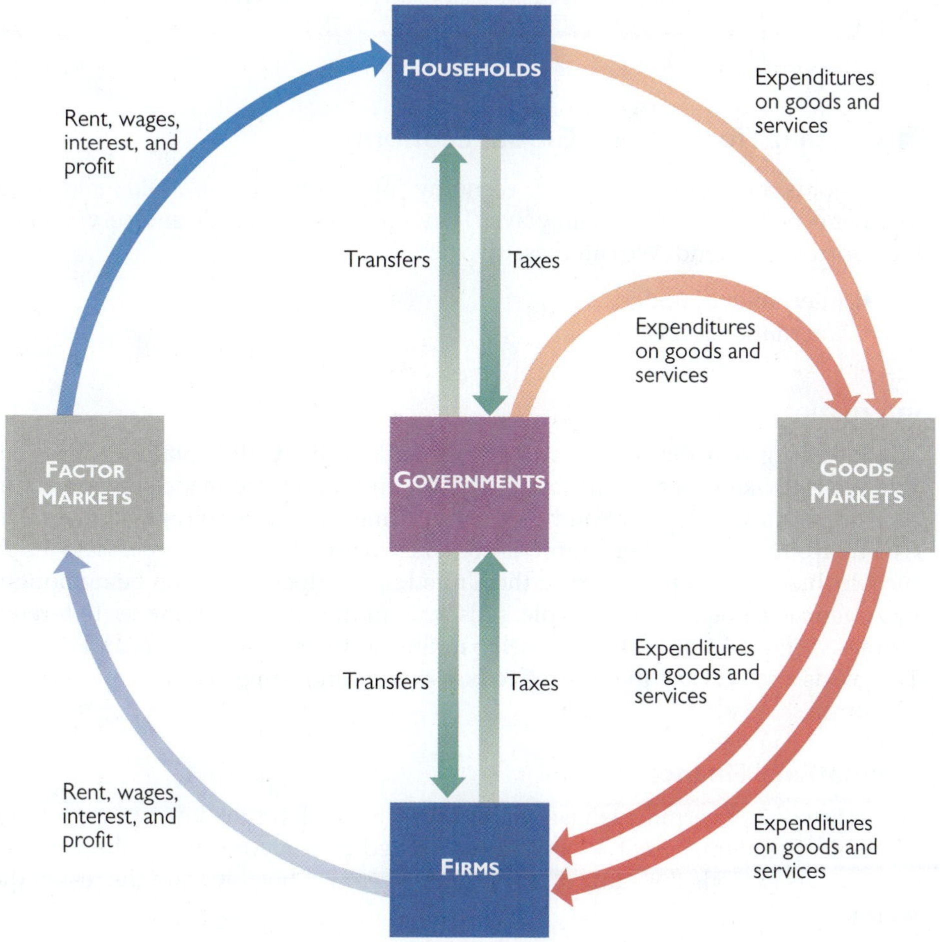

The green flows from households and firms to governments are taxes, and the green flows from governments to households and firms are money transfers.

The red flow from governments through the goods markets to firms is the expenditure on goods and services by governments.

# EYE on the PAST
## Growing Government

One hundred years ago in 1915, the federal government spent 2 cents out of each dollar earned. Today, the federal government spends 20 cents. Government grew during the two world wars and during the 1960s and 1970s as social programs expanded.

Only during the 1980s and 1990s did big government begin to shrink in a process begun by Ronald Reagan and continued by Bill Clinton. But 9-11 saw the start of a new era of growing government. Fiscal stimulus and bailouts to cope with the global financial crisis sent government spending soaring.

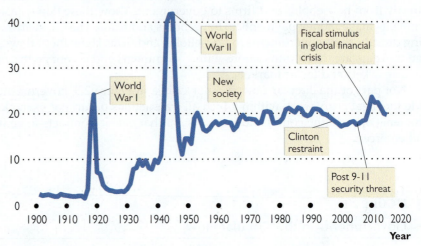

SOURCE OF DATA: Budget of the United States Government, Historical Tables, Table 1.1.

## ◼ Circular Flows in the Global Economy

Households and firms in the U.S. economy interact with households and firms in other economies in two main ways: They buy and sell goods and services and they borrow and lend. We call these two activities

- International trade
- International finance

### International Trade

Many of the goods that you buy were not made in the United States. Your iPod, Wii games, Nike shoes, smartphone, T-shirt, and bike were made somewhere in Asia or possibly Europe or South or Central America. The goods and services that we buy from firms in other countries are U.S. *imports.*

Much of what is produced in the United States doesn't end up being bought by Americans. Boeing, for example, sells most of the airplanes it makes to foreign airlines. The banks of Wall Street sell banking services to Europeans and Asians. The goods and services that we sell to households and firms in other countries are U.S. *exports.*

### International Finance

When firms or governments want to borrow, they look for the lowest interest rate available. Sometimes, that is outside the United States. Also, when the value of our imports exceeds the value of our exports, we must borrow from the rest of the world.

Firms and governments in the rest of the world behave in the same way. They look for the lowest interest rate at which to borrow and the highest at which to lend. They might borrow from or lend to Americans.

Figure 2.6 shows the flows through goods markets and financial markets in the global economy. Households and firms in the U.S. economy interact with those in the rest of the world (other economies) in goods markets and financial markets.

The red flow shows the expenditure by Americans on imports of goods and services, and the blue flow shows the expenditure by the rest of the world on U.S. exports (other countries' imports). The green flow shows U.S. lending to the rest of the world, and the orange flow shows U.S. borrowing from the rest of the world.

It is these international trade and international finance flows that tie nations together in the global economy and through which global booms and slumps are transmitted.

### ■ FIGURE 2.6

## Circular Flows in the Global Economy

U.S. lending

U.S. Economy

Expenditure on U.S. imports

U.S. borrowing

Expenditure on U.S. exports

FINANCIAL MARKETS

GOODS MARKETS

U.S. borrowing

Expenditure on U.S. exports

U.S. lending

REST OF WORLD ECONOMY

Expenditure on U.S. imports

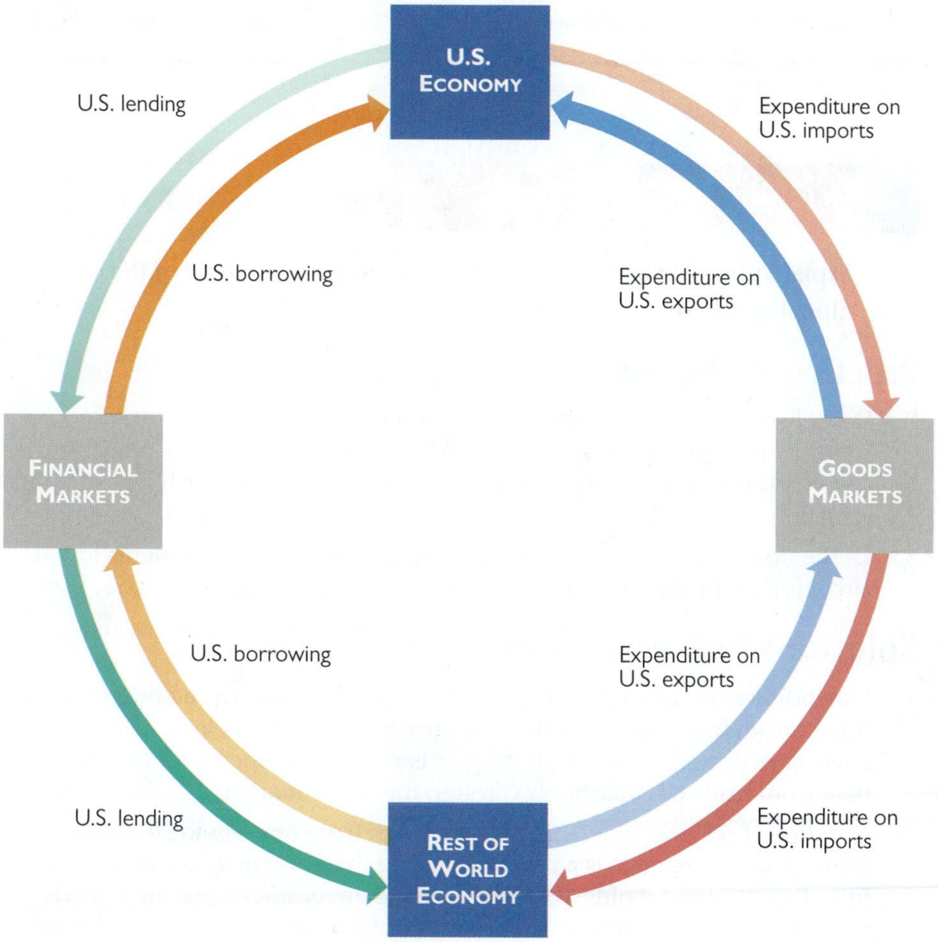

Households and firms in the U.S. economy interact with those in the rest of the world (other economies) in goods markets and financial markets.

The red flow shows the expenditure by Americans on imports of goods and services, and the blue flow shows the expenditure by the rest of the world on U.S. exports (other countries' imports).

The green flow shows U.S. lending to the rest of the world, and the orange flow shows U.S. borrowing from the rest of the world.

# EYE on the GLOBAL ECONOMY
## The Ups and Downs in International Trade

International trade expanded rapidly after China became a powerful player in the global economy.

At an average growth rate of close to 7 percent a year, world trade has doubled every decade and increased as a percentage of world production.

A mini-recession in 2001 slowed the growth in world trade to a crawl and the 2009 global recession reduced world trade.

After the recession of 2009, world trade bounced back to 27 percent of global production, where it remained in 2015.

**Global international trade (percentage of world GDP)**

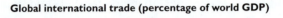
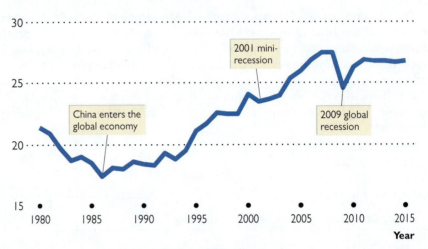

SOURCE OF DATA: International Monetary Fund, World Economic Outlook Database, October 2015.

# CHECKPOINT 2.3

**Explain the circular flow model of the U.S. economy and of the global economy.**

## Practice Problems

1. Describe the flows in the circular flow model in which expenditure on consumption goods and services, purchases of new national defense equipment, and payments for labor services appear. Through which market does each flow pass?

2. Of the flows that run between households, firms, and governments in the circular flow model, which ones are real flows and which are money flows?

## Solutions to Practice Problems

1. Expenditure on consumption goods and services flows from households to firms through the goods market. Purchases of national defense flow from governments to firms through the goods market. Payments for labor services flow from firms to households through the factor market.

2. The flow of services of factors of production from households to firms through factor markets is a real flow, as are the flows of goods and services from firms to households and from firms to governments through goods markets. The money flows are the flows of factor incomes, household and government expenditures on goods and services, taxes, and transfers.

**CHAPTER SUMMARY**

## Key Points

1. **Describe what, how, and for whom goods and services are produced in the United States.**

   - Consumption goods and services represent 85 percent of total production; capital goods represent 15 percent.
   - Goods and services are produced by using the four factors of production: land, labor, capital, and entrepreneurship.
   - The incomes people earn (rent for land, wages for labor, interest for capital, and profit for entrepreneurship) determine who gets the goods and services produced.

2. **Describe what, how, and for whom goods and services are produced in the global economy.**

   - Forty-three percent of the world's production (by value) comes from the advanced industrial countries and 57 percent comes from the emerging market and developing economies.
   - Production in the advanced economies uses more capital (both machines and human), but some developing economies use the latest capital and technologies.
   - The global distribution of income is more unequal than the U.S. distribution. Poverty has fallen in Asia, but it has increased in Africa.

3. **Explain the circular flow model of the U.S. economy and of the global economy.**

   - The circular flow model of the U.S. economy shows the real flows of factors of production and goods and the corresponding money flows of incomes and expenditures.
   - Governments in the circular flow receive taxes, make transfers, and buy goods and services.
   - The circular flow model of the global economy shows the flows of U.S. exports and imports and the international financial flows that result from lending to and borrowing from other countries.

## Key Terms

MyEconLab Key Terms Quiz

| | | |
|---|---|---|
| Capital, 37 | Factors of production, 36 | Labor, 37 |
| Capital goods, 34 | Firms, 48 | Land, 36 |
| Circular flow model, 48 | Goods markets, 48 | Market, 48 |
| Consumption goods and services, 34 | Households, 48 | Profit (or loss), 39 |
| Entrepreneurship, 38 | Human capital, 37 | Rent, 39 |
| Factor markets, 48 | Interest, 39 | Wages, 39 |

MyEconLab Chapter 2 Study Plan

# CHAPTER CHECKPOINT

## Study Plan Problems and Applications

1. Which of the following items are *not* consumption goods and services? Explain why not.
   - A chocolate bar
   - A ski lift
   - A golf ball

2. Which of the following items are *not* capital goods? Explain why not.
   - An auto assembly line
   - A shopping mall
   - A golf ball

3. Which of the following items are *not* factors of production? Explain why not.
   - Vans used by a baker to deliver bread
   - 1,000 shares of Amazon.com stock
   - Undiscovered oil in the Arctic Ocean

4. Which factor of production earns the highest percentage of total U.S. income? Define that factor of production. What is the income earned by this factor of production called?

5. With more job training and more scholarships to poor American students, which special factor of production is likely to grow faster than in the past?

6. Define the factor of production called capital. Give three examples of capital, different from those in the chapter. Distinguish between the factor of production capital and financial capital.

7. The pace at which new businesses are created in the U.S. economy and the percentage of U.S. jobs in young firms has fallen.

   > Ryan Decker and others, "The Role of Entrepreneurship in U.S. Job Creation and Economic Dynamism."
   > *Journal of Economic Perspectives*, 2014.

   Explain how you would expect these facts to influence *what, how,* and *for whom* goods and services are produced in the United States.

8. In the circular flow model, explain the real flow and/or the money flow in which each item in List 1 belongs. Illustrate your answers on a circular flow diagram.

9. **Why you can get a free college education in Germany but not in California** Even American students can get a free college degree in Germany, where high taxes pay for colleges. Despite college being free, fewer students in Germany earn college degrees than in the United States and more enter vocational apprenticeships.

   > Source: *Los Angeles Times*, October 29, 2015

   If California adopted the German model of higher education, how would that change *for whom* goods and services are produced?

10. Read *Eye on the Dreamliner* on p. 43 and then answer the following questions:
    - How many firms are involved in the production of the Dreamliner and how many are identified in the figure on p. 43?
    - Is the Dreamliner a capital good or a consumption good? Explain why.
    - State the factors of production that make the Dreamliner and provide an example of each.
    - Explain how the production of the Dreamliner influences *what, how,* and *for whom* goods and services are produced.
    - Use a diagram to show where in the circular flow model of the global economy the flows of the components listed on p. 43 appear and where the sales of Dreamliners appear.

---

**LIST 1**

- You buy a coffee at Starbucks.
- The government buys some Dell computers.
- A student works at a FedEx office.
- Donald Trump rents a building to Marriott hotels.
- You pay your income tax.

## Instructor Assignable Problems and Applications

MyEconLab Homework, Quiz, or Test if assigned by instructor

**1.** Boeing's Dreamliner has had a rocky start.
- Why doesn't Boeing manufacture all the components of the Dreamliner at its own factory in the United States?
- Describe some of the changes in *what, how,* and *for whom* that would occur if Boeing manufactured all the components of the Dreamliner at its own factories in the United States.
- State some of the tradeoffs that Boeing faces in making the Dreamliner.
- Why might Boeing's decisions in making the Dreamliner be in the social interest?

**2.** The global economy has seen a fall in the number of landlines and rapid growth in the number of smartphones. In the United States, 41 percent of households have no landline and 90 percent have a smartphone. In Africa, 33 percent have a smartphone. Describe the changes in *what, how,* and *for whom* telecommunication services are produced in the global economy.

**3.** Which of the entries in List 1 are consumption goods and services? Explain your choice.

**4.** Which of the entries in List 1 are capital goods? Explain your choice.

**5.** Which of the entries in List 1 are factors of production? Explain your choice.

**6.** In the African nation of Senegal, to enroll in school a child needs a birth certificate that costs $25. This price is several weeks' income for many families. Explain how this requirement is likely to affect the growth of human capital in Senegal.

**7. China's income gap widens**
The income gap has widened in China. In 2014, the pay of workers in the coastal regions increased by 9.7 percent while that of workers in the inland regions grew by 9 percent.
Source: *South China Morning Post,* May 28, 2015

Explain how the distribution of personal income in China can be getting more unequal even though the poorest are getting richer.

**8.** Compare the scale of agricultural production in the advanced and developing economies. In which is the percentage higher? In which is the total amount produced greater?

**9.** On a diagram of the circular flow model, indicate in which real or money flow each entry in List 2 belongs.

Use the following information to work Problems **10** and **11**.

**Poor India makes millionaires at fastest pace**
India, with the world's largest population of poor people, also paradoxically created millionaires at the fastest pace in the world. Millionaires increased by 22.7 percent to 123,000. In contrast, the number of Indians living on less than a dollar a day is 350 million and those living on less than $2 a day is 700 million. In other words, there are 7,000 very poor Indians for every millionaire.
Source: *The Times of India,* June 25, 2008

**10.** How is the personal distribution of income in India changing?

**11.** Why might incomes of $1 a day and $2 a day underestimate the value of the goods and services that these households actually consume?

**LIST 1**
- An interstate highway
- An airplane
- A school teacher
- A stealth bomber
- A garbage truck
- A pack of bubble gum
- President of the United States
- A strawberry field
- A movie
- An ATM

**LIST 2**
- General Motors pays its workers wages.
- IBM pays a dividend to its stockholders.
- You buy your groceries.
- Southwest rents some aircraft.
- Nike pays Serena Williams for promoting its sports shoes.

## Multiple Choice Quiz

**1.** Which of the following classifications is correct?

  A. City streets are consumption goods because they wear out with use.

  B. Stocks are capital goods because when people buy and sell them they make a profit.

  C. The coffee maker in the coffee shop at an airport is a consumption good because people buy the coffee it produces.

  D. White House security is a government service because it is paid for by the government.

**2.** Which of the following statements about U.S. production is correct?

  A. Construction accounts for a larger percentage of total production than does manufacturing.

  B. Real estate services account for 14.5 percent of the value of total production, larger than any other item of services or goods.

  C. Consumption goods and services represent 78.5 percent of U.S. production by value and that percentage doesn't fluctuate much.

  D. The manufacture of goods represents more than 50 percent of total production.

**3.** Which of the following items is *not* a factor of production?

  A. An oil rig in the Gulf of Mexico

  B. A ski jump in Utah

  C. A bank loan to a farmer

  D. An orange grove in Florida

**4.** What is human capital?

  A. A fruit picker

  B. Unskilled labor

  C. Your professor's knowledge of economics

  D. An auto assembly line robot

**5.** Which of the following statements is correct?

  A. Labor earns wages and entrepreneurship earns bonuses.

  B. Land earns interest and capital earns rent.

  C. Entrepreneurship earns interest and capital earns profit.

  D. Capital earns interest and labor earns wages.

**6.** How are goods and services produced in the global economy?

  A. Developing countries use less human capital but just as much physical capital as advanced economies.

  B. Emerging economies use more capital-intensive technology than do developing economies.

  C. Human capital in all economies is similar.

  D. Advanced economies use less capital than developing economies.

**7.** In the circular flow model, which of the following items is a real flow?

  A. The flow of government expenditures to firms for the goods bought

  B. The flow of income from firms to households for the services of the factors of production hired

  C. The flow of U.S. borrowing from the rest of the world

  D. The flow of labor services from households to firms

Is wind power free?

# The Economic Problem

**3**

When you have completed your study of this chapter,
you will be able to

**1** Explain and illustrate the concepts of scarcity, production efficiency,
and tradeoff using the production possibilities frontier.

**2** Calculate opportunity cost.

**3** Explain what makes production possibilities expand.

**4** Explain how people gain from specialization and trade.

MyEconLab Big Picture Video

## 3.1   PRODUCTION POSSIBILITIES

The wind is free, but wind power is not: it must be produced. It is one of the vast array of goods and services produced in the nation's farms, factories, stores, offices, and construction sites. In 2015, 280 billion hours of labor equipped with $55 trillion worth of capital produced $18 trillion worth of goods and services.

Our production capability is enormous, but it is limited by our available resources and by technology. At any given time, we have fixed quantities of the factors of production and a fixed state of technology, so there is a limit to what we can produce. The economic problem is that our wants exceed what it is possible for our resources to produce.

Your task in this chapter is to study a model of the economic problem. We begin with a piece of the model that describes the limits to production, which is called the production possibilities frontier.

### ■ Production Possibilities Frontier

**Production possibilities frontier**

The boundary between the combinations of goods and services that can be produced and the combinations that cannot be produced, given the available factors of production and the state of technology.

The **production possibilities frontier** is the boundary between the combinations of goods and services that can be produced and the combinations that cannot be produced, given the available factors of production—land, labor, capital, and entrepreneurship—and the state of technology.

Although we produce millions of different goods and services, we can visualize the limits to production most easily if we look at a model economy that produces just two goods. Imagine an economy that produces only bikes and smartphones. All the land, labor, capital, and entrepreneurship available gets used to produce these two goods.

Land can be used for bike factories or smartphone factories. Labor can be trained to work as bike makers or as smartphone makers. Capital can be used for building bike or smartphone assembly lines. Entrepreneurs can put their talents to making bikes or running smartphone businesses. In every case, the more resources that are used to produce bikes, the fewer are left to produce smartphones.

Suppose that if no factors of production are allocated to producing smartphones, the maximum number of bikes that can be produced is 15 million a year. So one production possibility is no smartphones and 15 million bikes. Another possibility is to allocate sufficient resources to produce 1 million smartphones a year. But these resources must be taken from bike factories. Suppose that the economy can now produce only 14 million bikes a year. As resources are moved from producing bikes to producing smartphones, the economy produces more smartphones but fewer bikes.

The table in Figure 3.1 illustrates these two combinations of smartphones and bikes as possibilities A and B. Suppose that C, D, E, and F are other combinations of the quantities of these two goods that the economy can produce. Possibility F uses all the resources to produce 5 million smartphones a year and allocates no resources to producing bikes. These six possibilities are alternative combinations of the quantities of the two goods that the economy can produce by *using all of its resources, given the technology.*

The graph in Figure 3.1 illustrates the production possibilities frontier, *PPF*, for smartphones and bikes. Each point on the graph labeled A through F represents the possibility in the table identified by the same letter. For example, point B represents the production of 1 million smartphones and 14 million bikes. These quantities also appear in the table as possibility B.

**FIGURE 3.1**

The Production Possibilities Frontier

MyEconLab Animation

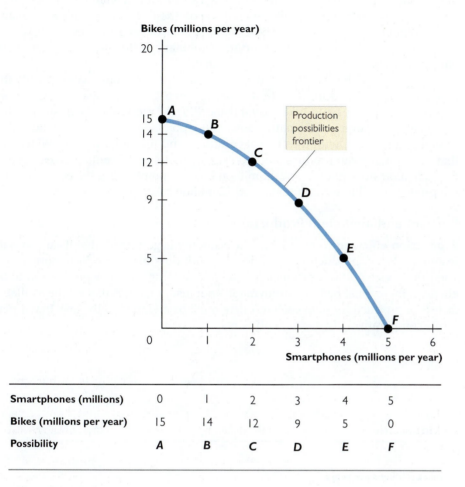

The table and the graph show the production possibilities frontier for smartphones and bikes.

Point *A* tells us that if the economy produces no smartphones, the maximum quantity of bikes it can produce is 15 million a year.

Each point *A, B, C, D, E,* and *F* on the graph represents the possibility in the table identified by the same letter.

The line passing through these points is the production possibilities frontier.

| Smartphones (millions) | 0 | 1 | 2 | 3 | 4 | 5 |
|---|---|---|---|---|---|---|
| Bikes (millions per year) | 15 | 14 | 12 | 9 | 5 | 0 |
| Possibility | **A** | **B** | **C** | **D** | **E** | **F** |

The *PPF* shows the limits to production *with the available resources and technology.* If either resources or technology change, the *PPF* shifts. If more resources or better technology become available, the *PPF* shifts outward. If resources are lost, for example in a natural disaster, the *PPF* shifts inward.

The *PPF* is a valuable tool for illustrating the effects of scarcity and its consequences. Let's see how.

## ■ How the *PPF* Illustrates Scarcity and Its Consequences

The *PPF* illustrates scarcity and some of its consequences by putting three distinctions in sharp focus. They are the distinctions between

- Attainable and unattainable combinations
- Efficient and inefficient production
- Tradeoffs and free lunches

## Attainable and Unattainable Combinations

Because the *PPF* shows the *limits* to production, it separates attainable combinations from unattainable ones. The economy can produce combinations of smartphones and bikes that are smaller than those on the *PPF*, and it can produce any of the combinations *on* the *PPF*. These combinations of smartphones and bikes are attainable. But it is impossible to produce combinations that are larger than those on the *PPF*. These combinations are unattainable.

Figure 3.2 emphasizes the attainable and unattainable combinations. Only the points on the *PPF* and inside it (in the orange area) are attainable. The combinations of smartphones and bikes beyond the *PPF* (in the white area), such as the combination at point *G*, are unattainable. These points illustrate combinations that cannot be produced with the current resources and technology. The *PPF* tells us that the economy can produce 4 million smartphones and 5 million bikes at point *E or* 2 million smartphones and 12 million bikes at point *C*. But the economy cannot produce 4 million smartphones and 12 million bikes at point *G*.

## Efficient and Inefficient Production

**Production efficiency**

A situation in which the economy is getting all that it can from its resources and cannot produce more of one good or service without producing less of something else.

**Production efficiency** occurs when the economy is getting all that it can from its resources. When production is efficient it is not possible to produce more of one good or service without producing less of something else. For production to be efficient, there must be full employment—not just of labor but of all the available factors of production—and each resource must be assigned to the task that it performs comparatively better than other resources can.

---

■ **FIGURE 3.2**

Attainable and Unattainable Combinations

MyEconLab Animation

The production possibilities frontier, *PPF*, separates attainable combinations from unattainable ones. The economy can produce at any point *inside* the *PPF* (the orange area) or at any point *on* the frontier. Any point outside the production possibilities frontier, such as point *G*, is unattainable.

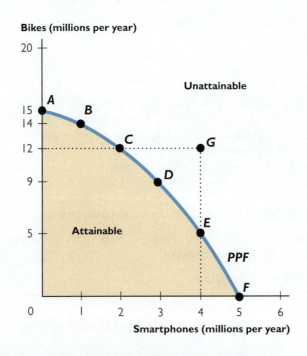

Figure 3.3 illustrates the distinction between efficient and inefficient production. With *inefficient* production, the economy might be producing 3 million smartphones and 5 million bikes at point *H*. With an *efficient* use of the economy's resources, it is possible to produce at a point on the *PPF* such as point *D* or *E*. At point *D*, there are more bikes and the same quantity of smartphones as at point *H*. And at point *E*, there are more smartphones and the same quantity of bikes as at point *H*. At points *D* and *E*, production is efficient.

## Tradeoffs and Free Lunches

A **tradeoff** is an exchange—giving up one thing to get something else. You trade off income for a better grade when you decide to cut back on the hours you spend on your weekend job and allocate the time to extra study. The Ford Motor Company faces a tradeoff when it cuts the production of trucks and uses the resources saved to produce more hybrid SUVs. The federal government faces a tradeoff when it cuts NASA's space exploration program and allocates more resources to homeland security. As a society, we face a tradeoff when we decide to cut down a forest and destroy the habitat of the spotted owl.

**Tradeoff**
An exchange—giving up one thing to get something else.

The production possibilities frontier illustrates the idea of a tradeoff. The *PPF* in Figure 3.3 shows how. If the economy produces at point *E* and people want to produce more bikes, they must forgo some smartphones. In the move from point *E* to point *D*, people trade off smartphones for bikes.

Economists often express the central idea of economics—that choices involve a tradeoff—with the saying "There is no such thing as a free lunch." A *free lunch* is a gift—getting something without giving up something else. What does the

**FIGURE 3.3**

Efficient and Inefficient Production, Tradeoffs, and Free Lunches

MyEconLab Animation

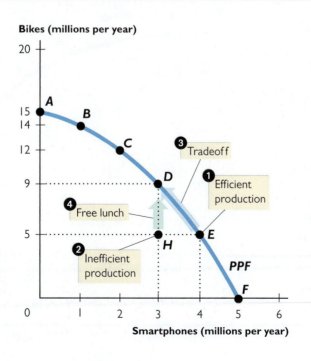

❶ When production occurs at a point on the *PPF*, such as point *E*, resources are used efficiently.

❷ When production occurs at a point inside the *PPF*, such as point *H*, resources are used inefficiently.

❸ When production is efficient— on the *PPF*—the economy faces a tradeoff. To move from point *E* to point *D* requires that some smartphones be given up for more bikes.

❹ When production is inefficient— inside the *PPF*—there is a free lunch. To move from point *H* inside the *PPF* to point *D* on the *PPF* does not involve a tradeoff.

famous saying mean? Suppose some resources are not being used or are not being used efficiently. Isn't it then possible to avoid a tradeoff and get a free lunch?

The answer is yes. You can see why in Figure 3.3. If production is taking place *inside* the *PPF* at point *H*, then it is possible to move to point *D* and increase the production of bikes by using currently unused resources or by using resources in their most productive way. Nothing is forgone to increase production—there is a free lunch.

When production is efficient—at a point on the *PPF*—choosing to produce more of one good involves a tradeoff. But if production is inefficient—at a point inside the *PPF*—there is a free lunch. More of some goods and services can be produced without producing less of any others.

So "there is no such thing as a free lunch" means that when resources are used efficiently, every choice involves a tradeoff. Because economists view people as making rational choices, they expect that resources will be used efficiently. That is why they emphasize the tradeoff idea and deny the existence of free lunches. We might *sometimes* get a free lunch, but we *almost always* face a tradeoff.

# EYE on YOUR LIFE
## Your Production Possibilities Frontier

MyEconLab Critical Thinking Exercise

Two "goods" that concern you a great deal are your grade point average (GPA) and the amount of time you have available for leisure or earning an income. You face a tradeoff. To get a higher GPA you must give up leisure or income. Your forgone leisure or forgone income is the opportunity cost of a higher GPA. Similarly, to get more leisure or more income, you must accept a lower grade. A lower grade is the opportunity cost of increased leisure or increased income.

The figure illustrates a student's *PPF*. Any point on or inside the *PPF* is attainable and any point outside the *PPF* is unattainable. A student who wastes time ends up with a lower GPA than the highest attainable from the time spent studying. But a student who works efficiently achieves a point *on* the *PPF* and achieves production efficiency.

The student in the figure allocates the scarce 168 hours a week between

studying (class and study hours) and other activities (work, leisure, and sleep hours). The student attends class and studies for 48 hours each week

and works or has fun (and sleeps) for the other 120 hours. With this allocation of time, and studying efficiently, the student's GPA is 3.

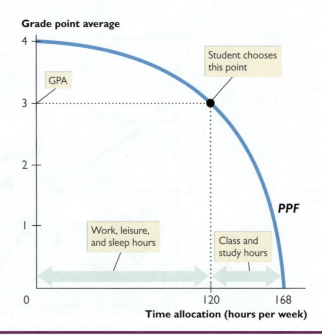

# CHECKPOINT 3.1

MyEconLab Study Plan 3.1
Key Terms Quiz
Solutions Video

**Explain and illustrate the concepts of scarcity, production efficiency, and tradeoff using the production possibilities frontier.**

## Practice Problems

1. Table 1 sets out the production possibilities of a small Pacific island economy. Draw the economy's *PPF*.

Figure 1 shows an economy's *PPF* and identifies some production points. Use this figure to work Problems **2** to **4**.

2. Which points are attainable? Explain why.
3. Which points are efficient and which points are inefficient? Explain why.
4. Which points illustrate a tradeoff? Explain why.

## In the News

**Honeybee decline linked to killer virus**
In 2007, the killer virus arrived in Hawaii, where almost all the queen bees used in the United States are bred. Bees are used to pollinate crops that are used in a third of the food we eat.

Source: *The Guardian*, June 8, 2012

Explain how a decline in bee population affects the U.S. *PPF*.

## Solutions to Practice Problems

1. The *PPF* is the boundary between attainable and unattainable combinations of goods. Figure 2 shows the economy's *PPF*. The graph plots each row of the table as a point with the corresponding letter.

2. Attainable points: Any point on the *PPF* is attainable and any point inside the *PPF* is attainable. Points outside the *PPF* (F and G) are unattainable. In Figure 1, the attainable points are A, B, C, D, and E.

3. Efficient points: Production is efficient when it is not possible to produce more of one good without producing less of another good. To be efficient, a point must be attainable, so points F and G can't be efficient. Points inside the *PPF* can't be efficient because more goods can be produced, so D and E are not efficient. The only efficient points are those *on* the *PPF*—A, B, and C.

   Inefficient points: Inefficiency occurs when resources are misallocated or unemployed. Such points are *inside* the *PPF*. These points are D and E.

4. Tradeoff: Begin by recalling that a tradeoff is an exchange—giving up something to get something else. A tradeoff occurs when moving along the *PPF* from one point to another point. So moving from any point *on* the *PPF*, point A, B, or C, to another point *on* the *PPF* illustrates a tradeoff.

## Solution to In the News

Honeybees are a resource used in the production of many food crops. Before 2007, the United States was at a point on its *PPF*. During the following years, with fewer queen bees, the number of honeybees declined and the quantity of food produced decreased. With no change in other resources and technology, and no change in the quantity of other goods and services produced, the U.S. *PPF* rotated inward.

**TABLE 1**

| Possibility | Fish (pounds) | | Berries (pounds) |
|---|---|---|---|
| A | 0 | and | 20 |
| B | 1 | and | 18 |
| C | 2 | and | 15 |
| D | 3 | and | 11 |
| E | 4 | and | 6 |
| F | 5 | and | 0 |

**FIGURE 1**

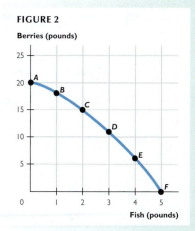

**FIGURE 2**

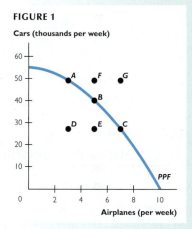

## 3.2   OPPORTUNITY COST

You've seen that moving from one point to another on the *PPF* involves a trade-off. But what are the terms of the tradeoff? *How much* of one item must be forgone to obtain an additional unit of another item—a large amount or a small amount? The answer is given by opportunity cost—the best thing you must give up to get something (see p. 8). We can use the *PPF* to calculate opportunity cost.

### ■ The Opportunity Cost of a Smartphone

The opportunity cost of producing a smartphone is the number of bikes forgone to get an additional smartphone. It is calculated as the number of bikes forgone divided by the number of smartphones gained.

Figure 3.4 illustrates the calculation. At point *A*, the quantities produced are zero smartphones and 15 million bikes; and at point *B*, the quantities produced are 1 million smartphones and 14 million bikes. To gain 1 million smartphones by moving from point *A* to point *B*, 1 million bikes are forgone, so the opportunity cost of 1 smartphone is 1 bike.

At point *C*, the quantities produced are 2 million smartphones and 12 million bikes. To gain 1 million smartphones by moving from point *B* to point *C*, 2 million bikes are forgone. Now the opportunity cost of 1 smartphone is 2 bikes.

If you repeat these calculations, moving from *C* to *D*, *D* to *E*, and *E* to *F*, you will obtain the opportunity costs shown in the table and the graph.

■ **FIGURE 3.4**

### Calculating the Opportunity Cost of a Smartphone

| Movement along *PPF* | Decrease in quantity of bikes | Increase in quantity of smartphones | Decrease in bikes divided by increase in smartphones |
|---|---|---|---|
| *A* to *B* | 1 million | 1 million | 1 bike per phone |
| *B* to *C* | 2 million | 1 million | 2 bikes per phone |
| *C* to *D* | 3 million | 1 million | 3 bikes per phone |
| *D* to *E* | 4 million | 1 million | 4 bikes per phone |
| *E* to *F* | 5 million | 1 million | 5 bikes per phone |

Along the *PPF* from *A* to *F*, the opportunity cost of a smartphone increases as the quantity of smartphones produced increases.

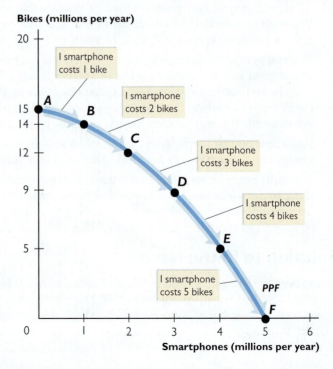

## ■ Opportunity Cost and the Slope of the *PPF*

Look at the numbers that we've just calculated for the opportunity cost of a smartphone and notice that they follow a striking pattern. The opportunity cost of a smartphone increases as the quantity of smartphones produced increases.

The magnitude of the *slope* of the *PPF* measures the opportunity cost. Because the *PPF* in Figure 3.4 is bowed outward, its slope changes and gets steeper as the quantity of smartphones produced increases.

When a small quantity of smartphones is produced—between points *A* and *B*—the *PPF* has a gentle slope and the opportunity cost of a smartphone is low. A given increase in the quantity of smartphones costs a small decrease in the quantity of bikes. When a large quantity of smartphones is produced—between points *E* and *F*—the *PPF* is steep and the opportunity cost of a smartphone is high. A given increase in the quantity of smartphones costs a large decrease in the quantity of bikes. Figure 3.5 shows the increasing opportunity cost of a smartphone.

## ■ Opportunity Cost Is a Ratio

The opportunity cost of a smartphone is the *ratio* of bikes forgone to smartphones gained. Similarly, the opportunity cost of a bike is the *ratio* of smartphones forgone to bikes gained. So the opportunity cost of producing a bike is equal to the inverse of the opportunity cost of producing a smartphone. For example, moving along the *PPF* in Figure 3.4 from *C* to *D* the opportunity cost of a smartphone is 3 bikes. Moving along the *PPF* in the opposite direction, from *D* to *C*, the opportunity cost of a bike is 1/3 of a smartphone.

## ■ FIGURE 3.5

### The Opportunity Cost of a Smartphone

MyEconLab Animation

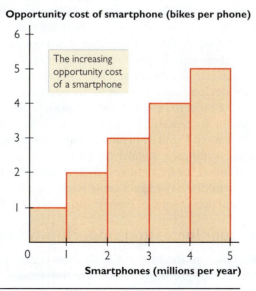

Because the *PPF* in Figure 3.4 is bowed outward, the opportunity cost of a smartphone increases as the quantity of smartphones produced increases.

| Smartphones (millions) | 0 to 1 | 1 to 2 | 2 to 3 | 3 to 4 | 4 to 5 |
|---|---|---|---|---|---|
| Opportunity cost (bikes per phone) | 1 | 2 | 3 | 4 | 5 |

# EYE on the ENVIRONMENT

MyEconLab Critical Thinking Exercise

## Is Wind Power Free?

Wind power is not free. To use it, we must give up other goods and services to build wind turbines and transmission lines.

Wind turbines can produce electricity only when the wind is strong enough, but advances in technology are enabling turbines to operate in lower wind conditions.

Some of the best wind farm locations are far from major population centers, so transmission lines can be long and power losses large.

If we produced most of our electricity using wind power, we would be operating inside the *PPF* at a point such as *Z*.

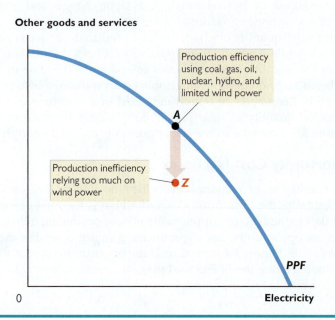

Other goods and services

Production efficiency using coal, gas, oil, nuclear, hydro, and limited wind power

A

Production inefficiency relying too much on wind power

● Z

*PPF*

0                                                    Electricity

---

## ■ Increasing Opportunity Costs Are Everywhere

Just about every production activity that you can think of has increasing opportunity cost. We allocate the most skillful farmers and the most fertile land to producing food, and we allocate the best doctors and the least fertile land to producing healthcare services. Some resources are equally productive in both activities. If we shift these equally productive resources away from farming to hospitals, we get an increase in healthcare at a low opportunity cost. But if we keep increasing healthcare services, we must eventually build hospitals on the most fertile land and get the best farmers to become hospital porters. The production of food drops drastically and the increase in the production of healthcare services is small. The opportunity cost of a unit of healthcare services rises. Similarly, if we shift resources away from healthcare toward farming, we must eventually use more skilled doctors and nurses as farmers and more hospitals as hydroponic vegetable factories. The decrease in the production of healthcare services is large, but the increase in food production is small. The opportunity cost of producing a unit of food rises.

## ■ Your Increasing Opportunity Cost

Flip back to the *PPF* in *Eye on Your Life* on p. 64 and think about its implications for your opportunity cost of a higher grade.

What is the opportunity cost of spending time with your friends in terms of the grade you might receive on your exam? What is the opportunity cost of a higher grade in terms of the activities you give up to study? Do you face increasing opportunity costs in these activities?

**CHECKPOINT 3.2**

MyEconLab Study Plan 3.2

Solutions Video

Calculate opportunity cost.

## Practice Problems

Table 1 shows Robinson Crusoe's production possibilities.

1.  What is his opportunity cost of a pound of berries when Crusoe increases the quantity of berries from 21 pounds to 26 pounds and production is efficient? Does this opportunity cost increase as he produces more berries?

2.  If Crusoe is producing 10 pounds of fish and 21 pounds of berries, what is his opportunity cost of an extra pound of berries? And what is his opportunity cost of an extra pound of fish? Explain your answers.

## In the News

**Cost of meeting 2021 vehicle emission standards**
Carbon dioxide emissions from cars must be cut from 130 grams to 95 grams per kilometer. To meet this new standard, the price of a car will rise by $1,350.

Source: *International Business Times*, November 9, 2015

Calculate the opportunity cost of reducing the carbon emission level by 1 gram.

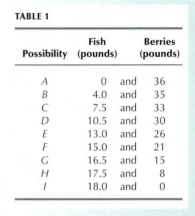

**TABLE 1**

| Possibility | Fish (pounds) | | Berries (pounds) |
|---|---|---|---|
| A | 0 | and | 36 |
| B | 4.0 | and | 35 |
| C | 7.5 | and | 33 |
| D | 10.5 | and | 30 |
| E | 13.0 | and | 26 |
| F | 15.0 | and | 21 |
| G | 16.5 | and | 15 |
| H | 17.5 | and | 8 |
| I | 18.0 | and | 0 |

## Solutions to Practice Problems

1.  If Crusoe's production is efficient, he is producing at a point *on* his *PPF*. His opportunity cost of an extra pound of berries is the quantity of fish he must give up to get the berries. It is calculated as the decrease in the quantity of fish divided by the increase in the quantity of berries as he moves along his *PPF*.

    To increase the quantity of berries from 21 pounds to 26 pounds (from row *F* to row *E* of Table 1), production of fish decreases from 15 pounds to 13 pounds. To gain 5 pounds of berries, Crusoe must forgo 2 pounds of fish. The opportunity cost of 1 pound of berries is the 2 pounds of fish forgone divided by 5 pounds of berries gained—2/5 of a pound of fish.

    Crusoe's opportunity cost of berries increases as he produces more berries. To see why, move Crusoe from row *E* to row *D* in Table 1. His production of berries increases by 4 pounds and his production of fish falls by 2.5 pounds. His opportunity cost of 1 pound of berries increases to 5/8 of a pound of fish.

2.  Figure 1 graphs the data in Table 1 and shows Crusoe's *PPF*. If Crusoe is producing 10 pounds of fish and 21 pounds of berries, he is producing at point *Z*. Point *Z* is a point *inside* Crusoe's *PPF*. When Crusoe produces 21 pounds of berries, he has enough time available to produce 15 pounds of fish at point *F* on his *PPF*. To produce more fish, Crusoe can move from *Z* toward *F* on his *PPF* and forgo no berries. His opportunity cost of a pound of fish is zero. Similiarly, his opportunity cost of a pound of berries is zero.

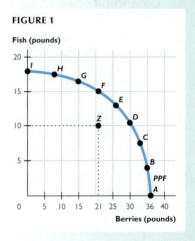

**FIGURE 1**

Fish (pounds)

## Solution to In the News

By spending $1,350 extra on a new car, you forgo $1,350 of other goods. With a new car, your emissions fall from 130 grams to 95 grams, a reduction of 35 grams. The opportunity cost of a 1-gram reduction in emissions is $1,350 of other goods divided by 35 grams, or $38.57 of other goods.

## 3.3 ECONOMIC GROWTH

**Economic growth**
The sustained expansion of production possibilities.

The *PPF* shows the limits to production with given resources and technology. But over time, resources and technology change and production possibilities expand. A process of sustained expansion of production possibilities is called **economic growth**. Our economy grows when we develop better technologies; improve the quality of labor by education, on-the-job training, and work experience; and acquire more machines (capital) to help us produce.

To study economic growth, we must look at the production possibilities for a consumption good—a smartphone—and a capital good—a smartphone factory. By using resources to produce smartphone factories, the economy can expand its future production possibilities. The greater the production of new capital—of new smartphone factories—the faster is the expansion of production possibilities.

Figure 3.6 shows how the *PPF* can expand. If no new factories are produced (at point *L*), production possibilities do not expand and the *PPF* stays at its original position. By producing fewer smartphones and using resources to produce 2 new smartphone factories (at point *K*), production possibilities expand once the new factories become operational. The *PPF* rotates outward to the new *PPF*.

But economic growth is *not* free. To make it happen, current consumption must decrease. The move from *L* to *K* in Figure 3.6 means forgoing 2 million smartphones now. The opportunity cost of producing new smartphone factories is the decrease in the number of smartphones produced today.

Also, economic growth does not end scarcity. It rotates the *PPF* outward, but on the new *PPF* we continue to face opportunity costs. To keep producing new capital, current consumption must be less than its maximum possible level.

■ **FIGURE 3.6**

### Expanding Production Possibilities

❶ If firms allocate no resources to producing smartphone factories and produce 5 million smartphones a year at point *L*, the *PPF* doesn't change.

❷ If firms decrease smartphone production to 3 million a year and produce 2 smartphone factories, at point *K*, production possibilities will expand. After a year, the *PPF* rotates outward to the new *PPF* and production can move to point *K'*.

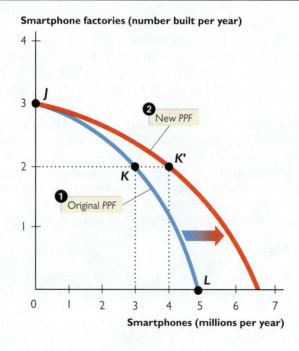

# EYE on the U.S. ECONOMY

## Expanding Our Production Possibilities

Horizontal drilling and hydraulic fracturing—fracking—combined with recent advances in remote sensing technology have made it possible to extract a large quantity of gas trapped in shale at low cost. The United States has an estimated 750 trillion cubic feet of this gas, enough for more than 90 years at today's extraction rate. The map below shows the locations of these gas deposits.

Figure 1 shows recent years of shale gas production. During 2010 and 2011, production doubled. The average growth rate since 2010 exceeds 30 percent per year.

Was this increase in gas production achieved by sliding along the PPF and producing less of other goods and servces? No! It was the result of advances in technology and the opening up of additional gas wells.

Figure 2 illustrates how these changes rotated the PPF outward from $PPF_{10}$ in 2010 to $PPF_{13}$ in 2013. Point J is the same on both curves because if we produced at that point (only other goods and services and no gas), we would not get the benefits of the technological advances in gas production. In 2010 we produced at point K, and in 2013 at point K'. Along $PPF_{13}$ the opportunity cost of gas is lower than along $PPF_{10}$.

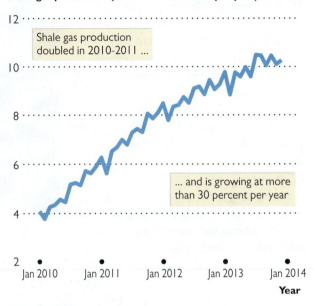

Shale gas production doubled in 2010-2011 ...

... and is growing at more than 30 percent per year

**Figure 1 Shale Gas Production**

**Natural Gas Shale Basins in the United States**

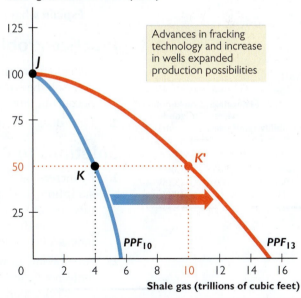

Advances in fracking technology and increase in wells expanded production possibilities

**Figure 2 Shale Gas Versus Other Goods and Services**

Source of data: Energy Information Administration.

# EYE on the GLOBAL ECONOMY
## Hong Kong's Rapid Economic Growth

Hong Kong's production possibilities per person were 25 percent of those of the United States in 1960. By 2015, they had grown to become equal to U.S. production possibilities per person. Hong Kong grew faster than the United States because it allocated more of its resources to accumulating capital and less to consumption than did the United States.

In 1960, the United States and Hong Kong produced at point A on their respective PPFs. In 2015, Hong Kong was at point B and the United States was at point C.

If Hong Kong continues to produce at any point on its PPF above C, it will grow more rapidly than the United States and its PPF will eventually shift out

beyond the PPF of the United States. But if Hong Kong produces at a point

below B, the pace of expansion of its PPF will slow.

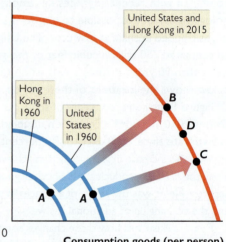

**Capital goods (per person)**

United States and Hong Kong in 2015

Hong Kong in 1960

United States in 1960

*B*

*D*

*C*

*A*   *A*

0

**Consumption goods (per person)**

---

MyEconLab Study Plan 3.3
Key Terms Quiz
Solutions Video

 CHECKPOINT 3.3

**Explain what makes production possibilities expand.**

## Practice Problems

**TABLE 1**

| Possibility | Education services (graduates) | Consumption goods (units) |
|---|---|---|
| A | 1,000 | 0 |
| B | 750 | 1,000 |
| C | 500 | 2,000 |
| D | 0 | 3,000 |

1. Table 1 shows an economy that produces education services and consumption goods. If the economy currently produces 500 graduates a year and 2,000 units of consumption goods, what is the opportunity cost of one additional graduate?

2. How does an economy grow? Explain why economic growth is not free.

## Solutions to Practice Problems

1. By increasing the number of graduates from 500 to 750, the quantity of consumption goods produced decreases from 2,000 to 1,000 units. The opportunity cost of a graduate is the decrease in consumption goods divided by the increase in the number of graduates. That is, the opportunity cost of a graduate is 1,000 units divided by 250, or 4 units of consumption goods.

2. An economy grows if it expands its production possibilities—if it develops better technologies; improves the quality of labor by education, on-the-job training, and work experience; and acquires more capital to use in production.

   Economic growth occurs when resources are used today to produce better technologies, higher-quality labor, or more machines. Those resources cannot be used to produce goods and services today, so the cost of economic growth is the goods and services forgone today. Economic growth is not free.

## 3.4    SPECIALIZATION AND TRADE

MyEconLab Concept Video

The next time you visit your favorite fast-food restaurant, watch what the workers are doing. You might see one person re-stocking the bread, salad materials, meat, sauces, boxes, and wrappers; another working the grill and another the fry maker; another assembling meals; and yet another taking orders and payments. Imagine how long you would wait for your burger if each worker performed all the tasks needed to fill each customer's not-so-fast-food order.

Specialization makes people more productive in two ways: It brings absolute advantage and comparative advantage.

*Specialization boosts productivity in a fast-food kitchen*

### ■ Absolute Advantage and Comparative Advantage

A person has an **absolute advantage** if that person is more productive than another. Being more productive means using fewer inputs or taking less time to produce a good or perform a production task. Being more productive also means being able to produce more with given inputs in a given amount of time.

The specialized workers at McDonald's have an *absolute advantage* over the same number of workers each performing all the tasks needed to make a burger.

A person has a **comparative advantage** in an activity if that person can perform the activity at a lower opportunity cost than anyone else. Recall that the opportunity cost of something is what you must give up to get it.

Notice the contrast between *absolute advantage* and *comparative advantage*. Absolute advantage is about *productivity*—how long does it take to produce a unit of a good. Comparative advantage is about *opportunity cost*—how much of some other good must be forgone to produce a unit of a good.

**Absolute advantage**

When one person (or nation) is more productive than another—needs fewer inputs or takes less time to produce a good or perform a production task.

**Comparative advantage**

The ability of a person to perform an activity or produce a good or service at a lower opportunity cost than anyone else.

# EYE on the U.S. ECONOMY
## No One Knows How to Make a Pencil

Not many products in today's world are as simple as a pencil. Yet the story of how the pencil in your hand got there illustrates the astonishing power of specialization and trade.

When you hold a pencil, you're holding cedar grown in Oregon, graphite mined in Sri Lanka, clay from Mississippi, wax from Mexico, rapeseed oil grown in the Dutch East Indies, pumice from Italy, copper from Arizona, and zinc from Alaska.

These materials were harvested and mined by thousands of workers

equipped with hundreds of specialized tools, all of which were manufactured by thousands of other workers using hundreds more specialized tools. These tools were in turn made of steel, itself made from iron ore, and from other minerals and materials.

Rail, road, and ocean transportation systems moved all these things to custom-built factories that made graphite "leads," erasers, brass to hold the erasers, paint, and glue.

Finally, all these components were bought by a pencil factory which, with

its millions of dollars' worth of custom machinery, put them all together.

Millions of people contributed to making that pencil, many of whom don't even know what a pencil is and *not one of whom knows how to make a pencil*. No one directed all these people. Each worker and business went about its self-interested specialized task trading with each other in markets.

Adapted from *I Pencil*, by Leonard Read, Foundation for Economic Education, 1958.

## ■ Comparative Advantage: A Model

We're going to explore the idea of comparative advantage and make it concrete by looking at a model economy with two smoothie bars: one operated by Liz and the other operated by Joe. You will see how we identify comparative advantage and how it creates an opportunity for Liz and Joe to gain from specialization and trade.

### Liz's Smoothie Bar

Liz operates a high-tech bar. She can turn out *either* a smoothie *or* a salad every 2 minutes. If she spends all her time making smoothies, she produces 30 an hour. If she spends all her time making salads, she also produces 30 an hour (Table 3.1). If she splits her time equally between the two, she can produce 15 smoothies *and* 15 salads an hour. For each additional smoothie Liz produces, she must decrease her production of salads by one, and for each additional salad Liz produces, she must decrease her production of smoothies by one. So

### Liz's opportunity cost of producing 1 smoothie is 1 salad,

and

### Liz's opportunity cost of producing 1 salad is 1 smoothie.

Liz's customers buy smoothies and salads in equal quantities, so Liz splits her time equally between the items and produces 15 smoothies and 15 salads an hour.

### Joe's Smoothie Bar

Joe produces smoothies and salads in a smaller bar than Liz's, and he has only one blender—a slow, old machine. Even if Joe uses all his resources to produce smoothies, he can produce only 6 an hour. But Joe is pretty good in the salad department. If he uses all his resources to make salads, he can produce 30 an hour (Table 3.2). Joe's ability to make smoothies and salads is the same regardless of how he splits an hour between the two tasks. He can make a salad in 2 minutes or a smoothie in 10 minutes. For each additional smoothie Joe produces, he must decrease his production of salads by 5. And for each additional salad Joe produces, he must decrease his production of smoothies by 1/5 of a smoothie. So

### Joe's opportunity cost of producing 1 smoothie is 5 salads,

and

### Joe's opportunity cost of producing 1 salad is 1/5 of a smoothie.

Joe's customers, like Liz's, buy smoothies and salads in equal quantities. Joe spends 50 minutes of each hour making smoothies and 10 minutes of each hour making salads. With this division of his time, Joe produces 5 smoothies and 5 salads an hour.

### Liz's and Joe's *PPFs*

The *PPF*s in Figure 3.7 illustrate the situation we've just described. In part (a), Liz faces a *PPF* that enables her to produce 15 smoothies and 15 salads. In part (b), Joe faces a *PPF* that enables him to produce 5 smoothies and 5 salads. On Liz's *PPF*, 1 smoothie costs 1 salad. On Joe's *PPF*, 1 smoothie costs 5 salads.

The *PPF*s in Figure 3.7 contrast with the outward-bowed *PPF*s that you've seen earlier in this chapter, which capture the general rule that the opportunity cost of a good increases as we increase its rate of production. It is easier to identify

**TABLE 3.1   LIZ'S PRODUCTION POSSIBILITIES**

| Item | Minutes to produce 1 | Quantity per hour |
|------|----------------------|-------------------|
| Smoothies | 2 | 30 |
| Salads | 2 | 30 |

**TABLE 3.2   JOE'S PRODUCTION POSSIBILITIES**

| Item | Minutes to produce 1 | Quantity per hour |
|------|----------------------|-------------------|
| Smoothies | 10 | 6 |
| Salads | 2 | 30 |

**FIGURE 3.7**

Production Possibilities Frontiers

MyEconLab Animation

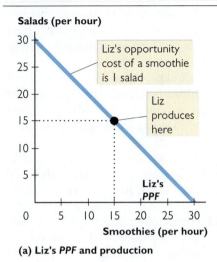

(a) Liz's *PPF* and production

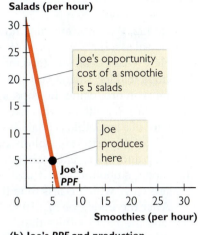

(b) Joe's *PPF* and production

Liz can produce 30 smoothies per hour or 30 salads per hour or any other combination along her *PPF* in part (a). Liz chooses to produce 15 smoothies and 15 salads per hour.

Joe can produce 6 smoothies per hour or 30 salads per hour or any other combination along his *PPF* in part (b). Joe chooses to produce 5 smoothies and 5 salads per hour.

comparative advantage and see the gains from trade when individuals have constant opportunity cost. And as you will soon see, the economy's *PPF* is outward-bowed even when individuals have constant opportunity cost and linear *PPFs*.

## Liz's Greater Productivity

You can see from the production numbers that Liz is three times as productive as Joe—her 15 smoothies and 15 salads an hour are three times Joe's 5 smoothies and 5 salads. Liz is more productive than Joe in producing both smoothies and salads, but Liz has a comparative advantage in only one of the activities.

## Liz's Comparative Advantage

In which of the two activities does Liz have a *comparative* advantage? Recall that comparative advantage is a situation in which one person's opportunity cost of producing a good is lower than another person's opportunity cost of producing that same good.

You've seen that Liz's opportunity cost of a smoothie is 1 salad, whereas Joe's opportunity cost of a smoothie is 5 salads. To produce 1 smoothie, Liz must forgo 1 salad while Joe must forgo 5 salads. So, because Liz forgoes fewer salads to make a smoothie, she has a comparative advantage in producing smoothies.

What about Joe? Doesn't he have a comparative advantage at anything? He does as you're about to see.

## Joe's Comparative Advantage

Look at the opportunity costs of producing salads. For Liz, that opportunity cost is 1 smoothie. But for Joe, a salad costs only 1/5 of a smoothie. Because Joe's opportunity cost of a salad is less than Liz's, Joe has a comparative advantage in producing salads.

It is always true that if one person has a comparative advantage in producing a good, others have a comparative advantage in producing some other good.

## ■ Achieving Gains from Trade

Liz and Joe run into each other in a bar, where Liz tells Joe about her smoothie business. Her only problem, she says, is that she wants to produce more because customers leave when her lines get too long. Joe describes his own smaller business to Liz. When he explains how he divides his hour between making smoothies and salads, Liz's eyes pop. "Have I got a deal for you!" she exclaims.

Here's Liz's deal. Joe stops making smoothies and produces 30 salads per hour. Liz stops making salads and produces 30 smoothies per hour. That is, they both specialize in producing the good in which they have a comparative advantage—see Table 3.3(b). They then trade: Liz sells Joe 10 smoothies and Joe sells Liz 20 salads—the price of a smoothie is 2 salads—see Table 3.3(c).

Trade at a price of 2 salads per smoothie (1/2 a smoothie per salad) enables both Liz and Joe to gain. Liz gets salads for 1/2 a smoothie each, which is less than the 1 smoothie that it costs her to produce a salad. Joe gets smoothies for 2 salads each, which is less than the 5 salads it costs him to produce a smoothie.

After the trade, Joe has 10 salads (the 30 he produces minus the 20 he sells to Liz) and the 10 smoothies that he buys from Liz. So Joe doubles the quantities of smoothies and salads he can sell. Liz has 20 smoothies (the 30 she produces minus the 10 she sells to Joe) and the 20 salads she buys from Joe. See Table 3.3(d). From specialization and trade, each gains 5 smoothies and 5 salads—see Table 3.3(e).

Liz draws the graphs in Figure 3.8 to illustrate her idea. The blue *PPF* is Liz's and the red *PPF* is Joe's. They are each producing at the points marked *A*. Liz's proposal is that they each produce at the points marked *B*.

After trading, each moves to the point marked *C*. At these points, Liz has 20 smoothies and 20 salads, 5 more of each than she was producing only for herself. Joe has 10 smoothies and 10 salads, also 5 more of each than he was producing only for himself. Because of the gains from specialization and trade, total production increases by 10 smoothies and 10 salads.

Notice that the points *C* are *outside* Liz's and Joe's *PPF*s. Everyone gains and enjoys greater quantities of goods than they can produce on their own.

**TABLE 3.3   LIZ AND JOE GAIN FROM TRADE**

| (a) Before Trade | Liz | Joe |
|---|---|---|
| Smoothies | 15 | 5 |
| Salads | 15 | 5 |

| (b) Specialization | Liz | Joe |
|---|---|---|
| Smoothies | 30 | 0 |
| Salads | 0 | 30 |

| (c) Trade | | |
|---|---|---|
| Smoothies | sell 10 | buy 10 |
| Salads | buy 20 | sell 20 |

| (d) After Trade | | |
|---|---|---|
| Smoothies | 20 | 10 |
| Salads | 20 | 10 |

| (e) Gains from Trade | | |
|---|---|---|
| Smoothies | +5 | +5 |
| Salads | +5 | +5 |

## ■ FIGURE 3.8

### The Gains from Specialization and Trade

MyEconLab Animation

❶ Before trade, Liz and Joe each produce at point *A* on their respective *PPF*s.

❷ Liz specializes in smoothies and Joe specializes in salads, so they each move to point *B* on their respective *PPF*s.

❸ They exchange smoothies for salads at a price of 2 salads per smoothie. After trade, each goes to point *C*—a point *outside* their individual *PPF*s. They each gain 5 salads and 5 smoothies—the quantities at point *C* minus the quantities at point *A*.

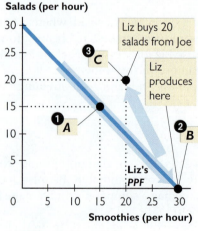

(a) Liz's gains from trade

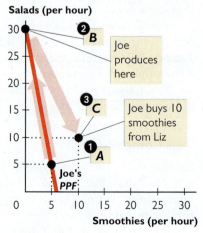

(b) Joe's gains from trade

## ■ The Economy's Production Possibilities Frontier

With specialization and trade, Liz and Joe get outside their individual *PPFs*, but they produce *on* the economy's *PPF*. Also, despite Liz and Joe having constant opportunity costs, along the economy's *PPF* opportunity cost is increasing—the economy's *PPF* is bowed outward. Figure 3.9 illustrates. The first 30 smoothies produced (by Liz) cost 1 salad each, but the 31st smoothie produced (by Joe) costs 5 salads. Similarly, the first 30 salads produced (by Joe) cost 1/5 smoothie each, but the 31st salad produced (by Liz) costs 1 smoothie. When Liz and Joe specialize, they produce efficiently on the economy's *PPF*. Without specialization and trade, they produce at an inefficient point *inside* the economy's *PPF*.

■ **FIGURE 3.9**

The Economy's Production Possibilities                     MyEconLab Animation

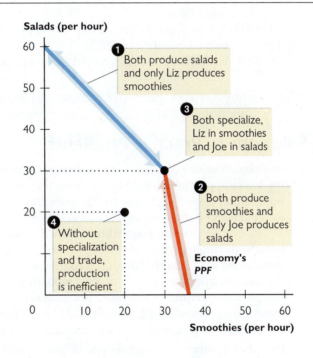

❶ When the economy produces more than 30 salads per hour, both Liz and Joe produce salads but only Liz produces smoothies.

❷ When the economy produces more than 30 smoothies per hour, both Liz and Joe produce smoothies but only Joe produces salads.

❸ When Liz and Joe specialize in their comparative advantage, the economy produces 30 salads and 30 smoothies at an efficient point on the economy's *PPF*.

❹ Without specialization and trade, Liz and Joe produce at an inefficient point inside the economy's *PPF*.

## EYE on YOUR LIFE
### Your Comparative Advantage

MyEconLab Critical Thinking Exercise

You are expanding your production possibilities by being in school and accumulating human capital.

By discovering your comparative advantage, you will be able to focus on producing the items that make you as well off as possible. Think hard about what you enjoy doing, and what you do comparatively better than others.

In today's world, it is a good idea to try to remain flexible so that you can switch jobs if you discover that your comparative advantage has changed.

Looking beyond your own self-interest, are you going to be a voice that supports or opposes offshore outsourcing?

You've learned in this chapter that

regardless of whether outsourcing remains inside the United States, as it does with Liz and Joe at their smoothie bars, or is global like the outsourcing of jobs by U.S. producers to India, both parties gain from trade.

Americans pay less for goods and services and Indians earn higher incomes.

MyEconLab Study Plan 3.4
Key Terms Quiz
Solutions Video

 CHECKPOINT 3.4

**Explain how people gain from specialization and trade.**

## Practice Problems

Tony and Patty produce skis and snowboards. Tables 1 and 2 show their production possibilities. Each week, Tony produces 5 snowboards and 40 skis and Patty produces 10 snowboards and 5 skis.

1.  Who has a comparative advantage in producing snowboards? Who has a comparative advantage in producing skis?
2.  If Tony and Patty specialize and trade, what are the gains from trade?

## In the News

**Sweet news after TPP sting**
Trans-Pacific Partnership (TPP) trade deal has kept tight restrictions on Australia's sugar exports to the United States. In 2015, U.S. sugar producers received 22¢ per pound while Australian growers received the world price of 12¢ per pound.
*Source: The Land, October 8, 2015*

Which country has a comparative advantage in producing sugar? Explain why both the United States and Australia can gain from free trade in sugar.

## Solutions to Practice Problems

1.  The person with a comparative advantage in snowboards is the one who has the lower opportunity cost of producing a snowboard. Tony's production possibilities show that to produce 5 more snowboards he must produce 10 fewer skis. So Tony's opportunity cost of a snowboard is 2 skis.

    Patty's production possibilities show that to produce 10 more snowboards, she must produce 5 fewer skis. So Patty's opportunity cost of a snowboard is 1/2 a ski. Patty has a comparative advantage in snowboards because her opportunity cost of a snowboard is less than Tony's. Tony's comparative advantage is in skis. For each ski produced, Tony must forgo making 1/2 a snowboard, whereas Patty must forgo making 2 snowboards for a ski. So Tony's opportunity cost of a ski is lower than Patty's.

2.  Patty has a comparative advantage in snowboards, so she specializes in snowboards. Tony has a comparative advantage in skis, so he specializes in skis. Patty makes 20 snowboards and Tony makes 50 skis. Before specializing, they made 15 snowboards and 45 skis. By specializing, total output increases by 5 snowboards and 5 skis. They share this gain by trading.

## Solution to In the News

The cost of producing sugar is less in Australia than in the United States, so Australia has a comparative advantage in producing sugar. If Australia specializes in producing sugar and the United States specializes in producing other goods (for example, movies or airplanes) and the two countries engage in free trade, each country can gain and get to a point outside its own *PPF*.

---

**TABLE 1   TONY'S PRODUCTION POSSIBILITIES**

| Snowboards (per week) | | Skis (per week) |
|---|---|---|
| 25 | and | 0 |
| 20 | and | 10 |
| 15 | and | 20 |
| 10 | and | 30 |
| 5 | and | 40 |
| 0 | and | 50 |

**TABLE 2   PATTY'S PRODUCTION POSSIBILITIES**

| Snowboards (per week) | | Skis (per week) |
|---|---|---|
| 20 | and | 0 |
| 10 | and | 5 |
| 0 | and | 10 |

CHAPTER SUMMARY

## Key Points

1. **Explain and illustrate the concepts of scarcity, production efficiency, and tradeoff using the production possibilities frontier.**

   - The production possibilities frontier, *PPF*, describes the limits to what can be produced by using all the available resources efficiently.
   - Points inside and on the *PPF* are attainable. Points outside the *PPF* are unattainable.
   - Production at any point on the *PPF* achieves production efficiency. Production at a point inside the *PPF* is inefficient.
   - When production is efficient—on the *PPF*—people face a tradeoff. If production is at a point inside the *PPF*, there is a free lunch to be had.

2. **Calculate opportunity cost.**

   - Along the *PPF*, the opportunity cost of *X* (the item measured on the *x*-axis) is the decrease in *Y* (the item measured on the *y*-axis) divided by the increase in *X*.
   - The opportunity cost of *Y* is the inverse of the opportunity cost of *X*.
   - The opportunity cost of producing a good increases as the quantity of the good produced increases.

3. **Explain what makes production possibilities expand.**

   - Technological change and increases in capital and human capital expand production possibilities.
   - The opportunity cost of economic growth is the decrease in current consumption.

4. **Explain how people gain from specialization and trade.**

   - A person has a comparative advantage in an activity if he or she can perform that activity at a lower opportunity cost than someone else.
   - People gain by increasing the production of the item in which they have a comparative advantage and trading.

## Key Terms

MyEconLab Key Terms Quiz

Absolute advantage, 73
Comparative advantage, 73
Economic growth, 70

Production efficiency, 62
Production possibilities frontier, 60
Tradeoff, 63

## CHAPTER CHECKPOINT

**TABLE 1**

| Corn (bushels) | | Beef (pounds) |
|---|---|---|
| 250 | and | 0 |
| 200 | and | 300 |
| 100 | and | 500 |
| 0 | and | 600 |

**TABLE 2**

| Labor (hours) | Entertainment (units) | | Good food (units) |
|---|---|---|---|
| 0 | 0 | or | 0 |
| 10 | 20 | or | 30 |
| 20 | 40 | or | 50 |
| 30 | 60 | or | 60 |
| 40 | 80 | or | 65 |
| 50 | 100 | or | 67 |

**FIGURE 1**

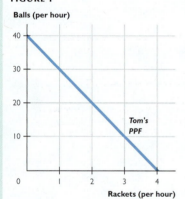

**FIGURE 2**

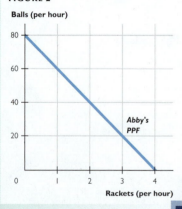

## Study Plan Problems and Applications

**1.** Table 1 shows the quantities of corn and beef that a farm can produce in a year. Draw a graph of the farm's *PPF*. Mark on the graph.

- An inefficient combination of corn and beef—label this point *A*.
- An unattainable combination of corn and beef—label this point *B*.
- An efficient combination of corn and beef—label this point *C*.

Use the following information to work Problems **2** and **3**.

The people of Leisure Island have 50 hours of labor a day that can be used to produce entertainment and good food. Table 2 shows the maximum quantity of *either* entertainment *or* good food that Leisure Island can produce with different quantities of labor.

**2.** Is an output of 50 units of entertainment and 50 units of good food attainable and efficient? With a production of 50 units of entertainment and 50 units of good food, do the people of Leisure Island face a tradeoff?

**3.** What is the opportunity cost of producing an additional unit of entertainment? Explain how the opportunity cost of producing a unit of entertainment changes as more entertainment is produced.

Use the following information to work Problems **4** and **5**.

**Malaria can be controlled**
The World Health Organization's malaria chief says that it is too costly to try to fully eradicate the disease. He says that by using nets, medicine, and DDT it is possible to eliminate 90 percent of malaria cases. But to eliminate 100 percent of cases would be extremely costly.

Source: *The New York Times*, March 4, 2008

**4.** Make a graph of the production possibilities frontier with malaria control on the *x*-axis and other goods and services on the *y*-axis.

**5.** Describe how the opportunity cost of controlling malaria changes as more resources are used to reduce the number of malaria cases.

**6.** Explain how the following events influence U.S. production possibilities:

- Some retail workers are re-employed building dams and wind farms.
- More people take early retirement.
- Drought devastates California's economy.

Use the following information to work Problems **7** and **8**.

Figures 1 and 2 show Tom's and Abby's production possibilities. Tom uses all his resources and produces 2 rackets and 20 balls an hour. Abby uses all her resources and produces 2 rackets and 40 balls an hour.

**7.** What is Tom's opportunity cost of producing a racket? What is Abby's opportunity cost of a racket? Who has a comparative advantage in producing rackets? Who has a comparative advantage in producing balls?

**8.** If Tom and Abby specialize and trade balls and rackets at the price of 15 balls per racket, what are Tom's and Abby's gains from trade?

**9.** Read *Eye on the Environment* on p. 68 and describe a tradeoff faced when deciding how to generate electricity and whether to use wind power.

## Instructor Assignable Problems and Applications

MyEconLab Homework, Quiz, or Test if assigned by instructor

Use the following information to work Problems **1** to **4**.

Representatives Waxman of California and Markey of Massachusetts proposed a law to limit greenhouse gas emissions from electricity generation and require electricity producers to generate a minimum percentage of power using renewable fuels, with some emission rights to be auctioned. The Congressional Budget Office estimated that the government would receive $846 billion from auctions and would spend $821 billion on incentive programs and compensation for higher energy prices. Electricity producers would spend $208 million a year to comply with the new rules. (Think of these dollar amounts as dollars' worth of other goods and services.)

1. Would the Waxman-Markey law achieve production efficiency?

2. Is the $846 billion that electricity producers would pay for the right to emit greenhouse gasses part of the opportunity cost of producing electricity?

3. Is the $821 billion that the government would spend on incentive programs and compensation for higher energy prices part of the opportunity cost of producing electricity?

4. Is the $208 million that electricity producers will spend to comply with the new rules part of the opportunity cost of producing electricity?

5. The people of Foodland have 40 hours of labor a day to bake pizza and bread. Table 1 shows the maximum quantity of *either* pizza *or* bread that Foodland can bake with different quantities of labor. Can Foodland produce 30 pizzas and 30 loaves of bread a day? If it can, is this output efficient, do the people of Foodland face a tradeoff, and what is the opportunity cost of producing an additional pizza?

**TABLE 1**

| Labor (hours) | Pizzas | | Bread (loaves) |
|---|---|---|---|
| 0 | 0 | or | 0 |
| 10 | 30 | or | 10 |
| 20 | 50 | or | 20 |
| 30 | 60 | or | 30 |
| 40 | 65 | or | 40 |

Use Table 2, which shows a farm's production possibilities, to work Problems **6** and **7**.

6. If the farm uses its resources efficiently, what is the opportunity cost of an increase in chicken production from 300 pounds to 500 pounds a year? Explain your answer.

7. If the farm adopted a new technology, which allows it to use fewer resources to fatten chickens, explain how the farm's production possibilities will change. Explain how the opportunity cost of producing a bushel of soybean will be affected.

**TABLE 2**

| Soybean (bushels per year) | | Chicken (pounds per year) |
|---|---|---|
| 500 | and | 0 |
| 400 | and | 300 |
| 200 | and | 500 |
| 0 | and | 600 |

8. In an hour, Sue can produce 40 caps or 4 jackets and Tessa can produce 80 caps or 4 jackets. Who has a comparative advantage in producing caps? If Sue and Tessa specialize and trade, who will gain?

Use the following opinion to work Problems **9** to **11**.

**Free Internet?**

Everyone should have free Internet access to education, news, jobs, and more.

9. Explain how Internet access has changed the production possibilities and the opportunity cost of producing education and news.

10. Sketch a *PPF* curve with education and news on the *x*-axis and other goods and services on the *y*-axis before and after the Internet.

11. Explain why it is not possible for everyone to have free Internet access to education, news, jobs, and more.

**TABLE 1**

| Possibility | Fish (pounds) | | Berries (pounds) |
|---|---|---|---|
| A | 0 | and | 40 |
| B | 1 | and | 36 |
| C | 2 | and | 30 |
| D | 3 | and | 22 |
| E | 4 | and | 12 |
| F | 5 | and | 0 |

# Multiple Choice Quiz

**1.** Table 1 shows the production possibilities of an island community. Choose the best statement.

A. This community has enough resources to produce 2 pounds of fish and 36 pounds of berries.

B. This community cannot produce 2 pounds of fish and 36 pounds of berries because this combination is inefficient.

C. This community will waste resources if it produces 2 pounds of fish and 22 pounds of berries.

D. This community can produce 2 pounds of fish and 30 pounds of berries but this combination is inefficient.

**2.** Table 1 shows the production possibilities of an island community. Choose the best statement.

A. Suppose that this community produces 3 pounds of fish and 20 pounds of berries. If it decides to gather more berries, it faces a tradeoff.

B. When this community produces 4 pounds of fish and 12 pounds of berries it faces a tradeoff, but it is inefficient.

C. Suppose that this community produces 5 pounds of fish and 0 pounds of berries. If it decides to gather some berries, it will get a free lunch.

D. If this community produces 3 pounds of fish and 22 pounds of berries, production is efficient but to produce more fish it faces a tradeoff.

**3.** Table 1 shows the production possibilities of an island community. This community's opportunity cost of producing 1 pound of fish _____.

A. is the increase in the quantity of berries gathered as the quantity of fish increases by 1 pound

B. increases as the quantity of berries gathered increases

C. is 10 pounds of berries if the quantity of fish increases from 2 to 3 pounds

D. increases as the quantity of fish caught increases

**4.** Table 1 shows the production possibilities of an island community. Choose the best statement.

A. When a drought hits the island, its *PPF* rotates outward.

B. When the islanders discover a better way of catching fish, the island's *PPF* rotates outward.

C. When islanders reduce the time they spend gathering berries, the *PPF* rotates inward.

D. If the islanders decide to spend more time gathering berries but continue to spend the same amount of time fishing, they face a tradeoff.

**5.** Mary makes 10 pies and 20 cakes a day and her opportunity cost of producing a cake is 2 pies. Tim makes 20 pies and 10 cakes a day and his opportunity cost of producing a cake is 4 pies. If Mary and Tim specialize in producing the good in which each has a comparative advantage, _____.

A. Mary produces only pies

B. Tim produces both pies and cakes

C. Mary produces only cakes while Tim produces only pies

D. Tim produces only cakes while Mary produces only pies

Why did the price of coffee rise in 2014?

# Demand and Supply

**4**

**When you have completed your study of this chapter, you will be able to**

**1** Distinguish between quantity demanded and demand, and explain what determines demand.

**2** Distinguish between quantity supplied and supply, and explain what determines supply.

**3** Explain how demand and supply determine price and quantity in a market, and explain the effects of changes in demand and supply.

**4** Explain how price floors, price ceilings, and sticky prices create surpluses, unemployment, and shortages.

MyEconLab Big Picture Video

## COMPETITIVE MARKETS

When you want a latte you go to a coffee shop. When a coffee shop needs to re-stock with beans and milk, it calls its suppliers of those items. You, your favorite coffee shop, and the shop's suppliers are trading in *markets*.

You learned in Chapter 2 that a market is any arrangement that brings buyers and sellers together. A market has two sides: demand (buyers) and supply (sellers). There are markets for *goods* such as a latte and a bagel, running shoes, apples, and hiking boots; for *services* such as airplane trips, haircuts, and tennis lessons; for *resources* such as coffee beans, computer programmers, and tractors; and for *manufactured components* such as memory chips and auto parts. There are also markets for money such as Japanese yen and for financial securities such as Facebook stock. Only imagination limits what can be traded in markets.

Some markets are physical places where buyers and sellers meet and where an auctioneer or a broker helps to determine the prices. Examples of this type of market are the New York Stock Exchange; wholesale fish, meat, and produce markets; and used car auctions.

Some markets are virtual spaces where buyers and sellers never meet face-to-face but connect over telephone lines or the Internet. Examples include currency markets, e-commerce Web sites such as Amazon.com and iTunes, auction sites such as eBay, and travel Web sites.

But most markets are unorganized collections of buyers and sellers. You do most of your trading in this type of market. An example is the market for coffee and snacks. The buyers in this $75-billion-a-year market are the more than 100 million Americans who regularly drink coffee. The sellers are the 55,000 coffee shops and snack bars. Each buyer can visit several different sellers, and each seller knows that the buyer has a choice of many alternatives.

Markets vary in the intensity of competition that buyers and sellers face. In this chapter, we're going to study a *competitive market* that has so many buyers and so many sellers that no single buyer or seller can influence the price.

*Markets for coffee and a bagel …*

*running shoes …*

*and airline travel.*

## 4.1  DEMAND

MyEconLab Concept Video

First, we'll study the behavior of buyers in a competitive market. The **quantity demanded** of any good, service, or resource is the amount that people are willing and able to buy during a specified period at a specified price. For example, when spring water costs $1 a bottle, you decide to buy 2 bottles a day. The 2 bottles a day is your quantity demanded of spring water.

The quantity demanded is measured as an amount *per unit of time*. For example, your quantity demanded of water is 2 bottles *per day*. We could express this quantity as 14 bottles per week, or some other number per month or per year. A particular number of bottles without a time dimension has no meaning.

Many things influence buying plans, and one of them is price. We look first at the relationship between quantity demanded and price. To study this relationship, we keep all other influences on buying plans the same and we ask: How, other things remaining the same, does the quantity demanded of a good change as its price varies? The law of demand provides the answer.

**Quantity demanded**
The amount of any good, service, or resource that people are willing and able to buy during a specified period at a specified price.

### ■ The Law of Demand

The **law of demand** states

> **Other things remaining the same, if the price of a good rises, the quantity demanded of that good decreases; and if the price of a good falls, the quantity demanded of that good increases.**

So the law of demand states that when all other things remain the same, if the price of an iPhone falls, people will buy more iPhones; or if the price of a baseball ticket rises, people will buy fewer baseball tickets.

Why does the quantity demanded increase if the price falls, all other things remaining the same?

The answer is that, faced with a limited budget, people always have an incentive to find the best deals available. If the price of one item falls and the prices of all other items remain the same, the item with the lower price is a better deal than it was before, so some people buy more of this item. Suppose, for example, that the price of bottled water fell from $2 a bottle to $1.50 a bottle while the price of Gatorade remained at $2 a bottle. Wouldn't some people switch from Gatorade to water? By doing so, they save 50¢ a bottle, which they can spend on other things they previously couldn't afford.

Think about the things that you buy and ask yourself: Which of these items does *not* obey the law of demand? If the price of a new textbook were lower, other things remaining the same (including the price of a used textbook), would you buy more new textbooks? Then think about all the things that you do not now buy but would if you could afford them. How cheap would a PC have to be for you to buy *both* a desktop and a laptop? There is a price that is low enough to entice you!

**Law of demand**
Other things remaining the same, if the price of a good rises, the quantity demanded of that good decreases; and if the price of a good falls, the quantity demanded of that good increases.

### ■ Demand Schedule and Demand Curve

**Demand** is the relationship between the quantity demanded and the price of a good when all other influences on buying plans remain the same. The quantity demanded is *one* quantity at *one* price. *Demand* is a *list of quantities at different prices* illustrated by a demand schedule and a demand curve.

**Demand**
The relationship between the quantity demanded and the price of a good when all other influences on buying plans remain the same.

**Demand schedule**

A list of the quantities demanded at each different price when all the other influences on buying plans remain the same.

**Demand curve**

A graph of the relationship between the quantity demanded of a good and its price when all the other influences on buying plans remain the same.

A **demand schedule** is a list of the quantities demanded at each different price when *all the other influences on buying plans remain the same*. The table in Figure 4.1 is a demand schedule for bottled water. It tells us that if the price of water is $2.00 a bottle, the quantity demanded is 8.5 million bottles a day. If the price of water is $1.50 a bottle, the quantity demanded is 9 million bottles a day. The quantity demanded increases to 10 million bottles a day at a price of $1.00 a bottle and to 12 million bottles a day at a price of 50¢ a bottle.

A **demand curve** is a graph of the relationship between the quantity demanded of a good and its price when all the other influences on buying plans remain the same. The points on the demand curve labeled *A* through *D* represent the rows *A* through *D* of the demand schedule. For example, point *B* on the graph represents row *B* of the demand schedule and shows that the quantity demanded is 9 million bottles a day when the price is $1.50 a bottle. Point *C* on the demand curve represents row *C* of the demand schedule and shows that the quantity demanded is 10 million bottles a day when the price is $1.00 a bottle.

The downward slope of the demand curve illustrates the law of demand. Along the demand curve, when the price of the good *falls*, the quantity demanded *increases*. For example, in Figure 4.1, when the price of a bottle of water falls from $1.00 to 50 cents, the quantity demanded increases from 10 million bottles a day to 12 million bottles a day. Conversely, when the price *rises*, the quantity demanded *decreases*. For example, when the price rises from $1.00 to $1.50 a bottle, the quantity demanded decreases from 10 million bottles a day to 9 million bottles a day.

**FIGURE 4.1**

Demand Schedule and Demand Curve

MyEconLab Animation

The table shows a demand schedule that lists the quantity of water demanded at each price if all other influences on buying plans remain the same. At a price of $1.50 a bottle, the quantity demanded is 9 million bottles a day.

The demand curve shows the relationship between the quantity demanded and price, other things remaining the same. The downward-sloping demand curve illustrates the law of demand. When the price falls, the quantity demanded increases; and when the price rises, the quantity demanded decreases.

| | Price (dollars per bottle) | Quantity demanded (millions of bottles per day) |
|---|---|---|
| A | 2.00 | 8.5 |
| B | 1.50 | 9.0 |
| C | 1.00 | 10.0 |
| D | 0.50 | 12.0 |

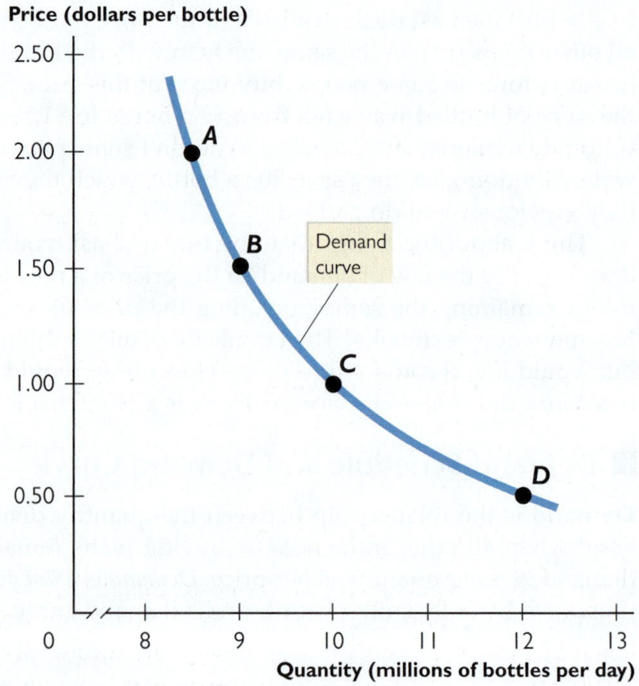

# ■ Changes in Demand

The demand curve shows how the quantity demanded changes when the price of the good changes but *all other influences on buying plans remain the same*. When the price of a good changes, we call the resulting change in buying plans a **change in the quantity demanded**. When any influence on buying plans other than the price of the good changes, there is a **change in demand**.

The main influences on buying plans that change demand are

- Prices of related goods
- Expected future prices
- Income
- Expectations
- Number of buyers
- Preferences

**Change in the quantity demanded**
A change in the quantity of a good that people plan to buy that results from a change in the price of the good with all other influences on buying plans remaining the same.

**Change in demand**
A change in the quantity that people plan to buy when any influence on buying plans other than the price of the good changes.

## Prices of Related Goods

Goods have substitutes and complements. A **substitute** for a good is another good that can be consumed in its place. Chocolate cake is a substitute for cheesecake, and bottled water is a substitute for Gatorade. The demand for a good and the price of one of its substitutes move in the *same direction*. The demand for a good *increases* if the price of one of its substitutes *rises*; the demand for a good *decreases* if the price of one of its substitutes *falls*. For example, the demand for cheesecake increases when the price of chocolate cake rises.

A **complement** of a good is another good that is consumed with it. A helmet is a complement of a bike, and bottled water is a complement of fitness center services. The demand for a good and the price of one of its complements move in *opposite directions*. The demand for a good *decreases* if the price of one of its complements *rises*; the demand for a good *increases* if the price of one of its complements *falls*. For example, the demand for helmets decreases when the price of a bike rises.

**Substitute**
A good that can be consumed in place of another good.

**Complement**
A good that is consumed with another good.

## Expected Future Prices

A rise in the expected *future* price of a good increases the *current* demand for that good and a fall in the expected *future* price decreases *current* demand. If you expect the price of noodles to rise next week, you buy a big enough stockpile to get you through the next few weeks. Your demand for noodles today has increased. If you expect the price of noodles to fall next week, you buy none now and plan to buy next week. Your demand for noodles today has decreased.

## Income

A rise in income brings an increase in demand and a fall in income brings a decrease in demand for a **normal good**. A rise in income brings a *decrease* in demand and a fall in income brings an *increase* in demand for an **inferior good**. For example, if your income increases and you decide to buy more chicken and less pasta, for you, chicken is a normal good and pasta is an inferior good.

**Normal good**
A good for which demand increases when income increases and demand decreases when income decreases.

**Inferior good**
A good for which demand decreases when income increases and demand increases when income decreases.

## Expectations

When income is expected to increase in the future, or when credit is easy to get and the cost of borrowing is low, the demand for some goods increases. And when income is expected to decrease in the future, or when credit is hard to get and the cost of borrowing is high, the demand for some goods decreases.

### Number of Buyers

The greater the number of buyers in a market, the larger is demand. For example, the demand for parking spaces, movies, bottled water, or just about anything is greater in New York City than it is in Boise, Idaho.

### Preferences

Tastes or *preferences,* as economists call them, influence demand. When preferences change, the demand for one item increases and the demand for another item (or items) decreases. For example, preferences have changed as people have become better informed about the health hazards of tobacco. This change in preferences has decreased the demand for cigarettes and has increased the demand for nicotine patches. Preferences also change when new goods become available. For example, the development of smartphones has decreased the demand for landlines and has increased the demand for Internet service.

### ■ Illustrating Changes in Buying Plans

Figure 4.2 illustrates and summarizes the distinction between a change in the quantity demanded and a change in demand. When the price of a good changes, there is a *change in the quantity demanded* shown by a *movement along the demand curve.* When any other influence on buying plans changes, there is a *change in demand,* which is shown by a *shift of the demand curve.* When demand *decreases,* the demand curve *shifts leftward* to $D_1$, and when demand *increases,* the demand curve *shifts rightward* to $D_2$.

---

**FIGURE 4.2**

Change in Quantity Demanded Versus Change in Demand             MyEconLab Animation

**❶ A decrease in the quantity demanded**

The quantity demanded decreases and there is a movement up along the demand curve $D_0$ if the price of the good rises and other things remain the same.

**❸ A decrease in demand**

Demand decreases and the demand curve shifts leftward (from $D_0$ to $D_1$) if

- The price of a substitute falls or the price of a complement rises.
- The price of the good is expected to fall.
- Income decreases.*
- Expected future income or credit decreases.
- The number of buyers decreases.

\* Bottled water is a normal good.

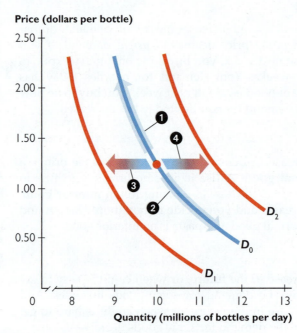

**❷ An increase in the quantity demanded**

The quantity demanded increases and there is a movement down along the demand curve $D_0$ if the price of the good falls and other things remain the same.

**❹ An increase in demand**

Demand increases and the demand curve shifts rightward (from $D_0$ to $D_2$) if

- The price of a substitute rises or the price of a complement falls.
- The price of the good is expected to rise.
- Income increases.
- Expected future income or credit increases.
- The number of buyers increases.

**CHECKPOINT 4.1**

MyEconLab Study Plan 4.1
Key Terms Quiz
Solutions Video

**Distinguish between quantity demanded and demand, and explain what determines demand.**

## Practice Problems

The following events occur one at a time in the market for smartphones:
- The price of a smartphone falls.
- Producers announce that smartphone prices will fall next month.
- The price of a call made from a smartphone falls.
- The price of a call made from a land-line phone increases.
- An increase in memory makes smartphones more popular.

1. Explain the effect of each event on the demand for smartphones.

2. Use a graph to illustrate the effect of each event.

3. Does any event (or events) illustrate the law of demand?

## In the News

**Airline profits soar yet no relief for passengers**
Airplanes are more crowded than ever and fares are at a five-year high.
Source: *USA Today*, January 27, 2015

Does this news clip imply that the law of demand doesn't work in the real world? Explain why or why not.

## Solutions to Practice Problems

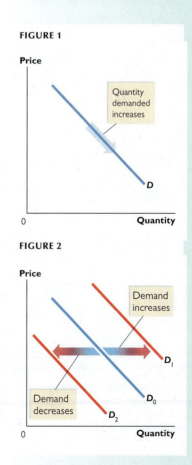

**FIGURE 1**

Price

Quantity demanded increases

$D$

0                          **Quantity**

**FIGURE 2**

Price

Demand increases

$D_1$

Demand decreases

$D_0$

$D_2$

0                          **Quantity**

1. A fall in the price of a smartphone increases the quantity of smartphones demanded but has no effect on the demand for smartphones.
   With the producers' announcement, the expected future price of a smartphone falls, which decreases the demand for smartphones today.
   A fall in the price of a call from a smartphone increases the demand for smartphones because a smartphone call and a smartphone are complements.
   A rise in the price of a call from a land-line phone increases the demand for smartphones because a land-line phone and a smartphone are substitutes.
   With smartphones more popular, the demand for smartphones increases.

2. Figure 1 illustrates the effect of a fall in the price of a smartphone as a movement along the demand curve $D$.
   Figure 2 illustrates the effect of an increase in the demand for smartphones as the shift of the demand curve from $D_0$ to $D_1$ and a decrease in the demand for smartphones as the shift of the demand curve from $D_0$ to $D_2$.

3. A fall in the price of a smartphone (other things remaining the same) illustrates the law of demand. Figure 1 illustrates the law of demand. The other events change demand and do not illustrate the law of demand.

## Solution to In the News

The law of demand states: If the price of an airline ticket rises, other things remaining the same, the quantity demanded of airline tickets will decrease. The demand curve for airline tickets slopes downward. The law of demand does work in the real world. Airlines can fill planes at high fares because "other things" have not remained the same. The demand for air travel has increased.

MyEconLab Concept Video

## 4.2 SUPPLY

A market has two sides. On one side are the buyers, or demanders, that we've just studied. On the other side of the market are the sellers, or suppliers. We now study the forces that determine suppliers' plans.

**Quantity supplied**

The amount of any good, service, or resource that people are willing and able to sell during a specified period at a specified price.

The **quantity supplied** of a good, service, or resource is the amount that people are willing and able to sell during a specified period at a specified price. For example, when the price of spring water is $1.50 a bottle, a spring owner decides to sell 2,000 bottles a day. The 2,000 bottles a day is the quantity supplied of spring water by this individual producer. (As in the case of demand, the quantity supplied is measured as an amount *per unit of time*.)

Many things influence selling plans, and one of them is the price. We look first at the relationship between quantity supplied of a good and its price. To study this relationship, we keep all other influences on selling plans the same, and we ask: Other things remaining the same, how does the quantity supplied of a good change as its price varies? The law of supply provides the answer.

### ■ The Law of Supply

**Law of supply**

Other things remaining the same, if the price of a good rises, the quantity supplied of that good increases; and if the price of a good falls, the quantity supplied of that good decreases.

The **law of supply** states

> **Other things remaining the same, if the price of a good rises, the quantity supplied of that good increases; and if the price of a good falls, the quantity supplied of that good decreases.**

So the law of supply states that when all other things remain the same, if the price of bottled water rises, spring owners will offer more water for sale; if the price of a flat-screen TV falls, Sony Corp. will offer fewer flat-screen TVs for sale.

Why, other things remaining the same, does the quantity supplied increase if the price rises and decrease if the price falls? Part of the answer lies in the principle of increasing opportunity cost (see p. 68). Because factors of production are not equally productive in all activities, as more of a good is produced, the opportunity cost of producing it increases. A higher price provides the incentive to bear the higher opportunity cost of increased production. Another part of the answer is that for a given cost, the higher price brings a larger profit, so sellers have greater incentive to increase production.

Think about the resources that you own and can offer for sale to others and ask yourself: Which of these items does *not* obey the law of supply? If the wage rate for summer jobs increased, would you have an incentive to work longer hours and bear the higher opportunity cost of forgone leisure? If the bank offered a higher interest rate on deposits, would you have an incentive to save more and bear the higher opportunity cost of forgone consumption? If the used book dealer offered a higher price for last year's textbooks, would you have an incentive to sell that handy math text and bear the higher opportunity cost of visiting the library (or finding a friend) whenever you needed the book?

### ■ Supply Schedule and Supply Curve

**Supply**

The relationship between the quantity supplied and the price of a good when all other influences on selling plans remain the same.

**Supply** is the relationship between the quantity supplied and the price of a good when all other influences on selling plans remain the same. The quantity supplied is *one* quantity at *one* price. *Supply* is a *list of quantities at different prices* illustrated by a supply schedule and a supply curve.

A **supply schedule** lists the quantities supplied at each different price when all the other influences on selling plans remain the same. The table in Figure 4.3 is a supply schedule for bottled water. It tells us that if the price of water is 50¢ a bottle, the quantity supplied is 8 million bottles a day. If the price of water is $1.00 a bottle, the quantity supplied is 10 million bottles a day. The quantity supplied increases to 11 million bottles a day at a price of $1.50 a bottle and to 11.5 million bottles a day at a price of $2.00 a bottle.

A **supply curve** is a graph of the relationship between the quantity supplied of a good and its price when all the other influences on selling plans remain the same. The points on the supply curve labeled *A* through *D* represent the rows *A* through *D* of the supply schedule. For example, point *C* on the supply curve represents row *C* of the supply schedule and shows that the quantity supplied is 10 million bottles a day when the price is $1.00 a bottle. Point *B* on the supply curve represents row *B* of the supply schedule and shows that the quantity supplied is 11 million bottles a day when the price is $1.50 a bottle.

The upward slope of the supply curve illustrates the law of supply. Along the supply curve, when the price of the good *rises*, the quantity supplied *increases*. For example, in Figure 4.3, when the price of a bottle of water rises from $1.50 to $2.00, the quantity supplied increases from 11 million bottles a day to 11.5 million bottles a day. And when the price *falls*, the quantity supplied *decreases*. For example, when the price falls from $1.50 to $1.00 a bottle, the quantity supplied decreases from 11 million bottles a day to 10 million bottles a day.

**Supply schedule**
A list of the quantities supplied at each different price when all the other influences on selling plans remain the same.

**Supply curve**
A graph of the relationship between the quantity supplied of a good and its price when all the other influences on selling plans remain the same.

### FIGURE 4.3

Supply Schedule and Supply Curve

MyEconLab Animation

| | Price (dollars per bottle) | Quantity supplied (millions of bottles per day) |
|---|---|---|
| **A** | 2.00 | 11.5 |
| **B** | 1.50 | 11.0 |
| **C** | 1.00 | 10.0 |
| **D** | 0.50 | 8.0 |

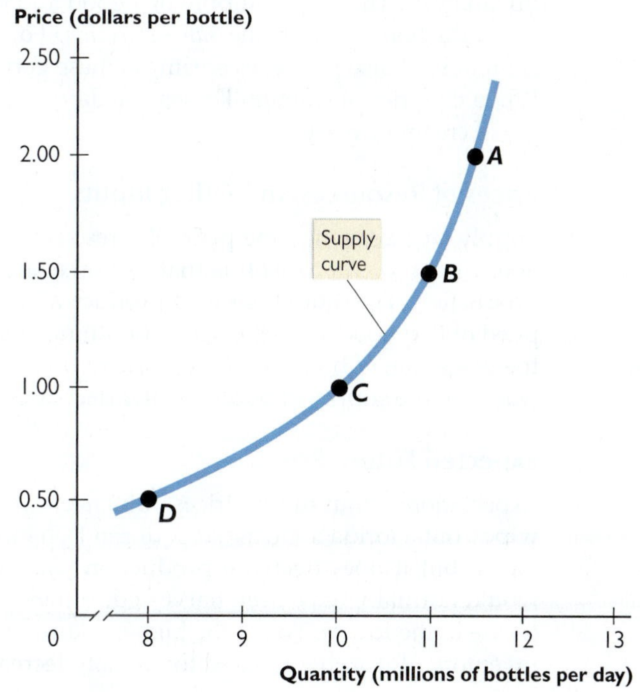

The table shows a supply schedule that lists the quantity of water supplied at each price if all other influences on selling plans remain the same. At a price of $1.50 a bottle, the quantity supplied is 11 million bottles a day.

The supply curve shows the relationship between the quantity supplied and price, other things remaining the same. The upward-sloping supply curve illustrates the law of supply. When the price rises, the quantity supplied increases; and when the price falls, the quantity supplied decreases.

**Change in the quantity supplied**

A change in the quantity of a good that suppliers plan to sell that results from a change in the price of the good.

**Change in supply**

A change in the quantity that suppliers plan to sell when any influence on selling plans other than the price of the good changes.

**Substitute in production**

A good that can be produced in place of another good.

**Complement in production**

A good that is produced along with another good.

## ■ Changes in Supply

The supply curve shows how the quantity supplied changes when the price of the good changes but *all other influences on selling plans remain the same*. When the price of the good changes, we call the resulting influence on selling plans a **change in the quantity supplied**. When any other influence on selling plans changes, there is a **change in supply**.

The main influences on selling plans that change supply are

- Prices of related goods
- Prices of resources and other inputs
- Expectations
- Number of sellers
- Productivity

### Prices of Related Goods

Related goods are either substitutes *in production* or complements *in production*. A **substitute in production** for a good is another good that can be produced in its place. Skinny jeans are substitutes in production for boot cut jeans in a clothing factory. The supply of a good *decreases* if the price of one of its substitutes in production *rises*; and the supply of a good *increases* if the price of one of its substitutes in production *falls*. That is, the supply of a good and the price of one of its substitutes in production move in *opposite directions*. For example, a clothing factory can produce cargo pants or button-fly jeans, so these goods are substitutes in production. When the price of button-fly jeans rises, the clothing factory switches production from cargo pants to button-fly jeans, so the supply of cargo pants decreases.

A **complement in production** of a good is another good that is produced along with it. Cream is a complement in production of skim milk in a dairy. The supply of a good *increases* if the price of one of its complements in production *rises*; and the supply of a good *decreases* if the price of one of its complements in production *falls*. That is, the supply of a good and the price of one of its complements in production move in the *same direction*. For example, when a dairy produces skim milk, it also produces cream, so these goods are complements in production. When the price of skim milk rises, the dairy produces more skim milk, so the supply of cream increases.

### Prices of Resources and Other Inputs

Supply changes when the price of a resource or other input used to produce the good changes. The reason is that resource and input prices influence the cost of production. The more it costs to produce a good, the smaller is the quantity supplied of that good at each price (other things remaining the same). For example, if the wage rate of bottling-plant workers rises, it costs more to produce a bottle of water, so the supply of bottled water decreases.

### Expected Future Prices

Expectations about future prices influence supply. For example, a severe frost that wipes out Florida's citrus crop doesn't change the production of orange juice today, but it does decrease production later in the year when the current crop would normally have been harvested. Sellers of orange juice will expect the price to rise in the future. To get the higher future price, some sellers will increase their inventory of frozen juice, and this action decreases the supply of juice today.

## Number of Sellers

The greater the number of sellers in a market, the larger is the supply. For example, many new sellers have developed springs and water-bottling plants in the United States, and the supply of bottled water has increased.

## Productivity

*Productivity* is output per unit of input. An increase in productivity lowers the cost of producing the good and increases its supply. A decrease in productivity has the opposite effect and decreases supply.

Technological change and the increased use of capital increase productivity. For example, advances in electronic technology have lowered the cost of producing a computer and increased the supply of computers. Technological change brings new goods such as the iPad, the supply of which was previously zero.

Natural events such as severe weather and earthquakes decrease productivity and decrease supply. For example, a four-year drought in California decreased the supply of agricultural products including nuts, fruits, and vegetables in 2015.

## ■ Illustrating a Change in Selling Plans

Figure 4.4 illustrates and summarizes the distinction between a change in the quantity supplied and a change in supply. When the price of a good changes, there is a *change in the quantity supplied* shown by a *movement along the supply curve*. When any other influence on buying plans changes, there is a *change in supply*, which is shown by a *shift of the supply curve*. When supply *decreases*, the supply curve *shifts leftward* to $S_1$ and when supply *increases*, the supply curve *shifts rightward* to $S_2$.

### ■ FIGURE 4.4

Change in Quantity Supplied Versus Change in Supply          MyEconLab Animation

**❶ A decrease in the quantity supplied**

The quantity supplied decreases and there is a movement down along the supply curve $S_0$ if the price of the good falls and other things remain the same.

**❸ A decrease in supply**

Supply decreases and the supply curve shifts leftward (from $S_0$ to $S_1$) if

- The price of a substitute in production rises.
- The price of a complement in production falls.
- A resource price or other input price rises.
- The price of the good is expected to rise.
- The number of sellers decreases.
- Productivity decreases.

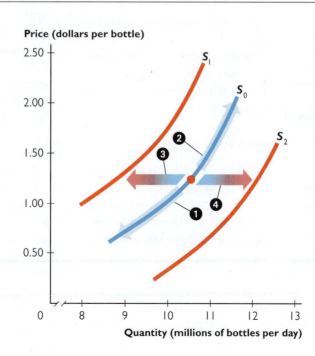

**❷ An increase in the quantity supplied**

The quantity supplied increases and there is a movement up along the supply curve $S_0$ if the price of the good rises and other things remain the same.

**❹ An increase in supply**

Supply increases and the supply curve shifts rightward (from $S_0$ to $S_2$) if

- The price of a substitute in production falls.
- The price of a complement in production rises.
- A resource price or other input price falls.
- The price of the good is expected to fall.
- The number of sellers increases.
- Productivity increases.

# EYE on YOUR LIFE

## Understanding and Using Demand and Supply

To truly understand the demand and supply model, it is a good idea to go beyond just memorizing the key terms and definitions and lists of factors that change demand or change supply. Take ownership of the model by seeing how it explains your buying plans and your selling plans.

### Your Buying Plans

Think about the things you buy: the quantities you buy and the prices you pay. These quantities and prices are points on your demand curves.

Now think about how some price changes would change your buying plans. How would your buying plans change if prices at the campus coffee shop increased? For which items would you change your quantity demanded? And for which items would you change your demand?

How would your buying plans change if you started a new job with a higher wage? What would you buy more of? What would you buy less of?

Suppose that you were just about to get a new smartphone when Apple and Samsung announce plans to launch new phones next month. You figure that the prices of the older models will fall. How will this fall in the expected future price of a smartphone influence your buying plans?

For each thought experiment we've just described, think about whether you are sliding along a demand curve or shifting a demand curve.

### Your Selling Plans

Most likely, you don't sell much stuff, but you own one precious resource that you might sell: your time.

If you have a job, think about the number of hours you work and the wage rate you earn. Are you working as many hours as you want to? If you are, you're at a point on the supply curve of your labor services.

How would you respond to a rise in the wage rate? Would you plan to work more hours or fewer hours?

Another thing you own is a pile of textbooks. Think about your selling plan for when your courses are over at the end of the semester. What is the lowest price at which you will sell this textbook? That price is a point on your supply curve of this book to the used book market.

You might also have a few old things that you'd like to sell on eBay. Again, think about your minimum supply-price—the point on your supply curve of these items.

By doing these thought experiments about your selling plans, you can make the idea of supply and the supply curve more concrete.

### From Plans to Actions

*Your* demand and supply curves and the *market* demand and supply curves describe *plans*. They are statements about "what-if." They describe the buying plans and the selling plans at different possible prices. But when you act on your plan and buy something, someone else must have a plan to sell that item. Your buying plan must match someone else's selling plan.

Neither demand nor supply on its own tells us what actually happens in a market. To find buying plans and selling plans that match, we must look at demand and supply together. That's what we look at in the next section of this chapter. You will see how prices adjust to balance the opposing forces of demand and supply.

### The Rest of Your Life

The demand and supply model is going to be a big part of the rest of your life! You will use it again and again during your economics course, so having a firm grasp of it will bring an immediate payoff.

But much more important, by understanding the laws of demand and supply and being aware of how prices adjust to balance these two opposing forces, you will have a much better appreciation of how your economic world works.

Every time you hear someone complaining about a price hike and blaming it on someone's greed, think about the market forces and how demand and supply determine that price.

As you shop for your favorite clothing, music, and food items, try to describe how supply and demand influence the prices of these goods.

## CHECKPOINT 4.2

MyEconLab Study Plan 4.2
Key Terms Quiz
Solutions Video

**Distinguish between quantity supplied and supply, and explain what determines supply.**

## Practice Problems

Lumber companies make timber beams from logs. In the process of making beams, the mill produces sawdust, which is made into pressed wood. In the market for timber beams, the following events occur one at a time:

- The wage rate of sawmill workers rises.
- The price of sawdust rises.
- The price of a timber beam rises.
- The price of a timber beam is expected to rise next year.
- A new law reduces the amount of forest that can be cut for timber.
- A new technology lowers the cost of producing timber beams.

1. Explain the effect of each event on the supply of timber beams.
2. Use a graph to illustrate the effect of each event.
3. Does any event (or events) illustrate the law of supply?

## In the News

**Pump prices slide as crude oil falls to six-year low**
The average price for regular gasoline at U.S. pumps fell almost 4¢ in March to $2.50 a gallon. The price of crude oil dropped to $43.46 per barrel on March 17, the lowest since March 2009.

Source: *Bloomberg Business*, March 23, 2015

Explain the effect of a lower oil price on the supply of gasoline.

## Solutions to Practice Problems

1. A rise in workers' wage rates increases the cost of producing a timber beam and decreases the supply of timber beams. A rise in the price of sawdust increases the supply of timber beams because sawdust and timber beams are complements in production. A rise in the price of a timber beam increases the quantity of timber beams supplied but has no effect on the supply of timber beams. An expected rise in the price of a timber beam decreases the supply of timber beams today as producers hold back and wait for the higher price. The new law decreases the supply of timber beams. The new technology increases the supply of timber beams.

2. In Figure 1, an increase in the supply shifts the supply curve from $S_0$ to $S_1$, and a decrease in the supply shifts the supply curve from $S_0$ to $S_2$. In Figure 2, the rise in the price of a beam creates a movement along the supply curve.

3. A rise in the price of a beam, other things remaining the same, is the only event that illustrates the law of supply—see Figure 2.

## Solution to In the News

Crude oil is refined to produce gasoline, so a fall in the price of crude oil lowers the cost of producing gasoline and increases the supply of gasoline.

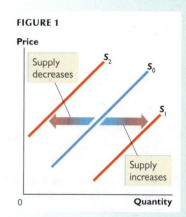
**FIGURE 1**

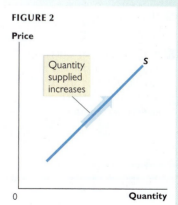
**FIGURE 2**

MyEconLab Concept Video

**Market equilibrium**
When the quantity demanded equals the quantity supplied—buyers' and sellers' plans are in balance.

**Equilibrium price**
The price at which the quantity demanded equals the quantity supplied.

**Equilibrium quantity**
The quantity bought and sold at the equilibrium price.

**Law of market forces**
When there is a surplus, the price falls; and when there is a shortage, the price rises.

# 4.3   MARKET EQUILIBRIUM

In everyday language, "equilibrium" means "opposing forces are in balance." In a market, demand and supply are the opposing forces. **Market equilibrium** occurs when the quantity demanded equals the quantity supplied—when buyers' and sellers' plans are in balance. At the **equilibrium price**, the quantity demanded equals the quantity supplied. The **equilibrium quantity** is the quantity bought and sold at the equilibrium price.

In the market for bottled water in Figure 4.5, equilibrium occurs where the demand curve and the supply curve intersect. The equilibrium price is $1.00 a bottle, and the equilibrium quantity is 10 million bottles a day.

## ■ Price: A Market's Automatic Regulator

When equilibrium is disturbed, market forces restore it. The **law of market forces** states

> **When there is a surplus, the price falls; and when there is a shortage, the price rises.**

A *surplus* is the amount by which the quantity supplied exceeds the quantity demanded. If there is a surplus, suppliers must cut the price to sell more. Buyers are pleased to take the lower price, so the price falls. Because a surplus arises when the price is above the equilibrium price, a falling price is exactly what the market needs to restore equilibrium.

A *shortage* is the amount by which the quantity demanded exceeds the quantity supplied. If there is a shortage, buyers must pay a higher price to get more. Sellers are pleased to take the higher price, so the price rises. Because a shortage arises when the price is below the equilibrium price, a rising price is exactly what is needed to restore equilibrium.

■ **FIGURE 4.5**

Equilibrium Price and Equilibrium Quantity

MyEconLab Animation

❶ Market equilibrium occurs at the intersection of the demand curve and the supply curve.

❷ The equilibrium price is $1.00 a bottle.

❸ At the equilibrium price, the quantity demanded and the quantity supplied are 10 million bottles a day, which is the equilibrium quantity.

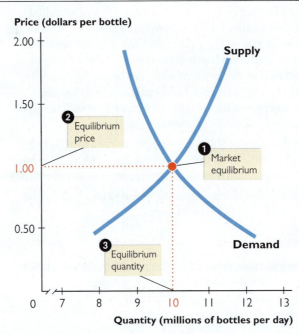

**FIGURE 4.6**

## The Forces That Achieve Equilibrium

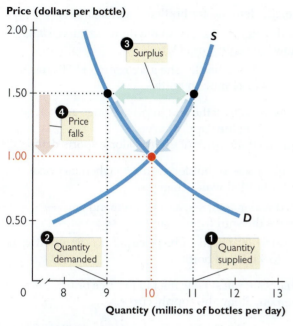

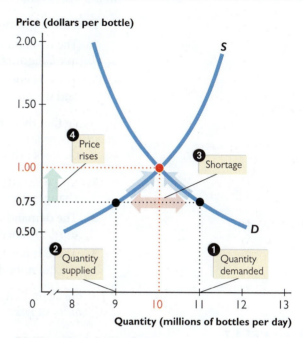

**(a)  Surplus and price falls**

**(b)  Shortage and price rises**

At $1.50 a bottle, ❶ the quantity supplied is 11 million bottles of water, ❷ the quantity demanded is 9 million bottles, ❸ the surplus is 2 million bottles of water, and ❹ the price falls.

At 75¢ a bottle, ❶ the quantity demanded is 11 million bottles of water, ❷ the quantity supplied is 9 million bottles, ❸ the shortage is 2 million bottles of water, and ❹ the price rises.

In Figure 4.6(a), at $1.50 a bottle, there is a surplus: The price falls, the quantity demanded increases, the quantity supplied decreases, and the surplus is eliminated at $1.00 a bottle.

In Figure 4.6(b), at 75¢ a bottle, there is a shortage of water: The price rises, the quantity demanded decreases, the quantity supplied increases, and the shortage is eliminated at $1.00 a bottle.

## ■ Predicting Price Changes: Three Questions

Because price adjustments eliminate shortages and surpluses, markets are normally in equilibrium. When an event disturbs an equilibrium, a new equilibrium soon emerges. To explain and predict changes in prices and quantities, we need to consider only changes in the *equilibrium* price and the *equilibrium* quantity. We can work out the effects of an event on a market by answering three questions:

1.  Does the event influence demand or supply?
2.  Does the event *increase* or *decrease* demand or supply—shift the demand curve or the supply curve *rightward* or *leftward*?
3.  What are the new *equilibrium* price and *equilibrium* quantity and how have they changed?

MyEconLab Concept Video

### ■ Effects of Changes in Demand

Let's practice answering the three questions by working out the effects of an event in the market for bottled water: A new study says that tap water is unsafe.

1.  With tap water unsafe, the demand for bottled water changes.
2.  The demand for bottled water *increases*, and the demand curve *shifts rightward*. Figure 4.7(a) shows the shift from $D_0$ to $D_1$.
3.  There is now a *shortage* at $1.00 a bottle. The *price rises* to $1.50 a bottle, and the quantity increases to 11 million bottles.

Note that there is *no change in supply*; the rise in price brings an *increase in the quantity supplied*—a movement along the supply curve.

Let's work out what happens if the price of a zero-calorie sports drink falls.

1.  The sports drink is a substitute for bottled water, so when its price changes, the demand for bottled water changes.
2.  The demand for bottled water *decreases*, and the demand curve *shifts leftward*. Figure 4.7(b) shows the shift from $D_0$ to $D_2$.
3.  There is now a *surplus* at $1.00 a bottle. The price *falls* to 75¢ a bottle, and the quantity decreases to 9 million bottles.

Note again that there is *no change in supply*; the fall in price brings a *decrease in the quantity supplied*—a movement along the supply curve.

■ **FIGURE 4.7**

## The Effects of a Change in Demand

MyEconLab Animation

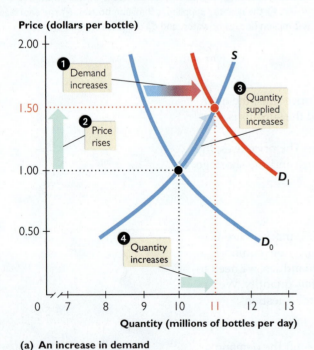

(a)  An increase in demand

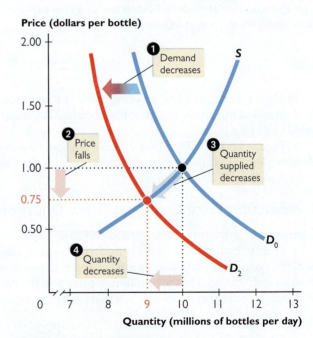

(b)  A decrease in demand

❶ An increase in demand shifts the demand curve rightward to $D_1$ and creates a shortage of water. ❷ The price rises, ❸ the quantity supplied increases, and ❹ the equilibrium quantity increases.

❶ A decrease in demand shifts the demand curve leftward to $D_2$ and creates a surplus of water. ❷ The price falls, ❸ the quantity supplied decreases, and ❹ the equilibrium quantity decreases.

# EYE on the GLOBAL ECONOMY
## The Markets for Cocoa and Chocolate

Fast-rising incomes in China and other developing economies and the sweet tooth of millions of newly rich middle classes are sending the consumption of chocolate soaring. With chocolate made from cocoa, the price of cocoa is soaring too.

Look at the data table below. It shows the quantities and prices of cocoa in 2010 and 2014, and it tells us that both the quantity of cocoa produced and the price of cocoa increased.

The quantity produced increased by 25 percent from 4 million tons in 2010 to 5 million tons in 2014.

The price of cocoa doubled from $1,500 a ton to $3,000 a ton.

Why did the price of cocoa increase? Was it because demand increased or supply decreased?

You can answer this question with the information in the table. You know that an increase in demand brings a rise in the price and an increase in the quantity bought, while a decrease in supply brings a rise in the price and a decrease in the quantity bought.

Because when the price of cocoa increased, the quantity of cocoa produced and consumed also increased, there must have been an increase in the demand for cocoa.

An increase in demand is consistent with the facts about rising incomes in China and other developing economies.

Cocoa is a normal good, so an increase in income brings an increase in the demand for cocoa. The fast-rising incomes in China and other developing economies brought an increase in the demand for cocoa.

The figure illustrates the global market for cocoa in 2010 and 2014. The supply curve $S$ shows the supply of cocoa, which we will assume didn't change between 2010 and 2014.

In 2010, the demand curve for cocoa was $D_{2010}$, the equilibrium price was $1,500 per ton and the equilibrium quantity of cocoa traded was 4 million tons.

By 2014, the higher incomes in China and other developing economies had increased the demand for cocoa to $D_{2014}$. The equilibrium price rose to $3,000 per ton and the equilibrium quantity traded increased to 5 million tons.

As the price of cocoa increased the quantity of cocoa supplied increased, which is shown by the movement up along the supply curve of cocoa.

| Year | Quantity of Cocoa (millions of tons per year) | Price of Cocoa (dollars per ton) |
|---|---|---|
| 2010 | 4 | 1,500 |
| 2014 | 5 | 3,000 |

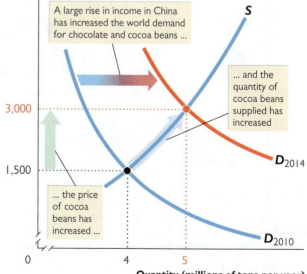

**Price (dollars per ton)**

A large rise in income in China has increased the world demand for chocolate and cocoa beans ...

... and the quantity of cocoa beans supplied has increased

... the price of cocoa beans has increased ...

**The Market for Cocoa Beans**

MyEconLab Concept Video

## ■ Effects of Changes in Supply

You can get more practice working out the effects of another event in the market for bottled water: European water bottlers buy springs and open new plants in the United States.

1. With more suppliers of bottled water, the supply changes.
2. The supply of bottled water *increases*, and the supply curve *shifts rightward*. Figure 4.8(a) shows the shift from $S_0$ to $S_1$.
3. There is now a *surplus* at $1.00 a bottle. The *price falls* to 75¢ a bottle, and the quantity increases to 11 million bottles.

Note that there is *no change in demand*; the fall in price brings an *increase in the quantity demanded*—a movement along the demand curve.

What happens if a drought dries up some springs?

1. The drought is a change in productivity, so the supply of water changes.
2. With fewer springs, the supply of bottled water *decreases*, and the supply curve *shifts leftward*. Figure 4.8(b) shows the shift from $S_0$ to $S_2$.
3. There is now a *shortage* at $1.00 a bottle. The *price rises* to $1.50 a bottle, and the quantity decreases to 9 million bottles.

Again, there is *no change in demand*; the rise in price brings a *decrease in the quantity demanded*—a movement along the demand curve.

■ **FIGURE 4.8**

## The Effects of a Change in Supply

MyEconLab Animation

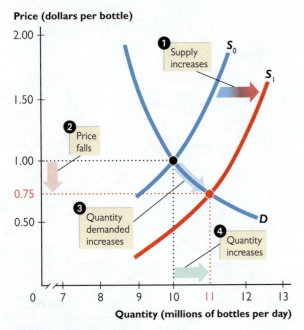

(a) An increase in supply

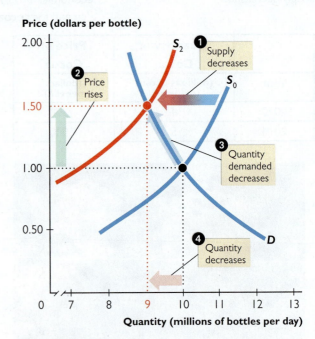

(b) A decrease in supply

❶ An increase in supply shifts the supply curve rightward to $S_1$ and creates a surplus of water. ❷ The price falls, ❸ the quantity demanded increases, and ❹ the equilibrium quantity increases.

❶ A decrease in supply shifts the supply curve leftward to $S_2$ and creates a shortage of water. ❷ The price rises, ❸ the quantity demanded decreases, and ❹ the equilibrium quantity decreases.

# EYE on the PRICE OF COFFEE

MyEconLab Critical Thinking Exercise

## Why Did the Price of Coffee Rise in 2014?

When a fungus called coffee rust swept through Brazil and other countries of South America in 2014, world coffee production decreased and the price of coffee beans increased.

The table below provides some data on the quantity and price of coffee in 2013 and 2014. What does the data table tell us?

It tells us that the quantity of coffee produced decreased by 3.6 percent from 19.4 billion pounds in 2013 to 18.7 billion pounds in 2014, and the price of coffee rose by more than 30 percent from $1.04 per pound to $1.35 per pound.

Did the price of coffee rise because demand increased or because supply decreased?

You can answer this question from the information provided. You know that an increase in demand brings a rise in the price and an increase in the quantity bought, while a decrease in supply brings a rise in the price and a decrease in the quantity bought.

Because the quantity of coffee decreased and the price increased, there must have been a decrease in the supply of coffee.

The supply of coffee decreases if the crop yields decrease or if producers decrease their plantings.

The information that coffee rust swept through Brazil and other countries of South America in 2014 suggests that coffee crop yields decreased, which decreased the supply.

The figure illustrates the global market for coffee in 2013 and 2014. The demand curve $D$ shows the demand for coffee, which we will assume was the same in both years.

In 2013, the supply curve was $S_{2013}$, the equilibrium price was $1.04 per pound and the equilibrium quantity traded was 19.4 billion pounds.

In 2014, decreased coffee production in Brazil and other countries decreased the supply of coffee to $S_{2014}$.

The equilibrium price rose to $1.35 per pound and the quantity traded decreased to 18.7 billion pounds.

The higher price brought a decrease in the quantity of coffee demanded, which is shown by the movement up along the demand curve.

| Year | Quantity of Coffee (billions of pounds per year) | Price of Coffee (dollars per pound) |
|------|--------------------------------------------------|-------------------------------------|
| 2013 | 19.4 | 1.04 |
| 2014 | 18.7 | 1.35 |

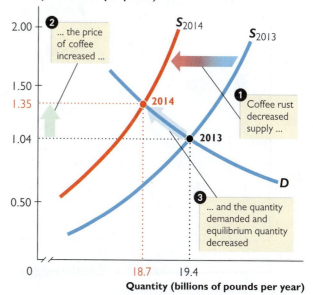

**The Market for Coffee in 2013–2014**

## ■ Effects of Changes in Both Demand and Supply

When events occur that change *both* demand and supply, you can find the resulting change in the equilibrium price and equilibrium quantity by combining the cases you've just studied.

### Both Demand and Supply Change in the Same Direction

When demand and supply change in the same direction, the equilibrium quantity changes in that same direction, but we need to know the magnitudes of the changes in demand and supply to predict whether the price rises or falls. If demand increases by more than supply increases, the price rises. But if supply increases by more than demand increases, the price falls.

Figure 4.9(a) shows the case when both demand and supply increase and by the same amount. The equilibrium quantity increases. But because the increase in demand equals the increase in supply, neither a shortage nor a surplus arises so the price doesn't change. A bigger increase in demand would have created a shortage and a rise in the price; a bigger increase in supply would have created a surplus and a fall in the price.

Figure 4.9(b) shows the case when both demand and supply decrease by the same amount. Here the equilibrium quantity decreases and again the price might either rise or fall.

### ■ FIGURE 4.9

The Effects of Change in *Both* Demand and Supply in the *Same Direction*          MyEconLab Animation

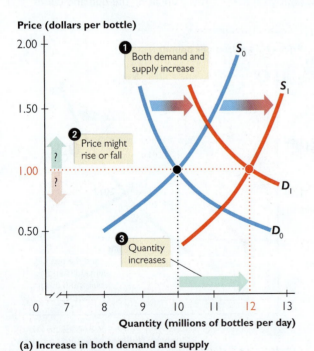

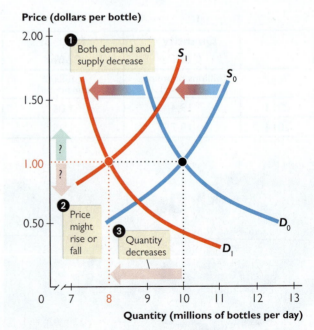

**(a) Increase in both demand and supply**

❶ An increase in demand shifts the demand curve rightward to $D_1$ and an increase in supply shifts the supply curve rightward to $S_1$.
❷ The price might rise or fall, but ❸ the quantity increases.

**(b) Decrease in both demand and supply**

❶ A decrease in demand shifts the demand curve leftward to $D_1$ and a decrease in supply shifts the supply curve leftward to $S_1$.
❷ The price might rise or fall, but ❸ the quantity decreases.

## Both Demand and Supply Change in Opposite Directions

When demand and supply change in opposite directions, we can predict how the price changes, but we need to know the magnitudes of the changes in demand and supply to say whether the equilibrium quantity increases or decreases. If demand changes by more than supply, the equilibrium quantity changes in the same direction as the change in demand. But if supply changes by more than demand, the equilibrium quantity changes in the same direction as the change in supply.

Figure 4.10(a) illustrates what happens when demand decreases and supply increases by the same amount. At the initial price, there is a surplus, so the price falls. A decrease in demand decreases the quantity and an increase in supply increases the quantity, so when these changes occur together, we can't say what happens to the quantity unless we know the magnitudes of the changes.

Figure 4.10(b) illustrates what happens when demand increases and supply decreases by the same amount. In this case, at the initial price, there is a shortage, so the price rises. An increase in demand increases the quantity and a decrease in supply decreases the quantity, so again, when these changes occur together, we can't say what happens to the quantity unless we know the magnitudes of the changes in demand and supply.

For all the cases in Figures 4.9 and 4.10 where you "can't say" what happens to price or quantity, draw some examples that go in each direction.

■ **FIGURE 4.10**

The Effects of Change in *Both* Demand and Supply in *Opposite Directions*    MyEconLab Animation

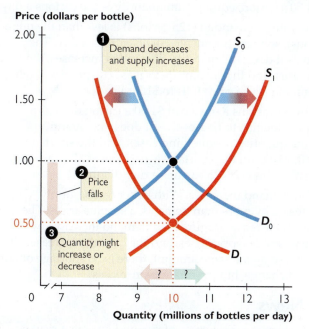

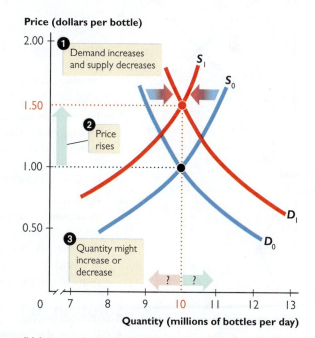

(a) Decrease in demand and increase in supply

(b) Increase in demand and decrease in supply

❶ A decrease in demand shifts the demand curve leftward to $D_1$ and an increase in supply shifts the supply curve rightward to $S_1$.
❷ The price falls, but ❸ the quantity might increase or decrease.

❶ An increase in demand shifts the demand curve rightward to $D_1$ and a decrease in supply shifts the supply curve leftward to $S_1$.
❷ The price rises, but ❸ the quantity might increase or decrease.

MyEconLab Study Plan 4.3

Key Terms Quiz

Solutions Video

# CHECKPOINT 4.3

**Explain how demand and supply determine price and quantity in a market, and explain the effects of changes in demand and supply.**

## Practice Problems

Table 1 sets out the demand and supply schedules for milk.

1.  What is the equilibrium price and equilibrium quantity of milk?
2.  Describe the situation in the milk market if the price were $1.75 a carton and explain how the market reaches equilibrium.
3.  A drought decreases the quantity supplied by 45 cartons a day at each price. What is the new equilibrium and how does the market adjust to it?
4.  If milk becomes more popular and better feeds increase milk production, describe how the equilibrium price and quantity of milk will change.

**TABLE 1**

| Price (dollars per carton) | Quantity demanded | Quantity supplied |
| --- | --- | --- |
| | (cartons per day) | |
| 1.00 | 200 | 110 |
| 1.25 | 175 | 130 |
| 1.50 | 150 | 150 |
| 1.75 | 125 | 170 |
| 2.00 | 100 | 190 |

## In the News

**El Niño takes toll on U.S. rice farmers**
Dry weather has delayed rice planting and harvests will be low. But wheat is enjoying a bumper crop.

*Source: The Guardian, September 27, 2015*

Using the demand and supply model, explain how the prices of rice and wheat will change and how the markets for rice and wheat will influence each other.

## Solutions to Practice Problems

1.  Equilibrium price is $1.50 a carton; equilibrium quantity is 150 cartons a day.
2.  At $1.75 a carton, the quantity demanded (125 cartons) is less than the quantity supplied (170 cartons), so there is a surplus of 45 cartons a day. The price begins to fall, and as it does, the quantity demanded increases, the quantity supplied decreases, and the surplus decreases. The price will fall until the surplus is eliminated. The price falls to $1.50 a carton.
3.  The supply decreases by 45 cartons a day so at $1.50 a carton there is a shortage of milk. The price begins to rise, and as it does, the quantity demanded decreases, the quantity supplied increases, and the shortage decreases. The price will rise until the shortage is eliminated. The new equilibrium occurs at $1.75 a carton and 125 cartons a day (Figure 1).
4.  With milk more popular, demand increases. With better feeds, supply increases. If supply increases by more than demand, a surplus arises. The price falls, and the quantity increases (Figure 2). If demand increases by more than supply, a shortage arises. The price rises, and the quantity increases. If demand and supply increase by the same amount, there is no shortage or surplus, so the price does not change, but the quantity increases.

## Solution to In the News

A fall in the rice harvest will decrease the supply of rice and raise its price. A bumper wheat harvest will increase the supply of wheat and lower its price. Wheat and rice are substitutes, so a higher price of rice will increase the demand for wheat and a lower price of wheat will decrease the demand for rice.

**FIGURE 1**

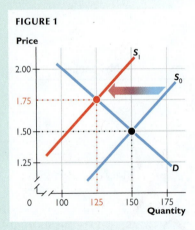

**FIGURE 2**

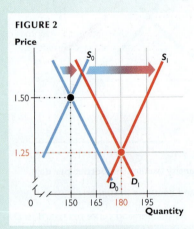

## 4.4    PRICE RIGIDITIES

MyEconLab Concept Video

You've seen that price adjustments bring market equilibrium. But suppose that for some reason, the price in a market does not adjust. What happens then? The answer depends on why the price doesn't adjust. There are three possibilities:

- Price floor
- Price ceiling or price cap
- Sticky price

### ■ Price Floor

A **price floor** is a government regulation that places a lower limit on the price at which a particular good, service, or factor of production may be traded. A **minimum wage law**—a government regulation that makes hiring labor for less than a specified wage illegal—is an example of a price floor. Firms are free to pay a wage rate that exceeds the minimum but may not pay less than the minimum. What are the effects of a minimum wage?

Firms hire labor, so they decide how much labor to demand. The lower the wage rate, the greater is the quantity of labor that firms demand. Households decide how much labor to supply. The higher the wage rate, the greater is the quantity of labor households are willing to supply. The wage rate adjusts to make the quantity of labor demanded equal to the quantity supplied.

Figure 4.11 shows the market for fast-food servers in Yuma, Arizona. In this market, the demand for labor curve is *D* and the supply of labor curve is *S*. Equilibrium occurs at a wage rate of $7 an hour with 6,000 people employed as servers.

**Price floor**
A government regulation that places a lower limit on the price at which a particular good, service, or factor of production may be traded.

**Minimum wage law**
A government regulation that makes hiring labor for less than a specified wage illegal.

■ **FIGURE 4.11**

A Market for Fast-Food Servers

MyEconLab Animation

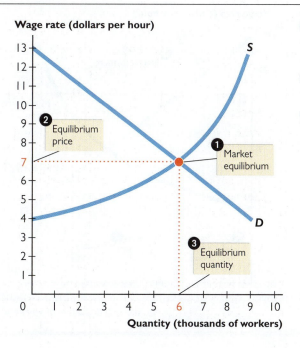

❶ Market equilibrium is determined by the demand for and the supply of fast-food servers.

❷ The equilibrium wage rate is $7 an hour.

❸ At the equilibrium wage rate, the equilibrium quantity of fast-food servers is 6,000.

Suppose that the government thinks that no one should have to work for a wage rate as low as $7 an hour and introduces a minimum wage. The effect of a minimum wage depends on whether it is set below or above the equilibrium wage. In Figure 4.11, the equilibrium wage rate is $7 an hour, and at this wage rate, firms hire 6,000 workers. If the government introduced a minimum wage below $7 an hour, nothing would change. The reason is that firms are already paying $7 an hour, and because this wage exceeds the minimum wage, the wage rate paid doesn't change. Firms continue to hire 6,000 workers.

Now suppose that the government introduces a minimum wage of $10 an hour. Figure 4.12 shows the effects of this law. Wage rates below $10 an hour are illegal, so we've shaded the illegal region below the minimum wage. Firms and workers are no longer permitted to operate at the equilibrium point in this market because it is in the illegal region. Market forces and the law are in conflict.

The government can set a minimum wage, but it can't tell employers how many workers to hire. If firms must pay $10 an hour for labor, they will hire only 3,000 workers. At the equilibrium wage rate of $7 an hour, firms hired 6,000 workers. So when the minimum wage is introduced, firms fire 3,000 workers.

But at $10 an hour, another 2,000 people who didn't want to work for $7 an hour now try to find work as servers. So at $10 an hour, the quantity of labor supplied is 8,000 workers. With 3,000 workers fired and another 2,000 looking for work at the higher wage rate, 5,000 people who would like to work as servers are unemployed.

Somehow, the 3,000 jobs available must be allocated among the 8,000 people who would like them. How is this allocation achieved? The answer is some combination of first-come, first-served and discrimination. When price doesn't allocate scarce resources, waiting lines and personal characteristics take over.

■ **FIGURE 4.12**

## A Minimum Wage Creates Unemployment

MyEconLab Animation

A minimum wage is introduced above the equilibrium wage rate. In this example, the minimum wage is $10 an hour.

❶ The quantity of labor demanded decreases to 3,000 workers.

❷ The quantity of labor supplied increases to 8,000 workers.

❸ With this minimum wage, 5,000 people are unemployed.

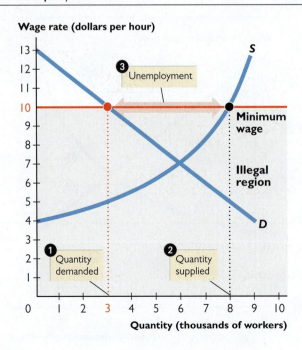

# EYE on the U.S. ECONOMY
## The Federal Minimum Wage

The *Fair Labor Standards Act* sets the federal minimum wage, but most states set their own minimum at a higher level than the federal minimum.

The minimum wage creates unemployment. But how much? Until recently, most economists believed that a 10 percent increase in the minimum wage decreased teenage employment by between 1 and 3 percent.

David Card of the University of California at Berkeley and Alan Krueger of Princeton University have challenged this view. They say that following a rise in the minimum wage in California, New Jersey, and Texas, the employment rate of low-income

workers *increased*, and they suggest three reasons why:

(1) Workers become more conscientious and productive.
(2) Workers are less likely to quit, so costly labor turnover is reduced.
(3) Managers make a firm's operations more efficient.

Most economists are skeptical about these ideas. They say that if higher wages make workers more productive and reduce labor turnover, firms will freely pay workers a higher wage. And they argue that there are other explanations for the employment increase that Card and Krueger found.

Daniel Hamermesh of the University of Texas at Austin says that

they got the timing wrong. Firms anticipated the minimum wage rise and so cut employment before it occurred. Looking at employment changes after the minimum wage increased missed its main effect. Finis Welch of Texas A&M University and Kevin Murphy of the University of Chicago say the employment effects that Card and Krueger found are caused by regional differences in economic growth, not changes in the minimum wage.

Also, looking only at employment misses the supply-side effect of the minimum wage. It brings an increase in the number of people who drop out of high school to look for work.

## ■ Price Ceiling or Price Cap

A **price ceiling** or **price cap** is a government regulation that places an *upper* limit on the price at which a particular good, service, or factor of production may be traded. You've probably encountered several price ceilings or price caps. One example is a ceiling on apartment rents—a rent ceiling. New York City has some notable rent ceilings that limit the rent that landlords can charge. Another example is a cap on college tuition. Student groups often lobby for tuition caps, and state legislatures sometimes deliver. A further example is a price cap on campus parking. College administrators think that parking must not be too expensive for students, so they keep the price low. A final example is a price cap—a zero price—on freeways.

To see how a price cap works, first imagine an unrestricted market in student parking. College administrators decide the quantity of parking spaces to make available, and the higher the price of a parking permit, the greater is the quantity of parking that the college is willing to supply.

Students decide the quantity of parking spaces to demand, and the lower the price of a permit, the greater is the quantity of parking spaces demanded. If the price of parking on campus is $100 a month, few students would drive to school. There would be a big increase in car-pooling, riding the bus, walking, and cycling.

Figure 4.13 illustrates a market for campus parking. The demand curve is $D$, and the supply curve is $S$. The price adjusts to an equilibrium of $80 a month, at which 2,000 parking spaces are demanded and supplied.

The effect of a price cap depends on whether it is imposed at a level above or below the equilibrium price. With a price cap *above* the equilibrium price, nothing would change. The reason is that people are already paying the equilibrium price, and because this price is below the price cap, the price paid doesn't change.

**Price ceiling** or **price cap**
A government regulation that places an *upper* limit on the price at which a particular good, service, or factor of production may be traded.

■ **FIGURE 4.13**

An Unregulated Market in Campus Parking Spaces

MyEconLab Animation

❶ Market equilibrium is determined by the demand for parking spaces and the supply of parking spaces.

❷ The equilibrium price is $80 a month.

❸ At the equilibrium price, 2,000 parking spaces are demanded and supplied.

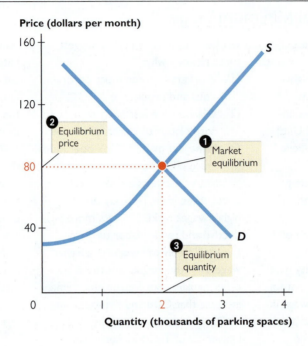

But a price cap set *below* the equilibrium price has powerful effects on the market. The reason is that it attempts to prevent the price from rising by enough to bring equality of the quantity demanded and the quantity supplied. The regulation and the market are in conflict, and one (or both) of them must yield.

Figure 4.14 shows the effects of a price cap that is set *below* the equilibrium price. The price cap is $40 a month. We've shaded the area above the price cap because any price in this region is unavailable. At a price cap of $40 a month, the quantity of spaces supplied is 1,000 and the quantity demanded is 3,000 spaces, so the price cap creates a shortage of 2,000 parking spaces.

The first effect, then, of a price cap is a shortage. Students are seeking a larger amount of parking than the college has an incentive to make available.

But the story does not end here. Somehow the 1,000 spaces that the college is willing to make available must be allocated among students who are seeking 3,000 spaces. Blocking price adjustments that bring the number of spaces demanded into equality with the number supplied doesn't end scarcity. When the college is unwilling to permit the price to rise and allocate scarce parking spaces, some other allocation mechanism must be used.

Some possibilities are a parking permit lottery; a first-come, first-served rule; a senior student priority rule; and issuing so many permits that students end up spending a large amount of time hunting for a space and sometimes end up missing class because they couldn't find a parking place.

Note that all of these alternative ways of rationing parking spaces impose costs on the students. When students don't pay the equilibrium price for parking, they pay in other ways—with their time or by being denied parking altogether.

**FIGURE 4.14**

A Price Cap in a Market for Campus Parking Spaces                    MyEconLab Animation

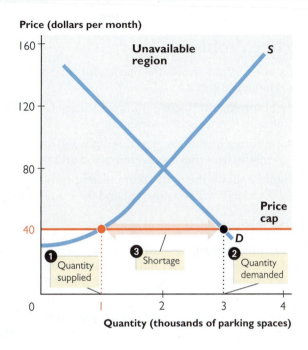

The college administration caps the price of parking at $40 a month.

❶ The number of parking spaces supplied is 1,000 spaces.

❷ The number of parking spaces demanded is 3,000.

❸ With this price cap, a shortage of 2,000 parking spaces is created.

## ■ Sticky Price

In most markets, a law or regulation does not restrict the price. But in some markets, the buyer and seller agree on a price for a fixed period; and in others, the seller sets a price that changes infrequently. For example, in some labor markets, firms enter into long-term contracts with labor unions that fix wage rates for at least one year and often for as many as three years. Borrowers and lenders often agree on an interest rate that is fixed for the term of a loan, which could be for as long as 30 years. And many commodities such as sugar, oil, and coal are traded on long-term contracts.

In these markets, the price adjustment process that is described in Figure 4.6 on p. 97 is slowed down. Prices do adjust, but not quickly enough to avoid shortages or surpluses.

If demand increases or if supply decreases after a price (or wage) contract is struck, a shortage arises. The quantity supplied is less than the quantity demanded at the contract price, so the quantity supplied determines the quantity that is actually traded. Buyers' plans are frustrated. The price gradually rises as contracts come up for renewal, but in the intervening period, a shortage persists.

Similarly, if demand decreases or if supply increases after a price (or wage) contract is struck, a surplus arises. The quantity demanded is less than the quantity supplied at the contract price, so the quantity demanded determines the quantity that is actually traded. Sellers' plans are frustrated. In the labor market, the sellers are workers and some of them become unemployed. The price (or wage rate) gradually falls as contracts come up for renewal, but in the intervening period, a surplus and above-normal unemployment persist.

MyEconLab Study Plan 4.4
Key Terms Quiz
Solutions Video

# CHECKPOINT 4.4

**Explain how price floors, price ceilings, and sticky prices create surpluses, unemployment, and shortages.**

## Practice Problems

Use Figure 1, which shows the market for fruit pickers in southern California, to work Problems **1** and **2**.

1. If California introduces a minimum wage for fruit pickers of $5 an hour, how many fruit pickers are employed and how many are unemployed?

2. If California introduces a minimum wage for fruit pickers of $8 an hour, how many fruit pickers are employed and how many are unemployed?

3. Figure 2 shows the market for on-campus housing. If a price cap is set at $600 a month, what is the rent and the number of apartments rented?

## In the News

**This city proposes highest minimum wage in America**
Berkeley Labor Council in California plans to increase the minimum wage rate each year from $9 an hour today until it hits $19 an hour in 2020.
Source: *Fortune*, September 15, 2015

Using the demand and supply model, explain how a doubling of the current minimum wage rate will influence employment in Berkeley.

## Solutions to Practice Problems

1. A minimum wage of $5 an hour is *below* the market equilibrium wage of $6 an hour, so pickers are paid $6 an hour, 4,000 fruit pickers are employed, and there are no unemployed fruit pickers.

2. A minimum wage rate of $8 an hour is *above* the market equilibrium wage of $6 an hour (Figure 3). At $8 an hour, 3,000 fruit pickers are demanded and 5,000 pickers would like jobs, so there is a surplus of pickers. Farms employ 3,000 fruit pickers at $8 an hour, but 2,000 pickers are unemployed.

3. The equilibrium rent is $800 a month. A price cap of $600 a month is *below* the equilibrium rent. With 1,000 apartments supplied and 4,000 demanded, a shortage arises. The rent is $600 a month and 1,000 apartments are rented (Figure 4).

## Solution to In the News

The current wage rate in Berkeley is the market equilibrium wage rate. The introduction of a $19 an hour minimum wage will decrease the quantity of workers demanded and increase the quantity supplied as people flock to Berkeley to try to find a high wage job. Employment will decrease and unemployment will increase.

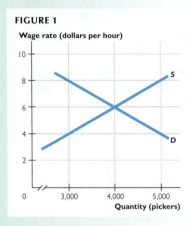
**FIGURE 1**

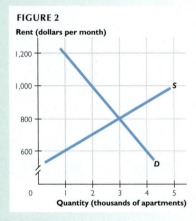
**FIGURE 2**

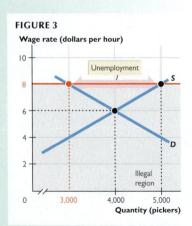
**FIGURE 3**

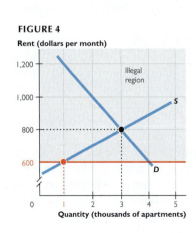
**FIGURE 4**

## CHAPTER SUMMARY

## Key Points

1. **Distinguish between quantity demanded and demand, and explain what determines demand.**

   • Other things remaining the same, the quantity demanded increases as the price falls and decreases as the price rises—the law of demand.

   • Changes in the prices of related goods, income, expectations about future prices and income, the number of buyers, and preferences change demand.

2. **Distinguish between quantity supplied and supply, and explain what determines supply.**

   • Other things remaining the same, the quantity supplied increases as the price rises and decreases as the price falls—the law of supply.

   • Changes in the prices of related goods, prices of resources and other inputs, expected future prices, the number of sellers, and productivity change supply.

3. **Explain how demand and supply determine price and quantity in a market, and explain the effects of changes in demand and supply.**

   • The price adjusts to maintain market equilibrium—to keep the quantity demanded equal to the quantity supplied. A surplus brings a fall in the price; a shortage brings a rise in the price.

   • An increase in demand increases both the price and the quantity; a decrease in demand decreases both the price and the quantity. An increase in supply increases the quantity but decreases the price; and a decrease in supply decreases the quantity but increases the price.

4. **Explain how price floors, price ceilings, and sticky prices create surpluses, unemployment, and shortages.**

   • A price floor above the equilibrium price creates a surplus (unemployment in the labor market).

   • A price ceiling below the equilibrium price creates a shortage.

   • A sticky price brings a temporary shortage or surplus.

## Key Terms

MyEconLab Key Terms Quiz

**CHAPTER CHECKPOINT**

## Study Plan Problems and Applications

1. Explain how each of the following events changes the demand for or supply of air travel.

   - Airfares tumble, while long-distance bus fares don't change.
   - The price of jet fuel rises.
   - Airlines reduce the number of flights each day.
   - People expect airfares to increase next summer.
   - The price of train travel falls.
   - The price of a pound of air cargo increases.

Use the laws of demand and supply to explain whether the statements in Problems **2** and **3** are true or false. In your explanation, distinguish between a change in demand and a change in the quantity demanded and between a change in supply and a change in the quantity supplied.

2. The United States does not allow oranges from Brazil (the world's largest producer of oranges) to enter the United States. If Brazilian oranges were sold in the United States, oranges and orange juice would be cheaper.

3. If the price of frozen yogurt falls, the quantity of ice cream consumed will decrease and the price of ice cream will rise.

4. Table 1 shows the demand and supply schedules for running shoes. What is the market equilibrium? If the price is $70 a pair, describe the situation in the market. Explain how market equilibrium is restored. If a rise in income increases the demand for running shoes by 100 pairs a day at each price, explain how the market adjusts to its new equilibrium.

5. "As more people buy fuel-efficient hybrid cars, the demand for gasoline will decrease and the price of gasoline will fall. The fall in the price of gasoline will decrease the supply of gasoline." Is this statement true? Explain.

6. Table 2 shows the demand and supply schedules for student workers at campus venues. If the college introduces a minimum wage of $11.50 an hour, how many students are employed and how many students want work at a campus venue but can't find a job?

7. **Rain delays to U.S. planting lift corn and soybean prices**
   Heavy rain has delayed the planting of corn and soybeans.
   Source: *Financial Times*, June 25, 2015

   Use the demand and supply model to explain how heavy rain will change the prices of corn and soybeans.

8. **Venezuelans organize to overcome food shortages**
   The government of Venezuela controls the price of food and there are shortages of milk, rice, coffee, pasta, sugar, and cooking oil. Eggs have disappeared. While people stand in line for milk, cheese and yogurt are abundant.
   Source: www.teleSURtv.net/english, November 27, 2015

   Are Venezuela's price controls price floors or price ceilings? Draw a graph to illustrate the shortages of food created by the price controls.

9. Read *Eye on the Price of Coffee* on p. 101 and explain how we know that the price increased in 2014 because the supply of coffee decreased and not because the demand for coffee increased.

**TABLE 1**

| Price (dollars per pair) | Quantity demanded | Quantity supplied |
|---|---|---|
| | (pairs per day) | |
| 60 | 1,000 | 400 |
| 70 | 900 | 500 |
| 80 | 800 | 600 |
| 90 | 700 | 700 |
| 100 | 600 | 800 |
| 110 | 500 | 900 |

**TABLE 2**

| Wage rate (dollars per hour) | Quantity demanded | Quantity supplied |
|---|---|---|
| | (student workers) | |
| 10.00 | 600 | 300 |
| 10.50 | 500 | 350 |
| 11.00 | 400 | 400 |
| 11.50 | 300 | 450 |
| 12.00 | 200 | 500 |
| 12.50 | 100 | 550 |

## Instructor Assignable Problems and Applications

MyEconLab Homework, Quiz, or Test if assigned by instructor

1. Why can we be confident that the market for coffee is competitive and that a decrease in supply rather than the greed of coffee growers is the reason for the 2014 rise in price?

2. What is the effect on the equilibrium price and equilibrium quantity of orange juice if the price of apple juice decreases and the wage rate paid to orange grove workers increases?

3. What is the effect on the equilibrium in the orange juice market if orange juice becomes more popular and a cheaper robot is used to pick oranges?

4. **Concerns over winter wheat may boost price**
   Concerns about the U.S. winter wheat crop and dry conditions in other wheat-producing nations have increased the price of wheat.
   Source: Agweb.com, July 6, 2015

   Explain how an upcoming harvest influences today's price of wheat.

Table 1 shows the demand and supply schedules for boxes of chocolates in an average week. Use this information to work Problems **5** and **6**.

5. If the price of chocolates is $17.00 a box, describe the situation in the market. Explain how market equilibrium is restored.

6. During Valentine's week, more people buy chocolates and chocolatiers offer their chocolates in special red boxes, which cost more to produce than the everyday box. Set out the three-step process of analysis and show on a graph the adjustment process to the new equilibrium. Describe the changes in the equilibrium price and the equilibrium quantity.

**TABLE 1**

| Price (dollars per box) | Quantity demanded | Quantity supplied |
|---|---|---|
| | (boxes per day) | |
| 13.00 | 1,600 | 1,200 |
| 14.00 | 1,500 | 1,300 |
| 15.00 | 1,400 | 1,400 |
| 16.00 | 1,300 | 1,500 |
| 17.00 | 1,200 | 1,600 |
| 18.00 | 1,100 | 1,700 |

7. **New York seals deal on $15 minimum fast-food wage**
   "Raising the minimum wage to $15 an hour will … bring dignity and respect to 2.2 million people, many of whom have been forced to live in poverty for too long," said Governor Andrew Cuomo. Between 135,000 and 200,000 workers will see their hourly wage rise gradually to $15 by the end of 2018 in New York City and by 2021 in the rest of the state.
   Source: CNNMoney, September 11, 2015

   On a graph of the market for fast-food workers, show the effect of the $15 an hour minimum wage on employment of fast-food workers.

8. **Bacon is 25 percent cheaper**
   Bacon is 25 percent cheaper now than a year ago and bacon sales are up 13 percent on the year. At the same time, the bird flu virus is killing millions of chickens and raising egg prices.
   Source: *CNN Money*, May 20, 2015

   Explain how this news clip illustrates the law of demand, why the price of bacon fell, and how the markets for bacon and eggs influence each other. Draw a graph to illustrate your explanations.

9. **China slowdown could bring good news**
   China's economic slowdown could help reduce the cost of steel used by U.S. auto makers.
   Source: *The Wall Street Journal*, September 8, 2015

   Explain how an economic slowdown in China influences the global steel market. What happens to the equilibrium price of steel?

# Multiple Choice Quiz

**1.** Which of the following events illustrates the law of demand? Other things remaining the same, a rise in the price of a good will _____.

A. decrease the quantity demanded of that good
B. increase the demand for a substitute of that good
C. decrease the demand for the good
D. increase the demand for a complement of that good

**2.** In the market for jeans, which of the following events increases the demand for a pair of jeans?

A. The wage rate paid to garment workers rises.
B. The price of a denim skirt (a substitute for jeans) rises.
C. The price of denim cloth falls.
D. New technology reduces the time it takes to make a pair of jeans.

**3.** Other things remaining the same, a fall in the price of peanuts will _____.

A. increase the supply of peanuts
B. decrease the supply of peanut butter
C. decrease the quantity supplied of peanuts
D. decrease the supply of peanuts

**4.** In the market for smartphones, which of the following events increases the supply of smartphones?

A. New technology lowers the cost of making a smartphone
B. A rise in the price of an e-book reader (a substitute in production)
C. An increase in people's incomes
D. A rise in the wage rate paid to electronics workers

**5.** When floods wiped out the banana crop in Central America, the equilibrium price of bananas _____ and the equilibrium quantity of bananas _____.

A. rose; increased
B. rose; decreased
C. fell; increased
D. fell; decreased

**6.** A decrease in the demand for chocolate with no change in supply will create a _____ of chocolate at today's price, but gradually the price will _____.

A. surplus; fall
B. shortage; fall
C. surplus; rise
D. shortage; rise

**7.** A minimum wage set above the market equilibrium wage rate _____.

A. increases both employment and the quantity of labor supplied
B. decreases unemployment and raises the wage rate of those employed
C. raises the wage rate of those employed and increases the supply of jobs
D. increases unemployment and decreases employment

**8.** A rent ceiling creates a _____ of housing if it _____ the equilibrium rent.

A. surplus; is less than
B. shortage; is less than
C. surplus; exceeds
D. shortage; exceeds

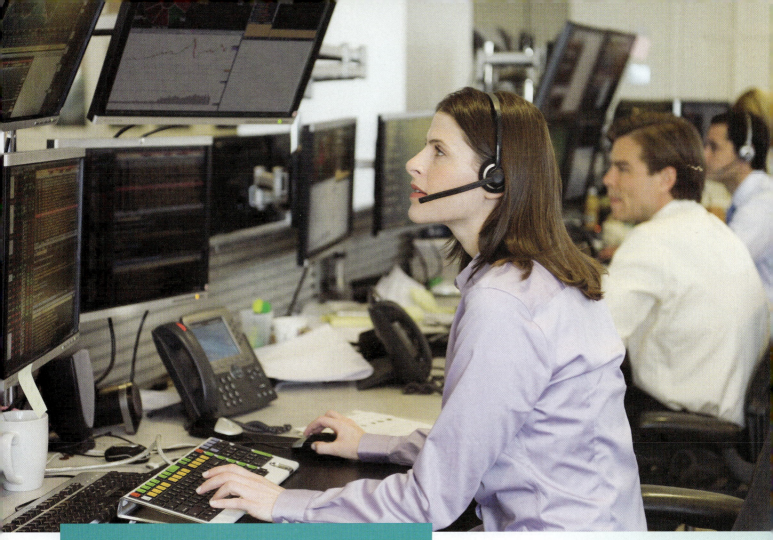

How do we track economic booms and busts?

# GDP: A Measure of Total Production and Income

**5**

**When you have completed your study of this chapter, you will be able to**

**1** Define GDP and explain why the value of production, income, and expenditure are the same for an economy.

**2** Describe how economic statisticians measure GDP and distinguish between nominal GDP and real GDP.

**3** Describe the uses of real GDP and explain its limitations as a measure of the standard of living.

MyEconLab **Big Picture Video**

MyEconLab Concept Video

## 5.1 GDP, INCOME, AND EXPENDITURE

Where is the U.S. economy heading? Will it remain weak, begin to expand more rapidly, or sink into a recession?

Everyone wants to know the answers to these questions. The people who make business decisions—homebuilders, auto producers, wireless service providers, airlines, oil producers, airplane makers, farmers, and retailers—want to know the answers so they can plan their production to align with demand. Governments want the answers because the amount of tax revenue that they collect depends on how much people earn and spend, which in turn depends on the state of the economy. Governments and the Federal Reserve want to know because they might be able to take actions that avoid excessive bust or boom. Ordinary citizens want the answers to plan their big decisions such as how long to remain in school, whether to rent or buy a new home, and how much to save toward retirement.

To assess the state of the economy we measure gross domestic product, or GDP. You're about to discover that GDP measures the value of total production, total income, and total expenditure.

### ■ GDP Defined

**Gross domestic product (GDP)**

The market value of all the final goods and services produced within a country in a given time period.

We measure total production as **gross domestic product**, or **GDP**, which is the market value of all the final goods and services produced within a country in a given time period. This definition has four parts, which we'll examine in turn.

### Value Produced

To measure total production, we must add together the production of apples and oranges, bats and balls. Just counting the items doesn't get us very far. Which is the greater total production: 100 apples and 50 oranges or 50 apples and 100 oranges?

GDP answers this question by valuing items at their *market value*—at the prices at which the items are traded in markets. If the price of an apple is 10 cents and the price of an orange is 20 cents, the market value of 100 apples plus 50 oranges is $20 and the market value of 50 apples and 100 oranges is $25. By using market prices to value production, we can add the apples and oranges together.

### What Produced

**Final good or service**

A good or service that is produced for its final user and not as a component of another good or service.

**Intermediate good or service**

A good or service that is used as a component of a final good or service.

A **final good or service** is something that is produced for its final user and not as a component of another good or service. A final good or service contrasts with an **intermediate good or service**, which is used as a component of a final good or service. For example, a Ford car is a final good, but a Firestone tire that Ford buys and installs on the car is an intermediate good. In contrast, if you buy a replacement Firestone tire for your car, then that tire is a final good. The same good can be either final or intermediate depending on how it is used.

GDP does not count the value of everything that is produced. With one exception, it includes only those items that are traded in markets and does not include the value of goods and services that people produce for their own use. For example, if you buy a car wash, the value produced is included in GDP. But if you wash your own car, your production is not counted as part of GDP. The exception is the market value of homes that people own. GDP puts a rental value on these homes and pretends that the owners rent their homes to themselves.

## Where Produced

Only goods and services that are produced *within a country* count as part of that country's GDP. Nike Corporation, a U.S. firm, produces sneakers in Vietnam, and the market value of those shoes is part of Vietnam's GDP, not part of U.S. GDP. Toyota, a Japanese firm, produces automobiles in Georgetown, Kentucky, and the value of this production is part of U.S. GDP, not part of Japan's GDP.

## When Produced

GDP measures the value of production *during a given time period.* This time period is either a quarter of a year—called the quarterly GDP data—or a year—called the annual GDP data. The Federal Reserve and others use the quarterly GDP data to keep track of the short-term evolution of the economy, and economists use the annual GDP data to examine long-term trends.

GDP measures not only the value of total production but also total income and total expenditure. The circular flow model that you studied in Chapter 2 explains why.

## ■ Circular Flows in the U.S. Economy

Four groups buy the final goods and services produced: households, firms, governments, and the rest of the world. Four types of expenditure correspond to these groups:

- Consumption expenditure
- Investment
- Government expenditure on goods and services
- Net exports of goods and services

## Consumption Expenditure

**Consumption expenditure** is the expenditure by households on consumption goods and services. It includes expenditures on *nondurable goods* such as orange juice and pizza, *durable goods* such as televisions and smartphones, and *services* such as rock concerts and haircuts. Consumption expenditure also includes house and apartment rents, including the rental value of owner-occupied housing.

**Consumption expenditure**
The expenditure by households on consumption goods and services.

## Investment

**Investment** is the purchase of new *capital goods* (tools, instruments, machines, and buildings) and additions to inventories. Capital goods are *durable goods* produced by one firm and bought by another. Examples are PCs produced by HP and bought by Ford Motor Company, and airplanes produced by Boeing and bought by United Airlines. Investment also includes the purchase of new homes by households.

**Investment**
The purchase of new *capital goods* (tools, instruments, machines, buildings) and additions to inventories.

At the end of a year, some of a firm's output might remain unsold. For example, if Ford produces 4 million cars and sells 3.9 million of them, the other 0.1 million (100,000) cars remain unsold. In this case, Ford's inventory of cars increases by 100,000. When a firm adds unsold output to inventory, we count those items as part of investment.

It is important to note that investment does *not* include the purchase of stocks and bonds. In macroeconomics, we reserve the term "investment" for the purchase of new capital goods and the additions to inventories.

## Government Expenditure on Goods and Services

**Government expenditure on goods and services** is expenditure by all levels of government on goods and services. For example, the U.S. Defense Department buys missiles and other weapons systems, the State Department buys travel services, the White House buys Internet services, and state and local governments buy cruisers for law enforcement officers.

## Net Exports of Goods and Services

**Net exports of goods and services** is the value of exports of goods and services minus the value of imports of goods and services. **Exports of goods and services** are items that firms in the United States produce and sell to the rest of the world. **Imports of goods and services** are items that households, firms, and governments in the United States buy from the rest of the world. Imports are produced in other countries, so expenditure on imports is not included in expenditure on U.S.-produced goods and services. If exports exceed imports, net exports are positive and expenditure on U.S.-produced goods and services increases. If imports exceed exports, net exports are negative and expenditure on U.S.-produced goods and services decreases.

## Total Expenditure

Total expenditure on goods and services produced in the United States is the sum of the four items that you've just examined. We call consumption expenditure $C$, investment $I$, government expenditure on goods and services $G$, and net exports of goods and services $NX$. So total expenditure, which is also the total amount received by the producers of final goods and services, is

$$\text{Total expenditure} = C + I + G + NX.$$

## Income

Labor earns wages, capital earns interest, land earns rent, and entrepreneurship earns profits. Households receive these incomes. Some part of total income, called *undistributed profit*, is a combination of interest and profit that firms retain and do not pay to households. But from an economic viewpoint, undistributed profit is income paid to households and then loaned to firms.

## ■ Expenditure Equals Income

Figure 5.1 shows the circular flows of income and expenditure that we've just described. The figure is based on Figures 2.4 and 2.5 (on p. 49 and p. 51), but it includes some more details and additional flows.

We call total income $Y$ and show it by the blue flow from firms to households. When households receive their incomes, they pay some in taxes and save some. Some households receive benefits from governments. **Net taxes** equal taxes paid minus cash benefits received and are the green flow from households to governments labeled $NT$. **Saving** is the amount of income that is not paid in net taxes or spent on consumption goods and services. Saving flows from households to financial markets and is the green flow labeled $S$. These two green flows are not expenditures on goods and services. They are just flows of money. Because households allocate all their incomes after paying net taxes to consumption and saving,

$$Y = C + S + NT.$$

The red flows show the four expenditure flows: consumption expenditure from households to firms, government expenditure from governments to firms, and net exports from the rest of the world to firms. Investment flows from the financial markets, where firms borrow, to the firms that produce capital goods.

Because firms pay out everything they receive as incomes to the factors of production, total expenditure equals total income. That is,

$$Y = C + I + G + NX.$$

From the viewpoint of firms, the value of production is the cost of production, which equals income. From the viewpoint of purchasers of goods and services, the value of production is the cost of buying it, which equals expenditure. So

### The value of production equals income equals expenditure.

The circular flow and the equality of income and expenditure provide two approaches to measuring GDP that we'll study in the next section.

■ **FIGURE 5.1**

The Circular Flow of Income and Expenditure                    MyEconLab Animation

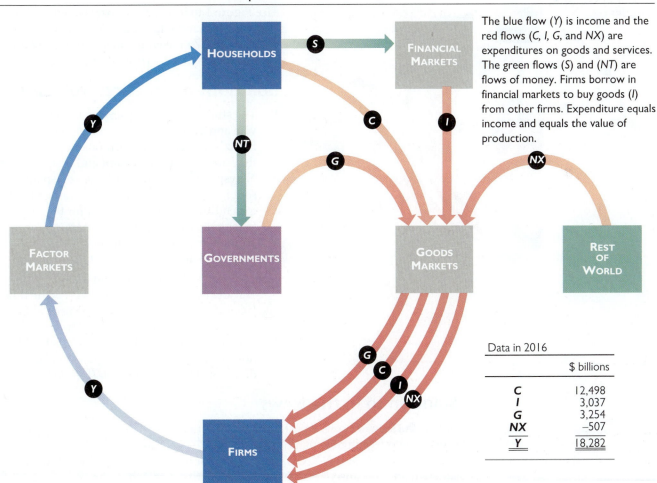

The blue flow (*Y*) is income and the red flows (*C, I, G,* and *NX*) are expenditures on goods and services. The green flows (*S*) and (*NT*) are flows of money. Firms borrow in financial markets to buy goods (*I*) from other firms. Expenditure equals income and equals the value of production.

Data in 2016

|  | $ billions |
|---|---|
| *C* | 12,498 |
| *I* | 3,037 |
| *G* | 3,254 |
| *NX* | −507 |
| *Y* | 18,282 |

MyEconLab Study Plan 5.1
Key Terms Quiz
Solutions Video

# CHECKPOINT 5.1

**Define GDP and explain why the value of production, income, and expenditure are the same for an economy.**

## Practice Problems

**LIST 1**

- Banking services bought by a student
- New cars bought by Hertz, the car rental firm
- Newsprint bought by *USA Today* from International Paper
- The purchase of a new aircraft for the vice president
- New house bought by Beyoncé

1. Classify each of the items in List 1 as a final good or service or as an intermediate good or service and identify which is a component of consumption expenditure, investment, or government expenditure on goods and services.

2. Figure 1 shows the flows of expenditure and income on Lotus Island. In 2016, $R$ was $10 billion; $W$ was $30 billion; $U$ was $12 billion; $J$ was $15 billion; and $Z$ was $3 billion. Calculate total expenditure and total income.

## In the News

**U.S. economy ended 2015 with slow growth**
GDP increased at an annual rate of 0.7 percent in the final quarter of 2015. Government expenditure grew at the same 0.7 percent rate, but consumption expenditure grew at a rate of 2.2 percent. Investment and net exports shrank.
Source: BEA News Release, January 29, 2016

Use Figure 1 to indicate the flows in which the items in the news clip occur. How can GDP increase by 0.7 percent if consumption expenditure increased at a 2.2 percent rate?

**FIGURE 1**

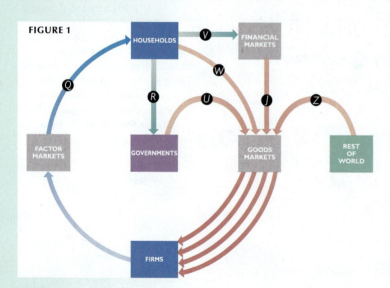

## Solutions to Practice Problems

1. The student's banking service is a final service and part of consumption expenditure. Hertz's new cars are additions to capital, so they are part of investment and final goods. Newsprint is an input into the newspaper, so it is an intermediate good and not a final expenditure. The new aircraft for the vice president is a final good and part of government expenditure. The new house is a final good and part of investment.

2. Total expenditure is the sum of $C$, $I$, $G$, and $NX$. In Figure 1, $C$ is the flow $W$; $I$ is the flow $J$; $G$ is the flow $U$; and $NX$ is the flow $Z$. So total expenditure equals $W + J + U + Z$, which is $60 billion. Total income is the blue flow, $Q$. But total income equals total expenditure, so total income is $60 billion.

## Solution to In the News

GDP is the sum of flows $W$, $J$, $U$, and $Z$. Investment is $J$; consumption expenditure is $W$; government expenditure is $U$; and exports are part of $Z$.
$GDP = C + I + G + NX$. GDP grew at the same rate as $G$ but GDP grew more slowly than $C$ because $I + NX$ grew at a negative rate—they shrank.

## 5.2  MEASURING U.S. GDP

MyEconLab Concept Video

U.S. GDP is the market value of all the final goods and services produced within the United States during a year. In 2016, U.S. GDP was $18.3 trillion. The Bureau of Economic Analysis in the U.S. Department of Commerce measures GDP by using two approaches:

- Expenditure approach
- Income approach

### ■ The Expenditure Approach

The expenditure approach measures GDP by using data on consumption expenditure, investment, government expenditure on goods and services, and net exports. This approach is like attaching a meter to the circular flow diagram on all the flows running through the goods markets to firms and measuring the magnitudes of those flows. Table 5.1 shows this approach. The first column gives the terms used in the U.S. National Income and Product Accounts. The next column gives the symbols we used in the previous section.

Using the expenditure approach, GDP is the sum of consumption expenditure on goods and services (*C*), investment (*I*), government expenditure on goods and services (*G*), and net exports of goods and services (*NX*). The third column gives the expenditures in 2016. GDP measured by the expenditure approach was $18,282 billion in the first quarter of 2016, expressed at an annual rate.

Net exports were negative in 2016 because imports exceeded exports. Imports were $2,686 billion and exports were $2,179 billion, so net exports—exports minus imports—were –$507 billion as shown in the table.

The fourth column in Table 5.1 shows the relative magnitudes of the expenditures. Consumption expenditure is by far the largest component of total expenditure; investment and government expenditure are the next largest and they are a similar size; and net exports is the smallest component. In 2016, consumption expenditure was 68.4 percent, investment was 16.6 percent, government expenditure was 17.8 percent, and net exports were a negative 2.8 percent of GDP.

### ■ TABLE 5.1

GDP: The Expenditure Approach

MyEconLab Real-time data

| Item | Symbol | Amount in 2016 (first quarter) (billions of dollars) | Percentage of GDP |
|---|---|---|---|
| Consumption expenditure | C | 12,498 | 68.4 |
| Investment | I | 3,037 | 16.6 |
| Government expenditure | G | 3,254 | 17.8 |
| Net exports | NX | −507 | −2.8 |
| GDP | Y | 18,282 | 100.0 |

The expenditure approach measures GDP by adding together consumption expenditure (*C*), investment (*I*), government expenditure (*G*), and net exports (*NX*).

In 2016, GDP measured by the expenditure approach was $18,282 billion.

SOURCE OF DATA: U.S. Department of Commerce, Bureau of Economic Analysis.

### Expenditures Not in GDP

Total expenditure (and GDP) does not include all the things that people and businesses buy. GDP is the value of *final goods and services*, so spending that is *not* on final goods and services is not part of GDP. Spending on intermediate goods and services is not part of GDP, although it is not always obvious whether an item is an intermediate good or a final good (see *Eye on the U.S. Economy* below). Also, we do not count as part of GDP spending on

- Used goods
- Financial assets

*Used Goods*   Expenditure on used goods is not part of GDP because these goods were part of GDP in the period in which they were produced and during which time they were new goods. For example, a 2015 automobile was part of GDP in 2015. If the car is traded on the used car market in 2017, the amount paid for the car is not part of GDP in 2017.

*Financial Assets*   When households buy financial assets such as bonds and stocks, they are making loans, not buying goods and services. The expenditure on newly produced capital goods is part of GDP, but the purchase of financial assets is not.

## EYE on the U.S. ECONOMY
### Is a Computer Program an Intermediate Good or a Final Good?

When American Airlines buys a new reservations software package, is that like General Motors buying tires? If it is, then software is an *intermediate good* and it is not counted as part of GDP. Airline ticket sales, like GM cars, are part of GDP, but the intermediate goods that are used to produce air transportation or cars are *not* part of GDP.

Or is American Airlines' purchase of new software like General Motors' purchase of a new assembly-line robot? If it is, then the software is a capital good and its purchase is the purchase of a final good. In this case, the software purchase is an *investment* and it *is* counted as part of GDP.

Brent Moulton worked as a government economist in the Bureau of Economic Analysis (BEA). Moulton's job was to oversee periodic adjustments to the GDP estimates to incorporate new data and new ideas about the economy.

The biggest change made was in how the purchase of computer software by firms is classified. Before 1999, it was regarded as an *intermediate good*. But since 1999, it has been treated as an *investment*.

How big a deal is this? When the BEA recalculated the 1996 GDP, the change increased the estimate of the 1996 GDP by $115 billion. That is a lot of money. To put it in perspective: GDP

in 1996 was $7,662 billion. So the adjustment was 1.5 percent of GDP.

This change is a good example of the ongoing effort by the BEA to keep the GDP measure as accurate as possible.

## ■ The Income Approach

To measure GDP using the income approach, the Bureau of Economic Analysis uses income data collected by the Internal Revenue Service and other agencies. The BEA takes the incomes that firms pay households for the services of the factors of production they hire—wages for labor services, interest for the use of capital, rent for the use of land, and profits for entrepreneurship—and sums those incomes. This approach is like attaching a meter to the circular flow diagram on all the flows running through factor markets from firms to households and measuring the magnitudes of those flows. Let's see how the income approach works.

The U.S. National Income and Product Accounts divide incomes into two big categories:

- Wage income
- Interest, rent, and profit income

### Wage Income

Wage income, called *compensation of employees* in the national accounts, is the total payment for labor services. It includes net wages and salaries plus fringe benefits paid by employers such as healthcare insurance, Social Security contributions, and pension fund contributions.

### Interest, Rent, and Profit Income

Interest, rent, and profit income, called *net operating surplus* in the national accounts, is the total income earned by capital, land, and entrepreneurship.

Interest income is the interest that households receive on capital. A household's capital is equal to its net worth—its assets minus its borrowing.

Rent includes payments for the use of land and other rented factors of production. It includes payments for rented housing and imputed rent for owner-occupied housing. (Imputed rent is an estimate of what homeowners would pay to rent the housing they own and use themselves. By including this item in the national accounts, we measure the total value of housing services, whether they are owned or rented.)

Profit includes the profits of corporations and the incomes of proprietors who run their own businesses. These incomes are a mixture of interest and profit.

Table 5.2 shows the relative magnitudes of these components of incomes.

### Net Domestic Product at Factor Cost

The sum of wages, interest, rent, and profit is *net domestic product at factor cost*. Net domestic product at factor cost is not GDP, and we must make two further adjustments to get to GDP: one from factor cost to market prices and another from net product to gross product.

### From Factor Cost to Market Price

The expenditure approach values goods and services at market prices, and the income approach values them at factor cost—the cost of the factors of production used to produce them. Indirect taxes (such as sales taxes) and subsidies (payments by government to firms) make these two values differ. Sales taxes make market prices exceed factor cost, and subsidies make factor cost exceed market prices. To convert the value at factor cost to the value at market prices, we must add indirect taxes and subtract subsidies.

### TABLE 5.2

### GDP: The Income Approach

The sum of all incomes equals net domestic product at factor cost. The income approach measure of GDP equals net domestic product at factor cost plus indirect taxes less subsidies plus depreciation (capital consumption).

In 2016, GDP measured by the income approach was $18,550 billion. This amount is $268 billion more than GDP measured by the expenditure approach—a statistical discrepancy of –$268 billion.

Wages are by far the largest part of total income.

| Item | Amount in 2016 (first quarter) (billions of dollars) | Percentage of GDP |
|---|---|---|
| Wages (compensation of employees) | 9,908 | 54.2 |
| Interest, rent, and profit (net operating surplus) | 4,576 | 25.0 |
| Net domestic product at factor cost | 14,484 | 79.2 |
| Indirect taxes less subsidies | 1,192 | 6.5 |
| Depreciation (capital consumption) | 2,874 | 15.7 |
| GDP (income approach) | 18,550 | 101.4 |
| Statistical discrepancy | −268 | −1.4 |
| GDP (expenditure approach) | 18,282 | 100.0 |

SOURCE OF DATA: U.S. Department of Commerce, Bureau of Economic Analysis.

## From Net Product to Gross Product

**Depreciation**
The decrease in the value of capital that results from its use and from obsolescence.

The income approach measures *net* product and the expenditure approach measures *gross* product. The difference is **depreciation**, which is the decrease in the value of capital that results from its use and from obsolescence. Firms' profits, which are included in the income approach, are net of depreciation, so the income approach gives a *net* measure. Investment, which is included in the expenditure approach, includes the purchase of capital to replace worn out or obsolete capital, so the expenditure approach gives a *gross* measure. To get *gross* domestic product from the income approach, we must *add* depreciation to total income.

## Statistical Discrepancy

The expenditure approach and income approach do not deliver exactly the same estimate of GDP. If a taxi driver doesn't report all his tips, they get missed in the income approach, but they get caught by the expenditure approach when he spends his income. So the sum of expenditures might exceed the sum of incomes. But most income gets reported to the Internal Revenue Service on tax returns while many items of expenditure are not recorded and must be estimated. So the sum of incomes might exceed the sum of estimated expenditures.

The discrepancy between the expenditure approach and the income approach estimates of GDP is called the *statistical discrepancy*, and it is calculated as the GDP expenditure total minus the GDP income total.

The two measures of GDP provide a check on the accuracy of the numbers. If the two are wildly different, we will want to know what mistakes we've made. Have we omitted some item? Have we counted something twice? The fact that the two estimates are close gives some confidence that they are reasonably accurate. But the expenditure total is regarded as the more reliable estimate of GDP, so the discrepancy is added to or subtracted from income to reconcile the two estimates.

Table 5.2 summarizes the calculation of GDP using the income approach and its reconciliation with GDP using the expenditure approach. The table also shows the relative magnitudes of the components of the income measure.

## ■ GDP and Related Measures of Production and Income

Although GDP is the main measure of total production, you will sometimes encounter another: gross *national* product or GNP.

### Gross National Product

A country's *gross national product*, or *GNP*, is the market value of all the final goods and services produced anywhere in the world in a given time period by the factors of production supplied by the residents of that country. For example, Nike's income from the capital that it supplies to its Vietnam shoe factory is part of U.S. GNP but not part of U.S. GDP. It is part of Vietnam's GDP. Similarly, Toyota's income on the capital it supplies to its Kentucky auto plant is part of U.S. GDP but not part of U.S. GNP. It is part of Japan's GNP.

GNP equals GDP plus net factor income received from or paid to other countries. The difference between U.S. GDP and GNP is small. But in an oil-rich Middle Eastern country such as Bahrain, where a large amount of capital is owned by foreigners, GNP is much smaller than GDP; and in a poor country such as Bangladesh, whose people work abroad and send income home, GNP is much larger than GDP.

### Disposable Personal Income

You've seen that consumption expenditure is the largest component of aggregate expenditure. The main influence on consumption expenditure is *disposable personal income*, which is the income received by households minus personal income taxes paid. Because disposable personal income plays an important role in influencing spending, the national accounts measure this item along with a number of intermediate totals that you can see in Figure 5.2. This figure shows how disposable personal income is calculated and how it relates to GDP and GNP.

### ■ FIGURE 5.2

GDP and Related Product and Income Measures                    MyEconLab Animation

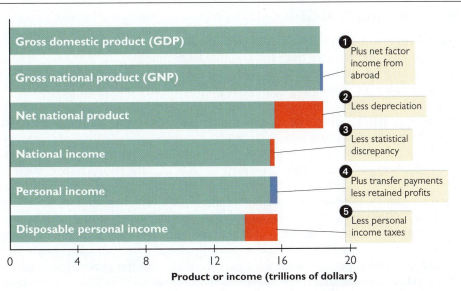

The bars show six related product and income measures and the relationship among them.

**1** Add net factor income from abroad to GDP to get GNP.

**2** Subtract depreciation from GNP to get net national product.

**3** Subtract the statistical discrepancy between the expenditure and income measures to get national income.

**4** Add transfer payments by governments less profits retained by firms to get personal income.

**5** Finally, subtract personal income taxes to get disposable personal income.

SOURCE OF DATA: U.S. Department of Commerce, Bureau of Economic Analysis.

## Real GDP and Nominal GDP

You've seen that GDP measures total expenditure on final goods and services in a given period. Suppose that we want to compare GDP in two periods, say 2009 and 2016. In 2009, GDP was $14,418 billion and by 2016, it was $18,282 billion—27 percent higher than in 2009. What does this 27 percent increase mean?

The answer is a combination of two things:

- We produced more goods and services.
- We paid higher prices for our goods and services.

Producing more goods and services contributes to an improvement in our standard of living. Paying higher prices means that our *cost of living* has increased but our standard of living has not. So it matters a great deal why GDP has increased. If the 27 percent increase is accounted for mainly by higher prices, our standard of living hasn't changed much. But if the 27 percent increase is accounted for mainly by the production of more goods and services, our standard of living might have increased a lot.

You're now going to see how economists at the Bureau of Economic Analysis isolate the effects on GDP of an increase in production. Their first step is to distinguish between two GDP concepts: real GDP and nominal GDP.

**Real GDP** is the value of the final goods and services produced in a given year expressed in terms of the prices in a *reference base year*. The *reference base year* is the year we choose against which to compare all other years. In the United States today, the *reference base year* is 2009.

Real GDP contrasts with **nominal GDP**, which is the value of the final goods and services produced in a given year expressed in terms of the prices of that same year. Nominal GDP is just a more precise name for GDP.

The method used to calculate real GDP has changed in recent years and is now a bit technical, but the essence of the calculation hasn't changed. Here, we describe the essence of the calculation. An appendix to this chapter describes the technical details of the method used by the Bureau of Economic Analysis.

## Calculating Real GDP

The goal of calculating *real GDP* is to measure the extent to which total production has increased and remove from the nominal GDP numbers the influence of price changes. To focus on the principles and keep the numbers easy to work with, we'll calculate real GDP for an economy that produces only one good in each of the GDP categories: consumption expenditure (*C*), investment (*I*), and government expenditure (*G*). We'll ignore exports and imports by assuming that net exports (exports minus imports) is zero.

Table 5.3 shows the quantities produced and the prices in 2009 (the *base year*) and in 2016. In part (a), we calculate nominal GDP in 2009. For each item, we multiply the quantity produced by its price to find the total expenditure on the item. We then sum the expenditures to find nominal GDP, which in 2009 is $100 million. Because 2009 is the base year, real GDP and nominal GDP are equal in 2009.

In part (b) of Table 5.3, we calculate nominal GDP in 2016. Again, we calculate nominal GDP by multiplying the quantity of each item produced by its price to find the total expenditure on the item. We then sum the expenditures to find nominal GDP, which in 2016 is $300 million. Nominal GDP in 2016 is three times its value in 2009. But by how much has the quantity of final goods and services produced increased? That's what real GDP will tell us.

**Real GDP**
The value of the final goods and services produced in a given year expressed in terms of the prices in a *reference base year*.

**Nominal GDP**
The value of the final goods and services produced in a given year expressed in terms of the prices of that same year.

**TABLE 5.3**

Calculating Nominal GDP and Real GDP in 2009 and 2016

| Item | | Quantity (millions of units) | Price (dollars per unit) | Expenditure (millions of dollars) |
|---|---|---|---|---|
| **(a) In 2009** | | | | |
| C | T-shirts | 10 | 5 | 50 |
| I | Computer chips | 3 | 10 | 30 |
| G | Security services | 1 | 20 | 20 |
| Y | Real GDP and Nominal GDP in 2009 | | | 100 |
| **(b) In 2016** | | | | |
| C | T-shirts | 4 | 5 | 20 |
| I | Computer chips | 2 | 20 | 40 |
| G | Security services | 6 | 40 | 240 |
| Y | Nominal GDP in 2016 | | | 300 |
| **(c) Quantities of 2016 valued at prices of 2009** | | | | |
| C | T-shirts | 4 | 5 | 20 |
| I | Computer chips | 2 | 10 | 20 |
| G | Security services | 6 | 20 | 120 |
| Y | Real GDP in 2016 | | | 160 |

The base year is 2009, so real GDP and nominal GDP are equal in that year.

Between 2009 and 2016, the production of security services (G) increased, but the production of T-shirts (C) and computer chips (I) decreased. In the same period, the price of a T-shirt remained constant, but the other two prices doubled.

Nominal GDP increased from $100 million in 2009 in part (a) to $300 million in 2016 in part (b).

Real GDP in part (c), which is calculated by using the quantities of 2016 in part (b) and the prices of 2009 in part (a), increased from $100 million in 2009 to $160 million in 2016, a 60 percent increase.

In part (c) of Table 5.3, we calculate real GDP in 2016. You can see that the quantity of each good and service produced in part (c) is the same as that in part (b). They are the quantities of 2016. You can also see that the prices in part (c) are the same as those in part (a). They are the prices of the base year—2009.

For each item, we now multiply the quantity produced in 2016 by its price in 2009 to find what the total expenditure would have been in 2016 if prices had remained the same as they were in 2009. We then sum these expenditures to find real GDP in 2016, which is $160 million.

Nominal GDP in 2016 is three times its value in 2009, but real GDP in 2016 is only 1.6 times its 2009 value—a 60 percent increase in *real* GDP.

## ■ Using the Real GDP Numbers

In the example that we've just worked through, we found the value of real GDP in 2016 based on the prices of 2009. This number alone enables us to compare production in two years only. By repeating the calculation that we have done for 2016 using the data for each year between 2009 and 2016, we can calculate the *annual* percentage change of real GDP—the annual growth rate of real GDP. This is the most common use of the real GDP numbers. Also, by calculating real GDP every three months—known as *quarterly real GDP*—the Bureau of Economic Analysis is able to provide valuable information that is used to interpret the current state of the economy. This information is used to guide both government macroeconomic policy and business production and investment decisions.

MyEconLab Study Plan 5.2

Key Terms Quiz

Solutions Video

## CHECKPOINT 5.2

**Describe how economic statisticians measure GDP and distinguish between nominal GDP and real GDP.**

## Practice Problems

**TABLE 1**

| Item | Amount (trillions of dollars) |
|---|---|
| Consumption expenditure | 12.1 |
| Government expenditure | 3.2 |
| Indirect taxes less subsidies | 1.2 |
| Depreciation | 2.8 |
| Net factor income from abroad | 0.2 |
| Investment | 3.0 |
| Net exports | −0.5 |
| Statistical discrepancy | −0.3 |

**TABLE 2**

**(a) In 2015:**

| Item | Quantity | Price |
|---|---|---|
| Apples | 60 | $0.50 |
| Oranges | 80 | $0.25 |

**(b) In 2016:**

| Item | Quantity | Price |
|---|---|---|
| Apples | 160 | $1.00 |
| Oranges | 220 | $2.00 |

Table 1 shows some of the items in the U.S. National Income and Product Accounts in 2015. Use Table 1 to work Problems **1** to **3**.

1.  Use the expenditure approach to calculate U.S. GDP in 2015.
2.  What was U.S. GDP as measured by the income approach in 2015? What was net domestic product at factor cost in 2015?
3.  Calculate U.S. GNP and U.S. national income in 2015.
4.  Table 2 shows some data for an economy. If the base year is 2015, calculate the economy's nominal GDP and real GDP in 2016.

## In the News

**Facebook is the reason for the productivity slowdown, no, really**
Facebook's WhatsApp is free and it sells no advertising. So WhatsApp's value of production in GDP is zero. Assume that WhatsApp's services are produced by 300 people all of whom earn $100,000 a year. By this measure, WhatsApp's value of production in GDP is $30 million.

Source: *Forbes*, February 13, 2016

What are the two approaches to measuring GDP described in the news clip? Why is one of these measures of the contribution of WhatsApp to GDP wrong?

## Solutions to Practice Problems

1.  GDP was $17.8 trillion. The expenditure approach sums the expenditure on final goods and services. That is, $Y = C + I + G + NX$.
    In 2015, U.S. GDP = $(12.1 + 3.0 + 3.2 − 0.5) trillion = $17.8 trillion.
2.  GDP as measured by the income approach was $18.1 trillion. GDP (income approach) = GDP (expenditure approach) *minus* Statistical discrepancy. In 2015, GDP (income approach) = $17.8 trillion − (−$0.3 trillion), or $18.1 trillion. Net domestic product at factor cost plus indirect taxes less subsidies plus depreciation equals GDP (income approach), so net domestic product at factor cost equals $(18.1 − 1.2 − 2.8) trillion, or $14.1 trillion.
3.  GNP = GDP + Net factor income from abroad. In 2015, GNP was $18.0 trillion ($17.8 trillion + $0.2 trillion). National income = GNP − Depreciation, which equals $18.0 trillion − $2.8 trillion, or $15.2 trillion.
4.  In 2016, nominal GDP equals (160 apples × $1) + (220 oranges × $2), or $600. Real GDP equals (160 apples × $0.50) + (220 oranges × $0.25), or $135.

## Solution to In the News

The two approaches to measuring GDP are the expenditure approach and the income approach. One of the measures in the news clip is wrong because the two approaches arrive at the same estimate of GDP. The news clip's income approach measure of $30 million is incorrect. The income approach measure is zero because Facebook incurs a a loss of $30 million when it pays its workers.

## 5.3    THE USES AND LIMITATIONS OF REAL GDP

MyEconLab Concept Video

We use estimates of real GDP for three main purposes:

- To compare the standard of living over time
- To track the course of the business cycle
- To compare the standard of living among countries

### ▪ The Standard of Living Over Time

A nation's *standard of living* is measured by the value of goods and services that its people enjoy, *on average*. Income per person determines what people can afford to buy and real GDP is a measure of real income. So *real GDP per person*—real GDP divided by the population—is a commonly used measure for comparing the standard of living over time.

Real GDP per person tells us the value of goods and services that the average person can enjoy. By using *real* GDP, we remove any influence that rising prices and a rising cost of living might have had on our comparison.

A handy way of comparing real GDP per person over time is to express it as a ratio of its value in some reference year. Table 5.4 provides the numbers for the United States that compare 2016 with 56 years earlier, 1960. In 1960, real GDP per person was $17,217 and in 2016 it was $56,200, or 3.3 times its 1960 level. To the extent that real GDP per person measures the standard of living, people in 2016 were 3.3 times as well off as their grandparents had been in 1960.

Figure 5.3 shows the entire 56 years of real GDP per person from 1960 to 2016 and displays two features of our changing standard of living:

1. The growth of potential GDP per person
2. Fluctuations of real GDP per person around potential GDP

**Potential GDP** is the level of real GDP when all the economy's factors of production—labor, capital, land, and entrepreneurial ability—are fully employed. When some factors of production are *unemployed*, real GDP is *below* potential GDP. And when some factors of production are *overemployed* and working harder and for longer hours than can be maintained in the long run, real GDP *exceeds* potential GDP.

You've seen that real GDP per person in 2016 was 3.3 times that of 1960. But in 2016, some labor and other factors of production were unemployed and the economy was producing less than potential GDP. To measure the trend in the standard of living, we must remove the influence of short-term fluctuations and focus on the path of potential GDP.

The growth rate of potential GDP fluctuates less than the growth rate of real GDP. During the 1960s, potential GDP per person grew at an average rate of 2.9 percent a year, but after 1970, its growth rate slowed to 2.1 percent a year. Then, after 2007, it slowed to 0.5 percent a year. This growth slowdown means that potential GDP is lower today (and lower by a large amount) than it would have been if the 1960s growth rate could have been maintained. If potential GDP had kept growing at the 1960s pace, potential GDP per person in 2016 would have been $36,000 more than it actually was. The cumulatively lost income from the growth slowdown of the 1970s is a staggering $509,000 per person (see Chapter 8, p. 194). Understanding the reasons for the growth slowdown is one of the major tasks of macroeconomists.

**TABLE 5.4    REAL GDP PER PERSON IN 1960 AND 2016**

| Year | 1960 | 2016 |
|---|---|---|
| Real GDP (billions) | $3,106 | $18,282 |
| Population (millions) | 180.4 | 325.3 |
| Real GDP per person | $17,217 | $56,200 |

**Potential GDP**
The value of real GDP when all the economy's factors of production—labor, capital, land, and entrepreneurial ability—are fully employed.

■ **FIGURE 5.3**

Real GDP and Potential GDP per Person in the United States: 1960–2016    MyEconLab Animation

Real GDP grows and fluctuates around the growth path of potential GDP. Potential GDP per person grew at an annual rate of 2.9 percent during the 1960s and slowed to 2.1 percent after 1970 and slowed again to 0.5 percent after 2007.

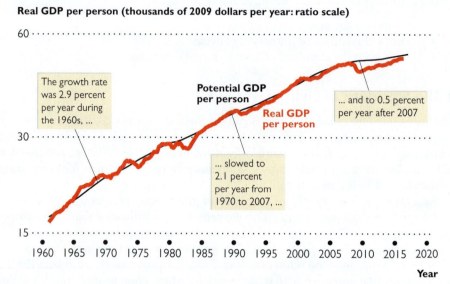

SOURCES OF DATA: Bureau of Economic Analysis and the Congressional Budget Office.

## ■ Tracking the Course of the Business Cycle

**Business cycle**

A periodic but irregular up-and-down movement of total production and other measures of economic activity.

We call the fluctuations in the pace of economic activity the business cycle. A **business cycle** is a periodic but irregular up-and-down movement of total production and other measures of economic activity such as employment and income. The business cycle isn't a regular, predictable, and repeating cycle like the phases of the moon. The timing and the intensity of the business cycle vary a lot, but every cycle has two phases:

1. Expansion
2. Recession

and two turning points:

1. Peak
2. Trough

Figure 5.4 shows these features of the most recent U.S. business cycle using real GDP as the measure of economic activity. An *expansion* is a period during which real GDP increases. In the early stage of an expansion, real GDP remains below potential GDP and as the expansion progresses, real GDP eventually exceeds potential GDP.

**Recession**

A period during which real GDP decreases for at least two successive quarters; or defined by the NBER as "a period of significant decline in total output, income, employment, and trade, usually lasting from six months to a year, and marked by contractions in many sectors of the economy."

A common definition of **recession** is a period during which real GDP decreases—its growth rate is negative—for at least two successive quarters. The National Bureau of Economic Research (NBER), which dates the U.S. business cycle phases and turning points, defines a recession more broadly as a significant decline in economic activity spread across the economy, lasting more than a few months,

**FIGURE 5.4**

The Most Recent U.S. Business Cycle

MyEconLab Real-time data

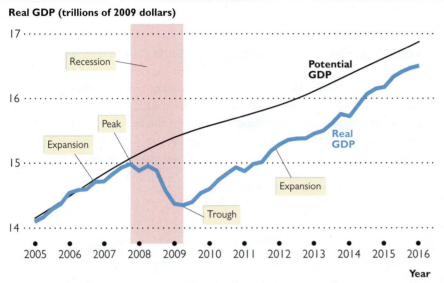

SOURCES OF DATA: Bureau of Economic Analysis, the Congressional Budget Office, and the National Bureau of Economic Research.

The most recent business cycle peak was in the fourth quarter of 2007 and the trough was in the second quarter of 2009 after which a new expansion began. Between the peak and the trough, the economy was in a recession. The recession was extremely deep and the expansion that followed was extremely weak—real GDP has remained a long way below potential GDP.

normally visible in real GDP, real income, employment, industrial production, and wholesale-retail sales. This definition means that sometimes the NBER declares a recession even though real GDP has not decreased for two successive quarters. A recession in 2001 was such a recession. An expansion ends and a recession begins at a business cycle peak. A peak is the highest level of real GDP that has been attained up to that time. A recession ends at a trough when real GDP reaches a low point and from which a new expansion begins.

The shaded bar in Figure 5.4 highlights the 2008–2009 recession. This recession was unusually severe. It lowered real GDP to its 2005 level. The end of a recession isn't the end of pain. When an expansion begins, real GDP is below potential GDP. And even after two years into the expansion that followed the 2008–2009 recession, real GDP had not returned to its previous peak level and the gap between real GDP and potential GDP was wide.

The period that began in 1991 following a severe recession and that ended with the global financial crisis of 2008 was so free from serious downturns in real GDP and other indicators of economic activity that it was called the *Great Moderation*, a name that contrasts it with the Great Depression. Some starry-eyed optimists even began to declare that the business cycle was dead. This long period of expansion also turned the attention of macroeconomists away from the business cycle and toward a focus on economic growth and the possibility of achieving faster growth.

But the 2008–2009 recession put the business cycle back on the agenda. Economists were criticized for not predicting it, and old divisions among economists that many thought were healed erupted in the pages of *The Economist* and *The New York Times* and online on a host of blogs.

We'll be examining the causes of recession and the alternative views among economists in greater detail as you progress through the rest of your study of macroeconomics.

# EYE on BOOMS AND BUSTS

MyEconLab Critical Thinking Exercise

## How Do We Track Economic Booms and Busts?

The National Bureau of Economic Research (NBER) Business Cycle Dating Committee determines the dates of U.S. business cycle turning points.

To identify the date of a business cycle peak, the NBER committee looks at data on industrial production, total employment, real GDP, and wholesale and retail sales.

Of these variables, real GDP is the most reliable measure of aggregate domestic production.

But when the NBER committee met in November 2008 to determine when the economy went into recession, the two measures of real GDP—the expenditure approach and the income approach—told conflicting stories.

For a few quarters in 2007 and 2008, because of the statistical discrepancy, the two estimates of real GDP did "not speak clearly about the date of a peak in activity."

So the NBER committee looked closely at the data on real personal income, real manufacturing, wholesale and retail sales, industrial production, and employment. All of these data peaked between November 2007 and June 2008. Weighing all the evidence, the committee decided that November 2007 was the peak.

But as the figure shows, real GDP didn't begin a sustained fall until the second quarter of 2008.

In contrast to the difficult task of dating the business cycle peak, the trough was clear. It occurred in the second quarter of 2009.

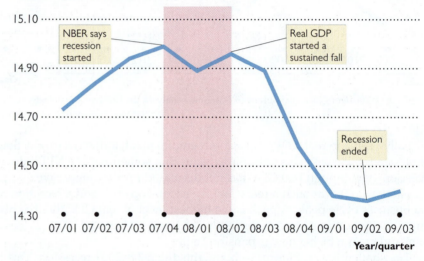

**Real GDP (trillions of 2009 dollars)**

SOURCES OF DATA: Bureau of Economic Analysis and the National Bureau of Economic Research.

Let's now leave comparisons of the standard of living over time and business cycles and briefly see how we compare the standard of living among countries.

## ■ The Standard of Living Among Countries

To use real GDP per person to compare the standard of living among countries, we must convert the numbers for other countries into U.S. dollars. To calculate real GDP, we must also use a common set of prices—called *purchasing power parity prices*—for all countries. The International Monetary Fund performs these calculations and if you turn back to Figure 2.3 on p. 46 you can see some comparisons based on these data. They tell, for example, that an average American has a standard of living (income per person) almost 6 times that of an average person in China.

Real GDP provides an easy way of comparing living standards. But real GDP doesn't include *all* the goods and services produced. Also, real GDP has nothing to say about factors other than the goods and services that affect the standard of living. Let's explore these limitations of real GDP.

# ■ Goods and Services Omitted from GDP

GDP measures the value of goods and services that are bought in markets. GDP excludes

- Household production
- Underground production
- Leisure time
- Environment quality

## Household Production

*Household production* is the production of goods and services (mainly services) in the home. Examples of this production are preparing meals, changing a light bulb, cutting grass, washing a car, and helping a student with homework. Because we don't buy these services in markets, they are not counted as part of GDP. The result is that GDP *underestimates* the value of the production.

Many items that were traditionally produced at home are now bought in the market. For example, more families now eat in fast-food restaurants—one of the fastest-growing industries in the United States—and use day-care services. These trends mean that food preparation and child-care services that were once part of household production are now measured as part of GDP. So real GDP grows more rapidly than does real GDP plus home production.

## Underground Production

*Underground production* is the production of goods and services hidden from the view of government because people want to avoid taxes and regulations or their actions are illegal. Because underground production is unreported, it is omitted from GDP.

Examples of underground production are the distribution of illegal drugs, farm work that uses illegal workers who are paid less than the minimum wage, and jobs that are done for cash to avoid paying income taxes. This last category might be quite large and includes tips earned by cab drivers, hairdressers, and hotel and restaurant workers.

Edgar L. Feige, an economist at the University of Wisconsin, estimates that U.S. underground production was about 16 percent of GDP during the early 1990s. Underground production in many countries, especially in most developing countries, is estimated to be larger than that in the United States.

## Leisure Time

Leisure time is an economic good that is not valued as part of GDP. Yet the marginal hour of leisure time must be at least as valuable to us as the wage we earn for working. If it were not, we would work instead. Over the years, leisure time has steadily increased as the workweek gets shorter, more people take early retirement, and the number of vacation days increases. These improvements in our standard of living are not measured in real GDP.

## Environment Quality

Pollution is an economic *bad* (the opposite of a *good*). The more we pollute our environment, other things remaining the same, the lower is our standard of living. This lowering of our standard of living is not measured by real GDP.

### ■ Other Influences on the Standard of Living

The quantity of goods and services consumed is a major influence on the standard of living. But other influences are

- Health and life expectancy
- Political freedom and social justice

#### Health and Life Expectancy

Good health and a long life—the hopes of everyone—do not show up directly in real GDP. A higher real GDP enables us to spend more on medical research, healthcare, a good diet, and exercise equipment. As real GDP has increased, our life expectancy has lengthened. But we face new health and life expectancy problems every year. Drug abuse is taking young lives at a rate that causes serious concern. When we take these negative influences into account, real GDP growth might overstate the improvements in the standard of living.

#### Political Freedom and Social Justice

A country might have a very large real GDP per person but have limited political freedom and social justice. For example, a small elite might enjoy political liberty and extreme wealth while the majority of people have limited freedom and live in poverty. Such an economy would generally be regarded as having a lower standard of living than one that had the same amount of real GDP but in which everyone enjoyed political freedom.

## EYE on YOUR LIFE
### Making GDP Personal

MyEconLab Critical Thinking Exercise

As you read a newspaper or business magazine, watch a TV news show, or browse a news Web site, you often come across reports about GDP.

What do these reports mean for you? Where in the National Income and Product Accounts do *your* transactions appear? How can you use information about GDP in your life?

#### Your Contribution to GDP

Your own economic transactions show up in the National Income and Product Accounts on both the expenditure side and the income side—as part of the expenditure approach and part of the income approach to measuring GDP.

Most of your expenditure is part of Consumption Expenditure. If you were to buy a new home, that item would appear as part of Investment. Because much of what you buy is produced in another country, expenditure on these goods shows up as part of Imports.

If you have a job, your income appears in Compensation of Employees.

Because the GDP measure of the value of production includes only market transactions, some of your own production of goods and services is most likely not counted in GDP.

What are the nonmarket goods and services that you produce? How would you go about valuing them?

#### Making Sense of the Numbers

To use the GDP numbers in a news report, you must first check whether the reporter is referring to *nominal* GDP or *real* GDP.

Using U.S. real GDP per person, check how your income compares with the average income in the United States. When you see GDP numbers for other countries, compare your income with that of a person in France, or Canada, or China.

# EYE on the GLOBAL ECONOMY
## Which Country Has the Highest Standard of Living?

You've seen that as a measure of the standard of living, GDP has limitations. To compare the standard of living across countries, we must consider other factors in addition to GDP.

GDP measures only the market value of all the final goods and services produced and bought in markets. GDP omits some goods and services (those produced in the home and in the hidden economy). It omits the value of leisure time, of good health and long life expectancy, as well as of political freedom and social justice. It also omits the damage (negative value) that pollution does to the environment.

These limitations of GDP as a measure of the standard of living apply in every country. So to make international comparisons of the standard of living, we must look at real GDP and other indicators. Nonetheless, real GDP per person is a major component of international comparisons.

Many alternatives to GDP have been proposed. One, called Green GDP, subtracts from GDP an estimate of the cost of greenhouse gas emissions and other negative influences on the environment. Another measure, called the Happy Planet Index, or HPI, goes further and subtracts from GDP an estimate of the cost of depleting nonrenewable resources.

Neither the Green GDP nor the HPI are reliable measures because they rely on guesses about the costs of pollution and resource depletion that are subjective and unreliable.

Taking an approach that focuses on the quality of life factors, the United Nations (UN) has constructed a Human Development Index (HDI), which combines income (GDP), life expectancy and health, and education.

The figure shows the relationship between the HDI and income per person in 2014. (In the figure, each dot represents a country.) These two measures of the standard of living tell a similar but not identical story.

The United States has a high HDI and a high income per person, but it doesn't have the highest of either.

Qatar is an example of a handful of countries with a higher income per person.

Australia and Norway are two of the countries with a higher HDI. In these countries, people live longer than do people in the United States and have universal access to healthcare.

The HDI doesn't include political freedom and social justice. If it did, the United States would score highly on that component of the index.

The bottom line is that we don't know which country has the highest standard of living, but we do know that GDP per person alone does not provide the complete answer.

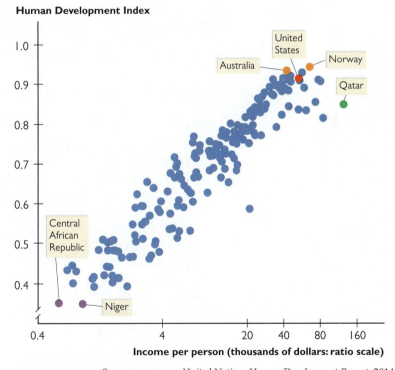

Source of data: *United Nations Human Development Report*, 2014.

MyEconLab Study Plan 5.3
Key Terms Quiz
Solutions Video

 CHECKPOINT 5.3

**Describe the uses of real GDP and explain its limitations as a measure of the standard of living.**

## Practice Problems

The United Nations Human Development Report gives the data for 2014 in Table 1. Other information suggests that household production is similar in Canada and the United States and smaller than in China and Russia. The underground economy is larger in Russia and China and a similar proportion of each of these economies. Canadians and Americans enjoy more leisure hours than do the Chinese and Russians. Canada and the United States spend significantly more on the environment than do China and Russia. Use this information and ignore any other influences to work Problems **1** and **2**.

**TABLE 1**

| Country | Real GDP per person |
|---|---|
| China | $12,547 |
| Russia | $22,352 |
| United States | $52,947 |
| Canada | $42,155 |

1. In which pair (or pairs) of countries is it easiest to compare the standard of living? And in which pair (or pairs) is it most difficult? Explain why.

2. Do the differences in real GDP per person correctly rank the standard of living in these four countries? What additional information would we need to be able to make an accurate assessment of the relative standard of living in these four countries?

## In the News

**Why GDP fails as a measure of well-being**

There is a new reason why GDP is a poor measure of economic well-being: It doesn't measure the benefits we gain from free apps and lots of other free stuff on the Internet. And none of the other indexes deal with this problem.

Source: *CBS News*, January 27, 2016

What are the other reasons why GDP is a poor measure of economic well-being?

## Solutions to Practice Problems

1. Two pairs—Canada and the United States, and China and Russia—are easy to compare because household production, the underground economy, leisure hours, and the environment are similar in the countries in each pair. The most difficult comparison is Canada and the United States with either China or Russia. Household production and the underground economy narrow the differences but leisure hours and the environment widen them.

2. Differences in real GDP per person probably correctly rank the standard of living because where the gap is small (Canada and the United States), other factors are similar, and where other factors differ, the gaps are huge. More information on the value of household production, the underground economy, the value of leisure, and the value of environmental differences is required to make an accurate assessment of relative living standards.

## Solution to In the News

Because GDP measures production that is traded in markets, it does not include household production, leisure time, health and life expectancy, political freedom, and social justice. These contributors to economic well-being are what other indexes such as green GDP and the HDI are designed to deal with.

**CHAPTER SUMMARY**

## Key Points

**1.** **Define GDP and explain why the value of production, income, and expenditure are the same for an economy.**

- GDP is the market value of all final goods and services produced within a country in a given time period.
- We can value goods and services either by what they cost to produce (incomes) or by what people are willing to pay (expenditures).
- The value of production equals income equals expenditure.

**2.** **Describe how economic statisticians measure GDP and distinguish between nominal GDP and real GDP.**

- BEA measures GDP by summing expenditures and by summing incomes. With no errors of measurement the two totals are the same, but in practice, a small statistical discrepancy arises.
- A country's GNP is similar to its GDP, but GNP is the value of production by factors of production supplied by the residents of a country.
- Nominal GDP is the value of production using the prices of the current year and the quantities produced in the current year.
- Real GDP is the value of production using the prices of a base year and the quantities produced in the current year.

**3.** **Describe the uses of real GDP and explain its limitations as a measure of the standard of living.**

- We use real GDP per person to compare the standard of living over time.
- We use real GDP to determine when the economy has reached a business cycle peak or trough.
- We use real GDP per person expressed in purchasing power parity dollars to compare the standard of living among countries.
- Real GDP omits some goods and services and ignores some factors that influence the standard of living.
- The Human Development Index takes some other factors into account.

## Key Terms

MyEconLab Key Terms Quiz

Business cycle, 130
Consumption expenditure, 117
Depreciation, 124
Exports of goods and services, 118
Final good or service, 116
Government expenditure on goods and services, 118

Gross domestic product (GDP), 116
Imports of goods and services, 118
Intermediate good or service, 116
Investment, 117
Net exports of goods and services, 118
Net taxes, 118

Nominal GDP, 126
Potential GDP, 129
Real GDP, 126
Recession, 130
Saving, 118

# CHAPTER CHECKPOINT

## Study Plan Problems and Applications

**1.** Figure 1 shows the flows of income and expenditure in an economy. In 2013, *U* was $2 trillion, *V* was $1.5 trillion, *W* was $7 trillion, *J* was $1.5 trillion, and *Z* was zero. Calculate total income, net taxes, and GDP.

**FIGURE 1**

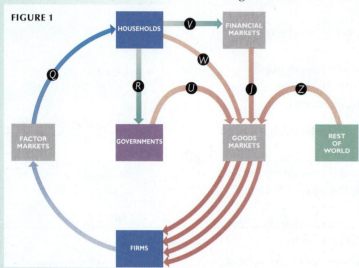

Use the following data to work Problems **2** and **3**.

The national accounts of Parchment Paradise are kept on (you guessed it) parchment. A fire in the statistics office destroys some accounts, leaving only the following data:

- GDP (income approach) $2,900
- Consumption expenditure $2,000
- Indirect taxes less subsidies $100
- Interest, rent, and profit $500
- Investment $800
- Government expenditure $400
- Wages $2,000
- Net factor income from abroad $50
- Net exports −$200

**2.** Calculate GDP (expenditure approach) and depreciation.

**3.** Calculate net domestic product at factor cost, the statistical discrepancy, and GNP.

Use the following information to work Problems **4** to **6**.

An economy produces only fun and food. Table 1 shows the prices and the quantities of fun and food produced in 2016 and 2017. The base year is 2016.

**4.** Calculate nominal GDP in 2016 and 2017.

**5.** Calculate the percentage increase in real GDP in 2017.

**6.** If potential GDP was $270 in 2016 and it grew by 1 percent in 2017, in which phase of the business cycle is the economy? Explain.

**TABLE 1**

**(a) In 2016:**

| Item | Quantity | Price |
|------|----------|-------|
| Fun  | 40       | $2    |
| Food | 60       | $3    |

**(b) In 2017:**

| Item | Quantity | Price |
|------|----------|-------|
| Fun  | 35       | $3    |
| Food | 65       | $2    |

Use the following information to work Problems **7** to **9**.

**Uncertain outlook**

The Commerce Department reported that in December 2015, retail sales rose by 0.2, net exports decreased, inventories held by businesses rose by 0.1 percent, and total sales by businesses fell by 0.6 percent.

Source: Commerce Department, February 2016

**7.** Which component of GDP changed because retail sales increased? Which component of GDP changed because business inventories increased?

**8.** Explain the effect of the fall in net exports on GDP.

**9.** Does the statement that total sales by businesses fell by 0.6 percent mean that GDP decreased by 0.6 percent? Explain your answer.

**10.** Read *Eye on Booms and Busts* on p. 132 and explain why the NBER reported that the 2008 recession began before real GDP had fallen for two successive quarters.

# Instructor Assignable Problems and Applications

**1.** In France, real GDP was the same in 2012 as it had been in 2011, but in the last quarter of 2012 and the first quarter of 2013, France's real GDP decreased. In the United States, real GDP increased in 2012, and in the first quarter of 2013, it was higher than in the last quarter of 2012.

Based on this information, which country was in a recession at the beginning of 2013? What features of the information provided led you to your conclusion?

**2.** Classify each of the items in List 1 as a final good or service or an intermediate good or service and identify it as a component of consumption expenditure, investment, or government expenditure on goods and services.

Use the following information to work Problems **3** and **4**.

Mitsubishi Heavy Industries makes the wings of the new Boeing 787 Dreamliner in Japan. Toyota assembles cars for the U.S. market in Kentucky.

**3.** Explain where these activities appear in the National Income and Product Accounts of the United States.

**4.** Explain where these activities appear in the National Income and Product Accounts of Japan.

Use the data on the economy of Iberia in Table 1 to work Problems **5** and **6**.

**5.** Calculate Iberia's GDP.

**6.** Calculate Iberia's imports of goods and services.

Use Table 2, which shows an economy's total production and the prices of the final goods it produced in 2016 and 2017, to work Problems **7** to **9**.

**7.** Calculate nominal GDP in 2016 and 2017.

**8.** The base year is 2016. Calculate real GDP in 2016 and 2017.

**9.** Calculate the percentage increase in real GDP in 2017.

Use the following information to work Problems **10** and **11**.

**New U.S. home sales surged**
Purchases of new U.S. homes surged in December and 2015 was the best year for housing since 2007. Existing-home sales also increased in the best year since 2006. The inventory of existing homes on the market was smaller than demand.
Source: Bloomberg, January 28, 2016

**10.** Where do new-home sales appear in the circular flow of expenditure and income? Explain how a surge in new home sales affects real GDP.

**11.** Where do sales and inventories of existing homes appear in the circular flow of expenditure and income? Explain how an increase in sales of existing homes and a low inventory of existing homes affects real GDP.

**12. Worries about China's slowing growth**
China reported that its real GDP grew by 6.9 percent in 2015, down from 7.3 percent in 2014. Experts think that China has overstated its true growth rate and many fear that its growth will slow further.
Source: *The Economist*, January 19, 2016

How does China's real GDP growth compare with that of the United States? If China's growth slows further, would that mean it was in a recession?

**LIST 1**

- Banking services bought by Target
- Security system bought by the White House
- Coffee beans bought by Starbucks
- New coffee machines bought by Starbucks
- Starbucks grande mocha frappuccino bought by a student
- New battle ship bought by the U.S. navy

**TABLE 1**

| Item | Amount |
|---|---|
| Net taxes | $18 billion |
| Government expenditure | $20 billion |
| Saving | $15 billion |
| Consumption expenditure | $67 billion |
| Investment | $21 billion |
| Exports | $30 billion. |

**TABLE 2**

**(a) In 2016:**

| Item | Quantity | Price |
|---|---|---|
| Fish | 100 | $2 |
| Berries | 50 | $6 |

**(b) In 2017:**

| Item | Quantity | Price |
|---|---|---|
| Fish | 75 | $5 |
| Berries | 65 | $10 |

# Multiple Choice Quiz

1. Gross domestic product is the market value of all the _____ in a given time period.

   A. goods and services bought by Americans
   B. goods and services produced by American companies in all countries
   C. final goods and services produced by all firms located in the United States
   D. U.S.-produced goods and services bought in the United States

2. A _____ is a final good and _____ is an intermediate good.

   A. new car bought by a student; a used SUV bought by a dealer
   B. new textbook; a used textbook
   C. new iPhone bought by a student; a new computer bought by Walmart
   D. tank of gasoline bought by you; jet fuel bought by Southwest Airlines

3. Saving equals _____.

   A. income minus consumption expenditure minus net taxes
   B. income minus net taxes
   C. total income minus total expenditure
   D. net taxes minus government expenditure

4. The expenditure approach to measuring U.S. GDP equals _____.

   A. the sum of U.S. consumption expenditure and U.S. investment
   B. U.S. government expenditure minus taxes paid by Americans
   C. all expenditure on final goods and services produced in the United States in a given time period
   D. all expenditure by Americans on goods and services produced in the United States in a given time period

5. When using the income approach to measure GDP at market prices, in addition to summing all factor incomes it is necessary to _____.

   A. subtract depreciation because profit is not reported as net profit
   B. add depreciation because capital depreciates when goods are manufactured
   C. add indirect taxes less subsidies to convert aggregate income from factor cost to market prices
   D. add a statistical discrepancy which is the sum of depreciation and indirect taxes less subsidies

6. The following statements about the business cycle are correct *except* _____.

   A. it is a regular predictable cycle in real GDP around potential GDP
   B. from the peak to the trough, the economy is in a recession
   C. from the trough to the peak, the economy is in an expansion
   D. it is a periodic movement in economic activity including employment

7. Real GDP per person is not an accurate measure of the standard of living because it _____.

   A. includes the goods and services that governments buy
   B. omits the goods and services that people produce for themselves
   C. includes goods and services bought by firms
   D. omits the goods and services imported from other countries

APPENDIX: MEASURING REAL GDP

This appendix explains the method used by the Bureau of Economic Analysis (BEA) to calculate real GDP using a measure called **chained-dollar real GDP**. We begin by explaining the problem that arises from using the prices of the base year (the method on pp. 126–127) and how the problem can be overcome.

**Chained-dollar real GDP**
The measure of real GDP calculated by the Bureau of Economic Analysis.

### ■ The Problem With Base Year Prices

When we calculated real GDP on pp. 126–127, we found that real GDP in 2016 was 60 percent greater than it was in 2009. But instead of using the prices of 2009 as the constant prices, we could have used the prices of 2016. In this case, we would have valued the quantities produced in 2009 at the prices of 2016. By comparing the values of real GDP in 2009 and 2016 at the constant prices of 2016, we get a different number for the percentage increase in production. If you use the numbers in Table 5.3 on p. 127 to value 2009 production at 2016 prices, you will get a real GDP in 2009 of $150 million (2016 dollars). Real GDP in 2016 at 2016 prices is $300 million. So by using the prices of 2016, production doubled—a 100 percent increase—from 2009 to 2016. Did production in fact increase by 60 percent or 100 percent?

The problem arises because to calculate real GDP, we weight the quantity of each item produced by its price. If all prices change by the same percentage, then the *relative* weight on each good or service doesn't change and the percentage change in real GDP from the first year to the second is the same regardless of which year's prices we use. But if prices change by different percentages, then the *relative* weight on each good or service *does* change and the percentage change in real GDP from the first year to the second depends on which prices we use. So which year's prices should we use: those of the first year or those of the second?

The answer given by the BEA method is to use the prices of both years. If we calculate the percentage change in real GDP twice, once using the prices of the first year and again using the prices of the second year, and then take the average of those two percentage changes, we get a unique measure of the change in real GDP and one that gives equal importance to the *relative* prices of both years.

To illustrate the calculation of the BEA measure of real GDP, we'll work through an example. The method has three steps:

- Value production in the prices of adjacent years.
- Find the average of two percentage changes.
- Link (chain) to the base year.

### ■ Value Production in the Prices of Adjacent Years

The first step is to value production in *adjacent* years at the prices of both years. We'll make these calculations for 2016, and its preceding year, 2015.

Table A5.1 shows the quantities produced and prices in the two years. Part (a) shows the nominal GDP calculation for 2015—the quantities produced in 2015 valued at the prices of 2015. Nominal GDP in 2015 is $145 million. Part (b) shows the nominal GDP calculation for 2016—the quantities produced in 2016 valued at the prices of 2016. Nominal GDP in 2016 is $172 million. Part (c) shows the value of the quantities produced in 2016 at the prices of 2015. This total is $160 million. Finally, part (d) shows the value of the quantities produced in 2015 at the prices of 2016. This total is $158 million.

■ **TABLE A5.1**

Real GDP Calculation Step 1: Value Production in Adjacent Years at Prices of Both Years

Step 1 is to value the production of adjacent years at the prices of both years.

Here, we value the production of 2015 and 2016 at the prices of both 2015 and 2016.

The value of 2015 production at 2015 prices, in part (a), is nominal GDP in 2015.

The value of 2016 production at 2016 prices, in part (b), is nominal GDP in 2016.

Part (c) calculates the value of 2016 production at 2015 prices, and part (d) calculates the value of 2015 production at 2016 prices.

We use these numbers in Step 2.

| Item | | Quantity (millions of units) | Price (dollars per unit) | Expenditure (millions of dollars) |
|---|---|---|---|---|
| **(a) In 2015** | | | | |
| C | T-shirts | 3 | 5 | 15 |
| I | Computer chips | 3 | 10 | 30 |
| G | Security services | 5 | 20 | 100 |
| Y | Nominal GDP in 2015 | | | 145 |
| **(b) In 2016** | | | | |
| C | T-shirts | 4 | 4 | 16 |
| I | Computer chips | 2 | 12 | 24 |
| G | Security services | 6 | 22 | 132 |
| Y | Nominal GDP in 2016 | | | 172 |
| **(c) Quantities of 2016 valued at prices of 2015** | | | | |
| C | T-shirts | 4 | 5 | 20 |
| I | Computer chips | 2 | 10 | 20 |
| G | Security services | 6 | 20 | 120 |
| Y | 2016 production at 2015 prices | | | 160 |
| **(d) Quantities of 2015 valued at prices of 2016** | | | | |
| C | T-shirts | 3 | 4 | 12 |
| I | Computer chips | 3 | 12 | 36 |
| G | Security services | 5 | 22 | 110 |
| Y | 2015 production at 2016 prices | | | 158 |

## Find the Average of Two Percentage Changes

The second step is to find the percentage change in the value of production based on the prices in the two adjacent years. Table A5.2 summarizes these calculations.

Valued at the prices of 2015, production increased from $145 million in 2015 to $160 million in 2016, an increase of 10.3 percent. Valued at the prices of 2016, production increased from $158 million in 2015 to $172 million in 2016, an increase of 8.9 percent. The average of these two percentage changes in the value of production is 9.6. That is, $(10.3 + 8.9) \div 2 = 9.6$.

We've now found the *growth rate* of real GDP in 2016. But we also want to calculate the *level* of real GDP. This level depends on the *reference base year*. The simplest example is when the previous year (2015 in this case) is the base year. In 2015, real GDP equals nominal GDP, which is $145 million. Real GDP in 2016, valued in 2015 dollars is 9.6 percent higher than in 2015 and equals $159 million.

Although the real GDP of $159 million is expressed in 2015 dollars, the calculation uses the average of the *relative prices* of the final goods and services that make up GDP in 2015 and 2016.

When the base year is not the previous year, we need to link or chain the current year to the base year. Let's see how we do this linking.

■ **TABLE A5.2**

**Real GDP Calculation Step 2: Find Average of Two Percentage Changes**

| Value of Production in Adjacent Years | | Millions of dollars |
|---|---|---|
| 2015 production at 2015 prices | | 145 |
| 2016 production at 2015 prices | | 160 |
| Percentage change in production at 2015 prices | 10.3 | |
| 2015 production at 2016 prices | | 158 |
| 2016 production at 2016 prices | | 172 |
| Percentage change in production at 2016 prices | 8.9 | |
| Average of two percentage changes in production | **9.6** | |

Using the numbers calculated in Step 1, we find the percentage change in production from 2015 to 2016 valued at 2015 prices, which is 10.3 percent.

We also find the percentage change in production from 2015 to 2016 valued at 2016 prices, which is 8.9 percent.

We then find the average of these two percentage changes, which is 9.6 percent.

## Link (Chain) to the Base Year

To link to the base year, we repeat the calculation that we've just described to obtain the real GDP growth rate each year. Real GDP equals nominal GDP in the base year, which currently is 2009. By applying the calculated growth rates to each successive year, we can obtain *chained-dollar real GDP* in 2009 dollars.

Figure A5.1 shows an example with real GDP equal to nominal GDP at $62 million in the base year, 2009, and assumed growth rates of real GDP for each year between 2008 and 2016. The 2016 growth rate is the 9.6 percent that we calculated in Table A5.2 above.

Starting with real GDP in the base year, we apply the calculated percentage change of 4.6 percent, so real GDP in 2010 was 4.6 percent higher than $62 million, which is $65 million. Repeating the calculation, real GDP in 2011 is 7.1 percent higher, which is $69 million, and in 2012, real GDP is 8.2 percent higher, which is $75 million. By 2015, real GDP has grown to $83 million. In 2016, real GDP is 9.6 percent higher than $83 million, which is $91 million.

The same method is used to chain-link the years before the base year. For example, real GDP in 2008 is 3.2 percent lower than in 2009 at $60 million.

■ **FIGURE A5.1**

**Real GDP Calculation Step 3: Link (Chain) to the Base Year**          MyEconLab Animation

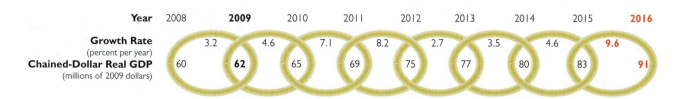

| Year | 2008 | **2009** | 2010 | 2011 | 2012 | 2013 | 2014 | 2015 | **2016** |
|---|---|---|---|---|---|---|---|---|---|
| **Growth Rate** (percent per year) | | 3.2 | 4.6 | 7.1 | 8.2 | 2.7 | 3.5 | 4.6 | **9.6** |
| **Chained-Dollar Real GDP** (millions of 2009 dollars) | 60 | **62** | 65 | 69 | 75 | 77 | 80 | 83 | **91** |

The growth rate of real GDP from one year to the next is calculated for every pair of years and then linked to the base year. Suppose that real GDP was $62 million in the base year, 2009. By applying the growth rate between each pair of years, we find the chained-dollar real GDP for each year, expressed in terms of the value of the dollar in the base year. Here, the percentages for 2008 through to 2016 are assumed. By 2016, the chained-dollar real GDP has increased to $91 million in 2009 dollars.

MyEconLab Chapter 5 Study Plan

 APPENDIX CHECKPOINT

## Study Plan Problems

An island economy produces only bananas and coconuts. Table 1 gives the quantities produced and prices in 2015 and in 2016. The base year is 2015.

**1.** Calculate nominal GDP in 2015 and nominal GDP in 2016.

**2.** Calculate the value of 2016 production in 2015 prices and the percentage increase in production when valued at 2015 prices.

**3.** Calculate the value of 2015 production in 2016 prices and the percentage increase in production when valued at 2016 prices.

**4.** Use the chained-dollar method to calculate real GDP in 2015 and 2016. In terms of what dollars is each of these two real GDPs measured?

**5.** Using the chained-dollar method, compare the growth rates of nominal GDP and real GDP in 2016.

**6.** If the base year is 2016, use the chained-dollar method to calculate real GDP in 2015 and 2016. In terms of what dollars is each of these two real GDPs measured?

**7.** If the base year is 2016, compare the growth rates of nominal GDP and real GDP in 2016.

**TABLE 1**

**(a) In 2015:**

| Item | Quantity | Price |
|---|---|---|
| Bananas | 100 | $10 |
| Coconuts | 50 | $12 |

**(b) In 2016:**

| Item | Quantity | Price |
|---|---|---|
| Bananas | 110 | $15 |
| Coconuts | 60 | $10 |

MyEconLab Homework, Quiz, or Test if assigned by instructor

## Instructor Assignable Problems

An economy produces only food and fun. Table 2 shows the quantities produced and prices in 2015 and 2016. The base year is 2016.

**1.** Calculate nominal GDP in 2015 and nominal GDP in 2016.

**2.** Calculate the value of 2016 production in 2015 prices and the percentage increase in production when valued at 2015 prices.

**3.** Calculate the value of 2015 production in 2016 prices and the percentage increase in production when valued at 2016 prices.

**4.** Using the chained-dollar method, calculate real GDP in 2015 and 2016. In terms of what dollars is each of these two real GDPs measured?

**5.** Using the chained-dollar method, compare the growth rates of nominal GDP and real GDP in 2016.

**6.** If the base year is 2015, use the chained-dollar method to calculate real GDP in 2015 and 2016. In terms of what dollars is each of these two real GDPs measured?

**7.** If the base year is 2015, compare the growth rates of nominal GDP and real GDP in 2016.

**TABLE 2**

**(a) In 2015:**

| Item | Quantity | Price |
|---|---|---|
| Food | 100 | $2 |
| Fun | 50 | $6 |

**(b) In 2016:**

| Item | Quantity | Price |
|---|---|---|
| Food | 75 | $5 |
| Fun | 65 | $10 |

## Key Term

Chained-dollar real GDP, 141

MyEconLab Key Terms Quiz

# Jobs and Unemployment

**When you have completed your study of this chapter,
you will be able to**

**6**

**1** Define the unemployment rate and other labor market indicators.

**2** Describe the trends and fluctuations in the indicators of the state of the U.S. labor market.

**3** Describe the types of unemployment, define full employment, and explain the link between unemployment and real GDP.

MyEconLab Big Picture Video

## 6.1 LABOR MARKET INDICATORS

Every month, 1,600 field interviewers and supervisors working on a joint project between the Bureau of Labor Statistics (or BLS) and the Bureau of the Census survey 60,000 households and ask a series of questions about the age and labor market status of their members. This survey is called the *Current Population Survey*. Let's look at the types of data collected by this survey.

### ■ Current Population Survey

Figure 6.1 shows the categories into which the BLS divides the population. It also shows the relationships among the categories. The first category divides the population into two groups: the working-age population and others. The **working-age population** is the total number of people aged 16 years and over who are not in jail, hospital, or some other form of institutional care or in the U.S. Armed Forces. In May 2016, the estimated population of the United States was 322.3 million, the working-age population was 252.9 million, and 69.4 million people were under 16 years of age, in the military, or living in institutions.

The second category divides the working-age population into two groups: those in the labor force and those not in the labor force. The **labor force** is the number of people employed plus the number unemployed. In May 2016, the U.S. labor force was 158.4 million and 94.5 million people were not in the labor force. Most of those not in the labor force were in school full time or had retired from work.

The third category divides the labor force into two groups: the employed and the unemployed. In May 2016 in the United States, 151.0 million people were employed and 7.4 million people were unemployed.

**Working-age population**
The total number of people aged 16 years and over who are not in jail, hospital, or some other form of institutional care or in the U.S. Armed Forces.

**Labor force**
The number of people employed plus the number unemployed.

### ■ Population Survey Criteria

The survey counts as *employed* all persons who, during the week before the survey, either

1.  Worked at least 1 hour as paid employees or worked 15 hours or more as unpaid workers in their family business or
2.  Were not working but had jobs or businesses from which they were temporarily absent.

The survey counts as *unemployed* all persons who, during the week before the survey,

1.  Had no employment,
2.  Were available for work,

and either

1.  Had made specific efforts to find employment during the previous four weeks or
2.  Were waiting to be recalled to a job from which they had been laid off.

People in the working-age population who by the above criteria are neither employed nor unemployed are classified as not in the labor force.

*To be counted as unemployed, a person must not only want a job but also have tried to find one.*

### FIGURE 6.1

Population Labor Force Categories

MyEconLab Real-time data

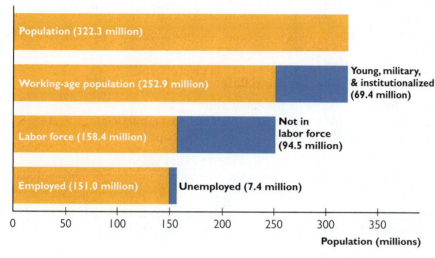

The U.S. population is divided into the working-age population and the young, military, and institutionalized. The working-age population is divided into the labor force and those not in the labor force. The labor force is divided into those employed and those unemployed. The figure shows the data for May 2016.

SOURCE OF DATA: Bureau of Labor Statistics.

## Three Labor Market Indicators

Using the numbers from the Current Population Survey, the BLS calculates several indicators of the state of the labor market. The three main labor market indicators are

- The unemployment rate
- The employment–population ratio
- The labor force participation rate

### The Unemployment Rate

The amount of unemployment—the number of people who want jobs but can't find them—is an indicator of unused labor resources. The BLS reports the absolute number of people unemployed and the **unemployment rate**, which is the percentage of the people in the labor force who are unemployed. That is,

$$\text{Unemployment rate} = \frac{\text{Number of people unemployed}}{\text{Labor force}} \times 100.$$

Table 6.1 shows the number of people unemployed and the number in the labor force in May 2016 and uses the formula above to calculate the unemployment rate in that month.

### The Employment–Population Ratio

The number of people of working age who have jobs is an indicator of both the availability of jobs and the degree of match between people's skills and the skills that employers demand. The BLS calculates the **employment–population ratio** as the percentage of the people of working age who are employed.

**Unemployment rate**
The percentage of the people in the labor force who are unemployed.

TABLE 6.1    UNEMPLOYMENT RATE: MAY 2016

| Unemployed | 7.4 million |
|---|---|
| Labor force | 158.4 million |
| Calculation | $\frac{7.4}{158.4} \times 100$ |
| Unemployment rate | 4.7 percent |

**Employment–population ratio**
The percentage of the people of working age who are employed.

**TABLE 6.2 EMPLOYMENT–POPULATION RATIO: MAY 2016**

| | |
|---|---|
| Employed | 151.0 million |
| Working-age population | 252.9 million |
| Calculation | $\frac{151.0}{252.9} \times 100$ |
| Employment–population ratio | 59.7 percent |

**Labor force participation rate**
The percentage of the working-age population in the labor force.

**TABLE 6.3 LABOR FORCE PARTICIPATION RATE: MAY 2016**

| | |
|---|---|
| Labor force | 158.4 million |
| Working-age population | 252.9 million |
| Calculation | $\frac{158.4}{252.9} \times 100$ |
| Labor force participation rate | 62.6 percent |

**Marginally attached worker**
A person who does not have a job, is available and willing to work, has not made specific efforts to find a job within the previous four weeks, but has looked for work sometime in the recent past.

**Discouraged worker**
A marginally attached worker who has not made specific efforts to find a job within the past four weeks because previous unsuccessful attempts to find a job were discouraging.

The BLS calculates the employment–population ratio using the formula:

$$\text{Employment–population ratio} = \frac{\text{Number of people employed}}{\text{Working-age population}} \times 100.$$

Table 6.2 uses this formula to calculate the employment–population ratio in May 2016.

### The Labor Force Participation Rate

The number of people in the labor force is an indicator of the willingness of working-age people to take jobs. The **labor force participation rate** is the percentage of the working-age population in the labor force. That is,

$$\text{Labor force participation rate} = \frac{\text{Labor force}}{\text{Working–age population}} \times 100.$$

Table 6.3 uses this formula with data on the number of people in the labor force and the working-age population to calculate the labor force participation rate in May 2016.

## ■ Alternative Measures of Unemployment

The official definition of unemployment omits two types of underused labor:

- Marginally attached workers
- Part-time workers who want full-time work

### Marginally Attached Workers

A **marginally attached worker** is a person who does not have a job, is available and willing to work, has not made specific efforts to find a job within the previous four weeks, but has looked for work sometime in the recent past. Marginally attached workers think of themselves as being in the labor force and unemployed. A **discouraged worker** is a person who is similar to an unemployed worker, but who has not made specific efforts to find a job within the previous four weeks because previous unsuccessful attempts were discouraging.

Other marginally attached workers differ from discouraged workers only in their reasons for not having looked for a job during the previous four weeks. For example, Martin doesn't have a job and is available for work, but he has not looked for work in the past four weeks because he was busy cleaning his home after a flood. He is a marginally attached worker but not a discouraged worker. Lena, Martin's wife, doesn't have a job and is available for work, but she hasn't looked for work in the past four weeks because she's been looking for six months and hasn't had a single job offer. She is a discouraged worker.

Neither the unemployment rate nor the labor force participation rate includes marginally attached workers. In May 2016, 538,000 people were discouraged workers. If we add them to both the number of people counted as unemployed and the labor force, the unemployment rate becomes 5.0 percent—a bit higher than the standard definition of the unemployment rate. Also in May 2016, 1,713,000 people were marginally attached workers. If we add them and the discouraged workers to both the number counted as unemployed and the labor force, the unemployment rate becomes 6.0 percent—1.3 percentage points higher than the standard definition.

# EYE on the U.S. ECONOMY
## The Current Population Survey

The Bureau of Labor Statistics and the Bureau of the Census go to great lengths to collect accurate labor force data. They constantly train and retrain around 1,600 field interviewers and supervisors. Each month, each field interviewer contacts 37 households and asks basic demographic questions about everyone living at the address and detailed labor force questions about those aged 16 or over.

Once a household has been selected for the survey, it is questioned for four consecutive months and then again for the same four months a year later. Each month, the addresses that have been in the panel eight times are removed and 6,250 new addresses are added. The rotation and overlap of households provide very reliable information about month-to-month and year-to-year changes in the labor market.

The first time that a household is in the panel, an interviewer, armed with a hand-held computer, visits it. If the household has a telephone, most of the subsequent interviews are conducted by phone, many of them from one of the three telephone interviewing centers in Hagerstown, Maryland; Jeffersonville, Indiana; and Tucson, Arizona.

For more information about the Current Population Survey, visit www.bls.gov/cps/cps_faq.htm.

## Part-Time Workers Who Want Full-Time Work

The Current Population Survey measures the number of full-time workers and part-time workers. **Full-time workers** are those who usually work 35 hours or more a week. **Part-time workers** are those who usually work less than 35 hours a week. Part-time workers are divided into two groups: part time for economic reasons and part time for noneconomic reasons.

People who work **part time for economic reasons** (also called *involuntary part-time workers)* are people who work 1 to 34 hours but are looking for full-time work. These people are unable to find full-time work because of unfavorable business conditions or seasonal decreases in the availability of full-time work.

People who work part time for noneconomic reasons do not want full-time work and are not available for such work. This group includes people with health problems, family or personal responsibilities, or education commitments that limit their availability for work.

The Bureau of Labor Statistics uses the data on full-time and part-time status to measure the slack in the labor market that results from people being underemployed—employed but not able to find as much employment as they would like.

In May 2016, when employment was 151.0 million, full-time employment was 123.1 million and part-time employment was 27.9 million. An estimated 6.4 million people worked part time for economic reasons. When this number, along with marginally attached workers, is added to the number unemployed, the unemployment rate becomes 9.6 percent.

**Full-time workers**
People who usually work 35 hours or more a week.

**Part-time workers**
People who usually work less than 35 hours a week.

**Part time for economic reasons**
People who work 1 to 34 hours per week but are looking for full-time work and cannot find it because of unfavorable business conditions.

MyEconLab Study Plan 6.1
    Key Terms Quiz
    Solutions Video
    Real-Time Data

# CHECKPOINT 6.1

**Define the unemployment rate and other labor market indicators.**

## Practice Problems

The BLS reported that in December 2015, the labor force was 157.8 million, employment was 149.9 million, and the working-age population was 252.0 million.

1. Calculate the unemployment rate and the labor force participation rate.

2. The BLS also reported that 18.3 percent of all employment in December 2015 was part time and that 6.0 million people worked part time for economic reasons. How many people worked part time for noneconomic reasons?

## In the News

**Summer 2015 youth labor market**
From April to July 2015, the number of employed youth 16 to 24 years old rose by 2.1 million to 20.3 million and youth unemployment increased from 2.1 million to 2.8 million. In July, the youth labor force grew by 2.8 million to a total of 23.1 million and the youth population was 38.5 million.

              Source: BLS Press Release, August 18, 2015

How did the youth unemployment rate change from April to July? Calculate the youth labor force participation rate in July.

## Solutions to Practice Problems

1. The unemployment rate is 5.0 percent. The labor force equals employment plus unemployment. So unemployment equals the labor force minus employment, which equals (157.8 million − 149.9 million), or 7.9 million. The unemployment rate equals unemployment as a percentage of the labor force. Unemployment rate = (7.9 ÷ 157.8) × 100 or 5 percent. The labor force participation rate is 65.5 percent. The labor force participation rate equals the labor force as a percentage of the working-age population. Labor force participation rate = (157.8 ÷ 252.0) × 100, or 62.6 percent.

2. 21.4 million people worked part time for noneconomic reasons. Employment was 149.9 million. Part-time employment was 18.3 percent of 149.9 million, which equals 27.4 million. Given that 6.0 million worked part time for economic reasons, then 27.4 million minus 6.0 million, or 21.4 million, worked part time for noneconomic reasons.

## Solution to In the News

The unemployment rate is the number unemployed as a percentage of the labor force. The April employment equals the July employment (20.3 million) minus the increase of 2.1 million from April to July, or 18.2 million. The labor force equals employed plus unemployed. The April labor force was (18.2 million + 2.1 million), or 20.3 million. In April, 2.1 million were unemployed, so the April unemployment rate was (2.1 ÷ 20.3) × 100, or 10.3 percent. In July, 2.8 million were unemployed and the labor force was 23.1 million, so the unemployment rate was 12.1 percent. From April to July, the unemployment rate rose from 10.3 percent to 12.1 percent. The July labor force participation rate equals the labor force (23.1 million) as a percentage of the youth population (38.5 million), or 60 percent.

## 6.2   LABOR MARKET TRENDS AND FLUCTUATIONS

MyEconLab Concept Video

What do we learn about the U.S. labor market from changes in the unemployment rate, the labor force participation rate, and the alternative measures of unemployment? Let's explore the trends and fluctuations in these indicators.

### ■ Unemployment Rate

Figure 6.2 shows the U.S. unemployment rate over the 88 years from 1929 to 2016. The most striking event visible in this figure is the **Great Depression**, a period of high unemployment, low incomes, and extreme economic hardship that lasted from 1929 to 1939. By 1933, the worst of the Great Depression years, real GDP had fallen by a huge 30 percent and as the figure shows, one in four of the people who wanted jobs couldn't find them. The horrors of the Great Depression led to the New Deal and shaped political attitudes that persist today.

During the 1960s, the unemployment rate gradually fell to 3.5 percent. These years saw a rapid rate of job creation, partly from the demands placed on the economy by the growth of defense production during the Vietnam War and partly from an expansion of consumer spending encouraged by an expansion of social programs. Another burst of rapid job creation driven by the "new economy"— the high-technology sector driven by the expansion of the Internet—lowered the unemployment rate to below average from 1995 through the early 2000s.

During the recessions of 1973–1975, 1981–1982, 1990–1991, and 2008–2009, the unemployment rate increased. While the popular representation of the 2008–2009 recession compares it with the Great Depression, you can see in Figure 6.2 that 2010 is strikingly different from 1933, the year in which the unemployment rate peaked during the Great Depression.

**Great Depression**
A period of high unemployment, low incomes, and extreme economic hardship that lasted from 1929 to 1939.

### ■ FIGURE 6.2

#### The U.S. Unemployment Rate: 1929–2016

MyEconLab Real-time data

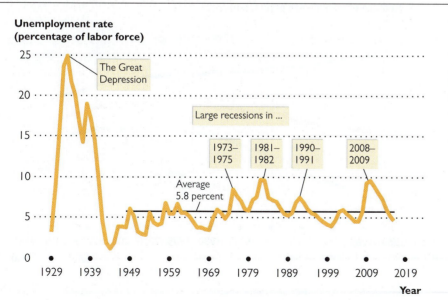

The average unemployment rate from 1948 to 2016 was 5.8 percent. The unemployment rate increases in recessions and decreases in expansions. Unemployment was at its lowest during World War II and the expansions of the 1950s, 1960s, and the 1990s and at its highest during the Great Depression and the recessions of 1981–1982 and 2008–2009.

SOURCE OF DATA: Bureau of Labor Statistics.

## ■ The Participation Rate

Figure 6.3 shows the labor force participation rate, which increased from 59 percent in 1960 to 67 percent at its peak in 1999. Why did the labor force participation rate increase? The main reason is an increase in the number of women who have entered the labor force.

Figure 6.3 shows that from 1960 to 1999, the participation rate of women increased from 37 percent to 60 percent. This increase is spread across women of all age groups and occurred for four main reasons. First, more women pursued a college education and so increased their earning power. Second, technological change in the workplace created a large number of white-collar jobs with flexible work hours that many women found attractive. Third, technological change in the home increased the time available for paid employment. And fourth, families looked increasingly to a second income to balance tight budgets.

Figure 6.3 also shows another remarkable trend in the U.S. labor force: The participation rate of men *decreased* from 83 percent in 1960 to 70 percent in 2016. Some of the decrease occurred as older men chose to retire earlier. But some arose from job loss at an age at which finding a new job is difficult. Decreased labor force participation of younger men occurred because more remained in school.

### Downward Trend Since 2000

The downward trend in the labor force participation rate that began in 2000 might arise in part from a mismeasurement of unemployment. Recall that the labor force is the sum of the employed and the unemployed. If we don't count all the people who are unemployed, then we don't count all the people in the labor force. Some new measures provide a broader view of unemployment.

■ **FIGURE 6.3**

The Changing Face of the Labor Market: 1960–2016                MyEconLab Real-time data

The labor force participation rate increased from 1960 to 1999 but then decreased slightly.

The labor force participation rate of women has driven these trends, increasing strongly from 37 percent in 1960 to 60 percent in 1999.

The labor force participation rate of men has decreased steadily.

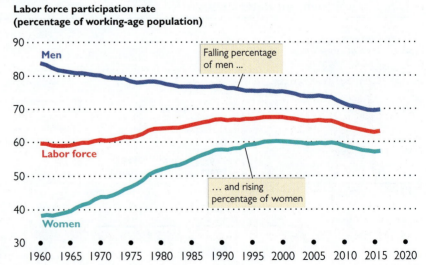

SOURCE OF DATA: Bureau of Labor Statistics.

# EYE on the GLOBAL ECONOMY
## Unemployment and Labor Force Participation

### Unemployment

U.S. unemployment falls inside the range experienced by other countries. The highest unemployment rates have been in the United Kingdom, Canada, and the Eurozone; and the lowest have been in Japan and the newly industrializing Asian economies.

Differences in unemployment rates were large during the early 1980s, narrowed through the 1990s and early 2000s, and widened after the 2008–2009 recession.

The Eurozone, with a higher average unemployment rate than the United States, also has higher unemployment benefits and more regulated labor markets.

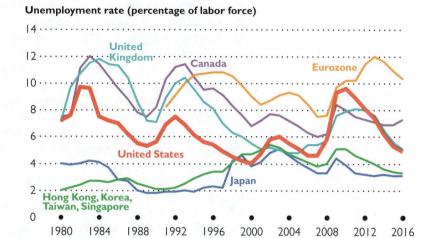

**Unemployment rate (percentage of labor force)**

**Figure 1  Unemployment**

Source of data: International Monetary Fund, *World Economic Outlook*, April 2016.

### Labor Force Participation

The labor force participation rate of women has increased in most advanced nations. But the participation rate of women in the labor force varies a great deal around the world. The figure compares eight other countries with the United States.

The U.S. rank is surprisingly low. Economists Francine D. Blau and Lawrence M. Kahn who have studied these data say that other countries have more "family-friendly" labor market policies. But they say these labor market policies encourage part-time work and U.S. women are more likely than women in other countries to have good full-time jobs as managers or professionals.

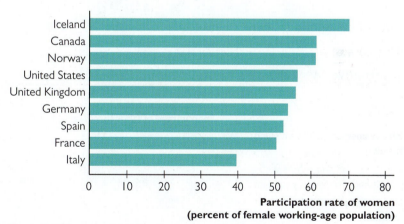

**Figure 2  Women in the Labor Force**

Source of data: OECD

Cultural factors play a central role in influencing national differences in women's work choices. But education, and particularly the percentage of women with a college degree, is the dominant source of international differences in women's and men's job market prospects.

## ■ Alternative Measures of Unemployment

You've seen that the official measure of unemployment does not include marginally attached workers and people who work part time for economic reasons. The Bureau of Labor Statistics (BLS) now provides three broader measures of the unemployment rate, known as U-4, U-5, and U-6, that include these wider groups of the jobless. The official unemployment rate (based on the standard definition of unemployment) is called U-3 and as these names imply, there are also U-1 and U-2 measures. The U-1 and U-2 measures of the unemployment rate are narrower than the official measure. U-1 is the percentage of the labor force that has been unemployed for 15 weeks or more and is a measure of long-term involuntary unemployment. U-2 is the percentage of the labor force that has been laid off and is another measure of involuntary unemployment.

Figure 6.4 shows the history of these six measures of unemployment since 1996. The relative magnitudes of the six measures are explained by what they include—the broader the measure, the higher the average. The gap between U-5 and U-6—part-time workers who want full-time work— is the largest. The six measures follow similar but not identical tracks: rising during recessions and falling in the expansion between recessions. But during the 2001 recession, U-1 barely rose while during the 2008–2009 recession, it more than doubled in less than a year.

Notice that the unemployment rate, on all six measures, keeps rising after a recession ends: It lags behind the business cycle. When an expansion begins, firms start hiring slowly. Some unemployed workers get jobs, but the labor force increases as marginally attached workers start to look for jobs. In the early stages of an expansion, the number of marginally attached workers looking for jobs exceeds the number of people hired and the unemployment rate increases.

**FIGURE 6.4**

Alternative Measures of Unemployment: 1996–2016          MyEconLab Real-time data

The alternative measures of unemployment are

U-1 People unemployed 15 weeks or longer

U-2 People laid off and others who completed a temporary job

U-3 Total unemployed (official measure)

U-4 Total unemployed plus discouraged workers

U-5 U-4 plus other marginally attached workers

U-6 U-5 plus employed part time for economic reasons

U-1, U-2, and U-3 are percentages of the labor force.

U-4, U-5, and U-6 are percentages of the labor force plus the unemployed in the added category.

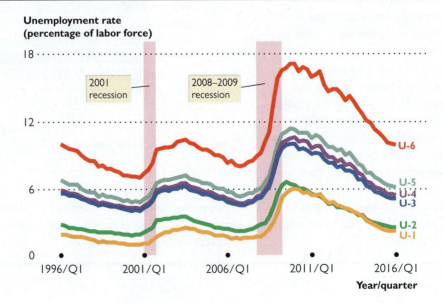

Source of data: Bureau of Labor Statistics.

CHECKPOINT 6.2

MyEconLab Study Plan 6.2
Key Terms Quiz
Solutions Video

**Describe the trends and fluctuations in the indicators of the state of the U.S. labor market.**

## Practice Problems

1. Figure 1 shows the unemployment rate in the United States from 1960 to 2016. In which decade—the 1960s, 1970s, 1980s, 1990s, or 2000s—was the average unemployment rate the lowest and what brought low unemployment in that decade? In which decade was the average unemployment rate the highest and what brought high unemployment in that decade?

2. Describe the trends in the labor force participation rates of men, women, and all working-age people.

## In the News

### Blue in red states

Unemployment is 4.9 percent—less than half of the Great Recession peak—but Bernie Sanders got a big cheer when he dismissed the official unemployment rate as not reflecting those who are involuntarily working part time, or those who have become so discouraged they have given up looking for employment.

Source: *U.S. News & World Report*, February 12, 2016

1. Which of the alternative measures of unemployment does Bernie Sanders think is more relevant than the official unemployment rate and what was its level at the start of 2016?

2. By how much did the broadest measure of unemployment change from its 2008–2009 "Great Recession" peak?

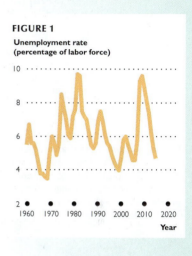

**FIGURE 1**

Unemployment rate
(percentage of labor force)

## Solutions to Practice Problems

1. Figure 1 shows that the unemployment rate was lowest during the 1960s when defense spending on the Vietnam War and expansion of social programs brought rapid expansions and lowered the unemployment rate.

   Figure 1 shows that the unemployment rate was highest during the 1980s. During the 1981–1982 recession it increased to almost 10 percent.

2. The labor force participation rate of women increased because (1) better-educated women earn more, (2) more white-collar jobs with flexible work hours were created, (3) people have more time for paid employment, and (4) families increasingly needed two incomes to balance their budgets. The labor force participation rate of men decreased because more men remained in school and some men took early retirement. The overall labor force participation rate increased.

## Solutions to In the News

1. Bernie Sanders prefers the U-6 measure of unemployment, which includes discouraged workers, other marginally attached workers, and part-time workers for economic reasons. At the start of 2016, U-6 was 10 percent.

2. The broadest measure of unemployment, U-6, peaked at about 17 percent during the 2008–2009 recession, so at the start of 2016, it was about 60 percent of its peak.

MyEconLab Concept Video

## 6.3  UNEMPLOYMENT AND FULL EMPLOYMENT

There is always someone without a job who is searching for one, so there is always some unemployment. The key reason is that the labor market is constantly churning. New jobs are created and old jobs die; and some people move into the labor force and some move out of it. This churning creates unemployment.

We distinguish among three types of unemployment:

- Frictional unemployment
- Structural unemployment
- Cyclical unemployment

### ■ Frictional Unemployment

**Frictional unemployment** is the unemployment that arises from people entering and leaving the labor force, from quitting jobs to find better ones, and from the ongoing creation and destruction of jobs—from normal labor turnover. Frictional unemployment is a permanent and healthy phenomenon in a dynamic, growing economy.

There is an unending flow of people into and out of the labor force as people move through the stages of life—from being in school to finding a job, to working, perhaps to becoming unhappy with a job and looking for a new one, and finally, to retiring from full-time work.

There is also an unending process of job creation and job destruction as new firms are born, firms expand or contract, and some firms fail and go out of business.

The flows into and out of the labor force and the processes of job creation and job destruction create the need for people to search for jobs and for businesses to search for workers. Businesses don't usually hire the first person who applies for a job, and unemployed people don't usually take the first job that comes their way. Instead, both firms and workers spend time searching for what they believe will be the best available match. By this process of search, people can match their own skills and interests with the available jobs and find a satisfying job and a good income.

**Frictional unemployment**
The unemployment that arises from people entering and leaving the labor force, from quitting jobs to find better ones, and from the ongoing creation and destruction of jobs—from normal labor turnover.

*A new graduate interviews for a job.*

### ■ Structural Unemployment

**Structural unemployment** is the unemployment that arises when changes in technology or international competition change the skills needed to perform jobs or change the locations of jobs. Structural unemployment usually lasts longer than frictional unemployment because workers must retrain and possibly relocate to find a job. For example, when banks introduced the automatic teller machine in the 1970s, many bank-teller jobs were destroyed. Meanwhile, new jobs for life-insurance salespeople and retail clerks were created. The former bank tellers remained unemployed for several months until they moved, retrained, and got one of these new jobs. Structural unemployment is painful, especially for older workers for whom the best available option might be to retire early but with a lower income than they had expected.

Sometimes, the amount of structural unemployment is small. At other times, it is large, and at such times, structural unemployment can become a serious long-term problem. It was especially large during the late 1970s and early 1980s.

**Structural unemployment**
The unemployment that arises when changes in technology or international competition change the skills needed to perform jobs or change the locations of jobs.

*Bank tellers lost jobs to computer technology.*

## ■ Cyclical Unemployment

The fluctuating unemployment over the business cycle—the higher than normal unemployment at a business cycle trough and the lower than normal unemployment at a business cycle peak—is called **cyclical unemployment**. A worker who is laid off because the economy is in a recession and who gets rehired some months later when the expansion begins has experienced cyclical unemployment.

## ■ "Natural" Unemployment

Natural unemployment is the unemployment that arises from frictions and structural change—when all the unemployment is frictional and structural and there is no cyclical unemployment. Natural unemployment as a percentage of the labor force is called the **natural unemployment rate**.

**Full employment** is defined as a situation in which the unemployment rate equals the natural unemployment rate.

What determines the natural unemployment rate? Is it constant or does it change over time?

The natural unemployment rate is influenced by many factors, but the most important ones are

- The age distribution of the population
- The pace of structural change
- The real wage rate
- Unemployment benefits

**Cyclical unemployment**
The fluctuating unemployment over the business cycle that increases during a recession and decreases during an expansion.

**Natural unemployment rate**
The unemployment rate when all the unemployment is frictional and structural and there is no cyclical unemployment.

**Full employment**
When the unemployment rate equals the natural unemployment rate.

# EYE on the U.S. ECONOMY
## How Long Does it Take to Find a Job?

The duration of unemployment spells varies over the business cycle. In 2000 at the business cycle peak, the median time to find a job was 6 weeks; in 2011 at the start of a weak expansion, it was 21 weeks; and in 2016 after a long but weak expansion, it was 11 weeks.

The figure provides more information: It shows the percentage of the unemployed at four unemployment durations. You can see that long-term unemployment (27 weeks and over) was much greater in 2011 than it was at the business cycle peak in 2000. The 2016 data lie between the extremes of 2000 and 2011.

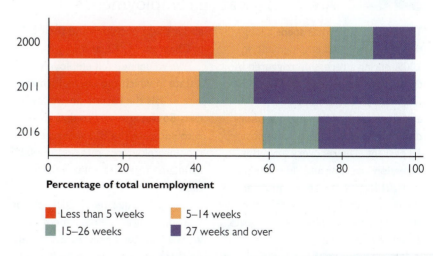

SOURCE OF DATA: Bureau of Labor Statistics.

### The Age Distribution of the Population

An economy with a young population has lots of new job seekers every year and a high level of frictional unemployment. An economy with an aging population has fewer new job seekers and less frictional unemployment.

### The Pace of Structural Change

The pace of structural change is sometimes slow, so the same jobs using the same machines remain in place for many years. But sometimes a technological upheaval sweeps aside the old ways, wipes out millions of jobs, and makes the skills once used to perform these jobs obsolete. The amount of structural unemployment fluctuates with the pace of technological change. The change is driven by fierce international competition, especially from fast-changing Asian economies. A high level of structural unemployment is present in some parts of the United States today.

### The Real Wage Rate

The natural unemployment rate is influenced by the real wage rate. Anything that raises the real wage above the market equilibrium creates a surplus of labor and increases the natural unemployment rate. The real wage might exceed the market equilibrium for two reasons: a minimum wage and an efficiency wage. The federal minimum wage creates unemployment because it is set above the equilibrium wage of low-skilled young workers. An efficiency wage is a wage set by firms above the going market wage to attract the most productive workers, get them to work hard, and discourage them from quitting. When firms set efficiency wages, some workers would like to work for these firms but can't get jobs.

## EYE on FULL EMPLOYMENT

MyEconLab Critical Thinking Exercise

### Are We Back at Full Employment?

The U.S. economy has spent a long time away from full employment. In 2009, during a recession triggered by the Global Financial Crisis, the unemployment rate soared to 10 percent and the broader U-6 measure of underutilized labor hovered at almost 18 percent. The recovery from this recession was long and slow. And in mid-2016, policy makers wanted answers to the following questions: Is the recovery now complete? Are we back at full employment?

The answers to these questions are a major input into the decisions of the Federal Reserve on the pace at which to raise interest rates. (You will learn about these decisions and their effects in Chapters 11, 12, and 17.)

We've defined full employment as a state in which the unemployment rate equals the natural unemployment rate. So the first way to find an answer is to compare the BLS measure of the unemployment rate and the CBO estimate of the natural unemployment rate.

In the first quarter of 2016, the actual and natural unemployment rates were equal at 4.9 percent. So based on these numbers, we're back at full employment.

But the natural unemployment rate is only an estimate. It varies over time and is influenced by many factors. Also, the employment–population ratio and the labor force participation rate data point to a different answer to the full-employment question. Both of these measures fell by 3 percentage points between 2007 and 2016. Three percent of the working-age population had disappeared from the labor force. Where did these people go? Did they represent hidden unemployment?

A way of answering this question has been suggested by economists at the Federal Reserve Bank of Atlanta. Their idea is to use an indicator they call the Z-Pop ratio, which is the percentage of the working-age population

## Unemployment Benefits

Unemployment benefits increase the natural unemployment rate by lowering the opportunity cost of job search. European countries have more generous unemployment benefits and higher natural unemployment rates than the United States. Extending unemployment benefits raises the natural unemployment rate.

There is no controversy about the existence of a natural unemployment rate. Nor is there disagreement that the natural unemployment rate changes. But economists don't know its exact size or the extent to which it fluctuates. The Congressional Budget Office estimates the natural unemployment rate and its estimate for 2016 was 4.9 percent—equal to the actual unemployment rate in that year.

## ◼ Unemployment and Real GDP

Cyclical unemployment is the fluctuating unemployment over the business cycle—unemployment that increases during a recession and decreases during an expansion. At full employment, there is *no* cyclical unemployment. At a business cycle trough, cyclical unemployment is *positive* and at a business cycle peak, cyclical unemployment is *negative*.

Figure 6.5(a) shows the unemployment rate in the United States between 1980 and 2016. It also shows the natural unemployment rate and cyclical unemployment. The natural unemployment rate in this figure was estimated by the Congressional Budget Office (CBO).

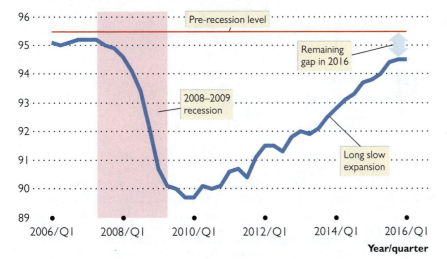

SOURCE OF DATA: Bureau of Labor Statistics, formula proposed by the Federal Reserve Bank of Atlanta, and authors' calculations.

that is fully utilized. The people counted as fully utilized are those working full-time, those working part-time for a noneconomic reason, and those who say they don't want a job.

The figure shows the Z-Pop ratio. Before the 2008–2009 recession, 95.2 percent of the population was fully utilized by this definition. The number fell to 89.7 percent and then slowly climbed. In 2016, 94.5 percent of the population was fully utilized.

So the Z-Pop ratio gives almost the same answer as that by comparing the unemployment rate with the natural unemployment rate, but not quite. It shows a small amount of underused labor remaining in 2016.

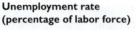

**FIGURE 6.5**

The Relationship Between Unemployment and the Output Gap       MyEconLab Real-time data

As the unemployment rate fluctuates around the natural unemployment rate in part (a), the output gap—real GDP minus potential GDP expressed as a percentage of potential GDP—fluctuates around a zero output gap in part (b).

When the unemployment rate *exceeds* the natural unemployment rate, real GDP is below potential GDP and the output gap is negative (the red sections in both parts).

When the unemployment rate is *below* the natural unemployment rate, real GDP is above potential GDP and the output gap is positive (the blue sections in both parts).

The natural unemployment rate shown in the graph is the Congressional Budget Office's estimate. It might turn out to be an underestimate for the years since 2008.

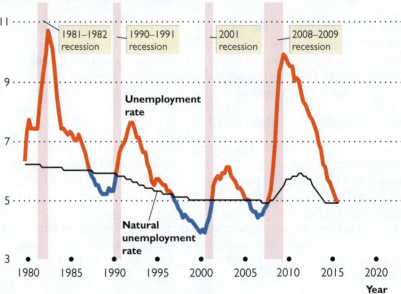

(a) Cyclical and natural unemployment

(b) The output gap

Sources of data: Bureau of Economic Analysis, Bureau of Labor Statistics, and Congressional Budget Office.

In Figure 6.5(a), you can see that during most of the 1980s, the early 1990s, early 2000s, and during 2008–2009, the unemployment rate was above the natural unemployment rate, so cyclical unemployment was positive (the red sections of the line). You can also see that during the late 1980s, from 1997 to 2001, and during 2005–2008 the unemployment rate was below the natural unemployment rate, so cyclical unemployment was negative (the blue sections of the line).

As the unemployment rate fluctuates around the natural unemployment rate, real GDP fluctuates around potential GDP. **Potential GDP** is the value of real GDP when the economy is at full employment—all the economy's factors of production (labor, capital, land, and entrepreneurial ability) are employed. Real GDP equals potential GDP when the economy is at full employment. Real GDP minus potential GDP expressed as a percentage of potential GDP is called the **output gap**.

Figure 6.5(b) shows the U.S. *output gap* from 1980 to 2016. You can see that as the unemployment rate fluctuates around the natural unemployment rate, the output gap also fluctuates. Most of the time, when the unemployment rate is above the natural unemployment rate, in part (a), the output gap is negative (real GDP is below potential GDP), in part (b); when the unemployment rate is below the natural unemployment rate, the output gap is positive (real GDP is above potential GDP); and when the unemployment rate equals the natural unemployment rate, the output gap is zero (real GDP equals potential GDP).

The general tendency for unemployment to be above the natural rate when real GDP is below potential GDP did not describe the situation in 2016. In that year, the unemployment rate had fallen to equal the natural rate but the output gap was about 2 percent below potential GDP. This discrepancy might arise from errors in estimating the natural unemployment rate and potential GDP.

**Potential GDP**
The value of real GDP when the economy is at full employment—all the economy's factors of production (labor, capital, land, and entrepreneurial ability) are employed.

**Output gap**
Real GDP minus potential GDP expressed as a percentage of potential GDP.

# EYE on YOUR LIFE
## Your Labor Market Status and Activity

MyEconLab Critical Thinking Exercise

You are going to spend a lot of your life in the labor market. Most of the time, you'll be supplying labor services. But first, you must find a job. Most likely, one job will not last your entire working life. You will want to find a new job when you decide to quit or when changing economic conditions destroy your current job.

As you look for a job, get a job, quit a job, or get laid off and look for a new job, you will pass through many and possibly all of the population categories used in the Current Population Survey that you've learned about in this chapter.

Think about your current labor market status while you are studying economics.

- Are you in the labor force or not?
- If you are in the labor force, are you employed or unemployed?
- If you are employed, are you a part-time or a full-time worker?

Now think about someone you know who is unemployed or has been unemployed. Classify the unemployment experienced by this person as

- frictional,
- structural, or
- cyclical.

How can you tell the type of unemployment experienced by this person?

The labor market conditions that you face today or when you graduate and look for a job depend partly on general national economic conditions—on whether the economy is in recession or booming.

Labor market conditions also depend on where you live. Visit the Bureau of Labor Statistics' Web site at www.bls.gov. There you can find information on employment and unemployment for your state and metropolitan area or county. By comparing the labor market conditions in your own region with those in other areas, you can figure out where it might be easier to find work.

MyEconLab Study Plan 6.3

Key Terms Quiz

Solutions Video

 **CHECKPOINT 6.3**

**Describe the types of unemployment, define full employment, and explain the link between unemployment and real GDP.**

## Practice Problems

**Recovery won't improve unemployment**

Despite some optimism about the seeds of recovery, the Congressional Budget Office (CBO) sees joblessness rising. The CBO sees unemployment peaking at 10.4% next year from an average of 9.3% this year, before it falls to 9.1% in 2011.

Source: *Fortune*, August 25, 2009

Before the recession began, the U.S. unemployment rate was about 6 percent.

1.  As a recession begins, firms quickly make layoffs. Is this rise in unemployment mostly a rise in frictional, structural, or cyclical unemployment?

2.  Why does unemployment continue to rise as an expansion begins?

## In the News

**The small but serious threat of a U.S. recession**

The unemployment rate is 4.9 percent, its level in 2008 before the recession. While it is unlikely that the United States will slip into recession this year, below-trend real GDP growth cannot be ruled out and some Wall Street economists say there is a 20 percent chance of recession in 2016.

Source: *The Financial Times*, February 5, 2016

1.  Using the information in the news clip along with that in Figure 6.5 (p. 160), how would you describe the state of the U.S. economy through 2014 and 2015 and at the beginning of 2016?

2.  How would "below-trend real GDP growth" change the unemployment rate and what type of unemployment would change?

## Solutions to Practice Problems

1.  When a recession starts, firms are quick to lay off workers. Most of the rise in unemployment is cyclical—related to the state of the economy. The unemployment rate rises quickly as the number of layoffs increases.

2.  The unemployment rate lags behind the business cycle. When an expansion begins, firms start hiring slowly. Some unemployed workers get jobs, but the labor force increases as marginally attached workers start to look for jobs. In the early stages of an expansion, the number of marginally attached workers looking for jobs exceeds the number of people hired and unemployment increases.

## Solutions to In the News

1.  In 2014 and 2015, the U.S. economy was recovering from the 2008–2009 recession. The unemployment rate was falling and the output gap was shrinking slowly. At the start of 2016, the unemployment rate was below its long-term average and the economy was close to full employment

2.  Below-trend real GDP growth would increase the unemployment rate and cyclical unemployment would increase.

**CHAPTER SUMMARY**

## Key Points

**1. Define the unemployment rate and other labor market indicators.**

- The unemployment rate is the number of people unemployed as a percentage of the labor force, and the labor force is the sum of the number of people employed and the number unemployed.
- The labor force participation rate is the labor force as a percentage of the working-age population.

**2. Describe the trends and fluctuations in the indicators of the state of the U.S. labor market.**

- The unemployment rate fluctuates with the business cycle, increasing in recessions and decreasing in expansions.
- The labor force participation rate of women has increased, and the labor force participation rate of men has decreased.

**3. Describe the types of unemployment, define full employment, and explain the link between unemployment and real GDP.**

- Unemployment can be frictional, structural, or cyclical.
- Full employment occurs when there is no cyclical unemployment and at full employment, the unemployment rate equals the natural unemployment rate.
- Potential GDP is the real GDP produced when the economy is at full employment.
- As the unemployment rate fluctuates around the natural unemployment rate, real GDP fluctuates around potential GDP and the output gap fluctuates between negative and positive values.

## Key Terms

MyEconLab Key Terms Quiz

Cyclical unemployment, 157
Discouraged worker, 148
Employment–population ratio, 147
Frictional unemployment, 156
Full employment, 157
Full-time workers, 149

Great Depression, 151
Labor force, 146
Labor force participation rate, 148
Marginally attached worker, 148
Natural unemployment rate, 157
Output gap, 161

Part time for economic reasons, 149
Part-time workers, 149
Potential GDP, 161
Structural unemployment, 156
Unemployment rate, 147
Working-age population, 146

MyEconLab Chapter 6 Study Plan

## CHAPTER CHECKPOINT

## Study Plan Problems and Applications

Use the following information gathered by a BLS labor market survey of four households to work Problems **1** and **2**.

- Household 1: Candy worked 20 hours last week setting up her Internet shopping business. The rest of the week, she completed application forms and attended two job interviews. Husband Jerry worked 40 hours at his job at GM. Daughter Meg, a student, worked 10 hours at her weekend job at Starbucks.
- Household 2: Joey, a full-time bank clerk, was on vacation. Wife, Serena, who wants a full-time job, worked 10 hours as a part-time checkout clerk.
- Household 3: Ari had no work last week but was going to be recalled to his regular job in two weeks. Partner Kosta, after months of searching for a job and not being able to find one, has stopped looking and will go back to school.
- Household 4: Mimi and Henry are retired. Son Hank is a professional artist, who painted for 12 hours last week and sold one picture.

**1.** Classify each of the 10 people into the labor market category used by the BLS. Who are part-time workers and who are full-time workers? Of the part-time workers, who works part time for economic reasons?

**2.** Calculate the unemployment rate and the labor force participation rate, and compare these rates with those in the United States in 2016.

**3.** Describe two examples of people who work part time for economic reasons and two examples of people who work part time for noneconomic reasons.

**4.** Explain the relationship between the percentage of employed workers who have part-time jobs and the business cycle.

**5.** Distinguish among the three types of unemployment: frictional, structural, and cyclical. Provide an example of each type of unemployment in the United States today.

**6.** Describe the relationship between the unemployment rate and the natural unemployment rate as the output gap fluctuates between being positive and being negative.

Use the following information to work Problems **7** and **8**.

**Unemployment falls to 4.9 percent, lowest in 8 years**
U.S. unemployment of 4.9 percent is full employment. Only 151,000 jobs were created in January, down from 262,000 in December. With falling oil prices, 7,000 energy jobs were lost in January but 29,000 manufacturing jobs were added.
Source: CNN Money, February 5, 2016

**7.** Using the information provided in the news clip, which types of unemployment were present in the U.S. economy in January 2016?

**8.** How would you expect a shrinking energy sector and an expanding manufacturing sector to influence the actual and natural unemployment rates?

**9.** Read *Eye on Full Employment* on pp. 158–159. In which year, 2000 or 2016, was real GDP below potential GDP? How can you tell from the graph on p. 160?

## Instructor Assignable Problems and Applications

MyEconLab Homework, Quiz, or Test if assigned by instructor
Real-Time Data

**1.** In the United States,

- Compare the duration of unemployment in 2016 with that in 2000 and explain whether the difference was most likely the result of frictions, structural change, or the business cycle.
- How does the unemployment of marginally attached workers influence the duration of unemployment in 2016 compared with that in 2000?

**2.** The Bureau of Labor Statistics reported that in the second quarter of 2008 the working-age population was 233,410,000, the labor force was 154,294,000, and employment was 146,089,000. Calculate for that quarter the labor force participation rate and the unemployment rate.

**3.** In July 2016, in the economy of Sandy Island, 10,000 people were employed and 1,000 were unemployed. During August 2016, 80 people lost their jobs and didn't look for new ones, 20 people quit their jobs and retired, 150 people who had looked for work were hired, 50 people became discouraged workers, and 40 new graduates looked for work. Calculate the change in the unemployment rate from July 2016 to August 2016.

**4.** The BLS survey reported the following data in a community of 320 people: 200 worked at least 1 hour as paid employees; 20 did not work but were temporarily absent from their jobs; 40 did not have jobs and didn't want to work; 10 were available for work and last week they had looked for work; and 6 were available for work and were waiting to be recalled to their previous job. Calculate the unemployment rate and the labor force participation rate.

**5.** Describe the trends and fluctuations in the unemployment rate in the United States from 1949 through 2016. In which periods was the unemployment rate above average and in which periods was it below average?

**6.** Describe how the labor force participation rate in the United States changed between 1960 and 2016. Contrast and explain the different trends in the labor force participation rates of women and men.

**7.** Explain why the natural unemployment rate is not zero and why the unemployment rate fluctuates around the natural unemployment rate.

Use the following information to work Problems **8** and **9**.

**The metro areas with the lowest and highest unemployment**
In December 2015, Ames, Iowa, had the lowest unemployment in the United States at 2.2 percent of the workforce. At the other end of the scale was El Centro, California, with 19.6 percent of its workforce unemployed.

Source: *Forbes*, February 9, 2016

In the depth of the 2008–2009 recession, the unemployment rate in Ames peaked at 5.7 percent. In El Centro, it peaked at 30.3 percent.

**8.** Use the information provided to estimate how much of the unemployment in Ames and El Centro in 2009 was cyclical and how much was natural. Explain your assumptions in arriving at your estimates.

**9.** How would you explain the difference in the unemployment rates in Ames and El Centro in December 2015? Why is the difference almost certainly not explained by different cyclical unemployment rates?

MyEconLab Chapter 6 Study Plan

## Multiple Choice Quiz

1. The BLS counts Jody as being unemployed if she _____.

   A. had a job last month but not this month
   B. doesn't have a job because the U.S. factory where she worked cannot compete with cheap Chinese imports
   C. wants a job and looked for a job last year but has now stopped looking
   D. wants a job and is willing to take a job but after searching last week cannot find a job

2. A marginally attached worker is a person who _____.

   A. works part time for economic reasons
   B. works part time for noneconomic reasons
   C. doesn't work, is available and willing to work, but hasn't looked for a job recently
   D. has no job but would like one and has gone back to school to retrain

3. If the BLS included all marginally attached workers as being unemployed, the _____ would be _____.

   A. unemployment rate; higher
   B. labor force; unchanged
   C. labor force participation rate; lower
   D. unemployment rate; lower

4. When the economy goes into recession, the biggest increase in unemployment is _____.

   A. structural because jobs are lost in most states
   B. cyclical because jobs are lost in many industries as they cut production
   C. frictional because the creation of jobs slows
   D. the combination of structural and frictional as few new jobs are created

5. The economy is at full employment when all unemployment is _____.

   A. structural
   B. cyclical
   C. structural and cyclical
   D. structural and frictional

6. Potential GDP is the value of real GDP when _____.

   A. the unemployment rate equals the natural unemployment rate
   B. there is no frictional unemployment
   C. there is no structural unemployment
   D. the unemployment rate is zero

7. When the unemployment rate_____ the natural unemployment rate, real GDP is _____ potential GDP and the output gap is _____.

   A. exceeds; below; negative
   B. is below; below; negative
   C. exceeds; above; positive
   D. is below; above; negative

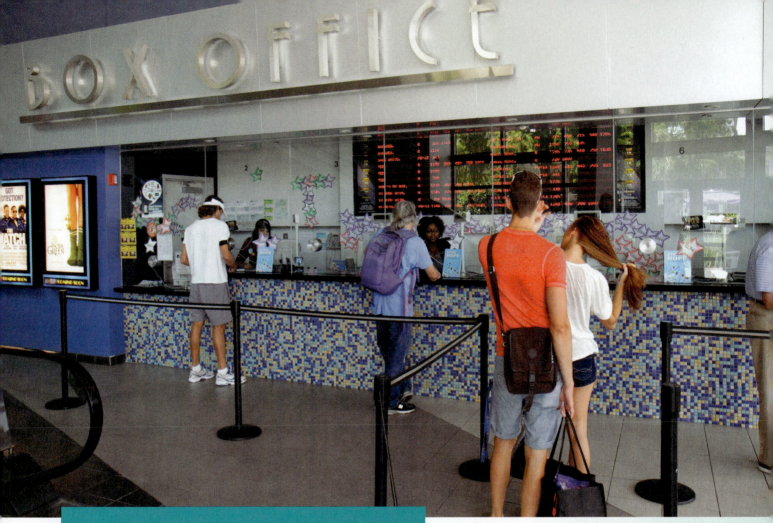

Which movie *really* was the biggest box office hit?

# The CPI and the Cost of Living

**7**

**When you have completed your study of this chapter, you will be able to**

**1** Explain what the Consumer Price Index (CPI) is and how it is calculated.

**2** Explain the limitations of the CPI and describe other measures of the price level.

**3** Adjust money values for inflation and calculate real wage rates and real interest rates.

MyEconLab Big Picture Video

MyEconLab Concept Video

**Consumer Price Index**
A measure of the average of the prices paid by urban consumers for a fixed market basket of consumption goods and services.

**Reference base period**
A period for which the CPI is defined to equal 100. Currently, the reference base period is 1982–1984.

## 7.1 THE CONSUMER PRICE INDEX

To see which movie was the biggest box office hit, we need a way of comparing prices in different periods. That's what the Consumer Price Index or CPI enables us to do. The **Consumer Price Index** is a measure of the average of the prices paid by urban consumers for a fixed market basket of consumption goods and services. The Bureau of Labor Statistics (BLS) calculates the CPI every month, and we can use these numbers to compare what the fixed market basket costs this month with what it cost in some previous month or other period.

### ■ Reading the CPI Numbers

The CPI is defined to equal 100 for a period called the **reference base period**. Currently, the reference base period is 1982–1984. That is, the CPI equals 100 on the average over the 36 months from January 1982 through December 1984.

In May 2016, the CPI was 240.2. This number tells us that the average of the prices paid by urban consumers for a fixed market basket of consumption goods and services was 140.2 percent higher in May 2016 than it was on the average during 1982–1984.

In April 2016, the CPI was 239.3. Comparing the CPI in May 2016 with the CPI in April 2016 tells us that the average of the prices paid by urban consumers for a fixed market basket of consumption goods and services *increased* by 0.9 percentage points in May 2016.

### ■ Constructing the CPI

Constructing the CPI is a huge operation that costs millions of dollars and involves three stages:

- Selecting the CPI market basket
- Conducting the monthly price survey
- Calculating the CPI

### ■ The CPI Market Basket

The first stage in constructing the CPI is to determine the *CPI market basket*. This "basket" contains the goods and services represented in the index and the relative importance, or weight, attached to each of them. The idea is to make the weight of the items in the CPI basket the same as in the budget of an average urban household. For example, if the average household spends 2 percent of its income on public transportation, then the CPI places a weight of 2 percent on the prices of bus, subway, and other transit system rides.

Although the CPI is calculated every month, the CPI market basket isn't updated every month. The information used to determine the CPI market basket comes from a survey, called the *Consumer Expenditure Survey*, that discovers what people actually buy. This survey is an ongoing activity, and the CPI market basket is being refreshed with increasing frequency. An astonishing 88,000 individuals and families contribute information.

The reference base period for the CPI has been fixed at 1982–1984 for more than 20 years and doesn't change when a new Consumer Expenditure Survey is used to update the market basket.

Figure 7.1 shows the CPI market basket in May 2016. The basket contains around 80,000 goods and services arranged in the eight large groups shown in the figure. The most important item in a household's budget is housing, which accounts for 42.1 percent of total expenditure. Transportation comes next at 15.4 percent. Third in relative importance is food and beverages at 14.8 percent. These three groups account for almost three quarters of the average household budget. Medical care takes 8.4 percent, education and communication takes 7.1 percent, recreation takes 5.8 percent, and apparel (clothing and footwear) takes 3.2 percent. Another 3.2 percent is spent on other goods and services.

The BLS breaks down each of these categories into smaller ones. For example, education and communication breaks down into textbooks and supplies, tuition, telephone services, and personal computer services.

As you look at these numbers, remember that they apply to the average household. Each individual household is spread around the average. Think about your own expenditure and compare it with the average.

## ■ The Monthly Price Survey

Each month, BLS employees check the prices of the 80,000 goods and services in the CPI market basket in 30 metropolitan areas. Because the CPI aims to measure price changes, it is important that the prices recorded each month refer to exactly the same items. For example, suppose the price of a box of jelly beans has increased but a box now contains more beans. Has the price of a jelly bean increased? The BLS employee must record the details of changes in quality, size, weight, or packaging so that price changes can be isolated from other changes.

Once the raw price data are in hand, the next task is to calculate the CPI.

### ■ FIGURE 7.1

The CPI Market Basket                                              MyEconLab Animation

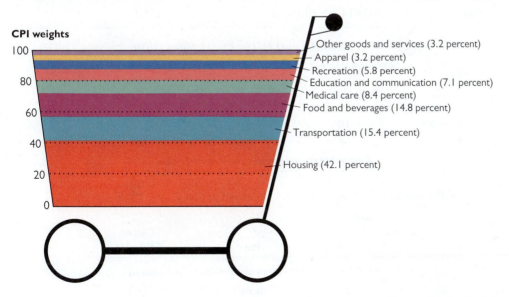

This shopping cart is filled with the items that an average urban household buys. Housing (42.1 percent), transportation (15.4 percent), and food and beverages (14.8 percent) take almost three quarters of household income.

CPI weights

Other goods and services (3.2 percent)
Apparel (3.2 percent)
Recreation (5.8 percent)
Education and communication (7.1 percent)
Medical care (8.4 percent)
Food and beverages (14.8 percent)

Transportation (15.4 percent)

Housing (42.1 percent)

SOURCE OF DATA: Bureau of Labor Statistics.

### ■ Calculating the CPI

The CPI calculation has three steps:

- Find the cost of the CPI market basket at reference base period prices.
- Find the cost of the CPI market basket at current period prices.
- Calculate the CPI for the reference base period and the current period.

We'll work through these three steps for a simple example. Suppose the CPI market basket contains only two goods and services: oranges and haircuts. We'll construct an annual CPI rather than a monthly CPI with the reference base period 2010 and the current period 2016.

Table 7.1 shows the quantities in the CPI market basket and the prices in the base period and the current period. Part (a) contains the data for the base period. In that period, consumers bought 10 oranges at $1 each and 5 haircuts at $8 each. To find the cost of the CPI market basket in the base period prices, multiply the quantities in the CPI market basket by the base period prices. The cost of oranges is $10 (10 at $1 each), and the cost of haircuts is $40 (5 at $8 each). So total expenditure in the base period on the CPI market basket is $50 ($10 + $40).

Part (b) contains the price data for the current period. The price of an orange increased from $1 to $2, which is a 100 percent increase ($1 ÷ $1 × 100 = 100 percent). The price of a haircut increased from $8 to $10, which is a 25 percent increase ($2 ÷ $8 × 100 = 25 percent).

The CPI provides a way of averaging these price increases by comparing the cost of the basket rather than the price of each item. To find the cost of the CPI market basket in the current period, 2016, multiply the quantities in the basket by their 2016 prices. The cost of oranges is $20 (10 at $2 each), and the cost of haircuts is $50 (5 at $10 each). So total expenditure on the fixed CPI market basket at current period prices is $70 ($20 + $50).

**TABLE 7.1**

The Consumer Price Index: A Simplified CPI Calculation

**(a) The cost of the CPI market basket at base period prices: 2010**

| Item | CPI market basket Quantity | Price | Cost of CPI basket |
|------|------|------|------|
| Oranges | 10 | $1 each | $10 |
| Haircuts | 5 | $8 each | $40 |
| | | Cost of CPI market basket at base period prices | $50 |

**(b) The cost of the CPI market basket at current period prices: 2016**

| Item | CPI market basket Quantity | Price | Cost of CPI basket |
|------|------|------|------|
| Oranges | 10 | $2 each | $20 |
| Haircuts | 5 | $10 each | $50 |
| | | Cost of CPI market basket at current period prices | $70 |

You've now taken the first two steps toward calculating the CPI. The third step uses the numbers you've just calculated to find the CPI for 2010 and 2016. The formula for the CPI is

$$\text{CPI} = \frac{\text{Cost of CPI basket at current period prices}}{\text{Cost of CPI basket at base period prices}} \times 100.$$

In Table 7.1, you established that the cost of the CPI market basket was $50 in 2010 and $70 in 2016. If we use these numbers in the CPI formula, we can find the CPI for 2010 and 2016. The base period is 2010, so

$$\text{CPI in 2010} = \frac{\$50}{\$50} \times 100 = 100.$$

$$\text{CPI in 2016} = \frac{\$70}{\$50} \times 100 = 140.$$

The principles that you've applied in this simplified CPI calculation apply to the more complex calculations performed every month by the BLS.

## ■ Measuring Inflation and Deflation

The CPI is a measure of the **price level**, an average of the *level* of prices during a given period. The **inflation rate** is a measure of the percentage *change* in the price level from one period to the next. To calculate the annual inflation rate using the CPI measure of the price level, we use the formula

$$\text{Inflation rate} = \frac{(\text{CPI in current year} - \text{CPI in previous year})}{\text{CPI in previous year}} \times 100.$$

**Price level**
An average of the *level* of prices during a given period.

**Inflation rate**
The percentage *change* in the price level from one period to the next.

Suppose that the current year is 2016 and the CPI for 2016 was 140. And suppose that in the previous year, 2015, the CPI was 120. Then in 2016,

$$\text{Inflation rate} = \frac{(140 - 120)}{120} \times 100 = 16.7 \text{ percent.}$$

If the inflation rate is *negative*, the CPI is *falling* and we have **deflation**. The United States has rarely experienced deflation, but 2009 was one of those rare years. You can check the latest data by visiting the BLS Web site. In July 2009, the CPI was 215.4, and in July 2008, it was 220.0. So during the year to July 2009,

**Deflation**
A situation in which the CPI is *falling* and the inflation rate is *negative*.

$$\text{Inflation rate} = \frac{(215.4 - 220.0)}{220.0} \times 100 = -2.1 \text{ percent.}$$

## ■ The Price Level, Inflation, and Deflation in the United States

Figure 7.2(a) on p. 172 shows the U.S. price level measured by the CPI between 1976 and 2016. The price level increased every year during this period until 2009 when it fell slightly. During the late 1970s and in 1980, the price level was increasing rapidly, but since the early 1980s, the rate of increase has slowed.

Figure 7.2(b) shows the U.S. inflation rate. When the price level rises rapidly, the inflation rate is high; when the price level rises slowly, the inflation rate is low; and when the price level is falling, the inflation rate is negative.

# EYE on the PAST
## 700 Years of Inflation and Deflation

These extraordinary data show that inflation became a persistent problem only after 1900. During the preceding 600 years, inflation was almost unknown. Inflation increased slightly during the sixteenth century after Europeans discovered gold in America. But this inflation barely reached 2 percent a year—less than we have today—and eventually subsided. The Industrial Revolution saw a temporary burst of inflation followed by a period of deflation.

SOURCES OF DATA: E.H. Phelps Brown and Sheila V. Hopkins, *Economica*, 1955, and Robert Sahr, http://oregonstate.edu/dept/pol_sci/fac/sahr/sahr.htm.

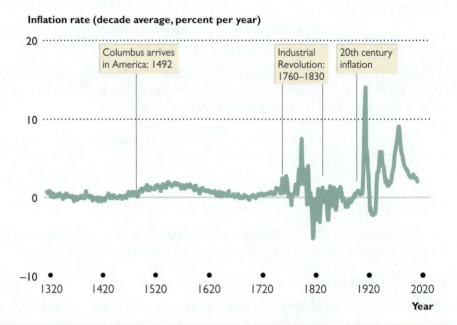

**Inflation rate (decade average, percent per year)**

Columbus arrives in America: 1492

Industrial Revolution: 1760–1830

20th century inflation

---

## FIGURE 7.2

### The CPI and the Inflation Rate: 1976–2016

MyEconLab Real-time data

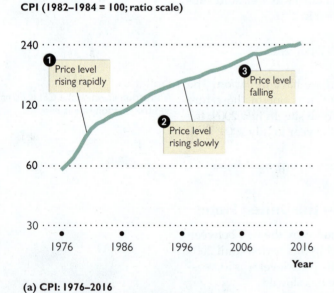

**CPI (1982–1984 = 100; ratio scale)**

① Price level rising rapidly

③ Price level falling

② Price level rising slowly

(a) CPI: 1976–2016

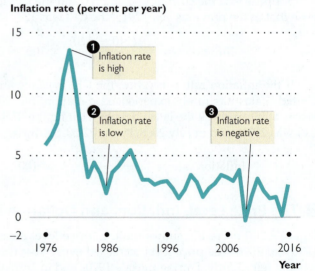

**Inflation rate (percent per year)**

① Inflation rate is high

② Inflation rate is low

③ Inflation rate is negative

(b) CPI inflation rate: 1976–2016

SOURCE OF DATA: Bureau of Labor Statistics.

① The price level in part (a) was rising rapidly during the 1970s and 1980s and the inflation rate in part (b) was high.

② The price level was rising slowly during the 1990s and 2000s and the inflation rate was low.

③ In 2009, the price level fell and the inflation rate was negative.

# CHECKPOINT 7.1

MyEconLab Study Plan 7.1
Key Terms Quiz
Solutions Video

**Explain what the Consumer Price Index (CPI) is and how it is calculated.**

## Practice Problems

A Consumer Expenditure Survey in Sparta shows that people buy only juice and cloth. In 2015, the year of the Consumer Expenditure Survey and also the reference base year, the average household spent $40 on juice and $25 on cloth. Table 1 sets out the prices of juice and cloth in 2015 and 2016.

1. Calculate the CPI market basket and the percentage of the average household budget spent on juice in the reference base year.
2. Calculate the CPI in 2016 and the inflation rate between 2015 and 2016.
3. Table 2 shows the CPI in Sparta. Calculate the inflation rates in 2015 and 2016. Did the CPI rise in 2016? Did the inflation rate increase in 2016?

**TABLE 1   PRICES**

|  | 2015 | 2016 |
|---|---|---|
| Juice | $4 a bottle | $4 a bottle |
| Cloth | $5 a yard | $6 a yard |

## In the News

**U.S. Consumer Price Index down 0.1 percent**
The U.S. CPI fell 0.1 percent in December 2015. The price of gasoline fell by 3.9 percent. Rents increased 0.2 percent, and medical care costs increased 0.1 percent.
                    Source: CNBC, Wednesday, January 20, 2016

Did the United States experience inflation or deflation in December 2015? Which of the items mentioned in the news clip has the highest weight in the CPI and which has the lowest weight?

**TABLE 2**

| Year | CPI |
|---|---|
| 2014 | 200 |
| 2015 | 219 |
| 2016 | 237 |

## Solutions to Practice Problems

1. The CPI market basket is the quantities bought during the Consumer Expenditure Survey year, 2015. The average household spent $40 on juice at $4 a bottle, so it bought 10 bottles of juice. The average household spent $25 on cloth at $5 a yard, so it bought 5 yards of cloth. The CPI market basket is made up of 10 bottles of juice and 5 yards of cloth.
   In the reference base year, the average household spent $40 on juice and $25 on cloth, so the household budget was $65. Expenditure on juice was 61.5 percent of the household budget: ($40 ÷ $65) × 100 = 61.5 percent.

2. To calculate the CPI in 2016, find the cost of the CPI market basket in 2015 and 2016. In 2015, the CPI basket costs $65 ($40 for juice + $25 for cloth). In 2016, the CPI market basket costs $70 (10 bottles of juice at $4 a bottle + 5 yards of cloth at $6 a yard). The CPI in 2016 is ($70 ÷ $65) × 100 = 107.7. The inflation rate is [(107.7 − 100) ÷ 100] × 100 = 7.7 percent.

3. The inflation rate in 2015 is [(219 − 200) ÷ 200] × 100 = 9.5 percent. The inflation rate in 2016 is [(237 − 219) ÷ 219] × 100 = 8.2 percent. In 2016, the CPI increased, but the inflation rate decreased.

## Solution to In the News

Deflation occurs when the CPI falls. The CPI fell by 0.1 percent in December 2015 so the United States experienced deflation. The weight in the CPI is highest on rents, which are part of housing (42.1 percent of CPI market basket). The weight on gasoline is part of transportation, the second largest category in the CPI market basket (15.4 percent). The smallest weight is on medical care (8.4 percent).

## 7.2  THE CPI AND OTHER PRICE LEVEL MEASURES

**Cost of living index**
A measure of the change in the amount of money that people need to spend to achieve a given standard of living.

The CPI is one of several alternative *price level* measures. Its purpose is to measure the cost of living or what amounts to the same thing, the *value of money*. The CPI is sometimes called a **cost of living index** —a measure of the change in the amount of money that people need to spend to achieve a given standard of living. The CPI is not a perfect measure of the cost of living (value of money) for two broad reasons.

First, the CPI does not try to measure all the changes in the cost of living. For example, the cost of living rises in a severe winter as people buy more natural gas and electricity to heat their homes. A rise in the prices of these items increases the CPI. But the increased quantities of natural gas and electricity bought don't change the CPI because the CPI market basket is fixed. So part of this increase in spending—the increase in the cost of maintaining a given standard of living—doesn't show up as an increase in the CPI.

Second, even those components of the cost of living that are measured by the CPI are not always measured accurately. The result is that the CPI is possibly a biased measure of changes in the cost of living.

Let's look at some of the sources of bias in the CPI and the ways the BLS tries to overcome them.

### ■ Sources of Bias in the CPI

The potential sources of bias in the CPI are

- New goods bias
- Quality change bias
- Commodity substitution bias
- Outlet substitution bias

### New Goods Bias

Every year, some new goods become available and some old goods disappear. Make a short list of items that you take for granted today that were not available 10 or 20 years ago. This list includes smartphones; tablet computers; and flat-panel, large-screen television sets. A list of items no longer available or rarely bought includes audiocassette players, vinyl records, photographic film, and typewriters.

When we want to compare the cost of living in 2016 with that in 2006, 1996, or 1986, we must do so by comparing the prices of different baskets of goods. We can't compare the same baskets because today's basket wasn't available 10 years ago and the basket of 10 years ago isn't available today.

To make comparisons, the BLS tries to measure the price of the service performed by yesterday's goods and today's goods. It tries to compare, for example, the price of listening to recorded music, regardless of the technology that delivers that service. But the comparison is hard to make. Today's smartphone delivers an improved quality of sound and level of convenience compared to yesterday's Walkman and Discman.

How much of a new product represents an increase in quantity and quality and how much represents a higher price? The BLS does its best to answer this question, but there is no sure way of making the necessary adjustment. It is believed that the arrival of new goods puts an upward bias into the CPI and its measure of the inflation rate.

*To measure the CPI, the BLS must compare the price of today's smartphone with that of the 1970s Walkman and 1980s Discman.*

### Quality Change Bias

Cars, smartphones, laptops, and many other items get better every year. For example, central locking, airbags, and antilock braking systems all add to the quality of a car. But they also add to the cost. Is the improvement in quality greater than the increase in cost? Or do car prices rise by more than can be accounted for by quality improvements? To the extent that a price rise is a payment for improved quality, it is not inflation. Again, the BLS does the best job it can to estimate the effects of quality improvements on price changes. But the CPI probably counts too much of any price rise as inflation and so overstates inflation.

*To compare the price of today's cars with those of earlier years, the BLS must value the improvements in features and quality.*

### Commodity Substitution Bias

Changes in relative prices lead consumers to change the items they buy. People cut back on items that become relatively more costly and increase their consumption of items that become relatively less costly. For example, suppose the price of carrots rises while the price of broccoli remains constant. Now that carrots are more costly relative to broccoli, you might decide to buy more broccoli and fewer carrots. Suppose that you switch from carrots to broccoli, spend the same amount on vegetables as before, and get the same enjoyment as before. Your cost of vegetables has not changed. The CPI says that the price of vegetables has increased because it ignores your substitution between goods in the CPI market basket.

*When consumers substitute lower priced broccoli for higher priced carrots, the CPI overstates the rise in the price of vegetables.*

### Outlet Substitution Bias

When confronted with higher prices, people use discount stores more frequently and convenience stores less frequently. This phenomenon is called *outlet substitution*. Suppose, for example, that gas prices rise by 10¢ a gallon. Instead of buying from your nearby gas station for $4.599 a gallon, you now drive farther to a gas station that charges $4.499 a gallon. Your cost of gas has increased because you must factor in the cost of your time and the gas that you use driving several blocks down the road. But your cost has not increased by as much as the 10¢ a gallon increase in the pump price. However, the CPI says that the price of gas has increased by 10¢ a gallon because the CPI does not measure outlet substitution.

*As consumers shop around for the lowest prices, outlet substitution occurs and the CPI overstates the rise in prices actually paid.*

The growth of online shopping in recent years has provided an alternative to discount stores that makes outlet substitution even easier and potentially makes this source of bias more serious.

## ■ The Magnitude of the Bias

You have reviewed the sources of bias in the CPI. But how big is the bias? When this question was tackled in 1996 by a Congressional Advisory Commission chaired by Michael Boskin, an economics professor at Stanford University, the answer was that the CPI overstated inflation by 1.1 percentage points a year. That is, if the CPI reports that inflation is 3.1 percent a year, most likely inflation is actually 2 percent a year.

In the period since the Boskin Commission reported, the BLS has taken steps to reduce the CPI bias. The more frequent Consumer Expenditure Survey that we described earlier in this chapter is one of these steps. Beyond that, the BLS uses ever more sophisticated models and methods to try to eliminate the sources of bias and make the CPI as accurate as possible.

## ■ Two Consequences of the CPI Bias

A bias in the CPI has two main undesirable consequences: It leads to

- Distortion of private contracts
- Increases in government outlays and decreases in taxes

### Distortion of Private Contracts

Suppose the United Automobile Workers union (UAW) and Ford Motor Company agree to a three-year wage deal to pay $30 an hour in the first year with increases equal to the percentage change in the CPI in the following years. If the CPI increases by 5 percent each year, the wage rate will increase to $31.50 in the second year and $33.08 in the third year.

Now suppose that the CPI is biased and the true increase in the cost of living is 3 percent a year. In the second year, $30.90 rather than $31.50, and in the third year, $31.83, not $33.08, compensates workers for the higher cost of living. So in the second year, the workers gain 60¢ an hour, or $21 for a 35-hour workweek. And in the third year, they gain $1.25 an hour, or $43.75 for a 35-hour workweek.

The workers' gain is Ford's loss. With a work force of a few thousand, the loss amounts to several thousand dollars a week and a few million dollars over the life of a 3-year wage contract.

### Increases in Government Outlays and Decreases in Taxes

The CPI is used to adjust the incomes of the 54 million Social Security beneficiaries, 47 million food stamp recipients, and 4 million retired former military personnel and federal civil servants (and their surviving spouses), and the budget for 3 million school lunches. Close to a third of federal government outlays are linked directly to the CPI. A bias in the CPI would increase all of these expenditures by more than required to compensate for the fall in the buying power of the dollar. Even a 1 percent bias would accumulate over a decade to almost a trillion dollars.

The CPI is also used to adjust the income levels at which higher tax rates apply. The tax rates on large incomes are higher than those on small incomes so, as incomes rise, if these adjustments were not made, the burden of taxes would rise relentlessly. To the extent that the CPI is biased upward, the tax adjustments over-compensate for rising prices and decrease the amount paid in taxes.

## ■ Alternative Consumer Price Indexes

Three alternative measures of the price level that we'll describe here aim to improve on the CPI. These measures are the

- Chained Consumer Price Index (C-CPI)
- Personal Consumption Expenditures Price Index (PCEPI)
- PCEPI Excluding Food and Energy

### Chained Consumer Price Index (C-CPI)

**Chained Consumer Price Index**
A measure of the price level calculated using current month and previous month prices and expenditures.

The **Chained Consumer Price Index (C-CPI)** is measure of the price level calculated using current month and previous month prices and expenditures. It is called a "chained" CPI because the inflation rate calculated for the current month is linked back, like the links in a chain, to a reference base month. (See pp. 141–143 for a description of chain linking). Because it uses current period expenditures that are updated every month, the C-CPI avoids the bias in the CPI. It takes account of new goods, quality change, and substitution effects. The only weakness of the C-CPI is that it gets revised several times as the data on recent expenditures get revised.

## Personal Consumption Expenditures Price Index (PCEPI)

The **Personal Consumption Expenditures Price Index (PCEPI)** is an average of the current prices of the goods and services included in the consumption expenditure component of GDP expressed as a percentage of base year prices. The PCEPI uses current quantities so, like the C-CPI, it avoids the sources of bias in the CPI.

## PCEPI Excluding Food and Energy

Food and energy prices fluctuate much more than other prices and their changes can obscure the underlying trend in the price level. By excluding these highly variable items, the underlying price level and inflation rate can be seen more clearly. The percentage change in the PCEPI excluding food and energy is called the **core inflation rate**.

Figure 7.3 shows the three alternative measures of the price level alongside the CPI since 2000. The two measures that use current period expenditures, the C-CPI and the PCEPI, are similar. They imply that the price level in 2015 was 132 percent higher than in 2000, which represents an annual inflation rate of 1.9 percent. The CPI rises above these two measures at an average annual inflation rate of 2.2 percent, which is an upward bias of 0.3 percentage points. The PCEPI excluding food and energy, the index used to calculate the core inflation rate, rises more slowly than the other measures. It is biased downward because, on average, food and energy prices rise faster than other prices. *Eye on the U.S. Economy* (on p. 178) looks at another way of identifying the underlying inflation rate.

**PCEPI**
An average of the current prices of the goods and services included in the consumption expenditure component of GDP expressed as a percentage of base year prices.

**Core inflation rate**
The annual percentage change in the PCEPI excluding the prices of food and energy.

### FIGURE 7.3

Four Measures of Consumer Prices

MyEconLab Real-time data

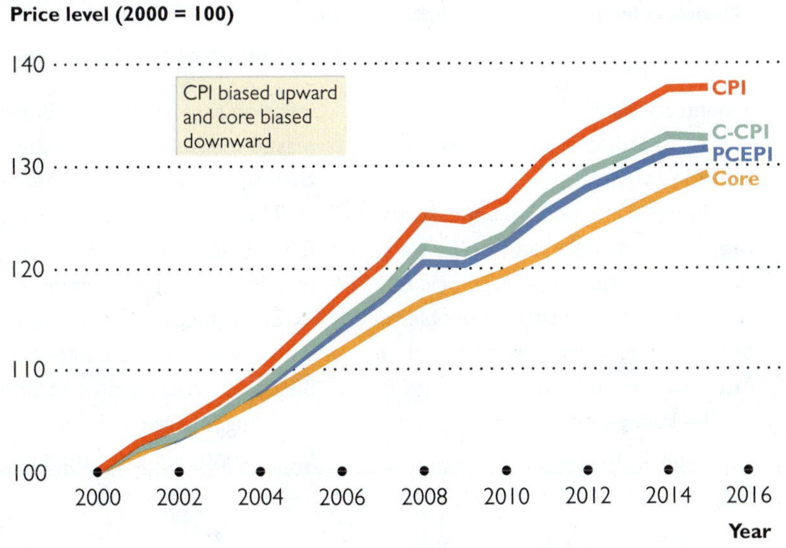

These four measures of the *price level* rise together.

The Chained Consumer Price Index, C-CPI, and the Personal Consumption Expenditures Price Index, PCEPI, provide the most accurate measure of the price level and inflation rate.

The CPI rises fastest reflecting its upward bias and the PCEPI excluding food and energy, the core inflation measure, rises the slowest reflecting its downward bias.

SOURCES OF DATA: Bureau of Labor Statistics and Bureau of Economic Analysis.

# EYE on the U.S. ECONOMY
## Measuring and Forecasting Inflation: The Sticky-Price CPI

The *sticky-price CPI* is a price index constructed from the items in the CPI whose prices change infrequently— whose prices are "sticky." These items contrast with the ones whose prices change frequently—whose prices are "flexible."

The table provides some examples. Among the 30 percent of the items in the CPI with flexible prices, the price of motor fuel changes most frequently—on average every 3 weeks. At the other extreme, among the 70 percent of items with sticky prices, the price of medical care services changes least frequently. It remains fixed for more than one year.

The figure shows the CPI inflation rate broken into its sticky-price and flexible-price components. The sticky prices respond to expectations about future market conditions and have small fluctuations. The flexible prices respond to current market conditions and fluctuate a lot.

The sticky-price inflation rate provides information about how expectations of future inflation are changing. Over the five years from 2011 to 2016, when the flexible-price inflation rate was falling, the sticky-price rate was rising. And in 2016, when flexible prices were *falling*, the sticky-price inflation rate exceeded 2 percent per year.

The sticky-price CPI solves three problems with other measures of the price level and inflation rate.

The first problem is volatility and the challenge of probing the underlying inflation rate and predicting its future level. The CPI inflation rate bounces

Examples of Flexible-Price and Sticky-Price Items

| Flexible-price items (30 percent of total) | Frequency of adjustment (weeks) | Sticky-price items (70 percent of total) | Frequency of adjustment (weeks) |
|---|---|---|---|
| Motor fuel | 3 | Recreation | 34 |
| Meats, poultry, fish, and eggs | 8 | Communication | 36 |
| New vehicles | 9 | Public transportation | 41 |
| Used cars and trucks | 9 | Rent of primary residence | 48 |
| Women's and girls' apparel | 10 | Education | 48 |
| Cereals and bakery products | 14 | Medical care services | 61 |

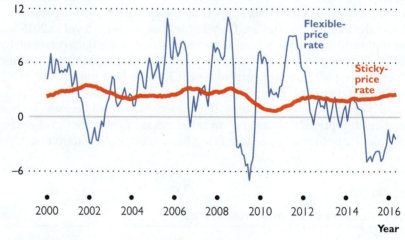

Flexible-price and sticky-price inflation rates

SOURCE OF DATA: Federal Reserve Bank of Atlanta.

around so much from month to month that it is hard to say what the current inflation rate is.

The core inflation rate measures the underlying inflation rate by excluding volatile food and energy prices, which leads to the second problem, bias. The CPI *overstates* the inflation rate and core inflation *understates* it.

The sticky-price CPI shares the small bias of the CPI because the average sticky-price and flexible-price

inflation rates are equal. But it is a less biased measure of underlying inflation than the core inflation rate.

The third problem is timing. The Chained CPI (C-CPI) overcomes the problem of bias but, along with the PCEPI, it measures the inflation rate with a delay as more information becomes available on consumer spending. In contrast, the sticky-price CPI is reported just hours after the BLS announces the CPI.

CHECKPOINT 7.2

MyEconLab Study Plan 7.2
Key Terms Quiz
Solutions Video

**Explain the limitations of the CPI and describe other measures of the price level.**

## Practice Problems

Economists in the Statistics Bureau decide to check the CPI substitution bias. To do so, they conduct a Consumer Expenditure Survey in both 2015 and 2016. Table 1 shows the results of the survey. It shows the items that consumers buy and their prices. The Statistics Bureau fixes the reference base year as 2015.

1. Calculate the CPI in 2016 if the CPI basket contains the 2015 quantities.
2. Calculate the CPI in 2016 if the CPI basket contains the 2016 quantities.
3. Is there any substitution bias in the CPI that uses the 2015 basket? Explain.

**TABLE 1**

| Item | 2015 Quantity | 2015 Price | 2016 Quantity | 2016 Price |
|------|------|------|------|------|
| Broccoli | 10 | $3.00 | 15 | $3.00 |
| Carrots | 15 | $2.00 | 10 | $4.00 |

## In the News

**News releases**

In 2015, the CPI increased by 0.7 percent, the C-CPI increased by 0.3 percent, and the PCEPI increased by 0.4 percent.

Sources: Bureau of Economic Analysis and Bureau of Labor Statistics, February, 2016

Why do these three measures of the price level give different inflation rates?

## Solutions to Practice Problems

1. Table 2 shows the calculation of the CPI in 2016 when the CPI basket is made of the 2015 quantities. The cost of the 2015 basket at 2015 prices is $60 and the cost of the 2015 basket at 2016 prices is $90. So the CPI in 2016 using the 2015 basket is ($90 ÷ $60) × 100 = 150.

2. Table 3 shows the calculation of the CPI in 2016 when the CPI basket is made of the 2016 quantities. The cost of the 2016 basket at 2015 prices is $65, and the cost of the 2016 basket at 2016 prices is $85. So the CPI in 2016 using the 2016 basket is ($85 ÷ $65) × 100 = 131.

3. The CPI that uses the 2015 basket displays some bias. With the price of broccoli constant and the price of carrots rising, consumers buy fewer carrots and more broccoli and they spend $85 on vegetables. But they would have spent $90 if they had not substituted broccoli for some carrots. The price of vegetables does not rise by 50 percent as shown by the CPI. Because of substitution, the price of vegetables rises by only 42 percent ($85 is 42 percent greater than $60). Using the 2016 basket, the price of vegetables rises by only 31 percent ($85 compared with $65). A CPI substitution bias exists.

**TABLE 2**

| Item | 2015 basket at 2015 prices | 2015 basket at 2016 prices |
|------|------|------|
| Broccoli | $30 | $30 |
| Carrots | $30 | $60 |
| Total | $60 | $90 |

**TABLE 3**

| Item | 2016 basket at 2015 prices | 2016 basket at 2016 prices |
|------|------|------|
| Broccoli | $45 | $45 |
| Carrots | $20 | $40 |
| Total | $65 | $85 |

## Solution to In the News

These three measures of the price level are based on the prices of different baskets of goods and services. The CPI basket contains only the goods and services that urban consumers buy in the year of the most recent consumer expenditure survey. The basket of the C-CPI contains the goods and services that urban consumers buy in the two most recent years. The basket of the PCEPI contains the goods and services in GDP that households buy in the two most recent years.

MyEconLab Concept Video

*Which postage stamp has the higher real price: the 2¢ stamp of 1916 or today's 47¢ stamp?*

## 7.3 NOMINAL AND REAL VALUES

In 2016, it cost 47 cents to mail a first-class letter. One hundred years earlier, in 1916, that same letter would have cost 2 cents to mail. Does it *really* cost you 23.5 times the amount that it cost your great-great-grandmother to mail a letter?

You know that it does not. You know that a dollar today buys less than what a dollar bought in 1916, so the cost of a stamp has not really increased to 23.5 times its 1916 level. But has it increased at all? Did it really cost you any more to mail a letter in 2016 than it cost your great-great-grandmother in 1916?

The CPI can be used to answer questions like these. In fact, that is one of the main reasons for constructing a price index. Let's see how we can compare the price of a stamp in 1916 and the price of a stamp in 2016.

### ■ Dollars and Cents at Different Dates

To compare dollar amounts at different dates, we need to know the CPI at those dates. Currently, the CPI equals 100 for reference base period 1982–1984. That is, the average of the CPI in 1982, 1983, and 1984 is 100. (The numbers for the three years are 96.4, 99.6, and 103.9, respectively. Calculate the average of these numbers and check that it is indeed 100.)

In 2016, the CPI was 240.2, and in 1916, it was 10.9. By using these two numbers, we can calculate the relative value of the dollar in 1916 and 2016. To do so, we divide the 2016 CPI by the 1916 CPI. That ratio is 240.2 divided by 10.9, or 22. That is, prices on average were 22 times higher in 2016 than in 1916.

We can use this ratio to convert the price of a 2-cent stamp in 1916 into its 2016 equivalent. The formula for this calculation is

$$\text{Price of stamp in 2016 dollars} = \text{Price of stamp in 1916 dollars} \times \frac{\text{CPI in 2016}}{\text{CPI in 1916}}$$

$$= 2 \text{ cents} \times \frac{240.2}{10.9} = 44 \text{ cents.}$$

So your great-great-grandmother did pay less than you pay! It really cost her 3 cents less to mail that first-class letter than it cost you in 2016. She paid the equivalent of 44 cents in 2016 money, and you paid 47 cents.

We've just converted the 1916 price of a stamp to its 2016 equivalent. We can do a similar calculation the other way around—converting the 2016 price to its 1916 equivalent. The formula for this alternative calculation is

$$\text{Price of stamp in 1916 dollars} = \text{Price of stamp in 2016 dollars} \times \frac{\text{CPI in 1916}}{\text{CPI in 2016}}$$

$$= 47 \text{ cents} \times \frac{10.9}{240.2} = 2.13 \text{ cents.}$$

The interpretation of this number is that you pay the *equivalent* of 2.13 cents in 1916 dollars. Your *real* price of a stamp is 2.13 cents expressed in 1916 dollars.

The calculations that we've just done are examples of converting a *nominal* value into a *real* value. A nominal value is one that is expressed in current dollars. A real value is one that is expressed in the dollars of a given year. We're now going to see how we convert other nominal macroeconomic variables into real variables using a similar method.

## ■ Nominal and Real Values in Macroeconomics

Macroeconomics makes a big issue of the distinction between the nominal value and the real value of a variable. Three nominal and real variables occupy a central position in macroeconomics. They are

- Nominal GDP and real GDP
- The nominal wage rate and the real wage rate
- The nominal interest rate and the real interest rate

We begin our examination of real and nominal variables in macroeconomics by reviewing what you've already learned about the distinction between nominal GDP and real GDP and interpreting that distinction in a new way.

## ■ Nominal GDP and Real GDP

When we calculated real GDP in 2016 in terms of 2009 dollars in Chapter 5 (pp. 126–127), we expressed the values of the goods and services produced in 2016 in terms of the prices that prevailed in 2009. We calculated real GDP directly. We didn't multiply nominal GDP in 2016 by the ratio of a price index in the two years.

But we can *interpret* real GDP in 2016 as nominal GDP in 2016 multiplied by the ratio of a price index in 2009 to its value in 2016. The price index that we would use is the **GDP price index**, which is an average of the current prices of all the goods and services included in GDP expressed as a percentage of the base year prices.

The GDP price index in 2009 (the base year) is defined to be 100, so we can interpret real GDP in any year as nominal GDP divided by the GDP price index in

**GDP price index**
An average of the current prices of all the goods and services included in GDP expressed as a percentage of base year prices.

# EYE on the U.S. ECONOMY
## Deflating the GDP Balloon

Nominal GDP increased every year between 1980 and 2016 except for 2009. Part of the increase reflects increased production, and part of it reflects rising prices.

You can think of GDP as a balloon that is blown up by growing production and rising prices. In the figure, the GDP price index or *GDP deflator* lets the inflation air—the contribution of rising prices—out of the nominal GDP balloon so that we can see what has happened to real GDP.

The small red balloon for 1980 shows real GDP in that year. The green balloon shows nominal GDP in 2016, and the red balloon for 2016 shows real GDP for that year.

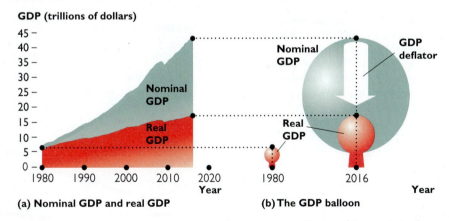

(a) Nominal GDP and real GDP

(b) The GDP balloon

SOURCE OF DATA: Bureau of Economic Analysis.

To see real GDP in 2016, we use the GDP price index to deflate nominal GDP. With the inflation air removed, we can see by how much real GDP grew from 1980 to 2016.

that year multiplied by 100. We don't calculate real GDP this way, but we can interpret it this way.

The GDP price index, or the CPI, or another price index might be used to convert a nominal variable to a real variable.

### ■ Nominal Wage Rate and Real Wage Rate

The price of labor services is the wage rate—the income that an hour of labor earns. In macroeconomics, we are interested in economy-wide performance, so we focus on the *average* hourly wage rate. The **nominal wage rate** is the average hourly wage rate measured in *current* dollars. The **real wage rate** is the average hourly wage rate measured in the dollars of a given reference base year.

To calculate the real wage rate relevant to a consumer, we divide the nominal wage rate by the CPI and multiply by 100. That is,

$$\text{Real wage rate in 2015} = \frac{\text{Nominal wage rate in 2015}}{\text{CPI in 2015}} \times 100.$$

In 2015, the nominal wage rate (average hourly wage rate) of production workers was $21.04 and the CPI was 237, so

$$\text{Real wage rate in 2015} = \frac{\$21.04}{237} \times 100 = \$8.88.$$

Because we measure the real wage rate in constant base period dollars, a change in the real wage rate measures the change in the quantity of goods and

**Nominal wage rate**
The average hourly wage rate measured in current dollars.

**Real wage rate**
The average hourly wage rate measured in the dollars of a given reference base year.

■ **FIGURE 7.4**

Nominal and Real Wage Rates: 1980–2015                                          MyEconLab Real-time data

The nominal wage rate has increased every year since 1980. The real wage rate decreased slightly from 1985 through the mid-1990s, after which it increased slightly. Over the entire 35-year period, the real wage rate remained steady.

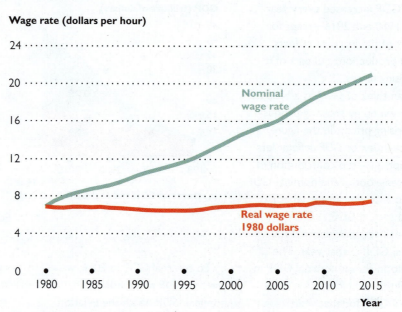

Source of data: Bureau of Labor Statistics.

services that an hour's work can buy. In contrast, a change in the nominal wage rate measures a combination of a change in the quantity of goods and services that an hour's work can buy and a change in the price level. So the real wage rate removes the effects of inflation from the changes in the nominal wage rate.

The real wage rate is a significant economic variable because it measures the real reward for labor services, which is a major determinant of the standard of living. The real wage rate is also significant because it measures the real cost of labor services, which influences the quantity of labor that firms are willing to hire.

Figure 7.4 shows what has happened to the nominal wage rate and the real wage rate in the United States between 1980 and 2015. The nominal wage rate is the average hourly earnings of production workers. This measure is just one of several different measures of average hourly earnings that we might have used.

The nominal wage rate increased from $6.85 an hour in 1980 to $21.04 an hour in 2015, but the real wage rate barely changed. In 1980 dollars, the real wage rate in 2015 was only $8.88 an hour.

The real wage rate barely changed as the nominal wage rate increased because the nominal wage rate grew at a rate almost equal to the inflation rate. When the effects of inflation are removed from the nominal wage rate, we can see what is happening to the buying power of the average wage rate.

You can also see that the real wage rate has fluctuated a little. It decreased slightly until the mid-1990s, after which it increased slightly.

# EYE on the PAST

## The Nominal and Real Wage Rates of Presidents of the United States

Who earned more, Barack Obama in 2016, or George Washington in 1788? George Washington's pay was $25,000 (on the green line), but in 2016 dollars it was $619,000 (on the red line). Barack Obama was paid $400,000 in 2016.

But presidential accommodations are more comfortable today, and presidential travel arrangements are a breeze compared to earlier times. So adding in the perks of the job, Barack Obama didn't get such a raw deal.

SOURCE OF DATA:
Robert Sahr, Oregon State University,
http://oregonstate.edu/cla/polisci/sahr/sahr.

### ■ Nominal Interest Rate and Real Interest Rate

You've just seen that we can calculate real values from nominal values by deflating them using the CPI. And you've seen that to make this calculation, we *divide* the nominal value by a price index. Converting a nominal interest rate to a real interest rate is a bit different. To see why, we'll start with their definitions.

A **nominal interest rate** is the dollar amount of interest expressed as a percentage of the amount loaned. For example, suppose that you have $1,000 in a bank deposit—a loan by you to a bank—on which you receive interest of $50 a year. The nominal interest rate is $50 as a percentage of $1,000, which is 5 percent a year.

A **real interest rate** is the goods and services forgone in interest expressed as a percentage of the amount loaned. Continuing with the above example, at the end of one year your bank deposit has increased to $1,050—the original $1,000 plus the $50 interest. Suppose that during the year prices increased by 3 percent, so now you need $1,030 to buy what $1,000 would have bought a year earlier. How much interest did you *really* receive? The answer is $20, or a real interest rate of 2 percent a year.

To convert a nominal interest rate to a real interest rate, we *subtract* the *inflation rate.* That is,

$$\text{Real interest rate} = \text{Nominal interest rate} - \text{Inflation rate.}$$

Put your numbers into this formula. Your nominal interest rate is 5 percent a year, and the inflation rate is 3 percent a year, so your real interest rate is 5 percent minus 3 percent, which equals 2 percent a year.

Figure 7.5 shows the nominal and the real interest rates in the United States between 1976 and 2016. When the inflation rate is high, the gap between the real interest rate and nominal interest rate is large. Sometimes, the real interest rate is negative (as it was during the late 1970s) and the lender pays the borrower!

**Nominal interest rate**
The dollar amount of interest expressed as a percentage of the amount loaned.

**Real interest rate**
The goods and services forgone in interest expressed as a percentage of the amount loaned and calculated as the nominal interest rate minus the inflation rate.

## EYE on BOX OFFICE HITS
MyEconLab Critical Thinking Exercise

### Which Movie *Really* Was the Biggest Box Office Hit?

*Gone with the Wind* is the answer to the question that we posed at the beginning of this chapter.

To get this answer, Box Office Mojo (www.boxofficemojo.com) calculates the amount that a movie *really* earns by converting the dollars earned to their equivalent in current year dollars. But rather than use the CPI, it uses the average prices of movie tickets as its price index.

*Gone with the Wind* was made in 1939. Looking only at its performance in the United States, the movie was rereleased in nine subsequent years and by 2015 it had earned a total box office revenue of almost $200 million.

*Star Wars: The Force Awakens*, released in 2015, earned $937 million. So the 2015 *Star Wars: The Force Awakens* earned almost five times the dollars earned by *Gone with the Wind*.

To convert the *Gone with the Wind* revenues into 2015 dollars, Box Office Mojo multiplies the dollars received each year by the 2015 ticket price and divides by the ticket price for the year in which the dollars were earned.

Valuing the tickets for *Gone with the Wind* at 2015 movie-ticket prices, it has earned $1,733 million, almost double *Star Wars: The Force Awakens* revenue.

Because Box Office Mojo uses average ticket prices, the real variable that it compares is the number of tickets sold. The average ticket price in 2015 was $8.43, which means 206 million have seen *Gone with the Wind* and 111 million have seen *Star Wars: The Force Awakens*. *Gone with the Wind* was the biggest hit because it was seen by the greatest number of people.

**FIGURE 7.5**

Nominal and Real Interest Rates: 1976–2016                    MyEconLab Real-time data

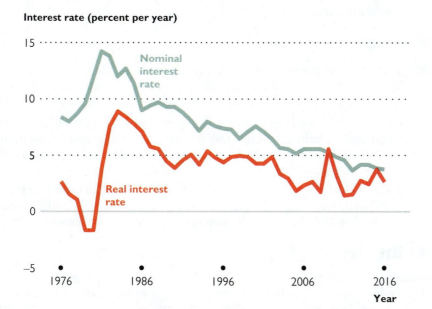

The interest rate shown here is that paid by the safest large corporations on long-term bonds (known as Moody's AAA).

The real interest rate equals the nominal interest rate minus the inflation rate, so the vertical gap between the nominal interest rate and the real interest rate is the inflation rate. The real interest rate is usually positive, but during the late 1970s, it became negative.

SOURCES OF DATA: Federal Reserve and Bureau of Labor Statistics.

# EYE on YOUR LIFE
## A Student's CPI

MyEconLab Critical Thinking Exercise

The CPI measures the percentage change in the average prices paid for the basket of goods and services bought by a typical urban household.

A student is not a typical household. How have the prices of a student's basket of goods and services changed? The answer is by a lot more than those of an average household.

Suppose that a student spends 25 percent of her income on rent, 25 percent on tuition, 25 percent on books and study supplies, 10 percent on food, 10 percent on transportation, and 5 percent on clothing.

We can use these weights and the data collected by the BLS on individual price categories to find the student's

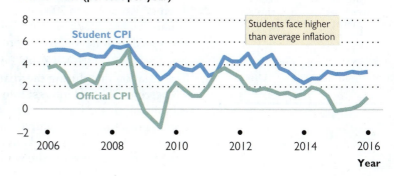

SOURCE OF DATA: Bureau of Labor Statistics.

CPI and the inflation rate that it implies.

The graph shows this student's inflation rate compared to that of the official CPI. Between 2006 and 2016,

the student's CPI rose 34 percent above the official CPI. Rent, textbooks, and tuition are the main items whose prices rose faster than average.

MyEconLab Study Plan 7.3
Key Terms Quiz
Solutions Video

# CHECKPOINT 7.3

**Adjust money values for inflation and calculate real wage rates and real interest rates.**

## Practice Problems

**TABLE 1**

| Year | Price of gasoline (cents per gallon) | CPI |
|------|------|------|
| 1985 | 112 | 107.6 |
| 1995 | 115 | 152.4 |
| 2005 | 230 | 195.3 |
| 2015 | 245 | 237.0 |

1. Table 1 shows the price of gasoline and the CPI for four years. The reference base period is 1982–1984. Calculate the real price of gasoline each year. In which year was this real price highest and in which year was it lowest?

2. Ford says it cut its labor costs by 35 percent between 2006 and 2011. Ford's wage rate, including benefits, was $80 an hour in 2006 and $58 an hour in 2011. The CPI was 202 in 2006 and 218 in 2011. Did the real wage rate fall by more or less than 35 percent?

3. Sally worked all year and put her savings into a mutual fund that paid a nominal interest rate of 7 percent a year. During the year, the CPI increased from 165 to 177. What was the real interest rate that Sally earned?

## In the News

**Negative interest rates**
The Federal Reserve has held interest rates close to zero percent for the past seven years. Even with low inflation, "real" interest rates have been negative.
Source: *San Diego Union Tribune*, February 5, 2016

Explain why with a zero interest rate, even low inflation makes the real interest rate negative. Can the real interest rate exceed the nominal interest rate?

## Solutions to Practice Problems

**TABLE 2**

| Year | Price of gasoline (cents per gallon) | CPI | Price of gasoline (1982–1984 cents per gallon) |
|------|------|------|------|
| 1985 | 112 | 107.6 | 104 |
| 1995 | 115 | 152.4 | 75 |
| 2005 | 230 | 195.3 | 118 |
| 2015 | 245 | 237.0 | 103 |

1. To calculate the real price, divide the nominal price by the CPI and multiply by 100. Table 2 shows the calculations. The real price was highest in 2005, when it was 118 cents (1982–1984 cents) per gallon. The real price was lowest in 1995, when it was 75 cents (1982–1984 cents) per gallon.

2. The real wage rate in 2006, expressed in dollars of the reference base year, equals ($80 ÷ 202) × 100, or $39.60 an hour. The real wage rate in 2011, expressed in dollars of the reference base year, equals ($58 ÷ 218) × 100, or $26.61 an hour. The real wage rate of these workers fell by 32.8 percent.

3. The inflation rate during the year equals [(177 − 165) ÷ 165] × 100, which is 7.3 percent. The real interest rate that Sally earned equals the nominal interest rate minus the inflation rate, which is 7.0 − 7.3, or −0.3 percent. Sally's real interest rate was negative. (If Sally had kept her savings in cash, her nominal interest rate would have been zero, and her real interest rate would have been −7.3 percent. She would have been worse off.)

## Solution to In the News

The real interest rate equals the nominal interest rate minus the inflation rate. So if the nominal interest rate equals zero, the real interest rate equals the negative of the inflation rate. If the inflation rate is 1 percent, the real interest rate is *minus* 1 percent, a negative number. The real interest rate exceeds the nominal interest rate if the inflation rate is negative (if there is deflation).

**CHAPTER SUMMARY**

## Key Points

**1. Explain what the Consumer Price Index (CPI) is and how it is calculated.**

- The Consumer Price Index (CPI) is a measure of the average of the prices of the goods and services that an average urban household buys.
- The CPI is calculated by dividing the cost of the CPI market basket in the current period by its cost in the base period and then multiplying by 100.

**2. Explain the limitations of the CPI and describe other measures of the price level.**

- The CPI does not include all the items that contribute to the cost of living.
- The CPI cannot provide an accurate measure of price changes because of new goods, quality improvements, and substitutions that consumers make when relative prices change.
- Other measures of the price level include the Chained Consumer Price Index (C-CPI), the Personal Consumption Expenditures Price Index (PCEPI), and the PCEPI Excluding Food and Energy.
- Both the C-CPI and the PCEPI use current information on quantities and to some degree overcome the sources of bias in the CPI.
- The PCEPI excluding food and energy is used to calculate the core inflation rate, which shows the inflation trend.

**3. Adjust money values for inflation and calculate real wage rates and real interest rates.**

- To adjust a money value (also called a nominal value) for inflation, we express the value in terms of the dollars of a given year.
- To convert a dollar value of year $B$ to the dollars of year $A$, multiply the value in year $B$ by the price level in year $A$ and divide by the price level in year $B$.
- The real wage rate equals the nominal wage rate divided by the CPI and multiplied by 100.
- The real interest rate equals the nominal interest rate minus the inflation rate.

## Key Terms

MyEconLab Key Terms Quiz

Chained Consumer Price Index, 176
Consumer Price Index, 168
Core inflation rate, 177
Cost of living index, 174
Deflation, 171

GDP price index, 181
Inflation rate, 171
Nominal interest rate, 184
Nominal wage rate, 182
PCEPI, 177

Price level, 171
Real interest rate, 184
Real wage rate, 182
Reference base period, 168

CHAPTER CHECKPOINT

## Study Plan Problems and Applications

**1.** In Canada, the reference base period for the CPI is 2002. By 2014, prices had risen by 25.2 percent since the base period. The inflation rate in Canada in 2015 was 1.1 percent. Calculate the CPI in Canada in 2015.

**2.** In Brazil, the reference base period for the CPI is 2000. By 2005, prices had risen by 51 percent since the base period. The inflation rate in Brazil in 2006 was 10 percent, and in 2007, the inflation rate was 9 percent. Calculate the CPI in Brazil in 2006 and 2007. Brazil's CPI in 2008 was 173. Did Brazil's cost of living increase or decrease in 2008?

**3.** Tables 1 and 2 show the quantities of the goods that Suzie bought and the prices she paid during two consecutive weeks. Suzie's CPI market basket contains the goods she bought in Week 1. Calculate the cost of Suzie's CPI market basket in Week 1 and in Week 2. What percentage of the CPI market basket is gasoline? Calculate the value of Suzie's CPI in Week 2 and her inflation rate in Week 2.

Use the following information to work Problems **4** and **5**.

The GDP price index in the United States in 2008 was about 99, and real GDP in 2008 was $14.8 trillion (2009 dollars). The GDP price index in 2013 was about 107, and real GDP in 2013 was $15.5 trillion (2009 dollars).

**4.** Calculate nominal GDP in 2008 and in 2013 and the percentage increase in nominal GDP between 2008 and 2013.

**5.** What was the percentage increase in production between 2008 and 2013, and by what percentage did the price level rise between 2008 and 2013?

**6.** Table 3 shows the prices that Terry paid for some of his expenditures in June and July 2016. Explain and discuss why these prices might have led to commodity substitution or outlet substitution.

**7.** In 2015, Annie, an 80-year-old, is telling her granddaughter Mary about the good old days. Annie says that in 1935, you could buy a nice house for $15,000 and a jacket for $5. Mary says that in 2015 such a house cost $220,000 and such a jacket cost $70. The CPI in 1935 was 16.7 and in 2015 it was 218.1. Which house has the lower real price? Which jacket has the lower real price?

Use the following information to work Problems **8** and **9**.

**Consumer prices drop as falling oil costs push inflation lower**
Falling oil prices pushed the CPI down 0.1 percent in December 2015. Energy prices fell 2.4 percent and the price of gasoline fell by 3.9 percent.
*Source: Los Angeles Times, January 20, 2016*

**8.** Given the further information that the weight on energy prices in the CPI is 8 percent, by how much would the CPI have changed in December 2015 if energy prices had not changed?

**9.** By what percentage did the prices of other items in the CPI basket change?

 **10.** Read *Eye on Box Office Hits* on p. 184 and using BLS data for the CPI in 1982 and 1997, determine which movie had the greater *real* box office revenues, *E.T.: The Extra-Terrestrial*, which earned $435 million in 1982 or *Titanic*, which earned $601 million in 1997.

**TABLE 1 DATA FOR WEEK 1**

| Item | Quantity | Price (per unit) |
|---|---|---|
| Coffee | 11 cups | $3.25 |
| DVDs | 1 | $25.00 |
| Gasoline | 15 gallons | $2.50 |

**TABLE 2 DATA FOR WEEK 2**

| Item | Quantity | Price (per unit) |
|---|---|---|
| Coffee | 11 cups | $3.25 |
| DVDs | 3 | $12.50 |
| Gasoline | 5 gallons | $3.00 |
| Concert | 1 ticket | $95.00 |

**TABLE 3**

| Item | Price in June | Price in July |
|---|---|---|
| | (dollars per unit) | |
| Steak | 4.11 | 4.01 |
| Bread | 3.25 | 3.12 |
| Bacon | 3.62 | 3.64 |
| Milk | 2.62 | 2.62 |
| Tomatoes | 1.60 | 1.62 |
| Apples | 1.18 | 1.19 |
| Bananas | 0.62 | 0.66 |
| Chicken | 1.28 | 1.26 |
| Lettuce | 1.64 | 1.68 |

## Instructor Assignable Problems and Applications

MyEconLab Homework, Quiz, or Test if assigned by instructor

1. Compare the method used by Box Office Mojo on p. 184 to calculate real box office receipts with the method used on p. 180 to calculate the real price of a postage stamp. Compare and contrast the real variables that each method calculates.

2. Pete is a student who spends 10 percent of his expenditure on books and supplies, 30 percent on tuition, 30 percent on rent, 10 percent on food and drink, 10 percent on transportation, and the rest on clothing. The price index for each item was 100 in 2006. Table 1 shows the prices in 2016.
What is Pete's CPI in 2016? (Hint: The contribution of each item to the CPI is its price weighted by its share of total expenditure.) Did Pete experience a higher or lower inflation rate between 2006 and 2016 than the student whose CPI is shown on p. 185?

3. The people on Coral Island buy only juice and cloth. The CPI market basket contains the quantities bought in 2016. The average household spent $60 on juice and $30 on cloth in 2016 when the price of juice was $2 a bottle and the price of cloth was $5 a yard. In the current year, 2017, juice is $4 a bottle and cloth is $6 a yard. Calculate the CPI and the inflation rate in 2017.

4. Tables 2 and 3 show the quantities of the goods that Harry bought and the prices he paid during two consecutive weeks. Harry's CPI market basket contains the goods he bought in Week 1. Calculate Harry's CPI in Week 2. What was his inflation rate in Week 2?

Use the following information to work Problems **5** and **6**.

The base year is 2012. Real GDP in 2012 was $15 trillion. The GDP price index in 2012 was 105, and real GDP in 2015 was $16 trillion.

5. Calculate nominal GDP in 2012 and in 2015 and the percentage increase in nominal GDP from 2012 to 2015.

6. What was the percentage increase in production from 2012 to 2015, and by what percentage did the price level rise from 2012 to 2015?

7. In 1988, the average wage rate was $9.45 an hour and in 2008 the average wage rate was $18.00 an hour. The CPI in 1988 was 118.3 and in 2008 it was 215.3. In which year was the real wage rate higher?

8. Imagine that you are given $1,000 to spend and told that you must spend it all buying items from a Sears catalog. But you do have a choice of catalog. You may select from the 1903 catalog or from Sears.com today. You will pay the prices quoted in the catalog that you choose.

Which catalog will you choose and why? Refer to any biases in the CPI that might be relevant to your choice.

Use the following information to work Problems **9** and **10**.

**Brazil keeps interest rates on hold**
Brazil's inflation rate climbed to 10.7 percent at the end of 2015 and the country's Monetary Policy Committee kept its benchmark interest rate at 14.25 percent.
Source: *The Financial Times*, January 20, 2016

9. Calculate the real interest rate in Brazil.

10. To maintain this real interest rate, how must the nominal interest rate change if the inflation rate falls to 4.5 percent a year?

**TABLE 1**

| Item | Price in 2016 |
|---|---|
| Books and supplies | 172.6 |
| Tuition | 169.0 |
| Rent | 159.0 |
| Food and drink | 129.8 |
| Transportation | 115.4 |
| Clothing | 92.9 |

**TABLE 2   DATA FOR WEEK 1**

| Item | Quantity | Price (per unit) |
|---|---|---|
| Coffee | 5 cups | $3.00 |
| iTunes songs | 5 | $1.00 |
| Gasoline | 10 gallons | $2.00 |

**TABLE 3   DATA FOR WEEK 2**

| Item | Quantity | Price (per unit) |
|---|---|---|
| Coffee | 4 cups | $3.25 |
| iTunes songs | 10 | $1.00 |
| Gasoline | 10 gallons | $3.00 |

MyEconLab Chapter 7 Study Plan

# Multiple Choice Quiz

1. The CPI measures the average prices paid by _____ for _____.

   A. urban consumers; a fixed basket of consumption goods and services
   B. urban consumers; the average basket of goods and services they buy
   C. all consumers; housing, transportation, and food
   D. everyone who earns an income; the necessities of life

2. The BLS reported that the CPI in July 2010 was 226. This news tells you that _____.

   A. consumer prices during July were 226 percent higher than they were during the base year
   B. the CPI inflation rate in July was 26 percent a year
   C. consumer prices rose by 26 percent during the month of July
   D. the prices of consumption goods and services have risen, on average, by 126 percent since the base year

3. When the price level _____ the inflation rate _____.

   A. rises rapidly; increases
   B. rises rapidly; is high
   C. falls; is zero
   D. rises slowly; falls

4. The CPI bias arises from all of the following items *except* _____.

   A. the introduction of new goods and services
   B. the improved quality of goods
   C. the goods and services bought by poor people
   D. consumers' responses to price changes

5. Of the alternative measures of the price level, the _____ overcomes the bias of the CPI and is a better measure of the inflation rate because it _____.

   A. GDP price index; uses a current basket
   B. PCEPI; uses a current basket of all consumption goods
   C. PCEPI excluding food and energy; is less volatile
   D. GDP price index; includes all goods and services bought by Americans

6. If nominal GDP increases by 5 percent a year and the GDP price index rises by 2 percent a year, then real GDP increases by _____.

   A. 7 percent a year
   B. 3 percent a year
   C. 2.5 percent a year
   D. 10 percent a year

7. When the CPI increases from 200 in 2016 to 210 in 2017 and the nominal wage rate is constant at $10 an hour, the real wage rate _____.

   A. increases by 10 percent
   B. increases to $15 an hour
   C. decreases by 5 percent
   D. is $10 an hour

8. When the price level is rising at _____ and the real interest rate is 1 percent a year, the nominal interest rate is 3 percent a year.

   A. 4 percent a year
   B. 3 percent a year
   C. 2 percent a year
   D. 1 percent a year

Why do Americans earn more and produce more than Europeans?

# Potential GDP and the Natural Unemployment Rate

**When you have completed your study of this chapter, you will be able to**

1 Explain what determines potential GDP.

2 Explain what determines the natural unemployment rate.

**8**

MyEconLab **Big Picture Video**

# MACROECONOMIC APPROACHES AND PATHWAYS

In the three previous chapters, you learned how economists define and measure real GDP, employment and unemployment, the price level, and the inflation rate—the key variables that *describe* macroeconomic performance. Your task in this chapter and those that follow is to learn the *macroeconomic theory* that *explains* macroeconomic performance and provides the basis for *policies* that might improve it.

The macroeconomic theory that we present is today's consensus view on how the economy works. But it isn't the view of all macroeconomists. Today's consensus is a merger of three earlier schools of thought that have contrasting views about the causes of recessions and the best policies for dealing with them. Some economists continue to identify with these schools of thought, and the severity of the 2008–2009 recession and slow recovery intensified debate and gave economists of all shades of opinion a platform from which to present their views.

We begin with an overview of the three schools of thought from which today's consensus has emerged.

## ■ The Three Main Schools of Thought

The three main schools of macroeconomic thought are

- Classical macroeconomics
- Keynesian macroeconomics
- Monetarist macroeconomics

## Classical Macroeconomics

**Classical macroeconomics**
The view that the market economy works well, that aggregate fluctuations are a natural consequence of an expanding economy, and that government intervention cannot improve the efficiency of the market economy.

According to **classical macroeconomics**, markets work well and deliver the best available macroeconomic performance. Aggregate fluctuations are a natural consequence of an expanding economy with rising living standards, and government intervention can only hinder the ability of the market to allocate resources efficiently. The first classical macroeconomists included Adam Smith, David Ricardo, and John Stuart Mill, all of whom worked in the 18th and 19th centuries. Modern day classical economists include the 2004 Nobel Laureates Edward C. Prescott of the University of Arizona and Finn E. Kydland of Carnegie-Mellon University and the University of California at Santa Barbara.

Classical macroeconomics fell into disrepute during the Great Depression of the 1930s, a time when many people believed that *capitalism*, the political system of private ownership, free markets, and democratic political institutions, could not survive and began to advocate *socialism*, a political system based on state ownership of capital and central economic planning.

Classical macroeconomics predicted that the Great Depression would eventually end but offered no method for ending it more quickly.

## Keynesian Macroeconomics

**Keynesian macroeconomics**
The view that the market economy is inherently unstable and needs active government intervention to achieve full employment and sustained economic growth.

According to **Keynesian macroeconomics**, the market economy is inherently unstable and requires active government intervention to achieve full employment and sustained economic growth. One person, John Maynard Keynes, and his book *The General Theory of Employment, Interest, and Money*, published in 1936, began this school of thought. Keynes' theory was that depression and high unemployment occur when households don't spend enough on consumption goods and services and businesses don't spend enough investing in new capital. That is, too little *private* spending is the cause of depression (and recession). To counter the problem of too little private spending, *government* spending must rise.

This Keynesian view picked up many followers and by the 1950s it was the mainstream, but it lost popularity during the inflationary 1970s when it seemed ever more remote from the problems of that decade. The global recession of 2008–2009 and the fear of another great depression revived interest in Keynesian ideas and brought a new wave of attacks on classical macroeconomics with Nobel Laureate Paul Krugman leading the charge in the columns of the *New York Times*.

## Monetarist Macroeconomics

According to **monetarist macroeconomics,** the *classical* view of the world is broadly correct but in addition to fluctuations that arise from the normal functioning of an expanding economy, fluctuations in the quantity of money generate the business cycle. A slowdown in the growth rate of money brings recession and a large decrease in the quantity of money brought the Great Depression.

Milton Friedman, intellectual leader of the Chicago School of economists during the 1960s and 1970s, was the most prominent monetarist. The view that monetary contractions are the sole source of recessions and depressions is held by few economists today. But the view that the quantity of money plays a role in economic fluctuations is accepted by all economists and is part of today's consensus.

**Monetarist macroeconomics**
The view that the market economy works well, that aggregate fluctuations are a natural consequence of an expanding economy, but that fluctuations in the quantity of money generate the business cycle.

## ■ Today's Consensus

Each of the earlier schools provides insights and ingredients that survive in today's consensus. *Classical* macroeconomics provides the story of the economy at or close to full employment. But the classical approach doesn't explain how the economy performs in the face of a major slump in spending.

*Keynesian* macroeconomics takes up the story in a recession or depression. When spending is cut and the demand for most goods and services and the demand for labor all decrease, prices and wage rates don't fall but the quantity of goods and services sold and the quantity of labor employed do fall and the economy goes into recession. In a recession, an increase in spending by governments, or a tax cut that leaves people with more of their earnings to spend, can help to restore full employment.

*Monetarist* macroeconomics elaborates the Keynesian story by emphasizing that a contraction in the quantity of money brings higher interest rates and borrowing costs, which are a major source of cuts in spending that bring recession. Increasing the quantity of money and lowering the interest rate in a recession can help to restore full employment. And keeping the quantity of money growing steadily in line with the expansion of the economy's production possibilities can help to keep inflation in check and can also help to moderate the severity of a recession.

Another component of today's consensus is the view that the *long-term* problem of economic growth is more important than the *short-term* problem of recessions. Take a look at *Eye on the U.S. Economy,* on p. 194, and you will see why. Even a small slowdown in economic growth brings a huge cost in terms of a permanently lower level of income per person. This cost is much larger than that arising from the income lost during recessions. But the costs of recessions are serious because they are concentrated on those who are unemployed.

# EYE on the U.S. ECONOMY
## The Lucas Wedge and the Okun Gap

During the 1960s, U.S. real GDP per person grew at a rate of 2.9 percent a year. The black line in part (a) shows the path that would have been followed if this growth rate had been maintained. After 1970, growth slowed to 2.0 percent per year and the blue line shows the path that real GDP per person followed. University of Chicago economist Robert E. Lucas, Jr. pointed out the large output loss that resulted from this growth slowdown. Part (a) shows this loss as the *Lucas wedge*, which is equivalent to a staggering $509,000 per person or 10 years' income.

Real GDP fluctuates around potential GDP and when the output gap is negative, output is lost. Brookings Institution economist Arthur B. Okun drew attention to this loss. Part (b) shows this loss as the *Okun gap*, which is equivalent to $34,000 per person or about 8 months' income.

Smoothing the business cycle and eliminating the Okun gap has a big payoff. But finding ways of restoring real GDP growth to its 1960s rate has a vastly bigger payoff.

SOURCES OF DATA: Bureau of Economic Analysis, the Congressional Budget Office, and authors' assumptions and calculations.

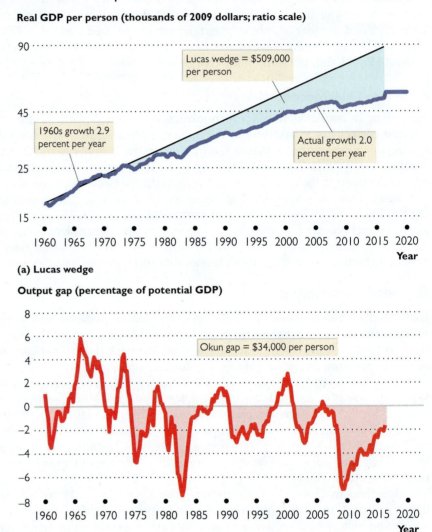

**Real GDP per person (thousands of 2009 dollars; ratio scale)**

Lucas wedge = $509,000 per person

1960s growth 2.9 percent per year

Actual growth 2.0 percent per year

**(a) Lucas wedge**

**Output gap (percentage of potential GDP)**

Okun gap = $34,000 per person

**(b) Okun gap**

## ■ The Road Ahead

This book bases your tour of macroeconomics on the new consensus. We begin in this chapter and the two that follow by explaining what determines potential GDP and the pace at which it grows. We then study money and explain what brings inflation. Finally, we explain how real and monetary forces interact to bring about the business cycle. We also explain the policy tools available to governments and central banks to improve macroeconomic performance.

## 8.1    POTENTIAL GDP

MyEconLab Concept Video

**Potential GDP** is the value of real GDP when all the economy's factors of production—labor, capital, land, and entrepreneurial ability—are fully employed. It is vital to understand the forces that determine potential GDP for three reasons. First, when the economy is *at* full employment, real GDP equals potential GDP; so actual real GDP is determined by the same factors that determine potential GDP. Second, real GDP can exceed potential GDP only temporarily as it approaches and then recedes from a business cycle peak. So potential GDP is the *sustainable* upper limit of production. Third, real GDP fluctuates around potential GDP, which means that on the average over the business cycle, real GDP equals potential GDP.

We produce the goods and services that make up real GDP by using the *factors of production*: labor and human capital, physical capital, land (and natural resources), and entrepreneurship. At any given time, the quantities of capital, land, and entrepreneurship and the state of technology are fixed. But the quantity of labor is not fixed. It depends on the choices that people make about the allocation of time between work and leisure. So with fixed quantities of capital, land, and entrepreneurship and fixed technology, real GDP depends on the quantity of labor employed. To describe this relationship between real GDP and the quantity of labor employed, we use a relationship that is similar to the production possibilities frontier, which is called the production function.

**Potential GDP**
The value of real GDP when all the economy's factors of production—labor, capital, land, and entrepreneurial ability—are fully employed.

# EYE on the GLOBAL ECONOMY
## Potential GDP in the United States and the European Union

In 2015, real GDP in the United States was $65 per hour worked. In the 28 countries of the European Union, real GDP averaged only $50 per hour worked—a gap of 25 percent. (Both numbers are measured in 2015 U.S. dollars.) Part (a) of the figure shows this difference.

Not only do Americans produce more per hour than Europeans, they work longer hours too. In 2015, Americans worked an average of almost 40 hours per week while Europeans worked an average of only 35 hours per week—a difference of 12.5 percent. Part (b) of the figure shows this difference.

Europeans achieve their shorter work hours by taking longer vacations and having more sick days than Americans.

The combination of greater production per hour and longer work hours translates into a substantially larger real GDP per worker in the United States than in Europe.

In 2015, real GDP per worker in the United States was $120,000 while in Europe it was only $75,000—a gap of almost 40 percent.

This chapter enables you to understand the sources of these differences in wage rates, work hours, and production.

SOURCE OF DATA: Organization for Economic Cooperation and Development.

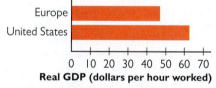

**(a) Real GDP per hour worked**

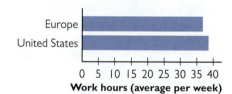

**(b) Average weekly hours**

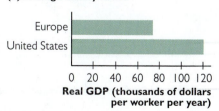

**(c) Real GDP per worker**

# ■ The Production Function

**Production function**

A relationship that shows the maximum quantity of real GDP that can be produced as the quantity of labor employed changes and all other influences on production remain the same.

The **production function** is a relationship that shows the maximum quantity of real GDP that can be produced as the quantity of labor employed changes and all other influences on production remain the same. Figure 8.1 shows a production function, which is the curve labeled *PF*.

In Figure 8.1, 100 billion labor hours can produce a real GDP of $11 trillion (at point *A*); 200 billion hours can produce a real GDP of $16 trillion (at point *B*); and 300 billion hours can produce a real GDP of $20 trillion (at point *C*).

The production function shares a feature of the *production possibilities frontier* that you studied in Chapter 3 (p. 62). Like the *PPF*, the production function is a boundary between the attainable and the unattainable. It is possible to produce at any point along the production function and beneath it in the shaded area. But it is not possible to produce at points above the production function. Those points are unattainable.

**Diminishing returns**

The tendency for each additional hour of labor employed to produce a successively smaller additional amount of real GDP.

The production function displays **diminishing returns**—each additional hour of labor employed produces a successively smaller additional amount of real GDP. The first 100 billion hours of labor produces $11 trillion of real GDP. The second 100 billion hours of labor increases real GDP from $11 trillion to $16 trillion, so the

■ **FIGURE 8.1**

The Production Function

MyEconLab Animation

The production function shows the maximum quantity of real GDP that can be produced as the quantity of labor employed changes and all other influences on production remain the same. In this example, 100 billion hours of labor can produce $11 trillion of real GDP at point A, 200 billion hours of labor can produce $16 trillion of real GDP at point B, and 300 billion hours of labor can produce $20 trillion of real GDP at point C.

The production function separates attainable combinations of labor hours and real GDP from unattainable combinations and displays diminishing returns: Each additional hour of labor produces a successively smaller additional amount of real GDP.

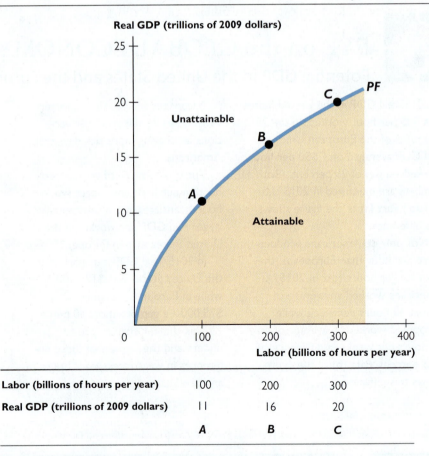

| Labor (billions of hours per year) | 100 | 200 | 300 |
|---|---|---|---|
| Real GDP (trillions of 2009 dollars) | 11 | 16 | 20 |
| | *A* | *B* | *C* |

second 100 billion hours produces only an additional $5 trillion of real GDP. The third 100 billion hours of labor increases real GDP from $16 trillion to $20 trillion, so the third 100 billion hours produces only an additional $4 trillion of real GDP.

Diminishing returns arise because the quantity of capital (and other factors of production) is fixed. As more labor is hired, the additional output produced decreases because the extra workers have less capital with which to work. For example, a forest service has three chain saws and an axe and hires three workers to clear roads and trails of fallen trees and debris during the spring thaw. Hiring a fourth worker will contribute less to the amount cleared than the amount that the third worker added, and hiring a fifth worker will add even less.

Because real GDP depends on the quantity of labor employed, potential GDP depends on the production function and the quantity of labor employed. To find potential GDP, we must understand what determines the quantity of labor employed.

## ■ The Labor Market

You've already studied the tool that we use to determine the quantity of labor employed: demand and supply. In macroeconomics, we apply the concepts of demand, supply, and market equilibrium to the economy-wide labor market.

The quantity of labor employed depends on firms' decisions about how much labor to hire (the demand for labor). It also depends on households' decisions about how to allocate time between employment and other activities (the supply of labor). And it depends on how the labor market coordinates the decisions of firms and households (labor market equilibrium). So we will study

- The demand for labor
- The supply of labor
- Labor market equilibrium

### The Demand for Labor

The **quantity of labor demanded** is the total labor hours that all the firms in the economy plan to hire during a given time period at a given real wage rate. The **demand for labor** is the relationship between the quantity of labor demanded and the real wage rate when all other influences on firms' hiring plans remain the same. The lower the real wage rate, the greater is the quantity of labor demanded.

The real wage rate is the *nominal wage rate* (the dollars per hour that people earn on average) divided by the price level (see Chapter 7, p. 182). We express the real wage rate in constant dollars—today in 2009 dollars. Think of the real wage rate as the quantity of real GDP that an hour of labor earns.

The lower the real wage rate, the greater is the quantity of labor that firms find it profitable to hire. The real wage rate influences the quantity of labor demanded because what matters to firms is not the number of dollars they pay for an hour of labor (the nominal wage rate) but how much output they must sell to earn those dollars. So firms compare the extra output that an hour of labor can produce with the real wage rate.

If an additional hour of labor produces at least as much additional output as the real wage rate, a firm hires that labor. At a small quantity of labor, an extra hour of labor produces more output than the real wage rate. But each additional hour of labor produces less additional output than the previous hour. As a firm hires more labor, eventually the extra output from an extra hour of labor equals the real wage rate. This equality determines the quantity of labor demanded at the real wage rate.

**Quantity of labor demanded**
The total labor hours that all the firms in the economy plan to hire during a given time period at a given real wage rate.

**Demand for labor**
The relationship between the quantity of labor demanded and the real wage rate when all other influences on firms' hiring plans remain the same.

***The Demand for Labor in a Soda Factory*** You might understand the demand for labor better by thinking about a single firm rather than the economy as a whole. Suppose that the money wage rate is $15 an hour and that the price of a bottle of soda is $1.50. For the soda factory, the real wage rate is a number of bottles of soda. To find the soda factory's real wage rate, divide the money wage rate by the price of its output—$15 an hour ÷ $1.50 a bottle. The real wage rate is 10 bottles of soda an hour. It costs the soda factory 10 bottles of soda to hire an hour of labor. As long as the soda factory can hire labor that produces more than 10 additional bottles of soda an hour, it is profitable to hire more labor. Only when the extra output produced by an extra hour of labor falls to 10 bottles an hour has the factory reached the profit-maximizing quantity of labor.

***Labor Demand Schedule and Labor Demand Curve*** We can represent the demand for labor as either a demand schedule or a demand curve. The table in Figure 8.2 shows part of a demand for labor schedule. It tells us the quantity of labor demanded at three different real wage rates. For example, if the real wage rate is $50 an hour (row *B*), the quantity of labor demanded is 200 billion hours a year. If the real wage rate rises to $80 an hour (row *A*), the quantity of labor demanded decreases to 100 billion hours a year. And if the real wage rate falls to $25 an hour (row *C*), the quantity of labor demanded increases to 300 billion hours a year.

Figure 8.2 shows the demand for labor curve. Points *A*, *B*, and *C* on the demand curve correspond to rows *A*, *B*, and *C* of the demand schedule.

### FIGURE 8.2

#### The Demand for Labor

MyEconLab Animation

Firms are willing to hire labor only if the labor produces more than its real wage rate. So the lower the real wage rate, the more labor firms can profitably hire and the greater is the quantity of labor demanded.

At a real wage rate of $50 an hour, the quantity of labor demanded is 200 billion hours at point *B*.

❶ If the real wage rate rises to $80 an hour, the quantity of labor demanded decreases to 100 billion hours at point *A*.

❷ If the real wage rate falls to $25 an hour, the quantity of labor demanded increases to 300 billion hours at point *C*.

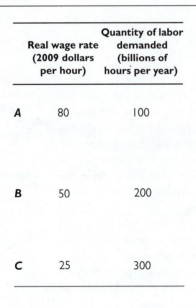

|   | Real wage rate (2009 dollars per hour) | Quantity of labor demanded (billions of hours per year) |
|---|---|---|
| A | 80 | 100 |
| B | 50 | 200 |
| C | 25 | 300 |

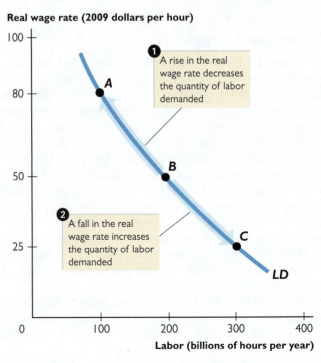

## The Supply of Labor

The **quantity of labor supplied** is the number of labor hours that all the households in the economy plan to work during a given time period at a given real wage rate. The **supply of labor** is the relationship between the quantity of labor supplied and the real wage rate when all other influences on work plans remain the same.

We can represent the supply of labor as either a supply schedule or a supply curve. The table in Figure 8.3 shows a supply of labor schedule. It tells us the quantity of labor supplied at three different real wage rates. For example, if the real wage rate is $50 an hour (row B), the quantity of labor supplied is 200 billion hours a year. If the real wage rate falls to $25 an hour (row A), the quantity of labor supplied decreases to 100 billion hours a year. And if the real wage rate rises to $75 an hour (row C), the quantity of labor supplied increases to 300 billion hours a year.

Figure 8.3 shows the supply of labor curve. It corresponds to the supply schedule, and the points A, B, and C on the supply curve correspond to the rows A, B, and C of the supply schedule.

The real wage rate influences the quantity of labor supplied because what matters to people is not the number of dollars they earn but what those dollars will buy. The quantity of labor supplied increases as the real wage rate increases for two reasons:

- Hours per person increase.
- Labor force participation increases.

**Quantity of labor supplied**
The number of labor hours that all the households in the economy plan to work during a given time period at a given real wage rate.

**Supply of labor**
The relationship between the quantity of labor supplied and the real wage rate when all other influences on work plans remain the same.

■ **FIGURE 8.3**

The Supply of Labor                                        MyEconLab Animation

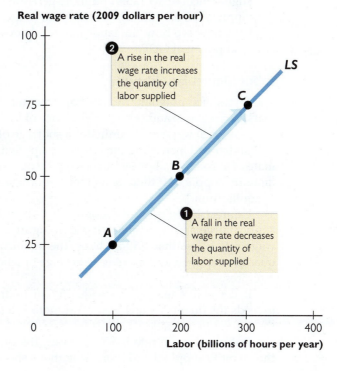

| Real wage rate (2009 dollars per hour) | Quantity of labor supplied (billions of hours per year) |
|---|---|
| C | 75 | 300 |
| B | 50 | 200 |
| A | 25 | 100 |

Households are willing to supply labor only if the real wage rate is high enough to attract them from other activities. The higher the real wage rate, the greater is the quantity of labor supplied.

At a real wage rate of $50 an hour, the quantity of labor supplied is 200 billion hours at point B.

❶ If the real wage rate falls to $25 an hour, the quantity of labor supplied decreases to 100 billion hours at point A.

❷ If the real wage rate rises to $75 an hour, the quantity of labor supplied increases to 300 billion hours at point C.

*Hours per Person* The real wage rate is the opportunity cost of taking leisure and not working. As the opportunity cost of taking leisure rises, other things remaining the same, households choose to work more. But other things don't remain the same. A higher real wage rate brings a higher income, which increases the demand for leisure and encourages less work.

So a rise in the real wage rate has two opposing effects. But for most households, the opportunity cost effect is stronger than the income effect, so a rise in the real wage rate brings an increase in the quantity of labor supplied.

*Labor Force Participation* Most people have productive opportunities outside the labor force and choose to work only if the real wage rate exceeds the value of other productive activities. For example, a parent might spend time caring for her or his child. The alternative is day care. The parent will choose to work only if he or she can earn enough per hour to pay the cost of day care and have enough left to make the work effort worthwhile. The higher the real wage rate, the more likely it is that a parent will choose to work and so the greater is the labor force participation rate.

*Other Influences on Labor Supply Decisions* Many factors other than the real wage rate influence labor supply decisions and influence the position of the labor supply curve. Income taxes and unemployment benefits are two of these factors.

The work-leisure decision depends on the *after-tax* wage rate—the wage rate actually received by the household. So, for a given wage rate, the income tax decreases the after-tax wage rate and the quantity of labor supplied decreases. The result is a decrease in the supply of labor. (The income tax rate doesn't change the demand for labor because for the employer, the cost of labor is the before-tax wage rate.)

Unemployment benefits lower the cost of searching for a job and encourage unemployed workers to take longer to find the best job available. The result is a decrease in the supply of labor.

Higher income tax rates and more generous unemployment benefits decrease the supply of labor—the labor supply curve lies farther to the left.

Let's now see how the labor market determines employment, the real wage rate, and potential GDP.

## Labor Market Equilibrium

The forces of supply and demand operate in labor markets just as they do in the markets for goods and services. The price of labor services is the real wage rate. A rise in the real wage rate eliminates a shortage of labor by decreasing the quantity demanded and increasing the quantity supplied. A fall in the real wage rate eliminates a surplus of labor by increasing the quantity demanded and decreasing the quantity supplied. If there is neither a shortage nor a surplus, the labor market is in equilibrium.

Figure 8.4(a) shows the labor market equilibrium. The demand curve and the supply curve are the same as those in Figures 8.2 and 8.3. In part (a), if the real wage rate is less than $50 an hour, the quantity of labor demanded exceeds the quantity supplied and there is a shortage of labor. In this situation, the real wage rate rises.

If the real wage rate exceeds $50 an hour, the quantity of labor supplied exceeds the quantity demanded and there is a surplus of labor. In this situation, the real wage rate falls.

If the real wage rate is $50 an hour, the quantity of labor demanded equals the quantity supplied and there is neither a shortage nor a surplus of labor. In this

■ **FIGURE 8.4**

Labor Market Equilibrium and Potential GDP                                   MyEconLab Animation

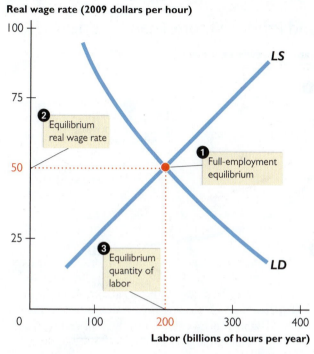

**(a) The labor market**

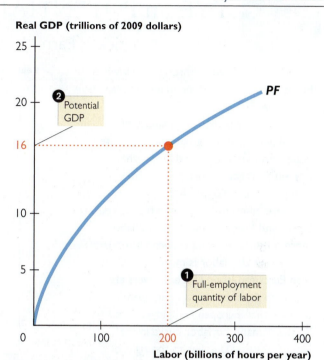

**(b) Potential GDP**

❶ Full employment occurs when the quantity of labor demanded equals the quantity of labor supplied. ❷ The equilibrium real wage rate is $50 an hour, and ❸ the equilibrium quantity of labor employed is 200 billion hours a year.

Potential GDP is the real GDP produced on the production function by the full-employment quantity of labor. ❶ The full-employment quantity of labor, 200 billion hours a year, produces a ❷ potential GDP of $16 trillion.

situation, the labor market is in equilibrium and the real wage rate remains constant. The equilibrium quantity of labor is 200 billion hours a year. When the equilibrium quantity of labor is employed, the economy is at full employment. So the full-employment quantity of labor is 200 billion hours a year.

## Full Employment and Potential GDP

When the labor market is in equilibrium, the economy is at full employment and real GDP equals potential GDP.

You've seen that the quantity of real GDP depends on the quantity of labor employed. The production function tells us how much real GDP a given amount of employment can produce. Now that we've determined the full-employment quantity of labor, we can find potential GDP.

Figure 8.4(b) shows the relationship between labor market equilibrium and potential GDP. The equilibrium quantity of labor employed in Figure 8.4(a) is 200 billion hours. The production function in Figure 8.4(b) tells us that 200 billion hours of labor produces $16 trillion of real GDP. This quantity of real GDP is potential GDP.

# EYE on POTENTIAL GDP

MyEconLab Critical Thinking Exercise

## Why Do Americans Earn More and Produce More Than Europeans?

Americans often work through lunch while Europeans take an extended lunch break. Why?

The answer is that the quantity of capital per worker is greater in the United States than in Europe, and U.S. technology, on average, is more productive than European technology.

These differences between the United States and Europe mean that U.S. labor is more productive than European labor.

Because U.S. labor is more productive than European labor, U.S. employers are willing to pay more for a given quantity of labor than European employers are. So the demand for labor curve in the United States, $LD_{US}$, lies to the right of the European demand for labor curve, $LD_{EU}$, in part (a) of the figure.

This difference in the productivity of labor also means that the U.S. production function, $PF_{US}$, lies above the European production function, $PF_{EU}$, in part (b) of the figure.

Higher income taxes and unemployment benefits in Europe mean that to induce a person to take a job, a firm in Europe must offer a higher wage rate than a firm in the United States has to offer. So the European labor supply curve, $LS_{EU}$, lies to the left of the U.S. labor supply curve, $LS_{US}$.

Equilibrium employment is greater in the United States than in Europe—Americans work longer hours—and the equilibrium real wage rate is higher in the United States than in Europe.

Potential GDP is higher in the United States than in Europe for two reasons: U.S. workers are more productive per hour of work and they work longer hours than Europeans.

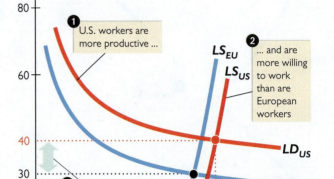

(a) Labor market in Europe and in the United States

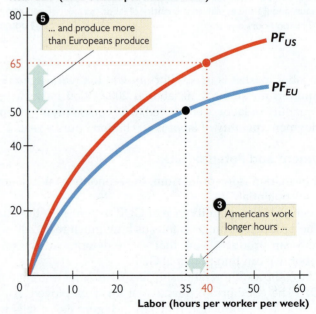

(b) Production function in Europe and in the United States

# CHECKPOINT 8.1

**Explain what determines potential GDP.**

## Practice Problem

1. Table 1 describes an economy's production function and demand for labor.

**TABLE 1**

| Quantity of labor demanded (billions of hours per year) | 0 | 1 | 2 | 3 | 4 |
|---|---|---|---|---|---|
| Real GDP (billions of 2009 dollars) | 0 | 40 | 70 | 90 | 100 |
| Real wage rate (2009 dollars per hour) | 50 | 40 | 30 | 20 | 10 |

Table 2 describes the supply of labor in this economy.

**TABLE 2**

| Quantity of labor supplied (billions of hours per year) | 0 | 1 | 2 | 3 | 4 |
|---|---|---|---|---|---|
| Real wage rate (2009 dollars per hour) | 10 | 20 | 30 | 40 | 50 |

Use the data in Tables 1 and 2 to make graphs of the labor market and production function. What are the equilibrium real wage rate and employment? What is potential GDP?

## In the News

**Tesla is recruiting**

Electric car maker Tesla is recruiting Nevadans with a high school diploma or equivalent to work in the battery gigafactory the company is building.

Source: *Reno Gazette Journal,* July 1, 2016

Explain how Tesla's huge project will influence potential GDP, employment, and the real wage rate in the United States.

## Solution to Practice Problem

1. The demand for labor is a graph of the first and last row of Table 1 and the supply of labor is a graph of the data in Table 2 (Figure 1). The production function is a graph of the first two rows of Table 1 (Figure 2).
Labor market equilibrium occurs when the real wage rate is $30 an hour and 2 billion hours of labor are employed (Figure 1). Potential GDP is the real GDP produced by the equilibrium quantity of labor (2 billion hours in Figure 1). Potential GDP is $70 billion (Figure 2).

## Solution to In the News

Potential GDP will increase. With increased capital equipment to manufacture batteries, the U.S. production function will shift upward. With no change in employment, potential GDP would increase. But Tesla's gigafactory project will increase the productivity of labor and increase the demand for labor. The increase in the demand for labor, with no change in the supply of labor, will increase the real wage rate. As the real wage rate rises, the quantity of labor supplied increases. The full-employment quantity of labor increases. Potential GDP, employment, and the real wage rate all increase.

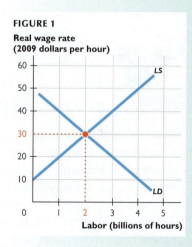

**FIGURE 1**

Real wage rate (2009 dollars per hour)

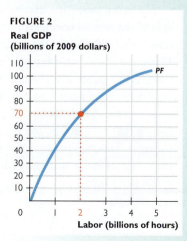

**FIGURE 2**

Real GDP (billions of 2009 dollars)

MyEconLab Concept Video

## 8.2   THE NATURAL UNEMPLOYMENT RATE

So far, we've focused on the forces that determine the real wage rate, the quantity of labor employed, and real GDP at full employment. We're now going to bring unemployment into the picture.

You learned in Chapter 6 that the BLS measures the amount of unemployment by counting the number of people who do not have a job, are willing to work, and have looked for work in the past 4 weeks. And you learned how we classify unemployment as frictional, structural, or cyclical. Finally, you learned that when the economy is at full employment, all the unemployment is frictional or structural and the unemployment rate is called the *natural unemployment rate.*

Measuring, describing, and classifying unemployment tell us a lot about it. But these activities do not *explain* the amount of unemployment that exists or why the unemployment rate changes over time and varies across economies.

Many forces interact to determine the unemployment rate. Understanding these forces is a challenging task. Economists approach this task in two steps. The first step is to understand what determines the natural unemployment rate—the unemployment rate when the economy is at full employment. The second step is to understand what makes unemployment fluctuate around the natural unemployment rate. In this chapter, we take the first of these steps. We take the second step in Chapters 13–15 when we study economic fluctuations.

# EYE on the PAST
## The Natural Unemployment Rate Over Seven Decades

If we look at the unemployment rate over the decades, we see the ups and downs of the business cycle. Most of the fluctuations are in cyclical unemployment—fluctuations around the natural unemployment rate. But the natural rate also fluctuates.

The figure shows the decade averages of the natural unemployment rate since 1950. During the 1950s and 1960s, the natural rate averaged a bit more than 5 percent. It climbed during the 1970s to more than 6 percent, and it remained high during the 1980s. During the1990s, 2000s, and 2010s, the natural unemployment rate fell to levels slightly lower than those of the 1950s and 1960s.

These changes resulted from the demographic and other influences that we describe in this section.

You will be a member of the labor force of the 2020s and the natural unemployment rate of the third decade of the 2000s will have a big effect on your job market outcome.

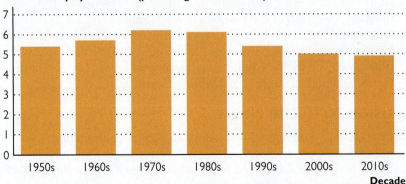

SOURCE OF DATA: Congressional Budget Office.

To understand the amount of frictional and structural unemployment that exists at the natural unemployment rate, economists focus on two fundamental causes of unemployment that cut across the frictional-structural classification. These two fundamental causes of unemployment are

- Job search
- Job rationing

## ■ Job Search

**Job search** is the activity of looking for an acceptable vacant job. Because the labor market is in a constant state of change, there are always some people who have not yet found suitable jobs and who are actively searching. The failure of businesses destroys jobs. The expansion of businesses and the startup of new businesses create jobs. As people pass through different stages of life, some enter or reenter the labor market, others leave their jobs to look for better ones, and others retire. This constant churning in the labor market means that there are always some people looking for jobs, and these people are part of the unemployed.

The amount of job search depends on a number of factors that change over time. The main ones are

- Demographic change
- Unemployment benefits
- Structural change

**Job search**
The activity of looking for an acceptable vacant job.

### Demographic Change

An increase in the proportion of the population that is of working age brings an increase in the entry rate into the labor force and an increase in the unemployment rate. This factor was important in the U.S. labor market during the 1970s. The bulge in the birth rate that occurred in the late 1940s and early 1950s increased the proportion of new entrants into the labor force during the 1970s and brought an increase in the unemployment rate.

As the birth rate declined, the bulge moved into higher age groups and the proportion of new entrants declined during the 1990s. During this period, the unemployment rate decreased.

Another source of demographic change has been an increase in the number of households with two incomes. When unemployment comes to one of these workers, it is possible, with income still flowing in, to take longer to find a new job. This factor might have increased frictional unemployment.

### Unemployment Benefits

The opportunity cost of job search influences the length of time that an unemployed person spends searching for a job. With no unemployment benefits, the opportunity cost of job search is high, and a person is likely to accept a job that is found quickly. With generous unemployment benefits, the opportunity cost of job search is low, and a person is likely to spend a considerable time searching for the ideal job.

Generous unemployment benefits are a large part of the story of high unemployment rates in Europe and some other countries such as Canada—see *Eye on the Global Economy* on p. 206.

# EYE on the GLOBAL ECONOMY
## Unemployment Benefits and the Natural Unemployment Rate

The gap between U.S. and Canadian unemployment rates provides information about the influence of unemployment benefits. The two unemployment rates followed similar cycles, but the Canadian unemployment rate exceeded the U.S. rate, which suggests that the natural unemployment rate was higher in Canada than in the United States.

Why? In 1980, Canadian unemployment benefits increased and are available to all the unemployed. In the United States only 38 percent of the unemployed receive benefits.

U.S. unemployment benefits were extended to provide a further 20 weeks of income to the unemployed during the 2008–2009 recession and this change contributed to narrowing

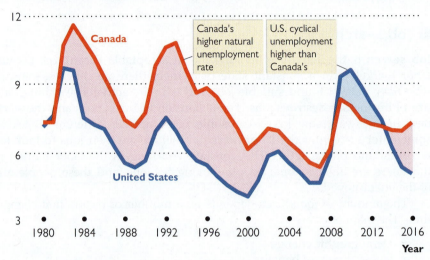

SOURCE OF DATA: Bureau of Labor Statistics and Statistics Canada.

the Canada–U.S. unemployment gap. But cyclical unemployment increased in the United States by more than in Canada and was the main source of the reversal of the gap between the two unemployment rates.

## Structural Change

Technological change influences unemployment. Sometimes it brings a structural slump, a condition in which some industries and even regions contract while other industries and regions flourish. When these events occur, labor turnover is high, job search increases, and the natural unemployment rate rises.

At other times, technological change brings a structural boom. It creates new jobs that are a good match for the people who are losing their jobs. When these events occur, labor turnover might be high, but job search decreases because new jobs are found quickly, and the natural unemployment rate falls. The Internet economy of the 1990s is an example of a structural boom. Lots of new jobs were created in every major population center, and those jobs were a good match for the skills available, so the natural unemployment rate decreased.

## ■ Job Rationing

**Job rationing**
A situation that arises when the real wage rate is above the full-employment equilibrium level.

**Job rationing** occurs when the real wage rate is above the full-employment equilibrium level. You have learned that markets allocate scarce resources by adjusting the market price to bring buying plans and selling plans into balance. You can think of the market as *rationing* scarce resources. In the labor market, the real wage rate rations employment and therefore rations jobs. Changes in the real wage rate keep the number of people seeking work and the number of jobs available in balance. But the real wage rate is not the only possible instrument for rationing jobs.

In some industries, the real wage rate is set above the full-employment equilibrium level, which brings a surplus of labor. In these labor markets, jobs are rationed by some other means.

The real wage rate might be set above the full-employment equilibrium level for three reasons:

- Efficiency wage
- Minimum wage
- Union wage

## Efficiency Wage

An **efficiency wage** is a real wage rate that is set above the full-employment equilibrium wage rate to induce a greater work effort. The idea is that if a firm pays only the going market average wage, employees have no incentive to work hard because they know that even if they are fired for slacking off, they can find a job with another firm at a similar wage rate. But if a firm pays *more* than the going market average wage, employees have an incentive to work hard because they know that if they are fired, they *cannot* expect to find a job with another firm at a similar wage rate.

**Efficiency wage**
A real wage rate that is set above the full-employment equilibrium wage rate to induce greater work effort.

Further, by paying an efficiency wage, a firm can attract the most productive workers. Also, its workers are less likely to quit their jobs, so the firm faces a lower rate of labor turnover and lower training costs. Finally, the firm's recruiting costs are lower because it always faces a steady stream of available new workers.

Paying an efficiency wage is costly, so only those firms that can't directly monitor the work effort of their employees use this device. For example, truck drivers and plant maintenance workers might receive efficiency wages. If enough firms pay an efficiency wage, the average real wage rate will exceed the full-employment equilibrium level.

## The Minimum Wage

A **minimum wage law** is a government regulation that makes hiring labor for less than a specified wage illegal. If the minimum wage is set below the equilibrium wage, the minimum wage has no effect. The minimum wage law and market forces are not in conflict. But if a minimum wage is set above the equilibrium wage, the minimum wage is in conflict with market forces and unemployment arises.

**Minimum wage law**
A government regulation that makes hiring labor for less than a specified wage illegal.

The current federal minimum wage is $7.25 an hour, and the minimum wage has a major effect in the markets for low-skilled labor. Because skill grows with work experience, teenage labor is particularly affected by the minimum wage.

## Union Wage

A **union wage** is a wage rate that results from collective bargaining between a labor union and a firm. Because a union represents a group of workers, it can usually achieve a wage rate that exceeds the level that would prevail in a competitive labor market.

**Union wage**
A wage rate that results from collective bargaining between a labor union and a firm.

For the United States, it is estimated that, on average, union wage rates are 30 percent higher than nonunion wage rates. But this estimate probably overstates the true effects of labor unions on the wage rate. In some industries, union wages are higher than nonunion wages because union members do jobs that require greater skill than nonunion jobs. In these cases, even without a union, those workers would earn a higher wage.

One way to calculate the effects of unions is to examine the wages of union and nonunion workers who do nearly identical work. For workers with similar skill levels, the union-nonunion wage difference is between 10 and 25 percent. For example, pilots who are members of the Air Line Pilots Association earn about 25 percent more than nonunion pilots with the same level of skill.

Labor unions are much more influential in Europe than in the United States. In Europe, unions not only achieve wage rates above those of a competitive market but also have broad political influence on labor market conditions.

### Job Rationing and Unemployment

Whether because of efficiency wages, a minimum wage law, or the actions of labor unions, if the real wage rate is above the full-employment equilibrium level, the natural unemployment rate increases. The above-equilibrium real wage rate decreases the quantity of labor demanded and increases the quantity of labor supplied.

Figure 8.5 illustrates job rationing and the frictional and structural unemployment it creates. The full-employment equilibrium real wage rate is $50 an hour, and the equilibrium quantity of labor is 200 billion hours a year. The existence of efficiency wages, the minimum wage, and union wages raises the economy's average real wage rate to $60 an hour. At this wage rate, the quantity of labor demanded decreases to 175 billion hours and the quantity of labor supplied increases to 240 billion hours. Firms ration jobs and choose the workers to hire on the basis of criteria such as education and previous job experience. The labor market is like a game of musical chairs in which a large number of chairs have been removed. So the quantity of labor supplied persistently exceeds the quantity demanded, and additional unemployment arises from job rationing.

■ **FIGURE 8.5**

Job Rationing Increases the Natural Unemployment Rate            MyEconLab Animation

The full-employment equilibrium real wage rate is $50 an hour. Efficiency wages, the minimum wage, and union wages put the average real wage rate above the full-employment equilibrium level—at $60 an hour.

❶ The quantity of labor demanded decreases to 175 billion hours.

❷ The quantity of labor supplied increases to 240 billion hours.

❸ A surplus of labor arises and increases the natural unemployment rate.

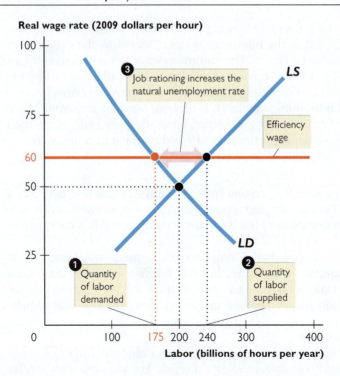

# EYE on the U.S. ECONOMY
## The Federal Minimum Wage

The *Fair Labor Standards Act* of 1938 set the federal minimum wage in the United States at 25¢ an hour. Over the years, the minimum wage has increased, and in 2016 it was $7.25 an hour. Although the minimum wage has increased, it hasn't kept up with the rising cost of living.

The figure shows the real minimum wage rate in 2009 dollars. You can see that during the late 1960s, the real minimum wage in 2009 dollars was $9 an hour. It decreased during the 1970s and 1980s and has fluctuated around an average of just under $6 an hour since the mid-1980s.

SOURCE OF DATA: Bureau of Labor Statistics.

# EYE on YOUR LIFE
## Natural Unemployment

MyEconLab Critical Thinking Exercise

You will encounter natural unemployment at many points in your life.

If you now have a job, you probably went through a spell of natural unemployment as you searched for the job.

When you graduate and look for a full-time job, you will most likely spend some more time searching for the best match for your skills and location preferences.

In today's world of rapid technological change, most of us must retool and change our jobs at least once and for many of us, more than once.

You might know an older worker who has recently lost a job and is going through the agony of figuring out what to do next.

Although natural unemployment can be painful for people who experience it, from a social perspective, it is productive. It enables scarce labor resources to be *re*-allocated to their most valuable uses.

MyEconLab Study Plan 8.2
Key Terms Quiz
Solutions Video

## CHECKPOINT 8.2

**Explain what determines the natural unemployment rate.**

## Practice Problems

During the past 50 years, Singapore has seen huge changes: rapid population growth and the introduction of newer and newer technologies. Singapore has modest unemployment benefits, no minimum wage, and weak labor unions.

1. Does Singapore's unemployment arise mainly from job search or job rationing?

2. Which of the factors listed above suggest that Singapore has a higher natural unemployment rate than the United States and which suggest that Singapore has a lower natural unemployment rate?

3. Figure 1 illustrates the labor market in an economy in which at full employment, 1,000 people a day job search. What is the equilibrium real wage rate and employment? Calculate the natural unemployment rate.

## In the News

**A mid-year burst of minimum-wage increases starts on July 1**
On July 1, the minimum wage will rise in Washington D.C., Los Angeles County, Chicago, and in cities in California, Kentucky, Maryland, and Oregon. San Francisco's minimum wage will rise to $13.00 an hour and Chicago's to $10.50.
Source: *The Wall Street Journal*, July 1, 2016

Explain why some part-time workers, low-skilled workers, and youth workers will gain and why unemployed teenagers will find it hard to get jobs.

## Solutions to Practice Problems

1. Singapore's unemployment arises mainly from job search. Of the sources of job rationing (efficiency wages, minimum wages, and union wages) only efficiency wages applies.

2. Singapore's rapid population growth and the introduction of new technologies increase the amount of job search —factors that increase the natural unemployment rate.

   Singapore has modest unemployment benefits, which limit the amount of job search, and no minimum wage and weak labor unions, which limit the amount of job rationing—factors that lower the natural unemployment rate

3. Labor market equilibrium determines the equilibrium real wage rate at $3 an hour and full employment at 3,000 workers. Unemployment is 1,000, so the labor force is 4,000 and the natural unemployment rate equals $(1,000 \div 4,000) \times 100$, or 25 percent.

## Solution to In the News

When the minimum wage rises, firms will retain those workers who produce at least as much output per hour as the minimum wage rate. Job experience helps part-time and low-skilled employees retain their jobs, but teenagers with no experience will find it hard to get jobs.

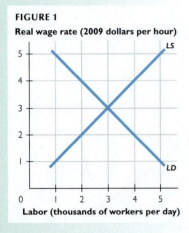

**FIGURE 1**

**Real wage rate (2009 dollars per hour)**

Labor (thousands of workers per day)

CHAPTER SUMMARY

## Key Points

**1. Explain what determines potential GDP.**

- Potential GDP is the quantity of real GDP that the full-employment quantity of labor produces.
- The production function describes the relationship between real GDP and the quantity of labor employed when all other influences on production remain the same. As the quantity of labor increases, real GDP increases.
- The quantity of labor demanded increases as the real wage rate falls, other things remaining the same.
- The quantity of labor supplied increases as the real wage rate rises, other things remaining the same.
- At full-employment equilibrium, the real wage rate makes the quantity of labor demanded equal the quantity of labor supplied.

**2. Explain what determines the natural unemployment rate.**

- The unemployment rate at full employment is the natural unemployment rate.
- Unemployment is always present because of job search and job rationing.
- Job search is influenced by demographic change, unemployment benefits, and structural change.
- Job rationing arises from an efficiency wage, the minimum wage, and a union wage.

## Key Terms

MyEconLab Key Terms Quiz

Classical macroeconomics, 192
Demand for labor, 197
Diminishing returns, 196
Efficiency wage, 207
Job rationing, 206

Job search, 205
Keynesian macroeconomics, 192
Minimum wage law, 207
Monetarist macroeconomics, 193
Potential GDP, 195

Production function, 196
Quantity of labor demanded, 197
Quantity of labor supplied, 199
Supply of labor, 199
Union wage, 207

## CHAPTER CHECKPOINT

## Study Plan Problems and Applications

Use the events in List 1, which occur in the United States one at a time, to work Problems **1** to **4**.

**LIST 1**

- Dell introduces a new supercomputer that everyone can afford.
- A major hurricane hits Florida.
- More high school graduates go to college.
- The CPI rises.
- An economic slump in the rest of the world decreases U.S. exports.

1. Sort the items into four groups: those that change the production function, those that change the demand for labor, those that change the supply of labor, and those that do not change the production function, the demand for labor, or the supply of labor. Say in which direction any changes occur.

2. Which of the events increase the equilibrium quantity of labor and which decrease it?

3. Which of the events raise the real wage rate and which lower it?

4. Which of the events increase potential GDP and which decrease it?

Use the information set out in Table 1 and Table 2 about the economy of Athabasca to work Problems **5** and **6**.

5. Calculate the quantity of labor employed, the real wage rate, and potential GDP.

6. If the labor force participation increases, explain how employment, the real wage rate, and potential GDP change.

Use the following information to work Problems **7** and **8**.

Suppose that the United States cracks down on illegal immigrants and returns millions of workers to their home countries.

7. Explain how the U.S. real wage rate, U.S. employment, and U.S. potential GDP would change.

8. In the countries to which the immigrants return, explain how employment, the real wage rate, and potential GDP would change.

9. Two island economies, Cocoa Island and Plantation Island, are identical in every respect except one. A survey tells us that at full employment, people on Cocoa Island spend 1,000 hours a day on job search, while the people on Plantation Island spend 2,000 hours a day on job search. Which economy has the greater potential GDP? Which has the higher real wage rate? And which has the higher natural unemployment rate?

10. **Where are all the workers?**
The baby boomers—people born between 1946 and 1964—are retiring and the percentage of adult Americans working or actively looking for a job is at its lowest level in nearly forty years.

Source: *U.S. News & World Report*, July 16, 2015

How would you expect the change in the labor force described in the news clip to affect potential GDP and the natural unemployment rate?

11. Read *Eye on Potential GDP* on p. 202 and then explain why potential GDP per worker per week is greater in the United States than in Europe. What could induce Europeans to work the same hours as Americans and would that close the gap between potential GDP per worker in the two economies?

**TABLE 1  PRODUCTION FUNCTION**

| Labor hours (millions) | Real GDP (millions of 2009 dollars) |
|---|---|
| 0 | 0 |
| 1 | 10 |
| 2 | 19 |
| 3 | 27 |
| 4 | 34 |
| 5 | 40 |

**TABLE 2  LABOR MARKET**

| Real wage rate (2009 dollars per hour) | Quantity of labor demanded | Quantity of labor supplied |
|---|---|---|
| | (millions of hours per year) | |
| 10 | 1 | 5 |
| 9 | 2 | 4 |
| 8 | 3 | 3 |
| 7 | 4 | 2 |
| 6 | 5 | 1 |

# Instructor Assignable Problems and Applications

MyEconLab Homework, Quiz, or Test if assigned by instructor

Use the following information to work Problems **1** and **2**.

In South Korea, real GDP per hour of labor is $22, the real wage rate is $15 per hour, and people work an average of 46 hours per week.

**1.** Draw a graph of the demand for and supply of labor in South Korea and the United States. Mark a point at the equilibrium quantity of labor per person per week and the real wage rate in each economy. Explain the difference in the two labor markets.

**2.** Draw a graph of the production functions in South Korea and the United States. Mark a point on each production function that shows potential GDP per hour of work in each economy. Explain the difference in the two production functions.

Use the following list of events that occur one at a time to work Problems **3** to **6**.

- The Middle East cuts supplies of oil to the United States.
- The New York Yankees win the World Series.
- U.S. labor unions negotiate wage hikes that affect all workers.
- A huge scientific breakthrough doubles the output that an additional hour of U.S. labor can produce.
- Migration to the United States increases the working-age population.

**3.** Sort the items into four groups: those that change the production function, those that change the demand for labor, those that change the supply of labor, and those that do not change the production function, the demand for labor, or the supply of labor. Say in which direction each change occurs.

**4.** Which of the events increase the equilibrium quantity of labor and which decrease the equilibrium quantity of labor?

**5.** Which of the events raise the real wage rate and which of the events lower the real wage rate?

**6.** Which of the events increase potential GDP and which decrease potential GDP?

Use the information set out in Table 1 and Table 2 about the economy of Nautica to work Problems **7** and **8**.

**7.** What is the quantity of labor employed, potential GDP, the real wage rate, and total labor income?

**8.** Suppose that the government introduces a minimum wage of $0.80 an hour. What is the real wage rate, the quantity of labor employed, potential GDP, and unemployment? Does the unemployment arise from job search or job rationing? Is the unemployment cyclical? Explain.

**9. Blizzard of 2016 ranks 4th among worst winter storms of past 100 years**
Millions of Americans were digging out after the Blizzard of 2016 blanketed 434,000 square miles of the mid-Atlantic and parts of the Northeast with several feet of snow. The storm, which disrupted the lives of 103 million people, ranks as the fourth worst winter storm to impact the Northeast.
Source: AccuWeather.com, January 31, 2016

Explain the effect of the Blizzard of 2016 on the economy of the mid-Atlantic and Northeast states. How did it impact the production function, the labor market, and potential GDP?

**TABLE 1   PRODUCTION FUNCTION**

| Labor (hours per day) | Real GDP (2009 dollars per year) |
|---|---|
| 0 | 0 |
| 10 | 100 |
| 20 | 180 |
| 30 | 240 |
| 40 | 280 |

**TABLE 2   LABOR MARKET**

| Real wage rate (2009 dollars per hour) | Quantity of labor demanded | Quantity of labor supplied |
|---|---|---|
| | (hours per day) | |
| 1.00 | 10 | 50 |
| 0.80 | 20 | 40 |
| 0.60 | 30 | 30 |
| 0.40 | 40 | 20 |

# Multiple Choice Quiz

1. U.S. potential GDP is the value of the goods and services produced in the United States _____.

   A. in the reference base year
   B. when the U.S. unemployment rate is zero
   C. when the U.S. economy is at full employment
   D. when the U.S. inflation rate is zero

2. The demand for labor curve shows the relationship between _____.

   A. the quantity of labor employed and firms' profits
   B. all households' willingness to work and the real wage rate
   C. the quantity of labor businesses are willing to hire and the real wage rate
   D. the labor force and the real wage rate

3. The supply of labor is the relationship between _____.

   A. the quantity of labor supplied and leisure time forgone
   B. the real wage rate and the quantity of labor supplied
   C. firms' willingness to supply jobs and the real wage rate
   D. the labor force participation rate and the real wage rate

4. Households' labor supply decisions are influenced by all of the following *except* _____.

   A. the opportunity cost of taking leisure and not working
   B. the after-tax wage rate
   C. unemployment benefits
   D. the number of full-time jobs available

5. The full-employment quantity of labor _____.

   A. increases if labor becomes more productive
   B. cannot increase because everyone who wants a job has one
   C. increases as the economy moves along its production function
   D. decreases if the income tax rate decreases

6. The natural unemployment rate _____.

   A. increases if unemployment benefits become more generous
   B. increases in a recession
   C. increases as the average age of the labor force rises
   D. decreases as firms outsource manufacturing jobs

7. Job rationing _____.

   A. increases the natural unemployment rate
   B. has no effect on the natural unemployment rate
   C. increases labor turnover as firms compete for high-quality labor
   D. decreases the demand for labor, which lowers the real wage rate

8. An efficiency wage results in all of the following *except* _____.

   A. a decrease in the rate of labor turnover
   B. an increase in the full-employment quantity of labor
   C. greater work effort
   D. an increase in the cost of monitoring work effort

Why are some nations rich and others poor?

# Economic Growth

**When you have completed your study of this chapter, you will be able to**

1 Define and calculate the economic growth rate, and explain the implications of sustained growth.

2 Explain the sources of labor productivity growth.

3 Review theories of the causes and effects of economic growth.

4 Describe policies that speed economic growth.

MyEconLab Big Picture Video

MyEconLab Concept Video

## 9.1 THE BASICS OF ECONOMIC GROWTH

**Economic growth**
A sustained expansion of production possibilities.

Some nations are rich and others poor because they have enjoyed or missed out on **economic growth**—a sustained expansion of production possibilities. Maintained over decades, rapid economic growth transforms a poor nation into a rich one. Such has been the experience of Hong Kong, South Korea, Taiwan, and some other Asian economies. Slow economic growth or the absence of growth can condemn a nation to devastating poverty. Such has been the fate of Sierra Leone, Somalia, Zambia, and much of the rest of Africa.

Economic growth is different from the rise in incomes that occurs during the recovery from a recession. Economic growth is a sustained trend, not a temporary cyclical expansion.

### ■ Calculating Growth Rates

**Economic growth rate**
The annual percentage change of real GDP.

We express the **economic growth rate** as the annual percentage change of real GDP. To calculate this growth rate, we use the formula:

$$\text{Growth rate of real GDP} \doteq \frac{\text{Real GDP in current year} - \text{Real GDP in previous year}}{\text{Real GDP in previous year}} \times 100.$$

For example, if real GDP in the current year is $8.4 trillion and if real GDP in the previous year was $8.0 trillion, then

$$\text{Growth rate of real GDP} = \frac{\$8.4 \text{ trillion} - \$8.0 \text{ trillion}}{\$8.0 \text{ trillion}} \times 100 = 5 \text{ percent.}$$

The growth rate of real GDP tells us how rapidly the total economy is expanding. This measure is useful for telling us about potential changes in the balance of economic power among nations, but it does not tell us about changes in the standard of living.

The standard of living depends on real GDP per person (also called *per capita real GDP*), which is real GDP divided by the population. So the contribution of real GDP growth to the change in the *standard of living* depends on the growth rate of real GDP per person. We use the above formula to calculate this growth rate, replacing real GDP with real GDP per person.

Suppose, for example, that in the current year, when real GDP is $8.4 trillion, the population is 202 million. Then real GDP per person in the current year is $8.4 trillion divided by 202 million, which equals $41,584. And suppose that in the previous year, when real GDP was $8.0 trillion, the population was 200 million. Then real GDP per person in that year was $8.0 trillion divided by 200 million, which equals $40,000.

Use these two values of real GDP per person with the growth formula to calculate the growth rate of real GDP per person. That is,

$$\text{Growth rate of real GDP per person} = \frac{\$41,584 - \$40,000}{\$40,000} \times 100 = 4 \text{ percent.}$$

# EYE on the PAST
## How Fast Has Real GDP per Person Grown?

If you're a middle-class American, you know what life is like in a household that spends (at least) $150 a day. Try to imagine life with only $1 a day to spend. That is the amount that a billion people in today's world struggle to live on. It is also the amount that our ancestors lived on for the first million years of human existence.

The figure shows estimates of incomes (real GDP per person) over more than a million years expressed in the value of the dollar in 2015. Real GDP per person averaged $330 a year—a bit less than $1 a day—until 1620! It rose to $400 a year when Aristotle and Plato were teaching in Athens, but slipped back during the next thousand years to $275 as the Roman Empire collapsed. When the Black Death gripped Europe in the 1340s, incomes fell to a 1-million-year low, and even when the Pilgrim Fathers began to arrive in America in

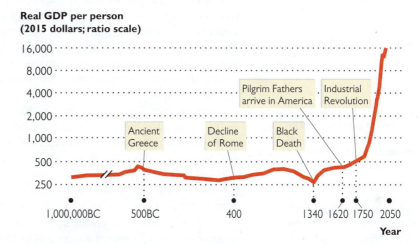

**Real GDP per person**
**(2015 dollars; ratio scale)**

SOURCE OF DATA: J. Bradford DeLong, *"Estimating World GDP, One Million B.C.–Present"* updated and converted to 2015 dollars.

the 1620s, incomes were still the same as those of Ancient Greece.

Beginning around 1750, first in England and then in Europe and the United States, an astonishing change known as the Industrial Revolution occurred. Real GDP per person

exploded. By 1850, it was twice its 1650 level. By 1950, it was more than five times its 1850 level, and by 2015, it was more than three times its 1950 level. This chapter explores the story of economic growth—of its causes and its effects.

We can also calculate the growth rate of real GDP per person by using the formula:

$$\frac{\text{Growth rate of}}{\text{real GDP per person}} = \frac{\text{Growth rate}}{\text{of real GDP}} - \frac{\text{Growth rate}}{\text{of population.}}$$

In the example you've just worked through, the growth rate of real GDP is 5 percent. The population changes from 200 million to 202 million, so

$$\text{Growth rate of population} = \frac{202\text{ million} - 200\text{ million}}{200\text{ million}} \times 100 = 1 \text{ percent.}$$

and

Growth rate of real GDP per person = 5 percent − 1 percent = 4 percent.

This formula makes it clear that real GDP per person grows only if real GDP grows faster than the population. If the growth rate of the population exceeds the growth of real GDP, then real GDP per person falls.

### ■ The Magic of Sustained Growth

Sustained growth of real GDP per person can transform a poor society into a wealthy one. The reason is that economic growth is like compound interest. If you put $100 in the bank and earn 5 percent a year interest on it, after one year, you have $105. If you leave that money in the bank for another year, you earn 5 percent interest on the original $100 and on the $5 interest that you earned last year. You are now earning interest on interest! The next year, things get even better. Then you earn 5 percent on the original $100 and on the interest earned in the first year and the second year. Your money in the bank is *growing* at a rate of 5 percent a year. Before too many years have passed, you'll have $200 in the bank. But after *how many* years?

The answer is provided by the **Rule of 70**, which states that the number of years it takes for the level of any variable to double is approximately 70 divided by the annual percentage growth rate of the variable. Using the Rule of 70, you can now calculate how many years it takes your $100 to become $200. It is 70 divided by 5, which is 14 years.

Table 9.1 shows the time it takes for real GDP per person to double at various growth rates. Growing at 1 percent a year, real GDP per person doubles in 70 years—an average human life span. But real GDP per person doubles in 35 years if its growth rate is 2 percent a year and in 10 years if its growth rate is 7 percent a year.

We can use the Rule of 70 to answer other questions about economic growth. For example, in 2015, U.S. real GDP per person was approximately 4 times that of China. China's recent growth rate of real GDP per person was 7 percent a year. If this growth rate were maintained, how long would it take China's real GDP per person to reach that of the United States in 2015? The answer, provided by the Rule of 70, is 20 years. China's real GDP per person doubles in 10 years and doubles again to 4 times its current level in another 10 years.

**Rule of 70**
The number of years it takes for the level of any variable to double is approximately 70 divided by the annual percentage growth rate of the variable.

**TABLE 9.1    GROWTH RATES**

| Growth rate (percent per year) | Years for level to double |
|---|---|
| 1 | 70 |
| 2 | 35 |
| 5 | 14 |
| 7 | 10 |
| 10 | 7 |

## EYE on the U.S. ECONOMY
### U.S. Growth Is Slowing

To achieve its transformative effects on the standard of living, the economic growth rate must be high and maintained over many years. You can see in the graph that the U.S. growth has not been maintained at a high rate.

The growth rate of potential GDP per person has slowed every decade since the 1960s with the consequence that the doubling period has blown out from 24 years in the 1960s to 125 years in the 2010s.

Why U.S. growth has slowed is not fully understood, but we will explore possible reasons in this chapter.

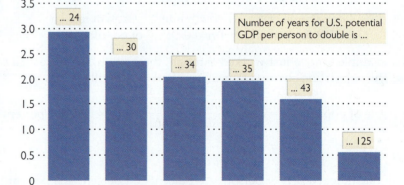

SOURCES OF DATA: Congressional Budget Office and authors' calculations.

# CHECKPOINT 9.1

MyEconLab Study Plan 9.1
Key Terms Quiz
Solutions Video

**Define and calculate the economic growth rate, and explain the implications of sustained growth.**

## Practice Problems

1. Mexico's real GDP was 13,769 billion pesos in 2014 and 14,120 billion pesos in 2015. Mexico's population growth rate in 2015 was 1.2 percent. Calculate Mexico's economic growth rate in 2015 and the growth rate of real GDP per person in Mexico in 2015.

2. Calculate the approximate number of years it will take for real GDP per person to double if an economy maintains an economic growth rate of 12 percent a year and a population growth rate of 2 percent a year.

3. Calculate the change in the number of years it will take for real GDP per person in India to double if the growth rate of real GDP per person increases from 8 percent a year to 10 percent a year.

## In the News

**China's economic growth in 2015 is slowest in 25 years**
China's growth rate slowed to an annual rate of 6.8 percent in the fourth quarter of 2015, down from 7.3 percent in 2014.

Source: *The Wall Street Journal*, January 19, 2016

If China's growth rate has slowed from 9 percent a year and remains at 6.8 percent a year, how many additional years will it take for China's real GDP to double?

## Solutions to Practice Problems

1. Mexico's economic growth rate in 2015 was 2.5 percent. The economic growth rate equals the percentage change in real GDP:
   [(Real GDP in 2015 − Real GDP in 2014) ÷ Real GDP in 2014] × 100, which is
   [(14,120 billion − 13,769 billion) ÷ 13,769 billion] × 100, or 2.5 percent.
   The growth rate of real GDP per person equals 1.3 percent.
   Growth rate of real GDP per person equals (Growth rate of real GDP − Population growth rate), which is (2.5 percent − 1.2 percent), or 1.3 percent.

2. It will take 7 years for real GDP per person to double. The growth rate of real GDP per person equals the economic growth rate minus the population growth rate. Real GDP per person grows at 12 percent minus 2 percent, which is 10 percent a year. The Rule of 70 tells us that the level of a variable that grows at 10 percent a year will double in 70 ÷ 10 years, or 7 years.

3. Two years. The Rule of 70 tells us that a variable that grows at 8 percent a year will double in 70 ÷ 8 years, which is approximately 9 years. By increasing its growth rate to 10 percent a year, the variable will double in 7 years.

## Solution to In the News

With a growth rate of 9 percent a year, real GDP per person will double in 8 years (70 ÷ 9). If the growth rate is maintained at 6.8 percent a year, real GDP per person will double in 10 years (70 ÷ 6.8)—taking an additional 2 years.

## 9.2   LABOR PRODUCTIVITY GROWTH

Real GDP grows when the quantities of the factors of production grow or when persistent advances in technology make them increasingly productive. To understand what determines the growth rate of real GDP, we must understand what determines the growth rates of the factors of production and the rate of increase in their productivity. You're going to see how saving and investment determine the growth rate of physical capital and how the growth of physical capital and human capital and advances in technology interact to determine the economic growth rate.

We are interested in real GDP growth because it contributes to improvements in our standard of living. But our standard of living improves only if we produce more goods and services with each hour of labor. So our main concern is to understand the forces that make our labor more productive. Let's start by defining labor productivity.

### ■ Labor Productivity

**Labor productivity**
The quantity of real GDP produced by one hour of labor.

**Labor productivity** is the quantity of real GDP produced by one hour of labor. It is calculated by using the formula:

$$\text{Labor productivity} = \frac{\text{Real GDP}}{\text{Aggregate hours}}.$$

For example, if real GDP is $8,000 billion and if aggregate hours are 200 billion, then we can calculate labor productivity as

$$\text{Labor productivity} = \frac{\$8,000 \text{ billion}}{200 \text{ billion hours}} = \$40 \text{ per hour.}$$

When labor productivity grows, real GDP per person grows. So the growth in labor productivity is the basis of the rising standard of living. What makes labor productivity grow? We'll answer this question by considering the influences on labor productivity growth under two broad headings:

- Saving and investment in physical capital
- Expansion of human capital and discovery of new technologies

These two broad influences on labor productivity growth interact and are the sources of the extraordinary growth in productivity during the past 200 years. Although they interact, we'll begin by looking at each on its own.

### ■ Saving and Investment in Physical Capital

Saving and investment in physical capital increase the amount of capital per worker and increase labor productivity. Labor productivity took a dramatic upturn when the amount of capital per worker increased during the Industrial Revolution. Production processes that use hand tools can create beautiful objects, but production methods that use large amounts of capital per worker, such as auto plant assembly lines, enable workers to be much more productive. The accumulation of capital on farms and building sites; in textile factories, iron foundries and steel mills, coal mines, chemical plants, and auto plants; and at banks and insurance companies added incredibly to the productivity of our labor.

A strong and experienced farm worker of 1830, using a scythe, could harvest 3 acres of wheat a day. A farm worker of 1831, using a mechanical reaper, could harvest 15 acres a day. And a farm worker of today, using a combine harvester, can harvest and thresh hundreds of acres a day.

The next time you see a movie set in the old West, look carefully at how little capital there is. Try to imagine how productive you would be in such circumstances compared with your productivity today.

## Capital Accumulation and Diminishing Marginal Returns

Although saving and investment in additional capital is a source of labor productivity growth, without the expansion of human capital and technological change, it would not bring sustained economic growth. Eventually growth would slow and most likely stop. The reason is a fundamental fact about capital known as the **law of diminishing marginal returns**, which states

> **If the quantity of capital is small, an increase in capital brings a large increase in production; and if the quantity of capital is large, an increase in capital brings a small increase in production.**

This law applies to all factors of production, not only to capital, and is the reason why the demand for labor curve slopes downward (see Chapter 8, p. 198).

You can see why the law of diminishing marginal returns applies to capital by thinking about how your own productivity is influenced by the capital you own. When you got your first computer your small quantity of capital increased and your productivity increased enormously. You most likely don't have two computers, but if you do, the productivity boost from your second computer was much smaller than that from the first. If you don't have two computers, one of the reasons is that you doubt it would be worth the expense because it would contribute such a small amount to your labor productivity.

*Farm labor productivity increased from harvesting 3 acres per day in 1830…*

*to harvesting hundreds of acres per day in the twenty-first century.*

**Productivity curve**
The relationship that shows how real GDP per hour of labor changes as the quantity of capital per hour of labor changes.

### Illustrating the Law of Diminishing Marginal Returns

Figure 9.1 illustrates the relationship between capital and productivity. The curve *PC* is a **productivity curve**, which shows how real GDP per hour of labor changes as the quantity of capital per hour of labor changes.

In Figure 9.1, when the quantity of capital (measured in real dollars) increases from $40 to $80 per hour of labor, real GDP per hour of labor increases from $30 to $50, a $20 or 67 percent increase. But when the quantity of capital increases from $180 to $220 per hour of labor, the same $40 increase as before, real GDP per hour of labor increases from $80 to $84, only a $4 or 5 percent increase. If capital per hour of labor keeps increasing, labor productivity increases by ever smaller amounts and eventually stops rising.

### ■ Expansion of Human Capital and Discovery of New Technologies

The expansion of human capital and the discovery of new technologies have a profoundly different effect on labor productivity than capital accumulation has. They don't display diminishing marginal returns.

***Expansion of Human Capital***  Human capital—the accumulated skill and knowledge of people—comes from three sources:

1. Education and training
2. Job experience
3. Health and diet

---

■ **FIGURE 9.1**

The Effects of an Increase in Capital                    MyEconLab Animation

---

When workers are equipped with more capital, they become more productive. The productivity curve *PC* shows how an increase in capital per hour of labor increases real GDP per hour of labor.

❶ When the quantity of capital per hour of labor increases from a low $40 to $80, real GDP per hour of labor increases by $20.

❷ When the quantity of capital per hour of labor increases from a high $180 to $220, real GDP per hour of labor increases by $4.

An equal-size increase in capital per hour of labor brings a diminishing increase in output, the greater is the quantity of capital.

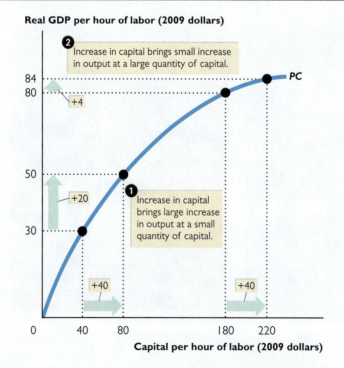

A hundred years ago, most people attended school for around eight years. A hundred years before that, most people had no formal education at all. Today, 90 percent of Americans complete high school and more than 60 percent go to college or university. Our ability to read, write, and communicate effectively contributes enormously to our productivity.

The education of thousands of scientists, engineers, mathematicians, biologists, computer programmers, and people equipped with a host of other specialist skills has made huge contributions to labor productivity and to the advance in technology.

While formal education is productive, school is not the only place where people acquire human capital. We also learn from on-the-job experience—from *learning by doing*. One carefully studied example illustrates the importance of learning by doing. Between 1941 and 1944 (during World War II), U.S. shipyards produced 2,500 Liberty Ships—cargo ships built to a standardized design. In 1941, it took 1.2 million person-hours to build a ship. By 1942, it took 600,000, and by 1943, it took only 500,000. Not much change occurred in the physical capital employed during these years, but an enormous amount of human capital was accumulated. Thousands of workers and managers learned from experience and their productivity more than doubled in two years.

Strong, healthy, well-nourished workers are much more productive than those who lack good nutrition, healthcare, and opportunties to exercise. This fact creates a virtuous circle. Improved healthcare, diet, and exercise increase labor productivity; and increased labor productivity brings the increased incomes that make these health improvements possible.

The expansion of human capital is the most fundamental source of economic growth because it directly increases labor productivity and is the source of the discovery of new technologies.

*Production using 1950s technology.*

***Discovery of New Technologies*** The growth of physical capital and the expansion of human capital have made large contributions to economic growth, but the discovery of new technologies has made an even greater contribution.

The development of writing, one of the most basic human skills, was the source of some of the earliest productivity gains. The ability to keep written records made it possible to reap ever-larger gains from specialization and trade. Imagine how hard it would be to do any kind of business if all the accounts, invoices, and agreements existed only in people's memories.

Later, the development of mathematics laid the foundation for the eventual extension of knowledge in physics, chemistry, and biology. This base of scientific knowledge was the foundation for the technological advances of the Industrial Revolution 200 years ago and of today's Information Revolution.

Since the Industrial Revolution, technological change has become a part of everyday life. Firms routinely conduct research to develop technologies that are more productive, and partnerships between business and the universities are commonplace in fields such as biotechnology and electronics.

## Illustrating the Effects of Human Capital and Technological Change

Figure 9.2 illustrates the effects of the expansion of human capital and the discovery of new technologies and labor productivity: They shift the *productivity curve* upward. In the figure, these influences shift the productivity curve from $PC_0$ to $PC_1$. Imagine that $PC_0$ is the productivity curve in 1960 and $PC_1$ is the productivity curve for 2015. With capital of \$180 per hour of labor, workers could

*Production using 2015 technology.*

■ **FIGURE 9.2**

The Effects of Human Capital and Technological Change                MyEconLab Animation

When human capital expands or technology advances, labor becomes more productive—a given amount of capital per hour of labor can produce more real GDP per hour of labor.

Here, with the technology of 1960 on $PC_0$, $180 of capital per hour of labor can produce $40 of goods and services—real GDP per hour of labor.

With the technology of 2015 on $PC_1$, the same $180 of capital per hour of labor can produce $80 of goods and services—real GDP per hour of labor.

The expansion of human capital and the discovery of new technologies shift the productivity curve upward and are not subject to diminishing marginal returns.

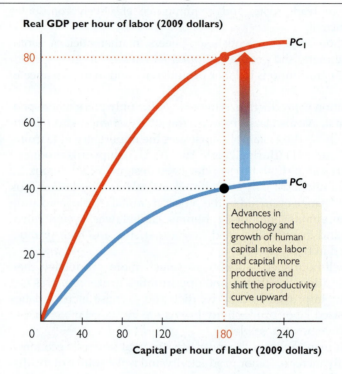

produce $80 of real GDP per hour of labor in 2015. If workers had been equipped with the same amount of capital but with the technology of 1960, they would have produced only $40 of real GDP per hour of labor. The upward shift of the productivity curve illustrates the fact that labor and capital become more productive at each quantity of capital per hour of labor. Capital is still subject to diminishing marginal returns but the overall level of productivity is higher with expanded human capital and more productive technologies.

■ **Combined Influences Bring Labor Productivity Growth**

To reap the benefits of technological change—to use new technologies to make labor productivity grow—capital must increase. Some of the most powerful and far-reaching technologies are embodied in human capital—for example, language, writing, mathematics, physics, biology, and engineering. But most technologies are embodied in physical capital. For example, to increase the productivity of transportation workers by using the discovery of the internal combustion engine, millions of horse-drawn carriages had to be replaced by automobiles and trucks; more recently, to increase the labor productivity of office workers by using the discovery of computerized word processing, millions of typewriters had to be replaced by computers and printers.

Figure 9.3 shows how the combined effects of capital accumulation, the expansion of human capital, and the discovery of new technologies bring labor productivity growth. In 1960, the productivity curve is $PC_0$, workers have $80 of capital per hour and produce $25 of real GDP per hour. By 2015, capital has increased to $180 per hour. With no expansion of human capital or technological

■ **FIGURE 9.3**

How Labor Productivity Grows                                   MyEconLab Animation

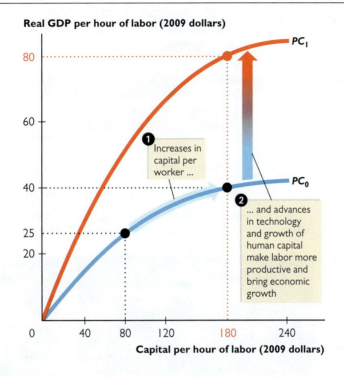

**Real GDP per hour of labor (2009 dollars)**

Increases in capital per worker ...

... and advances in technology and growth of human capital make labor more productive and bring economic growth

**Capital per hour of labor (2009 dollars)**

In 1960, workers had $80 of capital per hour of labor and produced real GDP per hour of $25 on $PC_0$.

❶ When the quantity of capital increased from $80 per hour of labor in 1960 to $180 per hour of labor in 2015, real GDP per hour of labor increased from $25 to $40 along $PC_0$.

❷ The expansion of human capital and discovery of new technologies shifted the productivity curve upward and increased real GDP per hour of labor from $40 to $80.

advance, real GDP per hour of labor would have increased to $40. But with the human capital and technology of 2015, output per hour increases to $80.

You've now seen what makes labor productivity grow. *Eye on the U.S. Economy* on p. 226 looks at the quantitative importance of the sources of growth since 1960. Real GDP grows because labor becomes more productive and also because the *quantity of labor* increases. Figure 9.4 summarizes the sources of economic growth and shows how the growth in labor productivity together with the growth in the quantity of labor bring real GDP growth.

■ **FIGURE 9.4**

The Sources of Economic Growth                                MyEconLab Animation

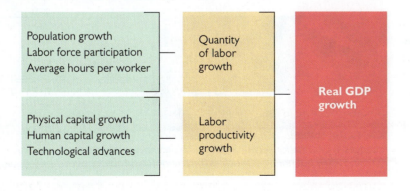

Population growth
Labor force participation
Average hours per worker

Physical capital growth
Human capital growth
Technological advances

Quantity of labor growth

Labor productivity growth

**Real GDP growth**

Real GDP depends on the quantity of labor and labor productivity.

The quantity of labor depends on the population, the labor force participation rate, and the average hours per worker.

Labor productivity depends on the amounts of physical capital and human capital and the state of technology.

Growth in the quantity of labor and growth in labor productivity bring real GDP growth.

# EYE on the U.S. ECONOMY

## U.S. Labor Productivity Growth Since 1960

The figure shows how labor productivity has grown since 1960. It also shows the contributions to productivity growth of advances in technology (the blue bars) and increases in physical capital and human capital (the red bars).

You can see that labor productivity growth during the 1960s was around double its later rate. Growth picked up a bit in the 1980s and 1990s and slowed again after 2007.

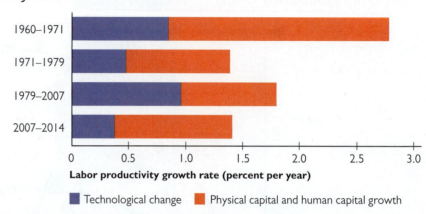

SOURCE OF DATA: Penn World Table 8.1 by Robert C. Feenstra, Robert Inklaar and Marcel P. Timmer, Congressional Budget Office, and authors' calculations.

## The Booming Sixties

Plastics, the laser, the computer, the transistor, the space race, the interstate highway system, the shopping mall, and passenger jet were among the technological advances that brought extraordinary labor productivity growth during the 1960s.

*Passenger jets and the construction of thousands of miles of interstate highways were among the technological advances that increased labor productivity during the 1960s.*

## The Stagnant Seventies

An oil price hike and oil embargo as well as higher taxes and expanded regulation slowed productivity growth during the 1970s and the higher cost of energy diverted the focus of technological change toward saving energy rather than increasing labor productivity.

*An embargo on oil exports to the United States and a higher cost of energy as well as tax hikes contributed to the productivity growth slowdown of the 1970s.*

## The Information Age

The Internet has transformed our lives and unlocking the human genome has opened the possibility of dramatic advances in healthcare. But the information age increase in labor productivity is lower than that of the 1960s; and after 2007, global financial turmoil lowered its rate to that of the stagnant 1970s.

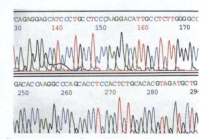

*Advances in information technologies and biotechnologies increased productivity during the 1990s and 2000s but not by as much as the technological advances of the 1960s did.*

**CHECKPOINT 9.2**

MyEconLab Study Plan 9.2
Key Terms Quiz
Solutions Video

Explain the sources of labor productivity growth.

## Practice Problems

Use the data in Table 1 to work Problems **1** and **2**.

**TABLE 1**

| Item | 2015 | 2016 |
|------|------|------|
| **Aggregate labor hours** (billions) | 25.0 | 25.6 |
| **Real GDP** (billions of 2009 dollars) | 1,000 | 1,050 |

1.  Calculate the growth rate of real GDP in 2016.
2.  Calculate labor productivity in 2015 and 2016, and the growth rate of labor productivity in 2016.

## In the News

**Labor productivity mixed**
The BLS reported the following data for the first quarter of 2016: In the nonfarm sector, output increased 0.9 percent as aggregate hours increased by 1.5 percent; in the manufacturing sector, output increased 0.6 percent as aggregate hours decreased by 0.7 percent.

Source: Productivity and Costs, Bureau of Labor Statistics, June 7, 2016

As aggregate hours and output changed, how did labor productivity in each sector change? In which sector was growth in labor productivity greater?

## Solutions to Practice Problems

1.  The growth rate of real GDP in 2016 was 5 percent. The growth rate equals [($1,050 billion − $1,000 billion) ÷ $1,000 billion] × 100 = 5 percent.
2.  Labor productivity is $40.00 an hour in 2015 and $41.02 an hour in 2016.

    Labor productivity equals real GDP divided by aggregate labor hours.

    In 2015, labor productivity was ($1,000 billion ÷ 25 billion) or $40.00 per hour of labor. In 2016, labor productivity was ($1,050 billion ÷ 25.6 billion) or $41.02 per hour of labor.

    The growth rate of labor productivity in 2016 was 2.55 percent.

    Labor productivity growth rate was [($41.02 − $40.00) ÷ $40.00] × 100 or 2.55 percent.

## Solution to In the News

In the nonfarm sector, output increased by less than the increase in aggregate hours, so labor productivity decreased. Output growth in manufacturing was less than that in the nonfarm sector, but aggregate hours decreased in manufacturing, so labor productivity increased. Because labor productivity increased in manufacturing and decreased in the nonfarm sector, labor productivity growth was greater in manufacturing.

**MyEconLab** Concept Video

## 9.3 CAUSES AND EFFECTS OF ECONOMIC GROWTH

You've seen that real GDP grows when labor productivity and the quantity of labor grow. You've also seen that labor productivity grows when saving and investment increase physical capital, when education and on-the-job training expand human capital, and when research leads to the discovery of new technologies. But what *causes* saving and investment in new capital, the expansion of human capital, the discovery of new technologies, and population growth? Economists have been trying to answer this question and understand why and how poor countries become rich and rich countries become richer since the time of Adam Smith in the eighteenth century. We'll look at two sets of ideas: old and new.

### ■ Old Growth Theory

**Classical growth theory**
The theory that the clash between an exploding population and limited resources will eventually bring economic growth to an end.

An old growth theory remains relevant today because some people believe that it might turn out to be correct. It is called **classical growth theory**, and it predicts that a clash between an exploding population and limited resources will eventually bring economic growth to an end. According to classical growth theory, labor productivity growth is temporary. When labor productivity rises and lifts real GDP per person above the subsistence level, which is the minimum real income needed to maintain life, a population explosion occurs. Eventually, the population grows so large that capital per worker and labor productivity fall and real GDP per person returns to the subsistence level.

Adam Smith, Thomas Robert Malthus, and David Ricardo, the leading economists of the late eighteenth and early nineteenth centuries, proposed this theory, but the view is most closely associated with Malthus and is sometimes called the *Malthusian theory*. It is also sometimes called the Doomsday theory.

Many people today are Malthusians. They say that if today's global population of 7 billion explodes to 11 billion by 2200, we will run out of many natural resources and the population will grow faster than the quantity of capital so labor productivity will fall and we will return to the primitive standard of living that was experienced before the Industrial Revolution. (You can see in *Eye on the Past* on p. 217 that for most of human history, people did live on the brink of subsistence.) We must act, say the Malthusians, to contain the population growth. This dismal implication led to economics being called the *dismal science*.

### ■ New Growth Theory

**New growth theory**
The theory that our unlimited wants will lead us to ever greater productivity and perpetual economic growth.

**New growth theory** predicts that our unlimited wants will lead us to ever greater productivity and perpetual economic growth. According to new growth theory, real GDP per person grows because of the choices people make in the pursuit of profit. Paul Romer of Stanford University developed this theory during the 1980s, building on ideas developed by Joseph Schumpeter during the 1930s and 1940s.

#### Choices and Innovation

The new growth theory emphasizes three facts about market economies:

- Human capital expands because of choices.
- Discoveries result from choices.
- Discoveries bring profit, and competition destroys profit.

*Human Capital Expansion and Choices*  People decide how long to remain in school, what to study, and how hard to study. And when they graduate from school, people make more choices about job training and on-the-job learning. All these choices govern the speed at which human capital expands.

*Discoveries and Choices*  When people discover a new product or technique, they consider themselves lucky. They are right, but chance does not determine the pace at which new discoveries are made—and at which technology advances. It depends on how many people are looking for a new technology and how intensively they are looking.

*Discoveries and Profits*  Profit is the spur to technological change. The forces of competition squeeze profits, so to increase profit, people constantly seek either lower-cost methods of production or new and better products for which people are willing to pay a higher price. Inventors can maintain a profit for several years by taking out a patent or copyright, but eventually a new discovery is copied and profits disappear.

Two other facts play a key role in the new growth theory:

- Many people can use discoveries at the same time.
- Physical activities can be replicated.

*Discoveries Used by All*  Once a profitable new discovery has been made, everyone can use it. For example, when Marc Andreeson created Mosaic, the Web browser that led to the creation of Netscape Navigator and Microsoft's Internet Explorer, everyone who was interested in navigating the Internet had access to a new and more efficient tool. One person's use of a Web browser does not prevent others from using it. This fact means that as the benefits of a new discovery spread, free resources become available. These resources are free because nothing is given up when an additional person uses them. They have a zero opportunity cost.

*Replicating Activities*  Production activities can be replicated. For example, there might be 2, 3, or 53 identical firms making fiber-optic cable by using an identical assembly line and production technique. If one firm increases its capital and output, that *firm* experiences diminishing returns. But the economy can increase its capital and output by adding another identical fiber cable factory, and the *economy* does not experience diminishing returns.

The assumption that capital does not experience diminishing returns is the central novel proposition of the new growth theory. The implication of this simple and appealing idea is astonishing. As capital accumulates, labor productivity grows indefinitely as long as people devote resources to expanding human capital and introducing new technologies.

## Perpetual Motion

Economic growth is like the perpetual motion machine in Figure 9.5. Growth is driven by insatiable wants that lead us to pursue profit and innovate. New and better products result from this process; new firms start up, and old firms go out of business. As firms start up and die, jobs are created and destroyed. New and better jobs lead to more leisure and more consumption. But our insatiable wants are still there, so the process continues—wants, profit incentives, innovation, and new products. The economic growth rate depends on the ability and the incentive to innovate.

**FIGURE 9.5**

A Perpetual Motion Machine

MyEconLab Animation

❶ People want a higher standard of living and are spurred by ❷ profit incentives to make the ❸ innovations that lead to ❹ new and better techniques and new and better products, which in turn lead to ❺ the birth of new firms and the death of some old firms, ❻ new and better jobs, and ❼ more leisure and more consumption goods and services. The result is ❽ a higher standard of living. But people want a yet higher standard of living, and the growth process continues.

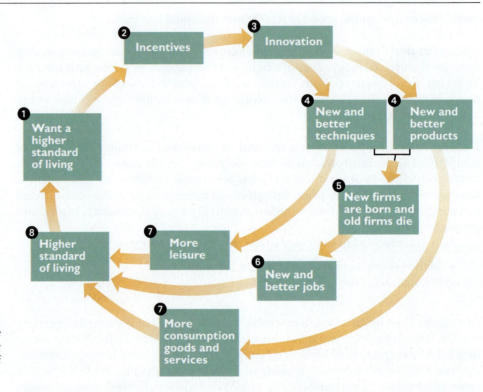

Based on a similar figure in *These Are the Good Old Days: A Report on U.S. Living Standards,* Federal Reserve Bank of Dallas 1993 Annual Report.

## ■ Economic Growth and the Distribution of Income

Does the gap between high and low incomes widen or narrow as real GDP grows? And what determines the long-term level and trends of income inequality? Economist Simon Kuznets posed these questions in the 1950s. He remarked that getting the answers was hampered by a scarcity of data and strongly held opinions. Over the years since the 1950s, more data have become available, but strongly held opinions continue to get in the way of clear thinking.

### The Data

Starting in the early 1980s, income inequality increased in a process that has been called the Great Divergence. The share of total income received by the top 1 percent of Americans moved up from 8 percent in 1980 to 18 percent in 2014. A similar trend is found in many other developed economies. Correspondingly, the income shares of lower income groups decreased.

The Great Divergence is the reverse of the Great Compression that preceded it. From 1913 to 1980, the income share of the top 1 percent *decreased* from 18 percent to 8 percent. Falling income inequality was the only trend known to Kuznets. His data showed that between 1880 and 1950, the share of total income going to the top 5 percent shrank from 31 percent to 20 percent in America and from 46 percent to 24 percent in Britain.

*Eye on the U.S. Economy* on p. 231 provides a striking perspective on these two contrasting episodes.

# EYE on the U.S. ECONOMY
## The Changing Shares in the Gains from Economic Growth

A common cry in recent years is that the economy is failing middle-class America. The rich are getting richer and the rest are standing still. Is this description accurate? If it is, the gains from economic growth have gone mainly to the rich.

To check this claim, we need to look at the incomes of the richest and poorest people and see how they have changed over the years. That's what the two figures do. They show the levels of income (per person) in different income groups as a percentage of incomes in 1970 (Figure 1) and 1929 (Figure 2).

Starting the story in 1970, Figure 1 shows that for about 10 years, the incomes of the rich (the top 1 percent) grew at a similar rate to those of other groups (the next top 19 percent and the bottom 20 percent).

Then, in 1983, the incomes of the top 1 percent started to outpace those of others. By 2007, the incomes of the top 1 percent were 5 times their 1970 level, of the next top 19 percent were double, and of the bottom 20 percent were only 1.8 times higher. And the bottom 20 percent made no progress at all from 1999 through 2014. It seems that there was indeed a Great Divergence.

Figure 2 tells a different story. From 1929 to 1970, while the incomes of 99 percent of people were rising to 3 times their 1929 level, those of the top 1 percent stagnated. When the incomes of the top 1 percent increased in the Great Divergence of Figure 1, they increased in a Great Convergence in Figure 2.

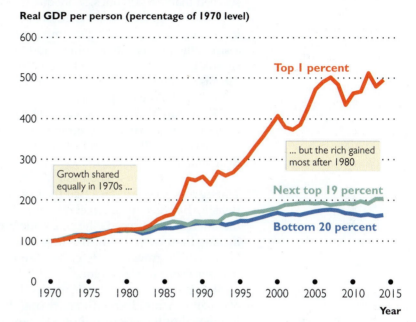

**Real GDP per person (percentage of 1970 level)**

Top 1 percent

... but the rich gained most after 1980

Growth shared equally in 1970s ...

Next top 19 percent

Bottom 20 percent

**Figure 1  The Unequal Shares Since 1980**

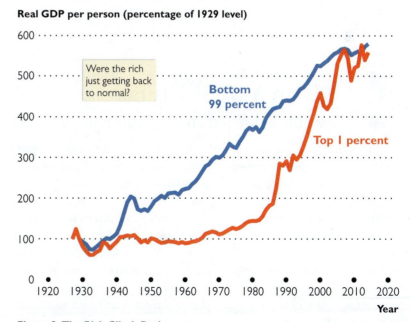

**Real GDP per person (percentage of 1929 level)**

Were the rich just getting back to normal?

Bottom 99 percent

Top 1 percent

**Figure 2  The Rich Climb Back**

SOURCES OF DATA: Bureau of Economic Analysis, U.S. Census Bureau, World Wealth and Income Database, and authors' calculations.

### The Explanations

Kuznets explained the decrease in inequality as incomes grow as resulting from market forces in a dynamic economy. Everyone is free to create a business. Some succeed and some fail. A greater number of hungry low-income entrepreneurs succeed than do rich ones, so inequality shrinks.

Paul Krugman says the Kuznets explanation of a compression driven by market forces does not fit the timing and that it was progressive income taxation, a strengthening of labor unions, and World War II wage and price controls that shrank the gap between the top and bottom earners. But timing poses a problem for this policy-induced explanation. The largest convergence occurred in the late 1930s, well before the political events that are claimed to have caused it.

Krugman also says the Great Divergence was caused by lower taxes on the rich, erosion of welfare programs, a decline in union membership, and soaring executive pay, all fostered by conservative economic policies initiated by Ronald Reagan.

French economist Thomas Piketty, the author of the best selling *Capital in the Twenty-First Century*, says that the Great Divergence is a consequence of the relationship between the interest rate, $r$, and the economic growth rate, $g$. He says that the interest rate exceeds the economic growth rate—$r > g$. The wealthy get their income from capital, which grows at rate $r$. The rest of us get our incomes from labor, which grows at rate $g$. Because $r > g$, the incomes of the rich grow faster than everyone else's income.

For Piketty, no automatic mechanism works against the steady concentration of wealth. A rapid growth spurt (rapid technological change) counters the rise in inequality temporarily. But only government redistribution can avoid rising inequality.

Economists do not yet have sound answers to the questions Simon Kuznets posed 60 years ago. We don't know enough to say where inequality is heading.

## EYE on YOUR LIFE
MyEconLab Critical Thinking Exercise
### How You Influence and Are Influenced by Economic Growth

Many of the choices that you make affect your personal economic growth rate—the pace of expansion of your own standard of living. And these same choices, in combination with similar choices made by millions of other people, have a profound effect on the economic growth of the nation and the world.

The most important of these choices right now is your choice to increase your human capital. By being in school, you have decided to expand your human capital.

You will continue to expand your human capital long after you finish school as your earning power rises with on-the-job experience. You might even decide to return to school at a later stage in your life.

A choice that will become increasingly important later in your life is to accumulate a retirement fund. This choice provides not only a source of income for you when you eventually retire but also financial resources that firms can use to finance the expansion of physical capital.

Not only do your choices influence economic growth; economic growth also has a big influence on you—on how you earn your income and on the standard of living that your income makes possible.

Because of economic growth, the jobs available today are more interesting and less dangerous and strenuous than those of 100 years ago; and jobs are hugely better paid. But for many of us, economic growth means that we must accept change and be ready to learn new skills and get new jobs.

## CHECKPOINT 9.3

MyEconLab Study Plan 9.3
Key Terms Quiz
Solutions Video

**Review theories of the causes and effects of economic growth.**

## Practice Problems

1. What is the classical growth theory and why does it predict that economic growth will eventually end?

2. What is the driving force of economic growth according to new growth theory? Why does it predict that economic growth will never end?

## In the News

**Graphene batteries may slash your phone recharge time to 15 minutes**
The world's first graphene battery pack puts more power in a smartphone and recharges in 13 to 15 minutes. Graphene also makes flexible screens possible, improves heart rate and fingerprint sensors, and holds the promise to revolutionize batteries for electric cars.

Source: *Digital Trends*, July 11, 2016

Graphene is a new material that can be 1 atom thick. Which of the growth theories that you've studied in this chapter is best supported by this news clip?

## Solutions to Practice Problems

1. The classical growth theory predicts that labor productivity growth is temporary: When labor productivity increases, real GDP per person increases and because it exceeds the real income needed to maintain life, a population explosion occurs. The population becomes so large that capital per worker and labor productivity decrease and real GDP per person returns to its subsistence level.

2. The driving force of economic growth according to new growth theory is a persistent pursuit of profit that is the incentive to innovate along with an absence of diminishing returns. New growth theory predicts that economic growth will never end because our unlimited wants will lead us to make choices that will bring ever-greater productivity and perpetual economic growth.

## Solution to In the News

The news clip describes an event that supports the new growth theory. According to this theory, real GDP per person grows because of the choices people make in the pursuit of profit. The perpetual pursuit of profit leads to innovations (graphene and its application to battery technology) that increase labor productivity and increase profit. The perpetual pursuit of profit through innovation will bring persistent economic growth.

MyEconLab Concept Video

## 9.4 ACHIEVING FASTER GROWTH

Why did it take more than a million years of human life before economic growth began? Why are some countries even today still barely growing? Why don't all societies save and invest in new capital, expand human capital, and discover and apply new technologies on a scale that brings rapid economic growth? What actions can governments take to encourage growth?

### ■ Preconditions for Economic Growth

The main reason economic growth is either absent or slow is that some societies lack the incentive system that encourages growth-producing activities. One of the fundamental preconditions for creating the incentives that lead to economic growth is economic freedom.

### Economic Freedom

**Economic freedom** is present when people are able to make personal choices, their private property is protected by the rule of law, and they are free to buy and sell in markets. The rule of law, an efficient legal system, and the ability to enforce contracts are essential foundations for creating economic freedom. Impediments to economic freedom are corruption in the courts and government bureaucracy; barriers to trade, such as import bans; high tax rates; stringent regulations on business, such as health, safety, and environmental regulation; restrictions on banks; labor market regulations that limit a firm's ability to hire and lay off workers; and illegal markets, such as those that violate intellectual property rights.

No unique political system is necessary to deliver economic freedom. Democratic systems do a good job, but the rule of law, not democracy, is the key requirement for creating economic freedom. Nondemocratic political systems that respect the rule of law can also work well. Hong Kong is the best example of a place with little democracy but a lot of economic freedom—and a lot of economic growth. No country with a high level of economic freedom is economically poor, but many countries with low levels of economic freedom stagnate.

### Property Rights

Economic freedom requires the protection of private property—the factors of production and goods that people own. The social arrangements that govern the protection of private property are called **property rights**. They include the rights to physical property (land, buildings, and capital equipment), to financial property (claims by one person against another), and to intellectual property (such as inventions). Clearly established and enforced property rights provide people with the incentive to work and save. If someone attempts to steal their property, a legal system will protect them. Such property rights also assure people that government itself will not confiscate their income or savings.

### Markets

Economic freedom also requires free markets. Buyers and sellers get information and do business with each other in *markets*. Market prices send signals to buyers and sellers that create incentives to increase or decrease the quantities demanded and supplied. Markets enable people to trade and to save and invest. But markets cannot operate without property rights.

**Economic freedom**
A condition in which people are able to make personal choices, their private property is protected by the rule of law, and they are free to buy and sell in markets.

**Property rights**
The social arrangements that govern the protection of private property.

Property rights and markets create incentives for people to specialize and trade, to save and invest, to expand their human capital, and to discover and apply new technologies. Early human societies based on hunting and gathering did not experience economic growth because they lacked property rights and markets. Economic growth began when societies evolved the institutions that create incentives. But the presence of an incentive system and the institutions that create it do not guarantee that economic growth will occur. They permit economic growth but do not make it inevitable.

Growth begins when the appropriate incentive system exists because people can specialize in the activities at which they have a comparative advantage and trade with each other. You saw in Chapter 3 how everyone gains from such activity. By specializing and trading, everyone can acquire goods and services at the lowest possible cost. Consequently, people can obtain a greater volume of goods and services from their labor.

As an economy moves from one with little specialization to one that reaps the gains from specialization and trade, its production and consumption grow. Real GDP per person increases, and the standard of living rises.

But for growth to be persistent, people must face incentives that encourage them to pursue the three activities that generate *ongoing* economic growth: saving and investment, expansion of human capital, and the discovery and application of new technologies.

## ■ Policies to Achieve Faster Growth

To achieve faster economic growth, we must increase the growth rate of capital per hour of labor, increase the growth rate of human capital, or increase the pace of technological advance. The main actions that governments can take to achieve these objectives are

- Create incentive mechanisms.
- Encourage saving.
- Encourage research and development.
- Encourage international trade.
- Improve the quality of education.

### Create Incentive Mechanisms

Economic growth occurs when the incentives to save, invest, and innovate are strong enough. These incentives require property rights enforced by a well-functioning legal system. Property rights and a legal system are the key ingredients that are missing in many societies. For example, they are absent throughout much of Africa. The first priority for growth policy is to establish these institutions so that incentives to save, invest, and innovate exist. Post-communist Russia is an example of a country that has attempted to take this step toward establishing the conditions in which economic growth can occur.

### Encourage Saving

Saving finances investment, which brings capital accumulation. So encouraging saving can increase the growth of capital and stimulate economic growth. The East Asian economies have the highest saving rates and the highest growth rates. Some African economies have the lowest saving rates and the lowest growth rates.

Tax incentives can increase saving. Individual Retirement Accounts (IRAs) are an example of a tax incentive to save. Economists claim that a tax on consumption rather than on income provides the best incentive to save.

### Encourage Research and Development

Everyone can use the fruits of basic research and development efforts. For example, all biotechnology firms can use advances in gene-splicing technology. Because basic inventions can be copied, the inventor's profit is limited and so the market allocates too few resources to this activity.

Governments can direct public funds toward financing basic research, but this solution is not foolproof. It requires a mechanism for allocating public funds to their highest-valued use. The National Science Foundation is one possibly efficient channel for allocating public funds to universities and public research facilities to finance and encourage basic research. Government programs such as national defense and space exploration also lead to innovations that have wide use. Laptop computers and nonstick coatings are two prominent examples of innovations that came from the U.S. space program.

### Encourage International Trade

Free international trade stimulates economic growth by extracting all the available gains from specialization and trade. The fastest-growing nations today are those with the fastest-growing exports and imports. The creation of the North American Free Trade Agreement and the integration of the economies of Europe through the formation of the European Union are examples of successful actions that governments have taken to stimulate economic growth through trade.

### Improve the Quality of Education

The free market would produce too little education because it brings social benefits beyond the benefits to the people who receive the education. By funding basic education and by ensuring high standards in skills such as language, mathematics, and science, governments can contribute enormously to a nation's growth potential. Education can also be expanded and improved by using tax incentives to encourage improved private provision. Singapore's Information Technology in Education program is one of the best examples of a successful attempt to stimulate growth through education.

## ■ How Much Difference Can Policy Make?

It is easy to make a list of policy actions that could increase a nation's economic growth rate. It is hard to convert that list into acceptable actions that make a big difference.

Political equilibrium arises from the balance of the interests of one group against the interests of another group. Change brings gains for some and losses for others, so change is slow. And even when change occurs, if the economic growth rate can be increased by even as much as half a percentage point, it takes many years for the full benefits to accrue.

A well-intentioned government cannot dial up a big increase in the economic growth rate, but it can pursue policies that will nudge the economic growth rate upward. Over time, the benefits from these policies will be large.

# EYE on RICH AND POOR NATIONS

## Why Are Some Nations Rich and Others Poor?

Political stability, property rights protected by the rule of law, and limited government intervention in markets: These are key features of the economies that enjoy high or rapidly rising incomes and they are the features missing in economies that remain poor. All the rich nations have possessed these growth-inducing characteristics for the many decades during which their labor productivity and standard of living have been rising.

The United States started to grow rapidly 150 years ago and overtook Europe in the early 20th century. In the past 50 years, the gaps between these countries haven't changed much. (See part (a) of the figure.)

In a transition from Communism to a market economy, Eastern Europe is now growing faster.

Tribal conflict in Africa and bureaucratic overload in Central and South America have kept growth slow and the gap between the United States and these regions has widened.

Real GDP per person in three Asian economies, in part (b), has converged toward that in the United States. These economies are like fast trains running on the same track at similar speeds with roughly constant gaps between them. Hong Kong is the lead train, and it runs about 15 years in front of Taiwan and almost 40 years in front of the People's Republic of China.

Between 1960 and 2015, Hong Kong and some other smaller countries of Asia transformed themselves from poor developing economies to take their places among the world's richest economies.

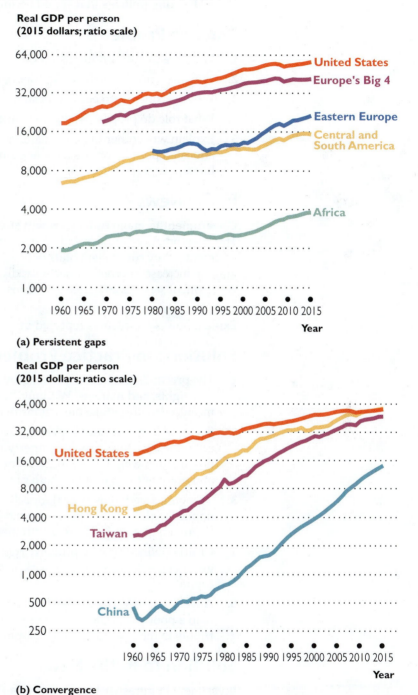

**Real GDP per person**
**(2015 dollars; ratio scale)**

(a) Persistent gaps

**Real GDP per person**
**(2015 dollars; ratio scale)**

(b) Convergence

SOURCES OF DATA: Penn World Table 8.1 by Robert C. Feenstra, Robert Inklaar and Marcel P. Timmer and International Monetary Fund, *World Economic Outlook Database.*

MyEconLab Study Plan 9.4

Key Terms Quiz

Solutions Video

# CHECKPOINT 9.4

### Describe policies that speed economic growth.

## Practice Problems

1. What are the preconditions for economic growth?
2. Why does much of Africa experience slow economic growth?
3. Why is economic freedom crucial for achieving economic growth?
4. What role do property rights play in encouraging economic growth?
5. Explain why, other things remaining the same, a country with a well-educated population has a faster economic growth rate than a country that has a poorly educated population.

## In the News

**Government to make India's growth sturdy**

The government of India is scaling up and better targeting its infrastructure investment. A key component of its policy is "digitalisation": an infrastructure program to increase Internet connectivity, digitally empower the country, and make government services available to citizens electronically.

Source: *Business Standard*, July 11, 2016

Explain how the measures reported in the news clip could lead to faster growth.

## Solutions to Practice Problems

1. The preconditions for economic growth are economic freedom, private property rights, and markets. Without these preconditions, people have little incentive to undertake the actions that lead to economic growth.

2. Some African countries experience slow economic growth because they lack economic freedom, private property rights are not enforced, and markets do not function well. People in these countries have little incentive to specialize and trade or to accumulate both physical and human capital.

3. Economic freedom is crucial for achieving economic growth because economic freedom allows people to make choices and gives them the incentives to pursue growth-producing activities.

4. Clearly defined private property rights and a legal system to enforce them give people the incentive to work, save, invest, and accumulate human capital.

5. A well-educated population has more skills and greater labor productivity than a poorly educated population. A well-educated population can contribute to the research and development that create new technology.

## Solution to In the News

Investment in infrastructure and Internet technology would increase India's stock of physical capital, which would increase labor productivity. Better electronic communication would increase human capital and again increase labor productivity. These measures could lead to faster growth in labor productivity and faster growth in real GDP per person in India.

# CHAPTER SUMMARY

## Key Points

**1. Define and calculate the economic growth rate, and explain the implications of sustained growth.**

- Economic growth is the sustained expansion of production possibilities. The annual percentage change in real GDP measures the economic growth rate.
- Real GDP per person must grow if the standard of living is to rise.
- Sustained economic growth transforms poor nations into rich ones.
- The Rule of 70 tells us the number of years in which real GDP doubles—70 divided by the percentage growth rate of real GDP.

**2. Explain the sources of labor productivity growth.**

- Real GDP grows when aggregate hours and labor productivity grow.
- Real GDP per person grows when labor productivity grows.
- The interaction of saving and investment in physical capital, expansion of human capital, and technological advances bring labor productivity growth.
- Saving and investment in physical capital alone cannot bring sustained steady growth because of diminishing marginal returns to capital.

**3. Review theories of the causes and effects of economic growth.**

- Classical growth theory predicts that economic growth will end because a population explosion will lower real GDP per person to its subsistence level.
- New growth theory predicts that capital accumulation, human capital growth, and technological change respond to incentives and can bring persistent growth in labor productivity.
- Theories about the effect of economic growth on the distribution of income are speculative and make no clear prediction about future trends.

**4. Describe policies that speed economic growth.**

- Economic growth requires an incentive system created by economic freedom, property rights, and markets.
- It might be possible to achieve faster growth by encouraging saving, subsidizing research and education, and encouraging international trade.

## Key Terms

MyEconLab Key Terms Quiz

Classical growth theory, 228
Economic freedom, 234
Economic growth, 216
Economic growth rate, 216

Labor productivity, 220
Law of diminishing marginal
  returns, 221
New growth theory, 228

Productivity curve, 222
Property rights, 234
Rule of 70, 218

CHAPTER CHECKPOINT

## Study Plan Problems and Applications

1. Explain why sustained growth of real GDP per person can transform a poor country into a wealthy one.

2. In 2015, India's real GDP grew by 7.3 percent a year and its population grew by 1.3 percent a year. If these growth rates are sustained, in what years would
   - Real GDP be twice what it was in 2015?
   - Real GDP per person be twice what it was in 2015?

3. Describe how U.S. potential GDP per person has grown since 1960.

4. Explain the link between labor hours, labor productivity, and real GDP.

5. Explain how saving and investment in capital change labor productivity. Why do diminishing returns arise? Provide an example of diminishing returns. Use a graph of the productivity curve to illustrate your answer.

6. Explain how advances in technology change labor productivity. Do diminishing returns arise? Provide an example of an advance in technology. Use a graph of the productivity curve to illustrate your answer.

7. Explain how an increase in human capital changes labor productivity. Do diminishing returns arise? Provide an example of an increase in human capital. Use a graph of the productivity curve to illustrate your answer.

8. What were the sources of labor productivity growth in the U.S. economy during the fifty years since 1960? How did the 1960s differ from the more recent decades?

9. Draw productivity curves to illustrate the changes in labor productivity that occurred in the U.S. economy in the 1960s and contrast the change with that after 2007. What were the new technologies that arrived in the 1960s?

10. What can governments in Africa do to encourage economic growth and raise the standard of living in their countries?

11. **As China's growth slows, income inequality speeds up**
    China's real GDP growth rate has fallen from 10 percent a year to 6.8 percent a year. At the same time, the distribution of income has become more unequal. Suggestions for dealing with these problems include encouraging the growth of small firms, expanding the services sector, and investing more in human capital and research.
    
    Source: Economywatch.com, June 16, 2016
    
    Compare China's growth slowdown and increased inequality with that of the United States. Would the suggestions for dealing with these problems work?

 12. Read *Eye on Rich and Poor Nations* on p. 237. Which nations are the richest and which are growing the fastest? What are the conditions that lead to higher incomes and faster-growing incomes?

## Instructor Assignable Problems and Applications

MyEconLab Homework, Quiz, or Test if assigned by instructor

1. Distinguish between low and high incomes and low and high economic growth rates. What are the key features of an economy that are present when incomes are high or fast growing and absent when incomes are low and stagnating or growing slowly? Provide an example of an economy with

   • Low income and slow growth rate.
   • Low income and rapid growth rate.
   • High income with sustained growth over many decades.

Use the following information to work Problems **2** and **3**.

China's growth rate of real GDP in 2005 and 2006 was 10.5 percent a year and its population growth rate was 0.5 percent a year.

2. If these growth rates continue, in what year would real GDP be twice what it was in 2006?

3. If these growth rates continue, in what year would real GDP per person be twice what it was in 2006?

4. Explain how an increase in physical capital and an increase in human capital change labor productivity. Use a graph to illustrate your answer.

5. Table 1 describes labor productivity in an economy. What must have occurred in this economy during year 1?

6. Describe and illustrate in a graph what happened in the economy in Table 1 if in year 1, capital per hour of labor was 30 and in year 2 it was 40.

7. China invests almost 50 percent of its annual production in new capital compared to 15 percent in the United States. Capital per hour of labor in China is about 25 percent of that in the United States. Explain which economy has the higher real GDP per hour of labor, has the faster growth rate of labor productivity, and experiences the more severe diminishing returns.

Use the following information to work Problems **8**, **9**, and **10**.

**Dear Silicon Valley: Forget flying cars, give us economic growth**
We have made enormous advances in computing technology. In Silicon Valley at Alphabet's X labs, people are working on transformative technologies that include driverless cars, high-altitude balloons that deliver the Internet to remote regions of the world, self-navigating drones, and flying wind turbines tethered to a ground station. But despite today's advances in technology, our economic growth rate has slowed.

Source: *MIT Technology Review*, June 21, 2016

8. How would you explain the disconnect between the advances in technology described in the news clip and the pace of real GDP growth?

9. Thinking about the perpetual motion machine of economic growth (Figure 9.5 on p. 230), what are the missing ingredients that make some of today's amazing technologies fail to deliver faster economic growth?

10. Of the preconditions for economic growth and the policies that might achieve faster growth, which are already present in Silicon Valley (and the rest of the U.S. economy), and which, if any, might need to be strengthened?

**TABLE 1   LABOR PRODUCTIVITY**

| Capital per hour of labor | Real GDP per hour of labor | |
|---|---|---|
| | in year 1 | in year 2 |
| 10 | 7 | 9 |
| 20 | 13 | 17 |
| 30 | 18 | 24 |
| 40 | 22 | 30 |
| 50 | 25 | 35 |
| 60 | 27 | 39 |
| 70 | 28 | 42 |

# Multiple Choice Quiz

**1.** If real GDP increases from $5 billion to $5.25 billion and the population increases from 2 million to 2.02 million, real GDP per person increases by _____ percent.

    A. 5.0
    B. 1.0
    C. 2.5
    D. 4.0

**2.** If the population growth rate is 2 percent, real GDP per person will double in 7 years if real GDP grows by _____ percent per year.

    A. 7
    B. 10
    C. 12
    D. 14

**3.** All of the following increase labor productivity *except* _____.

    A. the accumulation of skill and knowledge
    B. an increase in capital per hour of labor
    C. an increase in consumption
    D. the employment of a new technology

**4.** The increase in real GDP per hour of labor that results from an increase in capital per hour of labor _____.

    A. is constant and independent of the quantity of capital
    B. is larger at a small quantity of capital than at a large quantity of capital
    C. is smaller at a small quantity of capital than at a large quantity of capital
    D. decreases as technology advances

**5.** The increase in real GDP per hour of labor that results from an advance in technology makes labor _____ productive _____.

    A. more; at all quantities of capital
    B. less; and capital more productive
    C. more; only at a large quantity of capital
    D. more; and capital less productive

**6.** The classical growth theory is that real GDP per person _____.

    A. only temporarily rises and then returns to the subsistence level
    B. grows forever
    C. is constant and does not change
    D. increases as the population grows

**7.** In new growth theory, the source of economic growth is _____.

    A. more leisure
    B. new and better jobs
    C. the persistent want for a higher standard of living
    D. an ever increasing growth rate of capital per hour of labor

**8.** An economy can achieve faster economic growth *without* _____.

    A. markets and property rights
    B. people being willing to save and invest
    C. incentives to encourage the research for new technologies
    D. an increase in the population growth rate

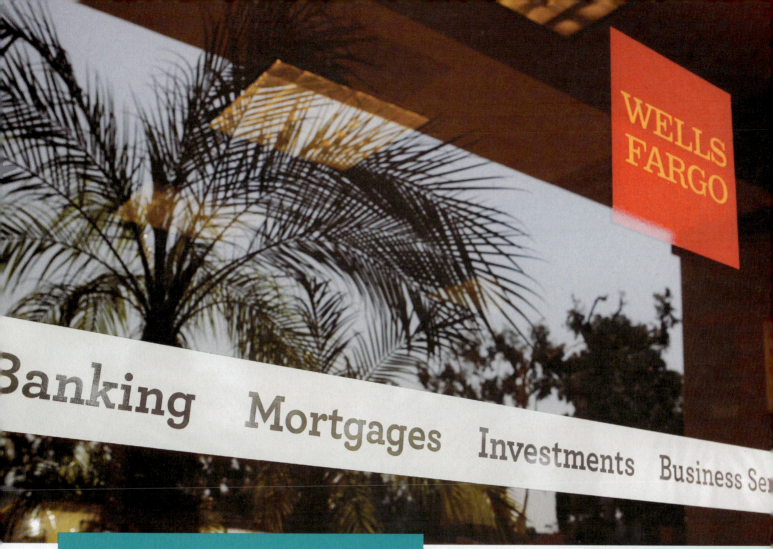

Why have interest rates been so low?

# Finance, Saving, and Investment

**10**

When you have completed your study of this chapter, you will be able to

**CHAPTER CHECKLIST**

**1** Describe the financial markets and the key financial institutions.

**2** Explain how borrowing and lending decisions are made and how these decisions interact in the loanable funds market.

**3** Explain how a government budget surplus or deficit influences the real interest rate, investment, and saving.

MyEconLab Big Picture Video

## 10.1 FINANCIAL INSTITUTIONS AND FINANCIAL MARKETS

To see what determines interest rates and why they have been so low, we need to understand how financial institutions function and financial markets work. The health of these institutions and markets affect saving and investment and the performance of every other market—of the labor market and the markets for goods and services—and the pace of economic growth.

### ■ Some Finance Definitions

First, we need to distinguish between two forms of capital: physical and financial. We also need to distinguish among investment, capital, wealth, and saving.

**Capital**—also called **physical capital**—is the tools, instruments, machines, buildings, and other items that have been produced in the past and that are used to produce goods and services. Inventories of raw materials, semifinished goods, and components are part of physical capital. The funds used to buy physical capital are called *financial capital*. You're going to see how decisions about investment and saving, along with borrowing and lending, influence the quantity of physical capital.

*Investment* (Chapter 5, p. 117) increases the quantity of capital and *depreciation* (Chapter 5, p. 124) decreases it. The total amount spent on new capital is called **gross investment**. The change in the quantity of capital is called **net investment**. Net investment equals gross investment minus depreciation. Figure 10.1 illustrates these concepts. Tom's end-of-year capital of $45,000 equals his initial capital of $30,000 plus net investment of $15,000; and net investment equals gross investment of $35,000 minus depreciation of $20,000.

**Capital or physical capital**
The tools, instruments, machines, buildings, and other items that have been produced in the past and that are used to produce goods and services.

**Gross investment**
The total amount spent on new capital.

**Net investment**
The change in the quantity of capital—equals gross investment minus depreciation.

■ **FIGURE 10.1**

Capital and Investment

MyEconLab Animation

On January 1, 2016, Tom's DVD Burning, Inc. had DVD-recording machines valued at $30,000.

During 2016, the value of Tom's machines fell by $20,000—depreciation—and he spent $35,000 on new machines—gross investment. Tom's net investment was $15,000, so at the end of 2016, Tom had capital valued at $45,000.

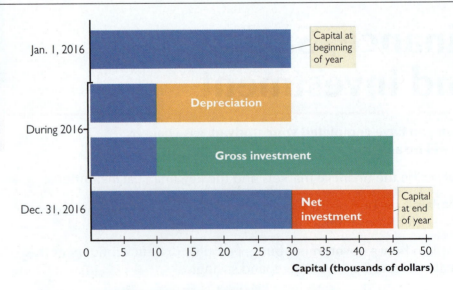

Capital (thousands of dollars)

**Wealth** is the value of all the things that people own. What people own is related to what they earn, but it is not the same thing. People earn an income, which is the amount they receive during a given time period from supplying the services of the resources they own. *Saving* (Chapter 5, p. 118), the amount of income that is not paid in taxes or spent on consumption, adds to wealth. Wealth also increases when the market value of assets rises—called *capital gains*.

**Wealth**
The value of all the things that people own.

If at the end of the school year, you have $250 in the bank and textbooks worth $300 and that's all that you own, your wealth is $550. If during the summer, you earn $5,000 (after-tax income) and spend $1,000 on consumption, your bank account increases to $4,250 and your wealth becomes $4,550. Your wealth has increased by $4,000, which equals your saving—your income of $5,000 minus your consumption expenditure of $1,000.

National wealth and national saving work like this personal example. The wealth of a nation at the end of a year equals its wealth at the start of the year plus its saving during the year, which equals income minus consumption expenditure.

To make real GDP grow, saving and wealth must be transformed into investment and capital. This transformation takes place in the markets for financial capital and through the activities of financial institutions that we now describe.

## ■ Markets for Financial Capital

Saving is the source of the funds that are used to finance investment, and these funds are supplied and demanded in three types of financial markets:

- Loan markets
- Bond markets
- Stock markets

### Loan Markets

Businesses often want short-term loans to buy inventories or to extend credit to their customers. Sometimes they get these funds in the form of a loan from a bank. Households often want funds to purchase big-ticket items, such as automobiles or household furnishings and appliances. They get these funds as bank loans, often in the form of outstanding credit card balances.

Households also get funds to buy new homes. (Expenditure on new homes is counted as part of investment.) These funds are usually obtained as a loan that is secured by a *mortgage*—a legal contract that gives ownership of a home to the lender in the event that the borrower fails to meet the agreed payment schedule (of loan repayments and interest). Mortgages were at the center of the U.S. credit crisis of 2007–2008.

All of these types of financing take place in loan markets.

### Bond Markets

When Walmart expands its business and opens new stores, it gets the funds it needs by selling bonds. Governments—federal, state, and municipal—also get the funds they need to finance a budget deficit by issuing bonds.

A **bond** is a promise to make specified payments on specified dates. For example, you can buy a Western Union bond that promises to pay $6.20 every year until 2035 and then to make a final payment of $100 in October 2036. Bonds issued by firms and governments are traded in the *bond market*.

**Bond**
A promise to pay specified sums of money on specified dates.

The term of a bond might be long (decades) or short (just a month or two). The U.S. Treasury issues very short-term bonds called *Treasury bills*.

The interest rate on a bond varies with its term to maturity. Usually, the longer the term, the higher is the interest rate. The relationship between the term of a bond and the interest rate is called the *yield curve*.

The interest rate on a bond also varies with its default risk—the risk that the bond issuer will not make the promised payments. The riskier the bond, the higher is its interest rate. Bonds are graded like students' tests on a scale from Aaa to Ccc. (See *Eye on the U.S. Economy* below.)

A special type of bond is a *mortgage-backed security*, which entitles its holder to the income from a package of mortgages. Mortgage lenders create mortgage-backed securities. They make mortgage loans to home buyers and then create securities that they sell to obtain more funds to make more mortgage loans. The holder of a mortgage-backed security is entitled to receive payments that derive from the payments received by the mortgage lender from the homebuyer–borrower. Mortgage-backed securities were at the center of a storm in the financial markets in 2007–2008.

### Stock Markets

**Stock**
A certificate of ownership and claim to the profits that a firm makes.

When Boeing wants to raise funds to expand its airplane-building business, it issues stock. A **stock** is a certificate of ownership and claim to a firm's profits. Boeing has issued about 900 million shares of its stock. If you owned 900 Boeing shares, you would own one millionth of Boeing and be entitled to receive one millionth of its profits.

A *stock market* is a financial market in which shares in corporations' stocks are traded. The New York Stock Exchange, the London Stock Exchange (in England), the Frankfurt Stock Exchange (in Germany), and the Tokyo Stock Exchange are all examples of stock markets.

# EYE on the U.S. ECONOMY
## Interest Rate Patterns

The *yield curve* shows that in 2016, the U.S. government could borrow by issuing 3-month Treasury Bills at 0.1 percent per year. But on 30-year bonds, it paid almost 2.5 percent. The higher *nominal* interest rate on longer-term bonds reflects inflation expectations.

The government is the least risky borrower and pays the lowest interest rate. The riskiest firms (Ccc) pay higher interest rates than the safest ones (Aaa).

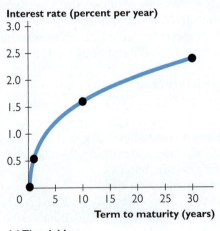

(a) The yield curve

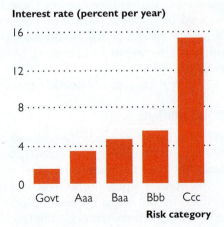

(b) The risk premiums

## ■ Financial Institutions

Financial markets are highly competitive because of the role played by financial institutions in those markets. A **financial institution** is a firm that operates on both sides of the markets for financial capital: It borrows in one market and lends in another. The key financial institutions are

- Investment banks
- Commercial banks
- Government-sponsored mortgage lenders
- Pension funds
- Insurance companies

**Financial institution**
A firm that operates on both sides of the markets for financial capital: It borrows in one market and lends in another.

### Investment Banks

Investment banks are firms that help other financial institutions and governments raise funds by issuing and selling bonds and stocks, as well as providing advice on transactions such as mergers and acquisitions. Until the late 1980s, the United States maintained a sharp separation between investment banking and commercial banking—a separation that was imposed by the Glass-Steagall Act of 1933. Until 2008, four big Wall Street firms—Goldman Sachs, Lehman Brothers, Merrill Lynch, and Morgan Stanley—provided investment banking services. But in the financial meltdown of 2008, Lehman disappeared and Merrill Lynch was taken over by the Bank of America, a commercial bank.

### Commercial Banks

The bank that you use for your own banking services and that issues your credit card is a commercial bank. We'll explain their role in Chapter 11 where we study the role of money in our economy.

### Government-Sponsored Mortgage Lenders

Two large financial institutions, the Federal National Mortgage Association, or Fannie Mae, and the Federal Home Loan Mortgage Corporation, or Freddie Mac, are government-sponsored enterprises that buy mortgages from banks, package them into *mortgage-backed securities*, and sell them. In September 2008, Fannie Mae and Freddie Mac owned or guaranteed $6 trillion worth of mortgages (half of the U.S. total of $12 trillion) and were taken over by the federal government.

### Pension Funds

Pension funds are financial institutions that use the pension contributions of firms and workers to buy bonds and stocks. The mortgage-backed securities of Fannie Mae and Freddie Mac are among the assets of pension funds. Some pension funds are very large and play an active role in the firms whose stock they hold.

### Insurance Companies

Insurance companies enter into agreements with households and firms to provide compensation in the event of accident, theft, fire, ill health, and a host of other misfortunes. Some companies, for example, provide insurance that pays out if a firm fails and cannot meet its bond obligations; and some insure other insurers in a complex network of reinsurance.

Insurance companies receive premiums from their customers, make payments against claims, and use the funds they have received but not paid out as claims to buy bonds and stocks on which they earn interest.

In normal times, insurance companies have a steady flow of funds coming in from premiums and interest on the financial assets they hold and a steady, but smaller, flow of funds paying claims. Their profit is the gap between the two flows. But in unusual times, when large and widespread losses are being incurred, insurance companies can run into difficulty in meeting their obligations. Such a situation arose in 2008 for one of the biggest insurers, AIG, and the firm was taken into public ownership.

### ■ Insolvency and Illiquidity

**Net worth**
The total market value of what a financial institution has lent minus the market value of what it has borrowed.

A financial institution's **net worth** is the total market value of what it has lent minus the market value of what it has borrowed. If net worth is positive, the institution is *solvent* and can remain in business. But if its net worth is negative, the institution is *insolvent* and must stop trading. The owners of an insolvent financial institution—usually its stockholders—bear the loss when the assets are sold and debts paid.

A financial institution both borrows and lends, so it is exposed to the risk that its net worth might become negative. To limit that risk, institutions are regulated and a minimum amount of their lending must be backed by their net worth.

Sometimes, a financial institution is solvent but illiquid. A firm is *illiquid* if it has made long-term loans with borrowed funds and is faced with a sudden demand to repay more of what it has borrowed than it has in available cash. In normal times, a financial institution that is illiquid can borrow from another institution. But if all financial institutions are short of cash, the market for loans among financial institutions dries up.

### ■ Interest Rates and Asset Prices

Stocks, bonds, short-term securities, and loans are collectively called *financial assets*. The *interest rate* on a financial asset is a percentage of the price of the asset.

Because the interest rate is a percentage of the price of an asset, if the asset price rises, other things remaining the same, the interest rate falls. And conversely, if the asset price falls, other things remaining the same, the interest rate rises.

To see this *inverse relationship* between an asset price and interest rate, look at the example of a Microsoft share. In September 2009, the price of a Microsoft share was $25 and each share entitled its owner to 50 cents of Microsoft profit. The interest rate on a Microsoft share as a percentage was

$$\text{Interest rate} = (\$0.50 \div \$25) \times 100 = 2 \text{ percent.}$$

If the price of a Microsoft share increased to $50 and each share still entitled its owner to 50 cents of Microsoft profit, the interest rate on a Microsoft share as a percentage would become

$$\text{Interest rate} = (\$0.50 \div \$50) \times 100 = 1 \text{ percent.}$$

This relationship means that an asset price and interest rate are determined simultaneously—one implies the other. In the next part of this chapter, we learn how asset prices and interest rates are determined in the financial markets.

**CHECKPOINT 10.1**

MyEconLab Study Plan 10.1
Key Terms Quiz
Solutions Video

### Describe the financial markets and the key financial institutions.

## Practice Problems

1. Michael is an Internet service provider. On December 31, 2015, he bought an existing business with servers and a building worth $400,000. During 2016, he bought new servers for $500,000. The market value of his older servers fell by $100,000. What was Michael's gross investment, depreciation, and net investment during 2016? What is Michael's capital at the end of 2016?

2. Lori is a student who teaches golf on the weekend and in a year earns $20,000 after paying her taxes. At the beginning of 2016, Lori owned $1,000 worth of books, DVDs, and golf clubs and she had $5,000 in a savings account at the bank. During 2016, the interest on her savings account was $300 and she spent a total of $15,300 on consumption goods and services. The market value of her books, DVDs, and golf clubs did not change. How much did Lori save in 2016? What was her wealth at the end of 2016?

## In the News

**Banks face increased capital requirements under new rule**

Regulators say that some of the world's biggest banks should not be permitted to rely on their own assessment of risk and must hold 40 percent more capital.

Source: *Financial Times*, March 4, 2016

What are the financial institutions that are required to raise more capital? What exactly is the "capital" referred to in the news clip? How might raising more capital make financial institutions safer?

## Solutions to Practice Problems

1. Michael's gross investment during 2016 was $500,000—the market value of the new servers he bought.

   Michael's depreciation during 2016 was $100,000—the fall in the market value of his older servers.

   Michael's net investment during 2016 was $400,000. Net investment equals gross investment minus depreciation, which is ($500,000 − $100,000).

   At the end of 2016, Michael's capital was $800,000. The capital grew during 2016 by the amount of net investment, so at the end of 2016 capital was $400,000 + $400,000, which equals $800,000.

2. Lori saved $5,000. Saving equals income (after tax) minus the amount spent. That is, Lori's saving was $20,300 minus $15,300, or $5,000.

   Lori's wealth at the end of 2016 was $11,000—the sum of her wealth at the start of 2016 ($6,000) plus her saving during 2016 ($5,000).

## Solution to In the News

The institutions are some of the world's biggest banks. "Capital" in the news clip is the banks' own funds. By using more of its own funds and less borrowed funds, a financial institution decreases its risk of insolvency in the event that its assets lose value.

**Loanable funds market**
The aggregate of all the individual financial markets.

## 10.2 THE LOANABLE FUNDS MARKET

In macroeconomics, we group all the individual financial markets into a single loanable funds market. The **loanable funds market** is the aggregate of the markets for loans, bonds, and stocks. In the loanable funds market, there is just one average interest rate that we refer to as *the* interest rate.

Thinking about financial markets as a single loanable funds market makes sense because the individual markets are highly interconnected with many common influences that move the interest rates on individual assets up and down together.

### ■ Flows in the Loanable Funds Market

The circular flow model (see Chapter 5, pp. 117–119) provides the accounting framework that describes the flows in the loanable funds market.

Loanable funds are used for three purposes:

1. Business investment
2. Government budget deficit
3. International investment or lending

And loanable funds come from three sources:

1. Private saving
2. Government budget surplus
3. International borrowing

Firms often use *retained earnings*—profits not distributed to stockholders—to finance business investment. These earnings belong to the firm's stockholders and are borrowed from the stockholders rather than being paid to them as dividends. To keep the accounts in the clearest possible way, we think of these retained earnings as being both a use and a source of loanable funds. They are part of business investment on the uses side and part of private saving on the sources side.

We measure all the flows of loanable funds in real terms—in constant 2009 dollars.

You're now going to see how these real flows and the real interest rate are determined in the loanable funds market by studying

- The demand for loanable funds
- The supply of loanable funds
- Equilibrium in the loanable funds market

### ■ The Demand for Loanable Funds

The *quantity of loanable funds demanded* is the total quantity of funds demanded to finance investment, the government budget deficit, and international investment or lending during a given period. Investment is the major item and the focus of our explanation of the forces that influence the demand side of the loanable funds market. The other two items—the government budget deficit and international investment and lending—can be thought of as amounts to be added to investment. (We study the effects of the government budget later in this chapter on pp. 260–263 and international borrowing and lending in Chapter 19.)

What determines investment and the demand for loanable funds? How does Amazon.com decide how much to borrow to build some new warehouses? Many details influence such a decision, but we can summarize them in two factors:

1. The real interest rate
2. Expected profit

The real interest rate is the opportunity cost of the funds used to finance the purchase of capital, and firms compare the real interest rate with the rate of profit they expect to earn on their new capital. Firms invest only when they expect to earn a rate of profit that exceeds the real interest rate. Fewer projects are profitable at a high real interest rate than at a low real interest rate, so:

**Other things remaining the same, the higher the real interest rate, the smaller is the quantity of loanable funds demanded; and the lower the real interest rate, the greater is the quantity of loanable funds demanded.**

## Demand for Loanable Funds Curve

The **demand for loanable funds** is the relationship between the quantity of loanable funds demanded and the real interest rate when all other influences on borrowing plans remain the same. Figure 10.2 illustrates the demand for loanable funds as a schedule and as a curve.

**Demand for loanable funds**
The relationship between the quantity of loanable funds demanded and the real interest rate when all other influences on borrowing plans remain the same.

■ **FIGURE 10.2**

The Demand for Loanable Funds                    MyEconLab Animation

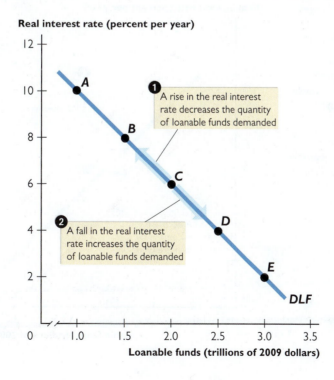

| | Real interest rate (percent per year) | Loanable funds demanded (trillions of 2009 dollars) |
|---|---|---|
| A | 10 | 1.0 |
| B | 8 | 1.5 |
| C | 6 | 2.0 |
| D | 4 | 2.5 |
| E | 2 | 3.0 |

The table shows the quantity of loanable funds demanded at five real interest rates. The graph shows the demand for loanable funds curve, DLF. Points A through E correspond to the rows of the table.

1. If the real interest rate rises, the quantity of loanable funds demanded decreases.

2. If the real interest rate falls, the quantity of loanable funds demanded increases.

To understand the demand for loanable funds, think about Amazon.com's decision to borrow $100 million to build some new warehouses. Suppose that Amazon expects to get a return of $5 million a year from this investment before paying interest costs. If the interest rate is less than 5 percent a year, Amazon expects to make a profit, so it builds the warehouses. If the interest rate is more than 5 percent a year, Amazon expects to incur a loss, so it doesn't build the warehouses. The quantity of loanable funds demanded is greater, the lower is the interest rate.

### Changes in the Demand for Loanable Funds

When the expected profit changes, the demand for loanable funds changes. Other things remaining the same, the greater the expected profit from new capital, the greater is the amount of investment and the greater is the demand for loanable funds.

The expected profit rises during a business cycle expansion and falls during a recession; rises when technological change creates profitable new products; rises as a growing population brings increased demand; and fluctuates with contagious swings of optimism and pessimism, called "animal spirits" by Keynes and "irrational exuberance" by Alan Greenspan.

Figure 10.3 shows how the demand for loanable funds curve shifts when the expected profit changes. With average profit expectations, the demand for loanable funds curve is $DLF_0$. A rise in expected profit shifts the demand curve rightward to $DLF_1$; a fall in expected profit shifts the demand curve leftward to $DLF_2$.

### FIGURE 10.3

Changes in the Demand for Loanable Funds

MyEconLab Animation

A change in expected profit changes the demand for loanable funds and shifts the demand for loanable funds curve.

❶ An increase in expected profit increases the demand for loanable funds and shifts the demand curve rightward to $DLF_1$.

❷ A decrease in expected profit decreases the demand for loanable funds and shifts the demand curve leftward to $DLF_2$.

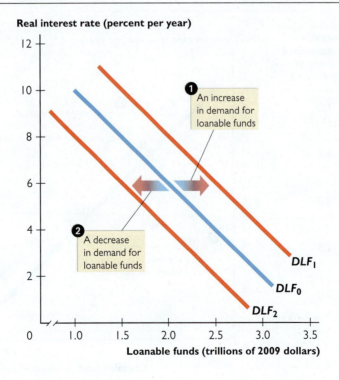

# ■ The Supply of Loanable Funds

The *quantity of loanable funds supplied* is the total funds available from private saving, the government budget surplus, and international borrowing during a given period. Saving is the main source of supply of loanable funds. A government budget surplus and international borrowing are other sources.

Saving and the supply of loanable funds are determined by decisions by people like you. Suppose that you've graduated and landed a great job that pays you $50,000 a year. How do you decide how much of your income to spend on consumption goods and how much to save and supply in the loanable funds market? Your decision will be influenced by many factors, but chief among them are

1. The real interest rate
2. Disposable income
3. Wealth
4. Expected future income
5. Default risk

We begin by focusing on the real interest rate.

> **Other things remaining the same, the higher the real interest rate, the greater is the quantity of loanable funds supplied; and the lower the real interest rate, the smaller is the quantity of loanable funds supplied.**

## The Supply of Loanable Funds Curve

The **supply of loanable funds** is the relationship between the quantity of loanable funds supplied and the real interest rate when all other influences on lending plans remain the same. Figure 10.4 illustrates the supply of loanable funds.

**Supply of loanable funds**
The relationship between the quantity of loanable funds supplied and the real interest rate when all other influences on lending plans remain the same.

The key reason the supply of loanable funds curve slopes upward is that the real interest rate is the *opportunity cost* of consumption expenditure. A dollar spent is a dollar not saved, so the interest that could have been earned on that saving is forgone. Forgone interest is the opportunity cost of consumption regardless of whether a person is a lender or a borrower. For a lender, saving less means receiving less interest. For a borrower, saving less means paying less off a loan (or increasing a loan) and paying more interest.

By thinking about student loans, you can see why the real interest rate influences saving and the supply of loanable funds. If the real interest rate on student loans jumped to 20 percent a year, graduates would save more (buying cheaper food and finding lower-rent accommodations) to pay off their loans as quickly as possible and avoid, as much as possible, paying the higher interest cost of their loan. If the real interest rate on student loans fell to 1 percent a year, graduates would save less and take longer to pay off their loans because the interest burden would be easier to bear.

## Changes in the Supply of Loanable Funds

A change in any influence on saving, other than the real interest rate, changes the supply of loanable funds. The other four factors listed above—disposable income, wealth, expected future income, and default risk—are the main things that change the supply of loanable funds.

## The Supply of Loanable Funds

The table shows the quantity of loanable funds supplied at five real interest rates. The graph shows the supply of loanable funds curve, *SLF*. Points *A* through *E* correspond to the rows of the table.

❶ If the real interest rate rises, the quantity of loanable funds supplied increases.

❷ If the real interest rate falls, the quantity of loanable funds supplied decreases.

| | Real interest rate (percent per year) | Loanable funds supplied (trillions of 2009 dollars) |
|---|---|---|
| A | 10 | 3.0 |
| B | 8 | 2.5 |
| C | 6 | 2.0 |
| D | 4 | 1.5 |
| E | 2 | 1.0 |

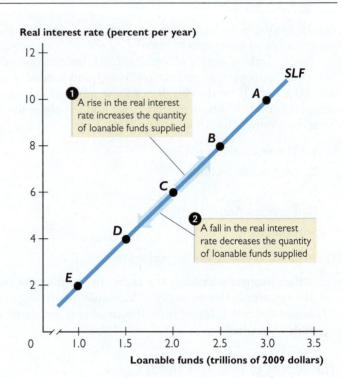

❶ A rise in the real interest rate increases the quantity of loanable funds supplied

❷ A fall in the real interest rate decreases the quantity of loanable funds supplied

*Disposable Income* A household's *disposable income* is the income earned minus net taxes. The greater a household's disposable income, other things remaining the same, the greater is its saving. For example, a student whose disposable income is $10,000 a year spends the entire $10,000 and saves nothing. An economics graduate whose disposable income is $50,000 a year spends $40,000 and saves $10,000.

*Wealth* A household's wealth is what it owns. The greater a household's wealth, other things remaining the same, the less it will save.

Patty is a department store executive who has $15,000 in the bank and no debts: She decides to spend $5,000 on a vacation and save nothing this year. Tony, another department store executive, has nothing in the bank and owes $10,000 on his credit card: He decides to cut consumption and start saving.

*Expected Future Income* The higher a household's expected future income, other things remaining the same, the smaller is its saving today: If two households have the same current disposable income, the household with the larger expected future disposable income will spend a larger portion of its current disposable income on consumption goods and services and so save less today.

Look at Patty and Tony again. Patty has just been promoted and will receive a $10,000 pay raise next year. Tony has just been told that he will be laid off at the end of the year. On receiving this news, Patty buys a new car—increases her consumption expenditure and cuts her saving—and Tony sells his car and takes the bus—decreases his consumption expenditure and increases his saving.

Most young households expect to have a higher future income for some years and then to have a lower income during retirement. Because of this pattern of income over the life cycle, young people save a small amount, middle-aged people save a lot, and retired people gradually spend their accumulated savings.

***Default Risk*** Default risk is the risk that a loan will not be repaid, or not repaid in full. The greater that risk, the higher is the interest rate needed to induce a person to lend and the smaller is the supply of loanable funds. In normal times, default risk is low but in times of financial crisis when asset prices tumble, default can become widespread as financial institutions become *illiquid* or *insolvent*.

### Shifts of the Supply of Loanable Funds Curve

When any of the four influences we've just described changes, the supply of loanable funds changes and the supply of loanable funds curve shifts. An increase in disposable income, or a decrease in wealth, expected future income, or default risk increases the supply of loanable funds.

Figure 10.5 shows how the supply of loanable funds curve shifts. Initially, the supply of loanable funds curve is $SLF_0$. Then disposable income increases or wealth, expected future income, or default risk decreases. The supply of loanable funds curve shifts rightward from $SLF_0$ to $SLF_1$. Changes in these factors in the opposite direction shift the supply curve leftward from $SLF_0$ to $SLF_2$.

■ **FIGURE 10.5**

Changes in the Supply of Loanable Funds                    MyEconLab Animation

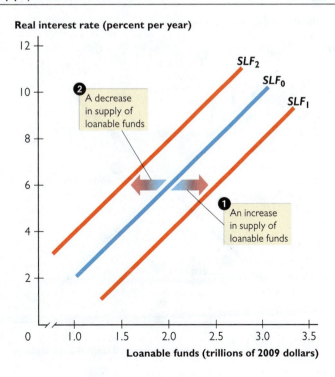

❶ An increase in disposable income or a decrease in wealth, expected future income, or default risk increases the supply of loanable funds and shifts the supply of loanable funds curve rightward from $SLF_0$ to $SLF_1$.

❷ A decrease in disposable income or an increase in wealth, expected future income, or default risk decreases the supply of loanable funds and shifts the supply of loanable funds curve leftward from $SLF_0$ to $SLF_2$.

### ■ Equilibrium in the Loanable Funds Market

You've seen that, other things remaining the same, the quantities of loanable funds demanded and supplied depend on the real interest rate. The higher the real interest rate, the greater is the amount of saving and the larger is the quantity of loanable funds supplied. But the higher the real interest rate, the smaller is the amount of investment and the smaller is the quantity of loanable funds demanded. There is one interest rate at which the quantities of loanable funds demanded and supplied are equal, and that interest rate is the equilibrium real interest rate.

Figure 10.6 shows how the demand for and supply of loanable funds determine the real interest rate. The *DLF* curve is the demand curve and the *SLF* curve is the supply curve. When the real interest rate exceeds 6 percent a year, the quantity of loanable funds supplied exceeds the quantity demanded. Borrowers have an easy time finding the funds they want, but lenders are unable to lend all the funds they have available. The real interest rate falls and continues to fall until the quantity of funds supplied equals the quantity of funds demanded.

Alternatively, when the interest rate is less than 6 percent a year, the quantity of loanable funds supplied is less than the quantity demanded. Borrowers can't find the funds they want, but lenders are able to lend all the funds they have available. So the real interest rate rises and continues to rise until the quantity of funds supplied equals the quantity demanded.

Regardless of whether there is a surplus or a shortage of loanable funds, the real interest rate changes and is pulled toward an equilibrium level. In Figure 10.6,

### ■ FIGURE 10.6

Equilibrium in the Loanable Funds Market

MyEconLab Animation

**1** If the real interest rate is 8 percent a year, the quantity of loanable funds demanded is less than the quantity supplied. There is a surplus of funds, and the real interest rate falls.

**2** If the real interest rate is 4 percent a year, the quantity of loanable funds demanded exceeds the quantity supplied. There is a shortage of funds, and the real interest rate rises.

**3** When the real interest rate is 6 percent a year, the quantity of loanable funds demanded equals the quantity supplied. There is neither a shortage nor a surplus of funds, and the real interest rate is at its equilibrium level.

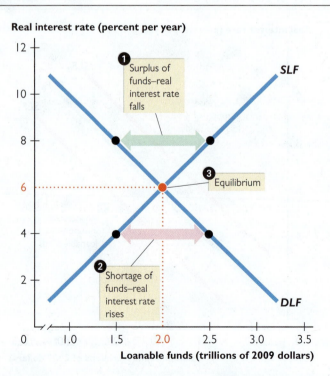

the equilibrium real interest rate is 6 percent a year. At this interest rate, there is neither a surplus nor a shortage of funds. Borrowers can get the funds they want, and lenders can lend all the funds they have available. The plans of borrowers (investors) and lenders (savers) are consistent with each other.

## ■ Changes in Demand and Supply

Fluctuations in either the demand for loanable funds or the supply of loanable funds bring fluctuations in the real interest rate and in the equilibrium quantity of funds lent and borrowed. Here we'll illustrate the effects of an increase in each.

An increase in expected profit increases the demand for loanable funds. With no change in supply, there is a shortage of funds and the interest rate rises until the equilibrium is restored. In Figure 10.7(a), the increase in the demand for loanable funds shifts the demand for loanable funds curve rightward from $DLF_0$ to $DLF_1$. At a real interest rate of 6 percent a year, there is a shortage of funds. The real interest rate rises to 8 percent a year, and the equilibrium quantity of funds increases.

If one of the influences on saving plans changes and increases saving, the supply of loanable funds increases. With no change in demand, there is a surplus of funds and the interest rate falls until the equilibrium is restored. In Figure 10.7(b), the increase in the supply of loanable funds shifts the supply of loanable funds curve rightward from $SLF_0$ to $SLF_1$. At a real interest rate of 6 percent a year, there is a surplus of funds. The real interest rate falls to 4 percent a year, and the equilibrium quantity of funds increases.

Over time, both demand and supply in the loanable funds market fluctuate and the real interest rate rises and falls. Both the supply of loanable funds and the demand for loanable funds tend to increase over time. On the average, they increase at a similar pace, so although demand and supply trend upward, the real interest rate has no trend. It fluctuates around a constant average level.

■ **FIGURE 10.7**

Changes in Demand and Supply in the Loanable Funds Market                MyEconLab Animation

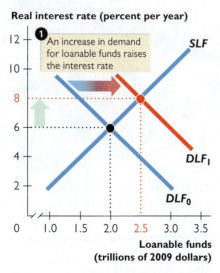

(a) An increase in investment

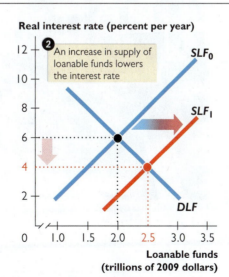

(b) An increase in saving

❶ If the demand for loanable funds increases and the supply of loanable funds remains the same, the real interest rate rises and the equilibrium quantity of funds increases.

❷ If the supply of loanable funds increases and the demand for loanable funds remains the same, the real interest rate falls and the equilibrium quantity of funds increases.

# EYE on the U.S. ECONOMY
## The Loanable Funds Market in a Financial Crisis

Financial markets can be turbulent and in 2007 and 2008, events in the loanable funds market created a financial crisis, the effects of which are still with us today.

An increase in default risk decreased supply; and the disappearance of some major Wall Street institutions and lowered profit expectations decreased demand.

Bear Stearns was absorbed by JP Morgan with help from the Federal Reserve; Lehman Brothers' assets were taken over by Barclays; Fannie Mae and Freddie Mac went into government oversight with U.S. taxpayer guarantees; Merrill Lynch became part of the Bank of America; AIG received an $85 billion lifeline from the Federal Reserve and sold off parcels of its business to financial institutions around the world; Wachovia was taken over by Wells Fargo and Washington Mutual by JP Morgan Chase.

But what caused the increase in default risk and the failure of so many financial institutions?

Between 2002 and 2005, interest rates were low. There were plenty of willing borrowers and plenty of willing lenders. Fueled by easy loans, home prices rose rapidly. Lenders bundled their loans into mortgage-backed securities and sold them to eager buyers around the world.

Then, in 2006, interest rates began to rise and home prices began to fall. People defaulted on mortgages; banks took losses and some became insolvent. A downward spiral of lending was under way.

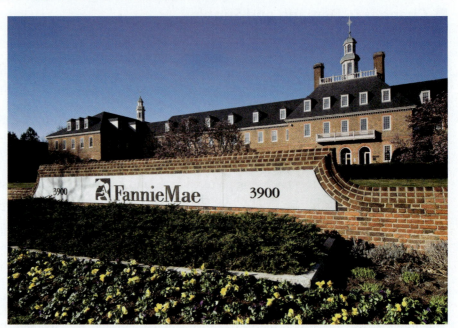

**CHECKPOINT 10.2**

MyEconLab Study Plan 10.2
Key Terms Quiz
Solutions Video

**Explain how borrowing and lending decisions are made and how these decisions interact in the loanable funds market.**

## Practice Problem

First Call, Inc. is a wireless service provider. It plans to build an assembly plant that costs $10 million if the real interest rate is 6 percent a year. If the real interest rate is 5 percent a year, First Call will build a larger plant that costs $12 million. And if the real interest rate is 7 percent a year, First Call will build a smaller plant that costs $8 million. Use this information to work Problems **1** and **2**.

1. Draw a graph of First Call's demand for loanable funds curve.

2. First Call expects its profit to double next year. If other things remain the same, explain how this increase in expected profit influences First Call's demand for loanable funds.

3. Draw graphs that illustrate how an increase in the supply of loanable funds and a decrease in the demand for loanable funds can lower the real interest rate and leave the equilibrium quantity of loanable funds unchanged.

## In the News

**The stock market is acting like everything is great**
Stock prices measured by the S&P 500 and Dow Jones Industrial Average set new highs this week. Company profits remain low, but investors are betting that higher profits are just around the corner.
Source: *The Washington Post*, July 14, 2016

Are the people who buy stocks suppliers or demanders of loanable funds? If stock prices rise, what happens to the interest rate on stocks? How would you explain the rise in stock prices in the news clip?

## Solutions to Practice Problems

1. The demand for loanable funds curve is the downward-sloping curve $DLF_0$ and passes through the points highlighted in Figure 1.

2. An increase in the expected profit increases investment today, which increases the quantity of loanable funds demanded at each real interest rate. The demand for loanable funds curve shifts rightward to $DLF_1$ (Figure 1).

3. The increase in the supply of loanable funds shifts the supply curve rightward. The decrease in the demand for loanable funds shifts the demand curve leftward. The real interest rate falls. If the shifts are of the same magnitude, the equilibrium quantity of funds remains unchanged (Figure 2). If the shift of the supply curve is greater (less) than that of the demand curve, then the equilibrium quantity of funds increases (decreases).

## Solution to In the News

The buyers of stocks are suppliers of loanable funds. When the price of a financial asset rises, the interest rate on that asset falls. In July 2016, the supply of loanable funds increased as more people bought stocks. The increase in supply lowered the interest rate and raised the prices of stocks.

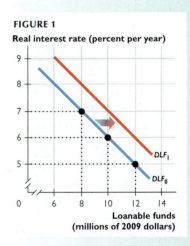

**FIGURE 1**
Real interest rate (percent per year)

Loanable funds
(millions of 2009 dollars)

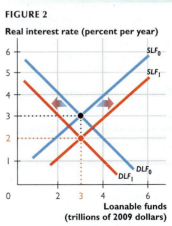

**FIGURE 2**
Real interest rate (percent per year)

Loanable funds
(trillions of 2009 dollars)

## 10.3 GOVERNMENT IN LOANABLE FUNDS MARKET

The government enters the loanable funds market when it has a budget surplus or budget deficit. So actions that change the government's budget balance influence the loanable funds market and the real interest rate. A change in the real interest rate influences both saving and investment. To complete our study of the forces that determine the quantity of investment and the real interest rate, we investigate the role played by the government's budget balance.

### ■ A Government Budget Surplus

A government budget surplus increases the supply of loanable funds. The real interest rate falls, which decreases private saving and decreases the quantity of private funds supplied. The lower real interest rate increases the quantity of loanable funds demanded and increases investment.

Figure 10.8 shows these effects of a government budget surplus. The private supply of loanable funds curve is *PSLF*. The supply of loanable funds curve, *SLF*, shows the sum of the private supply and the government budget surplus. Here, the government budget surplus is $1 trillion, so at each real interest rate the *SLF* curve lies $1 trillion to the right of the *PSLF* curve. That is, the horizontal distance between the *PSLF* curve and the *SLF* curve is the government budget surplus.

■ **FIGURE 10.8**

Government Budget Surplus

The demand for loanable funds curve is *DLF*, and the private supply of loanable funds curve is *PSLF*. With a balanced government budget, the real interest rate is 6 percent a year and investment is $2 trillion a year. Private saving and investment are $2 trillion a year.

❶ A government budget surplus of $1 trillion is added to private saving to determine the supply of loanable funds curve *SLF*.

❷ The real interest rate falls to 4 percent a year.

❸ The quantity of private saving decreases to $1.5 trillion.

❹ The quantity of loanable funds demanded and investment increase to $2.5 trillion.

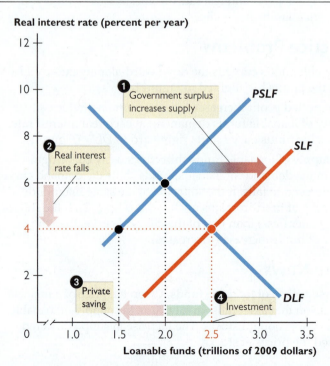

With no government budget surplus, the real interest rate is 6 percent a year, the quantity of loanable funds is $2 trillion a year and investment is $2 trillion a year. But with the government budget surplus of $1 trillion a year, the equilibrium real interest rate falls to 4 percent a year and the quantity of loanable funds increases to $2.5 trillion a year.

The fall in the real interest rate decreases private saving to $1.5 trillion, but investment increases to $2.5 trillion, which is financed by private saving and the government budget surplus (government saving).

## ■ A Government Budget Deficit

A government budget deficit increases the demand for loanable funds. The real interest rate rises, which increases private saving and increases the quantity of private funds supplied. But the higher real interest rate decreases investment and the quantity of loanable funds demanded by firms to finance investment.

Figure 10.9 shows these effects of a government budget deficit. The private demand for loanable funds curve is *PDLF*. The demand for loanable funds curve, *DLF*, shows the sum of the private demand and the government budget deficit. Here, the government budget deficit is $1 trillion, so at each real interest rate the *DLF* curve lies $1 trillion to the right of the *PDLF* curve. That is, the horizontal distance between the *PDLF* curve and the *DLF* curve equals the government budget deficit.

With no government budget deficit, the real interest rate is 6 percent a year, the quantity of loanable funds is $2 trillion a year and investment is $2 trillion a

### FIGURE 10.9

Government Budget Deficit

MyEconLab Animation

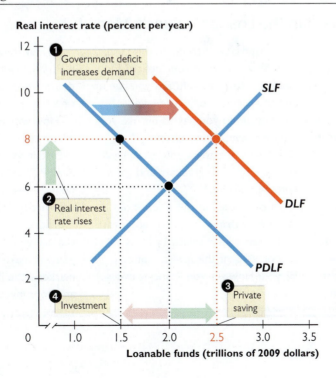

The supply of loanable funds curve is *SLF* and the private demand for loanable funds curve is *PDLF*. With a balanced government budget, the real interest rate is 6 percent a year and the quantity of loanable funds is $2 trillion a year. Private saving and investment are $2 trillion a year.

① A government budget deficit of $1 trillion is added to the private demand for funds to determine the demand for loanable funds curve *DLF*.

② The real interest rate rises to 8 percent a year.

③ Private saving and the quantity of loanable funds increase to $2.5 trillion.

④ Investment decreases to $1.5 trillion. Investment is crowded out.

year. But with the government budget deficit of $1 trillion, the real interest rate rises from 6 percent a year to 8 percent a year and the quantity of loanable funds increases from $2 trillion to $2.5 trillion.

The rise in the real interest rate increases private saving to $2.5 trillion, but investment decreases to $1.5 trillion. The tendency for a government budget deficit to raise the real interest rate and decrease investment is called the **crowding-out effect**. Investment does not decrease by the full amount of the government budget deficit because private saving increases. In this example, private saving increases by $0.5 trillion to $2.5 trillion.

**Crowding-out effect**
The tendency for a government budget deficit to raise the real interest rate and decrease investment.

### The Ricardo-Barro Effect

First suggested by the English economist David Ricardo in the eighteenth century and refined by Robert J. Barro of Harvard University during the 1980s, the Ricardo-Barro effect holds that the effects we've just shown are wrong and that the government budget deficit has no effect on the real interest rate or investment. Barro says that rational taxpayers can see that a deficit today means that future taxes will be higher and future disposable incomes will be smaller. With smaller expected future disposable incomes, saving increases. The increase in saving increases the supply of loanable funds—shifts the *SLF* curve rightward—by an amount equal to the government budget deficit. The supply of loanable funds might increase and lessen the influence of the government budget deficit on the real interest rate and investment, but most economists regard the full Ricardo-Barro effect as unlikely.

## EYE on YOUR LIFE
### Your Participation in the Loanable Funds Market

MyEconLab Critical Thinking Exercise

Think about the amount of saving that you do. How much of your disposable income do you save? Is it a positive amount or a negative amount?

If you save a positive amount, what do you do with your savings? Do you put them in a bank, in the stock market, in bonds, or just keep money at home? What is the interest rate you earn on your savings?

If you save a negative amount, just what does that mean? It means that you have a deficit (like a government deficit). You're spending more than your disposable income. In this case, how do you finance your deficit? Do you get a student loan? Do you run up an outstanding credit card balance? How much do you pay to finance your negative saving (your *dissaving*)?

How do you think your saving will change when you graduate and get a better-paying job?

Also think about the amount of investment that you do. You are investing in your human capital by being in school. What is this investment costing you? How are you financing this investment?

When you graduate and start a well-paying job, you will need to decide whether to buy an apartment or a house or to rent your home.

How would you make a decision whether to buy or rent a home? Would it be smart to borrow $300,000 to finance the purchase of a home? How would the interest rate influence your decision?

These examples show just some of the many decisions and transactions you will make in the loanable funds market—the link between your saving and your investment.

# EYE on FINANCIAL MARKETS

MyEconLab Critical Thinking Exercise

## Why Have Interest Rates Been So Low?

Interest rates were at record low levels from 2008 through 2013 and with what you have learned in this chapter, you can explain why.

The most recent normal year in the U.S. economy was 2007, the eve of the onset of a global financial crisis.

In 2007, the total amount borrowed in the U.S. loanable funds market was $51 trillion, and the real interest rate was 2 percent a year.

The figure illustrates this situation. The supply of loanable funds curve was $SLF_{07}$ and the demand for loanable funds curve was $DLF_{07}$. Both the demand curve and the supply curve include borrowing and lending decisions by households, firms, governments, the rest of the world, and financial institutions,

including the Federal Reserve (or the Fed). Loanable funds market equilibrium occurred at a real interest rate of 2 percent a year and a total quantity of loanable funds of $51 trillion.

Interest rates fell to a record low because the demand for loanable funds decreased and the supply increased.

On the demand side of the market, by mid-2009, expected profit had fallen, which decreased investment from $2.2 trillion in 2007 to $1.5 trillion and the demand for loanable funds by households and businesses had decreased sharply. But the federal government launched a massive rescue plan that increased its outlays and its demand for loanable funds.

Despite the large increase in government demand, the overall demand for loanable funds decreased: The demand by households, businesses, and financial institutions decreased by more than the demand by the federal government increased.

By 2013, the demand for loanable funds had decreased to $DLF_{13}$.

On the supply side of the market, the Fed continued to supply large quantities of funds. The Fed's goal was to lower the interest rate and stimulate investment. (You will study the actions that enable the Fed to increase the supply of loanable funds in Chapter 11.)

By 2013, the supply of loanable funds had increased to $SLF_{13}$.

The equilibrium real interest rate was 0.5 percent per year, and the equilibrium quantity of loanable funds was $55 trillion.

Even without the increase in supply, the real interest rate would have fallen, but the equilibrium quantity of loanable funds would also have fallen.

The increase in the supply of loanable funds limited the decrease in investment and lessened the severity of the recession triggered by the financial crisis.

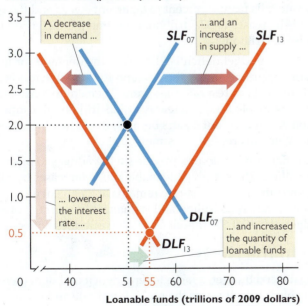

SOURCES OF DATA: Bureau of Economic Analysis and Federal Reserve. The interest rate is the average of the yield on Aaa equities, government bonds, mortgages, and federal funds, adjusted for inflation measured by the consumer price index.

MyEconLab Study Plan 10.3
Key Terms Quiz
Solutions Video

## CHECKPOINT 10.3

**Explain how a government budget surplus or deficit influences the real interest rate, investment, and saving.**

### Practice Problems

Table 1 shows the demand for loanable funds schedule and the supply of loanable funds schedule when the government budget is balanced.

1. If the government budget surplus is $1 trillion, what are the real interest rate, the quantity of investment, and the quantity of private saving?

2. If the government budget deficit is $1 trillion, what are the real interest rate, the quantity of investment, and the quantity of private saving? Is there any crowding out in this situation?

3. If the government budget deficit is $1 trillion and the Ricardo-Barro effect occurs, what are the real interest rate and the quantity of investment?

### In the News

**U.S. budget deficit expanded in April**
In the year to April 2016, the U.S. budget deficit increased to $511 billion, up from $460 billion a year earlier.

Source: *The Wall Street Journal*, May 11, 2016

Explain the effect of a large federal deficit and debt on economic growth.

### Solutions to Practice Problems

1. If the government budget surplus is $1 trillion, the supply of loanable funds increases. Figure 1 shows the supply of loanable funds *SLF*. The equilibrium real interest rate falls from 7 percent to 6 percent a year and the quantity of loanable funds increases to $2.5 trillion. Investment is $2.5 trillion and private saving is $1.5 trillion.

2. If the government budget deficit is $1 trillion, the demand for loanable funds increases. Figure 2 shows the demand for loanable funds curve *DLF*. The equilibrium real interest rate rises from 7 percent to 8 percent a year and the quantity of loanable funds increases to $2.5 trillion. Investment decreases to $1.5 trillion. Crowding out occurs because the deficit increases the real interest rate, which decreases investment.

3. If the Ricardo-Barro effect occurs, private saving adjusts to offset the budget deficit of $1 trillion. The supply of loanable funds increases by $1 trillion and the equilibrium real interest rate remains at 7 percent a year. The quantity of loanable funds is $3 trillion and it finances investment of $2 trillion and the budget deficit of $1 trillion. Crowding out does not occur.

### Solution to In the News

Compared to a balanced budget, a large federal deficit and debt increases the demand for loanable funds. It raises the real interest rate and lowers private investment. Investment increases the capital stock, which increases labor productivity and real GDP. The higher real interest rate slows the growth of the capital stock, slows labor productivity growth, and slows real GDP growth.

**TABLE 1**

| Real interest rate (percent per year) | Loanable funds demanded | Loanable funds supplied |
|---|---|---|
| | (trillions of 2009 dollars per year) | |
| 4 | 3.5 | 0.5 |
| 5 | 3.0 | 1.0 |
| 6 | 2.5 | 1.5 |
| 7 | 2.0 | 2.0 |
| 8 | 1.5 | 2.5 |
| 9 | 1.0 | 3.0 |
| 10 | 0.5 | 3.5 |

**FIGURE 1**

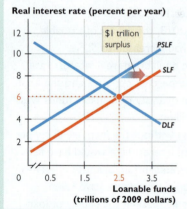

**FIGURE 2**

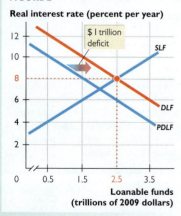

# CHAPTER SUMMARY

## Key Points

1. **Describe the financial markets and the key financial institutions.**

   - Firms use financial capital to buy and operate physical capital.
   - Gross investment is the total amount spent on physical capital in a given period. Net investment equals gross investment minus depreciation.
   - Wealth is the value of what people own; saving is the amount of disposable income that is not spent, and it adds to wealth.
   - The market for financial capital is a market made up of the markets for loans, bonds, and stocks.

2. **Explain how borrowing and lending decisions are made and how these decisions interact in the loanable funds market.**

   - Other things remaining the same, the lower the real interest rate or the higher the expected profit rate, the greater is the quantity of loanable funds demanded.
   - The demand for loanable funds changes when the expected profit rate changes.
   - Other things remaining the same, the higher the real interest rate, the greater is the quantity of loanable funds supplied.
   - The supply of loanable funds changes when disposable income, wealth, expected future income, or default risk changes.
   - Equilibrium in the loanable funds market determines the real interest rate.
   - At the equilibrium real interest rate, the quantity of loanable funds demanded equals the quantity of loanable funds supplied.

3. **Explain how a government budget surplus or deficit influences the real interest rate, investment, and saving.**

   - A government budget surplus increases the supply of loanable funds and a government budget deficit increases the demand for loanable funds.
   - With no change in private saving, an increase in the government budget deficit raises the real interest rate and crowds out investment.
   - A government budget deficit might increase private saving because it decreases expected future disposable income.

## Key Terms

MyEconLab Key Terms Quiz

Bond, 245
Capital or physical capital, 244
Crowding-out effect, 262
Demand for loanable funds, 251

Financial institution, 247
Gross investment, 244
Loanable funds market, 250
Net investment, 244

Net worth, 248
Stock, 246
Supply of loanable funds, 253
Wealth, 245

# CHAPTER CHECKPOINT

## Study Plan Problems and Applications

1. On January 1, 2016, Terry's Towing Service owned 4 tow trucks valued at $300,000. During 2016, Terry's bought 2 new trucks for a total of $180,000. At the end of 2016, the market value of all the firm's trucks was $400,000. What was Terry's gross investment? Calculate Terry's depreciation and net investment.

Use the following information to work Problems **2** and **3**.

The Bureau of Economic Analysis reported that the U.S. capital stock was $49.6 trillion at the end of 2012, $51.2 trillion at the end of 2013, and $53.6 trillion at the end of 2014. Depreciation in 2013 was $1.6 trillion, and gross investment during 2014 was $3.4 trillion.

2. Calculate U.S. net investment and gross investment during 2013.

3. Calculate U.S. depreciation and net investment during 2014.

4. Mike takes a summer job washing cars. During the summer, he earns an after-tax income of $3,000 and he spends $1,000 on goods and services. What was Mike's saving during the summer and the change, if any, in his wealth?

5. What is the market for financial capital? What is financial capital? Explain why, when the real interest rate rises, the demand for loanable funds does not change but the quantity of funds demanded decreases.

6. With an increase in political tension, many governments increased defense spending, which decreased government budget surpluses. Show, on a graph, the effects of a decrease in government budget surpluses if there is no Ricardo-Barro effect. Explain how the effects differ if there is a partial Ricardo-Barro effect.

7. **Rio declares financial emergency ahead of Olympics, requests federal funding**
   Rio de Janeiro requested federal funding to help pay for public services during the Olympics, at a time when Brazil's federal government revenue has fallen and created a large deficit.
   Source: *International Business Times*, July 15, 2016
   Draw a graph of the loanable funds market in Brazil. Suppose that the Brazilian government borrows the required funds in the loanable funds market. How will this borrowing change the real interest rate and the quantity of saving in Brazil?

8. **German government achieves budget surplus**
   The German government's budget was balanced in 2014 and moved into a surplus of $13 billion in 2015. Helped by higher tax revenues, the budget surplus was twice as high as expected.
   Source: *The Wall Street Journal*, January 13, 2016
   Explain the effect of Germany's budget surplus on the loanable funds market in Germany. How will the budget surplus influence economic growth?

9. Read *Eye on Financial Markets* on p. 263. What would the real interest rate and quantity of loanable funds have been in 2013 if the supply of loanable funds had been at its 2007 level? Explain your answer.

## Instructor Assignable Problems and Applications

MyEconLab Homework, Quiz, or Test if assigned by instructor

1. Explain why the supply of loanable funds and the demand for loanable funds decreased during the global financial crisis of 2007–2008. Draw a graph of the loanable funds market before the crisis and use your graph to illustrate the source and effects of the crisis on saving, investment, and the real interest rate.

2. On January 1, 2016, Sophie's Internet Cafe owned 10 computer terminals valued at $8,000. During 2016, Sophie's bought 5 new computer terminals at a cost of $1,000 each, and at the end of the year, the market value of all of Sophie's computer terminals was $11,000. What was Sophie's gross investment, depreciation, and net investment?

3. The numbers in the second column of Table 1 are the Federal Reserve's estimates of personal wealth at the end of each year. The numbers in the third column are the Bureau of Economic Analysis's estimates of personal saving each year. In which years did the change in wealth exceed saving? In which years did saving exceed the change in wealth? Given the definitions of saving and wealth, how can the change in wealth differ from saving?

4. Cindy takes a summer job and earns an after-tax income of $8,000. Her living expenses during the summer were $2,000. What was Cindy's saving during the summer and the change, if any, in her wealth?

5. A stock market boom of 2002–2007 increased wealth by trillions of dollars. Explain the effect of this increase in wealth on the equilibrium real interest rate, investment, and saving.

**TABLE 1**

| Year | Wealth | Saving |
|------|--------|--------|
| | (billions of dollars) | |
| 2011 | 63,544 | 785 |
| 2012 | 69,598 | 1,000 |
| 2013 | 79,383 | 662 |
| 2014 | 84,201 | 690 |

Use the following information to work Problems **6** and **7**.

The U.S. saving rate increased from −0.1 percent in 2011 to 2.0 percent in 2012, to 2.4 percent in 2013, to 2.9 percent in 2014, and to 3.0 percent in 2015.

6. How can the saving rate be negative? Why might a negative saving rate be something to worry about? How might U.S. saving be increased?

7. Explain why the U.S. saving rate might have increased and its effect on the supply of loanable funds.

Use the following information to work Problems **8** to **10**.

**IMF says it battled crisis well**

The International Monetary Fund (IMF) reported that it acted effectively in combating the global recession, especially in Eastern Europe. The IMF made $163 billion available to developing countries. The IMF required countries with large deficits to cut spending or not increase it, but it urged the United States, Western European countries, and China to run deficits to stimulate their economies.

Source: *The Wall Street Journal*, September 29, 2009

8. Explain how an increase in government expenditure will change the government's budget balance and the loanable funds market.

9. Why do you think the IMF required countries with large deficits, like those in Eastern Europe, to cut spending rather than increase it?

10. The Center for Economic and Policy Research in Washington, D.C., claims that the IMF didn't allow developing countries that were looking for loans to expand their deficits sufficiently. Would these countries have weathered the global recession better if they had obtained larger loans from the IMF?

# Multiple Choice Quiz

1. Financial capital is the _____.

   A. money used to buy stocks and bonds
   B. money used to buy physical capital
   C. funds that savers supply and buyers of physical capital borrow
   D. money in the bank

2. If the price of a U.S. government bond is $50 and the owner of the bond is entitled to $2.50 income each year, then the interest rate on the bond is _____.

   A. 0.2 percent
   B. 5 percent
   C. 10 percent
   D. 20 percent

3. In the loanable funds market, an increase in _____.

   A. the real interest rate increases the demand for loanable funds
   B. expected profit increases the demand for loanable funds
   C. expected profit doesn't change the demand for loanable funds, but the quantity of loanable funds demanded increases
   D. the real interest rate doesn't change the demand for loanable funds, but the quantity of loanable funds demanded increases

4. The supply of loanable funds increases _____.

   A. when the demand for loanable funds increases
   B. when people increase saving as the real interest rate rises
   C. when disposable income increases or wealth decreases
   D. if net taxes decrease or expected future income increases

5. An increase in expected profit _____ the real interest rate and _____ the quantity of loanable funds.

   A. decreases; decreases
   B. increases; decreases
   C. decreases; increases
   D. increases; increases

6. A government budget surplus _____.

   A. increases the supply of loanable funds
   B. raises the real interest rate
   C. decreases the demand for loanable funds and lowers the real interest rate
   D. decreases net taxes, increases disposable income, and increases saving

7. Crowding out occurs when _____.

   A. households' budgets are in deficit and saving decreases
   B. the government budget is in surplus, so people have paid too much tax
   C. the government budget is in deficit and the real interest rate rises
   D. the government budget is in deficit but taxpayers are rational and the Ricardo-Barro effect operates

8. An increase in the government budget deficit _____.

   A. increases private saving and investment
   B. increases private saving and decreases investment
   C. increases the supply of private saving and decreases investment
   D. decreases private saving and investment

How does the Fed create money
and regulate its quantity?

# The Monetary System

**When you have completed your study of this chapter,
you will be able to**

**1** Define money and describe its functions.

**2** Describe the functions of banks.

**3** Describe the functions of the Federal Reserve System (the Fed).

**4** Explain how the banking system creates money and how the Fed
controls the quantity of money.

MyEconLab Big Picture Video

## 11.1 WHAT IS MONEY?

Money, like fire and the wheel, has been around for a very long time. An incredible array of items has served as money. North American Indians used wampum (beads made from shells), Fijians used whales' teeth, and early American colonists used tobacco. Cakes of salt served as money in Ethiopia and Tibet. What do wampum, whales' teeth, tobacco, and salt have in common? Why are they examples of money? Today, when we want to buy something, we use coins or notes (dollar bills), write a check, send an e-check, present a credit or debit card, or use a smartphone app. Are all these things that we use today money? To answer these questions, we need a definition of money.

### ■ Definition of Money

**Money** is any commodity or token that is generally accepted as a *means of payment*. This definition has three parts that we'll examine in turn.

### A Commodity or Token

Money is always something that can be recognized and that can be divided up into small parts. So money might be an actual commodity, such as a bar of silver or gold. But it might also be a token, such as a quarter or a $10 bill. Money might also be a virtual token, such as an electronic record in a bank's database (more about this type of money later).

### Generally Accepted

Money is *generally* accepted, which means that it can be used to buy *anything and everything*. Some tokens can be used to buy some things but not others. For example, a bus pass is accepted as payment for a bus ride, but you can't use your bus pass to buy toothpaste. So a bus pass is not money. In contrast, you can use a $5 bill to buy either a bus ride or toothpaste—or anything else that costs $5 or less. So a $5 bill is money.

### Means of Payment

A **means of payment** is a method of settling a debt. When a payment has been made, the deal is complete. Suppose that Gus buys a car from his friend Ann. Gus doesn't have enough money to pay for the car right now, but he will have enough three months from now, when he gets paid. Ann agrees that Gus may pay for the car in three months' time. Gus buys the car with a loan from Ann and then pays off the loan. The loan isn't money. Money is what Gus uses to pay off the loan.

So what wampum, whales' teeth, tobacco, and salt have in common is that they have served as a generally accepted means of payment, and that is why they are examples of money.

### ■ The Functions of Money

Money performs three vital functions. It serves as a

- Medium of exchange
- Unit of account
- Store of value

**Money**
Any commodity or token that is generally accepted as a *means of payment*.

**Means of payment**
A method of settling a debt.

## Medium of Exchange

A **medium of exchange** is an object that is generally accepted in return for goods and services. Money is a medium of exchange. Without money, you would have to exchange goods and services directly for other goods and services—an exchange called **barter**. Barter requires a *double coincidence of wants*. For example, if you want a soda and have only a paperback novel to offer in exchange for it, you must find someone who is selling soda and who also wants your paperback novel. Money guarantees that there is a double coincidence of wants because people with something to sell will always accept money in exchange for it. Money acts as a lubricant that smoothes the mechanism of exchange. Money enables you to specialize in the activity in which you have a comparative advantage (see Chapter 3, pp. 73–75) instead of searching for a double coincidence of wants.

**Medium of exchange**
An object that is generally accepted in return for goods and services.

**Barter**
The direct exchange of goods and services for other goods and services, which requires a double coincidence of wants.

## Unit of Account

An agreed-upon measure for stating the prices of goods and services is called a *unit of account*. To get the most out of your budget, you have to figure out whether going to a rock concert is worth its opportunity cost. But that cost is not dollars and cents. It is the number of movies, cappuccinos, ice-cream cones, or sticks of gum that you must give up to attend the concert. It's easy to do such calculations when all these goods have prices in terms of dollars and cents (see Table 11.1). If a rock concert costs $64 and a movie costs $8, you know right away that going to the concert costs you 8 movies. If a cappuccino costs $4, going to the concert costs 16 cappuccinos. You need only one calculation to figure out the opportunity cost of any pair of goods and services. For example, the opportunity cost of the rock concert is 128 sticks of gum ($64 ÷ 50¢ = 128 sticks of gum).

Now imagine how troublesome it would be if the rock concert ticket agent posted its price as 8 movies, and if the movie theater posted its price as 2 cappuccinos, and if the coffee shop posted the price of a cappuccino as 2 ice-cream cones, and if the ice-cream shop posted its price as 4 sticks of gum! Now how much running around and calculating do you have to do to figure out how much that rock concert is going to cost you in terms of the movies, cappuccino, ice cream, or sticks of gum that you must give up to attend it? You get the answer for movies right away from the sign posted by the ticket agent. For all the other goods, you're going to have to visit many different places to establish the price of each commodity in terms of another and then calculate prices in units that are relevant for your own decision. Cover up the column labeled "price in money units" in Table 11.1 and see how hard it is to figure out the number of sticks of gum it costs to attend a rock concert. It's enough to make a person swear off rock! How much simpler it is using dollars and cents.

**TABLE 11.1  A UNIT OF ACCOUNT SIMPLIFIES PRICE COMPARISONS**

| Good | Price in money units | Price in units of another good |
|------|----------------------|--------------------------------|
| Rock concert | $64.00 | 8 movies |
| Movie | $8.00 | 2 cappuccinos |
| Cappuccino | $4.00 | 2 ice-cream cones |
| Ice-cream cone | $2.00 | 4 sticks of gum |
| Stick of gum | $0.50 | |

## Store of Value

Any commodity or token that can be held and exchanged later for goods and services is called a *store of value*. Money acts as a store of value. If it did not, it would not be accepted in exchange for goods and services. The more stable the value of a commodity or token, the better it can act as a store of value and the more useful it is as money. No store of value is completely stable. The value of a physical object, such as a house, a car, or a work of art, fluctuates over time. The value of the commodities and tokens that we use as money also fluctuates, and when there is inflation, money persistently falls in value.

**Fiat money**
Objects that are money because the law decrees or orders them to be money.

**Currency**
Notes (dollar bills) and coins.

**M1**
Currency held by individuals and businesses, traveler's checks, and checkable deposits owned by individuals and businesses.

**M2**
M1 plus savings deposits and small time deposits, money market funds, and other deposits.

## ■ Money Today

Money in the world today is called **fiat money**. *Fiat* is a Latin word that means decree or order. Fiat money is money because the law decrees it to be so. The objects used as money have value only because of their legal status as money.

Today's fiat money consists of

- Currency
- Deposits at banks and other financial institutions

### Currency

The notes (dollar bills) and coins that we use in the United States today are known as **currency**. The government declares notes to be money with the words printed on every dollar bill, "This note is legal tender for all debts, public and private."

### Deposits

Deposits at banks, credit unions, savings banks, and savings and loan associations are also money. Deposits are money because they can be used to make payments. You don't need to go to the bank to get currency to make a payment. You can write a check or use your debit card to tell your bank to move some money from your account to someone else's.

### Currency Inside the Banks Is Not Money

Although currency and bank deposits are money, currency *inside the banks* is *not money*. The reason is while currency is inside a bank, it isn't available as a means of payment. When you get some cash from the ATM, you convert your bank deposit into currency. You change the form of your money, but there is no change in the quantity of money that you own. Your bank deposit decreases, and your currency holding increases.

If we counted bank deposits and currency inside the banks as money, think about what would happen to the quantity of money when you get cash from the ATM. The quantity of money would appear to decrease. Your currency would increase, but both bank deposits and currency inside the banks would decrease.

You can see that counting both bank deposits and currency inside the banks as money would be double counting.

## ■ Official Measures of Money: M1 and M2

Figure 11.1 shows the items that make up two official measures of money. **M1** consists of currency held by individuals and businesses, traveler's checks, and checkable deposits owned by individuals and businesses. **M2** consists of M1 plus savings deposits and time deposits (less than $100,000), money market funds, and other deposits. Time deposits are deposits that can be withdrawn only after a fixed term. Money market funds are deposits that are invested in short-term securities.

### Are M1 and M2 Means of Payment?

The test of whether something is money is whether it is a generally accepted means of payment. Currency passes the test. Checkable deposits also pass the test because they can be transferred from one person to another by using a debit card or writing a check. So all the components of M1 serve as means of payment.

■ **FIGURE 11.1**

Two Measures of Money: June 2016                                    MyEconLab Real-time data

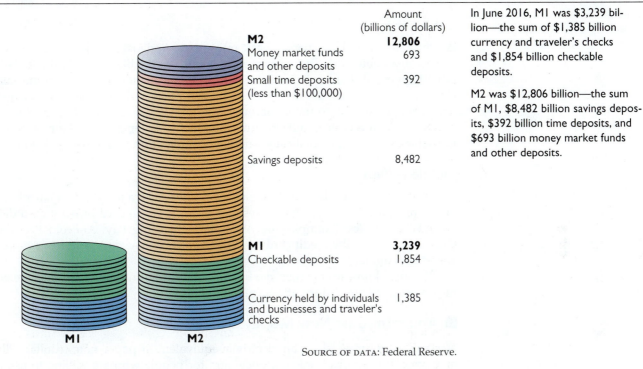

|  | Amount (billions of dollars) |
|---|---|
| **M2** | **12,806** |
| Money market funds and other deposits | 693 |
| Small time deposits (less than $100,000) | 392 |
| Savings deposits | 8,482 |
| **M1** | **3,239** |
| Checkable deposits | 1,854 |
| Currency held by individuals and businesses and traveler's checks | 1,385 |

In June 2016, M1 was $3,239 billion—the sum of $1,385 billion currency and traveler's checks and $1,854 billion checkable deposits.

M2 was $12,806 billion—the sum of M1, $8,482 billion savings deposits, $392 billion time deposits, and $693 billion money market funds and other deposits.

SOURCE OF DATA: Federal Reserve.

Some of the savings deposits in M2 are also instantly convertible into a means of payment. You can use the ATM to get currency to pay for your groceries or gas. But other savings deposits, time deposits, and money market funds are not instantly convertible and are *not* a means of payment.

## ■ Checks, Credit Cards, Debit Cards, and Mobile Wallets

In defining money and describing the things that serve as money today, we have not included checks, credit cards and debit cards, or mobile wallets. Aren't these things that we use when we buy something also money?

### Checks

A check is not money. It is an instruction to a bank to make a payment. The easiest way to see why a check is not money is to think about how the quantity of money you own changes if you write a check. You don't suddenly have more money because you've written a check to pay a bill. Your money is your bank deposit, not the value of the checks you've written.

### Credit Cards

A credit card is not money. It is a special type of ID card that gets you an instant loan. Suppose that you use your credit card to buy a textbook. You sign or enter your PIN and leave the store with your book. The book may be in your possession, but you've not yet paid for it. You've taken a loan from the bank that issued your credit card. Your credit card issuer pays the bookstore and you eventually get your credit card bill, which you pay using money.

### Debit Cards

A debit card works like a paper check, only faster. And just as a check isn't money, neither is a debit card. To see why a debit card works like a check, think about what happens if you use your debit card to buy your textbook. When the sales clerk swipes your card in the bookstore, the computer in the bookstore's bank gets a message: Take $100 from your account and put it in the account of the bookstore. The transaction is done in a flash. But again, the bank deposits are the money and the debit card is the tool that causes money to move from you to the bookstore.

### Mobile Wallets

A *mobile wallet* is an electronic version of a physical wallet. It is a smartphone, tablet, or smartwatch app that stores and accesses credit card or debit card data to make purchases. Examples are Apple Pay, Samsung Pay, Android Pay, and Current C. So like the credit cards and debit cards whose data it stores, a mobile wallet isn't money.

You now know that checks, credit and debit cards, and mobile wallets are not money, but one new information-age money is gradually emerging—e-cash.

### ■ An Embryonic New Money: E-Cash

*Electronic cash* (or *e-cash*) is an electronic equivalent of paper notes (dollar bills) and coins. It is an electronic currency, and for people who are willing to use it, e-cash works like other forms of money. But for e-cash to become a widely used form of money, it must evolve some of the characteristics of physical currency.

People use physical currency because it is portable, recognizable, transferable, untraceable, and anonymous and can be used to make change. The designers of e-cash aim to reproduce all of these features of notes and coins. Today's e-cash is portable, untraceable, and anonymous, but it has not yet reached the level of recognition that makes it *universally* accepted as a means of payment. E-cash doesn't yet meet the definition of money.

Like notes and coins, e-cash can be used in shops. It can also be used over the Internet. To use e-cash in a shop, the buyer uses a smart card that stores some e-cash and the shop uses a smart card reader. When a transaction is made, e-cash is transferred from the smart card directly to the shop's bank account. Users of smart cards receive their e-cash by withdrawing it from a bank account by using a special ATM or a smartphone.

Several versions of e-cash in U.S. dollars, euros, and other currencies are available on the Internet. The most popular and widely used e-cash system is PayPal, which is owned by eBay. The most sophisticated and secure e-cash is a currency called Bitcoin, which can be used to settle debts and be traded for dollars and other currencies on the Internet.

A handy advantage of e-cash over paper notes arises when you lose your wallet. If it is stuffed with dollar bills, you're out of luck. If it contains e-cash recorded on your smart card, your bank can cancel the e-cash stored on the card and issue you replacement e-cash.

Although e-cash is not yet universally accepted, it is likely that its use will grow and that it will gradually replace physical forms of currency.

# CHECKPOINT 11.1

MyEconLab Study Plan 11.1
Key Terms Quiz
Solutions Video

**Define money and describe its functions.**

## Practice Problems

1. In the United States today, which of the items in List 1 are money?

2. In January 2016, currency held by individuals and businesses and traveler's checks were $1,347 billion; checkable deposits owned by individuals and businesses were $1,764 billion; savings deposits were $8,189 billion; small time deposits were $400 billion; and money market funds and other deposits were $709 billion. Calculate M1 and M2 in January 2016.

3. In May 2016, M1 was $3,239 billion; M2 was $12,731 billion; checkable deposits owned by individuals and businesses were $1,861 billion; small time deposits were $393 billion; and money market funds and other deposits were $706 billion. Calculate currency held by individuals and businesses and traveler's checks. Calculate savings deposits.

> **LIST 1**
>
> - Your Visa card
> - The quarters inside vending machines
> - U.S. dollar bills in your wallet
> - The check that you have just written to pay for your rent
> - The loan you took out last August to pay for your tuition

## In the News

**Android Pay adds support for 115 new U.S. banks**
Android Pay now operates in the United States and the Uinted Kingdom and is expanding around the world. It supports CITI bank and AMEX and from today, 115 more banks and credit unions are joining the service.
Source: androidheadlines.com, June 30, 2016

As people use mobile wallets to make purchases, will currency disappear? How will the components of M1 change? Will credit cards and debit cards disappear?

## Solutions to Practice Problems

1. Money is defined as a means of payment. Only the quarters inside vending machines and U.S. dollar bills in your wallet are money.

2. M1 is $3,111 billion. M1 is the sum of currency held by individuals and businesses and traveler's checks ($1,347 billion) and checkable deposits owned by individuals and businesses ($1,764 billion).
M2 is $12,409 billion. M2 is the sum of M1 ($3,111 billion), savings deposits ($8,189 billion), small time deposits ($400 billion), and money market funds and other deposits ($709 billion).

3. Currency held by individuals and businesses and traveler's checks were $1,378 billion. Currency held by individuals and businesses and traveler's checks equals M1 ($3,239 billion) minus checkable deposits owned by individuals and businesses ($1,861 billion).
Savings deposits are $8,393 billion. Savings deposits equals M2 ($12,731 billion) minus M1 ($3,239 billion) minus small time deposits ($393 billion) minus money market funds and other deposits ($706 billion)

## Solution to In the News

Most people will probably carry less currency, but it won't disappear because currency is used in the underground economy. Most of M1 will be checkable deposits. Mobile wallets are digitized credit cards and debit cards, so these cards will not disappear.

## 11.2 THE BANKING SYSTEM

The banking system consists of the Federal Reserve and the banks and other institutions that accept deposits and that provide the services that enable people and businesses to make and receive payments. Sitting at the top of the system (see Figure 11.2), the Federal Reserve (or the Fed) sets the rules and regulates and influences the activities of banks and other institutions. Three types of financial institutions accept the deposits that are part of the nation's money:

- Commercial banks
- Thrift institutions
- Money market funds

Here, we describe the functions of these institutions, and in the next section, we describe the structure and functions of the Federal Reserve.

### ■ Commercial Banks

A *commercial bank* is a firm that is chartered by the Comptroller of the Currency in the U.S. Treasury (or by a state agency) to accept deposits and make loans. In 2016, about 5,260 commercial banks operated in the United States, down from 15,000 in the 1980s. The number of banks has shrunk because in 1997 the rules under which banks operate were changed, permitting them to open branches in every state. A wave of mergers followed this change of rules. Also, more than 130 banks failed during the financial crisis of 2008–2009.

### Bank Deposits

A commercial bank accepts three broad types of deposits: checkable deposits, savings deposits, and time deposits. A bank pays a low interest rate (sometimes zero) on checkable deposits, and it pays the highest interest rate on time deposits.

### ■ FIGURE 11.2

The Institutions of the Banking System                                                  MyEconLab Animation

The Federal Reserve regulates and influences the activities of the commercial banks, thrift institutions, and money market funds, whose deposits make up the nation's money.

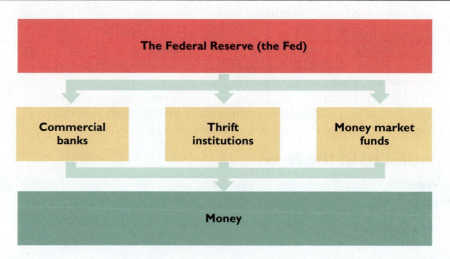

# EYE on the PAST
## The "Invention" of Banking

It is the sixteenth century somewhere in Europe: Because gold is valuable and easy to steal, goldsmiths have well-guarded safes in which people "deposit" their gold. The goldsmiths issue gold receipts entitling owners to reclaim their "deposits" on demand.

Isabella, who has a receipt for 100 ounces of gold deposited with Samuel Goldsmith, buys some land from Henry. She can pay for the land in one of two ways: She can visit Samuel, collect her gold, and hand the gold to Henry. Or she can give Henry her gold receipt, which enables Henry to claim the 100 ounces of gold.

It is a simpler and safer transaction to use the receipt. When Henry wants to buy something, he too can pass the receipt on to someone else.

So Samuel Goldsmith's gold receipt is circulating as a means of payment. It is money!

Because the receipts circulate while the gold remains in his safe, Samuel realizes that he can lend gold receipts and charge interest for doing so. Samuel writes receipts for gold that he doesn't own, but has on deposit, and lends these receipts. Samuel is one of the first bankers.

## Profit and Risk: A Balancing Act

Commercial banks try to maximize their stockholders' wealth by lending for long terms at high interest rates and borrowing from depositors and others. But lending is risky. Risky loans sometimes don't get repaid and the prices of risky securities sometimes fall. In either of these events, a bank incurs a loss that could even wipe out the stockholders' wealth. Also, when depositors see their bank incurring losses, mass withdrawals—called a run on the bank—might create a crisis. So a bank must perform a balancing act. It must be careful in the way it uses the depositors' funds and balance security for depositors and stockholders against high but risky returns. To trade off between risk and profit a bank divides its assets into four parts: reserves, liquid assets, securities, and loans.

## Reserves

A bank's **reserves** consist of currency in its vaults plus the balance on its reserve account at the Federal Reserve.

The currency in a bank's vaults is a reserve to meet its depositors' withdrawals. Your bank must replenish currency in its ATM every time you and your friends have raided it for cash for a midnight pizza.

A commercial bank's deposit at the Federal Reserve is similar to your own deposit at a bank. The bank uses its reserve account at the Fed to receive and make payments to other banks and to obtain currency. The Fed requires banks to hold a minimum percentage of deposits as reserves, called the *required reserve ratio*. Banks' *desired* reserves might exceed the required reserves, especially when the cost of borrowing reserves is high.

**Reserves**
The currency in the bank's vaults plus the balance on its reserve account at the Federal Reserve.

### Liquid Assets

Banks' *liquid assets* are short-term Treasury bills and overnight loans to other banks. The interest rates on liquid assets are low but they are low-risk assets. The interest rate on interbank loans, called the **federal funds rate**, is the central target of the Fed's monetary policy actions.

### Securities and Loans

*Securities* are bonds issued by the U.S. government and by other organizations. Some bonds have low interest rates and are safe. Some bonds have high interest rates and are risky. Mortgage-backed securities are examples of risky securities.

*Loans* are the provision of funds to businesses and individuals. Loans earn the bank a high interest rate, but they are risky and, even when not very risky, cannot be called in before the agreed date. Banks earn the highest interest rate on unpaid credit card balances, which are loans to credit card holders.

### Bank Assets and Liabilities: The Relative Magnitudes

Figure 11.3 shows the relative magnitudes of the banks' assets and liabilities—deposits and other borrowing—in 2016. After performing their profit-versus-risk balancing acts, the banks kept 17 percent of total assets in reserves (and liquid assets), 22 percent in securities, and 61 percent in loans. Checkable deposits (part of M1) and savings deposits and small time deposits (part of M2) were 75 percent of total funds. Another 13 percent of total funds were borrowed and the banks' own capital—net worth of its stock holders—was 12 percent of total funds.

The commercial banks' asset allocation in 2016 is a new normal and is a consequence of a financial crisis in 2008 and 2009. *Eye on the U.S. Economy* on p. 279 contrasts pre-crisis normal times with the depth of the crisis.

**Federal funds rate**
The interest rate on interbank loans (loans made in the federal funds market).

---

■ **FIGURE 11.3**

Commercial Banks' Assets, Liabilities, and Net Worth

MyEconLab Animation

In 2016, commercial bank loans were 61 percent of total assets, securities were 22 percent, and reserves were 17 percent.

The banks obtained the funds allocated to these assets from three sources: 75 percent from checkable deposits (part of M1) and savings deposits and small time deposits (part of M2); 13 percent borrowed from bond holders; and 12 percent from the banks' stock holders—the banks' net worth.

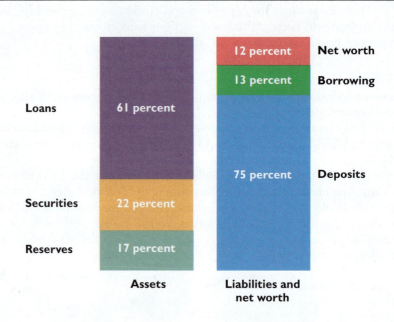

Source of data: Federal Reserve.

# EYE on the U.S. ECONOMY
## Commercial Banks Under Stress in the Financial Crisis

In normal times, bank reserves are less than 1 percent of total assets and liquid assets are less than 4 percent. Loans are 68 percent and securities 28 percent. July 2007 was such a normal time (the orange bars).

During the financial crisis that started in 2007 and intensified in September 2008, the banks took big hits as the value of their securities and loans fell.

Faced with a riskier world, the banks increased their liquid assets and reserves. In September 2009 (the blue bars), liquid assets were almost 10 percent of total assets and reserves were 8 percent.

The balancing act tipped away from risk-taking and toward security.

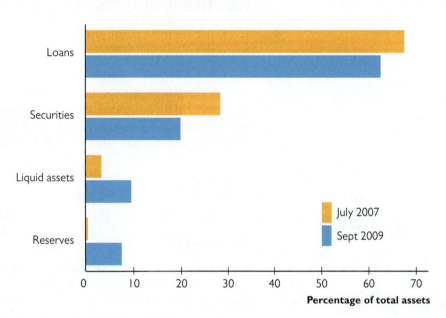

Source of data: Federal Reserve.

## ■ Thrift Institutions

The three types of thrift institutions are savings and loan associations, savings banks, and credit unions. A *savings and loan association (S&L)* is a financial institution that accepts checkable deposits and savings deposits and that makes personal, commercial, and home-purchase loans. A *savings bank* is a financial institution that accepts savings deposits and makes mostly consumer and home-purchase loans. The depositors own some savings banks (called mutual savings banks). A *credit union* is a financial institution owned by a social or economic group, such as a firm's employees, that accepts savings deposits and makes mostly consumer loans.

Like commercial banks, the thrift institutions hold reserves and must meet minimum reserve ratios set by the Fed.

## ■ Money Market Funds

A *money market fund* is a financial institution that obtains funds by selling shares and uses these funds to buy assets such as U.S. Treasury bills. Money market fund shares act like bank deposits. Shareholders can write checks on their money market fund accounts, but there are restrictions on most of these accounts. For example, the minimum deposit accepted might be $2,500 and the smallest check a depositor is permitted to write might be $500.

MyEconLab Study Plan 11.2
Key Terms Quiz
Solutions Video

 # CHECKPOINT 11.2

**Describe the functions of banks.**

## Practice Problems

1. What are the institutions that make up the banking system?

2. What is a bank's balancing act?

Use the following information to work Problems **3** and **4**.
A bank's deposits and assets are $320 in checkable deposits and $896 in savings deposits held by individuals and businesses; $840 in small time deposits; $990 in loans to businesses; $400 in outstanding credit card balances; $634 in government securities; $2 in currency in the bank's vault; and $30 in its reserve account at the Fed.

3. Calculate the bank's total deposits, deposits that are part of M1, and deposits that are part of M2.

4. Calculate the bank's loans, securities, and reserves.

## In the News

**Regulators close Georgia bank in 95th failure for the year**
Regulators shut down Atlanta-based Georgian Bank. On July 24, 2009, Georgian Bank had $2 billion in assets and $2 billion in deposits. By September 29, 2009, Georgian Bank had lost about $2 billion in home loans and other assets.
Source: *USA Today*, September 30, 2009

Explain how Georgian Bank's balancing act failed.

## Solutions to Practice Problems

1. The institutions that make up the banking system are the Fed, commercial banks, thrift institutions, and money market funds.

2. A bank makes a profit by borrowing from depositors at a low interest rate and lending at a higher interest rate. The bank must hold enough reserves to meet depositors' withdrawals. The bank's balancing act is to balance the risk of loans (profits for stockholders) against the security for depositors.

3. Total deposits are $320 + $896 + $840 = $2,056.
   Deposits that are part of M1 are checkable deposits, $320.
   Deposits that are part of M2 include all deposits, $2,056.

4. Loans are $990 + $400 = $1,390. Securities are $634.
   Reserves are $30 + $2 = $32.

## Solution to In the News

In July, Georgian Bank's $2 billion of assets (home loans and securities) balanced its deposits of $2 billion. The bank expected to make a profit on its assets that exceeded the interest it paid to depositors. The financial crisis increased the risk on all financial assets. The bank was now holding assets that were more risky than it had planned. As people defaulted on their home loans and the value of securities fell, the value of Georgian Bank's assets crashed to zero. With fewer assets than deposits, regulators had no choice other than to close the bank and sell its assets and deposits. The bank failed to balance risk against profit.

## 11.3 THE FEDERAL RESERVE SYSTEM

MyEconLab Concept Video

The **Federal Reserve System (the Fed)** is the central bank of the United States. A central bank is a public authority that provides banking services to banks and governments and regulates financial institutions and markets. A central bank does not provide banking services to businesses and individual citizens. Its only customers are banks such as Bank of America and Citibank and the U.S. government. The Fed is organized into 12 Federal Reserve districts shown in Figure 11.4.

The Fed's main task is to regulate the interest rate and quantity of money to achieve low and predictable inflation and sustained economic expansion.

**Federal Reserve System (the Fed)**
The central bank of the United States.

### ■ The Structure of the Federal Reserve

The key elements in the structure of the Federal Reserve are

- The Chair of the Board of Governors
- The Board of Governors
- The regional Federal Reserve Banks
- The Federal Open Market Committee

### The Chair of the Board of Governors

The Chair of the Board of Governors is the Fed's chief executive, public face, and center of power and responsibility. When things go right, the Chair gets the credit; when they go wrong, the Chair gets the blame. Janet Yellen, a former University of California, Berkeley, economics professor, is the Fed's current Chair.

*Fed Chair Janet Yellen*

### ■ FIGURE 11.4

The Federal Reserve Districts

MyEconLab Animation

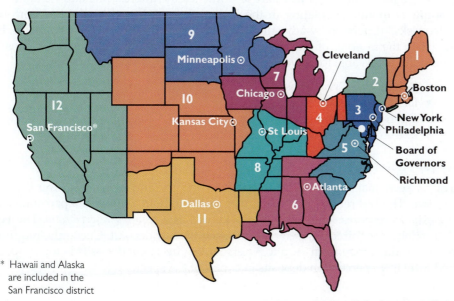

The nation is divided into 12 Federal Reserve districts, each having a Federal Reserve Bank. (Some of the larger districts also have branch banks.) The Board of Governors of the Federal Reserve System is located in Washington, D.C.

\* Hawaii and Alaska are included in the San Francisco district

SOURCE: *Federal Reserve Bulletin.*

### The Board of Governors

The Board of Governors has seven members (including the Chair), who are appointed by the President of the United States and confirmed by the Senate, each for a 14-year term. The terms are staggered so that one seat on the board becomes vacant every two years. The President appoints one of the board members as the Chair for a term of four years, which is renewable.

### The Regional Federal Reserve Banks

There are 12 regional Federal Reserve Banks, one for each of the 12 Federal Reserve districts shown in Figure 11.4. Each regional Federal Reserve Bank has nine directors, three of whom are appointed by the Board of Governors and six of whom are elected by the commercial banks in the Federal Reserve district. The directors of each regional Federal Reserve Bank appoint that Bank's president, and the Board of Governors approves this appointment.

The Federal Reserve Bank of New York (known as the New York Fed) occupies a special place because it implements some of the Fed's most important policy decisions.

### The Federal Open Market Committee

**Federal Open Market Committee**
The Fed's main policy-making committee.

The **Federal Open Market Committee** (FOMC) is the Fed's main policy-making committee. The FOMC consists of the following twelve members:

- The Chair and the other six members of the Board of Governors
- The president of the Federal Reserve Bank of New York
- Four presidents of the other regional Federal Reserve Banks (on a yearly rotating basis)

The FOMC meets approximately every six weeks to review the state of the economy and to decide the actions to be carried out by the New York Fed.

## ■ The Fed's Policy Tools

The Fed's most important tasks are to influence the interest rate and regulate the amount of money circulating in the United States. How does the Fed perform these tasks? It does so by adjusting the reserves of the banking system. Also, by adjusting the reserves of the banking system and standing ready to make loans to banks, the Fed is able to prevent bank failures. The Fed's policy tools are

- Required reserve ratios
- Discount rate
- Open market operations
- Extraordinary crisis measures

### Required Reserve Ratios

You've seen that banks hold reserves of currency and deposits at the Federal Reserve. The Fed requires the banks and thrifts to hold a minimum percentage of deposits as reserves. This minimum is known as a *required reserve ratio.* The Fed determines a required reserve ratio for each type of deposit. Currently, required reserve ratios range from zero to 3 percent on checkable deposits below a specified level to 10 percent on deposits in excess of the specified level.

### Discount Rate

The discount rate is the interest rate at which the Fed stands ready to lend reserves to commercial banks. A change in the discount rate begins with a proposal to the FOMC by at least one of the 12 Federal Reserve Banks. If the FOMC agrees that a change is required, it proposes the change to the Board of Governors for its approval.

### Open Market Operations

An **open market operation** is the purchase or sale of government securities—U.S. Treasury bills and bonds—by the Federal Reserve in the open market. When the Fed conducts an open market operation, it makes a transaction with a bank or some other business but it does not transact with the federal government. The New York Fed conducts the Fed's open market operations.

**Open market operation**
The purchase or sale of government securities—U.S. Treasury bills and bonds—by the New York Fed in the open market.

### Extraordinary Crisis Measures

The financial crisis of 2008, the slow recovery, and ongoing financial stress have brought three more tools into play. They are

- Quantitative easing (or QE)
- Credit easing
- Operation Twist

*Quantitative Easing (QE)*   When the Fed creates bank reserves by conducting a large-scale open market purchase at a low or possibly zero federal funds rate, the action is called *quantitative easing*. There have been three episodes of quantitative easing: QE1, QE2, and QE3—see *Eye on Creating Money* on pp. 292–293.

*Credit Easing*   When the Fed buys private securities or makes loans to financial institutions to stimulate their lending, the action is called *credit easing*.

*Operation Twist*   When the Fed buys long-term government securities and sells short-term government securities, the action is called *Operation Twist*. The idea is to lower long-term interest rates and stimulate long-term borrowing and invest-ment expenditure. An Operation Twist was conducted in September 2011.

### ■ How the Fed's Policy Tools Work

The Fed's normal policy tools work by changing either the demand for or the sup-ply of the monetary base, which in turn changes the interest rate. The **monetary base** is the sum of coins, Federal Reserve notes, and banks' reserves at the Fed.

**Monetary base**
The sum of coins, Federal Reserve notes, and banks' reserves at the Fed.

By increasing the required reserve ratio, the Fed can force the banks to hold a larger quantity of monetary base. By raising the discount rate, the Fed can make it more costly for the banks to borrow reserves—borrow monetary base. And by selling securities in the open market, the Fed can decrease the monetary base. All of these actions lead to a rise in the interest rate.

Similarly, by decreasing the required reserve ratio, the Fed can permit the banks to hold a smaller quantity of monetary base. By lowering the discount rate, the Fed can make it less costly for the banks to borrow monetary base. And by buying securities in the open market, the Fed can increase the monetary base. All of these actions lead to a decrease in the interest rate.

Open market operations are the Fed's main tool and in the next section you will learn in more detail how they work.

# CHECKPOINT 11.3

**Describe the functions of the Federal Reserve System (the Fed).**

## Practice Problems

1. What is the Fed and what is the FOMC?
2. Who is the Fed's chief executive, and what are the Fed's main policy tools?
3. What is the monetary base?
4. Suppose that at the end of December 2009, the monetary base in the United States was $700 billion, Federal Reserve notes were $650 billion, and banks' reserves at the Fed were $20 billion. Calculate the quantity of coins.

## In the News

**Helicopter Money Primer: The possible next frontier in quantitative easing**
Central banks—the Fed, the Bank of Japan, the European Central Bank, the People's Bank of China, and others—have bought trillions of dollars of bonds. The Fed alone has bought $4 trillion worth.

Source: DailyFX, July 15, 2016

What are the Fed's policy tools and which policy tool did the Fed use to increase its assets to $4 trillion?

## Solutions to Practice Problems

1. The Federal Reserve System (the Fed) is the U.S. central bank—a public authority that provides banking services to banks and the U.S. government and that regulates the quantity of money and the banking system. The FOMC is the Federal Open Market Committee—the Fed's main policy-making committee.

2. The Fed's chief executive is the Chair of the Board of Governors, currently Janet Yellen. The Fed's main policy tools are required reserve ratios, the discount rate, and open market operations. In unusual times, extraordinary crisis measures are an additional tool.

3. The monetary base is the sum of coins, Federal Reserve notes (dollar bills), and banks' reserves at the Fed.

4. To calculate the quantity of coins, we use the definition of the monetary base: coins plus Federal Reserve notes plus banks' reserves at the Fed.
   Quantity of coins = Monetary base − Federal Reserve notes − Banks' reserves at the Fed.
   So at the end of December 2009,
   Quantity of coins = $700 billion − $650 billion − $20 billion
   = $30 billion.

## Solution to In the News

The Fed's policy tools are the required reserve ratio, discount rate, open market operations, and extraordinary crisis measures called *quantitative easing* and *credit easing*. The policy tool used by the Fed to increase its assets to $4 trillion were large-scale open market operations called quantitative easing. These operations were conducted in three bursts known as QE1, QE2, and QE3.

## 11.4 REGULATING THE QUANTITY OF MONEY

Banks create money, but this doesn't mean that they have smoke-filled back rooms in which counterfeiters are busily working. Remember, most money is deposits, not currency. What banks create is deposits, and they do so by making loans.

### Creating Deposits by Making Loans

The easiest way to see that banks create deposits is to think about what happens when Andy, who has a Visa card issued by Citibank, uses his card to buy a tank of gas from Chevron. When Andy signs the card sales slip, he takes a loan from Citibank and obligates himself to repay the loan at a later date. At the end of the business day, a Chevron clerk takes a pile of signed credit card sales slips, including Andy's, to Chevron's bank. For now, let's assume that Chevron also banks at Citibank. The bank immediately credits Chevron's account with the value of the slips (minus the bank's commission).

You can see that these transactions have created a bank deposit and a loan. Andy has increased the size of his loan (his credit card balance), and Chevron has increased the size of its bank deposit. And because deposits are money, Citibank has created money.

If, as we've just assumed, Andy and Chevron use the same bank, no further transactions take place. But the outcome is essentially the same when two banks are involved. If Chevron's bank is the Bank of America, then Citibank uses its reserves to pay the Bank of America. Citibank has an increase in loans and a decrease in reserves; the Bank of America has an increase in reserves and an increase in deposits. The banking system as a whole has an increase in loans, an increase in deposits, and no change in reserves.

## EYE on YOUR LIFE
### Money and Your Role in Its Creation

Imagine a world without money in which you must barter for everything you buy. What kinds of items would you have available for these trades? Would you keep some stocks of items that you know lots of people are willing to accept? Would you really be bartering, or would you be using a commodity as money? How much longer would it take you to conduct all the transactions of a normal day?

Now think about your own holdings of money today. How much money do you have in your pocket or wallet? How much do you have in the bank? How does the money you hold change over the course of a month?

Of the money you're holding, which items are part of M1 and which are part of M2? Are all the items in M2 means of payment?

Now think about the role that *you* play in creating money. Every time you charge something to your credit card, you help the bank that issued it to create money. The increase in your credit card balance is a loan from the bank to you. The bank pays the seller right away. So the seller's bank deposit and your outstanding balance increase together. Money is created.

You contribute to the currency drain that limits the ability of your bank to create money when you visit the ATM and get some cash to pay for your late-night pizza.

Of course, your transactions are a tiny part of the total. But together, you and a few million other students like you play a big role in the money creation process.

If Andy had swiped his card at an automatic payment pump, all these transactions would have occurred at the time he filled his tank, and the quantity of money would have increased by the amount of his purchase (minus the bank's commission for conducting the transactions).

Three factors limit the quantity of deposits that the banking system can create:

- The monetary base
- Desired reserves
- Desired currency holding

## The Monetary Base

You've seen that the monetary base is the sum of coins, Federal Reserve notes, and banks' deposits at the Fed. The size of the monetary base limits the total quantity of money that the banking system can create because banks have a desired level of reserves and households and firms have a desired level of currency holding and both of these desired holdings of the monetary base depend on the quantity of money.

## Desired Reserves

A bank's *desired* reserves are the reserves that the bank chooses to hold. The *desired reserve ratio* is the ratio of reserves to deposits that a bank wants to hold. This ratio exceeds the *required reserve ratio* by an amount that the banks determine to be prudent on the basis of their daily business requirements.

A bank's *actual reserve ratio* changes when its customers make a deposit or a withdrawal. If a bank's customer makes a deposit, reserves and deposits increase by the same amount, so the bank's reserve ratio increases. Similarly, if a bank's customer makes a withdrawal, reserves and deposits decrease by the same amount, so the bank's reserve ratio decreases.

**Excess reserves**
A bank's actual reserves minus its desired reserves.

A bank's **excess reserves** are its actual reserves minus its desired reserves. When the banking system as a whole has excess reserves, banks can create money by making new loans. When the banking system as a whole is short of reserves, banks must destroy money by decreasing the quantity of loans.

## Desired Currency Holding

We hold our money in the form of currency and bank deposits. The proportion of money held as currency isn't constant but at any given time, people have a definite view as to how much they want to hold in each form of money.

Because households and firms want to hold some proportion of their money in the form of currency, when the total quantity of bank deposits increases, so does the quantity of currency that they want to hold.

Because desired currency holding increases when deposits increase, currency leaves the banks when loans are made and deposits increase. We call the leakage of currency from the banking system the *currency drain*. And we call the ratio of currency to deposits the *currency drain ratio*.

The greater the currency drain ratio, the smaller is the quantity of deposits and money that the banking system can create from a given amount of monetary base. The reason is that as currency drains from the banks, they are left with fewer reserves (and less excess reserves), so they make fewer loans.

## ■ How Open Market Operations Change the Monetary Base

When the Fed buys securities in an open market operation, it pays for them with newly created bank reserves and money. With more reserves in the banking system, the supply of interbank loans increases, the demand for interbank loans decreases, and the federal funds rate—the interest rate in the interbank loans market—falls.

Similarly, when the Fed sells securities in an open market operation, buyers pay for the securities with bank reserves and money. With smaller reserves in the banking system, the supply of interbank loans decreases, the demand for interbank loans increases, and the federal funds rate rises. The Fed sets a target for the federal funds rate and conducts open market operations on the scale needed to hit its target.

A change in the federal funds rate is only the first stage in an adjustment process that follows an open market operation. If banks' reserves increase, the banks can increase their lending and create even more money. If banks' reserves decrease, the banks must decrease their lending, which decreases the quantity of money. We'll study the effects of open market operations in some detail, beginning with an open market purchase.

### The Fed Buys Securities

Suppose the Fed buys $100 million of U.S. government securities in the open market. There are two cases to consider, depending on who sells the securities. A bank might sell some of its securities, or a person or business that is not a commercial bank—the general public—might sell. The outcome is essentially the same in the two cases. To convince you of this fact, we'll study the two cases, starting with the simpler case in which a commercial bank sells securities. (The seller will be someone who thinks the Fed is offering a good price for securities and it is profitable to make the sale.)

*FOMC meeting.*

***A Commercial Bank Sells*** When the Fed buys $100 million of securities from the Manhattan Commercial Bank, two things happen:

1. The Manhattan Commercial Bank has $100 million less in securities, and the Fed has $100 million more in securities.
2. To pay for the securities, the Fed increases the Manhattan Commercial Bank's reserve account at the New York Fed by $100 million.

Figure 11.5 shows the effects of these actions on the balance sheets of the Fed and the Manhattan Commercial Bank. Ownership of the securities passes from the commercial bank to the Fed, so the bank's securities decrease by $100 million and the Fed's securities increase by $100 million, as shown by the red-to-blue arrow running from the Manhattan Commercial Bank to the Fed.

The Fed increases the Manhattan Commercial Bank's reserves by $100 million, as shown by the green arrow running from the Fed to the Manhattan Commercial Bank. This action increases the reserves of the banking system.

The commercial bank's total assets remain constant, but their composition changes. Its holdings of government securities decrease by $100 million, and its reserves increase by $100 million. The bank can use these additional reserves to make loans. When the bank makes loans, it creates deposits and the quantity of money increases.

We've just seen that when the Fed buys government securities from a bank, the bank's reserves increase. What happens if the Fed buys government securities from the public—say, from AIG, an insurance company?

■ **FIGURE 11.5**

The Fed Buys Securities from a Commercial Bank                    MyEconLab Animation

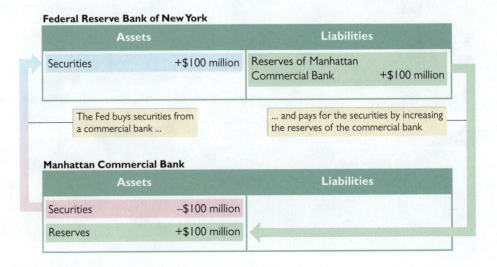

***The Nonbank Public Sells***   When the Fed buys $100 million of securities from AIG, three things happen:

1. AIG has $100 million less in securities, and the Fed has $100 million more in securities.

2. The Fed pays for the securities with a check for $100 million drawn on itself, which AIG deposits in its account at the Manhattan Commercial Bank.

3. The Manhattan Commercial Bank collects payment of this check from the Fed, and the Manhattan Commercial Bank's reserves increase by $100 million.

Figure 11.6 shows the effects of these actions on the balance sheets of the Fed, AIG, and the Manhattan Commercial Bank. Ownership of the securities passes from AIG to the Fed, so AIG's securities decrease by $100 million and the Fed's securities increase by $100 million (red-to-blue arrow). The Fed pays for the securities with a check payable to AIG, which AIG deposits in the Manhattan Commercial Bank. This payment increases Manhattan's reserves by $100 million (green arrow). It also increases AIG's deposit at the Manhattan Commercial Bank by $100 million (blue arrow). This action increases the reserves of the banking system.

**◼ FIGURE 11.6**

The Fed Buys Securities from the Public                    MyEconLab Animation

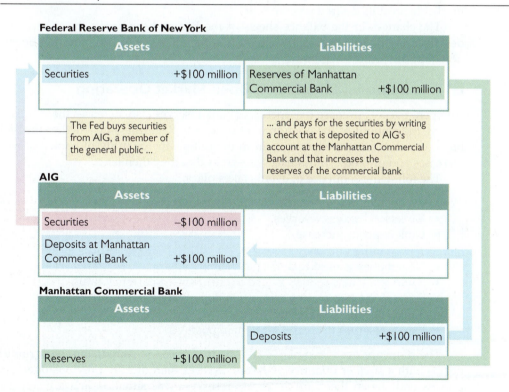

AIG has the same total assets as before, but their composition has changed. It now has more money and fewer securities. The Manhattan Commercial Bank's reserves increase, and so do its deposits—both by $100 million. Because bank reserves and deposits have increased by the same amount, the bank has excess reserves, which it can use to make loans. When it makes loans, the quantity of money increases.

We've worked through what happens when the Fed buys government securities from either a bank or the public. When the Fed sells securities, the transactions that we've just traced operate in reverse.

### The Fed Sells Securities

If the Fed sells $100 million of U.S. government securities in the open market, most likely a person or business other than a bank buys them. (A bank would buy them only if it had excess reserves and couldn't find a better use for its funds.)

When the Fed sells $100 million of securities to AIG, three things happen:

1. AIG has $100 million more in securities, and the Fed has $100 million less in securities.
2. AIG pays for the securities with a check for $100 million drawn on its deposit account at the Manhattan Commercial Bank.
3. The Fed collects payment of this check from the Manhattan Commercial Bank by decreasing its reserves by $100 million.

These actions decrease the reserves of the banking system. The Manhattan Commercial Bank is now short of reserves and must borrow in the federal funds market to meet its desired reserve ratio.

The changes in the balance sheets of the Fed and the banks that we've just described are not the end of the story about the effects of an open market operation; they are just the beginning.

## ■ The Multiplier Effect of an Open Market Operation

An open market purchase that increases bank reserves also increases the *monetary base* by the amount of the open market purchase. Regardless of whether the Fed buys securities from the banks or from the public, the quantity of bank reserves increases and gives the banks excess reserves that they then lend.

The following sequence of events takes place:

- An open market purchase creates excess reserves.
- Banks lend excess reserves.
- Bank deposits increase.
- The quantity of money increases.
- New money is used to make payments.
- Some of the new money is held as currency—a currency drain.
- Some of the new money remains in deposits in banks.
- Banks' desired reserves increase.
- Excess reserves decrease but remain positive.

The sequence described above repeats in a series of rounds, but each round begins with a smaller quantity of excess reserves than did the previous one. The process ends when there are no excess reserves. This situation arises when the increase in the monetary base resulting from the open market operation is willingly held—when the increase in desired reserves plus the increase in desired currency holding equals the increase in the monetary base. Figure 11.7 illustrates and summarizes the sequence of events in one round of the multiplier process.

An open market *sale* works similarly to an open market *purchase*, but the sale *decreases* the monetary base and sets off a multiplier process similar to that described in Figure 11.7. At the end of the process the quantity of money has decreased by an amount that lowers desired reserves and desired currency holding by an amount equal to the decrease in the monetary base resulting from the open market sale. (Make your own version of Figure 11.7 to trace the multiplier process when the Fed *sells* and the banks or public *buys* securities.)

The magnitude of the change in the quantity of money brought about by an open market operation is determined by the money multiplier that we now explain.

## The Money Multiplier

The **money multiplier** is the number by which a change in the monetary base is multiplied to find the resulting change in the quantity of money. It is also the ratio of the change in the quantity of money to the change in the monetary base.

The magnitude of the money multiplier depends on the desired reserve ratio and the currency drain ratio. The smaller are these two ratios, the larger is the money multiplier. Let's explore the money multiplier in more detail.

**Money multiplier**
The number by which a change in the monetary base is multiplied to find the resulting change in the quantity of money.

■ **FIGURE 11.7**

A Round in the Multiplier Process Following an Open Market Operation        MyEconLab Animation

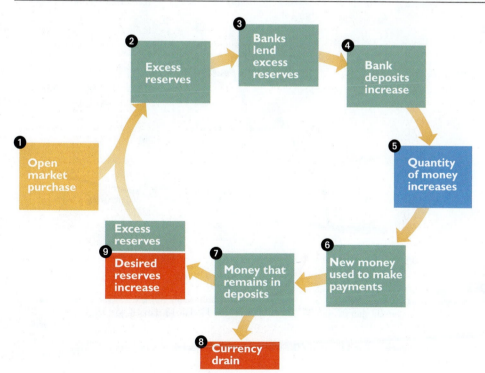

❶ An open market purchase increases bank reserves and ❷ creates excess reserves.

❸ Banks lend the excess reserves, ❹ new deposits are created, and ❺ the quantity of money increases.

❻ New money is used to make payments.

❼ Households and firms receiving payments keep some on deposit in banks and ❽ some in the form of currency—a currency drain.

❾ The increase in bank deposits increases banks' reserves but also increases banks' desired reserves.

Desired reserves increase by less than actual reserves, so the banks still have some excess reserves, but less than before. The process repeats until excess reserves have been eliminated.

To see how the desired reserve ratio and the currency drain ratio determine the size of the money multiplier, begin with two facts:

The quantity of money, $M$, is the sum of deposits, $D$, and currency, $C$, or $M = D + C$, and

The monetary base, $MB$, is the sum of desired reserves, $R$, and currency, $C$, or $MB = R + C$.

The money multiplier is equal to the quantity of money, $M$, divided by the monetary base, $MB$, that is,

$$\text{Money multiplier} = M/MB.$$

# EYE on CREATING MONEY

MyEconLab Critical Thinking Exercise

## How Does the Fed Create Money and Regulate Its Quantity?

During the Great Depression, many banks failed, bank deposits were destroyed, and the quantity of money crashed by 25 percent. Most economists believe that it was these events that turned an ordinary recession in 1929 into a deep and decade-long depression.

Former Fed Chair Ben Bernanke is one of the economists who has studied this tragic episode in U.S. economic history, and he had no intention of witnessing a similar event on his watch.

Figure 1 shows what the Fed did to pump reserves into the banking system. In the fall of 2008 in an episode called QE1 (see p. 283), the Fed doubled the monetary base. In 2010 and 2011, a more gradual but sustained QE2 took the monetary base to more than three times its pre-crisis level. And in 2012 and 2013, a further gradual QE3 raised the monetary base to four times its normal level.

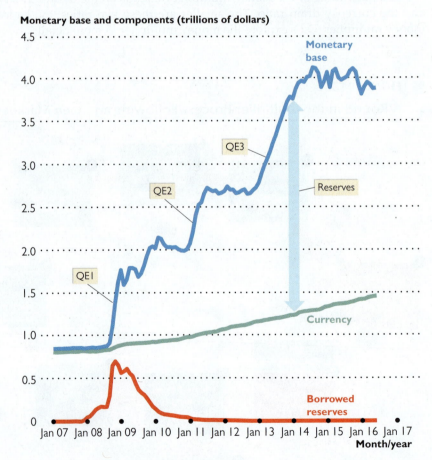

Figure 1 The Monetary Base in Financial Crisis

Because $M = D + C$ and $MB = R + C$,

$$\text{Money multiplier} = (D + C)/(R + C).$$

Now divide each item on the right-hand side of this equation by deposits, $D$, to get

$$\text{Money multiplier} = (1 + C/D)/(R/D + C/D).$$

Notice that $C/D$ is the currency drain ratio and $R/D$ is the desired reserve ratio. If the currency drain ratio is 50 percent, $C/D = 0.5$; and if the desired reserve ratio is 10 percent, $R/D = 0.1$, then the money multiplier is $1.5/0.6 = 2.5$.

The larger the desired reserve ratio and the larger the currency drain ratio, the smaller is the money multiplier.

The desired reserve ratio and the currency drain ratio that determine the magnitude of the money multiplier are not constant, so neither is the money multiplier constant. You can see in *Eye on Creating Money* below (Figure 2) that the desired reserve ratio and money multiplier changed dramatically in 2008.

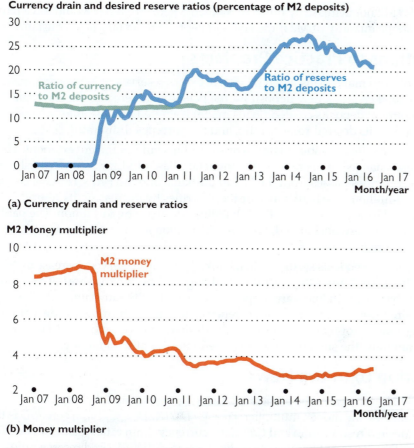

**(a) Currency drain and reserve ratios**

**(b) Money multiplier**

**Figure 2 The Changing Money Multiplier**

This extraordinary increase in the monetary base did not bring a similar increase in the quantity of money. Figure 2 shows the reason.

In 2008, the banks' desired reserve ratio, in part (a), increased tenfold from its normal level of 1.2 percent to 12 percent. This increase brought a crash in the money multiplier, in part (b), from a normal value of 9 to an unusually low value of 5.

The surge in the desired reserve ratio is the sole reason for the collapse in the money multiplier. You can see, in part (a), that the other influence on the multiplier, the currency drain ratio, barely changed.

The banks face an unusually high level of risk and this is the main source of the increase in the desired reserve ratio. As the risk faced by banks returns to normal, the desired reserve ratio will fall, and when this happens the Fed will decrease the monetary base or create an explosion in the quantity of money.

Sources of data: Federal Reserve and Bureau of Economic Analysis.

MyEconLab Study Plan 11.4

Key Terms Quiz

Solutions Video

 CHECKPOINT 11.4

**Explain how the banking system creates money and how the Fed controls the quantity of money.**

## Practice Problems

1.  How do banks create new deposits by making loans, and what factors limit the amount of deposits and loans that they can create?

2.  If the Fed makes an open market sale of $1 million of securities, who can buy the securities? What initial changes occur if the Fed sells to a bank?

3.  If the Fed makes an open market sale of $1 million of securities, what is the process by which the quantity of money changes? What factors determine the change in the quantity of money?

## In the News

**Fed doubles monetary base**

During the fourth quarter of 2008, the Fed doubled the monetary base but the quantity of money (M2) increased by only 5 percent.

Source: Federal Reserve

Why did M2 not increase by much more than 5 percent? What would have happened to the quantity of M2 if the Fed had kept the monetary base constant?

## Solutions to Practice Problems

1.  Banks can make loans when they have excess reserves. When a bank makes a loan, it creates a new deposit for the person who receives the loan. The amount of deposits created (loans made) is limited by the banks' excess reserves, its desired reserve ratio, and the currency drain ratio.

2.  The Fed sells securities to banks or the public, but not the government. The initial change is a decrease in the monetary base of $1 million. Ownership of the securities passes from the Fed to the bank, and the Fed's assets decrease by $1 million. The bank pays for the securities by decreasing its reserves at the Fed by $1 million. The Fed's liabilities decrease by $1 million. The bank's total assets are unchanged, but it has $1 million less in reserves and $1 million more in securities.

3.  When the Fed sells securities to a bank, the bank's reserves decrease by $1 million. The bank's deposits do not change, so the bank is short of reserves. The bank calls in loans and deposits decrease by the same amount. The desired reserve ratio and the currency drain ratio determine the decrease in the quantity of money. The larger the desired reserve ratio or the currency drain ratio, the smaller is the decrease in the quantity of money.

## Solution to In the News

When the Fed increases the monetary base, M2 increases and the increase is determined by the money multiplier, $(1 + C/D)/(R/D + C/D)$, where $R/D$ is the banks' desired reserve ratio and $C/D$ is the currency drain ratio. M2 didn't increase by more than 5 percent because the banks increased their desired reserve ratio, which decreased the money multiplier. If the Fed had kept the monetary base unchanged, M2 would have decreased because the money multiplier decreased.

CHAPTER SUMMARY

## Key Points

**1. Define money and describe its functions.**

- Money is anything that serves as a generally accepted means of payment.
- Money functions as a medium of exchange, unit of account, and store of value.
- M1 consists of currency held by individuals and businesses, traveler's checks, and checkable deposits owned by individuals and businesses.
- M2 consists of M1 plus savings deposits, small time deposits, and money market funds.

**2. Describe the functions of banks.**

- The deposits of commercial banks and thrift institutions are money.
- Banks borrow short term and lend long term and make a profit on the spread between the interest rates that they pay and receive.

**3. Describe the functions of the Federal Reserve System (the Fed).**

- The Federal Reserve is the central bank of the United States.
- The Fed influences the economy by setting the required reserve ratio for banks, by setting the discount rate, by open market operations, and by taking extraordinary measures in a financial crisis.

**4. Explain how the banking system creates money and how the Fed controls the quantity of money.**

- Banks create money by making loans.
- The maximum quantity of deposits the banks can create is limited by the monetary base, the banks' desired reserves, and desired currency holding.
- When the Fed buys securities in an open market operation, it creates bank reserves. When the Fed sells securities in an open market operation, it destroys bank reserves.
- An open market operation has a multiplier effect on the quantity of money.

## Key Terms

MyEconLab Key Terms Quiz

Barter, 271
Currency, 272
Excess reserves, 286
Federal funds rate, 278
Federal Open Market Committee, 282
Federal Reserve System (the Fed), 281

Fiat money, 272
M1, 272
M2, 272
Means of payment, 270
Medium of exchange, 271
Monetary base, 283

Money, 270
Money multiplier, 291
Open market operation, 283
Reserves, 277

## CHAPTER CHECKPOINT

## Study Plan Problems and Applications

**1.** What is money? Would you classify any of the items in List 1 as money?

**2.** What are the three functions that money performs? Which of the following items perform some but not all of these functions, and which perform all of these functions? Which of the items are money?

- A checking account at the Bank of America
- A dime
- A debit card

**3.** Monica transfers $10,000 from her savings account at the Bank of Alaska to her money market fund. What is the immediate change in M1 and M2?

**4.** Terry takes $100 from his checking account and deposits the $100 in his savings account. What is the immediate change in M1 and M2?

**5.** Suppose that banks had deposits of $500 billion, a desired reserve ratio of 4 percent and no excess reserves. The banks had $15 billion in notes and coins. Calculate the banks' reserves at the central bank.

**6.** Explain the Fed's policy tools and briefly describe how each works.

**7.** Table 1 shows a bank's balance sheet. The bank has no excess reserves and there is no currency drain. Calculate the bank's desired reserve ratio.

**8.** The Fed buys $2 million of securities from AIG. If AIG's bank has a desired reserve ratio of 0.1 and there is no currency drain, calculate the bank's excess reserves as soon as the open market purchase is made, the maximum amount of loans that the banking system can make, and the maximum amount of new money that the banking system can create.

Use the following information to work Problems **9** and **10**.

If the desired reserve ratio is 5 percent, the currency drain ratio is 20 percent of deposits, and the central bank makes an open market purchase of $1 million of securities, calculate the change in

**9.** The monetary base and the change in its components.

**10.** The quantity of money, and how much of the new money is currency and how much is bank deposits.

Use the following information to work Problems **11** and **12**.

**China conducts open market operations**
The People's Bank of China (the central bank of China) indicated it would lower interest rates and inject 685 billion yuan ($105 billion) into the banking system through open market operations.

Source: *Bloomberg News*, February 29, 2016

**11.** In the open market operation described in the news clip, explain whether the People's Bank of China buys or sells securities. Illustrate the effects of the open market operation on the balance sheets of the banks and the central bank.

**12.** Explain how the open market operation described in the news clip will change the quantity of money in China.

**13.** Read *Eye on Creating Money* on pp. 292–293. By how much did the monetary base increase and why didn't M2 increase by the same percentage?

**LIST 1**

- Store coupons for noodles
- A $100 Amazon.com gift certificate
- Frequent flier miles
- Credit available on your Visa card
- The dollar coins that a coin collector owns

**TABLE 1**

| Assets | | Liabilities | |
|---|---|---|---|
| (millions of dollars) | | | |
| Reserves at | | Checkable | |
| the Fed | 20 | deposits | 80 |
| Cash in vault | 5 | Savings | |
| Securities | 75 | deposits | 120 |
| Loans | 100 | | |

# Instructor Assignable Problems and Applications

MyEconLab Homework, Quiz, or Test if assigned by instructor

1. When the Fed increased the monetary base between 2008 and 2014, which component of the monetary base increased most: banks' reserves or currency? How did the banks' borrowed reserves change?

2. What happened to the money multiplier between 2008 and 2014? What would the money multiplier have been if the currency drain ratio had increased? What would the money multiplier have been if the banks' desired reserve ratio had not changed?

3. What are the three functions that money performs? Which of the items in List 1 perform some but not all of these functions and which of the items are money?

4. Naomi buys $1,000 worth of American Express traveler's checks and charges the purchase to her American Express card. What is the immediate change in M1 and M2?

5. A bank has $500 million in checkable deposits, $600 million in savings deposits, $400 million in small time deposits, $950 million in loans to businesses, $500 million in government securities, $20 million in currency, and $30 million in its reserve account at the Fed. Calculate the bank's deposits that are part of M1, deposits that are part of M2, and the bank's loans, securities, and reserves.

6. What can the Fed do to increase the quantity of money and keep the monetary base constant? Explain why the Fed would or would not

   - Change the currency drain ratio.
   - Change the required reserve ratio.
   - Change the discount rate.
   - Conduct an open market operation.

**LIST 1**

- An antique clock
- An S&L savings deposit
- Your credit card
- The coins in the Fed's museum
- Government securities

Use Table 1, which shows a bank's balance sheet, to work Problems **7** and **8**. The desired reserve ratio on all deposits is 5 percent and there is no currency drain.

7. Calculate the bank's excess reserves. If the bank uses all of these excess reserves to make a loan, what is the quantity of the loan and the quantity of total deposits after the bank has made the loan?

8. If there is no currency drain, what is the quantity of loans and the quantity of total deposits when the bank has no excess reserves?

Use the following information to work Problems **9**, **10**, and **11**.

**China lowers reserve requirements**
The People's Bank of China lowered the required reserve ratio from 17.5 percent to 17 percent, noting that it remained much higher than in other countries.
                    Source: *Bloomberg News*, February 29, 2016

9. Compare the required reserve ratio in China and the required reserve ratio on checkable deposits in the United States today.

10. If the currency drain ratio in China is 10 percent of deposits and the desired reserve ratio equals the required reserve ratio, calculate the money multipliers in China and compare it with the U.S. money multiplier.

11. If the currency drain ratio in China is 10 percent of deposits, by how much did the money multiplier change when the required reserve ratio changed as described in the news clip?

**TABLE 1**

| Assets | | Liabilities | |
|--------|---|------------|---|
| (millions of dollars) | | | |
| Reserves at | | Checkable | |
| the Fed | 25 | deposits | 90 |
| Cash in vault | 15 | Savings | |
| Securities | 60 | deposits | 110 |
| Loans | 100 | | |

MyEconLab Chapter 11 Study Plan

## Multiple Choice Quiz

1.  A commodity or token is money if it is _____.

    A. generally accepted as a means of payment
    B. a store of value
    C. used in a barter transaction
    D. completely safe as a store of value

2.  Money in the United States today includes _____.

    A. currency and deposits at both banks and the Fed
    B. the currency in people's wallets, stores' tills, and the bank deposits that people and businesses own
    C. currency in ATMs and people's bank deposits
    D. the banks' reserves and bank deposits owned by individuals and businesses

3.  Rick withdraws $500 from his savings account, keeps $100 as currency, and deposits $400 in his checking account.

    A. M1 increases by $400 and M2 decreases by $500.
    B. M1 does not change, but M2 decreases by $500.
    C. M1 does not change, but M2 decreases by $400.
    D. M1 increases by $500 and M2 does not change.

4.  Commercial banks' assets include _____.

    A. bank deposits of individuals and businesses and bank reserves
    B. loans to individuals and businesses and government securities
    C. bank reserves and the deposits in M2
    D. government securities and borrowed funds

5.  The Fed's policy tools include all the following *except* _____.

    A. required reserve ratio and open market operations
    B. quantitative easing
    C. discount rate
    D. taxing banks' deposits at the Fed

6.  A commercial bank creates money when it does all the following *except* _____.

    A. decreases its excess reserves
    B. makes loans
    C. creates deposits
    D. puts cash in its ATMs

7.  An open market _____ of $100 million of securities _____.

    A. purchase; increases bank reserves
    B. sale; increases bank reserves
    C. purchase; decreases the Fed's liabilities
    D. sale; increases the Fed's liabilities

8.  The money multiplier _____.

    A. increases if banks increase their desired reserve ratio
    B. increases if the currency drain ratio increases
    C. is 1 if the desired reserve ratio equals the currency drain ratio
    D. decreases if banks increase their desired reserve ratio

## What causes inflation?

# Money, Interest, and Inflation

**12**

**When you have completed your study of this chapter, you will be able to**

**CHAPTER CHECKLIST**

**1** Explain what determines the demand for money and how the demand for money and the supply of money determine the *nominal* interest rate.

**2** Explain how in the long run, the quantity of money determines the price level and money growth brings inflation.

**3** Identify the costs of inflation and the benefits of a stable value of money.

MyEconLab Big Picture Video

MyEconLab Concept Video

# WHERE WE ARE AND WHERE WE'RE HEADING

Before we explore the effects of money on the interest rate and the inflation rate, let's take stock of what we've learned and preview where we are heading.

## ■ The Real Economy

*Real* factors that are independent of the price level determine potential GDP and the natural unemployment rate (Chapter 8). The demand for labor and supply of labor determine the quantity of labor employed and the real wage rate at full employment. The full-employment equilibrium quantity of labor and the production function determine potential GDP. At full employment, real GDP equals potential GDP and the unemployment rate equals the natural unemployment rate.

Investment and saving along with population growth, human capital growth, and technological change determine the growth rate of real GDP (Chapter 9).

Investment and saving plans influence the demand for and supply of loanable funds, which in turn determine the real interest rate and the equilibrium amount of investment and saving (Chapter 10).

## ■ The Money Economy

Money consists of currency and bank deposits. Banks create deposits by making loans, and the Fed influences the quantity of money through its open market operations, which determine the monetary base and the federal funds rate—the interest rate on interbank loans (Chapter 11).

The effects of the Fed's actions and of changes in the quantity of money are complex. In the current chapter (Chapter 12), we focus on the immediate effects and on the long-run or ultimate effects of the Fed's actions.

The immediate effects are on the short-term nominal interest rate. If the Fed increases (or decreases) the quantity of money, the short-term nominal interest rate falls (or rises).

The long-run effects of the Fed's actions are on the price level and the inflation rate. In the long run, the loanable funds market determines the real interest rate and the Fed's actions determine only the price level and the inflation rate. If the Fed increases (or decreases) the quantity of money, the price level rises (or falls). And if the Fed speeds up (or slows down) the rate at which the quantity of money grows, the inflation rate increases (or decreases).

## ■ Real and Money Interactions and Policy

When the Fed changes the short-term nominal interest rate, other changes ripple through the economy. Expenditure plans change and real GDP, employment, unemployment, and the price level (and inflation rate) all change. In the long run, the real effects fade, leaving changes in only the price level and inflation rate. We lay the foundation for studying the ripple effects of the Fed's actions in Chapters 13–15. These chapters explain how the real and monetary factors interact and describe the short-run constraint on the Fed's choices.

Chapters 16 and 17 build on the foundation of all the preceding chapters. Chapter 16 explains how the government uses fiscal policy to sustain economic growth and stabilize output and employment. Chapter 17 explains how the Fed uses monetary policy to achieve those same goals and to control inflation.

## 12.1 MONEY AND THE INTEREST RATE

MyEconLab Concept Video

To understand the Fed's influence on the interest rate, we study the demand for money, the supply of money, and the forces that bring equilibrium in the market for money. We'll begin with the demand for money.

### ■ The Demand for Money

The amount of money that households and firms choose to hold is the **quantity of money demanded**. What determines the quantity of money demanded? The answer is the "price" of money. But what is that "price"?

Two possible answers, both correct, are the value of money and the opportunity cost of holding money. The value of money is the quantity of goods and services that a dollar will buy, which is related to the *price level*. We'll explore this "price" of money when we study the long-run effects of money in the next part of this chapter. The opportunity cost of holding money is the goods and services forgone by holding money rather than some other asset.

To determine the quantity of money to hold, households and firms compare the benefit from holding money to its opportunity cost. They choose to hold the quantity that balances the benefit of holding an *additional* dollar of money against its opportunity cost. What are the benefit and opportunity cost of holding money?

**Quantity of money demanded**
The amount of money that households and firms choose to hold.

#### Benefit of Holding Money

You've seen that money is the means of payment (Chapter 11, p. 270). The more money you hold, the easier it is for you to make payments. By holding enough money you can settle your bills at the end of each month without having to spend time and effort raising a loan or selling some other financial asset.

The marginal benefit of holding money is the change in total benefit that results from holding one more dollar as money. The marginal benefit of holding money diminishes as the quantity of money held increases. If you hold only a few dollars in money, then holding a few more dollars brings large benefits—you can buy a coffee or take a bus ride. If you hold enough money to make your normal weekly payments, then holding more dollars brings only a small benefit because you're not very likely to want to spend those extra dollars. Holding even more money brings only a small additional benefit. You barely notice the difference in the benefit of having $1,000 versus $1,001 in your bank account.

To get the most out of your assets, you hold money only up to the point at which its marginal benefit equals its opportunity cost.

#### Opportunity Cost of Holding Money

The opportunity cost of holding money is the interest rate forgone on an alternative asset. If you can earn 8 percent a year on a mutual fund account, then holding an additional $100 in money costs you $8 a year. Your opportunity cost of holding $100 in money is the goods and services worth $8 that you must forgo.

A fundamental principle of economics is that if the opportunity cost of something increases, people seek substitutes for it. Money is no exception. Other assets such as a mutual fund account are substitutes for money. The higher the opportunity cost of holding money—the higher the interest income forgone by not holding other assets—the smaller is the quantity of money demanded.

## Opportunity Cost: *Nominal* Interest Is a *Real* Cost

The opportunity cost of holding money is the nominal interest rate. In Chapter 7 (p. 184), you learned the distinction between the *nominal* interest rate and the *real* interest rate and that

$$\text{Real interest rate} = \text{Nominal interest rate} - \text{Inflation rate.}$$

We can use this equation to find the real interest rate for a given nominal interest rate and inflation rate. For example, if the nominal interest rate on a mutual fund account is 8 percent a year and the inflation rate is 2 percent a year, the real interest rate is 6 percent a year. Why isn't the real interest rate of 6 percent a year the opportunity cost of holding money? That is, why isn't the opportunity cost of holding $100 in money only $6 worth of goods and services forgone?

The answer is that if you hold $100 in money rather than in a mutual fund, your buying power decreases by $8, not by $6. With inflation running at 2 percent a year, on each $100 that you hold as money and that earns no interest, you lose $2 worth of buying power a year. On each $100 that you put into your mutual fund account, you gain $6 worth of buying power a year. So if you hold money rather than a mutual fund, you lose the buying power of $6 plus $2, or $8—equivalent to the nominal interest rate on the mutual fund, not the real interest rate.

Because the opportunity cost of holding money is the nominal interest rate on an alternative asset,

> **Other things remaining the same, the higher the nominal interest rate, the smaller is the quantity of money demanded.**

This relationship describes the decision made by an individual or a firm about how much money to hold. It also describes money-holding decisions for the economy—the sum of the decisions of every individual and firm.

We summarize the influence of the nominal interest rate on money-holding decisions in a demand for money schedule and curve.

## The Demand for Money Schedule and Curve

**Demand for money**
The relationship between the quantity of money demanded and the nominal interest rate, when all other influences on the amount of money that people wish to hold remain the same.

The **demand for money** is the relationship between the quantity of money demanded and the nominal interest rate, when all other influences on the amount of money that people wish to hold remain the same. We illustrate the demand for money with a demand for money schedule and a demand for money curve, such as those in Figure 12.1. If the interest rate is 5 percent a year, the quantity of money demanded is $1 trillion. The quantity of money demanded decreases to $0.98 trillion if the interest rate rises to 6 percent a year and increases to $1.02 trillion if the interest rate falls to 4 percent a year.

The demand for money curve is *MD*. When the interest rate rises, everything else remaining the same, the opportunity cost of holding money rises and the quantity of money demanded decreases—there is a movement up along the demand for money curve. When the interest rate falls, the opportunity cost of holding money falls and the quantity of money demanded increases—there is a movement down along the demand for money curve.

**FIGURE 12.1**

## The Demand for Money

MyEconLab Animation

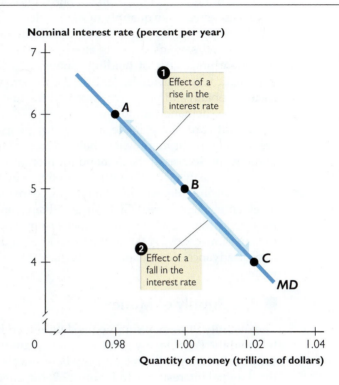

| | Nominal interest rate (percent per year) | Quantity of money demanded (trillions of dollars) |
|---|---|---|
| **A** | 6 | 0.98 |
| **B** | 5 | 1.00 |
| **C** | 4 | 1.02 |

The demand for money schedule is graphed as the demand for money curve, *MD*. Rows *A, B,* and *C* in the table correspond to points *A, B,* and *C* on the curve. The nominal interest rate is the opportunity cost of holding money.

Other things remaining the same, ❶ an increase in the nominal interest rate decreases the quantity of money demanded, and ❷ a decrease in the nominal interest rate increases the quantity of money demanded.

## ■ Changes in the Demand for Money

A change in the nominal interest rate brings a change in the quantity of money demanded and a movement along the demand for money curve. A change in any other influence on money holding changes the demand for money. The three main influences on the demand for money are

- The price level
- Real GDP
- Financial technology

### The Price Level

The demand for money is proportional to the price level—an *x* percent rise in the price level brings an *x* percent increase in the quantity of money demanded at each nominal interest rate. The reason is that we hold money to make payments: If the price level changes, the quantity of dollars that we need to make payments changes in the same proportion.

### Real GDP

The demand for money increases as real GDP increases. The reason is that when real GDP increases, expenditures and incomes increase. To make the increased expenditures and income payments, households and firms must hold larger average amounts of money.

### Financial Technology

Changes in financial technology change the demand for money. Most changes in financial technology come from advances in computing and record keeping. Some advances increase the quantity of money demanded, and some decrease it.

Daily interest checking deposits and automatic transfers between checkable deposits and savings deposits enable people to earn interest on money, lower the opportunity cost of holding money, and increase the demand for money. Automatic teller machines, debit cards, and smart cards, which have made money easier to obtain and use, have increased the marginal benefit from money and increased the demand for money.

Credit cards have made it easier for people to buy goods and services on credit and pay for them when their credit card account becomes due. This development has decreased the demand for money.

A change in any of the influences on money holdings that we've just reviewed other than the interest rate changes the demand for money. A rise in the price level, an increase in real GDP, or an advance in financial technology that lowers the opportunity cost of holding money or makes money more useful increases the demand for money. A fall in the price level, a decrease in real GDP, or a technological advance that creates a substitute for money decreases the demand for money.

### ■ The Supply of Money

**Supply of money**
The relationship between the quantity of money supplied and the nominal interest rate.

The quantity of money supplied is determined by the actions of the banking system and the Fed. On any given day, the quantity of money supplied is fixed. The **supply of money** is the relationship between the quantity of money supplied and the nominal interest rate. In Figure 12.2, the quantity of money supplied is $1 trillion regardless of the nominal interest rate, so the supply of money curve is the vertical line *MS*.

### ■ The Nominal Interest Rate

People hold some of their financial wealth as money and some in the form of other financial assets. You have seen that the amount of wealth that people hold as money depends on the nominal interest rate that they can earn on other financial assets. Demand and supply determine the nominal interest rate. We can study the forces of demand and supply in either the market for financial assets or the market for money. Because the Fed influences the quantity of money, we focus on the market for money.

On a given day, the price level, real GDP, and the state of financial technology are fixed. Because these influences on the demand for money are fixed, the demand for money curve is given.

The interest rate is the only influence on the quantity of money demanded that is free to fluctuate. Every day, the interest rate adjusts to make the quantity of money demanded equal the quantity of money supplied—to achieve money market equilibrium.

In Figure 12.2, the demand for money curve is *MD*. The equilibrium interest rate is 5 percent a year. At any interest rate above 5 percent a year, the quantity of money demanded is less than the quantity of money supplied. At any interest rate below 5 percent a year, the quantity of money demanded exceeds the quantity of money supplied.

**FIGURE 12.2**

## Money Market Equilibrium

MyEconLab Animation

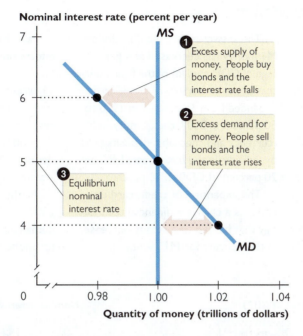

The supply of money curve is *MS*, and the demand for money curve is *MD*.

**1** If the interest rate is 6 percent a year, the quantity of money held exceeds the quantity demanded. People buy bonds, the price of a bond rises, and the interest rate falls.

**2** If the interest rate is 4 percent a year, the quantity of money held falls short of the quantity demanded. People sell bonds, the price of a bond falls, and the interest rate rises.

**3** If the interest rate is 5 percent a year, the quantity of money held equals the quantity demanded. The money market is in equilibrium.

***The Interest Rate and Bond Price Move in Opposite Directions***   When the government issues a bond, it specifies the dollar amount of interest that it will pay each year on the bond. Suppose that the government issues a bond that pays $100 of interest a year. The interest *rate* that you receive on this bond depends on the price that you pay for it. If the price is $1,000, the interest rate is 10 percent a year—$100 is 10 percent of $1,000.

If the price of the bond *falls* to $500, the interest rate *rises* to 20 percent a year. The reason is that you still receive an interest payment of $100, but this amount is 20 percent of the $500 price of the bond. If the price of the bond *rises* to $2,000, the interest rate *falls* to 5 percent a year. Again, you still receive an interest payment of $100, but this amount is 5 percent of the $2,000 price of the bond.

***Interest Rate Adjustment***   If the interest rate is above its equilibrium level, people would like to hold less money than they are actually holding. They try to get rid of some money by buying other financial assets such as bonds. The demand for financial assets increases, the prices of these assets rise, and the interest rate falls. The interest rate keeps falling until the quantity of money that people want to hold increases to equal the quantity of money supplied.

Conversely, when the interest rate is below its equilibrium level, people are holding less money than they would like to hold. They try to get more money by selling other financial assets. The demand for these financial assets decreases, the prices of these assets fall, and the interest rate rises. The interest rate keeps rising until the quantity of money that people want to hold decreases to equal the quantity of money supplied.

# EYE on the U.S. ECONOMY
## Credit Cards and Money

Today, 70 percent of U.S. households own a credit card. That's down a bit from a peak of 83 percent in 2002.

By using a credit card account to buy goods and services, it is possible to economize on money holding. Instead of holding and using money, a card holder buys with a card and then pays off the card account balance (or part of it) on her or his own pay day.

Back in 1970, only 18 percent of U.S. households had a credit card. How has the spread of credit cards affected the quantity of money that we hold?

The answer is that the quantity of M1 money has decreased as a percentage of GDP. Part (a) of the figure shows that as the ownership of credit cards expanded from 18 percent in 1970 to 80 percent in 2007, the quantity of M1 (currency and checkable deposits held by individuals and businesses) fell from 20 percent of GDP to 10 percent.

The expansion of credit card ownership is a change in financial technology that has led to a steady decrease in the demand for M1 money.

Part (b) of the figure shows the effects on the demand for money. Here, we graph the quantity of M1 as a percentage of GDP against the interest rate. As credit card use increased between 1970 and 2007, the demand for money decreased and the demand for money curve shifted leftward from $MD_0$ to $MD_1$.

As the interest rate fell between 2007 and 2014, the quantity of money demanded increased along the demand for money curve $MD_1$.

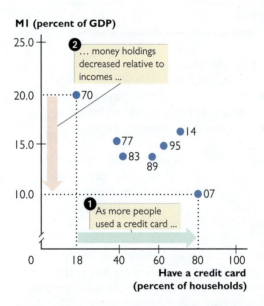

SOURCE OF DATA: Federal Reserve.

**(a) Changes in the use of credit cards and money**

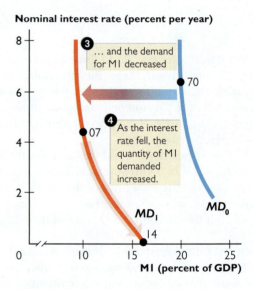

**(b) Changes in the demand for M1**

## ◼ Changing the Interest Rate

To change the interest rate, the Fed changes the quantity of money. Figure 12.3 illustrates two changes. The demand for money curve is *MD*. If the Fed increases the quantity of money to $1.02 trillion, the supply of money curve shifts rightward from $MS_0$ to $MS_1$ and the interest rate falls to 4 percent a year. If the Fed decreases the quantity of money to $0.98 trillion, the supply of money curve shifts leftward from $MS_0$ to $MS_2$ and the interest rate rises to 6 percent a year.

**FIGURE 12.3**

Interest Rate Changes

MyEconLab Animation

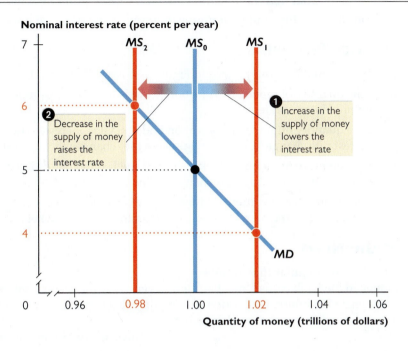

The demand for money is *MD*, and initially, the supply of money is $MS_0$. The interest rate is 5 percent a year.

**1** If the Fed increases the quantity of money and the supply of money curve shifts rightward to $MS_1$, the interest rate falls to 4 percent a year.

**2** If the Fed decreases the quantity of money and the supply of money curve shifts leftward to $MS_2$, the interest rate rises to 6 percent a year.

# EYE on YOUR LIFE
## Money Holding and Fed Watching

MyEconLab Critical Thinking Exercise

How much currency (cash) do you have in your wallet, on average? How much money do you keep in your bank account, on average?

Why don't you hold a larger average bank balance by paying off a smaller part of your credit card balance than you can afford to pay?

Wouldn't it be better to keep a bit more money in the bank?

Almost certainly, that would not be a smart idea. Why? Because the opportunity cost of holding that money would be too high.

If you have an outstanding credit card balance, the interest rate on that balance is the opportunity cost of holding money.

By paying off as much of your credit card balance as you can afford, you avoid a high interest rate on the outstanding balance.

Your demand for money is sensitive to this opportunity cost.

Do you watch the Fed? Probably not, but you can learn to become an effective Fed watcher. In the process, you will become much better informed about the state of the U.S. economy and the state of the economy in your region.

To become a Fed watcher, try to get into the habit of visiting the Fed's Web site at www.federalreserve.gov. Type "Beige Book" in the Search tool and look at the latest Beige Book to see what is happening in your region.

Also, keep an eye on the FOMC calendar for the dates of interest rate announcements. On these dates, check the media for opinions on what the Fed's interest rate decision will be. After the decision is made and announced, check the Fed's explanation as to why it made its decision.

MyEconLab Study Plan 12.1
Key Terms Quiz
Solutions Video

# CHECKPOINT 12.1

**Explain what determines the demand for money and how the demand for money and the supply of money determine the *nominal* interest rate.**

## Practice Problems

Use the demand for money curve in Figure 1 to work Problems **1** to **3**.

1. If the quantity of money is $4 trillion, what is the supply of money and the nominal interest rate?

2. If the quantity of money is $4 trillion and real GDP increases, how will the interest rate change? Explain the process that changes the interest rate.

3. If the quantity of money is $4 trillion and the Fed decreases it to $3.9 trillion, how will the price of a bond change? Why?

4. If banks increase the interest rate they pay on deposits, how will the demand for money and the nominal interest rate in the money market change?

## In the News

**Cash is more popular than bonds**

Money in the bank earns almost nothing. Even so, in the second half of 2015 an additional $208 billion was added to bank deposits and money market funds and billions of dollars were moved from bonds.

Source: CNN Money, February 5, 2016

What is the opportunity cost of holding money? If people move out of bonds and into money, how will the demand for money and the interest rate change?

## Solutions to Practice Problems

1. The supply of money is the curve *MS*. The interest rate is 4 percent a year, at the intersection of $MD_1$ and *MS* (Figure 2).

2. The demand for money increases, and the demand for money curve shifts from $MD_1$ to $MD_2$ (Figure 2). At an interest rate of 4 percent a year, people want to hold more money, so they sell bonds. The price of a bond falls, and the interest rate rises.

3. At 4 percent a year, people would like to hold $4 trillion. With only $3.9 trillion of money available, they sell bonds to get more money. The price of a bond falls, and the interest rate rises. The price will fall and the interest rate will rise until the quantity of money that people want to hold equals the $3.9 trillion available. The interest rate rises to 6 percent a year (Figure 3).

4. A higher interest rate on bank deposits lowers the opportunity cost of holding money, so the demand for money increases. As the demand for money increases, with no change in the supply of money, the nominal interest rate in the money market rises (as Figure 2 shows).

## Solution to In the News

The opportunity cost of holding money is the interest rate forgone by not holding bonds. If people sell bonds, the demand for money increases. The increase in the demand for money with no change in the supply of money raises the interest rate on bonds. (People sell bonds, so the price of a bond falls).

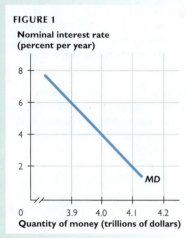

**FIGURE 1**

Nominal interest rate (percent per year)

Quantity of money (trillions of dollars)

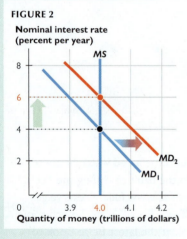

**FIGURE 2**

Nominal interest rate (percent per year)

Quantity of money (trillions of dollars)

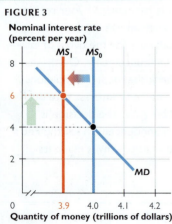

**FIGURE 3**

Nominal interest rate (percent per year)

Quantity of money (trillions of dollars)

A change in the nominal interest rate is the initial effect of a change in the quantity of money, but it is not the ultimate or long-run effect. When the interest rate changes, borrowing and lending and investment and consumption spending also change, which in turn change production and prices—change real GDP and the price level.

The details of this adjustment process are complex, and we explore them in the next two chapters. But the place where the process comes to rest—the *long-run* outcome—is easier to describe. It is crucial to understand the long-run outcome because that is where the economy is heading. We're now going to examine the long-run equilibrium in the money market.

## ■ The Money Market in the Long Run

The *long run* refers to the economy at full employment when real GDP equals potential GDP (Chapter 8, p. 195). Over the business cycle, real GDP fluctuates around potential GDP. But averaging over an expansion and recession and a peak and trough, real GDP equals potential GDP. That is, real GDP equals potential GDP *on average*. So another way to think about the *long run* is as a description of the economy *on average* over the business cycle.

### The Long-Run Demand for Money

In the long run, equilibrium in the loanable funds market determines the real interest rate (Chapter 10, pp. 250–257). The nominal interest rate that influences money holding plans equals the real interest rate plus the inflation rate. For now, we'll consider an economy that has no inflation, so the real interest rate equals the nominal interest rate. (We'll consider inflation later in this chapter.)

With the interest rate determined by real forces in the long run, what is the variable that adjusts to make the quantity of money that people plan to hold equal the quantity of money supplied? The answer is the "price" of money. The law of demand applies to money just as it does to any other object. The lower the "price" of money, the greater is the quantity of money that people are willing to hold. What is the "price" of money? It is the *value* of money.

### The Value of Money

The *value of money* is the quantity of goods and services that a unit of money will buy. It is the inverse of the *price level, P,* which equals the GDP price index divided by 100. That is,

$$\text{Value of money} \ = \ 1/P.$$

To see why, suppose that you have $100 in your wallet. If you spend that money, you can buy goods and services valued at $100. Now suppose that the price level rises by 10 percent. After the price rise, the quantity of goods and services that $100 can buy has fallen. Your $100 can now buy only $100 divided by 1.1 or $91 of goods and services. Yesterday's $100 is worth $91 today. The price level has risen and the value of money has fallen and each percentage change is the same. The higher the value of money, the smaller is the quantity of money that people plan to hold. If it seems strange that a higher value of money makes people want to hold less money, think about how much money you would plan to hold if the price of a restaurant meal was 20 cents and the price of a movie ticket was 10 cents. You would be happy to hold (say) $1 on average. But if the price of a meal is $20 and the price of a movie ticket is $10, you would want to hold $100 on average. The price level is lower and the value of money higher in the first case than in the second; and the amount of money you would plan to hold is lower in the first case than in the second.

## Money Market Equilibrium in the Long Run

In the long run, money market equilibrium determines the value of money. If the quantity of money supplied exceeds the long-run quantity demanded, people go out and spend their surplus money. The quantity of goods and services available is fixed equal to potential GDP, so the extra spending forces prices upward. As the price level rises, the value of money falls.

If the quantity of money supplied is less than the long-run quantity demanded, people lower their spending to build up the quantity of money they hold. The shortage of money translates into a surplus of goods and services, so the spending cut-back forces prices downward. The price level falls and the value of money rises. When the quantity of money supplied equals the long-run quantity demanded, the price level and the value of money are at their equilibrium levels.

Figure 12.4 illustrates long-run money market equilibrium. The long-run demand for money curve is *LRMD*. Its position depends on potential GDP and the equilibrium interest rate. The supply of money is *MS*. Equilibrium occurs when the value of money is 1.

■ **FIGURE 12.4**

Long-Run Money Market Equilibrium

MyEconLab Animation

The long-run demand for money is determined by potential GDP and the equilibrium interest rate.

The *LRMD* curve shows how the quantity of money that households and firms plan to hold, in the long run, depends on the value of money (or 1/P, the inverse of the price level).

The *MS* curve shows the quantity of money supplied, which is $1 trillion.

The price level adjusts to make the value of money equal 1 and achieve long-run money market equilibrium.

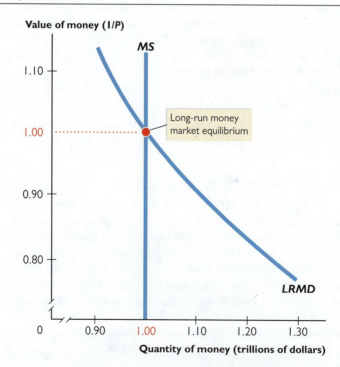

## ■ A Change in the Quantity of Money

Suppose that starting from a long-run equilibrium, the Fed increases the quantity of money by 10 percent. In the short run, the greater quantity of money lowers the nominal interest rate. With a lower interest rate, people and businesses borrow more and spend more. But with real GDP equal to potential GDP, there are no more goods and services to buy, so when people go out and spend, prices start to rise. Eventually, a new long-run equilibrium is reached at which the price level has increased in proportion to the increase in the quantity of money. Because the quantity of money increased by 10 percent, the price level has also risen by 10 percent from 1.0 to 1.1.

Figure 12.5 illustrates this outcome. Initially, the supply of money is $MS_0$ and the quantity of money is $1 trillion. The Fed increases the supply of money to $MS_1$ and the quantity of money is now $1.1 trillion—a 10 percent increase. There is now a surplus of money and people go out and spend it. The increased spending on the same unchanged quantity of goods and services raises the price level and lowers the value of money. Eventually, the price level has increased by 10 percent from 1.0 to 1.1 and the value of money has decreased by 10 percent from 1.00 to 0.91.

You've just seen a key proposition about the quantity of money and the price level.

**In the long run and other things remaining the same, a given percentage change in the quantity of money brings an equal percentage change in the price level.**

## ■ FIGURE 12.5

### The Long-Run Effect of a Change in the Quantity of Money                    MyEconLab Animation

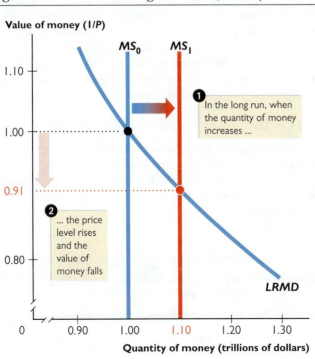

❶ The Fed increases the supply of money from $MS_0$ to $MS_1$ and the quantity of money increases from $1 trillion to $1.1 trillion, a 10 percent increase.

❷ The price level rises by 10 percent and the value of money falls by 10 percent to restore long-run money market equilibrium.

### ■ The Price Level in a Baby-Sitting Club

It is hard to visualize a long-run equilibrium and even harder to visualize and compare two long-run equilibrium situations like those that we've just described. An example of a simpler situation might help.

In an isolated neighborhood, there are no teenagers but lots of young children, and parents can't find any babysitters. So they form a club and sit for each other. The deal is that each time a parent sits for someone else, he or she receives a token that can be used to buy one babysitting session from another member of the club. The organizer notices that the club is inactive. Every member has a few unspent tokens, but they spend them infrequently. To make the club more active, the organizer decides to issue every member one token for each token that is currently held, so the supply of tokens doubles.

With more tokens to spend, parents start to plan more evenings out. Suddenly, the phones are ringing as parents seek babysitters. Every member of the club wants a sitter, but there are no more sitters than before. After making a few calls and finding no sitters available, anxious parents who really do need a sitter start to offer a higher price: two tokens per session. That does the trick. At the higher price, the quantity of baby-sitting services demanded decreases and the quantity supplied increases. Equilibrium is restored. Nothing real has changed, but the quantity of tokens and the price level have doubled.

Think of the equilibrium quantity of baby-sitting services as potential GDP, the quantity of tokens as the quantity of money, and the price of a baby-sitting session as the price level. You can then see how a given percentage change in the quantity of money at full employment brings an equal percentage change in the price level.

### ■ The Quantity Theory of Money

**Quantity theory of money**
The proposition that when real GDP equals potential GDP, an increase in the quantity of money brings an equal percentage increase in the price level.

The proposition that when real GDP equals potential GDP, an increase in the quantity of money brings an equal percentage increase in the price level is called the **quantity theory of money**. We've derived this proposition by looking at equilibrium in the money market in the long run. Another way of seeing the relationship between the quantity of money and the price level uses the concepts of *the velocity of circulation* and *the equation of exchange*. We're now going to explore the quantity theory. We're then going to see how ongoing money growth brings inflation and see what determines the inflation rate in the long run.

#### The Velocity of Circulation and Equation of Exchange

**Velocity of circulation**
The average number of times that each dollar of money is used during a year to buy final goods and services.

The **velocity of circulation** is the average number of times that each dollar of money is used during a year to buy final goods and services. The value of final goods and services is nominal GDP, which is real GDP, $Y$, multiplied by the price level, $P$. If we call the quantity of money $M$, then the velocity of circulation is determined by the equation:

$$V = (P \times Y) \div M.$$

In this equation, $P$ is the GDP price index divided by 100. If the GDP price index is 125, then the price level is 1.25. If the price level is 1.25, real GDP is $8 trillion, and the quantity of money is $2 trillion, then the velocity of circulation is

$$V = (1.25 \times \$8\,\text{trillion}) \div \$2\,\text{trillion, or}$$

$$V = 5.$$

That is, with $2 trillion of money, each dollar is used an average of 5 times during the year, so $2 trillion × 5 equals $10 trillion of goods and services bought.

The **equation of exchange** states that the quantity of money, $M$, multiplied by the velocity of circulation, $V$, equals the price level $P$, multiplied by real GDP, $Y$. That is,

$$M \times V = P \times Y.$$

The equation of exchange is *always* true because it is implied by the definition of the velocity of circulation. That is, if you multiply both sides of the equation on p. 312 that defines the velocity of circulation by $M$, you get the equation of exchange.

Using the above numbers—a price level of 1.25, real GDP of $8 trillion, the quantity of money of $2 trillion, and the velocity of circulation of 5—you can see that

$$M \times V = \$2\,\text{trillion} \times 5 = \$10\,\text{trillion},$$

and

$$P \times Y = 1.25 \times \$8\,\text{trillion} = \$10\,\text{trillion}.$$

So,

$$M \times V = P \times Y = \$10\,\text{trillion}.$$

**Equation of exchange**
An equation that states that the quantity of money multiplied by the velocity of circulation equals the price level multiplied by real GDP.

## The Quantity Theory Prediction

We can rearrange the equation of exchange to isolate the price level on the left side. To do so, divide both sides of the equation of exchange by real GDP to obtain

$$P = (M \times V) \div Y.$$

On the left side is the price level, and on the right side are all the things that influence the price level. But this equation is still just an implication of the definition of the velocity of circulation. To turn the equation into a theory of what determines the price level, we use two other facts: (1) At full employment, real GDP equals potential GDP, which is determined only by real factors and not by the quantity of money; and (2) the velocity of circulation is relatively stable and does not change when the quantity of money changes.

So with $V$ and $Y$ constant, if $M$ increases $P$ must increase, and the percentage increase in $P$ must equal the percentage increase in $M$.

We can use the above numbers to illustrate this prediction. Real GDP is $8 trillion, the quantity of money is $2 trillion, and the velocity of circulation is 5. Put these values into the equation:

$$P = (M \times V) \div Y.$$

to obtain

$$P = (\$2\,\text{trillion} \times 5) \div \$8\,\text{trillion} = 1.25.$$

Now increase the quantity of money from $2 trillion to $2.4 trillion. The percentage increase in the quantity of money is

$$(\$2.4\,\text{trillion} - \$2\,\text{trillion}) \div \$2\,\text{trillion} \times 100 = 20\,\text{percent}.$$

Now find the new price level. It is

$$P = (\$2.4 \text{ trillion} \times 5) \div \$8 \text{ trillion} = 1.50.$$

The price level rises from 1.25 to 1.50, and the percentage increase in the price level is

$$(1.50 - 1.25) \div 1.25 \times 100 = 20 \text{ percent}.$$

When the economy is at full employment (real GDP equals potential GDP) and the velocity of circulation is stable, the price level and the quantity of money increase by the same 20 percent.

## ■ Inflation and the Quantity Theory of Money

The equation of exchange tells us about the price *level*, the quantity of money, the quantity of real GDP, and the velocity of circulation. We can turn the equation into one that tells us about *rates of change* or *growth rates* of these variables. We want to make this conversion because we want to know what determines the inflation rate—the rate of change of the price level.

In rates of change or growth rates,

$$\text{Money growth} + \text{Velocity growth} = \text{Inflation rate} + \text{Real GDP growth,}$$

which means that

$$\text{Inflation rate} = \text{Money growth} + \text{Velocity growth} - \text{Real GDP growth.}$$

### Constant Inflation

Figure 12.6 illustrates three cases in which the inflation rate is constant—at zero, at a low or moderate rate, and at a high or rapid rate. In each case, the velocity growth rate is 1 percent a year and the real GDP growth rate is 3 percent a year. The money growth rate is the only thing that is different across the three cases, and it is this difference that brings the different inflation rates.

If the quantity of money grows at 2 percent a year, there is no inflation. That is,

$$\text{Inflation rate} = 2 \text{ percent} + 1 \text{ percent} - 3 \text{ percent} = 0 \text{ percent a year.}$$

With the quantity of money growing at 4 percent a year, the inflation rate is 2 percent a year. That is,

$$\text{Inflation rate} = 4 \text{ percent} + 1 \text{ percent} - 3 \text{ percent} = 2 \text{ percent a year.}$$

And with the quantity of money growing at 10 percent a year, the inflation rate is 8 percent a year. That is,

$$\text{Inflation rate} = 10 \text{ percent} + 1 \text{ percent} - 3 \text{ percent} = 8 \text{ percent a year.}$$

### A Change in the Inflation Rate

We've looked at three different inflation rates—zero, moderate, and rapid—with given growth rates of real GDP and velocity of circulation. We're now going to see what happens when the growth rate of money *changes*. We'll start with an increase in the money growth rate.

**■ FIGURE 12.6**

Money Growth and Inflation

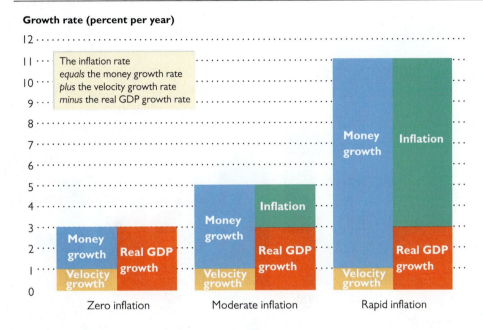

**Growth rate (percent per year)**

The inflation rate *equals* the money growth rate *plus* the velocity growth rate *minus* the real GDP growth rate

Zero inflation  Moderate inflation  Rapid inflation

The velocity of circulation grows at 1 percent a year (the orange block), and real GDP grows at 3 percent a year (the red block). The inflation rate (green block) is determined by money growth (blue block).

If the quantity of money grows at 2 percent a year, the inflation rate is zero.

If the quantity of money grows at 4 percent a year, the inflation rate is a moderate 2 percent a year.

But if the quantity of money grows at 10 percent a year, the inflation rate is a rapid 8 percent a year.

***Increase in Money Growth Rate***   When the money growth rate increases, the inflation rate increases slowly and there is a temporary (short-run) increase in the real GDP growth rate. The velocity of circulation increases as the inflation rate speeds up but this increase does not persist. Once the velocity has increased in response to a higher inflation rate, it remains constant at its new level. (You can see in *Eye on Inflation* on p. 316 that velocity growth has been zero for most of the past 40 years. It increased during the 1990s but decreased again during the 2000s.)

A faster inflation reduces potential GDP and slows real GDP growth (for reasons that we explore in the final section of this chapter) but for low inflation rates, these effects are small and are dominated by the main direct effect of money growth on the inflation rate. Eventually, real GDP growth slows to that of potential GDP, velocity growth returns to its long-run rate, and the inflation rate changes by the full amount of the change in the money growth rate.

***Decrease in Money Growth Rate***   When the money growth rate decreases, the effects that we've just described work in the opposite direction.

You can see in *Eye on Inflation* (p. 316) that changes in the growth rate of real GDP and changes in velocity growth have been small in comparison to the changes in the growth rate of money and the inflation rate. So,

**In the long run and other things remaining the same, a change in the *growth rate* of the quantity of money brings an equal change in the inflation rate.**

The relationship between the money growth rate and the inflation rate is at its clearest when inflation is rapid in *hyperinflation*.

# EYE on INFLATION

MyEconLab Critical Thinking Exercise

## What Causes Inflation?

According to the quantity theory of money, whether we face a future with inflation, deflation, or a stable price level depends entirely on the rate at which the Fed permits the quantity of money to grow.

But is the quantity theory correct? Does it explain our past inflation with enough accuracy to be a guide to future inflation?

The figure shows how the quantity theory performs in explaining decade-average inflation rates since the 1960s.

### The 1960s and 1970s

The 1960s had low inflation (the green bars) and in the 1970s, inflation increased to become a serious problem. The quantity theory does a perfect job of explaining inflation in these two decades. The inflation rate equaled the growth rate of M2 (the blue bars) minus the growth rate of real GDP (the red bars). The velocity of circulation (of M2) was constant.

During the 1970s, an increase in the growth rate of M2 accompanied by a slowdown in the growth rate of real GDP increased the inflation rate— exactly as predicted by the quantity theory of money.

### The 1980s and 1990s

The inflation rate fell in 1980s and again in 1990s. And again, the quantity theory does a good job of explaining why. During the 19680s, the M2 growth rate slowed and it slowed again in the 1990s. With the real GDP growth rate unchanged, the inflation

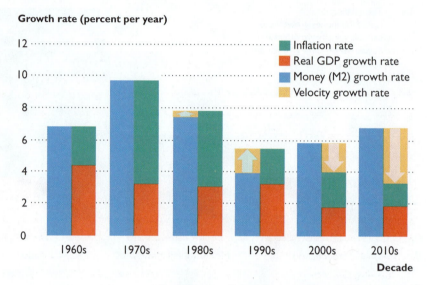

**Growth rate (percent per year)**

Legend:
- Inflation rate
- Real GDP growth rate
- Money (M2) growth rate
- Velocity growth rate

Decade: 1960s, 1970s, 1980s, 1990s, 2000s, 2010s

SOURCE OF DATA: Federal Reserve and Bureau of Economic Analysis.

rate fell as predicted by the quantity theory. But the inflation rate didn't fall by as much as the theory predicts. Why?

The answer is that the velocity of circulation was increasing (the yellow bars and up-arrows). Financial innovation enabled a given quantity of money to circulate more quickly.

### The 2000s and 2010s

During the 2000s and 2010s, the M2 growth rate increased but the inflation rate decreased. The changes in inflation in these two decades are the opposite of what the quantity theory predicts. The reason is that the velocity of circulation decreased (the yellow bars and down-arrows).

Velocity of circulation decreased because interest rates were lowered by the Fed to unprecedented levels.

At very low interest rates, the opportunity cost of holding money is low, so the quantity of money held increases and the velocity decreases.

### The Future

To predict future inflation rates, we must predict the future growth rate of M2 and the future real GDP and velocity growth. In the long run, real GDP growth doesn't stray far from 2 to 3 percent and velocity is constant. So the M2 growth rate is the source of possible changes in the inflation rate.

The Fed is able to influence the inflation rate and the money growth rate and, absent any pressures that the Fed finds impossible to resist, we can expect the Fed to do a good job of keeping inflation in check. That doesn't mean zero inflation. It means an inflation rate running at around 2 percent per year.

## ■ Hyperinflation

When the inflation rate exceeds 50 percent *a month,* it is called **hyperinflation**. An inflation rate of 50 percent per month translates to an inflation rate of 12,875 percent per year. Hyperinflation occurs when the quantity of money grows at a rapid pace. The reason money growth sometimes becomes rapid is that government expenditure gets out of control and exceeds what the government can collect in tax revenue or borrow. In such a situation, the government prints money to finance its spending and the quantity of money increases at an extraordinarily rapid and increasing rate.

Hyperinflation is rare but not unknown (see *Eye on the Past* below). The highest inflation in the world in recent times was in the African nation of Zimbabwe, where the inflation rate peaked at 231,150,888.87 percent a year in July 2008.

**Hyperinflation**
Inflation at a rate that exceeds 50 percent *a month* (which translates to 12,875 percent per year).

# EYE on the PAST
## Hyperinflation in Germany in the 1920s

An international treaty signed in 1919 required Germany to pay large amounts as compensation for war damage to other countries in Europe. To meet its obligations, Germany started to print money. The quantity of money increased by 24 percent in 1921, by 220 percent in 1922, and by 43 *billion* percent in 1923!

Not surprisingly, the price level increased rapidly. The figure shows you how rapidly.

In November 1923 when the hyperinflation reached its peak, the price level was more than doubling every day. Wages were paid twice a day, and people spent their morning's wages at lunchtime to avoid the loss in the value of money that the afternoon would bring.

Hyperinflation made bank notes more valuable as fire kindling than as money. The sight of people burning Reichmarks (the name of Germany's money at that time) was a common one, as the photo shows.

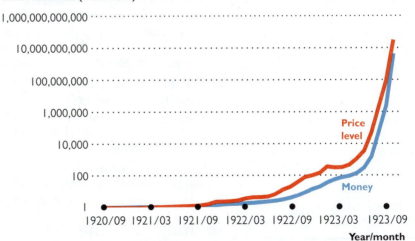

SOURCE OF DATA: Phillip Cagan, "The Monetary Dynamics of Hyperinflation," in Milton Friedman (editor), *Studies in the Quantity Theory of Money*, University of Chicago Press, 1956.

MyEconLab Study Plan 12.2
Key Terms Quiz
Solutions Video

 CHECKPOINT 12.2

**Explain how in the long run, the quantity of money determines the price level and money growth brings inflation.**

## Practice Problems

In 2016, the economy of Singapore was at full employment. In Singapore dollars, S$, real GDP was 400 billion. The nominal interest rate was 1.8 percent a year, the inflation rate was −1.6 percent a year (deflation), the price level was 1.02, and the velocity of circulation was 0.76. Use this data to work Problems **1** and **2**.

1. Calculate the real interest rate. If the real interest rate remains unchanged and the inflation rate increases to 2 percent a year and then remains constant, explain how the nominal interest rate will change in the long run.

2. What was the quantity of money in Singapore?

3. If the quantity of money grows at 8 percent a year, velocity of circulation is constant, and potential GDP grows at 6 percent a year, what is the inflation rate in the long run?

## In the News

**Argentina says consumer prices rose 3.1 percent in June**
Argentina's consumer prices increased by 3.1 percent in June and the government forecasts that the 2016 inflation rate will be 40 to 42 percent.
*Source: Reuters, July 13, 2016*

The quantity of money in Argentina is growing at a rate of 30 percent a year. How can the inflation rate exceed the money growth rate?

## Solutions to Practice Problems

1. The real interest rate equals the nominal interest rate minus the inflation rate. That is, the real interest rate equals 1.8 percent a year minus −1.6 percent a year, which equals 3.4 percent a year. If inflation increases to 2 percent a year and remains at 2 percent, then the nominal interest rate will rise from 1.8 percent a year to 5.4 percent a year, which equals the real interest rate (3.4 percent) plus the inflation rate (2 percent).

2. The quantity of money was S$536.8 billion.
   Velocity of circulation ($V$) = Nominal GDP ($P \times Y$) ÷ Quantity of money ($M$). Rewrite this equation as: $M = (P \times Y) \div V$
   $(P \times Y) = 1.02 \times$ S$400 billion, or S$408 billion, so $M =$ S$408 billion ÷ 0.76, or S$536.8 billion.

3. With velocity constant, velocity growth is zero. So the inflation rate in the long run equals the money growth rate minus the real GDP growth rate, which is 8 percent a year minus 6 percent a year, or 2 percent a year.

## Solution to In the News

The inflation rate equals the money growth rate plus the velocity growth rate minus the real GDP growth rate. If the inflation rate is 40 percent per year and the money growth rate is 30 percent per year, then the velocity growth rate minus the real GDP growth rate equals 10 percent per year.

## 12.3   THE COST OF INFLATION
MyEconLab Concept Video

Inflation decreases potential GDP, slows economic growth, and consumes leisure time. These outcomes occur for four reasons that we classify as the four costs of inflation:

- Tax costs
- Shoe-leather costs
- Confusion costs
- Uncertainty costs

### ■ Tax Costs

We've seen that inflation occurs when the quantity of money grows more rapidly than real GDP. But why would we ever want to make this happen? Why don't we keep the quantity of money growing at the same pace as real GDP grows? One part of the answer is that the government gets revenue from inflation.

#### Inflation Is a Tax

A government can pay its expenses with newly created money. But the things a government buys with this money aren't free. They are paid for by people and businesses in proportion to the amount of money they hold—by a tax on money holding that we call the inflation tax.

When the government spends newly created money, the quantity of money increases and, as predicted by the quantity theory, the price level rises. The inflation rate equals the growth rate of the quantity of money (other things remaining the same).

To see how the inflation tax gets paid, suppose that the Coca-Cola Company is holding $110,000 in money. The annual inflation rate is 10 percent, and the price level rises from 1.0 to 1.1. At the end of the year, Coca-Cola's money will buy only $100,000 of goods and services ($110,000 ÷ 1.1 = $100,000). The firm has lost $10,000—it has "paid" an inflation tax of $10,000.

Governments in today's world don't create new money by printing it. Money gets created when the central bank buys government bonds. In the United States, the Fed doesn't buy bonds directly from the government: it buys them in open market operations. When the Fed buys bonds, the monetary base increases and the quantity of money increases. The Fed pays the interest it receives on the bonds to the government, so the government ends up paying no interest on its bonds held by the Fed. By this process, the government "prints" money.

#### Inflation, Saving, and Investment

The income tax on interest income drives a wedge between the before-tax interest rate paid by borrowers and the after-tax interest rate received by lenders. A rise in the income tax rate increases the before-tax interest rate and decreases the after-tax interest rate. The increase in the before-tax interest rate decreases borrowing and investment, and the decrease in the after-tax interest rate decreases lending and saving.

An increase in the inflation rate increases the true tax rate on interest income, and strengthens the effect that we have just described. To see why, let's consider an example.

Suppose that the real interest rate is 4 percent a year and the income tax rate is 50 percent. With no inflation, the nominal interest rate is also 4 percent a year and the real after-tax interest rate is 2 percent a year (50 percent of 4 percent).

Now suppose the inflation rate rises to 4 percent a year, so the nominal interest rate rises to 8 percent a year. The after-tax nominal interest rate rises to 4 percent a year (50 percent of 8 percent). Subtract the 4 percent inflation rate from this amount, and you see that the after-tax real interest rate is zero! The true income tax rate has increased to 100 percent.

The fall in the after-tax real interest rate weakens the incentive to lend and save and the rise in the before-tax interest rate weakens the incentive to borrow and invest. With a fall in saving and investment, the rates of capital accumulation and real GDP growth slow down.

## ■ Shoe-Leather Costs

The "shoe-leather costs" of inflation are costs that arise from an increase in the velocity of circulation of money and an increase in the amount of running around that people do to try to avoid incurring losses from the falling value of money.

When money loses value at a rapid anticipated rate, it does not function well as a store of value and people try to avoid holding it. They spend their incomes as soon as they receive them, and firms pay out incomes—wages and dividends—as soon as they receive revenue from their sales. The velocity of circulation increases.

During the 1990s when inflation in Brazil was around 80 percent a year, people would end a taxi ride at the ATM closest to their destination, get some cash, pay the driver, and finish their journey on foot. The driver would deposit the cash in his bank account before looking for the next customer.

During the 1920s when inflation in Germany exceeded 50 percent a month—hyperinflation—wages were paid and spent twice in a single day!

Imagine the inconvenience of spending most of your time figuring out how to keep your money holdings close to zero.

One way of keeping money holdings low is to find other means of payment such as tokens, commodities, or even barter. All of these are less efficient than money as a means of payment. For example, in Israel during the 1980s, when inflation reached 1,000 percent a year, the U.S. dollar started to replace the increasingly worthless shekel. Consequently, people had to keep track of the exchange rate between the shekel and the dollar hour by hour and had to engage in many additional and costly transactions in the foreign exchange market.

## ■ Confusion Costs

We make economic decisions by comparing marginal cost and marginal benefit. Marginal cost is a real cost—an opportunity forgone. Marginal benefit is a real benefit—a willingness to forgo an opportunity. Although costs and benefits are real, we use money as our unit of account and standard of value to calculate them. Money is our measuring rod of value. Borrowers and lenders, workers and employers, all make agreements in terms of money. Inflation makes the value of money change, so it changes the units on our measuring rod.

Does it matter that our units of value keep changing? Some economists think it matters a lot. Others think it matters only a little.

Economists who think it matters a lot point to the obvious benefits of stable units of measurement in other areas of life. For example, suppose that we had not invented an accurate time-keeping technology and clocks and watches gained 5 to

15 minutes a day. Imagine the hassle you would have arriving at class on time or catching the start of the ball game. For another example, suppose that a tailor used an elastic tape measure. You would end up with a jacket that was either too tight or too loose, depending on how tightly the tape was stretched.

For a third example, recall the crash of the Mars Climate Orbiter.

> Mars Climate Orbiter…failed to achieve Mars orbit because of a navigation error….Spacecraft operating data needed for navigation were provided…in English units rather than the specified metric units. This was the direct cause of the failure. (Mars Program Independent Assessment Team Summary Report, March 14, 2000)

If rocket scientists can't make correct calculations that use just two units of measurement, what chance do ordinary people and business decision makers have of making correct calculations that involve money when its value keeps changing?

These examples of confusion and error that can arise from units of measurement don't automatically mean that a changing value of money is a big problem. But they raise the possibility that it might be.

## ■ Uncertainty Costs

A high inflation rate brings increased uncertainty about the long-term inflation rate. Will inflation remain high for a long time or will price stability be restored? This increased uncertainty makes long-term planning difficult and gives people a shorter-term focus. Investment falls, and so the economic growth rate slows.

But this increased uncertainty also misallocates resources. Instead of concentrating on the activities at which they have a comparative advantage, people find it more profitable to search for ways of avoiding the losses that inflation inflicts. As a result, inventive talent that might otherwise work on productive innovations works on finding ways of profiting from the inflation instead.

Uncertainty about inflation makes the economy behave a bit like a casino in which some people gain and some lose and no one can predict where the gains and losses will fall. Gains and losses occur because of unpredictable changes in the value of money. In a period of rapid, unpredictable inflation, resources get diverted from productive activities to forecasting inflation. It becomes more profitable to forecast the inflation rate correctly than to invent a new product. Doctors, lawyers, accountants, farmers—just about everyone—can make themselves better off, not by specializing in the profession for which they have been trained but by spending more of their time dabbling as amateur economists and inflation forecasters and managing their investment portfolios.

From a social perspective, this diversion of talent resulting from uncertainty about inflation is like throwing scarce resources onto the garbage heap. This waste of resources is a cost of inflation.

## ■ How Big Is the Cost of Inflation?

The cost of inflation depends on its rate and its predictability. The higher the inflation rate, the greater is the cost. And the more unpredictable the inflation rate, the greater is the cost. Peter Howitt of Brown University, building on work by Robert Barro of Harvard University, has estimated that if inflation is lowered from 3 percent a year to zero, the growth rate of real GDP will rise by between 0.06 and 0.09 percentage points a year. These numbers might seem small, but they are growth rates. After 30 years, real GDP would be 2.3 percent higher and the accumulated value of all the additional future output would be worth 85 percent of current GDP, or $15.5 trillion!

In hyperinflation, the costs are much greater. Hyperinflation is rare, but there have been some spectacular examples of it. Several European countries experienced hyperinflation during the 1920s after World War I and again during the 1940s after World War II. In these examples the costs of inflation were enormous.

Hyperinflation is more than just a historical curiosity. It has occurred in the recent past. In 1994, Brazil almost reached the hyperinflation stratosphere with a monthly inflation rate of 40 percent. A cup of coffee that cost 15 cruzeiros in 1980 cost 22 billion cruzeiros in 1994. Between 1989 and 1994, Russia experienced a near hyperinflation. In 2016, the inflation rate in Venezuela soared past 1,000 percent per year—not quite hyperinflation but a ripping 21 percent per month.

The most spectacular recent hyperinflation was in Zimbabwe, which peaked at 231,150,888.87 percent per year. At that point, the monetary system collapsed, the Zimbabwe dollar was taken out of circulation and replaced by the U.S. dollar, and economic life was at a near standstill.

ˈMyEconLab Study Plan 12.3

Solutions Video

# CHECKPOINT 12.3

### Identify the costs of inflation and the benefits of a stable value of money.

## Practice Problems

1.  Ben has $1,000 in his savings account and the bank pays an interest rate of 5 percent a year. The inflation rate is 3 percent a year. The government taxes the interest that Ben earns on his deposit at 20 percent. Calculate the after-tax nominal interest rate and the after-tax real interest rate that Ben earns.

2.  Economy *A* has a stable price level—no inflation. Economy *B* is in a hyperinflation—prices are rising at a rate of 50 percent per month. Describe and explain the differences between these two economies in the money growth rate, the velocity of circulation, the nominal interest rate, and the frequency of wage payments.

## Solutions to Practice Problems

1.  Ben's interest income equals 5 percent of $1,000, which is $50. The government takes $10 of his $50 of interest in tax, so the interest income Ben earns after tax is $40. The after-tax nominal interest rate is ($40 ÷ $1,000) × 100, which equals 4 percent a year.
    The after-tax real interest rate equals the after-tax nominal interest rate minus the inflation rate. The after-tax nominal interest rate is 4 percent a year. So the after-tax real interest rate equals 4 percent a year minus the inflation rate of 3 percent a year, which is 1 percent a year.

2.  The equation of exchange tells us that economy *B* has a higher money growth rate than economy *A*. With hyperinflation, the opportunity cost of holding money is higher in economy *B*, so economy *B* also has a higher velocity of circulation and more frequent wage payments than economy *A*. The nominal interest rate equals the real interest rate plus the expected inflation rate, so economy *B* has the higher nominal interest rate.

**CHAPTER SUMMARY**

## Key Points

1. **Explain what determines the demand for money and how the demand for money and the supply of money determine the *nominal* interest rate.**

   - The demand for money is the relationship between the quantity of money demanded and the nominal interest rate, other things remaining the same. The higher the nominal interest rate, other things remaining the same, the smaller is the quantity of money demanded.
   - Increases in real GDP increase the demand for money. Some advances in financial technology increase the demand for money, and some advances decrease it.
   - Each day, the price level, real GDP, and financial technology are given and money market equilibrium determines the nominal interest rate.
   - To lower the interest rate, the Fed increases the supply of money. To raise the interest rate, the Fed decreases the supply of money.

2. **Explain how in the long run, the quantity of money determines the price level and money growth brings inflation.**

   - In the long run, real GDP equals potential GDP and the real interest rate is the level that makes the quantity of loanable funds demanded equal the quantity of loanable funds supplied in the global financial market.
   - The nominal interest rate in the long run equals the equilibrium real interest rate plus the inflation rate.
   - Money market equilibrium in the long run determines the price level.
   - An increase in the quantity of money, other things remaining the same, increases the price level by the same percentage.
   - The inflation rate in the long run equals the growth rate of the quantity of money minus the growth rate of potential GDP.
   - The equation of exchange and the velocity of circulation provide an alternative way of viewing the relationship between the quantity of money and the price level (and money growth and inflation).

3. **Identify the costs of inflation and the benefits of a stable value of money.**

   - Inflation has four costs: tax costs, shoe-leather costs, confusion costs, and uncertainty costs.
   - The higher the inflation rate, the greater are these four costs.

## Key Terms

MyEconLab Key Terms Quiz

Demand for money, 302
Equation of exchange, 313
Hyperinflation, 317

Quantity of money demanded, 301
Quantity theory of money, 312
Supply of money, 304

Velocity of circulation, 312

# CHAPTER CHECKPOINT

## Study Plan Problems and Applications

1. Draw a graph to illustrate the demand for money. On the graph show the effect of an increase in real GDP and the effect of an increase in the number of families that have a credit card.

2. If the Fed makes a decision to cut the quantity of money, explain the short-run effects on the quantity of money demanded and the nominal interest rate.

3. The Fed conducts an open market purchase of securities. Explain the effects of this action on the nominal interest rate in the short run and the value of money in the long run.

In 2007, the United States was at full employment. The quantity of money was growing at 6.4 percent a year, the nominal interest rate was 4.4 percent a year, real GDP grew at 1.9 percent a year, and the inflation rate was 2.9 percent a year. Use this information to work Problems **4** and **5**.

4. Calculate the real interest rate.

5. Was the velocity of circulation constant? (Hint: Use the quantity theory of money.) If the velocity of circulation was not constant, how did it change and why might it have changed?

6. If the quantity of money is $3 trillion, real GDP is $10 trillion, the price level is 0.9, the real interest rate is 2 percent a year, and the nominal interest rate is 7 percent a year, calculate the velocity of circulation, the value of $M \times V$, and nominal GDP.

7. If the velocity of circulation is growing at 1 percent a year, the real interest rate is 2 percent a year, the nominal interest rate is 7 percent a year, and the growth rate of real GDP is 3 percent a year, calculate the inflation rate, the growth rate of money, and the growth rate of nominal GDP.

8. Suppose that the government passes a new law that sets a limit on the interest rate that credit card companies can charge on overdue balances. As a result, the nominal interest rate charged by credit card companies falls from 15 percent a year to 7 percent a year. If the average income tax rate is 30 percent, explain how the after-tax real interest rate on overdue credit card balances changes.

**Annualized inflation in Venezuela soars to 1,000 percent**
Inflation in Venezuela hit a monthly rate of 23.3 percent in June and it was feared that it would soon move into unstoppable hyperinflation. The country faced constant looting and social unrest.

Source: *PanAm Post*, July 15, 2016

9. What is hyperinflation? Is Venezuela in a hyperinflation?

10. Compare inflation in Venezuela in 2016 with that in Germany in 1923. Why did Germany print money in 1923 and create hyperinflation? Why is Venezuela printing money today? Why does a high inflation rate bring looting and social unrest?

11. Read *Eye on Inflation* on p. 316. Why did inflation increase during the 1970s? In which decades did velocity growth break the link between money growth and inflation?

# Instructor Assignable Problems and Applications

MyEconLab Homework, Quiz, or Test if assigned by instructor

1. Explain what causes inflation. Why is it easier to predict the decade-average inflation rate than the inflation rate in a single year?

2. If the Fed doubled the quantity of money and nothing else changed, what would happen to the price level in the short run and the long run? What would happen to the inflation rate?

3. Suppose that banks launch an aggressive marketing campaign to get everyone to use debit cards for every conceivable transaction. They offer prizes to new debit card holders and introduce a charge on using a credit card. How would the demand for money and the nominal interest rate change?

4. Draw a graph of the money market to illustrate equilibrium in the short run. If the growth rate of the quantity of money increases, explain what happens to the real interest rate and the nominal interest rate in the short run.

5. The Fed conducts an open market sale of securities. Explain the effects of this action in the short run on the nominal interest rate and in the long run on the value of money and the price level.

6. What is the quantity theory of money? Define the velocity of circulation and explain how it is measured.

7. If the velocity of circulation is constant, real GDP is growing at 3 percent a year, the real interest rate is 2 percent a year, and the nominal interest rate is 7 percent a year, calculate the inflation rate, the growth rate of money, and the growth rate of nominal GDP.

8. Sara has $200 in currency and $2,000 in a bank account on which the bank pays no interest. The inflation rate is 2 percent a year. Calculate the amount of inflation tax that Sara pays in a year.

Use the following information to work Problems **9** to **12**.

**Fed's easy money can't control price level**
Robert F. Stauffer, Emeritus Professor of Economics at Roanoke College, Salem, Virginia, argues that the Fed's monetary policy cannot closely control the price level, and an inflation target can be achieved only by chance. He takes issue with Harvard economist Martin Feldstein, who argues that the Fed's easy money policy will eventually raise the inflation rate to more than 3 percent.

Source: The Wall Street Journal, July 14, 2016

9. Why might Robert Stauffer be right? If he is right, what is he implying about the equation of exchange and the quantity theory of money?

10. Why might Martin Feldstein be right? If he is right, what is he implying about the equation of exchange and the quantity theory of money?

11. When Martin Feldstein describes the Fed's monetary policy as "easy," he means that the Fed has created a lot of money, has made money grow at a fast rate, and has pushed interest rates down. Looking at the graph in *Eye on Inflation* (p. 316), has money been "easy" during the 2010s? In which decade was it most "easy"?

12. If the money growth rate and real GDP growth rate of the 2010s are maintained and if the velocity growth rate is zero, will the inflation rate rise to 3 percent as predicted by Martin Feldstein?

# Multiple Choice Quiz

**1.** Holding money provides a benefit _____.

   A. because it is a means of payment
   B. because its opportunity cost is low
   C. which is constant no matter how much money is held
   D. because most money is in bank deposits

**2.** The opportunity cost of holding money _____.

   A. is determined by the inflation rate
   B. is zero because money earns no interest
   C. equals the nominal interest rate on bonds
   D. equals the real interest rate on bonds

**3.** The quantity of money demanded increases if _____.

   A. the supply of money increases
   B. the nominal interest rate falls
   C. banks increase the interest rate on deposits
   D. the price of a bond falls

**4.** If the Fed increases the quantity of money, people will be holding _____.

   A. too much money, so they buy bonds and the interest rate rises
   B. too much money, so they buy bonds and the interest rate falls
   C. the quantity of money they demand and banks will hold more money
   D. more money and will increase their demand for money

**5.** In the long run, money market equilibrium determines the _____.

   A. real interest rate
   B. price level
   C. nominal interest rate
   D. economic growth rate

**6.** If the quantity theory of money is correct and other things remain the same, an increase in the quantity of money increases _____.

   A. nominal GDP and the velocity of circulation
   B. the price level and potential GDP
   C. real GDP
   D. nominal GDP and the price level

**7.** In the long run with a constant velocity of circulation, the inflation rate _____.

   A. is constant and equals the money growth rate
   B. equals the money growth rate minus the growth rate of real GDP
   C. equals the growth rate of real GDP minus the growth rate of money
   D. is positive if the economic growth rate is positive

**8.** The costs of inflation do *not* include _____.

   A. the cost of running around to compare prices at different outlets
   B. the increased opportunity cost of holding money
   C. the tax on money held by individuals and businesses
   D. an increase in saving and investment

Why did the U.S. economy go into recession in 2008?

# Aggregate Supply and Aggregate Demand

**When you have completed your study of this chapter, you will be able to**

1 Define and explain the influences on aggregate supply.

2 Define and explain the influences on aggregate demand.

3 Explain how trends and fluctuations in aggregate demand and aggregate supply bring economic growth, inflation, and the business cycle.

**13**

CHAPTER CHECKLIST

MyEconLab Big Picture Video

## 13.1   AGGREGATE SUPPLY

The purpose of the aggregate supply–aggregate demand model is to explain how real GDP and the price level are determined. The model uses similar ideas to those that you encountered in Chapter 4 where you learned how the quantity and price are determined in a competitive market. But the *aggregate* supply–*aggregate* demand model (*AS-AD* model) isn't just an application of the competitive market model. Some differences arise because the *AS-AD* model is a model of an imaginary market for the total of all the final goods and services that make up real GDP. The quantity in this "market" is real GDP and the price is the price level measured by the GDP price index.

The *quantity of real GDP supplied* is the total amount of final goods and services that firms in the United States plan to produce and it depends on the quantities of

- Labor employed
- Capital, human capital, and the state of technology
- Land and natural resources
- Entrepreneurial talent

You saw in Chapter 8 that at full employment, real GDP equals *potential GDP*. The quantities of land, capital and human capital, the state of technology, and the amount of entrepreneurial talent are fixed. Labor market equilibrium determines the quantity of labor employed, which is equal to the quantity of labor demanded and the quantity of labor supplied at the equilibrium real wage rate.

Over the business cycle, real GDP fluctuates around potential GDP because the quantity of labor employed fluctuates around its full employment level. The aggregate supply–aggregate demand model explains these fluctuations.

We begin on the supply side with the basics of aggregate supply.

### ■ Aggregate Supply Basics

**Aggregate supply**
The relationship between the quantity of real GDP supplied and the price level when all other influences on production plans remain the same.

**Aggregate supply** is the relationship between the quantity of real GDP supplied and the price level when all other influences on production plans remain the same. This relationship can be described as follows:

> **Other things remaining the same, the higher the price level, the greater is the quantity of real GDP supplied, and the lower the price level, the smaller is the quantity of real GDP supplied.**

Figure 13.1 illustrates aggregate supply as an aggregate supply schedule and aggregate supply curve. The aggregate supply schedule lists the quantities of real GDP supplied at each price level, and the upward-sloping *AS* curve graphs these points.

The figure also shows potential GDP: $16 trillion in the figure. When the price level is 105, the quantity of real GDP supplied is $16 trillion, which equals potential GDP (at point *C* on the *AS* curve).

Along the aggregate supply curve, the price level is the only influence on production plans that changes. A rise in the price level brings an increase in the quantity of real GDP supplied and a movement up along the aggregate supply curve; a fall in the price level brings a decrease in the quantity of real GDP supplied and a movement down along the aggregate supply curve.

**FIGURE 13.1**

## Aggregate Supply Schedule and Aggregate Supply Curve

MyEconLab Animation

| | Price level (GDP price index, 2009 = 100) | Quantity of real GDP supplied (trillions of 2009 dollars) |
|---|---|---|
| E | 115 | 17.0 |
| D | 110 | 16.5 |
| C | 105 | 16.0 |
| B | 100 | 15.5 |
| A | 95 | 15.0 |

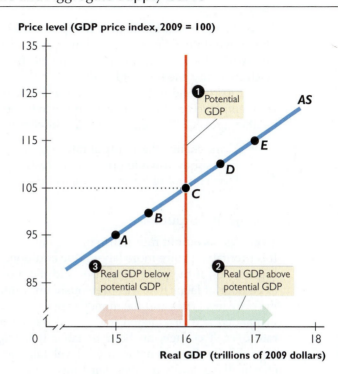

The aggregate supply schedule and aggregate supply curve, AS, show the relationship between the quantity of real GDP supplied and the price level when all other influences on production plans remain the same. Each point A through E on the AS curve corresponds to the row identified by the same letter in the schedule.

❶ Potential GDP is $16 trillion, and when the price level is 105, real GDP equals potential GDP.

❷ If the price level is above 105, real GDP exceeds potential GDP.

❸ If the price level is below 105, real GDP is less than potential GDP.

Among the other influences on production plans that remain constant along the *AS* curve are

- The money wage rate
- The money prices of other resources

In contrast, along the potential GDP line, when the price level changes, the money wage rate and the money prices of other resources change by the same percentage as the change in the price level to keep the real wage rate (and other real prices) at the full-employment equilibrium level.

### Why the *AS* Curve Slopes Upward

Why does the quantity of real GDP supplied increase when the price level rises and decrease when the price level falls? The answer is that a movement along the *AS* curve brings a change in the real wage rate (and changes in the real cost of other resources whose money prices are fixed). If the price level rises, the real wage rate falls, and if the price level falls, the real wage rate rises. When the real wage rate changes, firms change the quantity of labor employed and the level of production.

Think about a concrete example. A ketchup producer has a contract with its workers to pay them $20 an hour. The firm sells ketchup for $1 a bottle. The real wage rate of a ketchup bottling worker is 20 bottles of ketchup. That is, the firm must sell 20 bottles of ketchup to buy one hour of labor. Now suppose the price of ketchup falls to 50 cents a bottle. The real wage rate of a bottling worker has increased to 40 bottles—the firm must now sell 40 bottles of ketchup to buy one hour of labor.

If the price of a bottle of ketchup increased, the real wage rate of a bottling worker would fall. For example, if the price increased to $2 a bottle, the real wage rate would be 10 bottles per worker—the firm needs to sell only 10 bottles of ketchup to buy one hour of labor.

Firms respond to a change in the real wage rate by changing the quantity of labor employed and the quantity produced. For the economy as a whole, employment and real GDP change. There are three ways in which these changes occur:

- Firms change their output rate.
- Firms shut down temporarily or restart production.
- Firms go out of business or start up in business.

## Change in Output Rate

To change its output rate, a firm must change the quantity of labor that it employs. It is profitable to hire more labor if the additional labor costs less than the revenue it generates. If the price level rises and the money wage rate doesn't change, an extra hour of labor that was previously unprofitable becomes profitable. So when the price level rises and the money wage rate doesn't change, the quantity of labor demanded and production increase. If the price level falls and the money wage rate doesn't change, an hour of labor that was previously profitable becomes unprofitable. So when the price level falls and the money wage rate doesn't change, the quantity of labor demanded and production decrease.

## Temporary Shutdowns and Restarts

A firm that is incurring a loss might foresee a profit in the future. Such a firm might decide to shut down temporarily and lay off its workers.

The price level relative to the money wage rate influences temporary shutdown decisions. If the price level rises relative to wages, fewer firms decide to shut down temporarily; so more firms operate and the quantity of real GDP supplied increases. If the price level falls relative to wages, a larger number of firms find that they cannot earn enough revenue to pay the wage bill and so temporarily shut down. The quantity of real GDP supplied decreases.

## Business Failure and Startup

People create businesses in the hope of earning a profit. When profits are squeezed or when losses arise, more firms fail, fewer new firms start up, and the number of firms decreases. When profits are generally high, fewer firms fail, more firms start up, and the number of firms increases.

The price level relative to the money wage rate influences the number of firms in business. If the price level rises relative to wages, profits increase, the number of firms in business increases, and the quantity of real GDP supplied increases. If the price level falls relative to wages, profits fall, the number of firms in business decreases, and the quantity of real GDP supplied decreases.

In a severe recession, business failure can be contagious. The failure of one firm puts pressure on both its suppliers and its customers and can bring a flood of failures and a large decrease in the quantity of real GDP supplied.

## ■ Changes in Aggregate Supply

Aggregate supply changes when any influence on production plans other than the price level changes. In particular, aggregate supply changes when

- Potential GDP changes.
- The money wage rate changes.
- The money prices of other resources change.

### Change in Potential GDP

Anything that changes potential GDP changes aggregate supply and shifts the aggregate supply curve. Figure 13.2 illustrates such a shift. You can think of point $C$ as an anchor point. The $AS$ curve and potential GDP line are anchored at this point, and when potential GDP changes, aggregate supply changes along with it. When potential GDP increases from $16 trillion to $17 trillion, point $C$ shifts to point $C'$, and the $AS$ curve and potential GDP line shift rightward together. The $AS$ curve shifts from $AS_0$ to $AS_1$.

### Change in Money Wage Rate

A change in the money wage rate changes aggregate supply because it changes firms' costs. The higher the money wage rate, the higher are firms' costs and the smaller is the quantity that firms are willing to supply at each price level. So an increase in the money wage rate decreases aggregate supply.

### ■ FIGURE 13.2

An Increase in Potential GDP

MyEconLab Animation

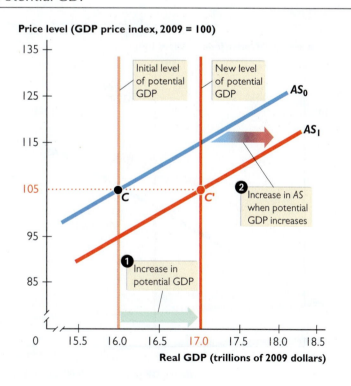

❶ An increase in potential GDP increases aggregate supply.

❷ When potential GDP increases from $16 trillion to $17 trillion, the aggregate supply curve shifts rightward from $AS_0$ to $AS_1$.

Suppose that the money wage rate is $52.50 an hour and the price level is 105. Then the real wage rate is $50 an hour ($52.50 × 100 ÷ 105 = $50)—see Chapter 7, p. 182. If the full-employment equilibrium real wage rate is $50 an hour, the economy is at full employment and real GDP equals potential GDP. In Figure 13.3, the economy is at point $C$ on the aggregate supply curve $AS_0$. The money wage rate is $52.50 an hour at all points on $AS_0$.

Now suppose the money wage rate rises to $57.50 an hour but the full-employment equilibrium real wage rate remains at $50 an hour. Real GDP now equals potential GDP when the price level is 115, at point $D$ on the aggregate supply curve $AS_2$. (If the money wage rate is $57.50 an hour and the price level is 115, the real wage rate is $57.50 × 100 ÷ 115 = $50 an hour.) The money wage rate is $57.50 an hour at all points on $AS_2$. The rise in the money wage rate *decreases* aggregate supply and shifts the aggregate supply curve leftward from $AS_0$ to $AS_2$.

A change in the money wage rate does not change potential GDP. The reason is that potential GDP depends only on the economy's real ability to produce and on the full-employment quantity of labor, which occurs at the equilibrium *real* wage rate. The equilibrium real wage rate can occur at any money wage rate.

### Change in Money Prices of Other Resources

A change in the money prices of other resources has a similar effect on firms' production plans to a change in the money wage rate. It changes firms' costs. At each price level, firms' real costs change and the quantity that firms are willing to supply changes so aggregate supply changes.

■ **FIGURE 13.3**

A Change in the Money Wage Rate                                    MyEconLab Animation

A rise in the money wage rate decreases aggregate supply. The aggregate supply curve shifts leftward from $AS_0$ to $AS_2$. A rise in the money wage rate does not change potential GDP.

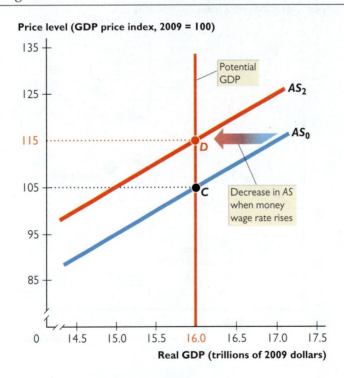

## CHECKPOINT 13.1

MyEconLab Study Plan 13.1
Key Terms Quiz
Solutions Video

**Define and explain the influences on aggregate supply.**

## Practice Problem

1.  Explain the influence of each of the events in List 1 on the quantity of real GDP supplied and aggregate supply in India and use a graph to illustrate.

## In the News

**A midyear burst of minimum-wage increases starts on July 1**
On July 1, 2016, the minimum wage will increase in 14 U.S. cities, states, and counties, and in the District of Columbia. In San Francisco, the minimum wage will rise to $13.00 by 2018.

Source: *The Wall Street Journal*, July 1, 2016

Explain how the widespread rise in the minimum wage will influence aggregate supply.

**LIST 1**

- Fuel prices rise.
- U.S. firms move their IT and data functions to India.
- Walmart and Starbucks open in India.
- Universities in India increase the number of engineering graduates.
- The money wage rate in India rises.
- The price level in India rises.

## Solution to Practice Problem

1.  As fuel prices rise, the quantity of real GDP supplied at the current price level decreases. The *AS* curve shifts leftward (Figure 1).

    As U.S. firms move their IT and data functions to India, real GDP supplied at the current price level increases. The *AS* curve shifts rightward (Figure 2).

    As Walmart and Starbucks open, the quantity of real GDP supplied at the current price level increases. The *AS* curve shifts rightward (Figure 2).

    With more graduates, the number of skilled workers increases, and production increases at the current price level. The *AS* curve shifts rightward (Figure 2).

    As the money wage rate rises, firms' costs increase and the quantity of real GDP supplied at the current price level decreases. The *AS* curve shifts leftward (Figure 1).

    As the price level increases, other things remaining the same, businesses become more profitable and increase the quantity of real GDP supplied along the *AS* curve (Figure 3). The *AS* curve does not shift.

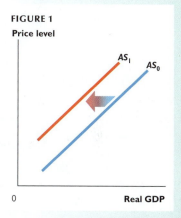
**FIGURE 1**
Price level

## Solution to In the News

The widespread rise in the minimum wage will increase the money wage rate. At the current price level, a rise in the money wage rate increases the real wage rate and decreases aggregate supply. If the rise in the minimum wage increases the natural unemployment rate, potential GDP decreases and aggregate supply decreases further.

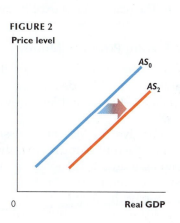
**FIGURE 2**
Price level

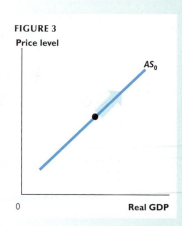
**FIGURE 3**
Price level

## 13.2 AGGREGATE DEMAND

The *quantity of real GDP demanded* (*Y*) is the total amount of final goods and services produced in the United States that people, businesses, governments, and foreigners plan to buy. This quantity is the sum of the real consumption expenditure (*C*), investment (*I*), government expenditure on goods and services (*G*), and exports (*X*) minus imports (*M*). That is,

$$Y = C + I + G + X - M.$$

Many factors influence expenditure plans. To study aggregate demand, we divide those factors into two parts: the price level and everything else. We'll first consider the influence of the price level on expenditure plans and then consider the other influences.

### ■ Aggregate Demand Basics

**Aggregate demand**
The relationship between the quantity of real GDP demanded and the price level when all other influences on expenditure plans remain the same.

**Aggregate demand** is the relationship between the quantity of real GDP demanded and the price level when all other influences on expenditure plans remain the same. This relationship can be described as follows:

> **Other things remaining the same, the higher the price level, the smaller is the quantity of real GDP demanded; and the lower the price level, the greater is the quantity of real GDP demanded.**

Figure 13.4 illustrates aggregate demand by using an aggregate demand schedule and aggregate demand curve. The aggregate demand schedule lists the quantities of real GDP demanded at each price level, and the downward-sloping *AD* curve graphs these points.

Along the aggregate demand curve, the only influence on expenditure plans that changes is the price level. A rise in the price level decreases the quantity of real GDP demanded and brings a movement up along the aggregate demand curve; a fall in the price level increases the quantity of real GDP demanded and brings a movement down along the aggregate demand curve.

The price level influences the quantity of real GDP demanded because a change in the price level brings a change in

- The buying power of money
- The real interest rate
- The real prices of exports and imports

#### The Buying Power of Money

A rise in the price level lowers the buying power of money and decreases the quantity of real GDP demanded. To see why, think about the buying plans in two economies—Russia and Japan—where the price level has changed a lot in recent years.

Anna lives in Moscow, Russia. She has worked hard all summer and has saved 20,000 rubles (the ruble is the currency of Russia), which she plans to spend attending graduate school after she has earned her economics degree. So Anna's money holding is 20,000 rubles. Anna has a part-time job, and her income from this job pays her expenses. The price level in Russia rises by 100 percent. Anna needs 40,000 rubles to buy what 20,000 rubles once bought. To make up some of the fall in the buying power of her money, Anna slashes her spending.

■ **FIGURE 13.4**

## Aggregate Demand Schedule and Aggregate Demand Curve

MyEconLab Animation

| | Price level (GDP price index, 2009 = 100) | Quantity of real GDP demanded (trillions of 2009 dollars) |
|---|---|---|
| A | 125 | 15.0 |
| B | 115 | 15.5 |
| C | 105 | 16.0 |
| D | 95 | 16.5 |
| E | 85 | 17.0 |

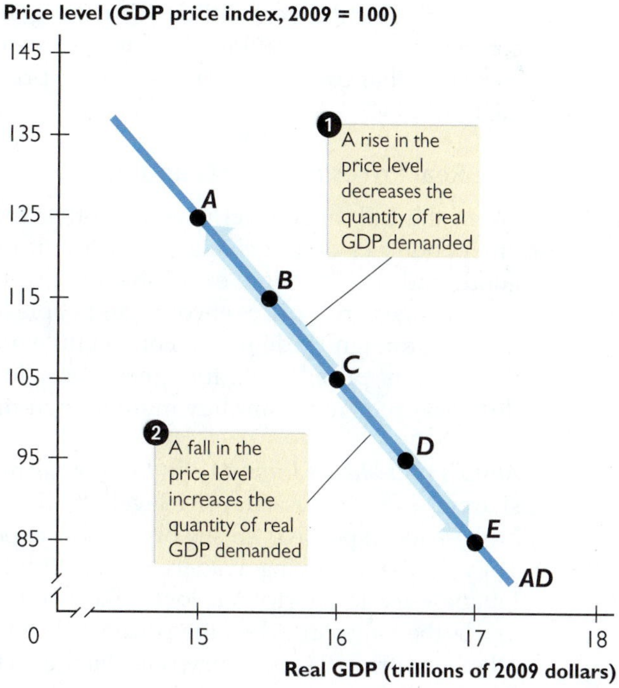

**Price level (GDP price index, 2009 = 100)**

① A rise in the price level decreases the quantity of real GDP demanded

② A fall in the price level increases the quantity of real GDP demanded

*AD*

**Real GDP (trillions of 2009 dollars)**

The aggregate demand schedule and aggregate demand curve, *AD*, show the relationship between the quantity of real GDP demanded and the price level when all other influences on expenditure plans remain the same. Each point *A* through *E* on the *AD* curve corresponds to the row identified by the same letter in the schedule.

The quantity of real GDP demanded

① decreases when the price level rises and

② increases when the price level falls.

Similarly, a fall in the price level, other things remaining the same, brings an increase in the quantity of real GDP demanded. To see why, think about the buying plans of Mika, who lives in Tokyo, Japan. She too has worked hard all summer and has saved 200,000 yen (the yen is the currency of Japan), which she plans to spend attending school next year. The price level in Japan falls by 10 percent; now Mika needs only 180,000 yen to buy what 200,000 yen once bought. With a rise in what her money buys, Mika decides to buy a smartphone.

### The Real Interest Rate

When the price level rises, the real interest rate rises. You saw in Chapter 12 (p. 303) that an increase in the price level increases the amount of money that people want to hold—increases the demand for money. When the demand for money increases, the nominal interest rate rises. In the short run, the inflation rate does not change, so a rise in the nominal interest rate brings a rise in the real interest rate. Faced with a higher real interest rate, businesses and people delay plans to buy new capital and consumer durable goods and they cut back on spending. As the price level rises, the quantity of real GDP demanded decreases.

*Anna and Mika Again*   Think about Anna and Mika again. Both of them want to buy a computer. In Moscow, a rise in the price level increases the demand for money and raises the real interest rate. At a real interest rate of 5 percent a year,

Anna was willing to borrow to buy the new computer. But at a real interest rate of 10 percent a year, she decides that the payments would be too high, so she delays buying it. The rise in the price level decreases the quantity of real GDP demanded.

In Tokyo, a fall in the price level lowers the real interest rate. At a real interest rate of 5 percent a year, Mika was willing to borrow to buy a low-performance computer. But at a real interest rate of close to zero, she decides to buy a fancier computer that costs more: The fall in the price level increases the quantity of real GDP demanded.

### The Real Prices of Exports and Imports

When the U.S. price level rises and other things remain the same, the prices in other countries do not change. So a rise in the U.S. price level makes U.S.-made goods and services more expensive relative to foreign-made goods and services. This change in real prices encourages people to spend less on U.S.-made items and more on foreign-made items. For example, if the U.S. price level rises relative to the foreign price level, foreigners buy fewer U.S.-made cars (U.S. exports decrease) and Americans buy more foreign-made cars (U.S. imports increase).

*Anna's and Mika's Imports*  In Moscow, Anna is buying some new shoes. With a sharp rise in the Russian price level, the Russian-made shoes that she planned to buy are too expensive, so she buys a less expensive pair imported from Brazil. In Tokyo, Mika is buying a smartphone. With the fall in the Japanese price level, a Japanese-made smartphone looks like a better buy than one made in Taiwan.

In the long run, when the price level changes by more in one country than in other countries, the exchange rate changes. The exchange rate change neutralizes the price level change, so this international price effect on buying plans is a short-run effect only. But in the short run, it is a powerful effect.

## ■ Changes in Aggregate Demand

A change in any factor that influences expenditure plans other than the price level brings a change in aggregate demand. When aggregate demand increases, the aggregate demand curve shifts rightward, which Figure 13.5 illustrates as the rightward shift of the $AD$ curve from $AD_0$ to $AD_1$. When aggregate demand decreases, the aggregate demand curve shifts leftward, which Figure 13.5 illustrates as the leftward shift of the $AD$ curve from $AD_0$ to $AD_2$. The factors that change aggregate demand are

- Expectations about the future
- Fiscal policy and monetary policy
- The state of the world economy

### Expectations

An increase in expected future income increases the amount of consumption goods (especially big-ticket items such as cars) that people plan to buy now. Aggregate demand increases. An increase in expected future inflation increases aggregate demand because people decide to buy more goods and services now before their prices rise. An increase in expected future profit increases the investment that firms plan to undertake now. Aggregate demand increases.

A decrease in expected future income, future inflation, or future profit has the opposite effect and decreases aggregate demand.

## Change in Aggregate Demand

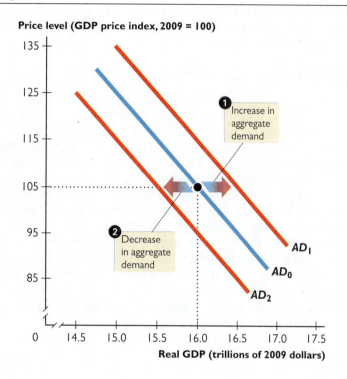

**❶ Aggregate demand *increases* if**

- Expected future income, inflation, or profits increase.
- The government or the Federal Reserve takes steps that increase planned expenditure.
- The exchange rate falls or the global economy expands.

**❷ Aggregate demand *decreases* if**

- Expected future income, inflation, or profits decrease.
- The government or the Federal Reserve takes steps that decrease planned expenditure.
- The exchange rate rises or the global economy contracts.

## Fiscal Policy and Monetary Policy

We study the effects of policy actions on aggregate demand in Chapters 16 and 17. Here, we'll just briefly note that the government can use **fiscal policy**—changing taxes, transfer payments, and government expenditure on goods and services—to influence aggregate demand. The Federal Reserve can use **monetary policy**—changing the quantity of money and the interest rate—to influence aggregate demand. A tax cut or an increase in either transfer payments or government expenditure on goods and services increases aggregate demand. A cut in the interest rate or an increase in the quantity of money increases aggregate demand.

**Fiscal policy**
Changing taxes, transfer payments, and government expenditure on goods and services.

**Monetary policy**
Changing the quantity of money and the interest rate.

## The World Economy

Two main influences that the world economy has on aggregate demand are the foreign exchange rate and foreign income. The foreign exchange rate is the amount of a foreign currency that you can buy with a U.S. dollar. Other things remaining the same, a rise in the foreign exchange rate decreases aggregate demand.

To see how the foreign exchange rate influences aggregate demand, suppose that $1 exchanges for 100 Japanese yen. A Fujitsu phone made in Japan costs 12,500 yen, and an equivalent Motorola phone made in the United States costs $110. In U.S. dollars, the Fujitsu phone costs $125, so people around the world buy the cheaper U.S. phone. Now suppose the exchange rate rises to 125 yen per dollar. At 125 yen per dollar, the Fujitsu phone costs $100 and is now cheaper than the Motorola phone. People will switch from the U.S. phone to the Japanese phone.

U.S. exports will decrease and U.S. imports will increase, so U.S. aggregate demand will decrease.

An increase in foreign income increases U.S. exports and increases U.S. aggregate demand. For example, an increase in income in Japan and Germany increases Japanese and German consumers' and producers' planned expenditures on U.S.-made goods and services.

### ■ The Aggregate Demand Multiplier

The aggregate demand multiplier is an effect that magnifies changes in expenditure plans and brings potentially large fluctuations in aggregate demand. When any influence on aggregate demand changes expenditure plans, the change in expenditure changes income; and the change in income induces a change in consumption expenditure. The increase in aggregate demand is the initial increase in expenditure plus the induced increase in consumption expenditure.

Suppose that an increase in expenditure induces an increase in consumption expenditure that is 1.5 times the initial increase in expenditure. Figure 13.6 illustrates the change in aggregate demand that occurs when investment increases by $0.4 trillion. Initially, the aggregate demand curve is $AD_0$. Investment then increases by $0.4 trillion ($\Delta I$) and the purple curve $AD_0 + \Delta I$ now describes aggregate spending plans at each price level. An increase in income induces an increase in consumption expenditure of $0.6 trillion, and the aggregate demand curve shifts rightward to $AD_1$. Chapter 14 (pp. 366–370) explains the expenditure multiplier in detail.

### ■ FIGURE 13.6

The Aggregate Demand Multiplier

MyEconLab Animation

❶ An increase in investment ❷ increases aggregate demand and increases income.

❸ A multiplier effect induces an increase in consumption expenditure, which ❹ increases aggregate demand by more than the initial increase in investment.

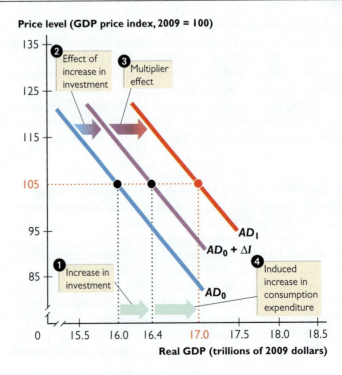

# CHECKPOINT 13.2

MyEconLab Study Plan 13.2
Key Terms Quiz
Solutions Video

**Define and explain the influences on aggregate demand.**

## Practice Problems

1. Mexico trades with the United States. Explain the effect of each of the following events on Mexico's aggregate demand.
   • The government of Mexico cuts income taxes.
   • The United States experiences strong economic growth.
   • Mexico sets new environmental standards that require factories to upgrade their production facilities.

2. Explain the effect of each of the following events on the quantity of real GDP demanded and aggregate demand in Mexico.
   • Europe trades with Mexico and goes into a recession.
   • The price level in Mexico rises.
   • Mexico increases the quantity of money.

## In the News

**Investment and government expenditure down and exports up**
The BEA announced that nonresidential investment and federal government spending decreased in the first quarter of 2016 while U.S. exports increased and U.S. imports decreased.

Source: Bureau of Economic Analysis, June 28, 2016

Explain how the items in the news clip influenced U.S. aggregate demand.

## Solutions to Practice Problems

1. A tax cut increases disposable income, which increases consumption expenditure, which increases aggregate demand. Strong U.S. growth increases the demand for Mexican-produced goods, which increases Mexico's aggregate demand. As factories upgrade their facilities, investment increases. Aggregate demand increases. In each case, the AD curve shifts rightward (Figure 1).

2. A recession in Europe decreases the demand for Mexico's exports, so aggregate demand decreases. The AD curve shifts leftward (Figure 2). A rise in the price level decreases the quantity of real GDP demanded along the AD curve, but the AD curve does not shift (Figure 3). An increase in the quantity of money increases aggregate demand, and the AD curve shifts rightward (Figure 1).

## Solution to In the News

The decrease in nonresidential investment and federal government expenditure decreased aggregate demand. The fall in U.S. imports and rise in U.S. exports increased the demand for U.S.-produced goods and services and increased U.S. aggregate demand.

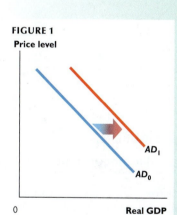

FIGURE 1
Price level

$AD_1$
$AD_0$

0                Real GDP

FIGURE 2
Price level

$AD_2$
$AD_0$

0                Real GDP

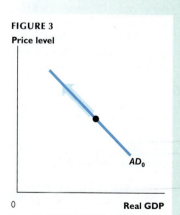

FIGURE 3
Price level

$AD_0$

0                Real GDP

## 13.3 EXPLAINING ECONOMIC TRENDS AND FLUCTUATIONS

The main purpose of the *AS-AD* model is to explain business cycle fluctuations in real GDP and the price level. But the model also helps our understanding of economic growth and inflation trends that we've studied in earlier chapters. The first step toward explaining economic trends and fluctuations is to combine aggregate supply and aggregate demand and determine macroeconomic equilibrium.

### ■ Macroeconomic Equilibrium

**Macroeconomic equilibrium**
When the quantity of real GDP demanded equals the quantity of real GDP supplied at the point of intersection of the *AD* curve and the *AS* curve.

Aggregate supply and aggregate demand determine real GDP and the price level. **Macroeconomic equilibrium** occurs when the quantity of real GDP demanded equals the quantity of real GDP supplied at the point of intersection of the *AD* curve and the *AS* curve. Figure 13.7 shows such an equilibrium at a price level of 105 and real GDP of $16 trillion.

To see why this position is the equilibrium, think about what happens if the price level is something other than 105. Suppose the price level is 95 and real GDP is $15 trillion (point *A* on the *AS* curve). The quantity of real GDP demanded exceeds $15 trillion, so firms are unable to meet the demand for their output. Inventories decrease, and customers clamor for goods and services. In this situation, firms increase production and raise prices. Eventually they can meet demand when real GDP is $16 trillion and the price level is 105.

Now suppose that the price level is 115 and that real GDP is $17 trillion (point *B* on the *AS* curve). The quantity of real GDP demanded is less than $17 trillion, so firms are unable to sell all their output. Unwanted inventories pile up. Firms cut production and lower prices until they can sell all their output, which occurs when real GDP is $16 trillion and the price level is 105.

### ■ FIGURE 13.7

Macroeconomic Equilibrium

Macroeconomic equilibrium occurs when the quantity of real GDP supplied on the *AS* curve equals the quantity of real GDP demanded on the *AD* curve.

❶ At a price level of 95, the quantity of real GDP supplied is $15 trillion at point A. The quantity of real GDP demanded exceeds the quantity supplied, so firms increase production and raise prices.

❷ At a price level of 115, the quantity of real GDP supplied is $17 trillion at point B. The quantity of real GDP demanded is less than the quantity supplied, so firms cut production and lower prices.

At a price level of 105, the quantity of real GDP supplied equals the quantity of real GDP demanded in macroeconomic equilibrium.

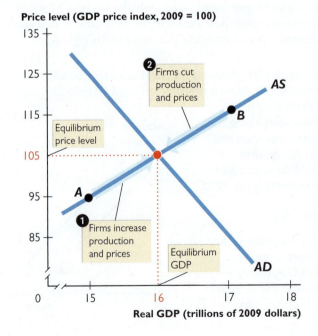

## ■ Three Types of Macroeconomic Equilibrium

In macroeconomic equilibrium, the economy might be at full employment or above or below full employment. Figure 13.8(a) shows these three possibilities. **Full-employment equilibrium**—when equilibrium real GDP equals potential GDP—occurs where the $AD$ curve intersects the aggregate supply curve $AS^*$.

At a higher money wage rate, aggregate supply is $AS_1$. Real GDP is $15.5 trillion and is less than potential GDP. The economy is *below full employment* and there is a **recessionary gap**. At a lower money wage rate, aggregate supply is $AS_2$. In this situation, real GDP is $16.5 trillion and is greater than potential GDP. The economy is *above full employment* and there is an **inflationary gap**.

### Adjustment toward Full Employment

When real GDP is below or above potential GDP, the money wage rate gradually changes to restore full employment. Figure 13.8(b) illustrates this adjustment.

In a *recessionary gap*, there is a surplus of labor and firms can hire new workers at a lower wage rate. As the money wage rate falls, the $AS$ curve shifts from $AS_1$ toward $AS^*$ and the price level falls and real GDP rises. The money wage continues to fall until real GDP equals potential GDP—full-employment equilibrium.

In an *inflationary gap*, there is a shortage of labor and firms must offer a higher wage rate to hire the labor they demand. As the money wage rate rises, the $AS$ curve shifts from $AS_2$ toward $AS^*$ and the price level rises and real GDP falls. The money wage rate continues to rise until real GDP equals potential GDP.

**Full-employment equilibrium**
When equilibrium real GDP equals potential GDP.

**Recessionary gap**
A gap that exists when potential GDP exceeds real GDP and that brings a falling price level.

**Inflationary gap**
A gap that exists when real GDP exceeds potential GDP and that brings a rising price level.

■ **FIGURE 13.8**

Output Gaps and Full-Employment Equilibrium

MyEconLab Animation

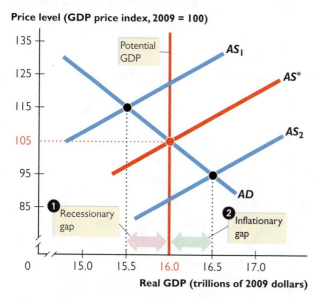

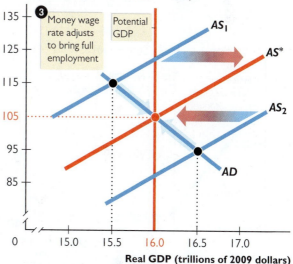

**(a) Three types of macroeconomic equilibrium**

**(b) Adjustment to full employment**

In part (a), when equilibrium real GDP is less than potential GDP, ➊ there is a recessionary gap; when equilibrium real GDP is greater than potential GDP, ➋ there is an inflationary gap; and when equilibrium real GDP equals potential GDP, the economy is at full employment.

In part (b), when an output gap exists ➌ the money wage rate adjusts to move the economy toward full employment. With a recessionary gap, the money wage rate falls and the $AS$ curve shifts rightward from $AS_1$ to $AS^*$. With an inflationary gap, the money wage rate rises and the $AS$ curve shifts leftward from $AS_2$ to $AS^*$.

## ■ Economic Growth and Inflation Trends

Economic growth results from a growing labor force and increasing labor productivity, which together make potential GDP grow (Chapter 9, pp. 220–225). Inflation results from a growing quantity of money that outpaces the growth of potential GDP (Chapter 12, pp. 312–316).

The *AS-AD* model can be used to understand economic growth and inflation trends. In the *AS-AD* model, economic growth is increasing potential GDP—a persistent rightward shift in the potential GDP line. Inflation arises from a persistent increase in aggregate demand at a faster pace than that of the increase in potential GDP—a persistent rightward shift of the *AD* curve at a faster pace than the growth of potential GDP. *Eye on the U.S. Economy* below shows how the *AS-AD* model explains U.S. economic growth and inflation trends.

# EYE on the U.S. ECONOMY
## U.S. Economic Growth, Inflation, and the Business Cycle

U.S. economic growth, inflation, and the business cycle result from changes in aggregate supply and aggregate demand.

A rightward movement in the U.S. potential GDP line brings economic growth and a greater rightward movement of the U.S. *AD* curve brings inflation. Part (a) shows the shifting curves that generate growth and inflation.

Part (b) shows the history of U.S. real GDP growth and inflation from 1970 to 2015. Each dot represents the real GDP and price level in a year—the black dot 1970 and the red dot 2015. The rightward movement of the dots is economic growth and the upward movement is a rising price level—inflation.

When the dots follow a path that is gently rising, as during the 1990s, the inflation rate is low and real GDP growth is quite rapid. When the dots follow a path that is steep, as during the 1970s, inflation is rapid and economic growth is slow.

Notice that the dots move rightward and upward in waves and occasionally

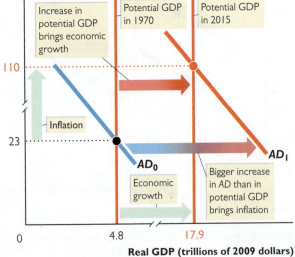

**(a) Economic growth and inflation**

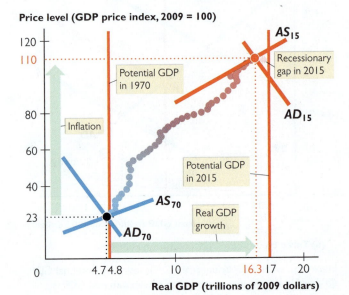

**(b) U.S. economic growth and inflation**

# ■ The Business Cycle

The business cycle results from fluctuations in aggregate supply and aggregate demand. Aggregate supply fluctuates because labor productivity grows at a variable pace, which brings fluctuations in the growth rate of potential GDP. The resulting cycle is called a **real business cycle**. But aggregate demand fluctuations are the main source of the business cycle. The key reason is that the swings in aggregate demand occur more quickly than changes in the money wage rate that change aggregate supply. The result is that the economy swings from inflationary gap to full employment to recessionary gap and back again.

*Eye on the U.S. Economy* below shows the most recent cycle interpreted as driven by aggregate demand fluctuations. But in the 2008–2009 recession, both aggregate demand and aggregate supply were at work as you can see on p. 347.

**Real business cycle**
A cycle that results from fluctuations in the pace of growth of labor productivity and potential GDP.

leftward. The pattern shows the business cycle expansions and recessions.

By comparing the dots with potential GDP, we can see that the economy was at full employment in 1970 and had a recessionary gap in 2015.

Part (c) shows how changes in aggregate demand create the business cycle, and part (d) shows the most recent cycle from 2000 to 2015.

When the *AD* curve is $AD_0$ in part (c), the economy is at point *A* and there is an inflationary gap. Part (d) identifies the actual gap in 2000 as *A*.

A decrease in aggregate demand to $AD_1$ lowers real GDP to potential GDP and the economy moves to point *B* in parts (c) and (d).

A further decrease in aggregate demand to $AD_2$ lowers real GDP to

below potential GDP and opens up a recessionary gap at point *C* in both parts (c) and (d).

In reality, *AD* rarely decreases. It increases at a slower pace than the increase in potential GDP. Also, in reality, *AS* fluctuates. But the relative positions of the *AS* and *AD* curves and the potential GDP line are like those shown in part (c).

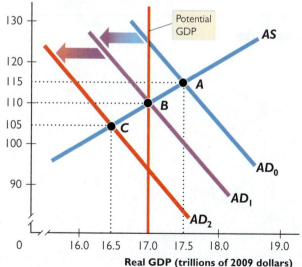

**(c) Aggregate demand fluctuations**

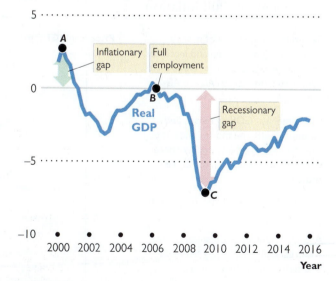

**(d) The U.S. output gap**

SOURCES OF DATA: Bureau of Labor Statistics, Bureau of Economic Analysis, and Congressional Budget Office.

## ■ Inflation Cycles

You've seen that inflation occurs if aggregate demand grows faster than potential GDP. But just as there are cycles in real GDP, there are also cycles in the inflation rate. And the two cycles are related. To study the interaction of real GDP and inflation cycles, we distinguish between two sources of inflation:

- Demand-pull inflation
- Cost-push inflation

### Demand-Pull Inflation

**Demand-pull inflation**

Inflation that starts because aggregate demand increases.

Inflation that starts because aggregate demand increases is called **demand-pull inflation**. Demand-pull inflation can be kicked off by any of the factors that change aggregate demand but the only thing that can sustain it is growth in the quantity of money.

Figure 13.9 illustrates the process of demand-pull inflation. Potential GDP is $16 trillion. Initially, the aggregate demand curve is $AD_0$, the aggregate supply curve is $AS_0$, and real GDP equals potential GDP. Aggregate demand increases, shifting the aggregate demand curve to $AD_1$. Real GDP increases and the price level rises. There is now an *inflationary gap*. A shortage of labor brings a rise in the money wage rate, which shifts the aggregate supply curve to $AS_1$. The price level rises further and real GDP returns to potential GDP.

The quantity of money increases again, and the aggregate demand curve shifts rightward to $AD_2$. The price level rises further, and real GDP again exceeds potential GDP. Yet again, the money wage rate rises and decreases aggregate supply. The $AS$ curve shifts to $AS_2$, and the price level rises further. As the quantity of money continues to grow, aggregate demand increases and the price level rises in an ongoing demand-pull inflation spiral.

### FIGURE 13.9

### A Demand-Pull Inflation

MyEconLab Animation

Each time the quantity of money increases, aggregate demand increases and the aggregate demand curve shifts rightward from $AD_0$ to $AD_1$ to $AD_2$, and so on.

Each time real GDP increases above potential GDP, the money wage rate rises and the aggregate supply curve shifts leftward from $AS_0$ to $AS_1$ to $AS_2$, and so on.

The price level rises from 105 to 108, 116, 120, 128, and so on.

A demand-pull inflation spiral results with real GDP fluctuating between $16 trillion and $16.5 trillion.

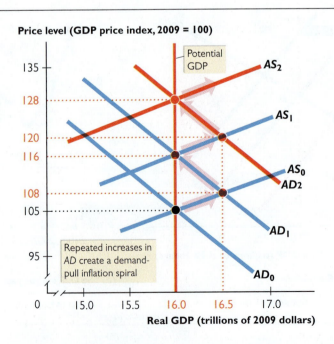

## Cost-Push Inflation

Inflation that begins with an increase in cost is called **cost-push inflation**. The two main sources of cost increases are increases in the money wage rate and increases in the money prices of raw materials such as oil.

Cost-push inflation can be kicked off by an increase in costs but the only thing that can sustain it is growth in the quantity of money.

Figure 13.10 illustrates cost-push inflation. The aggregate demand curve is $AD_0$, the aggregate supply curve is $AS_0$, and real GDP equals potential GDP. The world price of oil rises, which decreases aggregate supply. The aggregate supply curve shifts leftward to $AS_1$, the price level rises, and real GDP decreases so there is a *recessionary gap*.

When real GDP decreases, unemployment rises above its natural rate and the Fed increases the quantity of money to restore full employment. Aggregate demand increases and the $AD$ curve shifts rightward to $AD_1$. Real GDP returns to potential GDP but the price level rises further.

Oil producers now see the prices of everything they buy rising so they raise the price of oil again to restore its new higher relative price. The $AS$ curve now shifts to $AS_2$, the price level rises again, and real GDP decreases again.

If the Fed responds yet again with an increase in the quantity of money, aggregate demand increases and the $AD$ curve shifts to $AD_2$. The price level rises even higher and full employment is again restored. A cost-push inflation spiral results.

The combination of a decreasing real GDP and a rising price level is called **stagflation**. You can see that stagflation poses a dilemma for the Fed. If the Fed does not respond when producers raise the oil price, the economy remains below full employment. If the Fed increases the quantity of money to restore full employment, it invites another oil price hike that will call forth yet a further increase in the quantity of money.

**Cost-push inflation**
An inflation that begins with an increase in cost.

**Stagflation**
The combination of recession (decreasing real GDP) and inflation (rising price level).

■ **FIGURE 13.10**

A Cost-Push Inflation                    MyEconLab Animation

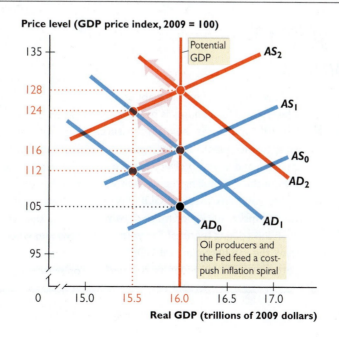

Each time a cost increase occurs, the aggregate supply curve shifts leftward from $AS_0$ to $AS_1$ to $AS_2$, and so on.

Each time real GDP decreases below potential GDP, the Fed increases the quantity of money and the aggregate demand curve shifts rightward from $AD_0$ to $AD_1$ to $AD_2$, and so on.

The price level rises from 105 to 112, 116, 124, 128, and so on.

A cost-push inflation spiral results with real GDP fluctuating between $16 trillion and $15.5 trillion.

## ■ Deflation and the Great Depression

When a financial crisis hit the United States in October 2008, many people feared a repeat of the dreadful events of the 1930s. From 1929 through 1933, the United States and most of the world experienced deflation and depression—the *Great Depression*. The price level fell by 22 percent and real GDP fell by 31 percent.

The recession of 2008–2009 turned out to be much less severe than the Great Depression. Real GDP fell by less than 4 percent and the price level continued to rise, although at a slower pace. Why was the Great Depression so bad and why was 2008–2009 so mild in comparison? You can answer these questions with what you've learned in this chapter.

During the Great Depression, banks failed and the quantity of money contracted by 25 percent. The Fed stood by and took no action to counteract the collapse of buying power, so aggregate demand also collapsed. Because the money wage rate didn't fall immediately, the decrease in aggregate demand brought a large fall in real GDP. The money wage rate and price level fell eventually, but not until employment and real GDP had shrunk to 75 percent of their 1929 levels.

In contrast, during the 2008 financial crisis, the Fed bailed out troubled financial institutions and doubled the monetary base. The quantity of money kept growing. Also, the government increased its own expenditures, which added to aggregate demand. The combined effects of continued growth in the quantity of money and increased government expenditure limited the fall in aggregate demand and prevented a large decrease in real GDP.

The challenge that now lies ahead is to unwind the monetary and fiscal stimulus as the components of private expenditure—consumption expenditure, investment, and exports—begin to increase and return to more normal levels and so bring an increase in aggregate demand. Too much stimulus will bring an inflationary gap and faster inflation. Too little stimulus will leave a recessionary gap.

You will explore these monetary and fiscal policy actions and their effects in Chapters 16 and 17.

## EYE on YOUR LIFE
### Using the *AS-AD* Model

MyEconLab Critical Thinking Exercise

Using all the knowledge that you have accumulated over the term, and by watching or reading the current news, try to figure out where the U.S. economy is in its business cycle right now.

First, can you determine if real GDP is currently above, below, or at potential GDP? Second, can you determine if real GDP is expanding or contracting in a recession?

Next, try to form a view about where the U.S. economy is heading. What do you see as the main pressures on aggregate supply and aggregate demand, and in which directions are they pushing or pulling the economy?

Do you think that real GDP will expand more quickly or more slowly over the coming months? Do you think the gap between real GDP and potential GDP will widen or narrow?

How do you expect the labor market to be affected by the changes in aggregate supply and aggregate demand that you are expecting? Do you expect the unemployment rate to rise, fall, or remain constant?

Talk to your friends in class about where they see the U.S. economy right now and where it is heading. Is there a consensus or is there a wide range of opinion?

# EYE on the BUSINESS CYCLE

## Why Did the U.S. Economy Go into Recession in 2008?

What causes the business cycle and what caused the 2008–2009 recession?

### Business Cycle Theory

The mainstream business cycle theory is that potential GDP grows at a steady rate while aggregate demand grows at a fluctuating rate.

Because the money wage rate is slow to change, if aggregate demand grows more quickly than potential GDP, real GDP moves above potential GDP and an inflationary gap emerges. The inflation rate rises and real GDP is pulled back toward potential GDP.

If aggregate demand grows more slowly than potential GDP, real GDP moves below potential GDP and a recessionary gap emerges. The inflation rate slows. Because the money wage rate responds very slowly to the recessionary gap, real GDP does not return to potential GDP until another increase in aggregate demand occurs.

Fluctuations in investment are the main source of fluctuations in aggregate demand. Consumption expenditure responds to changes in income.

A recession can also occur if aggregate supply decreases to bring stagflation. And a recession might occur because both aggregate demand and aggregate supply decrease.

### The 2008–2009 Recession

The 2008–2009 recession is an example of a recession caused by a decrease in both aggregate demand and aggregate supply. The figure illustrates these two contributing forces.

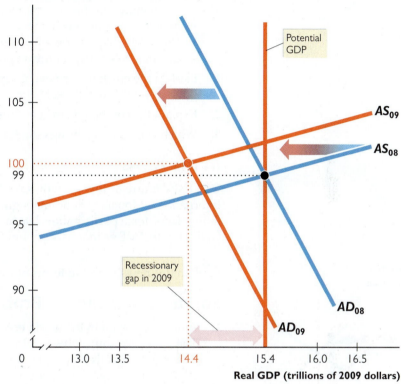

SOURCES OF DATA: Bureau of Economic Analysis and Congressional Budget Office.

At the peak in 2008, real GDP was $15.4 trillion and the price level was 99. In the second quarter of 2009, real GDP had fallen to $14.4 trillion and the price level had risen to 100.

The financial crisis that began in 2007 and intensified in 2008 decreased the supply of loanable funds and investment fell. In particular, construction investment collapsed.

Recession in the global economy decreased the demand for U.S. exports, so this component of aggregate demand also decreased.

The decrease in aggregate demand was moderated by a large injection of spending by the U.S. government, but this move was not enough to stop aggregate demand from decreasing.

We cannot account for the combination of a rise in the price level and a decrease in real GDP with a decrease in aggregate demand alone. Aggregate supply must also have decreased. The rise in oil prices in 2007 and a rise in the money wage rate were the two factors that brought about the decrease in aggregate supply.

MyEconLab Study Plan 13.3
Key Terms Quiz
Solutions Video

# CHECKPOINT 13.3

**Explain how trends and fluctuations in aggregate demand and aggregate supply bring economic growth, inflation, and the business cycle.**

## Practice Problems

The U.S. economy is at full employment when the following events occur:
- A deep recession hits the world economy.
- The world oil price rises by a large amount.
- U.S. businesses expect future profits to fall.

1. Explain the effect of each event separately on aggregate demand and aggregate supply. How will real GDP and the price level change in the short run?

2. Explain the combined effect of these events on real GDP and the price level.

3. Which event, if any, brings stagflation?

## In the News

**U.S. risks future of low growth, says IMF**
International Monetary Fund managing director Christine Lagarde says that a falling labor force participation rate and falling productivity will slow U.S. real GDP growth. IMF economists say business investment will also slow.
Source: *Financial Times*, June 22, 2016

Explain this news report in terms of the *AS-AD* model.

## Solutions to Practice Problems

1. A deep recession in the world economy decreases U.S. aggregate demand. The *AD* curve shifts leftward. In the short run, U.S. real GDP decreases and the price level falls (Figure 1). A rise in the world oil price decreases U.S. aggregate supply. The *AS* curve shifts leftward. In the short run, U.S. real GDP decreases and the price level rises (Figure 2). A fall in expected future profits decreases U.S. aggregate demand. The *AD* curve shifts leftward. In the short run, U.S. real GDP decreases and the price level falls (Figure 1).

2. All three events decrease U.S. real GDP (Figures 1 and 2). The deep world recession and the fall in expected future profits decrease the price level (Figure 1). The rise in the world oil price increases the price level (Figure 2). So the combined effect on the price level is ambiguous.

3. Stagflation is a rising price level and a decreasing real GDP together. The rise in the world oil price brings stagflation because it decreases aggregate supply, decreases real GDP, and raises the price level (Figure 2).

## Solution to In the News

The news report contains information about likely future developments in U.S. aggregate supply and aggregate demand. A falling labor force participation rate and falling productivity will slow the growth rate of U.S. potential GDP and aggregate supply. A slowdown in business investment will slow the growth rate of aggregate demand. The combination of these changes will slow the growth rate of real GDP. Their effects on the price level depend on whether aggregate supply or aggregate demand slows most.

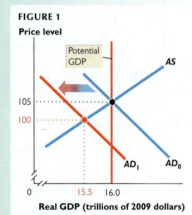

**FIGURE 1**

Price level

**FIGURE 2**

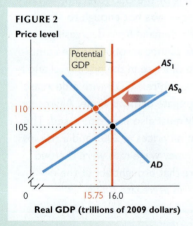

Price level

**CHAPTER SUMMARY**

## Key Points

**1. Define and explain the influences on aggregate supply.**

- Aggregate supply is the relationship between the quantity of real GDP supplied and the price level when all other influences on production plans remain the same.
- The *AS* curve slopes upward because with a given money wage rate, a rise in the price level lowers the real wage rate, increases the quantity of labor demanded, and increases the quantity of real GDP supplied.
- A change in potential GDP, a change in the money wage rate, or a change in the money price of other resources changes aggregate supply.

**2. Define and explain the influences on aggregate demand.**

- Aggregate demand is the relationship between the quantity of real GDP demanded and the price level when all other influences on expenditure plans remain the same.
- The *AD* curve slopes downward because a rise in the price level decreases the buying power of money, raises the real interest rate, raises the real price of domestic goods compared with foreign goods, and decreases the quantity of real GDP demanded.
- A change in expected future income, inflation, and profits; a change in fiscal policy and monetary policy; and a change in the foreign exchange rate and foreign real GDP all change aggregate demand—the aggregate demand curve shifts.

**3. Explain how trends and fluctuations in aggregate demand and aggregate supply bring economic growth, inflation, and the business cycle.**

- Aggregate demand and aggregate supply determine real GDP and the price level in macroeconomic equilibrium, which can occur at full employment or above or below full employment.
- Away from full employment, gradual changes in the money wage rate move real GDP toward potential GDP.
- Economic growth is a persistent increase in potential GDP, and inflation occurs when aggregate demand grows at a faster rate than potential GDP.
- Business cycles occur because aggregate demand and aggregate supply fluctuate.
- Demand-pull and cost-push forces bring inflation and real GDP cycles.

## Key Terms

MyEconLab Key Terms Quiz

**CHAPTER CHECKPOINT**

## Study Plan Problems and Applications

**1.** As more people in India have access to higher education, explain how potential GDP and aggregate supply will change in the long run.

**2.** Explain the effect of each of the following events on the quantity of U.S. real GDP demanded and the demand for U.S. real GDP:

- The world economy goes into a strong expansion.
- The U.S. price level rises.
- Congress raises income taxes.

**3.** The United States is at full employment when the Fed cuts the quantity of money, other things remaining the same. Explain the effect of the cut in the quantity of money on aggregate demand in the short run.

**4.** Table 1 sets out an economy's aggregate demand and aggregate supply schedules. What is the macroeconomic equilibrium? If potential GDP is $600 billion, what is the type of macroeconomic equilibrium? Explain how real GDP and the price level will adjust in the long run.

**5.** Suppose that the U.S. economy has a recessionary gap and the world economy goes into an expansion. Explain the effect of the expansion on U.S. real GDP and unemployment in the short run.

**6.** Explain the effect of the Fed's action that increases the quantity of money on the macroeconomic equilibrium in the short run. Explain the adjustment process that returns the economy to full employment.

Use Figure 1 to work Problems **7** to **9**. Initially, the economy is at point *B*.

**7.** Some events change aggregate demand from $AD_0$ to $AD_1$. Describe two possible events. What is the new equilibrium point? If potential GDP is $1 trillion, describe the type of macroeconomic equilibrium.

**8.** Some events change aggregate supply from $AS_0$ to $AS_1$. Describe two possible events. What is the new equilibrium point? If potential GDP is $1 trillion, does the economy have an inflationary gap, a recessionary gap, or no gap?

**9.** Some events change aggregate demand from $AD_0$ to $AD_1$ and aggregate supply from $AS_0$ to $AS_1$. What is the new macroeconomic equilibrium?

**10.** "Brexit" expected to rattle U.S. economy
The United Kingdom vote to leave the European Union (known as Brexit) is expected to affect the U.S. economy by driving up the value of the dollar. But it is not thought that Brexit alone will shrink the U.S. economy.

Source: *The Wall Street Journal*, June 24, 2016

Explain how a high value of the dollar affects U.S. real GDP and on an *AS-AD* graph show the macroeconomic equilibrium in the U.S. economy with and without the effects of Brexit.

**11.** Read *Eye on the Business Cycle* on p. 347. What caused the 2008–2009 recession and how do we know that a decrease in aggregate supply played a role?

**TABLE 1**

| Price level (GDP price index) | Real GDP demanded | Real GDP supplied |
|---|---|---|
| | (billions of 2009 dollars) | |
| 90 | 900 | 600 |
| 100 | 850 | 700 |
| 110 | 800 | 800 |
| 120 | 750 | 900 |
| 130 | 700 | 1,000 |

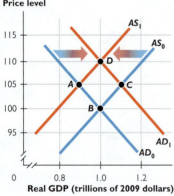

**FIGURE 1**

## Instructor Assignable Problems and Applications

MyEconLab Homework, Quiz, or
Test if assigned by instructor

1. What, according to the mainstream theory of the business cycle, is the most common source of recession: a decrease in aggregate demand, a decrease in aggregate supply, or both? Which is the most likely component of aggregate demand to start a recession? How does the aggregate demand multiplier influence a recession?

2. Suppose that the United States is at full employment. Explain the effect of each of the following events on aggregate supply:
   • Union wage settlements push the money wage rate up by 10 percent.
   • The price level increases.
   • Potential GDP increases.

3. Suppose that the United States is at full employment. Then the federal government cuts taxes, and all other influences on aggregate demand remain the same. Explain the effect of the tax cut on aggregate demand in the short run.

Use the following information to work Problems **4** and **5**.

Because fluctuations in the world oil price make the U.S. short-run macroeconomic equilibrium fluctuate, someone suggests that the government should vary the tax rate on oil, lowering the tax when the world oil price rises and increasing the tax when the world oil price falls, to stabilize the oil price in the U.S. market.

4. How would such an action influence aggregate demand?

5. How would such an action influence aggregate supply?

6. Table 1 sets out the aggregate demand and aggregate supply schedules in Japan. Potential GDP is 600 trillion yen. What is the short-run macroeconomic equilibrium? Does Japan have an inflationary gap or a recessionary gap and what is its magnitude?

7. Suppose that the world price of oil rises. On an *AS-AD* graph, show the effect of the world oil price rise on U.S. macroeconomic equilibrium in the short run. Explain the adjustment process that restores the economy to full employment.

8. Explain the effects of a global recession on the U.S. macroeconomic equilibrium in the short run. Explain the adjustment process that restores the economy to full employment.

TABLE 1

| Price level<br>(GDP<br>price index) | Real GDP<br>demanded | Real GDP<br>supplied |
|---|---|---|
| | (trillions of 2005 yen) | |
| 75 | 600 | 400 |
| 85 | 550 | 450 |
| 95 | 500 | 500 |
| 105 | 450 | 550 |
| 115 | 400 | 600 |
| 125 | 350 | 650 |
| 135 | 300 | 700 |

Use the following information to work Problems **9** and **10**.

**Brexit means a bumpy road ahead for the U.K. economy**
The decision by the U.K. people to leave the European Union has already brought a sharp fall in the value of the pound and is expected to lower business and household spending.

Source: *Financial Times*, June 24, 2016

9. Explain the effects of a fall in the value of the U.K. pound and lower spending by businesses and households on U.K. aggregate demand and aggregate supply.

10. The U.K. economy in 2016 was close to full employment. Use the *AS-AD* model to show the effect on U.K. real GDP of the effects of Brexit described in the news clip.

## Multiple Choice Quiz

**1.** Aggregate supply increases when _____.

  A. the price level rises
  B. the money wage rate falls
  C. consumption increases
  D. the money price of oil increases

**2.** When potential GDP increases, _____.

  A. aggregate demand increases
  B. aggregate supply increases
  C. both aggregate demand and aggregate supply increase
  D. the price level rises

**3.** The quantity of real GDP demanded increases if _____.

  A. the buying power of money increases
  B. the money wage rate rises
  C. the price level falls
  D. the nominal interest rate falls

**4.** An increase in expected future income increases _____.

  A. consumption expenditure, which increases current aggregate demand
  B. investment, which increases current aggregate supply
  C. the demand for money, which decreases current aggregate demand
  D. future consumption expenditure and has no effect on current aggregate demand

**5.** Macroeconomic equilibrium occurs when the quantity of real GDP _____ equals the quantity of _____.

  A. demanded; real GDP supplied
  B. demanded; potential GDP
  C. supplied; potential GDP
  D. demanded; real GDP supplied and potential GDP

**6.** If the economy is at full employment and the Fed increases the quantity of money, _____.

  A. aggregate demand increases, a recessionary gap appears, and the money wage rate starts to rise
  B. aggregate supply increases, the price level starts to fall, and an expansion begins
  C. aggregate demand increases, an inflationary gap appears, and the money wage rate starts to rise
  D. potential GDP and aggregate supply increase together and the price level does not change

**7.** Over the past decade, the demand for goods produced in China has brought a sustained increase in the demand for China's exports that has outstripped the growth of supply. As a result, China has experienced a _____.

  A. period of stable prices and sustained economic growth
  B. rising price level and demand-pull inflation
  C. rising price level and cost-push inflation
  D. rising price level and a falling real wage rate

# Aggregate Expenditure
# Multiplier

# 14

## CHAPTER CHECKLIST

**When you have completed your study of this chapter,
you will be able to**

**1** Explain how real GDP influences expenditure plans.

**2** Explain how real GDP adjusts to achieve equilibrium expenditure.

**3** Explain the expenditure multiplier.

**4** Derive the *AD* curve from equilibrium expenditure.

MyEconLab **Big Picture Video**

## 14.1 EXPENDITURE PLANS AND REAL GDP

When the government spends $1 million on a highway construction project, does that expenditure stimulate consumption expenditure in a multiplier effect? This question lies at the core of this chapter.

To answer the question, we use the *aggregate expenditure model*, a model that explains what determines the quantity of real GDP demanded and changes in that quantity *at a given price level.*

The aggregate expenditure model—also known as the *Keynesian model*—was originally designed to explain what happens in an economy in deep recession when firms can't cut their prices any further but can increase production without raising their prices, so the price level is actually fixed. The severity of the global recession of 2008–2009 gave the model a rebirth and the question of the size of the government expenditure multiplier became a hot issue.

You learned in Chapter 5 (pp. 117–119) that aggregate expenditure equals the sum of consumption expenditure, *C*, investment, *I*, government expenditure on goods and services, *G*, and net exports, *NX*. **Aggregate planned expenditure** is the sum of the spending plans of households, firms, and governments. We divide expenditure plans into autonomous expenditure and induced expenditure. *Autonomous expenditure* does not respond to changes in real GDP and *induced expenditure* does respond to changes in real GDP. We start by looking at induced expenditure and its main component, consumption expenditure.

**Aggregate planned expenditure**
Planned consumption expenditure plus planned investment, plus planned government expenditure, plus planned exports minus planned imports.

### ■ The Consumption Function

**Consumption function**
The relationship between consumption expenditure and disposable income, other things remaining the same.

The **consumption function** is the relationship between consumption expenditure and disposable income, other things remaining the same. *Disposable income* is aggregate income—GDP—minus net taxes. (Net taxes are taxes paid to the government minus transfer payments received from the government.)

Households must either spend their disposable income on consumption or save it. A decision to spend a dollar on consumption is a decision not to save a dollar. The consumption decision and the saving decision is one decision.

#### Consumption Plans

For households and the economy as a whole, as disposable income increases, planned consumption expenditure increases. But the increase in planned consumption is less than the increase in disposable income. The table in Figure 14.1 shows a consumption schedule. It lists the consumption expenditure that people plan to undertake at each level of disposable income.

Figure 14.1 shows a consumption function based on the consumption schedule. Along the consumption function, the points labeled *A* through *E* correspond to the columns of the table. For example, when disposable income is $9 trillion at point *D*, consumption expenditure is $8 trillion. Along the consumption function, as disposable income increases, consumption expenditure increases.

At point *A* on the consumption function, consumption expenditure is $2 trillion even though disposable income is zero. This consumption expenditure is called *autonomous consumption*, and it is the amount of consumption expenditure that would take place in the short run even if people had no current income. This consumption expenditure would be financed either by spending past savings or by borrowing.

■ **FIGURE 14.1**

The Consumption Function

MyEconLab Animation

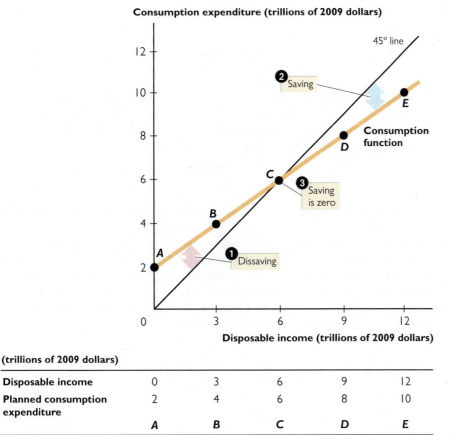

**Consumption expenditure (trillions of 2009 dollars)**

The table shows consumption expenditure (and saving) plans at various levels of disposable income. The figure graphs these data as the consumption function. The figure also shows a 45° line along which consumption expenditure equals disposable income.

❶ When the consumption function is above the 45° line, saving is negative (dissaving occurs).

❷ When the consumption function is below the 45° line, saving is positive.

❸ At the point where the consumption function intersects the 45° line, all disposable income is consumed and saving is zero.

| (trillions of 2009 dollars) | | | | | |
| --- | --- | --- | --- | --- | --- |
| **Disposable income** | 0 | 3 | 6 | 9 | 12 |
| **Planned consumption expenditure** | 2 | 4 | 6 | 8 | 10 |
| | *A* | *B* | *C* | *D* | *E* |

Figure 14.1 also shows a 45° line. Because the scale on the *x*-axis measures disposable income and the scale on the *y*-axis measures consumption expenditure, and because the two scales are equal, along the 45° line consumption expenditure equals disposable income. So the 45° line serves as a reference line for comparing consumption expenditure and disposable income. Between *A* and *C*, consumption expenditure exceeds disposable income; between *C* and *E*, disposable income exceeds consumption expenditure; and at point *C*, consumption expenditure equals disposable income.

You can see saving in Figure 14.1. When consumption expenditure exceeds disposable income (and the consumption function is above the 45° line), saving is negative—called *dissaving*. When consumption expenditure is less than disposable income (the consumption function is below the 45° line), saving is positive. And when consumption expenditure equals disposable income (the consumption function intersects the 45° line), saving is zero.

When consumption expenditure exceeds disposable income, past savings are used to pay for current consumption. Such a situation cannot last forever, but it can and does occur if disposable income falls temporarily.

**Marginal propensity to consume**

The fraction of a change in disposable income that is spent on consumption—the change in consumption expenditure divided by the change in disposable income that brought it about.

## Marginal Propensity to Consume

The **marginal propensity to consume** (*MPC*) is the fraction of a change in disposable income that is spent on consumption. It is calculated as the change in consumption expenditure divided by the change in disposable income that brought it about. That is,

$$MPC = \frac{\text{Change in consumption expenditure}}{\text{Change in disposable income}}.$$

Suppose that when disposable income increases from $6 trillion to $9 trillion, consumption expenditure increases from $6 trillion to $8 trillion. The $3 trillion increase in disposable income increases consumption expenditure by $2 trillion. Using these numbers in the formula to calculate the *MPC*,

$$MPC = \frac{\$2 \text{ trillion}}{\$3 \text{ trillion}} = 0.67.$$

The marginal propensity to consume tells us that when disposable income increases by $1, consumption expenditure increases by 67¢.

Figure 14.2 shows that the *MPC* equals the slope of the consumption function. A $3 trillion increase in disposable income from $6 trillion to $9 trillion is the base of the red triangle. The increase in consumption expenditure that results from this increase in income is $2 trillion and is the height of the triangle. The slope of the consumption function is given by the formula "slope equals rise over run" and is $2 trillion divided by $3 trillion, which equals 0.67—the *MPC*.

### FIGURE 14.2

## Marginal Propensity to Consume

MyEconLab Animation

The marginal propensity to consume, *MPC*, is equal to the change in consumption expenditure divided by the change in disposable income, other things remaining the same.

The slope of the consumption function measures the *MPC*.

In the figure:

**1** A $3 trillion change in disposable income brings

**2** a $2 trillion change in consumption expenditure, so

**3** the *MPC* equals
$2 trillion ÷ $3 trillion = 0.67.

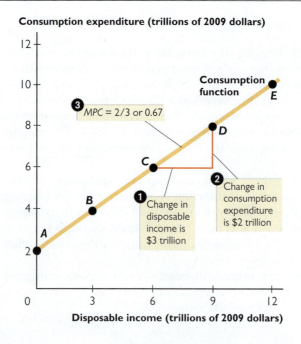

## Other Influences on Consumption Expenditure

Consumption plans are influenced by many factors other than disposable income. The more important influences are

- Real interest rate
- Wealth
- Expected future income

***Real Interest Rate***   When the real interest rate falls, consumption expenditure increases (and saving decreases) and when the real interest rate rises, consumption expenditure decreases (and saving increases).

***Wealth and Expected Future Income***   When either wealth or expected future income decreases, consumption expenditure also decreases and when wealth or expected future income increases, consumption expenditure also increases.

Figure 14.3 shows the effects of these influences on the consumption function. When the real interest rate falls or when wealth or expected future income increases, the consumption function shifts upward from $CF_0$ to $CF_1$. Such a shift occurs during the expansion phase of the business cycle if a stock market boom increases wealth and expected future income increases.

When the real interest rate rises, or when wealth or expected future income decreases, the consumption function shifts downward from $CF_0$ to $CF_2$. Such a shift occurs during a recession if a stock market crash decreases wealth and expected future income decreases.

---

### FIGURE 14.3

Shifts in the Consumption Function

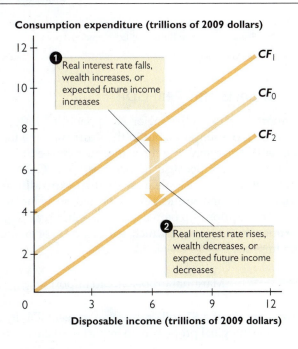

❶ A fall in the real interest rate or an increase in either wealth or expected future income increases consumption expenditure and shifts the consumption function upward from $CF_0$ to $CF_1$.

❷ A rise in the real interest rate or a decrease in either wealth or expected future income decreases consumption expenditure and shifts the consumption function downward from $CF_0$ to $CF_2$.

# EYE on the U.S. ECONOMY
## The U.S. Consumption Function

Each dot in the figure represents consumption expenditure and disposable income in the United States for a year between 1960 and 2015 (some labeled).

The lines labeled $CF_{60}$ and $CF_{15}$ are estimates of the U.S. consumption function in 1960 and 2015, respectively.

The slope of these consumption functions—the marginal propensity to consume—is 0.87, which means that a $1 increase in disposable income brings an 87¢ increase in consumption expenditure.

The consumption function shifted upward from 1960 to 2015—autonomous consumption increased—because as economic growth brought higher expected future income and greater wealth, people chose to increase consumption expenditure from a given disposable income.

During the recession of 2009, the consumption function temporarily shifted downward as a fall in house prices lowered wealth and encouraged people to save more.

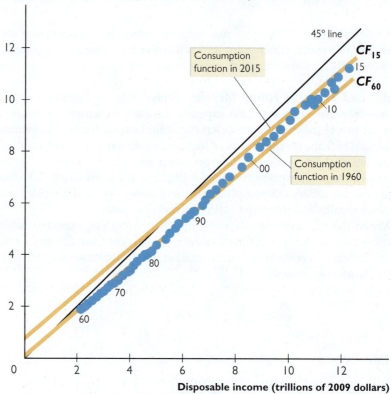

SOURCE OF DATA: Bureau of Economic Analysis.

## ■ Imports and Real GDP

Imports are the other major component of induced expenditure. Many factors influence U.S. imports, but in the short run, one factor dominates: U.S. real GDP. Other things remaining the same, an increase in U.S. real GDP brings an increase in U.S. imports. Because an increase in real GDP is also an increase in income, as incomes increase, people increase their expenditures on most goods and services. Many goods and services are imported, so as incomes increase imports increase.

The relationship between imports and real GDP is described by the **marginal propensity to import**, which is the fraction of an increase in real GDP that is spent on imports.

**Marginal propensity to import**

The fraction of an increase in real GDP that is spent on imports—the change in imports divided by the change in real GDP.

$$\text{Marginal propensity to import} = \frac{\text{Change in imports}}{\text{Change in real GDP}}.$$

For example, if a $1 trillion increase in real GDP increases imports by $0.2 trillion, then the marginal propensity to import is $0.2 trillion ÷ $1 trillion, which is 0.2.

# CHECKPOINT 14.1

MyEconLab Study Plan 14.1
Key Terms Quiz
Solutions Video

**Explain how real GDP influences expenditure plans.**

## Practice Problems

1. Suppose that the marginal propensity to consume is 0.8. If disposable income increases by $0.5 trillion, by how much will consumption expenditure change?

2. Explain how each of the following events influences the U.S. consumption function:
   • The marginal propensity to consume decreases.
   • U.S. autonomous consumption decreases.
   • Americans expect an increase in future income.

3. Figure 1 shows the consumption function. What is the marginal propensity to consume, and what is autonomous consumption?

## In the News

**Spending rises by more than personal income**
Personal disposable income increased $68.6 billion in April and $33.9 billion in May. Personal consumption expenditures increased $141.2 in April and $53.5 billion in May.

Source: Bureau of Economic Analysis News Release, June 29, 2016

How can consumers increase spending by more than the increase in personal income?

## Solutions to Practice Problems

1. Consumption expenditure will increase by $0.4 trillion, which is 0.8 multiplied by the change in disposable income of $0.5 trillion.

2. The marginal propensity to consume equals the slope of the consumption function. So when the marginal propensity to consume decreases, the consumption function becomes flatter.
   Autonomous consumption is the $y$-axis intercept of the consumption function. So when autonomous expenditure decreases, the consumption function shifts downward.
   When expected future income increases, current consumption expenditure increases and the consumption function shifts upward.

3. When disposable income increases by $100 billion, consumption expenditure increases by $80 billion. The *MPC* is $80 billion ÷ $100 billion = 0.8.
   Autonomous consumption (consumption expenditure that is independent of disposable income) equals the $y$-axis intercept and is $80 billion (Figure 2).

## Solution to In the News

Other things remaining the same, a rise in personal income brings a smaller rise in consumption expenditure in a movement along the consumption function. When consumption expenditure rises by more than the rise in personal income, the consumption function has shifted upward. Autonomous consumption expenditure increased as households spent part of their past savings or increased their debt and spent part of their expected future income.

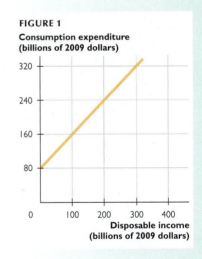

**FIGURE 1**
Consumption expenditure
(billions of 2009 dollars)

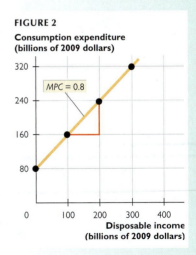

**FIGURE 2**
Consumption expenditure
(billions of 2009 dollars)

MyEconLab Concept Video

## 14.2 EQUILIBRIUM EXPENDITURE

You are now going to discover how, with a fixed price level, aggregate expenditure plans interact to determine real GDP. We will study the relationship between aggregate planned expenditure and real GDP; and we'll study the forces that make aggregate planned expenditure and actual expenditure equal.

But first we'll return to the distinction between *induced* expenditure and *autonomous* expenditure.

### ■ Induced Expenditure and Autonomous Expenditure

Aggregate planned expenditure is the sum of *induced* expenditure and *autonomous* expenditure. *Induced* expenditure equals consumption expenditure minus imports. You've seen that consumption expenditure increases when disposable income increases. But disposable income equals aggregate income—real GDP—minus net taxes. So disposable income and consumption expenditure increase when real GDP increases. You've also seen that imports increase when real GDP increases. An increase in real GDP brings a larger increase in consumption expenditure than in imports, so induced expenditure—consumption expenditure minus imports—increases as real GDP increases.

*Autonomous* expenditure—expenditure that does not respond directly to changes in real GDP—consists of investment, government expenditure on goods and services, exports, and autonomous consumption expenditure. These items of aggregate expenditure do change but in response to influences other than real GDP. For example, investment responds to the real interest rate and expected profit. Government expenditure on goods and services depends on the government's policy priorities. And exports depend on global demand for U.S.-produced goods and services.

We combine induced expenditure plans and autonomous expenditure to determine aggregate planned expenditure and equilibrium real GDP.

### ■ Aggregate Planned Expenditure and Real GDP

An aggregate expenditure schedule and an aggregate expenditure curve describe the relationship between aggregate planned expenditure and real GDP. The table in Figure 14.4 sets out an aggregate expenditure schedule. The columns are the components of aggregate expenditure, $C$, $I$, $G$, $X$, and $M$, and aggregate planned expenditure, $AE$, equals $C + I + G + X - M$.

Figure 14.4 plots an aggregate expenditure curve. The aggregate expenditure curve is the red line $AE$. Points $A$ through $F$ on that curve correspond to the rows of the table. The $AE$ curve is a graph of aggregate planned expenditure (the last column) plotted against real GDP (the first column).

The horizontal lines in Figure 14.4 show the components of autonomous expenditure $I$, $G$, and $X$. The line labeled $C + I + G + X$ adds consumption expenditure to these components of autonomous expenditure. Aggregate expenditure is expenditure on U.S.-produced goods and services, but the line $C + I + G + X$ includes expenditure on imports. So the $AE$ curve is the $C + I + G + X$ line minus imports. For example, if a student buys a Honda motorbike made in Japan, the student's expenditure is part of $C$, but it is not an expenditure on a U.S.-produced good. To find the expenditure on U.S.-produced goods, we subtract the value of the imported motorbike.

### FIGURE 14.4

## Aggregate Expenditure

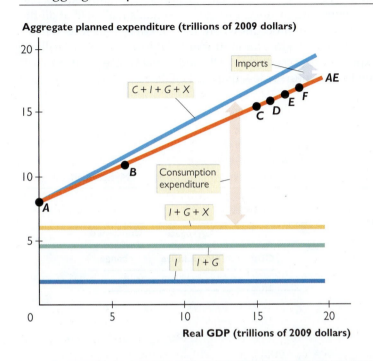

**Aggregate planned expenditure (trillions of 2009 dollars)**

The aggregate expenditure schedule shows the relationship between aggregate planned expenditure and real GDP. For example, in row B of the table, when real GDP is $6 trillion, aggregate planned expenditure is $11.0 trillion ($5.60 + $1.75 + $2.75 + $1.50 − $0.60). As real GDP increases, aggregate planned expenditure increases.

This relationship is graphed as the aggregate expenditure curve AE. The components of aggregate expenditure that increase with real GDP are consumption expenditure and imports.

The other components—investment, government expenditure, and exports—do not vary with real GDP.

| | Real GDP (Y) | Consumption expenditure (C) | Investment (I) | Government expenditure (G) | Exports (X) | Imports (M) | Aggregate planned expenditure (AE = C + I + G + X − M) |
|---|---|---|---|---|---|---|---|
| | | | | (trillions of 2009 dollars) | | | |
| **A** | 0 | 2.00 | 1.75 | 2.75 | 1.50 | 0 | 8.00 |
| **B** | **6.00** | **5.60** | **1.75** | **2.75** | **1.50** | **0.60** | **11.00** |
| **C** | 15.00 | 11.00 | 1.75 | 2.75 | 1.50 | 1.50 | 15.50 |
| **D** | 16.00 | 11.60 | 1.75 | 2.75 | 1.50 | 1.60 | 16.00 |
| **E** | 17.00 | 12.20 | 1.75 | 2.75 | 1.50 | 1.70 | 16.50 |
| **F** | 18.00 | 12.80 | 1.75 | 2.75 | 1.50 | 1.80 | 17.00 |

Figure 14.4 shows that aggregate planned expenditure increases as real GDP increases. But notice that for each $1 increase in real GDP, aggregate planned expenditure increases by less than $1. For example, when real GDP increases by $1 trillion, from $15 trillion in row C to $16 trillion in row D of the table, aggregate planned expenditure increases by $0.5 trillion, from $15.5 trillion to $16.0 trillion. This feature of the AE curve is important and plays a big role in determining equilibrium expenditure and the effect of a change in autonomous expenditure.

The AE curve summarizes the relationship between aggregate planned expenditure and real GDP. But what determines the point on the AE curve at which the economy operates? What determines actual aggregate expenditure?

## ■ Equilibrium Expenditure

**Equilibrium expenditure**
The level of aggregate expenditure that occurs when aggregate *planned* expenditure equals real GDP.

**Equilibrium expenditure** occurs when aggregate *planned* expenditure equals real GDP. In Figure 14.5(a) aggregate planned expenditure equals real GDP at all the points on the 45° line. Equilibrium occurs where the *AE* curve intersects the 45° line at point *D* with real GDP at $16 trillion. If real GDP is less than $16 trillion, aggregate planned expenditure exceeds real GDP; and if real GDP exceeds $16 trillion, aggregate planned expenditure is less than real GDP.

■ **FIGURE 14.5**

### Equilibrium Expenditure

MyEconLab Animation

**Aggregate planned expenditure (trillions of 2009 dollars)**

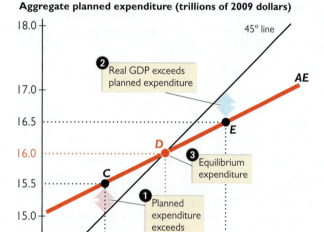

(a) Equilibrium expenditure

**Unplanned inventory change (trillions of 2009 dollars)**

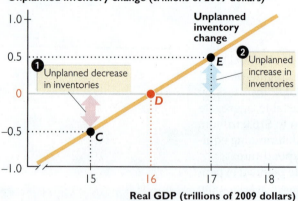

(b) Unplanned inventory change

|  | Real GDP | Aggregate planned expenditure | Unplanned inventory change |
|---|---|---|---|
|  |  | (trillions of 2009 dollars) |  |
| *C* | 15.0 | 15.5 | −0.5 |
| *D* | **16.0** | **16.0** | **0.0** |
| *E* | 17.0 | 16.5 | 0.5 |

The table shows expenditure plans and unplanned changes in inventories at different levels of real GDP. Part (a) of the figure illustrates equilibrium expenditure, and part (b) shows the unplanned inventory changes that bring changes in real GDP.

❶ When aggregate planned expenditure exceeds real GDP, an unplanned decrease in inventories occurs. Firms increase production, and real GDP increases.

❷ When real GDP exceeds aggregate planned expenditure, an unplanned increase in inventories occurs. Firms decrease production, and real GDP decreases.

❸ When aggregate planned expenditure equals real GDP, there are no unplanned inventory changes and real GDP remains at its equilibrium level.

# ■ Convergence to Equilibrium

At equilibrium expenditure, production plans and spending plans agree, and there is no reason for production or spending to change. But when aggregate planned expenditure and actual aggregate expenditure are unequal, production plans and spending plans are misaligned, and a process of convergence toward equilibrium expenditure occurs. Throughout this convergence process, real GDP adjusts.

What are the forces that move aggregate expenditure toward equilibrium? To answer this question, we look at a situation in which aggregate expenditure is away from equilibrium.

## Convergence from Below Equilibrium

Suppose that in Figure 14.5, real GDP is $15 trillion. At this level of real GDP, actual aggregate expenditure is also $15 trillion, but aggregate planned expenditure is $15.5 trillion—point C in Figure 14.5(a). Aggregate planned expenditure exceeds actual expenditure. When people spend $15.5 trillion and firms produce goods and services worth $15 trillion, firms' inventories decrease by $0.5 trillion—point C in Figure 14.5(b). This change in inventories is *unplanned*. Because the change in inventories is part of investment, the decrease in inventories decreases actual investment. So actual investment is $0.5 trillion less than planned investment.

Real GDP doesn't remain at $15 trillion for long. Firms have inventory targets based on their sales, and when inventories fall below target, firms increase production. Firms keep increasing production as long as unplanned decreases in inventories occur.

Eventually firms will have increased production by $1 trillion, so real GDP will have increased to $16 trillion. At this real GDP, aggregate planned expenditure rises to $16 trillion—point D in Figure 14.5(a). With aggregate planned expenditure equal to actual expenditure, the unplanned change in inventories is zero and firms hold production constant. The economy has converged on equilibrium expenditure.

## Convergence from Above Equilibrium

Now suppose that in Figure 14.5, real GDP is $17 trillion. Actual aggregate expenditure is also $17 trillion, but aggregate planned expenditure is $16.5 trillion—point E in Figure 14.5(a). Actual expenditure exceeds planned expenditure and firms' inventories pile up by an unwanted $0.5 trillion—point E in Figure 14.5(b).

Real GDP doesn't remain at $17 trillion. Firms now want to lower their inventories, so they decrease production.

Eventually firms will have decreased production by $1 trillion, so real GDP will have decreased to $16 trillion. At this real GDP, aggregate planned expenditure falls to $16 trillion—point D in Figure 14.5(a). With aggregate planned expenditure equal to actual expenditure, the unplanned change in inventories is zero and firms hold production constant. The economy has converged on equilibrium expenditure.

Starting from below equilibrium, unplanned decreases in inventories induce firms to increase production; starting from above equilibrium, unplanned increases in inventories induce firms to decrease production. In both cases, production is pulled toward the equilibrium level at which there are no unplanned inventory changes.

# EYE on the PAST
## Say's Law and Keynes' Principle of Effective Demand

During the Industrial Revolution, which began around 1760 and lasted for 70 years, technological change was rapid. People have talked about the "new economy" of the 1990s, but the 1990s was just another phase of a process that began in the truly new economy of the late 1700s. The pace of change in economic life during those years was unprecedented. Never before had old jobs been destroyed and new jobs created on such a scale. In this environment of rapid economic change, people began to wonder whether the economy could create enough jobs and a high enough level of demand to ensure that people would buy all the things that the new industrial economy could produce.

A French economist, Jean-Baptiste Say, provided the assurance that people were looking for. Born in 1767 (he was 9 years old when Adam Smith's *Wealth of Nations* was published—see Chapter 1, p. 18), Say suffered the wrath of Napoleon for his conservative call for smaller and leaner government and was the most famous economist of his era. His book *A Treatise on Political Economy (Traité d'économie politique),* published in 1803, became the best-selling university economics textbook in both Europe and America.

In this book, Say reasoned that *supply creates its own demand*—an idea that came to be called *Say's Law*.

You've seen Say's Law at work in the full-employment economy. The real wage rate adjusts to ensure that the quantity of labor demanded equals the quantity of labor supplied and real

GDP equals potential GDP. The real interest rate adjusts to ensure that the quantity of investment that firms plan equals the quantity of saving. Because saving equals income minus consumption expenditure, the equilibrium real interest rate ensures that consumption expenditure plus investment exactly equals potential GDP.

Say's Law came under attack at various times during the nineteenth century. But it came under an onslaught during the Great Depression of the 1930s. With a quarter of the labor force unemployed and real GDP at around three quarters of potential GDP, it seemed like a stretch to argue that supply creates its own demand. But there was no simple principle or slogan with which to replace Say's Law.

In the midst of the Great Depression, in 1936, a British economist, John Maynard Keynes, provided the catch phrase that the world was looking for: *effective demand.*

Born in England in 1883, Keynes was one of the outstanding people of the twentieth century. He was a prolific writer on economic issues, represented Britain at the Versailles peace conference at the end of World War I, and played a prominent role in creating the International Monetary Fund, which monitors the global macroeconomy today.

Keynes revolutionized macroeconomic thinking by turning Say's Law on its head. In Keynes' view, supply does *not* create its own demand, and *effective demand* determines real GDP. If businesses spend less on new capital than the amount that people save,

equilibrium expenditure will be less than potential GDP. Prices and wages are sticky, and resources can become unemployed and remain unemployed indefinitely.

The aggregate expenditure model in this chapter is the modern distillation of Keynes' idea.

*Jean-Baptiste Say*

*John Maynard Keynes*

# CHECKPOINT 14.2

MyEconLab Study Plan 14.2
Key Terms Quiz
Solutions Video

**Explain how real GDP adjusts to achieve equilibrium expenditure.**

## Practice Problems

Table 1 gives real GDP ($Y$) and its components in billions of dollars.

1. Calculate aggregate planned expenditure when real GDP is $200 billion and when real GDP is $600 billion.

2. Calculate equilibrium expenditure.

3. If real GDP is $200 billion, explain the process that moves the economy toward equilibrium expenditure.

4. If real GDP is $600 billion, explain the process that moves the economy toward equilibrium expenditure.

**TABLE 1**

| | A | B | C | D | E | F | G |
|---|---|---|---|---|---|---|---|
| 1 | | Y | C | I | G | X | M |
| 2 | A | 100 | 110 | 50 | 60 | 60 | 15 |
| 3 | B | 200 | 170 | 50 | 60 | 60 | 30 |
| 4 | C | 300 | 230 | 50 | 60 | 60 | 45 |
| 5 | D | 400 | 290 | 50 | 60 | 60 | 60 |
| 6 | E | 500 | 350 | 50 | 60 | 60 | 75 |
| 7 | F | 600 | 410 | 50 | 60 | 60 | 90 |

## In the News

**Retailers scale back after inventory buildups**

Big retailers are lowering inventories built up earlier this year. Economists say the buildup of inventories increased economic growth and a pullback by retailers and manufacturers may slow economic growth for the rest of the year.

Source: *The Wall Street Journal*, September 25, 2015

Explain why a fall in inventories might slow economic growth and a buildup of inventories might boost economic growth.

## Solutions to Practice Problems

1. Aggregate planned expenditure equals $C + I + G + X - M$. When real GDP is $200 billion (row $B$ of Table 1), aggregate planned expenditure is $310 billion. When real GDP is $600 billion (row $F$), aggregate planned expenditure is $490 billion.

2. Equilibrium expenditure occurs when aggregate planned expenditure equals real GDP. Equilibrium expenditure is $400 billion (row $D$ of Table 1).

3. If real GDP is $200 billion, aggregate planned expenditure is $310 billion, which exceeds real GDP. Firms' inventories decrease by $110 billion. Firms' expenditure plans are not fulfilled, so they increase production to restore their inventories. Real GDP increases. As long as aggregate planned expenditure exceeds real GDP, firms increase production and real GDP increases.

4. If real GDP is $600 billion, aggregate planned expenditure is $490 billion, which is less than real GDP. Firms' inventories increase by $110 billion. Firms cut production and try to reduce their inventories. Real GDP decreases. As long as aggregate planned expenditure is less than real GDP, firms' inventories will increase. Firms will cut production as they try to reduce their inventories to their target level. Real GDP decreases.

## Solution to In the News

When firms reduce their target level of inventories, planned investment falls and equilibrium expenditure and real GDP decrease. Economic growth will slow. When firms plan to build up their inventories, the reverse occurs. Equilibrium expenditure and real GDP increase and economic growth might pick up.

**Multiplier**
The amount by which a change in any component of autonomous expenditure is magnified or multiplied to determine the change in equilibrium expenditure and real GDP that it generates.

## 14.3 EXPENDITURE MULTIPLIERS

When autonomous expenditure (investment, government expenditure, or exports) increases, aggregate expenditure and real GDP also increase. A **multiplier** determines the amount by which a change in any component of autonomous expenditure is magnified or multiplied to determine the change in equilibrium expenditure and real GDP that it generates.

### ■ The Basic Idea of the Multiplier

An increase in investment increases real GDP, which increases disposable income and consumption expenditure. The increase in consumption expenditure adds to the increase in investment and a multiplier determines the magnitude of the resulting increase in aggregate expenditure.

Figure 14.6 illustrates the multiplier. The initial aggregate expenditure schedule graphs as $AE_0$. Equilibrium expenditure and real GDP are $16 trillion. You can see this equilibrium in row $B$ of the table and where the curve $AE_0$ intersects the 45° line at point $B$ in the figure.

Suppose that investment increases by $0.5 trillion. This increase in investment increases aggregate planned expenditure by $0.5 trillion at each level of real GDP. The new $AE$ curve is $AE_1$. The new equilibrium expenditure (row $D'$) occurs where $AE_1$ intersects the 45° line and is $18 trillion (point $D'$). At this real GDP, aggregate planned expenditure equals real GDP. The increase in equilibrium expenditure ($2 trillion) is *larger* than the increase in investment ($0.5 trillion).

### ■ FIGURE 14.6

The Multiplier

| Real GDP (Y) | Aggregate planned expenditure | | | | |
|---|---|---|---|---|---|
| | Original (AE₀) | | New (AE₁) | | |
| (trillions of 2009 dollars) | | | | | |
| 15.00 | A | 15.25 | A' | 15.75 | |
| 16.00 | B | 16.00 | B' | 16.50 | |
| 17.00 | C | 16.75 | C' | 17.25 | |
| 18.00 | D | 17.50 | D' | 18.00 | |
| 19.00 | E | 18.25 | E' | 18.75 | |

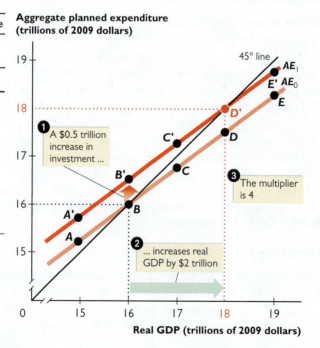

❶ A $0.5 trillion increase in investment shifts the AE curve upward by $0.5 trillion from AE₀ to AE₁.

❷ Equilibrium expenditure increases by $2 trillion, from $16 trillion to $18 trillion.

❸ The increase in equilibrium expenditure is 4 times the increase in autonomous expenditure, so the multiplier is 4.

## ■ The Size of the Multiplier

The multiplier is the amount by which a change in autonomous expenditure is multiplied to determine the change in equilibrium expenditure that it generates. To calculate the multiplier, we divide the change in equilibrium expenditure by the change in autonomous expenditure that generated it. That is,

$$\text{Multiplier} = \frac{\text{Change in equilibrium expenditure}}{\text{Change in autonomous expenditure}}.$$

The change in equilibrium expenditure also equals the change in real GDP, which we'll call $\Delta Y$. In Figure 14.6, the change in autonomous expenditure is a change in investment, which we'll call $\Delta I$. The multiplier is

$$\text{Multiplier} = \frac{\Delta Y}{\Delta I}.$$

In Figure 14.6, equilibrium expenditure increases by \$2 trillion ($\Delta Y = \$2$ trillion) and investment increases by \$0.5 trillion ($\Delta I = \$0.5$ trillion), so

$$\text{Multiplier} = \frac{\Delta Y}{\Delta I} = \frac{\$2 \text{ trillion}}{\$0.5 \text{ trillion}} = 4.$$

The multiplier is 4—real GDP changes by 4 times the change in investment.

Why is the multiplier greater than 1? It is because an increase in autonomous expenditure induces further increases in aggregate expenditure—induced expenditure increases. If the State of California spends \$10 million on a new highway, aggregate expenditure and real GDP immediately increase by \$10 million. Highway construction workers now have more income, and they spend part of it on cars, vacations, and other goods and services. Real GDP now increases by the initial \$10 million plus the extra consumption expenditure. The producers of cars, vacations, and other goods now have increased incomes, and they in turn spend part of the increase on consumption goods and services. Additional income induces additional expenditure, which creates additional income.

## ■ The Multiplier and the *MPC*

Ignoring imports and income taxes, the magnitude of the multiplier depends only on the marginal propensity to consume. To see why, let's do a calculation. The change in real GDP ($\Delta Y$) equals the change in consumption expenditure ($\Delta C$) plus the change in investment. ($\Delta I$) That is,

$$\Delta Y = \Delta C + \Delta I.$$

But with no income taxes, the change in consumption expenditure is determined by the change in real GDP and the marginal propensity to consume. It is

$$\Delta C = MPC \times \Delta Y.$$

Now substitute $MPC \times \Delta Y$ for $\Delta C$ in the previous equation:

$$\Delta Y = MPC \times \Delta Y + \Delta I.$$

Now solve for $\Delta Y$ as

$$(1 - MPC) \times \Delta Y = \Delta I,$$

and rearrange the equation:

$$\Delta Y = \frac{1}{(1 - MPC)} \Delta I.$$

Finally, divide both sides of the equation by $\Delta I$ to give

$$\text{Multiplier} = \frac{\Delta Y}{\Delta I} = \frac{1}{(1 - MPC)}.$$

In Figure 14.6, the $MPC$ is 0.75. So if we use this value of $MPC$,

$$\text{Multiplier} = \frac{\Delta Y}{\Delta I} = \frac{1}{(1 - 0.75)} = \frac{1}{0.25} = 4.$$

The greater the marginal propensity to consume, the larger is the multiplier. For example, with a marginal propensity to consume of 0.9, the multiplier would be 10. Let's now look at the influence of imports and income taxes.

## ■ The Multiplier, Imports, and Income Taxes

The size of the multiplier depends on imports and income taxes, both of which make the multiplier smaller.

When an increase in investment increases real GDP and consumption expenditure, part of the increase in expenditure is on imports, not U.S.-produced goods and services. Only expenditure on U.S.-produced goods and services increases U.S. real GDP. The larger the marginal propensity to import, the smaller is the multiplier.

When an increase in investment increases real GDP, income tax payments increase, so disposable income increases by less than the increase in real GDP and consumption expenditure increases by less than it would if income tax payments had not changed. The marginal tax rate determines the extent to which income tax payments change when real GDP changes. The **marginal tax rate** is the fraction of a change in real GDP that is paid in income taxes. The larger the marginal tax rate, the smaller are the changes in disposable income and real GDP that result from a given change in autonomous expenditure.

The marginal propensity to import and the marginal tax rate together with the marginal propensity to consume determine the multiplier, and their combined influence determines the slope of the $AE$ curve. The general formula for the multiplier is

$$\text{Multiplier} = \frac{\Delta Y}{\Delta I} = \frac{1}{(1 - \text{Slope of } AE \text{ curve})}.$$

Figure 14.7 compares two situations. In Figure 14.7(a), there are no imports and no income taxes. The slope of the $AE$ curve equals $MPC$, which is 0.75, so the multiplier is 4 (as we calculated above). In Figure 14.7(b), imports and income taxes decrease the slope of the $AE$ curve to 0.5. In this case,

$$\text{Multiplier} = \frac{\Delta Y}{\Delta I} = \frac{1}{(1 - 0.5)} = 2.$$

Over time, the value of the multiplier changes as the marginal tax rate, the marginal propensity to consume, and the marginal propensity to import change. These ongoing changes make the multiplier hard to predict.

**Marginal tax rate**
The fraction of a change in real GDP that is paid in income taxes—the change in tax payments divided by the change in real GDP.

■ **FIGURE 14.7**

The Multiplier and the Slope of the *AE* Curve                    MyEconLab Animation

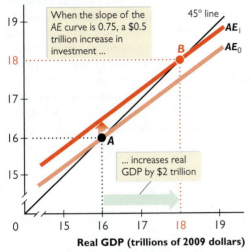

(a) Multiplier is 4

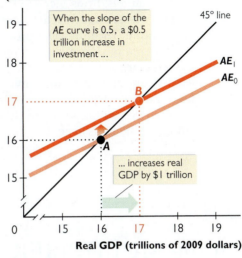

(b) Multiplier is 2

In part (a), with no imports and no income taxes, the slope of the *AE* curve equals the marginal propensity to consume, which in this example is 0.75. The multiplier is 4.

In part (b), with imports and income taxes, the slope of the *AE* curve is less than the marginal propensity to consume. In this example, the slope of the *AE* curve is 0.5 and the multiplier is 2.

# EYE on YOUR LIFE
## Looking for Multipliers

MyEconLab Critical Thinking Exercise

You can see multipliers in your daily life if you look in the right places and in the right way.

Look for an event in your home city or state that brings new economic activity. It might be a major construction project that is going on near your home or school. It might be a major sporting event that occurs infrequently and brings a large number of people to a city. Or it might be a major new business that moves into an area or expands its activity level.

What supplies do you see being delivered to the site, event, or new business? How many people do you estimate have jobs at this new activity? Where do the supplies and the workers come from?

This new economic activity sets off a multiplier process. What are the first round multiplier effects? Whose incomes are higher because of the purchase of these supplies and the expenditure of the workers hired by the project?

Where do the workers buy their coffee and lunch? Do their purchases create new jobs for students and others in local coffee shops and fast-food outlets?

Where do the workers and suppliers spend the rest of their incomes?

Now think about the second round and subsequent round effects. Where do the students hired by coffee shops spend their incomes and what additional jobs do those expenditures create?

The process goes on and on.

### ■ Business-Cycle Turning Points

When an expansion is triggered by an increase in autonomous expenditure, as the economy turns the corner into expansion, aggregate planned expenditure exceeds real GDP. Firms see their inventories taking an unplanned dive. To meet their inventory targets, firms increase production, and real GDP begins to increase. This initial increase in real GDP brings higher incomes, which stimulate consumption expenditure. The multiplier process kicks in, and the expansion picks up speed.

When a recession is triggered by a decrease in autonomous expenditure, as the economy turns the corner into recession, real GDP exceeds aggregate planned expenditure and unplanned inventories pile up. To cut inventories, firms produce less, and real GDP falls. This initial fall in real GDP brings lower incomes. People cut their consumption expenditure. The multiplier process reinforces the initial cut in autonomous expenditure, and the recession takes hold.

## EYE on the MULTIPLIER                    MyEconLab Critical Thinking Exercise

### How Big Is the Government Expenditure Multiplier?

Christina Romer, former Chair of the President's Council of Economic Advisers, has estimated the government expenditure multiplier to be 1.6. This number led administration economists to predict that the stimulus plan that increased government expenditure would prevent the unemployment rate from rising much above 8 percent. This prediction turned out to be optimistic and one reason might be that the multiplier assumption is also too optimistic.

Robert Barro, a leading macroeconomist at Harvard University, has studied the effects of very large increases in government expenditure during wars. He finds that the multiplier is only 0.8, which means that real GDP increases by *less than* the increase in government expenditure. The reason is that some private expenditure, mainly investment, gets "crowded out" and real GDP falls.

John Taylor of Stanford University, another leading macroeconomist, agrees with Barro that the government expenditure multiplier is less than 1. He says that crowding out gets more severe as time passes, so the multiplier gets smaller after two years and smaller still after three years.

A big multiplier can occur only if there is substantial slack in the economy—when the recessionary gap is large.

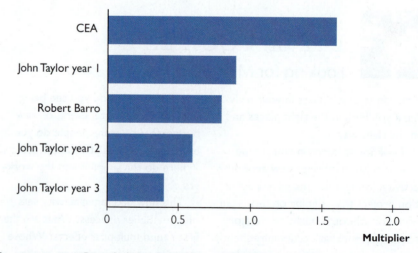

SOURCES OF DATA: Council of Economic Advisers (CEA), Christina Romer and Jared Bernstein, "The Job Impact of the American Recovery and Reinvestment Plan," January 2009; Robert J. Barro, "Government Spending Is No Free Lunch," *The Wall Street Journal*, January 22, 2009; John F. Cogan, Tobias Cwik, John B. Taylor, Volker Wieland, "New Keynesian versus Old Keynesian Government Spending Multipliers," February 2009.

# CHECKPOINT 14.3

MyEconLab Study Plan 14.3
Key Terms Quiz
Solutions Video

### Explain the expenditure multiplier.

## Practice Problems

An economy has no imports and no income taxes, *MPC* is 0.80, and real GDP is $150 billion. Businesses increase investment by $5 billion. Use this information to answer Problems **1** and **2**.

1. Calculate the multiplier and the change in real GDP.

2. Calculate the new level of real GDP and explain why real GDP increases by more than $5 billion.

3. In an economy with no imports and no income taxes, an increase in autonomous expenditure of $2 trillion increases equilibrium expenditure by $8 trillion. Calculate the multiplier and the marginal propensity to consume. What happens to the multiplier if an income tax is introduced?

## In the News

**Infrastructure spending as a catalyst of growth**
Government infrastructure spending has a large multiplier. Expenditure on construction projects goes directly back into the economy through wages. And improved infrastructure boosts productivity and economic growth.
   Source: European Bank for Reconstruction and Development, August 5, 2015

Explain what determines the size of the multiplier effect of infrastructure spending.

## Solutions to Practice Problems

1. The multiplier equals $1/(1 - MPC)$. *MPC* is 0.8, so the multiplier is 5. Real GDP increases by $25 billion. The increase in investment increases real GDP by the multiplier (5) times the change in investment ($5 billion).

2. Real GDP increases from $150 billion to $175 billion. Real GDP increases by more than $5 billion because the increase in investment induces an increase in consumption expenditure.

3. The multiplier is the increase in equilibrium expenditure ($8 trillion) divided by the increase in autonomous expenditure ($2 trillion). The multiplier is 4.

   The marginal propensity to consume is 0.75.
   The multiplier is $1/(1 - MPC)$. So $4 = 1/(1 - MPC)$, and *MPC* is 0.75.

   If the government introduces an income tax, the slope of the *AE* curve becomes smaller and the multiplier becomes smaller.

## Solution to In the News

Expenditure on infrastructure projects of $1 billion will increase real GDP by more than $1 billion—a multiplier effect—because when a new project begins, jobs are created and wage payments increase. Workers spend part of the higher incomes on consumption, which creates more jobs. These workers earn an income and spend part of it on consumption. The size of the expenditure multiplier depends on the slope of the *AE* curve, which in turn depends on the *MPC*, the marginal propensity to import, and the marginal tax rate.

## 14.4   THE *AD* CURVE AND EQUILIBRIUM EXPENDITURE

In this chapter, we've studied the aggregate expenditure model, in which firms change production when sales and inventories change but they don't change their prices. The aggregate expenditure model determines equilibrium expenditure and real GDP at a given price level. In Chapter 13, we studied the simultaneous determination of real GDP and the price level using the *AS-AD* model. The aggregate demand curve and equilibrium expenditure are related, and this section shows you how.

### ■ Deriving the *AD* Curve from Equilibrium Expenditure

The *AE* curve is the relationship between aggregate planned expenditure and real GDP when all other influences on expenditure plans remain the same. A movement along the *AE* curve arises from a change in real GDP.

The *AD* curve is the relationship between the quantity of real GDP demanded and the price level when all other influences on expenditure plans remain the same. A movement along the *AD* curve arises from a change in the price level.

Equilibrium expenditure depends on the price level. When the price level rises, other things remaining the same, aggregate planned expenditure decreases and equilibrium expenditure decreases. And when the price level falls, other things remaining the same, aggregate planned expenditure increases and equilibrium expenditure increases. The reason is that a change in the price level changes the buying power of money, the real interest rate, and the real prices of exports and imports (see Chapter 13, pp. 334–336).

When the price level rises, each of these effects decreases aggregate planned expenditure at each level of real GDP, so the *AE* curve shifts downward. A fall in the price level has the opposite effect. When the price level falls, the *AE* curve shifts upward.

Figure 14.8(a) shows the effects of a change in the price level on the *AE* curve and equilibrium expenditure. When the price level is 105, the *AE* curve is $AE_0$, and it intersects the 45° line at point *B*. Equilibrium expenditure is $16 trillion. If the price level rises to 125, aggregate planned expenditure decreases and the *AE* curve shifts downward to $AE_1$. Equilibrium expenditure decreases to $15 trillion at point *A*. If the price level falls to 85, aggregate planned expenditure increases and the *AE* curve shifts upward to $AE_2$. Equilibrium expenditure increases to $17 trillion at point *C*.

The changes in the price level that shift the *AE* curve and change equilibrium expenditure bring movements along the *AD* curve. Figure 14.8(b) shows these movements. At a price level of 105, the quantity of real GDP demanded is $16 trillion—point *B* on the *AD* curve. If the price level rises to 125, the quantity of real GDP demanded decreases along the *AD* curve to $15 trillion at point *A*. If the price level falls to 85, the quantity of real GDP demanded increases along the *AD* curve to $17 trillion at point *C*.

The two parts of Figure 14.8 are connected and illustrate the relationship between the *AE* curve and the *AD* curve. Each point of equilibrium expenditure corresponds to a point on the *AD* curve. The equilibrium expenditure points *A*, *B*, and *C* (part a) correspond to the points *A*, *B*, and *C* on the *AD* curve (part b).

◼ **FIGURE 14.8**

## Equilibrium Expenditure and Aggregate Demand

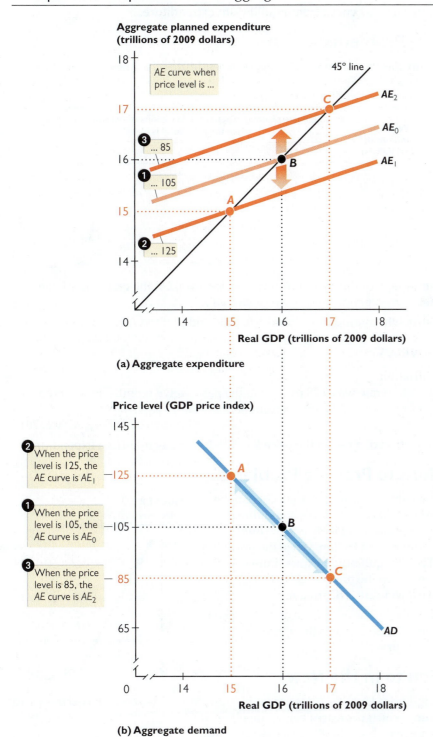

**(a) Aggregate expenditure**

**(b) Aggregate demand**

A change in the price level shifts the *AE* curve and results in a movement along the *AD* curve.

**❶** When the price level is 105, equilibrium expenditure is $16 trillion at point *B* on the *AE* curve $AE_0$ and the quantity of real GDP demanded is $16 trillion at point *B* on the *AD* curve.

**❷** When the price level rises to 125, the *AE* curve shifts downward to $AE_1$ and equilibrium expenditure decreases to $15 trillion at point *A*. The quantity of real GDP demanded decreases along the *AD* curve to point *A*.

**❸** When the price level falls to 85, the *AE* curve shifts upward to $AE_2$ and equilibrium expenditure increases to $17 trillion at point *C*. The quantity of real GDP demanded increases along the *AD* curve to point *C*.

Points *A*, *B*, and *C* on the *AD* curve in part (b) correspond to the equilibrium expenditure points *A*, *B*, and *C* in part (a).

MyEconLab Study Plan 14.4

Solutions Video

# CHECKPOINT 14.4

**Derive the *AD* curve from equilibrium expenditure.**

## Practice Problems

An economy has the following aggregate expenditure schedules:

**TABLE 1**

| Real GDP (trillions of 2009 dollars) | Aggregate planned expenditure in trillions of 2009 dollars when the price level is | | |
|---|---|---|---|
| | 115 | 105 | 95 |
| 0 | 1.0 | 1.5 | 2.0 |
| 1.0 | 1.5 | 2.0 | 2.5 |
| 2.0 | 2.0 | 2.5 | 3.0 |
| 3.0 | 2.5 | 3.0 | 3.5 |
| 4.0 | 3.0 | 3.5 | 4.0 |
| 5.0 | 3.5 | 4.0 | 4.5 |
| 6.0 | 4.0 | 4.5 | 5.0 |

1. Make a graph of the *AE* curve at each price level. On the graph, mark the equilibrium expenditure at each price level.
2. Construct the aggregate demand schedule and plot the *AD* curve.

## In the News

**Brazil's inflation**
Brazil's inflation rate was 9.28 percent in the past twelve months. Food and beverage prices rose more than one percent per month.

Source: Bloomberg, May 6, 2016

Explain the effect of a rise in the price level on Brazil's equilibrium expenditure.

**FIGURE 1**

Aggregate planned expenditure (trillions of 2009 dollars)

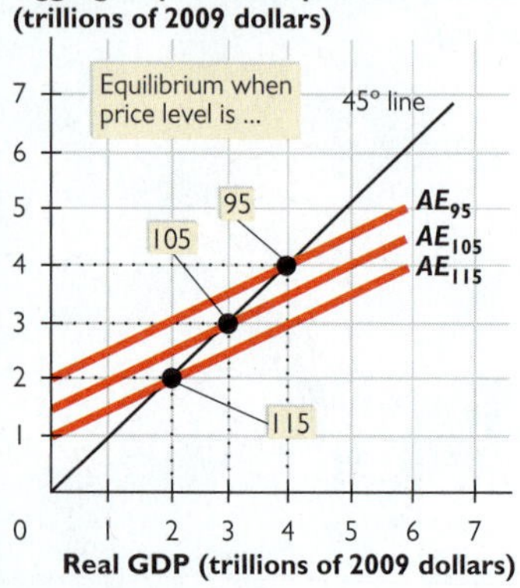

**TABLE 2**

| Price level | Real GDP demanded (trillions of 2009 dollars) |
|---|---|
| 95 | 4 |
| 105 | 3 |
| 115 | 2 |

## Solutions to Practice Problems

1. Figure 1 shows the three *AE* curves and the three levels of equilibrium expenditure. When the price level is 95, equilibrium expenditure is $4 trillion. When the price level is 105, equilibrium expenditure is $3 trillion. When the price level is 115, equilibrium expenditure is $2 trillion.
2. Table 2 shows the aggregate demand schedule, and Figure 2 shows the aggregate demand curve.

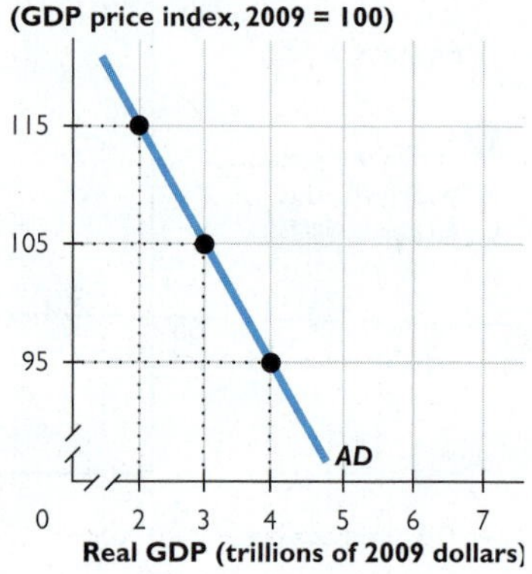

## Solution to In the News

A rise in the price level decreases consumption expenditure, which decreases aggregate planned expenditure and shifts the *AE* curve downward. Brazil's equilibrium expenditure decreases.

**FIGURE 2**

Price level (GDP price index, 2009 = 100)

**CHAPTER SUMMARY**

## Key Points

**1. Explain how real GDP influences expenditure plans.**

- Autonomous expenditure is the sum of the components of aggregate expenditure that real GDP does not influence directly.
- Induced expenditure is the sum of the components of aggregate expenditure that real GDP influences.
- Consumption expenditure varies with disposable income and real GDP and depends on the marginal propensity to consume.
- Imports vary with real GDP and depend on the marginal propensity to import.

**2. Explain how real GDP adjusts to achieve equilibrium expenditure.**

- Actual aggregate expenditure equals real GDP, but when aggregate planned expenditure differs from real GDP, firms have unplanned inventory changes.
- If aggregate planned expenditure exceeds real GDP, firms increase production and real GDP increases. If real GDP exceeds aggregate planned expenditure, firms decrease production and real GDP decreases.
- Real GDP changes until aggregate planned expenditure equals real GDP.

**3. Explain the expenditure multiplier.**

- When autonomous expenditure changes, equilibrium expenditure changes by a larger amount: There is a multiplier.
- The multiplier is greater than 1 because a change in autonomous expenditure changes induced expenditure.
- The larger the marginal propensity to consume, the larger is the multiplier.
- Income taxes and imports make the multiplier smaller.

**4. Derive the *AD* curve from equilibrium expenditure.**

- The *AD* curve is the relationship between the quantity of real GDP demanded and the price level when all other influences on expenditure plans remain the same.
- The quantity of real GDP demanded on the *AD* curve is the equilibrium real GDP when aggregate planned expenditure equals real GDP.

## Key Terms

MyEconLab Key Terms Quiz

Aggregate planned expenditure, 354
Consumption function, 354
Equilibrium expenditure, 362
Marginal propensity to consume, 356

Marginal propensity to import, 358
Marginal tax rate, 368
Multiplier, 366

# CHAPTER CHECKPOINT

## Study Plan Problems and Applications

Table 1 shows disposable income and saving in an economy. Use Table 1 to answer Problems **1** and **2**.

1. Calculate consumption expenditure at each level of disposable income. Over what range of disposable income is there dissaving? Estimate the level of disposable income at which saving is zero.

2. Calculate the marginal propensity to consume. If wealth increases by $10 trillion, in which direction will the consumption function change?

Use Table 2 to work Problems **3**, **4**, and **5**. Table 2 shows real GDP, $Y$, the components of planned expenditure, and aggregate planned expenditure (in millions of dollars) in an economy in which taxes are constant.

**TABLE 1**

| Disposable income | Saving |
|---|---|
| (trillions of dollars) | |
| 0 | −5 |
| 10 | −3 |
| 20 | −1 |
| 30 | 1 |
| 40 | 3 |
| 50 | 5 |

**TABLE 2**

| Y | Planned expenditure | | | | | |
|---|---|---|---|---|---|---|
| | C | I | G | X | M | AE |
| 0 | 2.0 | 1.75 | 1.0 | 1.25 | 0 | 6.0 |
| 2 | Q | 1.75 | 1.0 | 1.25 | 0.4 | 6.8 |
| 4 | 4.4 | R | 1.0 | 1.25 | 0.8 | 7.6 |
| 6 | 5.6 | 1.75 | S | 1.25 | 1.2 | 8.4 |
| 8 | 6.8 | 1.75 | 1.0 | T | 1.6 | 9.2 |
| 10 | 8.0 | 1.75 | 1.0 | 1.25 | U | 10.0 |
| 12 | 9.2 | 1.75 | 1.0 | 1.25 | 2.4 | V |

3. Find the value of Q, R, S, T, U, and V.

4. Calculate the marginal propensity to consume and the marginal propensity to import. What is equilibrium expenditure?

5. If investment crashes to $0.55 million but nothing else changes, what is equilibrium expenditure and what is the multiplier?

6. Figure 1 shows aggregate planned expenditure when the price level is 100. When the price level increases to 110, aggregate planned expenditure changes by $0.5 trillion. What is the quantity of real GDP demanded when the price level is 100 and 110?

Use this information to work Problems **7** and **8**.

**U.S. durable goods orders rebound strongly**

The Commerce Department reported that orders for durable goods increased 4.9 percent in January. Civilian aircraft orders surged 54.2 percent.

Source: Reuters, February 25, 2016

7. Explain the process by which an increase in durable goods orders at a constant price level changes equilibrium expenditure and real GDP.

8. What determines the increase in aggregate demand resulting from an increase in durable goods orders?

9. Read *Eye on the Multiplier* on p. 370. Why do multiplier estimates differ? What conditions would be consistent with a large multiplier?

**FIGURE 1**

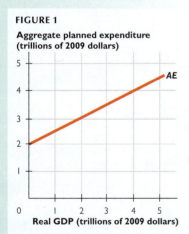

Aggregate planned expenditure (trillions of 2009 dollars)

## Instructor Assignable Problems and Applications

MyEconLab Homework, Quiz, or Test if assigned by instructor

1. The output gap in the second quarter of 2009 was $0.8 trillion. How much fiscal stimulus would be required to close the output gap if the multiplier was as large as the Obama team believes? How much fiscal stimulus would be required if the multiplier was as large as Robert Barro believes?

Table 1 shows disposable income and consumption expenditure in an economy. Use Table 1 to work Problems **2** and **3**.

2. Calculate saving at each level of disposable income. Over what range of disposable income does consumption expenditure exceed disposable income? Calculate autonomous consumption expenditure.

3. Calculate the marginal propensity to consume. At what level of disposable income will saving be zero? If expected future income increases, in which direction will the consumption function change?

Use the following information to work Problems **4** to **6**.

In an economy with no exports and no imports, autonomous consumption is $1 trillion, the marginal propensity to consume is 0.8, investment is $5 trillion, and government expenditure on goods and services is $4 trillion. Taxes are $4 trillion and do not vary with real GDP.

4. If real GDP is $30 trillion, calculate disposable income, consumption expenditure, and aggregate planned expenditure. What is equilibrium expenditure?

5. If real GDP is $30 trillion, explain the process that takes the economy to equilibrium expenditure. If real GDP is $40 trillion, explain the process that takes the economy to equilibrium expenditure.

6. If investment increases by $0.5 trillion, calculate the change in equilibrium expenditure and the multiplier.

Use the following information to work Problems **7** and **8**.

Figure 1 shows the aggregate demand curve in an economy. Suppose that aggregate planned expenditure increases by $0.75 trillion for each $1 trillion increase in real GDP.

7. If investment increases by $1 trillion, calculate the change in the quantity of real GDP demanded if the price level is constant at 105.

8. Compare the shift of the *AD* curve with the $1 trillion increase in investment. Explain the magnitude of the shift of the *AD* curve.

Use the following information to work Problems **9** and **10**.

**U.S. durable goods orders slump most in three years**
The Commerce Department reported that orders for U.S. durable goods fell in January by the most in three years. Orders for commercial aircraft and business equipment fell most. Machinery orders dropped 10.4 percent.
Source: Bloomberg, February 29, 2012

9. Explain the process by which a decrease in durable goods orders at a constant price level changes equilibrium expenditure and real GDP.

10. What determines the decrease in aggregate demand resulting from a decrease in durable goods orders?

**TABLE 1**

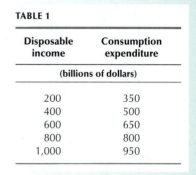

| Disposable income | Consumption expenditure |
|---|---|
| (billions of dollars) | |
| 200 | 350 |
| 400 | 500 |
| 600 | 650 |
| 800 | 800 |
| 1,000 | 950 |

**FIGURE 1**

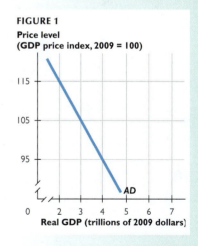

## Multiple Choice Quiz

**1.** The consumption function shows how an increase in _____ influences _____.

   A. income; households' aggregate planned expenditure
   B. nominal GDP; consumption expenditure
   C. disposable income; consumption expenditure
   D. consumption as a fraction of income; real GDP

**2.** The marginal propensity to consume tells us by how much _____ changes when _____ changes.

   A. consumption expenditure; wealth
   B. the real interest rate; planned consumption
   C. expected future income; the percentage of income spent
   D. consumption expenditure; disposable income

**3.** Induced expenditure includes _____.

   A. consumption expenditure, government expenditure, and exports
   B. investment, exports, and imports
   C. consumption expenditure and imports
   D. consumption expenditure, investment, and government expenditure

**4.** The aggregate planned expenditure curve _____ increases.

   A. slopes upward because induced expenditure increases as income
   B. is horizontal because autonomous expenditure is constant when income
   C. shifts upward if induced expenditure increases as income
   D. slopes upward because autonomous expenditure

**5.** If real GDP _____ planned expenditure, the economy converges to equilibrium expenditure because inventories _____ and firms increase production.

   A. exceeds; pile up
   B. exceeds; are run down
   C. is less than; are run down
   D. is less than; pile up

**6.** The multiplier equals _____ divided by _____.

   A. the marginal propensity to consume; autonomous expenditure
   B. 1; (1 − Slope of the *AE* curve)
   C. 1; Slope of the *AE* curve
   D. Slope of the *AE* curve; the marginal propensity to consume

**7.** The multiplier will increase if the marginal propensity to consume _____ or the marginal tax rate _____.

   A. increases; decreases
   B. increases; increases
   C. decreases; increases
   D. decreases; decreases

**8.** A rise in the price level shifts the *AE* curve _____.

   A. upward and creates a movement up along the *AD* curve
   B. downward and creates a movement up along the *AD* curve
   C. upward and shifts the *AD* curve rightward
   D. downward and shifts the *AD* curve leftward

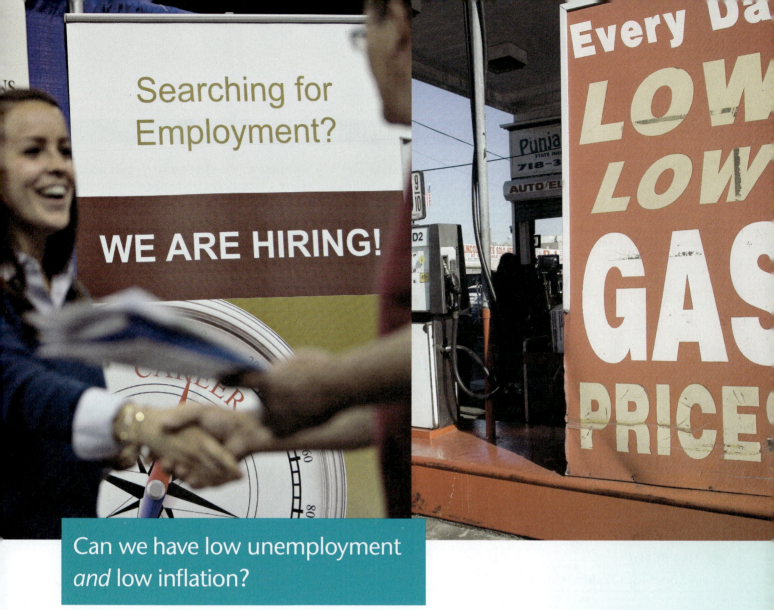

Can we have low unemployment *and* low inflation?

# The Short-Run Policy Tradeoff

**15**

CHAPTER CHECKLIST

**When you have completed your study of this chapter, you will be able to**

**1** Describe the short-run tradeoff between inflation and unemployment.

**2** Distinguish between the short-run and the long-run Phillips curves and describe the shifting tradeoff between inflation and unemployment.

**3** Explain how the Fed can influence the inflation rate and the unemployment rate.

MyEconLab **Big Picture Video**

379

## 15.1   THE SHORT-RUN PHILLIPS CURVE

**Short-run Phillips curve**
The relationship between the inflation rate and the unemployment rate when the natural unemployment rate and the expected inflation rate remain constant.

We *can* have low inflation and low unemployment. To see why, you need to understand the long-run Phillips curve and a temporary tradeoff called the short-run Phillips curve. The **short-run Phillips curve** shows the relationship between the inflation rate and the unemployment rate when the natural unemployment rate and the expected inflation rate remain constant.

Figure 15.1 illustrates the short-run Phillips curve. Here, the natural unemployment rate is 6 percent and the expected inflation rate is 3 percent a year. At full employment, the unemployment rate equals the natural unemployment rate and the inflation rate equals the expected inflation rate at point *B*. This point is the anchor point for the short-run Phillips curve.

In an expansion, the unemployment rate decreases and the inflation rate rises. For example, the economy might move to a point such as *A*, where the unemployment rate is 5 percent and the inflation rate is 4 percent a year.

In a recession, the unemployment rate increases and the inflation rate falls. For example, the economy might move to a point such as *C*, where the unemployment rate is 7 percent and the inflation rate is 2 percent a year.

The short-run Phillips curve presents a *tradeoff* between inflation and unemployment. A lower unemployment rate can be achieved only by paying the cost of a higher inflation rate, and a lower inflation rate can be achieved only by paying the cost of a higher unemployment rate. For example, in Figure 15.1, a decrease in the unemployment rate from 6 percent to 5 percent costs a 1-percentage-point increase in the inflation rate from 3 percent a year to 4 percent a year.

■ **FIGURE 15.1**

A Short-Run Phillips Curve

❶ If the natural unemployment rate is 6 percent, and ❷ the expected inflation rate is 3 percent a year, then ❸ point *B* is at full employment on a short-run Phillips curve.

❹ The short-run Phillips curve (*SRPC*) shows the tradeoff between inflation and unemployment at the given natural unemployment rate and expected inflation rate.

A higher unemployment rate brings a lower inflation rate, and a lower unemployment rate brings a higher inflation rate.

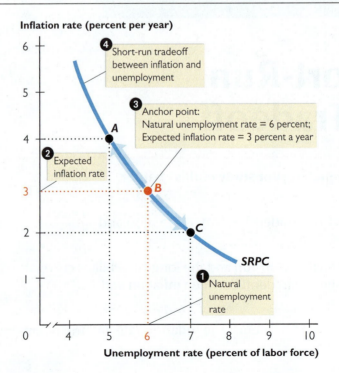

# ■ Aggregate Supply and the Short-Run Phillips Curve

The short-run Phillips curve is another way of looking at the upward-sloping aggregate supply curve that you learned about in Chapter 13—see pp. 328–332.

Both the short-run Phillips curve and the aggregate supply curve arise because the money wage rate is fixed in the short run.

Along an aggregate supply curve, the money wage rate is fixed. So when the price level rises, the *real wage rate* falls, and a fall in the real wage rate increases the quantity of labor employed and increases the quantity of real GDP supplied.

The events that we've just described also play out along a short-run Phillips curve. The rise in the price level means that the inflation rate has (perhaps temporarily) increased. The increase in the quantity of labor employed means a decrease in the number unemployed and a fall in the unemployment rate.

So a movement along an aggregate supply curve is equivalent to a movement along a short-run Phillips curve. Let's explore these connections between the aggregate supply curve and the short-run Phillips curve a bit more closely.

## Unemployment and Real GDP

In a given period, with a fixed amount of capital and a given state of technology, real GDP depends on the quantity of labor employed. At full employment, the quantity of real GDP is *potential GDP* and the unemployment rate is the natural unemployment rate. If real GDP exceeds potential GDP, employment exceeds its full-employment level and the unemployment rate falls below the natural unemployment rate. Similarly, if real GDP is less than potential GDP, employment is less than its full-employment level and the unemployment rate rises above the natural unemployment rate.

The quantitative relationship between the unemployment rate and real GDP was first estimated by economist Arthur M. Okun and is called **Okun's Law**. Okun's Law states that for each percentage point that the unemployment rate is above (below) the natural unemployment rate, real GDP is 2 percent below (above) potential GDP. For example, if the natural unemployment rate is 6 percent and potential GDP is $10 trillion, then when the actual unemployment rate is 7 percent, real GDP is $9.8 trillion—98 percent of potential GDP, or 2 percent below potential GDP. And when the actual unemployment rate is 5 percent, real GDP is $10.2 trillion—102 percent of potential GDP, or 2 percent above potential GDP. Table 15.1 summarizes this relationship.

## Inflation and the Price Level

The inflation rate is the percentage change in the price level. So starting from last period's price level, the higher the inflation rate, the higher is the current period's price level. Suppose that last year, the price level was 100. If the inflation rate is 2 percent, the price level rises to 102; if the inflation rate is 3 percent, the price level rises to 103; and if the inflation rate is 4 percent, the price level rises to 104.

With these relationships between the unemployment rate and real GDP (in Table 15.1) and between the inflation rate and the price level, we can establish the connection between the short-run Phillips curve and the aggregate supply curve. Figure 15.2 shows this connection.

First suppose that in the current year, real GDP equals potential GDP and the unemployment rate equals the natural unemployment rate. In Figure 15.2, real

**Okun's Law**
For each percentage point that the unemployment rate is above (below) the natural unemployment rate, real GDP is 2 percent below (above) potential GDP.

TABLE 15.1

| | Unemployment rate (percent) | Real GDP (trillions of 2009 dollars) |
|---|---|---|
| A | 5 | 10.2 |
| B | 6 | 10.0 |
| C | 7 | 9.8 |

GDP is $10 trillion and the unemployment rate is 6 percent. The economy is at point *B* on the short-run Phillips curve in part (a) and point *B* on the aggregate supply curve in part (b). The inflation rate is 3 percent a year (its expected rate) in part (a), and the price level is 103 (also its expected level) in part (b).

Next suppose that instead of being at full employment, the economy is above full employment with real GDP of $10.2 trillion at point *A* on the aggregate supply curve in Figure 15.2(b). In this case, the unemployment rate is 5 percent in Table 15.1 and the economy is at point *A* on the short-run Phillips curve in Figure 15.2(a). The inflation rate is 4 percent a year (higher than expected) in part (a), and the price level is 104 (also higher than expected) in part (b).

Finally, suppose that the economy is below full employment with real GDP of $9.8 trillion at point *C* on the aggregate supply curve in Figure 15.2(b). In this case, the unemployment rate is 7 percent in Table 15.1 and the economy is at point *C* on the short-run Phillips curve in Figure 15.2(a). The inflation rate is 2 percent a year (lower than expected) in part (a), and the price level is 102 (also lower than expected) in part (b).

**■ FIGURE 15.2**

## The Short-Run Phillips Curve and the Aggregate Supply Curve

MyEconLab Animation

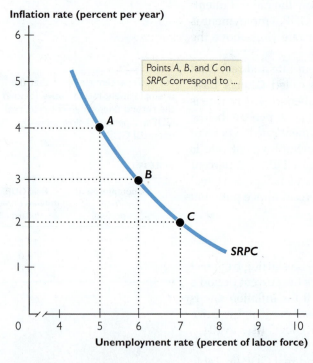

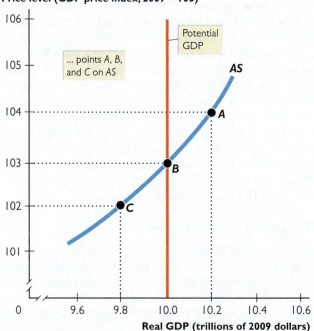

**(a) The short-run Phillips curve**

**(b) The aggregate supply curve**

Point *A* on the Phillips curve corresponds to point *A* on the aggregate supply curve: The unemployment rate is 5 percent and the inflation rate is 4 percent a year in part (a), and real GDP is $10.2 trillion and the price level is 104 in part (b).

Point *B* on the Phillips curve corresponds to point *B* on the aggregate supply curve: The unemployment rate is 6 percent and the inflation rate is 3 percent a year in part (a), and real GDP is $10 trillion and the price level is 103 in part (b).

Point *C* on the Phillips curve corresponds to point *C* on the aggregate supply curve: The unemployment rate is 7 percent and the inflation rate is 2 percent a year in part (a), and real GDP is $9.8 trillion and the price level is 102 in part (b).

## ■ Aggregate Demand Fluctuations

A decrease in aggregate demand that brings a movement down along the aggregate supply curve from point $B$ to point $C$ lowers the price level and decreases real GDP. That same decrease in aggregate demand brings a movement down along the Phillips curve from point $B$ to point $C$.

Similarly, an increase in aggregate demand that brings a movement up along the aggregate supply curve from point $B$ to point $A$ raises the price level and increases real GDP relative to what they would have been. That same increase in aggregate demand brings a movement up along the Phillips curve from point $B$ to point $A$.

# EYE on the GLOBAL ECONOMY
## Inflation and Unemployment

The Phillips curve is so named because New Zealand economist A. W. (Bill) Phillips discovered the relationship in about 100 years of unemployment and wage inflation data for the United Kingdom.

The figure shows data on inflation and unemployment in the United Kingdom over most of the twentieth century—1900 to 1997. The data reveal no neat, tight tradeoff. The short-run tradeoff shifts around a great deal.

The highest inflation rate in 1975 did not occur at the lowest unemployment rate, and the lowest inflation rate in 1922 did not occur at the highest unemployment rate. But the lowest unemployment rate in 1917 did bring a high inflation rate. And the highest unemployment rate during the Great Depression of the 1930s brought a gently falling price level.

A.W. (Bill) Phillips

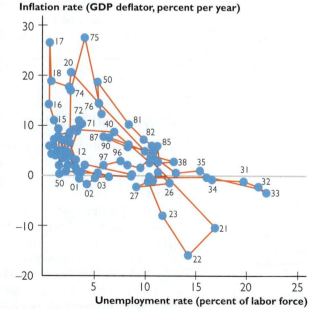

SOURCE: Michael Parkin, "Unemployment, Inflation, and Monetary Policy," *Canadian Journal of Economics*, November 1998.

# EYE on the PAST
## The U.S. Phillips Curve

Phillips made his discovery in 1958, two years before the election of John F. Kennedy as President of the United States. Very soon thereafter, two young American economists, Paul A. Samuelson and Robert M. Solow, both at MIT and eager to help the new Kennedy administration to pursue a low-unemployment strategy, looked for a Phillips curve in the U.S. data. The figure shows what they found: The red line joining the blue dots shows no recognizable relationship between inflation and unemployment for the 20 or so years that they studied.

Giving more weight to the 1950s experience, Samuelson and Solow proposed the Phillips curve shown in the figure. They believed that the U.S. Phillips curve provided support for the then growing view that the new Kennedy administration could pursue a low unemployment policy with only a moderate rise in the inflation rate.

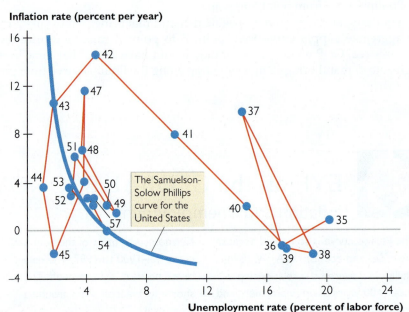

SOURCE OF DATA: Paul A. Samuelson and Robert M. Solow, "Problem of Achieving and Maintaining a Stable Price Level, Analytical Aspects of Anti-Inflation Policy." *American Economic Review*, 50(2), May 1960.

As the 1960s unfolded, the Samuelson-Solow version of the Phillips curve began to look like a permanent tradeoff between inflation and unemployment. But in the late 1960s and early 1970s, the relationship disappeared in the face of rising inflation expectations.

## ■ Why Bother with the Phillips Curve?

You've seen that the short-run Phillips curve is another way of looking at the aggregate supply curve. And you might be wondering, why bother with the short-run Phillips curve? Isn't the aggregate supply curve adequate for describing the short-run tradeoff?

The Phillips curve is useful for two reasons. First, it focuses directly on two policy targets: the inflation rate and the unemployment rate. Second, the aggregate supply curve shifts whenever the money wage rate or potential GDP changes. Such changes occur every day, so the aggregate supply curve is not a stable tradeoff. The short-run Phillips curve isn't a stable tradeoff either, but it is more stable than the aggregate supply curve. The short-run Phillips curve shifts only when the natural unemployment rate changes or when the expected inflation rate changes.

## CHECKPOINT 15.1

MyEconLab Study Plan 15.1
Key Terms Quiz
Solutions Video

**Describe the short-run tradeoff between inflation and unemployment.**

## Practice Problems

Table 1 describes five possible outcomes in a country for 2017, depending on the level of aggregate demand in that year. Potential GDP is $10 trillion, and the natural unemployment rate is 5 percent.

1. Calculate the inflation rate for each possible outcome.
2. Use Okun's Law to find real GDP at each unemployment rate in Table 1.
3. What are the expected price level and the expected inflation rate in 2017?
4. Plot the short-run Phillips curve for 2017. Mark the points A, B, C, D, and E that correspond to the data in Table 1 and that you have calculated.
5. Plot the aggregate supply curve for 2017. Mark the points A, B, C, D, and E that correspond to the data in Table 1.

**TABLE 1**

| | Price level (2016 = 100) | Unemployment rate (percentage) |
|---|---|---|
| A | 102.5 | 9 |
| B | 105.0 | 6 |
| C | 106.0 | 5 |
| D | 107.5 | 4 |
| E | 110.0 | 3 |

## In the News

**U.K. unemployment rate hit lowest since 2005**
The unemployment rate in the United Kingdom fell to 4.9 percent in the three months to May, its lowest level since 2005. In the same three months, wages rose by 2.3 percent, their biggest increase since October 2015.

Source: Reuters, July 20, 2016

With the expected inflation rate steady, did the U.K. economy move along its short-run Phillips curve? If so, in which direction? Or did the economy move off its short-run Phillips curve?

## Solutions to Practice Problems

1. The inflation rate in 2017 equals the price level in 2017 minus the price level in 2016. So for A, the inflation rate is 102.5 − 100, which equals 2.5 percent per year. Calculate the inflation rate at the other points in the same way.
2. Okun's Law: For each 1 percentage point the unemployment rate U exceeds the natural unemployment rate U* (5 percent), real GDP is below potential GDP by 2 percent. So for A, U exceeds U* by 4 percentage points, so real GDP is 8 percent below potential GDP, equal to $9.2 trillion. Calculate real GDP at the other points in the same way.
3. The expected price level is the price level at full employment—row C. The expected price level is 106, and the expected inflation rate is 6 percent.
4. Plot the inflation rate (Solution 1) against the unemployment rate (Table 1) to get the short-run Phillips curve (Figure 1).
5. Plot the price level (Table 1) against real GDP (Solution 2) to get the aggregate supply curve (Figure 2).

## Solution to In the News

With the expected inflation rate steady, the increase in wage inflation and decrease in unemployment imply that the U.K. economy remained on its short-run Phillips curve and moved leftward up along it as the wage inflation rate rose and the unemployment rate fell.

**FIGURE 1**

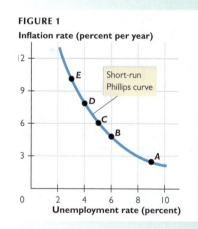

**FIGURE 2**

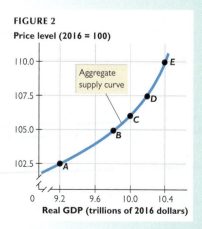

## 15.2 SHORT-RUN AND LONG-RUN PHILLIPS CURVES

The short-run Phillips curve shows the *tradeoff* between inflation and unemployment when the natural unemployment rate and expected inflation rate remain the same. Changes in the natural unemployment rate and the expected inflation rate change the short-run tradeoff and changes in the expected inflation rate give rise to a *long-run* Phillips curve that we'll now examine.

### ■ The Long-Run Phillips Curve

**Long-run Phillips curve**
The relationship between inflation and unemployment when the economy is at full employment. The long-run Phillips curve is a vertical line at the natural unemployment rate.

The **long-run Phillips curve** shows the relationship between inflation and unemployment when the economy is at full employment. At full employment, the unemployment rate is the *natural unemployment rate,* so on the long-run Phillips curve, there is only one possible unemployment rate: the natural unemployment rate.

In contrast, the inflation rate can take on any value at full employment. You learned in Chapter 12 (pp. 312–315) that at full employment, for a given real GDP growth rate, the greater the money growth rate, the greater is the inflation rate.

This description of the economy at full employment tells us the properties of the long-run Phillips curve: It is a vertical line located at the natural unemployment rate. In Figure 15.3, the long-run Phillips curve is *LRPC* along which the unemployment rate equals the natural unemployment rate and any inflation rate is possible.

### ■ FIGURE 15.3

The Long-Run Phillips Curve

The long-run Phillips curve is a vertical line at the natural unemployment rate. In the long run, there is no unemployment–inflation tradeoff.

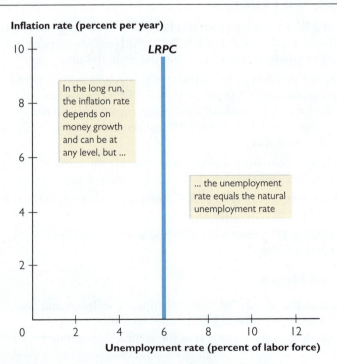

Inflation rate (percent per year)

*LRPC*

In the long run, the inflation rate depends on money growth and can be at any level, but ...

... the unemployment rate equals the natural unemployment rate

Unemployment rate (percent of labor force)

# ■ Expected Inflation

The **expected inflation rate** is the inflation rate that people forecast and use to set the money wage rate and other money prices. Suppose there is full employment and McDonald's servers earn $10 an hour. With no inflation, a money wage rate of $10 an hour keeps the market for servers in equilibrium. But with 10 percent inflation, a constant money wage rate means a falling real wage rate and a shortage of servers. Now, a 10 percent rise in the money wage rate to $11 is needed to keep the market for servers in equilibrium. If McDonald's and everyone else expect 10 percent inflation, the money wage rate will rise by 10 percent to prevent a labor shortage from arising.

If expectations about the inflation rate turn out to be correct, the price level rises by the 10 percent expected and the real wage rate remains constant at its full-employment equilibrium level and unemployment remains at the natural unemployment rate.

Because the actual inflation rate equals the expected inflation rate at full employment, we can interpret the long-run Phillips curve as the relationship between inflation and unemployment when the inflation rate equals the expected inflation rate.

Figure 15.4 shows short-run Phillips curves for two expected inflation rates. A short-run Phillips curve shows the tradeoff between inflation and unemployment at *a particular expected inflation rate.* When the expected inflation rate changes, the short-run Phillips curve shifts to intersect the long-run Phillips curve at the new expected inflation rate.

**Expected inflation rate**
The inflation rate that people forecast and use to set the money wage rate and other money prices.

## ■ FIGURE 15.4

### Short-Run and Long-Run Phillips Curves

MyEconLab Animation

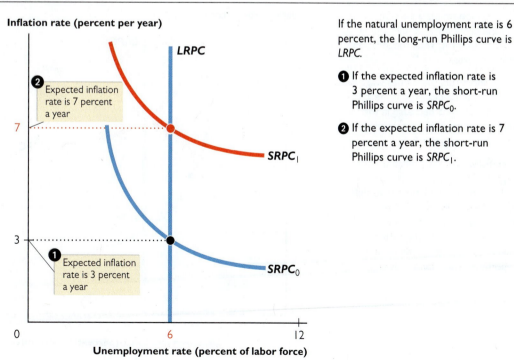

If the natural unemployment rate is 6 percent, the long-run Phillips curve is *LRPC.*

❶ If the expected inflation rate is 3 percent a year, the short-run Phillips curve is $SRPC_0$.

❷ If the expected inflation rate is 7 percent a year, the short-run Phillips curve is $SRPC_1$.

In Figure 15.4, when the expected inflation rate is 3 percent a year, the short-run Phillips curve is $SRPC_0$ and when the expected inflation rate is 7 percent a year, the short-run Phillips curve is $SRPC_1$.

## ■ The Natural Rate Hypothesis

**Natural rate hypothesis**
The proposition that when the inflation rate changes, the unemployment rate changes *temporarily* and eventually returns to the natural unemployment rate.

The **natural rate hypothesis** is the proposition that when the inflation rate changes, the unemployment rate changes *temporarily* and eventually returns to the natural unemployment rate. The temporary change in the unemployment rate occurs because the real wage rate changes, which leads to a change in the quantity of labor demanded. The unemployment rate returns to the natural rate because eventually, the money wage rate changes to catch up with the change in the price level and return the real wage rate to its full-employment level.

Figure 15.5 illustrates the natural rate hypothesis. Initially, the inflation rate is 3 percent a year and the economy is at full employment, at point $A$. Then the quantity of money grows more rapidly, at a rate that will generate inflation at 7 percent a year in the long run. In the short run, with a fixed money wage rate, the real wage rate falls, the quantity of labor employed increases and the unemployment rate falls. The inflation rate rises to 5 percent a year, and the economy moves from point $A$ to point $B$. When the higher inflation rate is expected, the money wage rate increases. As the expected inflation rate increases from 3 percent to 7 percent a year, the short-run Phillips curve shifts upward from $SRPC_0$ to $SRPC_1$. Inflation speeds up and the unemployment rate returns to the natural unemployment rate. In Figure 15.5, the economy moves from point $B$ to point $C$.

■ **FIGURE 15.5**

The Natural Rate Hypothesis

MyEconLab Real-time data

The inflation rate is 3 percent a year, and the economy is at full employment, at point A. Then the inflation rate increases.

In the short run, the money wage rate is fixed and the increase in the inflation rate brings a decrease in the unemployment rate—a movement along SRPC₀ to point B.

Eventually, the higher inflation rate is expected, the money wage rate rises, and the short-run Phillips curve shifts upward gradually to SRPC₁. At the higher expected inflation rate, unemployment returns to the natural unemployment rate—the natural rate hypothesis. The economy is at point C.

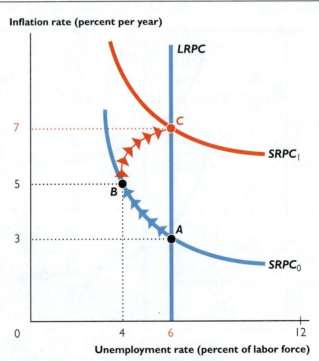

# EYE on the PAST

## A Live Test of the Natural Rate Hypothesis

The figure describes the U.S. economy from 1960 to 1971 and shows that the natural rate hypothesis describes these years well.

The natural unemployment rate was around 6 percent, so the long-run Phillips curve, *LRPC*, was located at that unemployment rate.

In 1960, the inflation rate and the expected inflation rate were around 1 percent a year. The short-run Phillips curve was $SRPC_0$.

Through 1966, the expected inflation rate remained at 1 percent a year but the actual inflation rate edged up and the unemployment rate decreased below the natural unemployment rate. The economy moved up along $SRPC_0$ from point *A* to point *B*.

Then, from 1967 to 1969, the inflation rate increased and so did the expected inflation rate. As the expected inflation rate rose. the short-run Phillips curve shifted upward. By 1969, the economy had moved to point *C*.

By 1970, the expected inflation rate was around 5 percent a year. As the higher inflation rate came to be expected, the unemployment rate increased.

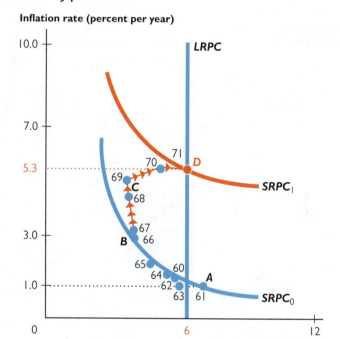

SOURCE OF DATA: Bureau of Labor Statistics and Bureau of Economic Analysis.

By 1971, the unemployment rate had returned to the natural unemployment rate, the short-run Phillips curve had shifted upward to $SRPC_1$, and the economy had moved to point *D*.

Notice the similarity between the actual events during this period and

the natural rate hypothesis, which Figure 15.5 illustrates.

Edmund S. Phelps of Columbia University and Milton Friedman of the University of Chicago proposed the natural rate hypothesis and predicted these events *before* they occurred.

## ■ Changes in the Natural Unemployment Rate

If the natural unemployment rate changes, both the long-run Phillips curve and the short-run Phillips curve shift. When the natural unemployment rate increases, both the long-run Phillips curve and the short-run Phillips curve shift rightward; and when the natural unemployment rate decreases, both the long-run Phillips curve and the short-run Phillips curve shift leftward.

Figure 15.6 illustrates these changes. When the natural unemployment rate is 6 percent, the long-run Phillips curve is $LRPC_0$. If the expected inflation rate is 3 percent a year, the short-run Phillips curve is $SRPC_0$. A decrease in the natural

■ **FIGURE 15.6**

Changes in the Natural Unemployment Rate

The natural unemployment rate is 6 percent, and the long-run Phillips curve is $LRPC_0$. The expected inflation rate is 3 percent a year, and the short-run Phillips curve is $SRPC_0$.

A decrease in the natural unemployment rate shifts both Phillips curves leftward to $LRPC_1$ and $SRPC_1$.

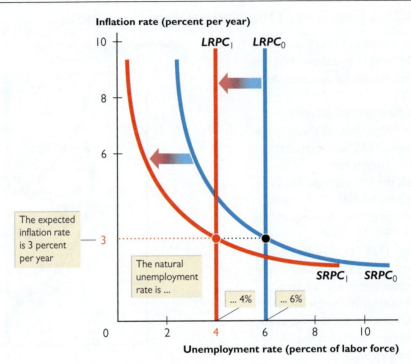

unemployment rate, with no change in the expected inflation rate, shifts both Phillips curves leftward to $LRPC_1$ and $SRPC_1$.

## ■ Have Changes in the Natural Unemployment Rate Changed the Tradeoff?

Changes in the natural unemployment rate have changed the tradeoff. According to the Congressional Budget Office, the natural unemployment rate increased from about 5 percent in 1950 to more than 6 percent in the mid-1970s and then decreased to 4.8 percent by 2000. It has been constant at this level through 2009.

You learned about the factors that influence the natural unemployment rate in Chapter 8 (pp. 205–208). Those factors divide into two groups: influences on job search and influences on job rationing. Job search is influenced by demographic change, unemployment compensation, and structural change. Job rationing arises from efficiency wages, the minimum wage, and union wages.

A bulge in the birth rate (known as the "baby boom") that occurred after World War II in the late 1940s and early 1950s, brought a bulge in the number of young people entering the labor force during the late 1960s and early 1970s. This bulge in the number of new entrants increased the amount of job search and increased the natural unemployment rate.

Structural change during the 1970s and 1980s, much of it a response to massive hikes in the world price of oil, also contributed to the increase in the natural unemployment rate during the 1970s and early 1980s.

# EYE on the TRADEOFF

MyEconLab Critical Thinking Exercise

## Can We Have Low Unemployment *and* Low Inflation?

In the short run, we can have low unemployment only if we permit the inflation rate to rise. And we can have low inflation only if we permit the unemployment rate to increase. In the long run, we can improve the unemployment–inflation tradeoff.

We can have low unemployment if we can lower the natural unemployment rate, but that is hard to do.

We can have low inflation if we can lower the expected inflation rate. That, too, is hard to do, but it isn't as hard as lowering the natural unemployment rate. The expected inflation rate does change frequently and sometimes by large amounts.

The years 2000–2015 show how changes in the expected inflation rate change the short-run tradeoff.

During these years, the natural unemployment rate was constant at 5 percent, so the long-run Phillips curve remained fixed at *LRPC*.

The expected inflation rate was 2.5 percent a year in 2000–2002 and the short-run Phillips curve was $SRPC_0$. The expected inflation rate then increased to 3.5 percent a year, where

it remained until 2005, and the short-run Phillips curve shifted to $SRPC_1$.

In 2006, the expected inflation rate decreased to 2.5 percent a year and the short-run Phillips curve shifted back from $SRPC_1$ to $SRPC_0$. The tradeoff improved.

In 2015, the expected inflation rate decreased again to zero percent a year and the short-run Phillips curve shifted downward from $SRPC_0$ to $SRPC_2$. The tradeoff improved still further. The 2015 data show that we can have low inflation and low unemployment.

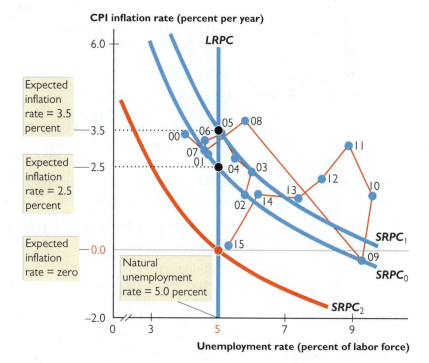

SOURCE OF DATA: Bureau of Labor Statistics and Congressional Budget Office.

As the baby boom generation approached middle age during the 1980s and 1990s, the number of new labor market entrants decreased and the natural unemployment rate decreased too. Also, during the 1990s, rapid technological change brought an increase in productivity and an increase in the demand for labor that shortened the time people spent on job search and lowered the natural unemployment rate yet further. During the 2000s, the natural unemployment rate remained steady.

The changes in the natural unemployment rate that we've just described shifted the short-run and long-run Phillips curves rightward during the 1960s and 1970s and shifted them leftward during the 1980s and 1990s.

MyEconLab Study Plan 15.2
Key Terms Quiz
Solutions Video

## CHECKPOINT 15.2

**Distinguish between the short-run and the long-run Phillips curves and describe the shifting tradeoff between inflation and unemployment.**

### Practice Problems

Figure 1 shows a short-run Phillips curve and a long-run Phillips curve.

1. Identify the curves and label them. What is the expected inflation rate and what is the natural unemployment rate?

2. If the expected inflation rate increases to 7.5 percent a year, show the new short-run and long-run Phillips curves.

3. If the natural unemployment rate increases to 8 percent, show the new short-run and long-run Phillips curves.

4. If aggregate demand starts to grow more rapidly and the inflation rate eventually hits 10 percent a year, how do unemployment and inflation change?

### In the News

**U.S. jobs and inflation data**

The number of Americans filing for unemployment benefits in June was unchanged at a 43-year low of 248,000. Producer prices recorded their biggest gain in a year in June.

Source: Reuters, July 14, 2016

Did the U.S. economy move along its short-run Phillips curve? If so, how? Or did the short-run Phillips curve shift? If so, how?

### Solutions to Practice Problems

1. The long-run Phillips curve is the vertical curve, *LRPC*, and the short-run Phillips curve is the downward-sloping curve, $SRPC_0$ (Figure 2). The expected inflation rate is 5 percent a year—the inflation rate at which *LRPC* and $SRPC_0$ intersect. The natural unemployment rate is 6 percent. The *LRPC* is vertical at the natural unemployment rate.

2. The short-run Phillips curve shifts upward, but the long-run Phillips curve does not change (Figure 2).

3. Both the short-run and long-run Phillips curves shift rightward (Figure 3).

4. Figure 4 shows that as expectations change, the inflation rate rises to 10 percent a year and unemployment falls and then gradually returns to its natural rate.

### Solution to In the News

The facts about unemployment and inflation in the news clip are consistent with an increase in the expected inflation rate and an upward shift in the short-run Phillips curve. With the number of Americans unemployed unchanged, the economy did not move along a short-run Phillips curve.

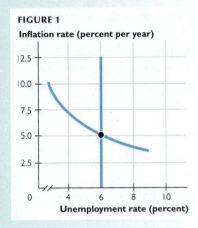

**FIGURE 1**

Inflation rate (percent per year)

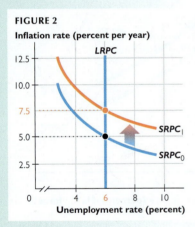

**FIGURE 2**

Inflation rate (percent per year)

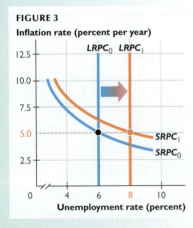

**FIGURE 3**

Inflation rate (percent per year)

**FIGURE 4**

Inflation rate (percent per year)

## 15.3  INFLUENCING INFLATION AND UNEMPLOYMENT

MyEconLab Concept Video

How can the Fed influence the inflation rate and the unemployment rate and achieve low levels of both? The basic answer is that the Fed can try to lower the expected inflation rate. When the expected inflation rate is low, as it was in 2000, the tradeoff is more favorable than when the expected inflation rate is high, as it was in 1980.

### ■ Influencing the Expected Inflation Rate

The *expected inflation rate* is the inflation rate that people forecast and use to set the money wage rate and other money prices. To forecast the inflation rate, people use the same basic method that they use to forecast other variables that affect their lives.

Data make up the first ingredient in forecasting—data about the past behavior of the phenomenon that we want to forecast. When people lay heavy bets that the Detroit Lions will win a game, they base their forecast on the performance of the Lions and the other teams in recent games.

Science is the second ingredient in forecasting—the specific science that seeks to understand the phenomenon that we wish to forecast. If we want to know whether it is likely to rain tomorrow, we turn to the science of meteorology. Science tells people how to interpret data.

So to forecast inflation, people use data about past inflation and other relevant variables and the science of economics, which seeks to understand the forces that cause inflation.

You already know the relevant economics: the *AS-AD* model. You know that the money growth rate determines the growth of aggregate demand in the long run. And you know that the trend growth rate of real GDP is the growth rate of aggregate supply in the long run. So the trend money growth rate minus the trend real GDP growth rate determines the trend inflation rate.

The inflation rate fluctuates around its trend as the demand-pull and cost-push forces generate the business cycle. In an expansion, the inflation rate rises above trend, and in a recession, the inflation rate falls below trend as aggregate demand fluctuates to bring movements along the aggregate supply curve. And you know that the money growth rate is one of the influences on these aggregate demand fluctuations.

The Fed determines the money growth rate, so the major ingredient in a forecast of inflation is a forecast of the Fed's actions. Professional Fed watchers and economic forecasters use these ideas along with a lot of data and elaborate statistical models of the economy to forecast the inflation rate.

When all the relevant data and economic science are used to forecast inflation, the resulting forecast is called a **rational expectation**. The rational expectation of the inflation rate is a forecast based on the Fed's forecasted monetary policy along with forecasts of the other forces that influence aggregate demand and aggregate supply. But the dominant factor is the Fed's monetary policy.

**Rational expectation**
The forecast that results from the use of all the relevant data and economic science.

To lower the expected inflation rate, the Fed must conduct its monetary policy in a manner that creates confidence about future inflation. Chapter 17 explores some of the strategies that might achieve such an outcome. If the Fed can lower inflation expectations, it might achieve lower inflation but not a lower unemployment rate. That is constrained by the natural unemployment rate. If the Fed targets the unemployment rate, trouble lies ahead as you're now about to see.

## ■ Targeting the Unemployment Rate

Suppose the Fed decides that it wants to lower the unemployment rate. To do so, it speeds up the growth rate of aggregate demand by speeding up the growth rate of money and lowering interest rates. With the expected inflation rate anchored at a low level, the first effect of this action is a lower unemployment rate and a slightly higher inflation rate. But if the Fed drives the unemployment rate below the natural unemployment rate, the inflation rate will continue to rise.

As a higher inflation rate becomes expected, wages and prices start to rise more rapidly, so the actual inflation rate rises further. If the Fed keeps aggregate demand (and the quantity of money) growing fast enough, the inflation rate will keep rising and the unemployment rate will remain below the natural unemployment rate. But eventually, both inflation and unemployment will rise in a return to full employment and the natural rate of unemployment.

Figure 15.7 illustrates the sequence of changes that we've just described. The economy is below full employment with low inflation. Inflation expectations are well anchored at 3 percent per year. Unemployment is above the natural unemployment rate of 6 percent. The economy is on its short-run Phillips curve, $SRPC_0$ at point $A$, to the right of its long-run Phillips curve, $LRPC$.

Now the Fed speeds up the money growth rate and lowers interest rates. Aggregate demand begins to increase at a faster pace. With no change in expected inflation, money wage rates continue to rise by the same amount as before. As the unemployment rate falls and the inflation rate rises, the economy moves up along

## FIGURE 15.7

Targeting the Unemployment Rate                                         MyEconLab Animation

The economy starts out at point $A$.

The Fed wants to lower the unemployment rate, so it makes aggregate demand grow faster and the economy slides leftward and upward along $SRPC_0$. The unemployment rate falls but the inflation rate rises.

If the Fed makes aggregate demand keep growing after the unemployment rate has fallen below the natural unemployment rate, the inflation rate keeps rising and the higher inflation becomes expected.

A rising expected inflation rate shifts the short-run Phillips curve upward toward $SRPC_1$ (red arrows). The unemployment rate remains below the natural unemployment rate throughout the adjustment to point $B$.

The unemployment rate has fallen but only temporarily, and the cost is permanently higher inflation.

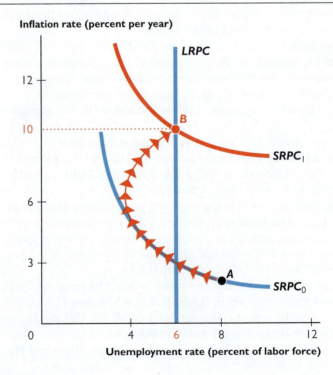

$SRPC_0$. When the expected inflation rate rises, the short-run Phillips curve shifts upward toward $SRPC_1$. The Fed's action lowers the unemployment rate but only temporarily and at the cost of permanently higher inflation. The economy follows the path of the red arrows—and unemployment remains below its natural unemployment rate until, eventually, the economy arrives at point $B$.

### Reversing the Policy to Lower Inflation

If the inflation that results from targeting unemployment becomes unacceptably high, the only way in which low inflation can be restored is to reverse the sequence of events just described. By lowering the growth rate of aggregate demand by slowing money growth and raising interest rates, the Fed can induce a recession. The unemployment rate moves above the natural unemployment rate but inflation eventually subsides and full employment returns.

### Inflation Reduction in Practice

It was back in 1981 that the Fed was last faced with a high inflation rate, and to slow it, we paid a high price. The Fed's policy action was unexpected. Money wage rates had been set too high for the path that the Fed followed. The consequence was recession—a decrease in real GDP and increased unemployment. Because it is difficult to lower the inflation rate without bringing on a recession, it is dangerous to use monetary policy to directly target unemployment. Keeping inflation low and stable is the best that monetary policy can do to keep unemployment low.

## EYE on YOUR LIFE
### The Short-Run Tradeoff in Your Life

MyEconLab Critical Thinking Exercise

The short-run tradeoff enters your life in three distinct ways:

1) It helps you to interpret and understand the current state of the U.S. economy.
2) It helps you to understand the policy decisions taken by the Fed.
3) It encourages you to take a stand on the relative weight that should be given to unemployment or inflation.

### The State of the Economy

Consider the change in the U.S. unemployment rate and inflation rate over the past year. Did they change in the same direction or in opposite directions? Can you interpret the change as a movement along a short-run Phillips curve or as a shifting short-run Phillips curve? Can you think of reasons why the short-run Phillips curve might have shifted? Did the natural unemployment rate change? Did the expected inflation rate change?

Was your expected inflation rate the same as what people on the average expected?

### The Fed's Recent Decisions

What has the Fed been doing to the interest rate over the past year? How do you think the changes in unemployment and inflation affected the Fed's policy decisions?

### Unemployment or Inflation

You've seen that in the long run, there is no tradeoff between unemployment and inflation. But in the short run, there is a tradeoff. If the inflation rate is high, how much unemployment is worth putting up with, and for how long, to lower the inflation rate?

Economists don't agree on the answer to this question. Some say that if inflation is too high, it must be lowered quickly. Some even say that no unemployment is worth enduring to lower inflation.

What is your view? Which is worse, too much inflation or too much unemployment?

MyEconLab Study Plan 15.3
Key Terms Quiz
Solutions Video

## CHECKPOINT 15.3

**Explain how the Fed can influence the inflation rate and the unemployment rate.**

### Practice Problems

Figure 1 shows the Phillips curves. Suppose that the current inflation rate is 5 percent a year and the Fed announces that it will slow the money growth rate so that inflation will fall to 2.5 percent a year.

1. If no one believes the Fed and inflation is expected to be 5 percent a year, explain how the Fed's action will affect inflation and unemployment next year.

2. If everyone believes the Fed, explain the effect of the Fed's action on inflation and unemployment next year.

3. If no one believes the Fed but the Fed keeps inflation at 2.5 percent for many years, explain the effect of the Fed's action on inflation and unemployment.

### In the News

**FOMC press release, June 15, 2016**
The FOMC expects inflation to remain low in the near term, but to rise to 2 percent over the medium term.
                                Source: Board of Governors of the Federal Reserve System

Where on the short-run Phillips curve does the Fed believe the economy to be? What is the Fed anticipating will happen to the short-run Phillips curve?

### Solutions to Practice Problems

1. The inflation rate falls and the unemployment rate rises as the economy moves down along its short-run Phillips curve (see Figure 2).

2. The inflation rate falls to 2.5 percent a year, and unemployment remains at 6 percent. People believe the Fed so expected inflation falls to 2.5 percent a year. The short-run Phillips curve shifts downward to $SRPC_1$ (Figure 3).

3. Initially, inflation falls below 5 percent a year and unemployment rises above 6 percent. The longer the Fed maintains this policy, the lower the expected inflation will be and the short-run Phillips curve will shift downward. The unemployment rate will decrease. Eventually, inflation will be 2.5 percent a year when the unemployment rate returns to 6 percent (Figure 4).

### Solution to In the News

With low inflation, the Fed believes that the economy is on a short-run Phillips curve with low expected inflation. The Fed anticipates that the expected inflation rate will rise, so the $SRPC$ will shift upward and the actual inflation rate will rise. This forecast implies that the unemployment rate is slightly below the natural rate.

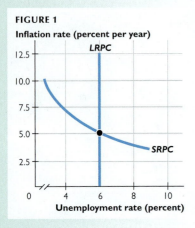

**FIGURE 1**

Inflation rate (percent per year)

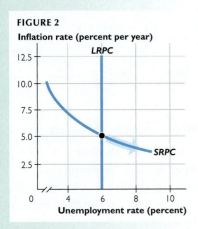

**FIGURE 2**

Inflation rate (percent per year)

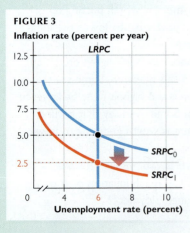

**FIGURE 3**

Inflation rate (percent per year)

**FIGURE 4**

Inflation rate (percent per year)

**CHAPTER SUMMARY**

## Key Points

**1.** **Describe the short-run tradeoff between inflation and unemployment.**

- The short-run Phillips curve is the downward-sloping relationship between the inflation rate and the unemployment rate when all other influences on these two variables remain the same.
- The short-run Phillips curve presents a *tradeoff* between inflation and unemployment.
- The short-run Phillips curve is another way of looking at the aggregate supply curve.

**2.** **Distinguish between the short-run and the long-run Phillips curves and describe the shifting tradeoff between inflation and unemployment.**

- The long-run Phillips curve shows the relationship between inflation and unemployment when the unemployment rate equals the natural unemployment rate and the inflation rate equals the expected inflation rate.
- The long-run Phillips curve is vertical at the *natural unemployment rate,* and there is no long-run tradeoff between unemployment and inflation.
- When the expected inflation rate changes, the short-run Phillips curve shifts to intersect the long-run Phillips curve at the new expected inflation rate.
- When the money growth rate changes, the unemployment rate changes temporarily and eventually returns to the natural unemployment rate—the natural rate hypothesis.
- Changes in the natural unemployment rate shift both the *SRPC* and the *LRPC.*

**3.** **Explain how the Fed can influence the inflation rate and the unemployment rate.**

- The rational expectation of the inflation rate is based on forecasts of the Fed's monetary policy and its influence on aggregate demand growth.
- A fall in the expected inflation rate improves the short-run tradeoff.
- Targeting the unemployment rate can only bring temporarily lower unemployment and at the cost of permanently higher inflation.

## Key Terms

MyEconLab Key Terms Quiz

Expected inflation rate, 387
Long-run Phillips curve, 386
Natural rate hypothesis, 388

Okun's Law, 381
Rational expectation, 393
Short-run Phillips curve, 380

398    Part 5 • ECONOMIC FLUCTUATIONS

MyEconLab Chapter 15 Study Plan

# CHAPTER CHECKPOINT

## Study Plan Problems and Applications

Table 1 describes four situations that might arise in 2018, depending on the level of aggregate demand. Table 2 describes four situations that might arise in 2019. Use Tables 1 and 2 to work Problems **1** to **4**.

**TABLE 1    DATA 2018**

| | Price level (2017 = 100) | Real GDP (trillions of 2017 dollars) | Unemployment rate (percent) |
|---|---|---|---|
| A | 102 | 11.0 | 9 |
| B | 104 | 11.1 | 7 |
| C | 106 | 11.2 | 5 |
| D | 110 | 11.4 | 3 |

**TABLE 2    DATA 2019**

| | Price level (2017 = 100) | Real GDP (trillions of 2017 dollars) | Unemployment rate (percent) |
|---|---|---|---|
| A | 108 | 11.1 | 9 |
| B | 110 | 11.2 | 7 |
| C | 112 | 11.3 | 5 |
| D | 116 | 11.5 | 3 |

1. Plot the short-run Phillips curve and aggregate supply curve for 2018 and mark the points *A*, *B*, *C*, and *D* on each curve that correspond to the data in Table 1.

2. In 2019, the outcome turned out to be row *C* of Table 1. Plot the short-run Phillips curve for 2019 and mark the points *A*, *B*, *C*, and *D* that correspond to the data in Table 2.

3. Compare the short-run Phillips curve of 2019 with that of 2018.

4. What is Okun's Law? If the natural unemployment rate is 6 percent, does this economy behave in accordance with Okun's Law?

5. Suppose that the natural unemployment rate is 7 percent in 2016 and it decreases to 6 percent in 2017 with no change in expected inflation. Explain how the short-run and long-run tradeoffs change.

6. Suppose that the natural unemployment rate is 7 percent and the expected inflation rate in 2017 is 3 percent a year. If the inflation rate is expected to rise to 5 percent a year in 2018, explain how the short-run and the long-run Phillips curves will change.

7. The inflation rate is 2 percent a year, and the quantity of money is growing at a pace that will maintain that inflation rate. The natural unemployment rate is 7 percent, and the current unemployment rate is 9 percent. In what direction will the unemployment rate change? How will the short-run Phillips curve and the long-run Phillips curve shift?

8. From 1991 until 2013, the average inflation rate in Russia was 151.48 percent per year. Explain how a history of rapid inflation might influence the short-run and long-run Phillips curves in Russia.

Use the following information to work Problems **9** and **10**.

**India seeks more reserved central bank**

There is a conflict in India between politicians who want faster growth and lower unemployment, and the central bank governor who wants price stability. The government is replacing the central bank governor and possibly increasing its inflation target.

Source: *The Wall Street Journal*, July 5, 2016

9. Sketch India's short-run and long-run Phillips curves if the expected inflation rate rises from 5 percent per year to 7 percent per year and the natural unemployment rate is constant at 8 percent.

10. If the government replaces the central bank governer and pursues faster growth by increasing aggregate demand, how will inflation and unemployment change? How will India's Phillips curves change?

11. Read *Eye on the Tradeoff* on p. 391. How can the Phillips curve account for the combination of inflation and unemployment in 2015? Do the data for that year mean that there is no tradeoff?

# Instructor Assignable Problems and Applications

1. Suppose that the U.S. economy fully recovers from the 2008–2009 recession, but the natural unemployment rate has risen to 8 percent and the expected inflation rate is zero. How would the short-run and long-run Phillips curves change? Would the tradeoff be more favorable or less favorable than that of 2015? Draw a graph to illustrate your answer.

2. In an economy, the natural unemployment rate is 4 percent and the expected inflation rate is 3 percent a year. Draw a graph of the short-run and long-run Phillips curves that display this information. Label each curve.

Table 1 describes four possible situations that might arise in 2017, depending on the level of aggregate demand in 2017. Table 2 describes four possible situations that might arise in 2018. Use Tables 1 and 2 to work Problems **3** and **4**.

3. Plot the short-run Phillips curve and aggregate supply curve for 2017 and mark the points A, B, C, and D on each curve that correspond to the data in Table 1.

4. In 2017, the outcome turned out to be row D of Table 1. Plot the short-run Phillips curve for 2018 and mark the points A, B, C, and D that correspond to the data in Table 2.

5. Explain the relationship between the long-run Phillips curve and potential GDP and the short-run Phillips curve and the aggregate supply curve.

6. The inflation rate is 3 percent a year, and the quantity of money is growing at a pace that will maintain the inflation rate at 3 percent a year. The natural unemployment rate is 4 percent, and the current unemployment rate is 3 percent. In what direction will the unemployment rate change? How will the short-run Phillips curve and the long-run Phillips curve shift?

7. The inflation rate is 6 percent a year, the unemployment rate is 4 percent, and the economy is at full employment. The Fed announces that it intends to slow the money growth rate to keep the inflation rate at 3 percent a year for the foreseeable future. People believe the Fed. Explain how unemployment and inflation change in the short run and in the long run.

Use the following information to work Problems **8** to **10**.

**Brazilian inflation and growth get worse**

Brazil's central bank has increased its inflation forecast to 9 percent and cut its forecast for real GDP growth, which it now says will be minus 1.1 percent.

Source: *The Wall Street Journal*, June 24, 2015

8. According to Okun's Law, how would you expect Brazil's fall in real GDP (negative growth rate) to change the unemployment rate?

9. Draw two short-run Phillips curves and a long-run Phillips curve for Brazil. On your graph, place two points, one for Brazil in 2014 and one for the central bank's expectations about the outcome in 2015. Explain any assumptions you make.

10. Explain and illustrate with a graph the effects of the central bank of Brazil trying to lower the inflation rate by unexpectedly slowing the money growth rate. Explain how the unemployment rate will change in the short run and in the long run if the central bank persists with a lower money growth rate. Contrast the outcome with that for an expected slowing of money growth.

**TABLE 1   DATA 2017**

| Price level (2016 = 100) | Real GDP (trillions of 2016 dollars) | Unemployment rate (percent) |
|---|---|---|
| A  102 | 10.0 | 8 |
| B  104 | 10.1 | 6 |
| C  106 | 10.2 | 4 |
| D  110 | 10.4 | 2 |

**TABLE 2   DATA 2018**

| Price level (2016 = 100) | Real GDP (trillions of 2016 dollars) | Unemployment rate (percent) |
|---|---|---|
| A  108 | 10.3 | 8 |
| B  110 | 10.4 | 6 |
| C  112 | 10.5 | 4 |
| D  116 | 10.7 | 2 |

# Multiple Choice Quiz

1. The short-run Phillips curve shows that, other things remaining the same, _____.

   A. an increase in expected inflation will lower the unemployment rate
   B. a fall in unemployment will lower the inflation rate
   C. the inflation rate rises by 1 percent when unemployment falls by 1 percent
   D. a rise in the inflation rate and a fall in the unemployment rate occur together

2. The long-run Phillips curve _____.

   A. is a horizontal curve at the expected inflation rate
   B. is a vertical curve at the natural unemployment rate
   C. slopes downward as the inflation rate falls
   D. slopes upward as the unemployment rate falls

3. The short-run Phillips curve intersects the long-run Phillips curve at _____.

   A. the expected inflation rate and the current unemployment rate
   B. the current inflation rate and the natural unemployment rate
   C. the expected inflation rate and the natural unemployment rate
   D. the current inflation rate and the current unemployment rate

4. An increase in the expected inflation rate, other things remaining the same, _____.

   A. shifts the short-run Phillips curve upward
   B. creates a movement up along the short-run Phillips curve
   C. decreases the natural unemployment rate and shifts the long-run Phillips curve leftward
   D. creates a movement up along the long-run Phillips curve with no change in the short-run Phillips curve

5. A decrease in the natural unemployment rate _____.

   A. shifts both the short-run and the long-run Phillips curves leftward
   B. shifts the short-run Phillips curve leftward but the long-run Phillips curve does not change
   C. creates a movement along the short-run Phillips curve
   D. increases the expected inflation rate and shifts the short-run Phillips curve upward

6. Suppose that the unemployment rate exceeds the natural unemployment rate and the Fed increases the money growth rate. If the Fed's action is _____.

   A. unexpected, the unemployment rate falls but the inflation rate rises
   B. unexpected, the inflation rate doesn't change but the unemployment rate falls
   C. expected, the inflation rate rises but the unemployment rate doesn't change
   D. expected, the unemployment rate doesn't change and the inflation rate equals the expected inflation rate

Can fiscal stimulus end
a recession?

# Fiscal Policy

## CHAPTER CHECKLIST

**When you have completed your study of this chapter,
you will be able to**

1  Describe the federal budget, the process that creates it, and a challenge that it faces.

2  Explain how fiscal stimulus is used to fight a recession.

3  Explain the supply-side effects of fiscal policy on employment, potential GDP, and the economic growth rate.

MyEconLab Big Picture Video

## 16.1 THE FEDERAL BUDGET

The federal budget is an annual statement of the tax revenues, outlays, and surplus or deficit of the government of the United States, together with the laws and regulations that authorize these revenues and outlays.

The federal budget has two purposes: to finance the activities of the federal government and to achieve macroeconomic objectives. The first purpose of the federal budget was its only purpose before the Great Depression years of the 1930s. The second purpose evolved as a response to the Great Depression and was initially based on the ideas of *Keynesian macroeconomics* (described in Chapter 8, pp. 192–193). **Fiscal policy** is the use of the federal budget to achieve the macroeconomic objectives of high and sustained economic growth and full employment.

**Fiscal policy**
The use of the federal budget to achieve the macroeconomic objectives of high and sustained economic growth and full employment.

### ■ The Institutions and Laws

The President and Congress make the budget and develop fiscal policy on a fixed annual time line and fiscal year. The U.S. fiscal year runs from October 1 this year to September 30 in the next calendar year. Fiscal 2018 is the fiscal year that begins on October 1, 2017.

### The Roles of the President and Congress

The President *proposes* a budget to Congress each February. After Congress has passed the budget acts in September, the President either signs those acts into law or vetoes the entire budget bill. The President does not have the veto power to eliminate specific items in a budget bill and approve others—known as a line-item veto. Although the President proposes and ultimately approves the budget, the task of making the tough decisions on spending and taxes rests with Congress.

Congress begins its work on the budget with the President's proposal. The House of Representatives and the Senate develop their own budget ideas in their respective House and Senate Budget Committees. Formal conferences between the two houses eventually resolve differences of view, and a series of spending acts and an overall budget act are usually passed by both houses before the start of the fiscal year.

Figure 16.1 summarizes the budget time line and the roles of the President and Congress in the budget process.

### ■ Budget Balance and Debt

**Budget balance**
Tax revenues minus outlays.

The government's **budget balance** is equal to tax revenues minus outlays. That is,

$$\text{Budget balance} = \text{Tax revenues} - \text{Outlays}$$

If tax revenues equal outlays, the government has a *balanced budget*. The government has a *budget surplus* if tax revenues exceed outlays. The government has a *budget deficit* if outlays exceed tax revenues.

The budget projections for the 2017 fiscal year were tax revenues of $3,477 billion, outlays of $4,089 billion, and a budget deficit of $612 billion. You can see that $3,477 - \$4,089 = -\$612$.

The government budget balance is equal to government saving, which might be zero (balanced budget), positive (budget surplus), or negative (budget deficit). When the government has a budget deficit, it incurs debt. That is, the government

■ **FIGURE 16.1**

The Federal Budget Time Line for Fiscal 2018                    MyEconLab Animation

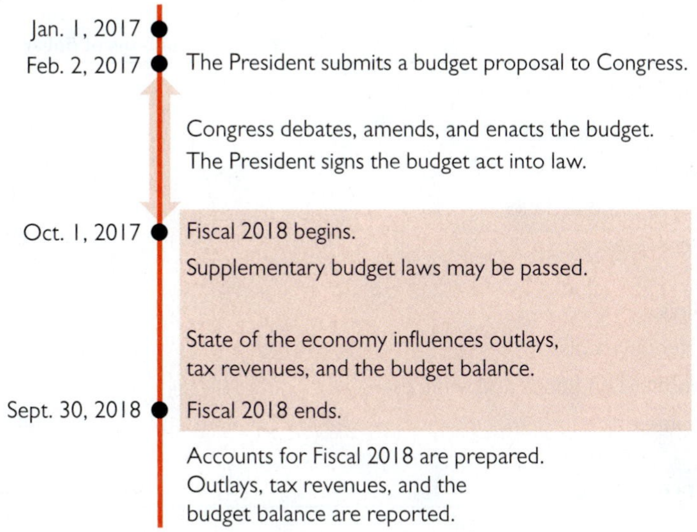

Jan. 1, 2017 ●
Feb. 2, 2017 ●   The President submits a budget proposal to Congress.

Congress debates, amends, and enacts the budget.
The President signs the budget act into law.

Oct. 1, 2017 ●   Fiscal 2018 begins.
Supplementary budget laws may be passed.

State of the economy influences outlays,
tax revenues, and the budget balance.

Sept. 30, 2018 ●   Fiscal 2018 ends.

Accounts for Fiscal 2018 are prepared.
Outlays, tax revenues, and the
budget balance are reported.

The federal budget process begins with the President's proposals in February.

Congress debates and amends the President's proposals and enacts a budget before the start of the fiscal year on October 1.

The President signs the budget act into law.

Throughout the fiscal year, Congress might pass supplementary budget laws. The budget outcome is calculated after the end of the fiscal year.

borrows to finance its budget deficit. When the government has a budget surplus, it repays some of its debt. The amount of government debt outstanding—debt that has arisen from past budget deficits—is called **national debt**.

The national debt at the end of a fiscal year equals the national debt at the end of the previous fiscal year plus the budget deficit or minus the budget surplus. For example,

Debt at the end of 2017 = Debt at the end of 2016 + Budget deficit in 2017.

At the end of the 2016 fiscal year, national debt was $19,433 billion. With a budget deficit of $612 billion in 2017, national debt at the end of the 2017 fiscal year becomes $20,045 billion. That is, $20,045 = $19,433 + $612.

### A Personal Analogy

The government's budget and debt are like your budget and debt, only bigger. If you take a student loan each year to go to school, you have a budget deficit and a growing debt. After graduating, if you have a job and repay some of your loan each year, you have a budget surplus each year and a shrinking debt.

### ■ The Federal Budget in Fiscal 2017

Table 16.1 (on p. 404) shows the magnitudes of the main items in the federal budget in 2017. Personal income taxes and Social Security taxes are the major sources of revenue. **Transfer payments**—Social Security benefits, Medicare and Medicaid benefits, unemployment benefits, and other cash benefits paid to individuals and firms—take the largest share of the government's financial resources. Expenditure on goods and services, which includes the government's defense and homeland security budgets, is also large.

*Eye on the Global Economy* and *Eye on the Past* put the government's revenues, outlays, and deficit in a global and historical perspective.

**National debt**
The amount of government debt outstanding–debt that has arisen from past budget deficits.

**Transfer payments**
Social Security benefits, Medicare and Medicaid benefits, unemployment benefits, and other cash benefits.

■ **TABLE 16.1**

### The Federal Budget in Fiscal 2017

MyEconLab Real-time data

The federal budget for 2017 was expected to be in a deficit. Tax revenues of $3,477 billion were expected to be $612 billion less than outlays of $4,089 billion.

Personal income taxes are the largest revenue source and transfer payments are the largest outlay.

SOURCE OF DATA: *Budget of the United States Government, Fiscal Year 2017.*

| Item | Projections (billions of dollars) |
|---|---|
| **Tax Revenues** | **3,477** |
| Personal income taxes | 1,724 |
| Social Security taxes | 1,185 |
| Corporate income taxes | 343 |
| Indirect taxes | 225 |
| **Outlays** | **4,089** |
| Transfer payments | 2,574 |
| Expenditure on goods and services | 1,211 |
| Debt interest | 304 |
| **Balance** | **−612** |

# EYE on the GLOBAL ECONOMY
## The U.S. Budget in Global Perspective

The United States is not alone in having a government budget deficit. All the major countries share this experience. But the United States has one of the largest budget deficits as a percentage of GDP.

To compare the budget deficits across countries, we use the concept of the "general government" deficit, which combines all levels of government: federal, state, and local.

Japan, the United Kingdom, and the United States have large deficits while Australia, Canada, the newly industrialized Asian economies, and even the Euro area have smaller deficits. New Zealand has a small budget surplus.

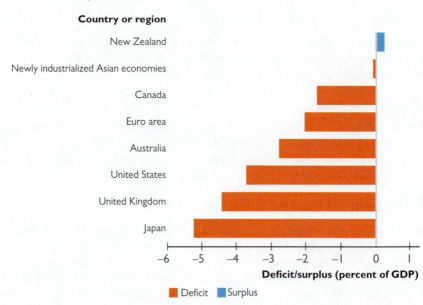

SOURCE OF DATA: International Monetary Fund, *World Economic Outlook*, April 2016.

# EYE on the PAST
## Federal Tax Revenues, Outlays, Deficits, and Debt

Except for a few years at the end of the 1990s, the U.S. federal government has had a budget deficit every year since 1970. You can see this fact in Figure 1, which shows the budget balance along with tax revenues and outlays from 1950 to 2015 all measured as percentages of GDP.

Figure 2 shows national debt as a percentage of GDP—the debt-to-GDP ratio. Gross debt equals Net debt held by the public plus debt held in federal government accounts.

Enormous deficits during World War II had left a legacy of debt equal to more than a year's GDP.

During the 1950s and 1960s, the government's debt-to-GDP ratio tumbled as balanced budgets combined with rapid real GDP growth. By 1974, the debt-to-GDP ratio had fallen to a low of 23 percent.

Budget deficits returned during the 1970s and swelled in the 1980s as the defense budget increased and some tax rates were cut. The result was a growing debt-to-GDP ratio that climbed to almost 50 percent by 1995.

Expenditure restraint combined with sustained real GDP growth lowered the debt-to-GDP ratio during the 1990s, but a surge in expenditures on defense and homeland security, further tax cuts, and a spending surge in 2009 and 2010 to fight the global financial crisis and recession, all combined to raise the debt-to-GDP ratio again.

Since 2010, the government has striven to keep spending under control and gradually shrink the deficit.

Revenues and outlays (percentage of GDP)

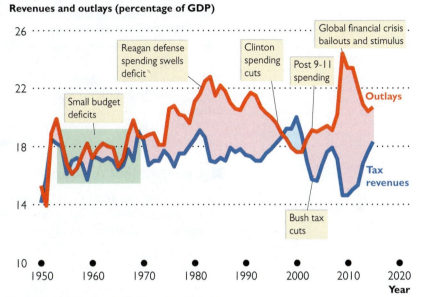

**Figure 1  Tax Revenues, Outlays, and Deficits**

Debt (percentage of GDP)

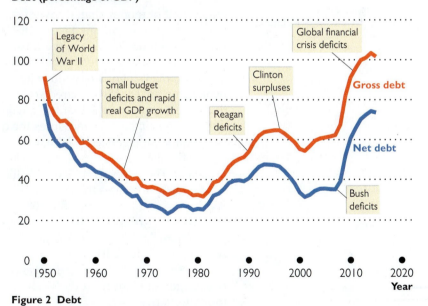

**Figure 2  Debt**

SOURCE OF DATA: *Budget of the U.S. Government, Fiscal Year 2017*, Historical Tables, Tables 7.1 and 14.1.

# ■ A Fiscal Policy Challenge

You've seen that the U.S. government has run a budget deficit and piled up debt for most of the past 40 years. That debt is going to keep growing as deficits become harder to avoid.

The age distribution of the U.S. population is the source of the problem. A surge in the birth rate after World War II created what is called the "baby boom generation." There are 77 million "baby boomers" and the first of them started collecting Social Security pensions in 2008 and became eligible for Medicare benefits in 2011. By 2030, all the baby boomers will be supported by Social Security and, under the existing laws, Medicare benefit payments will have doubled. The aging of the population is going to keep the government's debt rising for many future years.

How big is this debt? And who's going to bear its burden? Will it be borne by the current generation or will it be passed on for a future generation to bear?

# ■ Generational Accounting

To determine the true scale of government obligations and their distribution across generations, we use a tool called *generational accounting*—an accounting system that measures two indicators of the true state of the government's budget::

- Fiscal imbalance
- Generational imbalance

## Fiscal Imbalance

**Fiscal imbalance**
The *present value* of the government's commitments to pay future benefits minus the *present value* of its future tax revenues..

**Fiscal imbalance** is the *present value* of the government's commitments to pay future benefits minus the *present value* of its future tax revenues. A *present value* is an amount of money that, if invested today, will earn interest and grow to equal a required future amount. Fiscal imbalance measures the government's true debt. It measures today's value of the future cost of the programs to which the government is committed minus today's value of the future taxes it will collect.

The government's obligation to pay Social Security pensions and Medicare benefits on an already declared scale are a debt owed by the government and are just as real as the bonds that the government issues to finance its current budget deficit. Fiscal imbalance measures the dollar value of this obligation.

Economist Jagadeesh Gokhale of the Cato Institute has reported an estimate of U.S. fiscal imbalance in his book *The Government Debt Iceberg* (see *Eye on the U.S. Economy*). The government's debt is like an iceberg because most of it is hidden.

Gokhale estimates that the Social Security and Medicare fiscal imbalance was $68 trillion in 2014. To put the $68 trillion in perspective, note that U.S. GDP in 2014 was $17 trillion. So the fiscal imbalance was 4 times the value of one year's production. And the fiscal imbalance grows every year by an amount that in 2014 was approaching $2 trillion.

These are enormous numbers and point to a catastrophic future. How can the federal government meet its Social Security and Medicare obligations? There are four alternative ways:

1. Raise income taxes
2. Raise Social Security taxes
3. Cut Social Security benefits
4. Cut other federal government spending

Because the fiscal imbalance grows every year, delaying a start on tackling the problem increases the scale of the changes needed. If we had started addressing the fiscal imbalance in 2003 and made only one of the four possible changes, income taxes would need to be raised by 69 percent, or Social Security taxes raised by 95 percent, or Social Security benefits cut by 56 percent. Cutting other government spending turns out not to be an effective alternative. Even if the government stopped *all* its other spending, including that on national defense, the saving would not eliminate the imbalance. By combining the four measures, the pain from each could be lessened, but the pain would still be severe.

Why isn't there a fifth option: keep borrowing by selling government bonds? At the current scale of deficit and debt, that option is viable. But at some point, bond holders would see that the government's debt was so large that the government would not be able to pay the interest on it. If that point were reached, the U.S. and global economies would collapse and go into deep recession or even depression.

## Generational Imbalance

A fiscal imbalance must eventually be corrected and when it is, people either pay higher taxes or receive lower benefits. The concept of generational imbalance tells us who will pay. **Generational imbalance** is the division of the fiscal imbalance between the current and future generations.

In the estimates of generational imbalance, the current generation is people born before 1988, and the future generation those born in or after 1988. With division of the population, the current generation will bear most of the cost but the next generation will pick up a big chunk of the Medicare tab.

*Eye on the U.S. Economy* shows an estimate of the scale of fiscal imbalance and how it is distributed across the current and next generation.

**Generational imbalance**
The division of the fiscal imbalance between the current and future generations.

# EYE on the U.S. ECONOMY
## Fiscal and Generational Imbalances

The figure shows how the fiscal imbalance is divided between Social Security benefits and Medicare, and how it is distributed across the current and the next (your) generation.

Medicare is by far the major source of the imbalance.

The current generation will pay for almost all its Social Security but it will not pay for all its Medicare, and much will fall on future generations. If we sum both items, the current generation will pay 83 percent and future generations will pay 17 percent of the fiscal imbalance.

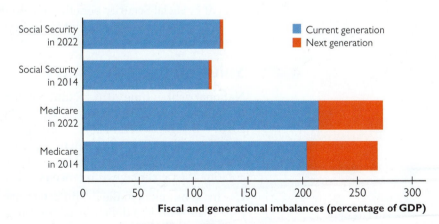

SOURCE OF DATA: Jagadeesh Gokhale, *The Government Debt Iceberg*, The Institute of Economic Affairs, London, 2014.

MyEconLab Study Plan 16.1
Key Terms Quiz
Solutions Video

 # CHECKPOINT 16.1

**Describe the federal budget, the process that creates it, and a challenge that it faces.**

## Practice Problems

1. What are the tax revenues and outlays in the federal budget, and what was the projected budget balance for Fiscal 2017?

2. At the end of Fiscal 2016 national debt was $19.4 trillion. If the budget deficit remains at its Fiscal 2017 level for two years, what will the national debt be at the end of Fiscal 2018?

3. What are the three ways in which the U.S. fiscal imbalance might be successfully addressed?

## In the News

**U.S. budget deficit widens to near two-year high**
Over the year to June 2016, the U.S. federal government deficit totaled $523 billion, which is 20.6 percent higher than a year earlier.
Source: *The Wall Street Journal*, July 13, 2016

Given the information in the news clip, by how much did U.S. national debt change between June 2014 and June 2016?

## Solutions to Practice Problems

1. The tax revenues are personal income taxes, Social Security taxes, corporate income taxes, and indirect taxes; the outlays are transfer payments, expenditure on goods and services, and debt interest. The projected budget balance for Fiscal 2017 was a deficit of $612 billion.

2. At the end of 2016, national debt was $19.4 trillion. The budget deficit in 2017 was $612 billion or $0.6 trillion. Adding $0.6 trillion per year to the 2016 national debt for two years takes the debt to $20.6 trillion at the end of 2018.

3. The three ways in which the U.S. fiscal imbalance might be successfully addressed are 1) a rise in income taxes, 2) a rise in Social Security taxes, and 3) a cut in Social Security benefits. The fourth way of cutting the deficit—cutting other spending—would not be successful because there isn't enough other spending to cut.

## Solution to In the News

National debt in June 2016 = National debt in June 2014 + Budget deficit in 2015 + Budget deficit in 2016. So the change in the national debt from June 2014 to June 2016 = Budget deficit in 2015 + Budget deficit in 2016. The budget deficit in 2016 was $523 billion. The budget deficit in 2015 was 20.6 percent lower than $523 billion, which is $523 billion divided by 1.206 and equals $434 billion. (Check by calculating the percentage difference between $523 and $434.)

Use these numbers in the formula: Change in the national debt from June 2014 to June 2016 = Budget deficit in 2015 + Budget deficit in 2016 = $434 billion + $523 billion = $957 billion.

## 16.2  FISCAL STIMULUS

MyEconLab Concept Video

We've described the federal budget and the institutions that make fiscal policy, and now we're going to study the *effects* of fiscal policy. We begin by exploring its effects on aggregate demand.

### ■ Fiscal Policy and Aggregate Demand

A number of different fiscal policy actions might be used in an attempt to stimulate aggregate demand. Government expenditure on goods and services or government transfer payments might be increased and taxes might be cut. And these changes might occur as an automatic response to the state of the economy or as a result of new spending or tax decisions by Congress.

A fiscal policy action that is triggered by the state of the economy is called an **automatic fiscal policy**. For example, an increase in unemployment induces an increase in transfer payments, and a fall in incomes induces a decrease in tax revenues.

A fiscal policy action that is initiated by an act of Congress is called a **discretionary fiscal policy**. A discretionary fiscal policy action requires a change in a spending program or in a tax law. Increases in defense spending or cuts in the income tax rates are examples of discretionary fiscal policy.

**Automatic fiscal policy**
A fiscal policy action that is triggered by the state of the economy.

**Discretionary fiscal policy**
A fiscal policy action that is initiated by an act of Congress.

### ■ Automatic Fiscal Policy

Automatic fiscal policy is a consequence of tax revenues and outlays that fluctuate with real GDP. These features of fiscal policy are called **automatic stabilizers** because they work to stabilize real GDP without explicit action by the government.

**Automatic stabilizers**
Features of fiscal policy that stabilize real GDP without explicit action by the government.

#### Induced Taxes

On the revenue side of the budget, tax laws define tax *rates*, not tax *dollars*. Tax dollars paid depend on tax rates and incomes. But incomes vary with real GDP, so tax revenues depend on real GDP. Taxes that vary with real GDP are called **induced taxes**. When real GDP increases in an expansion, wages and profits rise, so the taxes paid on these incomes—induced taxes—rise. When real GDP decreases in a recession, wages and profits fall, so the induced taxes on these incomes fall.

**Induced taxes**
Taxes that vary with real GDP.

#### Needs-Tested Spending

On the expenditure side of the budget, the government creates programs that entitle suitably qualified people and businesses to receive benefits. The spending on such programs is called *needs-tested spending*, and it results in transfer payments that depend on the economic state of individual citizens and businesses. In a recession, as the unemployment rate increases, needs-tested spending on unemployment benefits and food stamps increases. In an expansion, the unemployment rate falls and needs-tested spending decreases.

#### Automatic Stimulus

Because government tax revenues fall and outlays increase in a recession, automatic stabilizers provide stimulus that helps to shrink the recessionary gap. Similarly, because tax revenues rise and outlays decrease in a boom, automatic stabilizers shrink an inflationary gap.

### ■ Cyclical and Structural Budget Balances

To identify the government budget deficit that arises from the business cycle, we distinguish between the budget's structural balance and its cyclical balance. The **structural surplus or deficit** is the budget balance that would occur if the economy were at full employment. That is, the structural balance is the balance that the full-employment level of real GDP would generate given the spending programs and tax laws that Congress has created. The **cyclical surplus or deficit** is the budget balance that arises purely because tax revenues and outlays are not at their full-employment levels. That is, the cyclical balance is the balance that arises because tax revenues rise and outlays fall in an inflationary gap and tax revenues fall and outlays rise in a recessionary gap.

The *actual* budget balance equals the sum of the structural balance and cyclical balance. A cyclical deficit corrects itself when full employment returns, but a structural deficit requires action by Congress. *Eye on the U.S. Economy* below looks at the recent history of the U.S. structural and cyclical balances.

**Structural surplus or deficit**
The budget balance that would occur if the economy were at full employment.

**Cyclical surplus or deficit**
The budget balance that arises because tax revenues and outlays are not at their full-employment levels.

## EYE on the U.S. ECONOMY
### The U.S. Structural and Cyclical Budget Balances

The U.S. federal budget balance in 2015 was a deficit of $1 trillion and the recessionary gap was close to $1 trillion. With such a large recessionary gap, you would expect some of the deficit to be cyclical. But how much of the 2015 deficit was cyclical? How much was structural?

According to the Congressional Budget Office (CBO), a quarter of the 2015 deficit was cyclical. The figure shows the actual and cyclical balances as percentages of GDP from 1990 through 2015.

The structural balance equals the actual balance minus the cyclical balance. You can see that the structural deficit was small in 2007, increased in 2008, and exploded in 2009. The 2009 fiscal stimulus package created most of this structural deficit.

When full employment returns, which the CBO says will be in 2018, the cyclical deficit will vanish, but the structural deficit must be addressed by further acts of Congress. No one knows the discretionary measures that will be taken to reduce the structural deficit and this situation creates uncertainty.

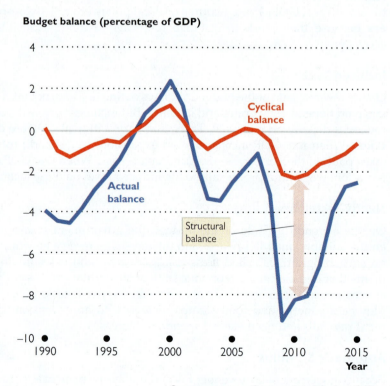

SOURCE OF DATA: Congressional Budget Office.

# ■ Discretionary Fiscal Policy

Discretionary fiscal policy can take the form of a change in government outlays or a change in tax revenues. And a change in government outlays can take the form of a change in expenditure on goods and services or a change in transfer payments. *Other things remaining the same*, a change in any of the items in the government budget changes aggregate demand and has a multiplier effect—aggregate demand changes by a greater amount than the initial change in the item in the government budget. These multiplier effects are similar to the ones that you studied in Chapters 13 and 14. (Other things might not remain the same, and we'll look at some possible offsetting factors after we've explained the basic Keynesian idea.)

## The Government Expenditure Multiplier

The **government expenditure multiplier** is the effect of a change in government expenditure on goods and services on aggregate demand. Government expenditure is a component of aggregate expenditure, so when government expenditure increases, aggregate demand increases. Real GDP increases and induces an increase in consumption expenditure, which brings a further increase in aggregate expenditure. A multiplier process like the one described in Chapter 14 (pp. 366–370) ensues.

**Government expenditure multiplier**
The effect of a change in government expenditure on goods and services on aggregate demand.

## The Tax Multiplier

The **tax multiplier** is the magnification effect of a change in taxes on aggregate demand. A *decrease* in taxes *increases* disposable income, which increases consumption expenditure. A decrease in taxes works like an increase in government expenditure. But the magnitude of the tax multiplier is smaller than the government expenditure multiplier because a $1 tax cut generates *less than* $1 of additional expenditure. The marginal propensity to consume determines the initial increase in expenditure induced by a tax cut and the magnitude of the tax multiplier. For example, if the marginal propensity to consume is 0.75, then the initial increase in consumption expenditure induced by a $1 tax cut is only 75 cents. In this case, the tax multiplier is 0.75 times the magnitude of the government expenditure multiplier.

**Tax multiplier**
The effect of a change in taxes on aggregate demand.

## The Transfer Payments Multiplier

The **transfer payments multiplier** is the effect of a change in transfer payments on aggregate demand. This multiplier works like the tax multiplier but in the opposite direction. An *increase* in transfer payments *increases* disposable income, which *increases* consumption expenditure. The magnitude of the transfer payments multiplier is similar to that of the tax multiplier. Just as a $1 tax cut generates *less than* $1 of additional expenditure, so also does a $1 increase in transfer payments. Again, it is the marginal propensity to consume that determines the increase in expenditure induced by an increase in transfer payments.

**Transfer payments multiplier**
The effect of a change in transfer payments on aggregate demand.

## The Balanced Budget Multiplier

The **balanced budget multiplier** is the magnification effect on aggregate demand of a *simultaneous* change in government expenditure and taxes that leaves the budget balance unchanged. The balanced budget multiplier is not zero. It is greater than zero because a $1 increase in government expenditure injects a dollar more into aggregate demand while a $1 tax rise (or decrease in transfer payments) takes less than $1 from aggregate demand. So when both government expenditure and taxes increase by $1, aggregate demand increases.

**Balanced budget multiplier**
The effect on aggregate demand of a *simultaneous* change in government expenditure and taxes that leaves the budget balance unchanged.

### ■ A Successful Fiscal Stimulus

If real GDP is below potential GDP, the government might pursue a fiscal stimulus by increasing its expenditure on goods and services, increasing transfer payments, cutting taxes, or doing some combination of all three. Figure 16.2 shows us how these actions increase aggregate demand for a successful stimulus package.

In Figure 16.2(a), potential GDP is $16 trillion but real GDP is only $15 trillion. The economy is at point $A$ and there is a *recessionary gap* (see Chapter 13, p. 341).

To eliminate the recessionary gap and restore full employment, the government introduces a fiscal stimulus. An increase in government expenditure or a tax cut increases aggregate expenditure by $\Delta E$. If this were the only change in spending plans, the $AD$ curve would become $AD_0 + \Delta E$ in Figure 16.2(b). But the initial increase in government expenditure sets off a multiplier process, which increases consumption expenditure. As the multiplier process plays out, aggregate demand increases and the $AD$ curve shifts rightward to $AD_1$.

With no change in the price level, the economy would move from the initial point $A$ to point $B$ on $AD_1$. But the increase in aggregate demand combined with the upward-sloping aggregate supply curve brings a rise in the price level, and the economy moves to a new equilibrium at point C. The price level rises to 105, real GDP increases to $16 trillion, and the economy returns to full employment.

*The "Cash for Clunkers" program stimulated aggregate demand.*

### ■ FIGURE 16.2

Fiscal Stimulus in the *AS-AD* Model

MyEconLab Animation

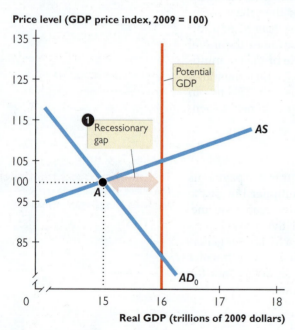

**(a) Below full-employment equilibrium**

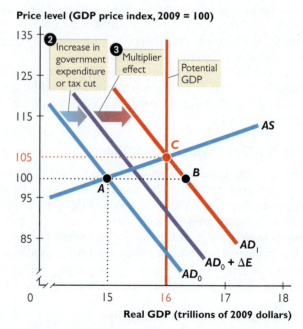

**(b) Potential GDP**

Potential GDP is $16 trillion. At point $A$, real GDP is $15 trillion, and ❶ there is a $1 trillion recessionary gap. ❷ An increase in government expenditure or a tax cut increases expenditure by $\Delta E$.

❸ The multiplier increases induced expenditure. The $AD$ curve shifts rightward to $AD_1$, the price level rises to 105, real GDP increases to $16 trillion, and the recessionary gap is eliminated.

# EYE on FISCAL STIMULUS

MyEconLab Critical Thinking Exercise

## Can Fiscal Stimulus End a Recession?

In February 2009, in the depths of the 2008–2009 recession, Congress passed the American Recovery and Reinvestment Act, a $787 billion fiscal stimulus package that the President signed at an economic forum in Denver.

This act of Congress is an example of discretionary fiscal policy. Did this action by Congress contribute to ending the 2008–2009 recession and making the recession less severe than it might have been?

The Obama Administration economists are confident that the answer is yes: The stimulus package made a significant contribution to easing and ending the recession.

But many, and perhaps most, economists think that the stimulus package played a small role and that the truly big story is not discretionary fiscal policy but the role played by automatic stabilizers.

Let's take a closer look at the fiscal policy actions and their likely effects.

### Discretionary Fiscal Policy

In a number of speeches, President Obama promised that fiscal stimulus would save or create 650,000 jobs by the end of the 2009 summer. In October 2009, the Administration economists declared the promise fulfilled. Fiscal stimulus had saved or created the promised 650,000 jobs.

This claim of success might be correct but it isn't startling and it isn't a huge claim. To see why, start by asking

how much GDP 650,000 people would produce. In 2009, each employed person produced $100,000 of real GDP on average. So 650,000 people would produce $65 billion of GDP.

Although the fiscal stimulus passed by Congress totalled $787 billion, by October 2009 only 20 percent of the stimulus had been spent (or taken in tax breaks). So the stimulus was about $160 billion.

If government outlays of $160 billion created $65 billion of GDP, the multiplier was 0.4 (65/160 = 0.4).

This multiplier is much smaller than the 1.6 that the Obama economists say will eventually occur. They believe, like Keynes, that the multiplier starts out small and gets larger over time as spending plans respond to rising incomes. An initial increase in expenditure increases aggregate expenditure. But the increase in aggregate expenditure generates higher incomes, which in turn induces greater consumption expenditure.

### Automatic Fiscal Policy

Government revenue is sensitive to the state of the economy. When personal incomes and corporate profits fall, income tax revenues fall too. When unemployment increases, outlays on unemployment benefits and other social welfare benefits increase. These fiscal policy changes are automatic. They occur with speed and without help from Congress.

The scale of automatic fiscal policy changes depends on the depth of recession. In 2009, real GDP sank to 6 percent below potential GDP—a recessionary gap of $800 billion.

Responding to this deep recession, tax revenues crashed and transfer payments skyrocketed. The figure below shows the magnitudes as percentages of GDP. You can see that the automatic stabilizers were much bigger than the discretionary actions—six times as large. This automatic action, not the stimulus package, played the major role in limiting job losses.

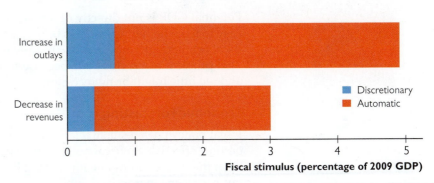

SOURCES OF DATA: Budget of the United States, 2010, Bureau of Economic Analysis, and White House press releases.

# ■ Limitations of Discretionary Fiscal Policy

Discretionary fiscal stabilization policy looks easy. Calculate the output gap and the multiplier, and determine the direction and size of the change in government expenditure or taxes that will eliminate the gap. In reality, discretionary fiscal policy is seriously hampered by many factors, four of which are

- Lawmaking time lag
- Shrinking area of lawmaker discretion
- Estimating potential GDP
- Economic forecasting

## Lawmaking Time Lag

The lawmaking time lag is the amount of time it takes Congress to pass the laws needed to change taxes or spending. This process takes time because each member of Congress has a different idea about what is the best tax or spending program to change, so long debates and committee meetings are needed to reconcile conflicting views. The economy might benefit from fiscal stimulation today, but by the time Congress acts, a different fiscal medicine might be needed.

## Shrinking Area of Lawmaker Discretion

During the 2000s, federal spending increased faster than in any other peacetime period. This growth in spending was driven by two forces: increased security threats and an aging population.

The increased security threat resulted in a large increase in expenditure on the military and homeland security. The aging population brought a very large increase in expenditure on entitlement programs such as Medicare.

The growth of this spending has reduced the areas in which Congress can act to change either taxes or outlays. Around 80 percent of the federal budget is effectively off limits for discretionary policy action, and the remaining 20 percent of items are very hard to cut.

So even if the state of the economy calls for a change in fiscal policy, Congress's room to maneuver is severely limited.

## Estimating Potential GDP

Potential GDP is not directly observed, so it must be estimated. Because it is not easy to tell whether real GDP is below, above, or at potential GDP, a discretionary fiscal action might move real GDP *away* from potential GDP instead of toward it. This problem is a serious one because too large a fiscal stimulus brings inflation and too little might bring recession.

## Economic Forecasting

Fiscal policy changes take a long time to enact in Congress and yet more time to become effective. So fiscal policy must target forecasts of where the economy will be in the future. Economic forecasting has improved enormously in recent years, but it remains inexact and subject to error. So for a second reason, discretionary fiscal action might move real GDP *away* from potential GDP and create the very problems that it seeks to correct.

Further problems with discretionary fiscal policy actions arise from their supply-side effects that we will examine in the next section.

# CHECKPOINT 16.2

**Explain how fiscal stimulus is used to fight a recession.**

## Practice Problems

1. Classify the following items as automatic fiscal policy, discretionary fiscal policy, or not part of fiscal policy.
   - A decrease in tax revenues in a recession
   - Additional government expenditure to upgrade highways
   - An increase in the public education budget
   - A cut in infrastructure expenditure during a boom

2. Explain how aggregate demand changes when government expenditure on national defense increases by $100 billion.

3. Explain how aggregate demand changes when the government increases taxes by $100 billion.

4. Explain how aggregate demand changes when the government increases both expenditure on goods and services and taxes by $100 billion.

## In the News

**Clinton and Trump on fiscal policy**
In the 2016 Presidential election campaign, both Hillary Clinton and Donald Trump committed to big government infrastructure spending and tax cuts.
Source: *The Wall Street Journal*, July 27, 2016

What policy will change aggregate demand the most: an increase in infrastructure spending or a cut in taxes?

## Solutions to Practice Problems

1. A decrease in tax revenues in a recession is an automatic fiscal policy.
   Expenditure to upgrade highways is a discretionary fiscal policy.
   An increase in the public education budget is a discretionary fiscal policy.
   A cut in infrastructure expenditure is a discretionary fiscal policy.

2. Aggregate demand increases by more than $100 billion because government expenditure increases induced expenditure.

3. Aggregate demand decreases but by less than $100 billion because the tax increase decreases disposable income, which decreases induced expenditure.

4. An increase in government expenditure of $100 billion increases aggregate demand by more than $100 billion. An increase in taxes of $100 billion decreases aggregate demand by less than $100 billion. The increase is greater than the decrease, so together aggregate demand increases. The balanced budget multiplier is positive.

## Solution to In the News

Infrastructure spending is expenditure on goods and services and its effect on aggregate demand is determined by the *government expenditure multiplier*. The effect of a decrease in taxes on aggregate demand is determined by the *tax multiplier*. The magnitude of the government expenditure multiplier exceeds the tax multiplier, so infrastructure spending will increase aggregate demand by more than a tax cut of the same magnitude.

MyEconLab Concept Video

# 16.3 THE SUPPLY SIDE: POTENTIAL GDP AND GROWTH

You've seen how fiscal policy can influence the output gap by changing aggregate demand and real GDP relative to potential GDP. But fiscal policy also influences potential GDP and the growth rate of potential GDP. These influences on potential GDP and economic growth arise because the government provides public goods and services that increase productivity and because taxes change the incentives that people face. These influences, called **supply-side effects**, operate more slowly than the demand-side effects emphasized by Keynesians. Supply-side effects are often ignored in times of recession when the focus is on fiscal stimulus and restoring full employment. But in the long run, the supply-side effects of fiscal policy dominate and determine potential GDP.

We'll begin an account of the supply side with a brief explanation of how full employment and potential GDP are determined in the absence of government services and taxes. Then we'll see how government services and taxes change employment and potential GDP.

**Supply-side effects**
The effects of fiscal policy on potential GDP and the economic growth rate.

## ■ Full Employment and Potential GDP

The quantity of labor demanded and the quantity of labor supplied depend on the real wage rate. The higher the real wage rate, other things remaining the same, the smaller is the quantity of labor demanded and the greater is the quantity of labor supplied. When the real wage rate has adjusted to make the quantity of labor demanded equal to the quantity of labor supplied, there is full employment. And when the quantity of labor is the full-employment quantity, real GDP equals potential GDP.

This brief description of how potential GDP and the full-employment quantity of labor are determined is a summary of the more detailed account in Chapter 8 (pp. 195–201).

How do taxes and the provision of government services—the elements of fiscal policy—influence employment and potential GDP?

## ■ Fiscal Policy, Employment, and Potential GDP

Both sides of the government budget influence potential GDP. The expenditure side provides public goods and services that enhance productivity and make labor more productive. The revenue side levies taxes that modify incentives that change the full-employment quantities of labor, as well as the amount of saving and investment.

### Public Goods and Productivity

Governments provide a legal system and other infrastructure services such as roads and highways, fire-fighting and policing services, and national security, all of which increase the nation's productive potential. Today's world provides a vivid demonstration of the role that good government plays in enhancing productivity. Compare the chaos and absence of productivity in parts of the Middle East and Africa with the order and calm and the productivity they permit in the United States and other industrialized countries.

Public goods and services, financed by the government budget, increase the real GDP that a given amount of labor can produce. So the provision of public goods and services increases potential GDP.

## Taxes and Incentives

A tax drives a wedge—called the **tax wedge**—between the price paid by a buyer and the price received by a seller. In the labor market, the income tax drives a wedge between the cost of labor to employers and the take-home pay of workers and decreases the equilibrium quantity of labor employed. A smaller quantity of labor produces a smaller amount of real GDP, so taxes lower potential GDP.

The income tax wedge is only a part of the tax wedge that affects decisions to supply labor. Taxes on expenditure also create a tax wedge that affects employment and potential GDP.

Taxes on consumption expenditure add to the tax wedge that lowers potential GDP. The reason is that a tax on consumption expenditure raises the prices paid for consumption goods and services and is equivalent to a cut in the real wage rate. The incentive to supply labor depends on the goods and services that an hour of labor can buy. The higher the tax on consumption expenditure, the smaller is the quantity of goods and services that an hour of labor buys and the weaker is the incentive to supply labor.

The expenditure tax rate must be added to the income tax rate to find the total tax wedge. If the income tax rate is 25 percent and the tax rate on consumption expenditure is 10 percent, a dollar earned buys only 65 cents worth of goods and services. The tax wedge is 35 percent.

**Tax wedge**
The gap created by a tax between what a buyer pays and what a seller receives. In the labor market, it is the gap between the before-tax wage rate and the after-tax wage rate.

# EYE on the GLOBAL ECONOMY
## Some Real-World Tax Wedges

Edward C. Prescott of the Arizona State University, who shared the 2004 Nobel Prize for Economic Science, has estimated the tax wedges for a number of countries. The U.S. tax wedge is a combination of consumption taxes, income taxes, and Social Security taxes.

Among the industrial countries, the U.S. tax wedge is relatively small. Prescott estimates that in France, (marginal) taxes on consumption are 33 percent and taxes on incomes are 49 percent. The estimates for the United Kingdom fall between those for France and the United States. The figure shows these components of the tax wedges in the three countries.

According to Prescott's estimates, the tax wedge has a powerful effect on

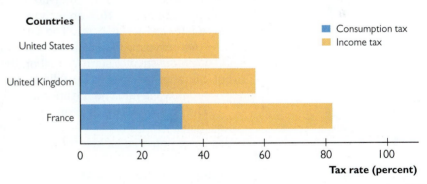

SOURCE OF DATA: Edward C. Prescott, *American Economic Review*, 2003.

employment and potential GDP. Potential GDP per person in France is lower than that of the United States, and the entire difference can be attributed to the difference in the tax wedge in the two countries.

Potential GDP per person in the United Kingdom is lower than that of the United States, and about a third of the difference arises from the different tax wedges. (The rest is due to different productivities.)

## ■ Fiscal Policy and Potential GDP: A Graphical Analysis

Figure 16.3 illustrates the effects of fiscal policy on potential GDP. It begins with the economy at full employment and with no income tax.

### Full Employment With No Income Tax

In part (a), the demand for labor curve is *LD*, and the supply of labor curve is *LS*. The equilibrium real wage rate is $30 an hour, and 250 billion hours of labor a year are employed. The economy is at full employment. In Figure 16.3(b), the production function is *PF*. (This production function incorporates the productivity of an efficient provision of public services.) When 250 billion hours of labor are employed, real GDP—which is also potential GDP—is $18 trillion.

Let's now see how an income tax changes potential GDP.

### The Effects of the Income Tax

The tax on labor income influences potential GDP by changing the full-employment quantity of labor. The income tax weakens the incentive to work and drives a wedge between the take-home wage of workers and the cost of labor to firms. The result is a smaller quantity of labor employed and a smaller potential GDP. Figure 16.3 shows this outcome.

In the labor market in part (a), the income tax has no effect on the demand for labor because the quantity of labor that firms plan to hire depends only on how productive labor is and what labor costs—the real wage rate. The demand for labor curve remains at *LD*.

But the income tax changes the supply of labor. With no income tax, the real wage rate is $30 an hour and 250 billion hours of labor a year are employed. An income tax weakens the incentive to work. Workers must pay the government part of each dollar of the before-tax wage rate, as determined by the income tax code. Workers look at the after-tax wage rate when they decide how much labor to supply. In Figure 16.3, an income tax of $15 an hour shifts the supply of labor curve leftward to *LS* + *tax*. The vertical distance between the *LS* curve and the *LS* + *tax* curve measures the $15 of income tax.

With the smaller supply of labor, the before-tax wage rate rises to $35 an hour but the after-tax wage rate falls to $20 an hour. The gap created between the before-tax wage rate and the after-tax wage rate is the *tax wedge*.

The new equilibrium quantity of labor employed is 200 billion hours a year—less than in the no-tax case. This decrease in the full-employment quantity of labor decreases potential GDP as shown in Figure 16.3(b).

### Changes in the Tax Rate

A change in the income tax rate changes equilibrium employment and potential GDP. In the example that you've just worked through, the tax rate is about 43 percent—a $15 tax on a $35 wage rate. If the income tax rate is increased, the supply of labor decreases yet more and the *LS* + *tax* curve shifts farther leftward. Equilibrium employment and potential GDP decrease.

If the income tax rate is decreased, the supply of labor increases and the *LS* + *tax* curve shifts rightward. Equilibrium employment and potential GDP increase.

You can now see that a tax cut has two effects: It increases aggregate demand by boosting consumption expenditure and it increases potential GDP.

■ **FIGURE 16.3**

Fiscal Policy and Potential GDP

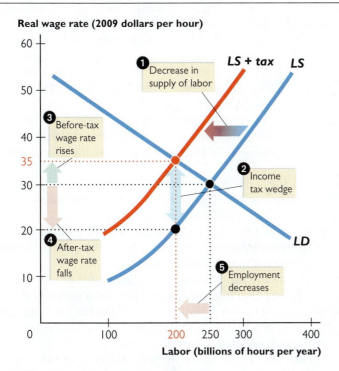

**(a) Income tax in the labor market**

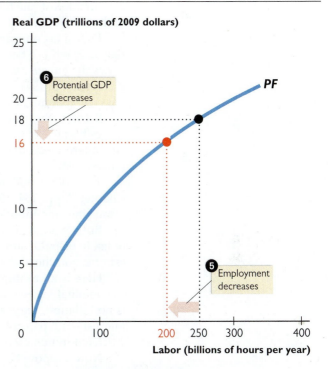

**(b) Income tax and potential GDP**

In part (a), the demand for labor is *LD* and the supply of labor is *LS*. With no income tax, the equilibrium real wage rate is $30 an hour and employment is 250 billion hours. In part (b), the production function, *PF*, tells us that 250 billion hours of labor (full employment of labor) produces a potential GDP of $18 trillion.

An income tax ❶ decreases the supply of labor and creates ❷ an income tax wedge between the wage that firms pay and the wage that workers receive. ❸ The before-tax wage rate paid by employers rises and ❹ the after-tax wage rate received by workers falls. ❺ Employment decreases and ❻ potential GDP decreases.

■ **Taxes, Deficits, and Economic Growth**

You've just seen how taxes can change incentives in the labor market and influence potential GDP. Taxes also affect the market for financial capital, which influences the amount of saving and investment; and saving and investment in turn affect the pace of capital accumulation and the economic growth rate.

Fiscal policy influences the economic growth rate in two ways:

First, taxes drive a wedge between the interest rate paid by borrowers and the interest rate received by lenders. This wedge lowers the amount of saving and investment and slows the economic growth rate.

Second, if the government has a budget deficit, then government borrowing to finance the deficit competes with firms' borrowing to finance investment and to some degree, government borrowing "crowds out" private investment.

Let's examine these two influences on economic growth a bit more closely.

### Interest Rate Tax Wedge

Lenders pay an income tax on the interest they receive from borrowers, which creates an interest rate tax wedge. The effects of this tax wedge are analogous to those of the tax wedge on labor income. But they are more serious for two reasons.

First, a tax on wages lowers the quantity of labor employed and lowers potential GDP, while a tax on interest lowers the quantity of saving and investment and slows the *growth rate of real GDP*. A tax on interest income creates a Lucas wedge (Chapter 8, p. 194)—an ever-widening gap between potential GDP and the potential GDP that might have been.

Second, the true tax rate on interest income is much higher than that on wages because of the way in which inflation and taxes on the interest rate interact. The interest rate that influences investment and saving plans is the *after-tax real interest rate*.

The *real interest rate* equals the *nominal interest rate* minus the *inflation rate* (see Chapter 7, pp. 184–185). The *after-tax real interest rate* equals the *real interest rate* minus the amount of *income tax paid on interest income*.

But the nominal interest rate, not the real interest rate, determines the amount of tax to be paid; and the higher the inflation rate, the higher is the nominal interest rate, and the higher is the true tax rate on interest income.

Here is an example. Suppose the tax rate on interest income is 40 percent of the nominal interest rate. If the nominal interest rate is 4 percent a year and there is no inflation, the real interest rate is also 4 percent a year. The tax on 4 percent interest is 1.6 percent (40 percent of 4 percent), so the after-tax real interest rate is 4 percent minus 1.6 percent, which equals 2.4 percent a year.

Now suppose that the nominal interest rate is 10 percent a year and the inflation rate is 6 percent a year, so the real interest rate is still 4 percent a year. The tax on 10 percent interest is 4 percent (40 percent of 10 percent), so now the after-tax real interest rate is 4 percent minus 4 percent, which equals zero. The true tax rate in this case is not 40 percent but 100 percent!

Even modest inflation makes the true tax rate on interest income extremely high and results in a smaller equilibrium quantity of saving and investment, a slower rate of capital accumulation, and a slower growth rate of real GDP.

### Deficits and Crowding Out

With no change in the government's outlays, a tax cut that increases the budget deficit brings an increase in the demand for loanable funds. (You learned about this effect of a government budget deficit in Chapter 10, pp. 261–262.) An increase in the demand for loanable funds raises the real interest rate and crowds out private investment. There is uncertainty about the magnitude of the crowding-out effect but no doubt about its presence.

You can see that this effect of an income tax cut works against the incentive effect. A lower income tax rate shrinks the tax wedge and stimulates employment, saving, and investment, but a higher budget deficit crowds out some investment.

## ◼ The Supply-Side Debate

Before 1980, few economists paid attention to the supply-side effects of taxes on employment and potential GDP. Then, when Ronald Reagan took office as President, a group of supply-siders began to argue the virtues of cutting taxes. Arthur Laffer was one of them. Laffer and his supporters were not held in high esteem among mainstream economists, but they did become influential for a period. They correctly argued that tax cuts would increase employment and increase output. But they incorrectly argued that tax cuts would increase tax revenues by enough to decrease the budget deficit. Given that U.S. tax rates are among the lowest in the industrial world, it is unlikely that tax cuts would increase tax revenues. When the Reagan administration did cut taxes, the budget deficit increased, a fact that reinforces this view.

Supply-side economics became tarnished because of its association with Laffer and came to be called "voodoo economics." But mainstream economists, including Martin Feldstein, a Harvard professor who was Reagan's chief economic adviser, recognized the power of tax cuts as incentives but took the standard view that tax cuts without spending cuts would swell the budget deficit and bring a crowding-out effect. This view is now widely accepted by economists on both sides of the political debate.

## ■ Long-Run Fiscal Policy Effects

The long-run consequences of fiscal policy are the most profound ones. If investment is crowded out by a large budget deficit, the economic growth rate slows and potential GDP gets ever farther below what it might have been as the Lucas wedge widens. If a large budget deficit persists so that debt increases, confidence in the value of money is eroded and inflation erupts. History provides many examples of this consequence of a fiscal stimulus that gets out of control. It is these long-run effects of fiscal policy that make it vital to keep government outlays and budget deficits under control and to have a plan for restoring a balanced budget at full employment.

## EYE on YOUR LIFE

MyEconLab Critical Thinking Exercise

### Your Views on Fiscal Policy and How Fiscal Policy Affects You

Consider the U.S. economy right now. Using all the knowledge that you have accumulated during your course and by reading or watching the current news, try to determine the macroeconomic policy issues that face the U.S. economy today.

Do we have a business-cycle problem? Does the economy have a recessionary gap or an inflationary gap, or is the economy back at full employment?

Do we have a productivity problem? Is potential GDP either too low or growing too slowly?

In light of your assessment of the current state of the U.S. economy, what type of fiscal policy would you recommend and vote for?

Are you more concerned about the provision of public services, the size of the budget deficit, or the size of the tax wedge?

If you are more concerned about the provision of public services, would your preferred package include increased spending? If so, on what programs? How would you pay for the expenditure?

If you are more concerned about the size of the budget deficit, how would you propose lowering it?

If you are more concerned about the tax wedge, would your preferred fiscal package include tax cuts? If it would, what public services would you cut to achieve lower taxes?

Consider recent changes in fiscal policy that you have seen reported in the media. What do you think these changes say about the federal government's views of the state of the economy? Do these views agree with yours?

Thinking further about the recent changes in fiscal policy: How do you expect these changes to affect you? How might your spending, saving, and labor supply decisions change?

Using your own responses to fiscal policy changes as an example, are these policy changes influencing aggregate demand, aggregate supply, or both? How do you think they will change real GDP?

MyEconLab Study Plan 16.3

Key Terms Quiz

Solutions Video

 # CHECKPOINT 16.3

**Explain the supply-side effects of fiscal policy on employment, potential GDP, and the economic growth rate.**

## Practice Problems

1.  The government cuts the income tax rate. Explain the effects of this action on the supply of labor, demand for labor, equilibrium employment, the real wage rate, and potential GDP.

2.  What is the true income tax rate on interest income if the nominal interest rate is 8 percent a year, the inflation rate is 5 percent a year, and the tax rate on nominal interest is 25 percent?

3.  If the government cuts its outlays but tax revenue is unchanged, explain the effects on saving, investment, the real interest rate, and the growth rate of real GDP.

## In the News

### New Social Security bill raises payroll tax cap

Currently the 12.4 percent Social Security tax applies only on earnings up to $118,500. The House of Representatives wants to expand the tax and make it apply to higher earnings and eventually, by 2021, to apply it to earnings up to $308,750.

Source: *Investopedia*, July 29, 2016

Explain how the expanded payroll tax will influence employment and potential GDP.

## Solutions to Practice Problems

1.  When the government cuts the income tax rate, the supply of labor increases but the demand for labor does not change. The equilibrium level of employment increases. The real wage rate paid by employers decreases and the real wage rate received by workers increases—the tax wedge shrinks. With increased employment, potential GDP increases.

2.  The true tax is 66.67 percent. With a nominal interest rate of 8 percent a year and a tax rate of 25 percent, the tax paid is 25 percent of 8 percent, which is 2 percent. The before-tax real interest rate is 8 percent minus 5 percent, which is 3 percent a year. The true tax paid is 2 percent tax divided by 3 percent before-tax real interest rate, or 66.67 percent.

3.  If the government cuts outlays but tax revenue is unchanged, the budget deficit decreases or the budget surplus increases. Either way, in the loanable funds market, the real interest rate falls and private saving decreases, but total saving and investment increase. With greater investment, capital grows more quickly, and so does real GDP.

## Solution to In the News

The expanded payroll tax will increase the tax wedge and raise the cost of labor. It will decrease the quantity of labor demanded and decrease the equilibrium employment. With a decrease in employment, potential GDP will decrease.

CHAPTER SUMMARY

## Key Points

**1. Describe the federal budget, the process that creates it, and a challenge that it faces.**

- The federal budget is an annual statement of the outlays, tax revenues, and budget surplus or deficit of the government of the United States.
- Fiscal policy is the use of the federal budget to finance the federal government and to influence macroeconomic performance.
- An ever rising national debt and large fiscal imbalance is a major fiscal policy challenge.

**2. Explain how fiscal stimulus is used to fight a recession.**

- Fiscal policy can be either discretionary or automatic.
- Changes in government expenditure and changes in taxes have multiplier effects on aggregate demand and can be used to try to keep real GDP at potential GDP.
- In practice, lawmaking time lags, a shrinking area of lawmaker discretion, the difficulty of estimating potential GDP, and the limitations of economic forecasting seriously hamper discretionary fiscal policy.
- Automatic stabilizers arise because tax revenues and outlays fluctuate with real GDP.

**3. Explain the supply-side effects of fiscal policy on employment, potential GDP, and the economic growth rate.**

- The provision of public goods and services increases productivity and increases potential GDP.
- Income taxes create a wedge between the wage rate paid by firms and received by workers and lower both employment and potential GDP.
- Income taxes create a wedge between the interest rate paid by firms and received by lenders and lower saving and investment and the growth rate of real GDP.
- A government budget deficit raises the real interest rate and crowds out some private investment, which slows real GDP growth.

## Key Terms

MyEconLab Key Terms Quiz

Automatic fiscal policy, 409
Automatic stabilizers, 409
Balanced budget multiplier, 411
Budget balance, 402
Cyclical surplus or deficit, 410
Discretionary fiscal policy, 409
Fiscal imbalance, 406

Fiscal policy, 402
Generational imbalance, 407
Government expenditure multiplier, 411
Induced taxes, 409
National debt, 403
Structural surplus or deficit, 410

Supply-side effects, 416
Tax multiplier, 411
Tax wedge, 417
Transfer payments, 403
Transfer payments multiplier, 411

CHAPTER CHECKPOINT

## Study Plan Problems and Applications

1. Suppose that in an economy, investment is $400 billion, saving is $400 billion, tax revenues are $500 billion, exports are $300 billion, and imports are $200 billion. Calculate government expenditure and the government's budget balance.

2. Classify the following items as automatic fiscal policy actions, discretionary fiscal policy actions, or neither.
   - An increase in expenditure on homeland security
   - An increase in unemployment benefits paid during a recession
   - Decreased expenditures on national defense during peace time
   - An increase in Medicaid expenditure brought about by a flu epidemic
   - A cut in farm subsidies

3. The U.S. economy is in recession and has a large recessionary gap. Describe what automatic fiscal policy might occur. Describe a fiscal stimulus that could be used that would not increase the budget deficit.

OilPatch is a mineral rich economy in which the government gets most of its tax revenue from oil royalties. But OilPatch has an income tax. Table 1 describes the labor market in OilPatch and Table 2 describes the economy's production function. The government introduces an income tax of $2 per hour worked. Use Tables 1 and 2 to work Problems 4 to 6.

4. What are the levels of employment and potential GDP in OilPatch, what is the real wage rate paid by employers, and what is the after-tax real wage rate received by workers?

5. If OilPatch eliminates its income tax, what then are the levels of employment and potential GDP and what is the real wage rate in OilPatch?

6. If OilPatch doubles its income tax to $4 an hour, what then are the levels of employment and potential GDP? What is the real wage rate paid by employers and the after-tax real wage rate received by workers?

7. The income tax rate on all forms of income is 40 percent and there is a tax of 10 percent on all consumption expenditure. The nominal interest rate is 7 percent a year and the inflation rate is 5 percent a year. What is the size of the tax wedge on wages and what is the true tax rate on interest income?

8. **The global economy is in bad shape and getting worse**
   The world economy is growing slowly and productive public investment that boosts both the demand and supply sides of the economy is not being used, either because debts are high or because governments are misguidedly pursuing austerity.

   Source: *MarketWatch*, May 2, 2016
   Explain the effects of public investment on aggregate demand and supply.

9. The Canadian Prime Minister Stephen Harper warned on November 6, 2008, that if policy makers adopt too strong a fiscal stimulus, then long-term growth might be jeopardized. Explain what he meant.

10. Read *Eye on Fiscal Stimulus* on p. 413. How big was the fiscal stimulus package of 2008–2009, how many jobs was it expected to create, and how large was the multiplier implied by that expectation? Did the stimulus work?

### TABLE 1  LABOR MARKET

| Real wage rate (dollars per hour) | Quantity of labor demanded (thousands of hours) | supplied (thousands of hours) |
|---|---|---|
| 10 | 6 | 2 |
| 11 | 5 | 3 |
| 12 | 4 | 4 |
| 13 | 3 | 5 |
| 14 | 2 | 6 |
| 15 | 1 | 7 |

### TABLE 2  PRODUCTION FUNCTION

| Employment (thousands of hours) | Real GDP (millions of dollars) |
|---|---|
| 2 | 6 |
| 3 | 11 |
| 4 | 15 |
| 5 | 18 |
| 6 | 20 |
| 7 | 21 |

# Instructor Assignable Problems and Applications

MyEconLab Homework, Quiz, or Test if assigned by instructor

**1.** From the peak in 1929 to the Great Depression trough in 1933, government tax revenues fell by 1.9 percent of GDP and government expenditure increased by 0.3 percent. Real GDP fell by 25 percent. Compare and contrast this experience with the fiscal policy that accompanied the 2008–2009 recession. What did fiscal policy do to moderate the last recession that was largely absent during the Great Depression?

**2.** Suppose that the U.S. government increases its expenditure on highways and bridges by $100 billion. Explain the effect that this expenditure would have on aggregate demand and real GDP.

**3.** Suppose that the U.S. government increases its expenditure on highways and bridges by $100 billion. Explain the effect that this expenditure would have on needs-tested spending and the government's budget balance.

Table 1 describes the labor market in LowTaxLand and Table 2 describes the economy's production function. LowTaxLand introduces an income tax of $1 per hour worked. Use Tables 1 and 2 to work Problems **4** to **6**.

**4.** What are the levels of employment and potential GDP in LowTaxLand, what is the real wage rate paid by employers, and what is the after-tax real wage rate received by workers?

**5.** If LowTaxLand eliminates its income tax, what then are the levels of employment and potential GDP and what is the real wage rate in LowTaxLand?

**6.** If LowTaxLand doubles its income tax to $2 an hour, what then are the levels of employment and potential GDP? What is the real wage rate paid by employers and the after-tax real wage rate received by workers?

**7.** Describe the supply-side effects of a fiscal stimulus and explain how a tax cut will influence potential GDP.

**8.** Use an aggregate supply–aggregate demand graph to illustrate the effects on real GDP and the price level of a fiscal stimulus when the economy is in recession.

Use the following information to work Problems **9** to **11**.

**CBO expects higher long-term deficits**
The Congressional Budget Office (CBO) says the national debt is on an upward path and will hit 122 percent of GDP in 2040. Healthcare programs and Social Security benefits are the large drivers of spending over the coming decades.
Source: *The Wall Street Journal*, July 12, 2016

**9.** Explain why the national debt does not measure the federal government's true indebtedness. How does the nation's fiscal imbalance provide a more accurate account of government's debt?

**10.** If the government decided to slow the growth of debt by cutting transfer payments and raising taxes by the same amount, how would this fiscal policy influence the budget deficit and real GDP?

**11.** How do healthcare programs and Social Security benefits drive spending and the deficit and how do they create fiscal imbalance and generational imbalance?

**TABLE 1  LABOR MARKET**

| Real wage rate (dollars per hour) | Quantity of labor demanded | supplied |
|---|---|---|
| | (thousands of hours) | |
| 10.00 | 18 | 6 |
| 10.50 | 15 | 9 |
| 11.00 | 12 | 12 |
| 11.50 | 9 | 15 |
| 12.00 | 6 | 18 |
| 12.50 | 3 | 21 |

**TABLE 2  PRODUCTION FUNCTION**

| Employment (thousands of hours) | Real GDP (millions of dollars) |
|---|---|
| 6 | 7 |
| 9 | 12 |
| 12 | 16 |
| 15 | 19 |
| 18 | 21 |
| 21 | 22 |

MyEconLab Chapter 16 Study Plan

## Multiple Choice Quiz

**1.** The federal government's major outlay in its budget is _____ and its major source of revenue is _____.

    A. debt interest; sales of government bonds
    B. expenditure on goods and services; taxes on goods and services
    C. Social Security and other benefits; personal income taxes
    D. subsidies to farmers; corporate taxes

**2.** U.S. national debt _____ when the federal government's _____.

    A. increases; outlays exceed tax revenue
    B. decreases; outlays exceed tax revenue
    C. increases; tax revenue rises faster than outlays
    D. decreases; tax revenue rises faster than outlays

**3.** Discretionary fiscal policy to stimulate the economy includes _____.

    A. lowering the tax rate paid by households with middle incomes
    B. raising the tax on gasoline
    C. the fall in tax revenue as the economy goes into recession
    D. the rise in tax revenue collected from businesses as their profits increase

**4.** Automatic fiscal policy _____.

    A. requires an action of the government
    B. is weak unless the government cuts its outlays to reduce the deficit
    C. operates as the economy moves along its business cycle
    D. reduces the deficit as the economy goes into recession

**5.** Needs-tested spending is _____ fiscal policy because it _____.

    A. automatic; increases in recession and decreases in expansion
    B. discretionary; increases when tax revenue increases
    C. automatic; increases when the government's budget deficit falls
    D. discretionary; is determined by economic hardship

**6.** A government expenditure multiplier _____.

    A. equals 1
    B. is less than the tax multiplier
    C. exceeds 1
    D. equals the tax multiplier

**7.** When the government lowers the income tax rate, _____.

    A. employment increases and potential GDP increases
    B. employment does not change but labor productivity falls
    C. labor productivity rises and employment decreases
    D. both labor productivity and potential GDP increase

**8.** A tax cut increases _____.

    A. aggregate demand but has no effect on aggregate supply
    B. aggregate demand because it increases disposable income and increases aggregate supply because it is an incentive to supply more labor
    C. aggregate demand because it increases consumption expenditure and decreases aggregate supply because labor productivity falls
    D. aggregate supply but has no effect on aggregate demand

Did the Fed save us from
another Great Depression?

# Monetary Policy

**When you have completed your study of this chapter,
you will be able to**

**1** Describe the objectives of U.S. monetary policy, the framework for achieving those objectives, and the Fed's monetary policy actions.

**2** Explain the transmission channels through which the Fed influences real GDP and the inflation rate.

**3** Explain and compare alternative monetary policy strategies.

MyEconLab Big Picture Video

# 17.1   HOW THE FED CONDUCTS MONETARY POLICY

A nation's monetary policy objectives and the framework for setting and achieving those objectives stem from the relationship between the central bank and the government. We'll describe the objectives of U.S. monetary policy and the framework and assignment of responsibility for achieving those objectives.

## ■ Monetary Policy Objectives

The objectives of monetary policy are ultimately political. In the United States, these objectives are set out in the mandate of the Board of Governors of the Federal Reserve System, which is defined by the Federal Reserve Act of 1913 and its subsequent amendments.

### Federal Reserve Act

The Fed's mandate was most recently clarified in an amendment to the Federal Reserve Act passed by Congress in 2000, which states that

> The Board of Governors of the Federal Reserve System and the Federal Open Market Committee shall maintain long-run growth of the monetary and credit aggregates commensurate with the economy's long-run potential to increase production, so as to promote effectively the goals of maximum employment, stable prices, and moderate long-term interest rates.

This description of the Fed's monetary policy objectives has two distinct parts: a statement of goals and a prescription of the means by which to pursue the goals.

### Goals: The Dual Mandate

The Fed's goals are often described as a "dual mandate" to achieve stable prices and also maximum employment.

The goal of "stable prices" doesn't mean a constant price level. Rather, it is interpreted to mean keeping the inflation rate low and predictable. Success in achieving this goal also ensures "moderate long-term interest rates."

The goal of "maximum employment" means attaining the maximum sustainable growth rate of potential GDP, keeping real GDP close to potential GDP, and keeping the unemployment rate close to the natural unemployment rate.

In the *long run*, these goals are in harmony and reinforce each other. Price stability is the key goal. It provides the best available environment for households and firms to make the saving and investment decisions that bring economic growth. So price stability encourages the maximum sustainable growth rate of potential GDP.

Price stability delivers moderate long-term interest rates because the nominal interest rate equals the real interest rate plus the inflation rate. With stable prices, the nominal interest rate is close to the real interest rate and, most of the time, this rate is likely to be moderate.

While the Fed's goals are in harmony in the long run, the Fed faces a tradeoff in the short run. For example, by taking an action that is designed to lower the inflation rate and achieve stable prices, the unemployment rate rises in the short run and slows real GDP growth. And using monetary policy to try to lower the unemployment rate and boost real GDP growth brings the risk of a rising inflation rate. (See Chapter 15, pp. 394–395.)

## Means for Achieving the Goals

The 2000 law instructs the Fed to pursue its goals by "maintain[ing] long-run growth of the monetary and credit aggregates commensurate with the economy's long-run potential to increase production." You can perhaps recognize this statement as being consistent with the quantity theory of money that you studied in Chapter 12 (see pp. 312–315). The "economy's long-run potential to increase production" is the growth rate of potential GDP. The "monetary and credit aggregates" are the quantities of money and loans. By keeping the growth rate of the quantity of money in line with the growth rate of potential GDP, the Fed is expected to be able to maintain full employment and keep the price level stable.

## Prerequisite for Achieving the Goals

The financial crisis that started in the summer of 2007 and intensified in the fall of 2008 brought the problem of financial instability to the top of the Fed's agenda. The focus of policy became the single-minded pursuit of **financial stability**—of enabling financial markets and institutions to resume their normal functions of allocating capital resources and risk.

**Financial stability**
A situation in which financial markets and institutions function normally to allocate capital resources and risk.

The pursuit of financial stability by the Fed is not an abandonment of the mandated goals of maximum employment and stable prices. Rather, it is a prerequisite for attaining those goals. Financial instability has the potential to bring severe recession and deflation—falling prices—and undermine the attainment of the mandated goals.

To pursue its mandated monetary policy goals, the Fed must make the general concepts of maximum employment and stable prices precise and operational.

## ■ Operational "Maximum Employment" Goal

The Fed pays close attention to the business cycle and tries to steer a steady course between inflation and recession. To gauge the state of output and employment relative to full employment, the Fed looks at a large number of indicators that include the labor force participation rate, the unemployment rate, measures of capacity utilization, activity in the housing market, the stock market, and regional information gathered by the regional Federal Reserve Banks. All these data are summarized in the Fed's *Beige Book*.

The *output gap*—the percentage deviation of real GDP from potential GDP—summarizes the state of aggregate demand relative to potential GDP. A positive output gap—an *inflationary gap*—brings rising inflation. A negative output gap—a *recessionary gap*—results in lost output and unemployment above the natural unemployment rate. The Fed tries to minimize the output gap.

## ■ Operational "Stable Prices" Goal

The Fed believes that core inflation provides the best indication of whether price stability is being achieved. The *core inflation rate* is the annual percentage change in the Personal Consumption Expenditure Price Index (PCEPI) *excluding* the prices of food and energy (see Chapter 7, p. 177).

Since January 2012, the Fed has regarded price stability as being achieved when the core inflation rate is 2 percent a year. Before 2012, the Fed avoided a numerical target for the core inflation rate. Former Fed Chair Alan Greenspan said that "price stability is best thought of as an environment in which inflation is so low and stable over time that it does not materially enter into the decisions of households and firms."

## ■ Responsibility for Monetary Policy

Who is responsible for monetary policy in the United States? What are the roles of the Fed, Congress, and the President?

### The Role of the Fed

The Federal Reserve Act makes the Board of Governors of the Federal Reserve System and the Federal Open Market Committee (FOMC) responsible for the conduct of monetary policy. We described the composition of the FOMC in Chapter 11 (see p. 282). The FOMC makes a monetary policy decision at eight scheduled meetings a year and publishes its minutes three weeks after each meeting.

### The Role of Congress

Congress plays no role in making monetary policy decisions, but the Federal Reserve Act requires the Board of Governors to report on monetary policy to Congress. The Fed makes two reports each year, one in February and another in July. These reports, along with the Fed Chair's testimony before Congress and the minutes of the FOMC, communicate the Fed's thinking on monetary policy to lawmakers and the public.

### The Role of the President

The formal role of the President of the United States is limited to appointing the members and the Chair of the Board of Governors. But some Presidents—Richard Nixon was one—have tried to influence the Fed's decisions.

You now know the objectives of monetary policy and can describe the framework and assignment of responsibility for achieving those objectives. Your next task is to see how the Fed conducts its monetary policy.

## ■ Policy Instrument

**Monetary policy instrument**
A variable that the Fed can directly control or closely target and that influences the economy in desirable ways.

To conduct its monetary policy, the Fed must select a **monetary policy instrument**, a variable that the Fed can directly control or closely target and that influences the economy in desirable ways.

### The Federal Funds Rate

**Federal funds rate**
The interest rate at which banks can borrow and lend reserves in the federal funds market.

The Fed's choice of monetary policy instrument is the **federal funds rate**, which is the interest rate on loans of reserves among banks. These interbank loans are made in what is called the federal funds market.

How does the Fed decide the appropriate level for the federal funds rate? And how, having made that decision, does the Fed move the federal funds rate to its target level?

### Interest Rate Decision-Making

The Federal Open Market Committee (FOMC) sets the federal funds rate target at the level that gets its forecasts of inflation and the output gap as close as possible to their desired levels. Before making its decision, the FOMC gathers and processes a large amount of information about the economy, the way it responds to shocks, and the way it responds to policy. The FOMC then processes all these data and comes to a judgment about the best level for the federal funds rate.

The Fed does not pursue formal published targets: It has implicit targets but the economy deviates from these targets most of the time. When it does, the Fed

■ **FIGURE 17.1**

The Fed's Key Monetary Policy Instrument: The Federal Funds Rate                          MyEconLab Real-time data

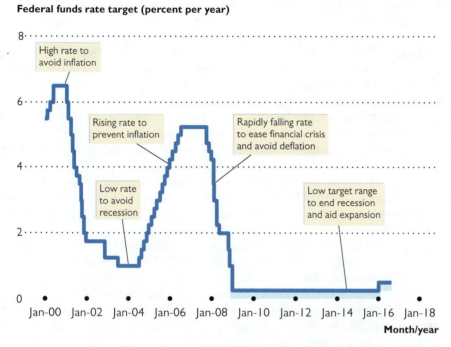

**Federal funds rate target (percent per year)**

The Fed sets a target for the federal funds rate and then takes actions to keep the rate close to the target.

When the Fed wants to slow inflation, it raises the federal funds rate target.

When the inflation rate is below the target and the Fed wants to avoid recession, it lowers the federal funds rate target.

When the Fed focused on restoring financial stability during the global financial crisis, it cut the federal funds rate target aggressively to almost zero. The Fed also set the target as a range, which is shown in light blue.

SOURCE OF DATA: Board of Governors of the Federal Reserve System.

places relative weights on its two objectives and, constrained by the short-run tradeoff (see Chapter 15), decides how quickly to try to get inflation back on track or the economy back to full employment.

Figure 17.1 shows the federal funds rate since 2000. You can see that the federal funds rate was 5.5 percent at the beginning of 2000, and during 2000 and 2001 the Fed increased the rate to 6.5 percent. The Fed raised the interest rate to this high level to lower the inflation rate.

Between 2002 and 2004, the federal funds rate was set at historically low levels. The reason is that with inflation well anchored at close to 2 percent a year, the Fed was less concerned about inflation than it was about recession, so it wanted to lean in the direction of avoiding recession.

From mid-2004 through early 2006, the Fed was increasingly concerned about the build-up of inflation pressures and it raised the federal funds rate target on 17 occasions to take it to 5.25 percent, a level that was held until September 2007.

When the global financial crisis began, the Fed acted cautiously in cutting the federal funds rate target. But as the crisis intensified, rate cuts became more frequent and larger, ending in December 2008 with an interest rate close to zero. The normal changes of a quarter of a percentage point (also called 25 *basis points*) were abandoned as the Fed slashed the rate, first by an unusual 50 basis points and finally, in December 2008, by an unprecedented 100 basis points. Since the end of 2008, the federal funds rate has been close to zero.

You've now seen how the Fed sets the federal funds rate target and your next task is to see how the Fed makes the federal funds rate hit its target.

## ◼ Hitting the Federal Funds Rate Target

The federal funds rate is the interest rate that banks earn (or pay) when they lend (or borrow) reserves. The federal funds rate is also the opportunity cost of holding reserves. Holding a larger quantity of reserves is the alternative to lending reserves to another bank, and holding a smaller quantity of reserves is the alternative to borrowing reserves from another bank. So the quantity of reserves that banks are willing to hold varies with the federal funds rate: The higher the federal funds rate, the smaller is the quantity of reserves that the banks plan to hold.

The Fed controls the quantity of reserves supplied, and the Fed can change this quantity by conducting an open market operation. You learned in Chapter 11 (pp. 287–290) how an open market purchase increases reserves and an open market sale decreases reserves. To hit the federal funds rate target, the New York Fed conducts open market operations until the supply of reserves is at just the right quantity to hit the target federal funds rate.

Figure 17.2 illustrates this outcome in the market for bank reserves. The x-axis measures the quantity of bank reserves on deposit at the Fed, and the y-axis measures the federal funds rate. The demand for reserves—the willingness of the banks to hold reserves—is the curve labeled *RD*.

The Fed's open market operations determine the supply of reserves, which is the supply curve *RS*. To decrease reserves, the Fed conducts an open market sale. To increase reserves, the Fed conducts an open market purchase.

Equilibrium in the market for bank reserves determines the federal funds rate where the quantity of reserves demanded by the banks equals the quantity of reserves supplied by the Fed. By using open market operations, the Fed adjusts the quantity of reserves supplied to keep the federal funds rate on target.

◼ **FIGURE 17.2**

### Equilibrium in the Market for Bank Reserves

MyEconLab Animation

The federal funds rate (on the y-axis) is the opportunity cost of holding reserves: The higher the federal funds rate, the smaller is the quantity of reserves that banks want to hold. The demand curve for bank reserves is *RD*.

❶ The FOMC sets the federal funds rate target at 5 percent a year.

❷ The New York Fed conducts open market operations to make the quantity of reserves supplied equal to $50 billion and the supply of reserves curve is *RS*.

❸ Equilibrium in the market for bank reserves occurs at the target federal funds rate.

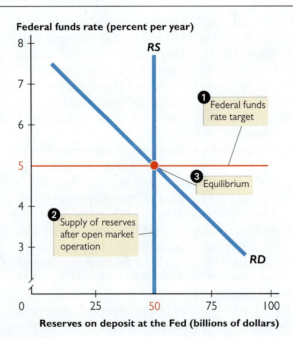

## ■ Restoring Financial Stability in a Financial Crisis

During the global financial crisis, the Fed took extraordinary steps to restore financial stability. Chapter 11 describes the tools of quantitative easing and credit easing employed by the Fed (p. 283) and *Eye on Creating Money* (pp. 292–293) shows the enormous surge in bank reserves and the monetary base brought about by "quantitative easing"—QE1—in 2008.

Figure 17.3 illustrates the Fed's QE1 action in the market for bank reserves. In normal times, the demand for reserves is $RD_0$ and the supply of reserves is $RS_0$. The federal funds rate is 5 percent and bank reserves are $50 billion.

At a time of financial instability and panic, banks' assessment of risk increases and they decide to hold more of their assets in safe, reserve deposits at the Fed. The demand for reserves increases and the demand curve becomes $RD_1$. If the Fed took no actions, the federal funds rate would rise, bank lending would shrink, the quantity of money would decrease, and a recession would intensify.

To avoid this outcome, the Fed's lending programs pump billions of dollars into the banks. The supply of reserves increases to $RS_1$, and the federal funds rate falls to zero. The banks don't start lending their increased reserves. They hang on to them. But flush with reserves, banks don't call in loans and deepen the recession. The Fed's action averted a worsening financial crisis.

Although the Fed avoided a more severe financial crisis, we don't know how bad things would have become without the extraordinary action. *Eye on the Fed in a Crisis* on p. 434 compares some features of the 2008–2009 recession with the Great Depression of the early 1930s.

## FIGURE 17.3

### The Market for Bank Reserves in a Financial Crisis

MyEconLab Animation

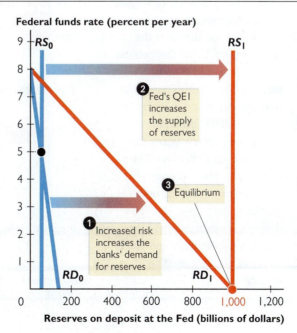

In a normal time, the demand for bank reserves is $RD_0$ and the supply of reserves is $RS_0$. The federal funds rate is 5 percent per year.

In a financial crisis:

❶ The banks face increased risk, so they increase their demand for reserves and the demand curve shifts to $RD_1$.

❷ The Fed's QE1 and other actions increase the supply of reserves and the supply curve shifts to $RS_1$.

❸ The equilibrium federal funds rate falls to zero and the quantity of reserves explodes to $1,000 billion.

# EYE on the FED IN A CRISIS

MyEconLab Critical Thinking Exercise

## Did the Fed Save Us From Another Great Depression?

The story of the Great Depression is complex and even today, after almost 80 years of research, economists are not in full agreement on its causes. But one part of the story is clear and it is told by Milton Friedman and Anna J. Schwartz: The Fed got it wrong.

An increase in financial risk drove the banks to increase their holdings of reserves and everyone else to lower their bank deposits and hold more currency.

Between 1929 and 1933, (Figure 1) the banks' desired reserve ratio increased from 8 percent to 12 percent and the currency drain ratio increased from 9 percent to 19 percent.

The money multiplier (Figure 2) fell from 6.5 to 3.8.

The quantity of money (Figure 3) crashed by 35 percent.

This massive contraction in the quantity of money was accompanied by a similar contraction of bank loans and by the failure of many banks.

Friedman and Schwartz say that this contraction of money and bank loans and the failure of banks could (and should) have been avoided by a more alert and wise Fed.

The Fed could have injected reserves into the banks to accommodate their desire for

greater security by holding more reserves and to offset the rise in currency holdings as people switched out of bank deposits.

Ben Bernanke's Fed did almost exactly what Friedman and Schwartz said the Fed needed to do in the Great Depression.

At the end of 2008, when the banks faced increased financial risk, the Fed flooded them with the reserves that they wanted to hold (Figure 1).

The money multiplier fell from 9.1 in 2008 to 3.3 in 2013 (Figure 2)—much more than it had fallen between 1929 and 1933—but there was no contraction of the quantity of money (Figure 3). Rather, the quantity of M2 increased by 37.5 percent in the 5 years to August 2013, a 6.6 percent annual rate.

We can't be sure that the Fed averted a Great Depression in 2009, but we can be confident that the Fed's actions helped to limit the depth and duration of the 2008–2009 recession.

For the past few years, the Fed has faced a dilemma. The recovery is slow but unemployment is close to the natural unemployment rate. The Fed's dilemma is when to stop fighting the slow recovery and start worrying about unleashing inflation.

*Milton Friedman and Anna J. Schwartz, authors of A Monetary History of the United States, who say the Fed turned an ordinary recession into the Great Depression.*

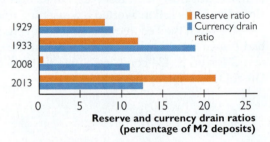

**Figure 1  The Flight to Safety: Reserve and Currency Ratios Increase**

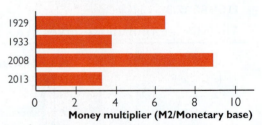

**Figure 2  The Collapsing Money Multiplier**

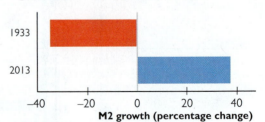

**Figure 3  Money Contraction Versus Growth**

SOURCE OF DATA: Federal Reserve Board.

# CHECKPOINT 17.1

MyEconLab Study Plan 17.1
Key Terms Quiz
Solutions Video

**Describe the objectives of U.S. monetary policy, the framework for achieving those objectives, and the Fed's monetary policy actions.**

## Practice Problems

1. What are the objectives of U.S. monetary policy?
2. What is core inflation and how does it differ from total PCEPI inflation?
3. What is the Fed's monetary policy instrument and what influences the level at which the Fed sets it?
4. Figure 1 shows the demand curve for bank reserves, *RD*. The current quantity of reserves supplied is $20 billion. The Fed wants to set the federal funds rate at 4 percent a year. Illustrate the target on the graph and show the supply of reserves that will achieve the target. Does the Fed conduct an open market operation and if so, does it buy or sell securities?

## In the News

### Fed defines price stability
The FOMC announced that it judges a 2 percent inflation rate to be consistent with the Fed's statutory mandate. The committee did not think it appropriate to specify a fixed goal for employment.

Source: Federal Reserve Monetary Policy Release, January 25, 2012

Explain why the FOMC might be willing to define price stability but not think it appropriate to specify a fixed employment goal.

## Solutions to Practice Problems

1. The objectives of U.S. monetary policy are to achieve stable prices (interpreted as a core inflation rate of about 2 percent per year) and maximum employment (interpreted as full employment).
2. Core inflation excludes the changes in the prices of food and fuel. The total PCEPI inflation rate includes the changes in all consumer prices. The core inflation rate fluctuates less than the total PCEPI inflation rate.
3. The federal funds rate is the Fed's monetary policy instrument and the inflation rate and output gap are two of the influences on the level at which the Fed sets the federal funds rate.
4. Figure 2 shows the market for bank reserves. With the initial quantity of reserves of $20 billion, the federal funds rate must have been 5 percent a year at point *A*. To set the federal funds rate at 4 percent a year, the Fed must conduct an open market purchase to increase the supply of reserves to *RS*. With supply *RS*, the federal funds rate equals the 4 percent target rate.

## Solution to In the News

Many factors influence employment and the FOMC looks at a large number of indicators to judge whether the maximum-employment goal is being achieved. The price level is influenced by monetary policy alone in the long run and is measured by one preferred price index, so the FOMC can give a fixed quantitative definition of the price-stability goal.

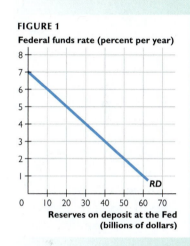

**FIGURE 1**
Federal funds rate (percent per year)

Reserves on deposit at the Fed
(billions of dollars)

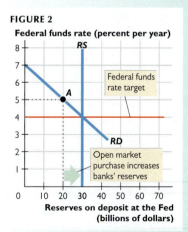

**FIGURE 2**
Federal funds rate (percent per year)

Reserves on deposit at the Fed
(billions of dollars)

# 17.2 MONETARY POLICY TRANSMISSION

You've seen that the Fed's goal is to keep the inflation rate around 2 percent a year and to keep the output gap close to zero. You've also seen how the Fed uses its market power to set the federal funds rate at the level that is designed to achieve these objectives. We're now going to trace the events that follow a change in the federal funds rate and see how those events lead to the ultimate policy goals. We'll begin with a quick overview of the transmission process and then look a bit more closely at each step.

## ■ Quick Overview

When the Fed lowers the federal funds rate, other short-term interest rates and the exchange rate also fall. The quantity of money and the supply of loanable funds increase. The long-term real interest rate falls. The lower real interest rate increases consumption expenditure and investment. The lower exchange rate makes U.S. exports cheaper and imports more costly, so net exports increase. Easier bank loans reinforce the effect of lower interest rates on aggregate expenditure. Aggregate demand increases, which increases real GDP and the price level relative to what they would have been. Real GDP growth and inflation speed up.

When the Fed raises the federal funds rate, as the sequence of events that we've just reviewed plays out, the effects are in the opposite directions.

Figure 17.4 provides a schematic summary of these ripple effects for both a cut and a rise in the federal funds rate. These ripple effects stretch out over a period of between one and two years. The interest rate and exchange rate effects are immediate. The effects on money and bank loans follow in a few weeks and run for a few months. Real long-term interest rates change quickly and often in anticipation of the short-term rate changes. Spending plans change and real GDP growth changes after about one year. The inflation rate changes between one year and two years after the change in the federal funds rate. But these time lags are not entirely predictable and can be longer or shorter. We're going to look at each stage in the transmission process, starting with the interest rate effects.

## ■ Interest Rate Changes

The first effect of a monetary policy decision by the FOMC is a change in the federal funds rate. Other interest rates then change. These interest rate effects occur quickly and relatively predictably.

The interest rate on U.S. government 3-month Treasury bills is immediately affected by a change in the federal funds rate. A powerful *substitution effect* keeps these two rates close to each other. Banks have a choice about how to hold their short-term liquid assets and a loan to another bank is a close substitute for holding Treasury bills. If the interest rate on Treasury bills is higher than the federal funds rate, the banks increase the quantity of Treasury bills held and decrease loans to other banks. The price of a Treasury bill rises and the interest rate falls. Similarly, if the interest rate on Treasury bills is lower than the federal funds rate, the banks decrease the quantity of Treasury bills held and increase loans to other banks. The price of a Treasury bill falls, and the interest rate rises. When the interest rate on Treasury bills is close to the federal funds rate, there is no incentive for a bank to switch between making loans to other banks and holding Treasury bills. Both the Treasury bill market and the federal funds market are in equilibrium.

**FIGURE 17.4**

Ripple Effects of the Fed's Actions    MyEconLab Animation

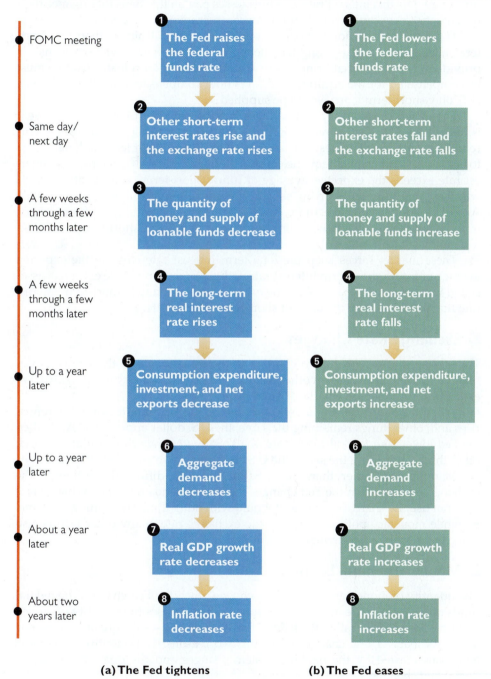

(a) The Fed tightens    (b) The Fed eases

The Fed changes its interest rate target and conducts open market operations to ❶ change the federal funds rate. The same day ❷ other short-term interest rates change and so does the exchange rate. A few weeks through a few months after the FOMC meeting, ❸ the quantity of money and supply of loanable funds change, which ❹ changes the long-term real interest rate.

Up to a year after the FOMC meeting, ❺ consumption expenditure, investment, and net exports change, which ❻ changes aggregate demand.

Eventually, the change in the federal funds rate has ripple effects that ❼ change real GDP and about two years after the FOMC meeting, ❽ the inflation rate changes.

Long-term interest rates also change, but not by as much as short-term rates. The long-term corporate bond rate, the interest rate paid on bonds issued by large corporations, is the most significant interest rate to be influenced by the federal funds rate. It is this interest rate that businesses pay on the loans that finance their purchases of new capital and that influences their investment decisions.

The long-term corporate bond rate is generally a bit higher than the short-term interest rate because long-term loans are riskier than short-term loans. To provide the incentive that brings forth a supply of long-term loans, lenders must be compensated for the additional risk. Without compensation for the additional risk, only short-term loans would be supplied.

The long-term interest rate fluctuates less than the short-term rate because it is influenced by expectations about future short-term interest rates as well as current short-term interest rates. The alternative to borrowing or lending long term is to borrow or lend using a sequence of short-term securities. If the long-term interest rate exceeds the expected average of future short-term interest rates, people will lend long term and borrow short term. The long-term interest rate will fall. And if the long-term interest rate is below the expected average of future short-term interest rates, people will borrow long term and lend short term. The long-term interest rate will rise.

These market forces keep the long-term interest rate close to the expected average of future short-term interest rates (plus a premium for the extra risk associated with long-term loans). And the expected average future short-term interest rate fluctuates less than the current short-term interest rate.

## ■ Exchange Rate Changes

The exchange rate responds to changes in the interest rate in the United States relative to the interest rates in other countries—the *U.S. interest rate differential*. We explain this influence in Chapter 19 (see pp. 490, 493, 495).

When the Fed raises the federal funds rate, the U.S. interest rate differential rises and, other things remaining the same, the U.S. dollar appreciates. And when the Fed lowers the federal funds rate, the U.S. interest rate differential falls and, other things remaining the same, the U.S. dollar depreciates.

Many factors other than the U.S. interest rate differential influence the exchange rate, so when the Fed changes the federal funds rate, the exchange rate does not usually change exactly as it would with other things remaining the same. So while monetary policy influences the exchange rate, many other factors also make the exchange rate change.

## ■ Money and Bank Loans

The quantity of money and bank loans change when the Fed changes the federal funds rate target. A rise in the federal funds rate decreases the quantity of money and bank loans; and a fall in the federal funds rate increases the quantity of money and bank loans. These changes occur for two reasons: The quantity of deposits and loans created by the banking system changes and the quantity of money demanded changes.

You've seen that to change the federal funds rate, the Fed must change the quantity of bank reserves. A change in the quantity of bank reserves changes the monetary base, which in turn changes the quantity of deposits and loans that the banking system can create. A rise in the federal funds rate decreases reserves and decreases the quantity of deposits and bank loans created; and a fall in the federal funds rate increases reserves and increases the quantity of deposits and bank loans created.

The quantity of money created by the banking system must be held by households and firms. The change in the interest rate changes the quantity of money demanded. A fall in the interest rate increases the quantity of money demanded and a rise in the interest rate decreases the quantity of money demanded.

A change in the quantity of money and the supply of bank loans directly affects consumption and investment plans. With more money and easier access to loans, consumers and firms spend more. With less money and loans harder to get, consumers and firms spend less.

## ■ The Long-Term Real Interest Rate

Demand and supply in the market for loanable funds determine the long-term real interest rate, which equals the long-term nominal interest rate minus the expected inflation rate. The long-term real interest rate influences expenditure decisions.

In the long run, demand and supply in the loanable funds market depend only on real forces—on saving and investment decisions. But in the short run, when the price level is not fully flexible, the supply of loanable funds is influenced by the supply of bank loans. Changes in the federal funds rate change the supply of bank loans, which changes the supply of loanable funds and changes the real interest rate in the loanable funds market.

A fall in the federal funds rate that increases the supply of bank loans increases the supply of loanable funds and lowers the equilibrium real interest rate. A rise in the federal funds rate that decreases the supply of bank loans decreases the supply of loanable funds and raises the equilibrium real interest rate.

These changes in the real interest rate, along with the other factors we've just described, change expenditure plans.

## ■ Expenditure Plans

The ripple effects that follow a change in the federal funds rate change three components of aggregate expenditure:

- Consumption expenditure
- Investment
- Net exports

Other things remaining the same, the lower the real interest rate, the greater is the amount of consumption expenditure and the smaller is the amount of saving.

Again, other things remaining the same, the lower the real interest rate, the greater is the amount of investment.

Finally, and again other things remaining the same, the lower the interest rate, the lower is the exchange rate and the greater are exports and the smaller are imports.

A cut in the federal funds rate increases all the components of aggregate expenditure; a rise in the federal funds rate decreases all the components of aggregate expenditure. These changes in aggregate expenditure plans change aggregate demand, which in turn changes real GDP and the inflation rate.

MyEconLab Concept Video

■ **The Fed Fights Recession**

We're now going to pull all the steps in the transmission story together. We'll start with inflation below target and real GDP below potential GDP. The Fed takes actions that are designed to restore full employment. Figure 17.5 shows the effects of the Fed's actions, starting in the market for bank reserves and ending in the market for real GDP.

In Figure 17.5(a), which shows the market for bank reserves, the FOMC lowers the target federal funds rate from 5 percent to 4 percent a year. To achieve the new target, the New York Fed buys securities and increases the supply of reserves in the banking system from $RS_0$ to $RS_1$.

With increased reserves, the banks create deposits by making loans and the supply of money increases. The short-term interest rate falls and the quantity of money demanded increases. In Figure 17.5(b), the supply of money increases from $MS_0$ to $MS_1$, the interest rate falls from 5 percent to 4 percent a year, and the quantity of money increases from $3 trillion to $3.1 trillion. The interest rate in the money market and the federal funds rate are kept close to each other by the powerful substitution effect described on p. 436.

■ **FIGURE 17.5**

The Fed Fights Recession

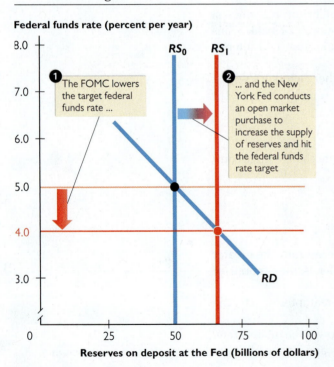

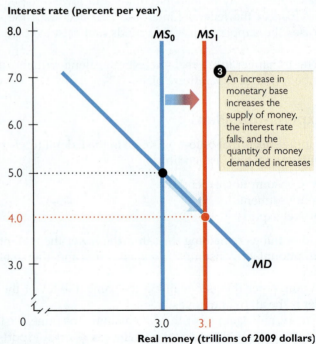

(a) Market for bank reserves

(b) Money market

❶ The FOMC lowers the federal funds rate target from 5 percent to 4 percent a year. ❷ The New York Fed buys securities in an open market operation and increases reserves from $RS_0$ to $RS_1$ to hit the new federal funds rate target.

❸ The supply of money increases from $MS_0$ to $MS_1$, the short-term interest rate falls, and the quantity of money demanded increases. The short-term interest rate and the federal funds rate change by similar amounts.

Banks create money by making loans. In the long run, an increase in the supply of bank loans is matched by a rise in the price level and the quantity of real loans is unchanged. But in the short run, with a sticky price level, an increase in the supply of bank loans increases the supply of (real) loanable funds. In Figure 17.5(c), the supply of loanable funds curve shifts rightward from $SLF_0$ to $SLF_1$. With the demand for loanable funds at $DLF$, the real interest rate falls from 6 percent to 5.5 percent a year.

Figure 17.5(d) shows aggregate demand and aggregate supply and the recessionary gap that triggered the Fed's action. The increase in money and loans and the decrease in the real interest rate increase aggregate planned expenditure. (Not shown in the figure, a fall in the interest rate lowers the exchange rate, which increases net exports and aggregate planned expenditure.) The increase in aggregate expenditure, $\Delta E$, increases aggregate demand and shifts the aggregate demand curve rightward to $AD_0 + \Delta E$. A multiplier process begins. The increase in expenditure increases income, which induces an increase in consumption expenditure. Aggregate demand increases further, and the aggregate demand curve shifts rightward, eventually to $AD_1$. The new equilibrium is at full employment but with a higher price level (and faster inflation).

MyEconLab Animation

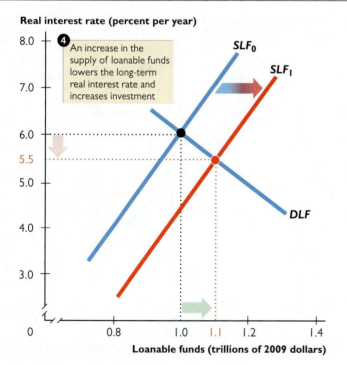

**(c) Market for loanable funds**

An increase in the quantity of money increases the supply of loans. ❹ An increase in the supply of bank loans increases the supply of loanable funds from $SLF_0$ to $SLF_1$ and the real interest rate falls. Investment increases.

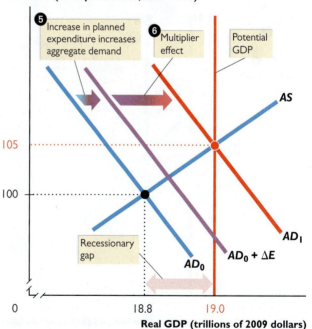

**(d) Real GDP and the price level**

❺ Aggregate planned expenditure increases and the aggregate demand curve shifts to $AD_0 + \Delta E$. ❻ A multiplier effect increases aggregate demand to $AD_1$. Real GDP increases and the price level rises (inflation speeds up).

## ■ The Fed Fights Inflation

If the inflation rate is too high and real GDP is above potential GDP, the Fed takes actions that are designed to lower the inflation rate and restore price stability. Figure 17.6 shows the effects of the Fed's actions starting in the market for reserves and ending in the market for real GDP.

In Figure 17.6(a), which shows the market for bank reserves, the FOMC raises the target federal funds rate from 5 percent to 6 percent a year. To achieve the new target, the New York Fed sells securities and decreases the supply of reserves in the banking system from $RS_0$ to $RS_1$.

With decreased reserves, the banks shrink deposits by decreasing loans and the supply of money decreases. The short-term interest rate rises and the quantity of money demanded decreases. In Figure 17.6(b), the supply of money decreases from $MS_0$ to $MS_1$, the interest rate rises from 5 percent to 6 percent a year, and the quantity of money decreases from $3 trillion to $2.9 trillion.

With a decrease in reserves, banks must decrease the supply of loans. The supply of (real) loanable funds decreases, and the supply of loanable funds curve shifts leftward in Figure 17.6(c) from $SLF_0$ to $SLF_1$. With the demand for loanable funds at $DLF$, the real interest rate rises from 6 percent to 6.5 percent a year.

## ■ FIGURE 17.6

### The Fed Fights Inflation

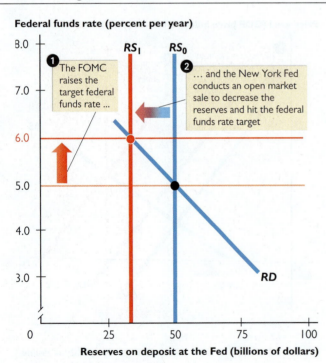

**(a) Market for bank reserves**

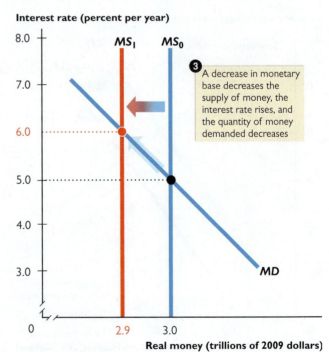

**(b) Money market**

❶ The FOMC raises the federal funds rate target from 5 percent to 6 percent a year. ❷ The New York Fed sells securities in an open market operation and decreases reserves from $RS_0$ to $RS_1$ to hit the new federal funds rate target.

❸ The supply of money decreases from $MS_0$ to $MS_1$, the short-term interest rate rises, and the quantity of money demanded decreases. The short-term interest rate and the federal funds rate change by similar amounts.

Figure 17.6(d) shows aggregate demand and aggregate supply in the market for real GDP and the inflationary gap to which the Fed is reacting. The decrease in the quantity of money and loans and the rise in the real interest rate decrease aggregate planned expenditure. The decrease in aggregate expenditure, $\Delta E$, decreases aggregate demand and shifts the aggregate demand curve leftward to $AD_0 - \Delta E$. A multiplier process begins. The decrease in expenditure decreases income, which induces a decrease in consumption expenditure. Aggregate demand decreases further, and the aggregate demand curve shifts leftward, eventually to $AD_1$. The economy returns to full employment. Real GDP is equal to potential GDP. The price level falls (the inflation rate slows).

In both of the examples, we have given the Fed a perfect hit at achieving full employment and keeping the price level stable. If the Fed changed aggregate demand by too little and too late, or by too much and too early, the economy would not have returned to full employment. Too little action would leave a recessionary or an inflationary gap. Too much action would overshoot the objective. If the Fed hits the brakes too hard, it pushes the economy from inflation to recession. If it stimulates too much, it turns recession into inflation.

MyEconLab Animation

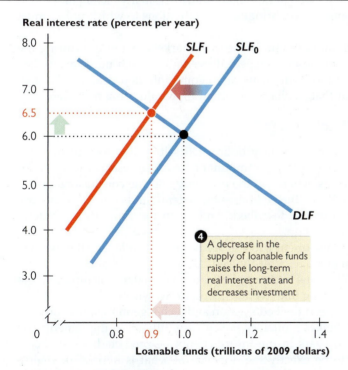

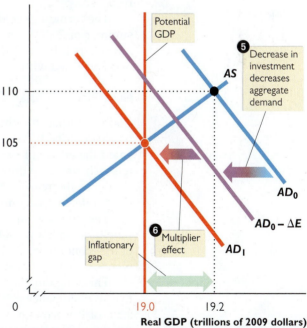

**(c) Market for loanable funds**

A decrease in the quantity of money decreases the supply of loans. ❹ A decrease in the supply of bank loans decreases the supply of loanable funds from $SLF_0$ to $SLF_1$ and the real interest rate rises. Investment decreases.

**(d) Real GDP and the price level**

❺ Aggregate planned expenditure decreases and the aggregate demand curve shifts to $AD_0 - \Delta E$. ❻ A multiplier effect decreases aggregate demand to $AD_1$. Real GDP decreases and the price level falls (inflation slows down).

## ■ Loose Links and Long and Variable Lags

The ripple effects of monetary policy that we've just analyzed with the precision of an economic model are, in reality, very hard to predict and influence.

To achieve its goals of price stability and full employment, the Fed needs a combination of good judgment and good luck. Too large an interest rate cut in an underemployed economy can bring inflation, as it did during the 1970s. And too large an interest rate rise in an inflationary economy can create unemployment, as it did in 1981 and 1991.

Loose links in the chain that runs from the federal funds rate to the ultimate policy goals make unwanted policy outcomes inevitable. And time lags that are both long and variable add to the Fed's challenges.

### Loose Links from Federal Funds Rate to Spending

The long-term real interest rate that influences spending plans is linked only loosely to the federal funds rate. Also, the response of the long-term real interest rate to a change in the nominal rate depends on how inflation expectations change. The response of expenditure plans to changes in the real interest rate depends on many factors that make the response hard to predict.

### Time Lags in the Adjustment Process

The Fed is especially handicapped by the fact that the monetary policy transmission process is long and drawn out. Also, the economy does not always respond in exactly the same way to a given policy change. Further, many factors other than policy are constantly changing and bringing new situations to which policy must respond.

The turmoil in credit markets and home loan markets that began during the summer of 2007 is an example of unexpected events to which monetary policy must respond. The Fed found itself facing an ongoing inflation risk, but that risk was combined with a fear that a collapse of spending would bring recession.

## ■ A Final Reality Check

You've studied the theory of monetary policy. Does it really work in the way we've described? It does. An enormous amount of statistical research has investigated the effects of the Fed's actions on the economy and the conclusions of this research are not in doubt. When the Fed raises the federal funds rate, the economy slows for the reasons that we've described. And when the Fed cuts the federal funds rate, the economy speeds up.

The time lags in the adjustment process are not predictable, but the average time lags are known. On average, after the Fed takes action to change the course of the economy, real GDP begins to change about one year later. The inflation rate responds with a longer time lag that averages around two years.

This long time-lag between the Fed's action and a change in the inflation rate, the ultimate policy goal, makes monetary policy very difficult to implement. The state of the economy two years in the future cannot be predicted, so the Fed's actions might turn out to be exactly the opposite of what is needed to steer a steady course between recession and inflation.

You've now seen how the Fed operates and studied the effects of its actions. We close this chapter by looking at alternative approaches to monetary policy.

# CHECKPOINT 17.2

MyEconLab Study Plan 17.2

Solutions Video

**Explain the transmission channels through which the Fed influences real GDP and the inflation rate.**

## Practice Problems

1. List the sequence of events in the transmission from a rise in the federal funds rate to a change in the inflation rate.

The economy has slipped into recession and the Fed takes actions to lessen its severity. Use this information to work Problems **2** and **3**.

2. What action does the Fed take? Illustrate the effects of the Fed's actions in the money market and the loanable funds market.

3. Explain how the Fed's actions change aggregate demand and real GDP.

## In the News

**Strong U.S. employment report brightens economic outlook**
The U.S. economy added more jobs than expected in both June and July. Wages increased more rapidly and real GDP was expected to grow faster. These developments raise the likelihood of a Fed interest rate increase.
Source: Reuters, August 5, 2016

What are the ripple effects and time lags that the Fed must consider in deciding when to raise the interest rate?

## Solutions to Practice Problems

1. When the Fed raises the federal funds rate, other short-term interest rates rise and the exchange rate rises; the quantity of money and supply of loanable funds decrease and the long-term real interest rate rises; consumption, investment, and net exports decrease; aggregate demand decreases; and eventually the real GDP growth rate and the inflation rate decrease.

2. The Fed lowers the federal funds rate, which lowers the short-term interest rate, and increases the supply of money (Figure 1). The supply of loans and the supply of loanable funds increase. The real interest rate falls (Figure 2).

3. A lower real interest rate (and exchange rate) and greater quantity of money and loanable funds increase aggregate expenditure and the $AD$ curve shifts to $AD_0 + \Delta E$. A multiplier effect increases aggregate demand and the $AD$ curve shifts to $AD_1$. Real GDP increases and recession is avoided (Figure 3).

## Solution to In the News

Following a change in the interest rate: several months later the quantity of money and loans respond; up to a year later, expenditure plans and real GDP respond; and up to two years later the inflation rate responds.

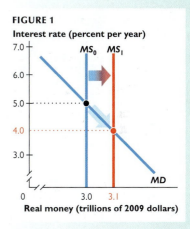

**FIGURE 1**

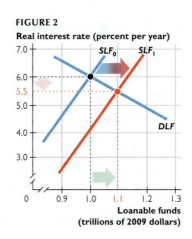

**FIGURE 2**

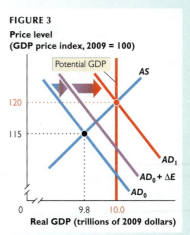

**FIGURE 3**

MyEconLab Concept Video

## 17.3 ALTERNATIVE MONETARY POLICY STRATEGIES

We're going to end our discussion of monetary policy by examining alternative strategies that the Fed might have chosen, and that some economists believe would improve macroeconomic outcomes. All the possible monetary policy strategies can be placed in two broad categories: *discretionary* and *rule-based*.

The Fed's monetary policy is discretionary. A central bank that pursues a **discretionary monetary policy** sets its policy instrument at the level it believes will best achieve its mandated policy goals. To make its interest rate decision, the FOMC gathers and analyzes a vast amount of data and comes to a judgment about the level that will best achieve price stability and full employment.

The alternative to discretionary monetary policy is rule-based policy. A **rule-based monetary policy** is one based on a rule for setting the policy instrument. Supporters of a rule-based policy say it is more predictable than discretionary policy and it reduces uncertainty about future policy decisions. Less uncertainty boosts business investment and economic growth. And less uncertainty about future inflation promotes the efficient working of capital markets and labor markets where agreements are based on long-term contracts.

Two alternative monetary policy rules have been proposed. They are

- An interest rate rule
- A monetary base rule

### ■ An Interest Rate Rule

John B. Taylor of Stanford University has proposed a rule for setting the federal funds rate—the *Taylor Rule*. The goal of this rule is to achieve 2 percent inflation and full employment. If the inflation rate is at the target of 2 percent and there is no output gap, the Taylor Rule sets the federal funds rate to neutral at 4 percent a year. A 1-percent deviation of the inflation rate from the target and a 1-percent deviation of real GDP from potential GDP moves the federal funds rate up or down by 0.5 percent.

The Taylor Rule was derived by crunching a large amount of U.S. macroeconomic data to construct a statistical model of the economy. The rule was then tested in this model and shown to be more effective than the Fed's decisions at attaining the mandated monetary policy goals.

### ■ A Monetary Base Rule

Bennett T. McCallum of Carnegie-Mellon University has proposed a rule for setting the monetary base—the *McCallum Rule*—with the same goal as the Taylor Rule: 2 percent inflation and full employment.

The *quantity theory of money* (Chapter 12, p. 312) provides the foundation for the McCallum Rule. The quantity theory links inflation to the money growth rate, the velocity growth rate, and the real GDP growth rate. In the McCallum Rule, money is the monetary base, so the quantity theory equation becomes

Inflation rate = Monetary base growth rate + Velocity growth rate − Real GDP growth rate

where velocity is the velocity of circulation of the monetary base.

The rule determines a growth rate for the monetary base that responds to changes in velocity growth and real GDP growth to deliver the 2 percent target inflation rate.

**Discretionary monetary policy**
A monetary policy that sets a central bank's policy instrument at the level it believes will best achieve its mandated policy goals.

**Rule-based monetary policy**
A monetary policy that is based on a rule for setting the policy instrument.

# EYE on the U.S. ECONOMY
## The Fed's Decisions Versus Two Rules

### The Taylor Rule

Figure 1 shows the Fed's decisions and the federal funds rate that the *Taylor Rule* would have set. If the rule delivers the best path for the federal funds rate, then the Fed kept the interest rate too low for too long in 2004 and 2005 and then raised it too quickly and by too much in 2006. John Taylor says the Fed's deviation from the rule contributed to the global financial crisis of 2007. Over the years since 2009, the Fed has again kept the federal funds rate well below what the Taylor Rule would have set. If the rule is correct, the Fed is stoking inflation.

### The McCallum Rule

Figure 2 shows the Fed's decision and the monetary base that the *McCallum Rule* would have delivered. If the rule delivers the best path for the monetary base, then the Fed wandered around too much. It increased the base by too much too quickly in each of the quantitative easing episodes (see Chapter 11, p. 283). The McCallum Rule agrees with the Taylor Rule: If the rules are correct, then the Fed is fuelling a future outbreak of inflation.

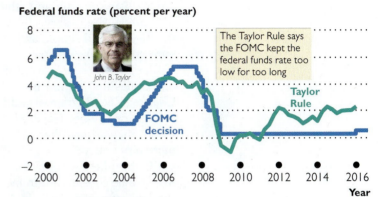

**Figure 1 Taylor Rule Versus FOMC**

**Figure 2 McCallum Rule Versus FOMC**

---

*Eye on the U.S. Economy* compares the Fed's decisions with the Taylor and McCallum rules. Two other strategies that the Fed might use are discretionary policies that are constrained by tightly defined objectives. They are

- Inflation targeting
- Money growth targeting

## ■ Inflation Targeting

**Inflation targeting** is a monetary policy regime in which the central bank makes a public agreement with the government to achieve an explicit inflation target and to explain how its policy actions will achieve that target.

The idea of inflation targeting is to state clearly and publicly the goals of monetary policy, to establish a framework of accountability, and to keep the inflation rate low and stable while maintaining a high and stable level of employment.

Inflation targets are usually specified in terms of a range for the CPI inflation rate. This range is typically between 1 percent and 3 percent a year, with an aim to achieve an average inflation rate of 2 percent a year. Because the lags in the

**Inflation targeting**
A monetary policy strategy in which the central bank makes a public agreement with the government to achieve an explicit inflation target and to explain how its policy actions will achieve that target.

operation of monetary policy are long, if the inflation rate falls outside the target range, the expectation is that the central bank will move the inflation rate back to the target over the next two years.

Several major central banks practice inflation targeting and have done so since the mid-1990s. The most committed inflation-targeting central banks are the Bank of England (the central bank of the United Kingdom), the Bank of Canada, the Reserve Bank of Australia, the Reserve Bank of New Zealand, the Swedish Riksbank, and the European Central Bank (the central bank of the euro countries).

Japan and the United States are the most prominent major industrial economies that do not use this monetary policy strategy. But when former Fed Chairman Ben Bernanke and former Fed Governor Frederic S. Mishkin were economics professors (at Princeton University and Columbia University, respectively) they argued that inflation targeting is a sensible way in which to conduct monetary policy.

Of the alternatives to the Fed's current strategy, inflation targeting is the most likely to be considered. In fact, some economists see it as a small step from what the Fed currently does. In November 2007, the Fed took a major step toward greater transparency, a central feature of inflation targeting, by publishing FOMC members' detailed forecasts of inflation, real GDP growth, and unemployment. And in 2012, the Fed defined an inflation rate of 2 percent as consistent with price stability.

There is wide agreement that inflation targeting achieves its goals. It's also clear that the inflation reports of inflation targeters have raised the level of discussion and understanding of the monetary policy process.

It is less clear whether inflation targeting does better than the implicit targeting that the Fed currently pursues in achieving low and stable inflation. The Fed's own record, without a formal inflation target agreement with the government, had been impressive until the global financial crisis raised questions about its strategy.

# EYE on the GLOBAL ECONOMY
## Inflation Targeting Around the World

Five advanced economies and the Eurozone have inflation targets (shown by the green bars) designed to anchor inflation expectations.

In four of the economies, the inflation targets have been achieved (orange lines), and the other two economies achieved near misses.

In all six cases, high-quality central bank inflation reports encourage an enhanced level of public discussion about inflation and awareness of each central bank's views and policy decisions

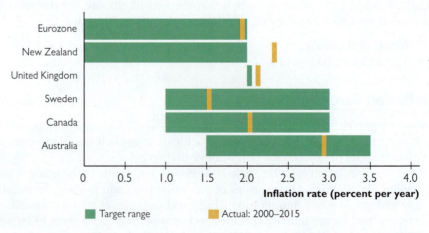

SOURCES OF DATA: National central banks and World Economic Outlook database, April 2016.

## ■ Money Targeting Rule

As long ago as 1948, Nobel Laureate Milton Friedman proposed a targeting rule for the quantity of money. Friedman's **k-percent rule** makes the quantity of money grow at a rate of $k$ percent a year, where $k$ equals the growth rate of potential GDP. Friedman's $k$-percent rule relies on a stable demand for money, which translates to a stable velocity of circulation. Friedman had examined data on money and nominal GDP and argued that the velocity of circulation of money was one of the most stable macroeconomic variables and that it could be exploited to deliver a stable price level and small business cycle fluctuations.

Friedman's idea remained just that until the 1970s, when inflation increased to more than 10 percent a year in the United States and to much higher rates in some other major countries.

During the mid-1970s, in a bid to end the inflation, the central banks of most major countries adopted the $k$-percent rule for the growth rate of the quantity of money. The Fed, too, began to pay close attention to the growth rates of money aggregates, including M1 and M2.

Inflation rates fell during the early 1980s in the countries that had adopted a $k$-percent rule. But one by one, these countries abandoned the $k$-percent rule.

Money targeting works when the demand for money curve is stable and predictable—when the velocity of circulation is stable. But in the world of the 1980s, and possibly in the world of today, technological change in the banking system leads to large and unpredictable shifts in the demand for money curve, which make the use of monetary targeting unreliable.

With money targeting, aggregate demand fluctuates because the demand for money fluctuates. With interest rate targeting, aggregate demand is insulated from fluctuations in the demand for money (and the velocity of circulation).

Monetary policy is a work in progress supported by the Fed and other central banks engaging in an ongoing research program and sharing of experience and ideas.

**k-percent rule**
A monetary policy rule that makes the quantity of money grow at $k$ percent per year, where $k$ equals the growth rate of potential GDP.

# EYE on YOUR LIFE
## Your Views on Monetary Policy and How Monetary Policy Affects You

MyEconLab Critical Thinking Exercise

Using the knowledge that you have accumulated during your course and by reading or watching the current news, try to determine the monetary policy issues that face the U.S. economy today.

What is the greater monetary policy risk: inflation or recession? If the risk is inflation, what action do you expect the Fed to take? If the risk is

recession, what do you expect the Fed to do?

Which of these problems, inflation or recession, do you care most about? Do you want the Fed to be more cautious about inflation and keep the interest rate high, or more cautious about recession and keep the interest rate low?

When Ben Bernanke was an economics professor at Princeton, he

studied inflation targeting and found that it works well.

Do you think the United States should join the ranks of inflation targeters? Should the Fed announce an inflation target?

Watch the media for commentary on the Fed's interest rate decisions and evolving monetary policy strategy.

MyEconLab Study Plan 17.3
Key Terms Quiz
Solutions Video

 CHECKPOINT 17.3

**Explain and compare alternative monetary policy strategies.**

## Practice Problems

1. What is the Fed's monetary policy strategy and what are the alternative strategies that it could have adopted?

2. Why does the Fed not target the quantity of money?

3. Which countries practice inflation targeting? How does this monetary policy strategy work and does it achieve a lower inflation rate?

## In the News

**The failed oracles of economic growth**

For nearly a decade, central bankers have been promising to raise growth and create jobs. The oracles of monetary policy have failed. We need some new ones. One such alternative is offered by John Taylor, the Stanford University economist who long ago proposed rules to govern central bank strategies.

Source: Terence Corcoran, *Financial Post*, July 21, 2016

What is the rule for monetary policy proposed by John Taylor and why might it do a better job than the monetary policy of the past decade?

## Solutions to Practice Problems

1. The Fed's monetary policy has mandated goals but it is free to use its discretion in achieving it goals. The Fed could have adopted four alternative monetary policy strategies. It could use one of two rule-based policies: an interest rate rule or a monetary base rule. It could adopt one of two alternative targeting policies: inflation targeting, or $k$-percent money targeting. The Fed's discretionary policy is only a short step away from inflation targeting.

2. The Fed does not target the quantity of money because it believes that the demand for money is too unstable and fluctuations in demand would bring unwanted fluctuations in interest rates, aggregate demand, real GDP, and the inflation rate.

3. The countries that practice inflation targeting are the United Kingdom, Canada, Australia, New Zealand, Sweden, and the European countries that use the euro. Inflation targeting works by announcing a target inflation rate, setting the overnight interest rate (equivalent to the U.S. federal funds rate) to achieve the target, and publishing reports that explain how and why the central bank believes that its current policy actions will achieve its ultimate policy goals. New Zealand and the United Kingdom have narrowly missed their inflation targets, but the other inflation targeters have achieved their goals.

## Solution to In the News

The Taylor Rule is a formula for setting the federal funds rate. The rule makes the interest rate respond to departures from an inflation target and an output gap in a predictable way. Employing a rule brings greater certainty and provides a stronger anchor for inflation expectations, which improves the short-run policy tradeoff. Greater certainty might also stimulate investment to speed economic growth and job creation.

## CHAPTER SUMMARY

## Key Points

1. **Describe the objectives of U.S. monetary policy, the framework for achieving those objectives, and the Fed's monetary policy actions.**

   - The Federal Reserve Act requires the Fed to use monetary policy to achieve the "dual mandate" of maximum employment and stable prices.
   - The Fed's goals can come into conflict in the short run.
   - The Fed translates the goal of stable prices as a core inflation rate of between 1 and 2 percent a year.
   - The Fed's monetary policy instrument is the federal funds rate.
   - The Fed sets the federal funds rate at the level that makes its forecast of inflation and other goals equal to their targets.
   - The Fed hits its federal funds rate target by using open market operations and in times of financial crisis by quantitative easing and credit easing.

2. **Explain the transmission channels through which the Fed influences real GDP and the inflation rate.**

   - A change in the federal funds rate changes other interest rates, the exchange rate, the quantity of money and loans, aggregate demand, and eventually real GDP and the inflation rate.
   - Changes in the federal funds rate change real GDP about one year later and change the inflation rate with an even longer time lag.

3. **Explain and compare alternative monetary policy strategies.**

   - The main alternatives to the Fed's discretionary policy are an interest rate rule, a monetary base rule, inflation targeting, and money growth targeting.
   - Rules dominate discretion in monetary policy because they bring greater certainty about future policy actions and better enable the central bank to manage inflation expectations.

## Key Terms

MyEconLab Key Terms Quiz

Discretionary monetary policy, 446
Federal funds rate, 430
Financial stability, 429
Inflation targeting, 447

k-percent rule, 449
Monetary policy instrument, 430
Rule-based monetary policy, 446

# CHAPTER CHECKPOINT

## Study Plan Problems and Applications

1. **Central bankers warn of QE threat to budget discipline**
   The German and Dutch central bank presidents warn that quantitative easing and low interest rates make discipline in government budgeting more important. Debt and deficits must be cut.
   
   Source: *Financial Times*, March 13, 2015
   
   How might a government budget deficit and debt threaten financial stability and make the central bank's job harder?

Use the following information to work Problems **2** to **4**.

Suppose that the U.S. economy is at full employment when strong economic growth in Asia increases the demand for U.S.-produced goods and services.

2. Explain how the U.S. price level and real GDP will change in the short run.

3. Explain how the U.S. price level and real GDP will change in the long run if the Fed takes monetary policy actions that are consistent with its objectives as set out in the Federal Reserve Act of 2000.

4. Explain whether the Fed faces a tradeoff in the short run.

5. What is the Fed's "dual mandate" for the conduct of monetary policy? What are the means to achieving the goals of the dual mandate?

6. What is financial stability? What actions has the Fed taken since 2007 in pursuit of financial stability? Use a graph to illustrate the effects of the Fed's actions.

Use the following information to work Problems **7** to **9**.

Figure 1 shows the aggregate demand curve, *AD*, and the short-run aggregate supply curve, *AS*, in the economy of Artica. Potential GDP is $300 billion.

7. What are the price level and real GDP? Does Artica have an unemployment problem or an inflation problem? Why?

8. What do you predict will happen if the central bank takes no monetary policy actions? What monetary policy action would you advise the central bank to take and what do you predict will be the effect of that action?

9. Suppose that a drought decreases potential GDP in Artica to $250 billion. Explain what happens if the central bank lowers the federal funds rate. Do you recommend that the central bank lower the interest rate? Why?

10. **Premature to rule out an interest rate increase this year**
    Federal Reserve Bank of New York President William Dudley says that in the current state of the economy, it would be worse for the Fed to raise rates too soon than moving slightly too late and adjusting by raising rates more quickly.
    
    Source: *Wall Street Journal*, August 1, 2016
    
    What are some of the problems that could arise if the Fed raises interest rates too soon or too late?

11. Read *Eye on the Fed in a Crisis* on p. 434. What are the key differences in monetary policy between the Great Depression and the slow recovery from the 2008–2009 recession?

**FIGURE 1**

Price level
(GDP price index, 2009 = 100)

Real GDP (billions of 2009 dollars)

# Instructor Assignable Problems and Applications

MyEconLab Homework, Quiz, or Test if assigned by instructor

1. In which episode, the Great Depression or the 2008–2009 recession, did the banks' desired reserve ratio and the currency drain ratio increase by the larger amount and the money multiplier fall by the larger amount?

2. Compare and contrast the Fed's monetary policy response to the surge in desired reserves and currency holdings in the Great Depression and the 2008–2009 recession.

Use the following information to work Problems **3** to **5**.

The U.S. economy is at full employment when the world price of oil begins to rise sharply. Short-run aggregate supply decreases.

3. Explain how the U.S. price level and real GDP will change in the short run.

4. Explain how the U.S. price level and real GDP will change in the long run if the Fed takes monetary policy actions that are consistent with its objectives as set out in the Federal Reserve Act of 2000.

5. Does the Fed face a tradeoff in the short run? Explain why or why not.

Use the following information to work Problems **6** to **9**.

Figure 1 shows the aggregate demand curve, *AD*, and the short-run aggregate supply curve, *AS*, in the economy of Freezone. Potential GDP is $300 billion.

6. What are the price level and real GDP? Does Freezone have an unemployment problem or an inflation problem? Why?

7. What do you predict will happen in Freezone if the central bank takes no monetary policy actions? What monetary policy action would you advise the central bank to take and what do you predict will be the effect of that action?

8. What happens in Freezone if the central bank lowers the federal funds rate? Do you recommend that the central bank lower the interest rate? Why?

9. What happens in Freezone if the central bank conducts an open market sale of securities? How will the interest rate change? Do you recommend that the central bank conduct an open market sale of securities? Why?

10. Suppose that inflation is rising toward 5 percent a year, and the Fed, Congress, and the White House are discussing ways of containing inflation without damaging employment and output. The President wants to cut aggregate demand but to do so in a way that will give the best chance of keeping investment high to encourage long-term economic growth. Explain the Fed's best action for meeting the President's objectives.

Use the following information to work Problems **11** and **12**.

**What the U.S. jobs report means for the Fed**

Despite U.S. job creation exceeding forecasts in July, experts believe that with weak output growth, the Fed will not raise the interest rate until after the U.S. presidential election.

Source: *Financial Times*, August 5, 2016

11. Explain why the Fed might be cautious about raising interest rates despite strong jobs growth.

12. What is the problem that might arise if the Fed keeps the interest rate too low for too long?

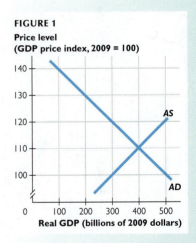

**FIGURE 1**

Price level
(GDP price index, 2009 = 100)

# Multiple Choice Quiz

**1.** The Fed's "dual mandate" is to achieve _____.

   A. a government budget surplus and low interest rates
   B. low inflation and maximum employment
   C. a stable quantity of money and stable prices
   D. zero unemployment and a stable means of payment

**2.** The Fed's operational goals include _____.

   A. a core inflation rate between 1 and 2 percent a year and an output gap as small as possible
   B. an economic growth rate of 3 percent a year and an unemployment rate equal to the natural unemployment rate
   C. a strong U.S. dollar on foreign exchange markets and a positive output gap
   D. maximum growth of stock prices and a low core inflation rate

**3.** The Fed's monetary policy instrument is the _____.

   A. inflation rate
   B. federal funds rate
   C. long-term interest rate
   D. monetary base

**4.** The Fed fights inflation by _____.

   A. lowering the federal funds rate, which lowers interest rates and decreases aggregate demand
   B. raising the federal funds rate, which raises interest rates and decreases aggregate demand
   C. decreasing the monetary base, which raises the interest rate and increases saving
   D. lowering the long-term real interest rate, which increases investment and spurs economic growth

**5.** To fight unemployment and close a recessionary gap, the Fed _____.

   A. stimulates aggregate demand by lowering the federal funds rate, which increases the quantity of money
   B. stimulates aggregate supply by lowering the federal funds rate, which increases potential GDP
   C. increases employment, which increases real GDP
   D. increases bank reserves, which banks use to make new loans to businesses, which increases aggregate supply

**6.** The Fed's choice of monetary policy strategy is _____.

   A. discretionary monetary policy
   B. the *k*-percent rule for money growth
   C. adjusting the federal funds rate to best fulfill its dual mandate
   D. setting the foreign exchange rate of the dollar

**7.** A monetary policy rule is _____ to discretionary monetary policy because _____.

   A. superior; discretion limits what the Fed can do in a financial crisis
   B. inferior; a rule makes it harder for people to forecast the inflation rate
   C. superior; a rule keeps inflation expectations anchored
   D. equivalent; the Fed uses its discretion to set the rule

Who wins and who loses from globalization?

# International Trade Policy

## 18

**When you have completed your study of this chapter, you will be able to**

**1** Explain how markets work with international trade and identify the gains from international trade and its winners and losers.

**2** Explain the effects of international trade barriers.

**3** Explain and evaluate arguments used to justify restricting international trade.

MyEconLab Big Picture Video

MyEconLab Concept Video

**Imports**
The goods and services that people and firms in one country buy from firms in other countries.

**Exports**
The goods and services that firms in one country sell to people and firms in other countries.

## 18.1 HOW GLOBAL MARKETS WORK

Because we trade with firms in other countries, the goods and services that we buy and consume are not limited to what we produce. The goods and services that we buy from firms in other countries are our **imports**; the goods and services that we sell to people and firms in other countries are our **exports**.

### ◼ International Trade Today

Global trade today is enormous. In 2015, global exports and imports (the two numbers are the same because what one country exports another imports) were about $23 trillion, which is 31 percent of the value of global production. The United States is the world's largest international trader and accounts for 10 percent of world exports and 12 percent of world imports. Germany and China, which rank 2 and 3 behind the United States, lag by a large margin.

In 2015, total U.S. exports were $2.3 trillion, which is about 13 percent of the value of U.S. production. Total U.S. imports were $2.8 trillion, which is about 16 percent of the value of total expenditure in the United States.

The United States trades both goods and services. In 2015, exports of services were $0.75 trillion (33 percent of total exports) and imports of services were $0.5 trillion (16 percent of total imports).

Our largest exports are private services such as banking, insurance, and business consulting. Our largest exports of goods are automobile parts and industrial and service machinery. Our largest import used to be crude oil, and it remains a large item. But in 2015, computers were our largest import. *Eye on the U.S. Economy* (p. 457) provides a bit more detail on our ten largest exports and imports.

### ◼ What Drives International Trade?

*Comparative advantage* is the fundamental force that drives international trade. We defined comparative advantage in Chapter 3 (p. 73) as the ability of a person to perform an activity or produce a good or service at a lower opportunity cost than anyone else. This same idea applies to nations. We can define *national comparative advantage* as the ability of a *nation* to perform an activity or produce a good or service at a lower opportunity cost than *any other nation*.

The opportunity cost of producing a T-shirt is lower in China than in the United States, so China has a comparative advantage in producing T-shirts. The opportunity cost of producing an airplane is lower in the United States than in China, so the United States has a comparative advantage in producing airplanes.

You saw in Chapter 3 how Liz and Joe reaped gains from trade by specializing in the production of the good at which they have a comparative advantage and then trading. Both were better off. This same principle applies to trade among nations.

China has a comparative advantage at producing T-shirts and the United States has a comparative advantage at producing airplanes, so the people of both countries can gain from specialization and trade. China can buy airplanes from the United States at a lower opportunity cost than that at which it can produce them. And Americans can buy T-shirts from China for a lower opportunity cost than that at which U.S. firms can produce them. Also, through international trade, Chinese producers can get higher prices for their T-shirts and Boeing can sell airplanes for a higher price. Both countries gain from international trade.

We're going to illustrate the gains from trade that we've just described by studying demand and supply in the global markets for T-shirts and airplanes.

# EYE on the U.S. ECONOMY
## U.S. Exports and Imports

The blue bars in part (a) of the figure show the ten largest U.S. exports and the red bars in part (b) show the ten largest U.S. imports. Some items appear in both parts (a) and (b) because the United States exports and imports items in many of the broad categories.

Three of the leading U.S. exports are services—private services, which include financial, business, professional and technical services (such as the sale of advertising by Google to Adidas, a European sportswear maker), and education (foreign students in our colleges and universities); travel (such as the expenditure on a Florida vacation by a visitor from England); and royalties and license fees (such as fees received by Hollywood movie producers on films shown abroad).

Computers such as laptops and tablets are the largest import. We also import large quantities of industrial ands service machinery, automobiles and parts, clothing, crude oil, and travel. Private services also feature as a large imports category.

Although we import a large quantity of computers, we export some too. We also export the semiconductors (computer chips) inside those imported computers. The Intel chip in a Lenovo laptop built in China and imported into the United States is an example. This chip is made in the United States and exported to China.

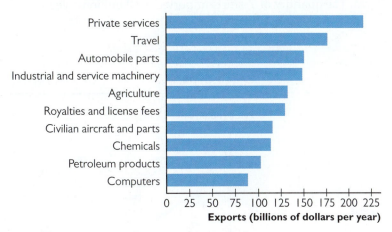

**(a) Ten large U.S. exports**

*The United States exports airplanes …*

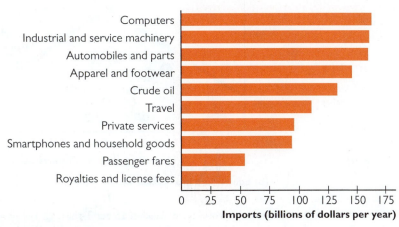

**(b) Ten large U.S. imports**

SOURCE OF DATA: Bureau of Economic Analysis.

*and imports computers.*

### ■ Why the United States Imports T-Shirts

Figure 18.1 illustrates the effects of international trade in T-shirts. The demand curve $D_{US}$ and the supply curve $S_{US}$ show the demand and supply in the U.S. domestic market only. The demand curve tells us the quantity of T-shirts that Americans are willing to buy at various prices. The supply curve tells us the quantity of T-shirts that U.S. garment makers are willing to sell at various prices.

Figure 18.1(a) shows what the U.S. T-shirt market would be like with no international trade. The price of a T-shirt would be $8 and 40 million T-shirts a year would be produced by U.S. garment makers and bought by U.S. consumers.

Figure 18.1(b) shows the market for T-shirts *with* international trade. Now the price of a T-shirt is determined in the world market, not the U.S. domestic market. The world price is *less than* $8 a T-shirt, which means that the rest of the world has a comparative advantage in producing T-shirts. The world price line shows the world price as $5 a T-shirt.

The U.S. demand curve, $D_{US}$, tells us that at $5 a T-shirt, Americans buy 60 million T-shirts a year. The U.S. supply curve, $S_{US}$, tells us that at $5 a T-shirt, U.S. garment makers produce 20 million T-shirts. To buy 60 million T-shirts when only 20 million are produced in the United States, we must import T-shirts from the rest of the world. The quantity of T-shirts imported is 40 million a year.

■ **FIGURE 18.1**

A Market with Imports                                                    MyEconLab Animation

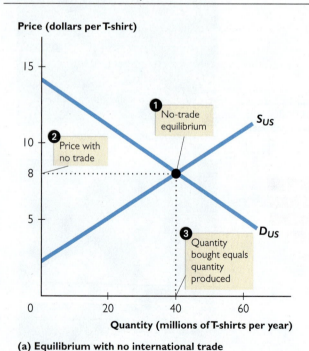

(a) Equilibrium with no international trade

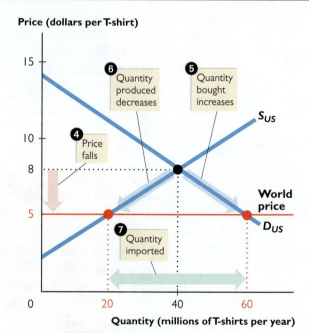

(b) Equilibrium in a market with imports

With no international trade, in part (a), ❶ domestic demand and domestic supply determine ❷ the equilibrium price at $8 a T-shirt and ❸ the quantity at 40 million T-shirts a year.
With international trade, in part (b), world demand and world supply determine the world price, which is $5 per T-shirt. ❹ The domestic price falls to $5 a T-shirt. ❺ Domestic purchases increase to 60 million T-shirts a year, and ❻ domestic production decreases to 20 million T-shirts a year. ❼ 40 million T-shirts a year are imported.

# ■ Why the United States Exports Airplanes

Figure 18.2 illustrates the effects of international trade in airplanes. The demand curve $D_{US}$ and the supply curve $S_{US}$ show the demand and supply in the U.S. domestic market only. The demand curve tells us the quantity of airplanes that U.S. airlines are willing to buy at various prices. The supply curve tells us the quantity of airplanes that U.S. aircraft makers are willing to sell at various prices.

Figure 18.2(a) shows what the U.S. airplane market would be like with no international trade. The price of an airplane would be $100 million and 400 airplanes a year would be produced by U.S. aircraft makers and bought by U.S. airlines.

Figure 18.2(b) shows the U.S. airplane market *with* international trade. Now the price of an airplane is determined in the world market, not the U.S. domestic market. The world price is *higher than* $100 million, which means that the United States has a comparative advantage in producing airplanes. The world price line shows the world price as $150 million.

The U.S. demand curve, $D_{US}$, tells us that at $150 million an airplane, U.S. airlines buy 200 airplanes a year. The U.S. supply curve, $S_{US}$, tells us that at $150 million an airplane, U.S. aircraft makers produce 700 airplanes a year. The quantity produced in the United States (700 a year) minus the quantity purchased by U.S. airlines (200 a year) is the quantity of U.S. exports, which is 500 airplanes a year.

■ **FIGURE 18.2**

A Market with Exports                                                                                  MyEconLab Animation

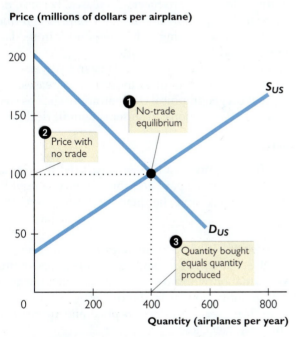

**(a) Equilibrium with no international trade**

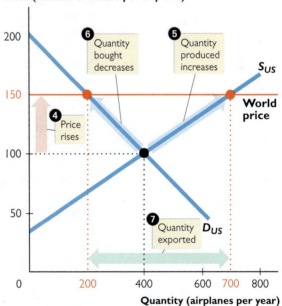

**(b) Equilibrium in a market with exports**

With no international trade, in part (a), ❶ domestic demand and domestic supply determine ❷ the equilibrium price at $100 million an airplane and ❸ the quantity at 400 airplanes a year. With international trade, in part (b), world demand and world supply determine the world price, which is $150 million an airplane. ❹ The domestic price rises. ❺ Domestic production increases to 700 airplanes a year, ❻ domestic purchases decrease to 200 airplanes a year, and ❼ 500 airplanes a year are exported.

MyEconLab Concept Video

# ■ Winners, Losers, and Net Gains From Trade

International trade has winners and it has losers. It is because some people lose, that we often hear complaints about international competition. We're now going to see who wins and who loses from international trade. You will then be able to understand who complains about international competition and why. You will learn why we hear producers complaining about cheap foreign imports. You will also see why we never hear consumers of imported goods and services complaining and why we never hear exporters complaining, except when they want greater access to foreign markets.

## Gains and Losses from Imports

We measure the gains and losses from imports by examining their effect on the price paid and quantity bought by domestic consumers and their effect on the price received and quantity sold by domestic producers.

**Consumers Gain from Imports**   When a country freely imports something from the rest of the world, it is because the rest of the world has a comparative advantage at producing that item. Compared to a situation with no international trade, the price paid by the consumer falls and the quantity bought increases. It is clear that the consumer gains. The greater the fall in price and increase in quantity bought, the greater is the gain to the consumer.

**Domestic Producers Lose from Imports**   Compared to a situation with no international trade, the price received by domestic producers of an item that is imported falls. Also, the quantity sold by these domestic producers decreases. Because domestic producers of this item sell a smaller quantity and for a lower price, producers lose from international trade. Import-competing industries shrink in the face of competition from cheaper foreign-produced imports.

The profits of firms that produce import-competing goods and services fall, these firms cut their workforce, unemployment in these industries increases, and wages fall. When these industries have a geographical concentration, such as steel production around Gary, Indiana, an entire region can suffer economic decline.

## Gains and Losses from Exports

We measure the gains and losses from exports just like we measured those from imports, by examining their effect on the price paid and the quantity bought by domestic consumers and the price received and the quantity sold by domestic producers.

**Domestic Consumers Lose from Exports**   When a country exports something to the rest of the world, it is because the country has a comparative advantage at producing that item. Compared to a situation with no international trade, the price paid by consumers rises and the quantity bought in the domestic economy decreases. Domestic consumers lose. The greater the rise in price and decrease in quantity bought, the greater is the consumers' loss.

**Domestic Producers Gain from Exports**   Compared to a situation with no international trade, the price received by domestic producers of an item that is exported rises. Also, the quantity sold by domestic producers of this good or service increases. Because these domestic producers sell a larger quantity and for a higher

# EYE on GLOBALIZATION

MyEconLab Critical Thinking Exercise

## Who Wins and Who Loses from Globalization?

Economists generally agree that the gains from globalization vastly outweigh the losses, but there are both winners and losers.

The U.S. consumer is a big winner. Globalization has brought iPads, Wii games, Nike shoes, and a wide range of other products to our shops at ever lower prices.

The Indian (and Chinese and other Asian) worker is another big winner. Globalization has brought a wider range of more interesting jobs and higher wages.

The U.S. (and European) textile workers and furniture makers are big losers. Their jobs have disappeared and many of them have struggled to find new jobs, even when they've been willing to take a pay cut.

But one of the biggest losers is the African farmer. Blocked from global agricultural markets by trade restrictions and subsidies in the United States and Europe, globalization is leaving much of Africa on the sidelines.

*The U.S. consumer …*

*and Indian workers gain from globalization.*

*But some U.S. workers and …*

*African farmers lose.*

price, producers of exported goods and services gain from international trade. Export industries expand in the face of global demand for their product.

The profits of firms that produce exports rise, these firms expand their workforce, unemployment in these industries decreases, and wages rise. When these industries have a geographical concentration, such as software production in Silicon Valley, an entire region can boom.

## Net Gain

Export producers and import consumers gain, and export consumers and import producers lose, but the gains exceed the losses. In the case of imports, consumers gain what producers lose and then gain even more from the cheaper imports. In the case of exports, producers gain what consumers lose and then gain even more from the items exported. So international trade provides a net gain for a country.

MyEconLab Study Plan 18.1
        Key Terms Quiz
        Solutions Video

# CHECKPOINT 18.1

**Explain how markets work with international trade and identify the gains from international trade and its winners and losers.**

## Practice Problems

Before the 1980s, China did not trade internationally: It was self-sufficient. Then China began to trade internationally in, among other items, coal and shoes. The world price of coal was less than China's domestic price and the world price of shoes was higher than its domestic price.

1.  Does China import or export coal? Who, in China, gains and who loses from international trade in coal? Does China gain from this trade in coal?

2.  On a graph of the market for coal in China show the gains, losses, and net gain or loss from international trade in coal.

3.  Does China import or export shoes? Who, in China, gains and who loses from international trade in shoes? Does China gain from this trade in shoes?

4.  On a graph of the market for shoes in China, show the gains, losses, and net gain or loss from international trade in shoes.

## In the News

**The great American shale boom**
In the past five years, U.S. oil output has doubled. In 2014, the United States and a few smaller countries added 2.4 million barrels a day to total world supply. Thanks to incredible advances in technology, instead of having to import more oil we've cut our reliance on foreign oil

Source: *Forbes*, November 20, 2015

Describe the comparative advantage that the United States has in producing oil, and explain why its comparative advantage has changed.

## Solutions to Practice Problems

1.  The rest of the world has a comparative advantage in producing coal. China imports coal, Chinese coal users gain more than Chinese coal producers lose, so China gains from international trade in coal.

2.  Figure 1 shows the market for coal in China. With international trade, the price falls, the quantity produced decreases, and the quantity bought increases. Consumers gain and producers lose.

3.  China has a comparative advantage in producing shoes. China exports shoes, Chinese shoe producers gain more than Chinese shoe consumers lose, so China gains from international trade in shoes.

4.  Figure 2 shows the shoe market in China. With international trade, the price rises, the quantity produced increases, and the quantity bought decreases. Producers gain and consumers lose.

## Solution to In the News

Before new fracking technology was developed, the opportunity cost of producing oil in the United States was higher than the world market price, so the United States imported most of its oil. With the development of fracking, the cost of producing a barrel of oil in the United States is below the world price. Now the United States has a comparative advantage in the production of oil.

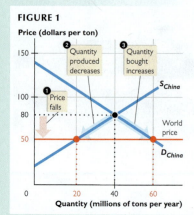

**FIGURE 1**

**Price (dollars per ton)**

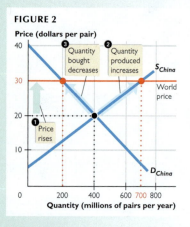

**FIGURE 2**

**Price (dollars per pair)**

## 18.2 INTERNATIONAL TRADE RESTRICTIONS

Governments use four sets of tools to influence international trade and protect domestic industries from foreign competition. They are

- Tariffs
- Import quotas
- Other import barriers

### ■ Tariffs

A **tariff** is a tax that is imposed on a good when it is imported. For example, the government of India imposes a 100 percent tariff on wine imported from California. When an Indian firm imports a $10 bottle of Californian wine, it pays the Indian government a $10 import duty.

The incentive for governments to impose tariffs is strong. First, they provide revenue to the government. Second, they enable the government to satisfy the self-interest of people who earn their incomes in import-competing industries. As you will see, tariffs and other restrictions on free international trade decrease the gains from trade and are not in the social interest. Let's see how.

**Tariff**

A tax imposed on a good when it is imported.

# EYE on the PAST
## The History of U.S. Tariffs

The figure shows the average tariff rate on U.S. imports since 1930. Tariffs peaked during the 1930s when Congress passed the Smoot-Hawley Act. With other nations, the United States signed the General Agreement on Tariffs and Trade (GATT) in 1947. In a series of rounds of negotiations, GATT achieved widespread tariff cuts for the United States and many other nations. Today, the World Trade Organization (WTO) continues the work of GATT and seeks to promote unrestricted trade among all nations.

The United States is a party to many trade agreements with individual countries or regions. These include the North American Free Trade Agreement (NAFTA) and the Central American Free Trade Agreement (CAFTA). These agreements have eliminated tariffs on most goods traded between the United States and the countries of North and Central America.

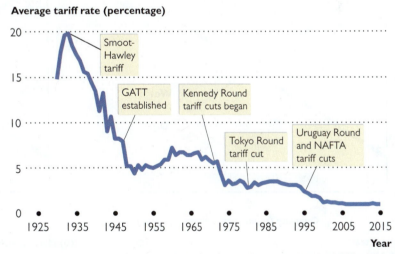

SOURCES OF DATA: The Budget for Fiscal Year 2013, Historical Tables, Table 2.5 and Bureau of Economic Analysis.

### The Effects of a Tariff

To see the effects of a tariff, let's return to the example in which, with free international trade, the United States imports T-shirts. The T-shirts are imported and sold at the world price. Then, under pressure from U.S. garment makers, the U.S. government imposes a tariff on imported T-shirts. Buyers of T-shirts must now pay the world price plus the tariff. Several consequences follow in the market for T-shirts. Figure 18.3 illustrates these consequences.

Figure 18.3(a) is the same as Figure 18.1(b) and shows the situation with free international trade. The United States produces 20 million T-shirts and imports 40 million T-shirts a year at the world price of $5 a T-shirt.

Figure 18.3(b) shows what happens with a tariff, which is set at $2 per T-shirt. The following changes occur in the U.S. market for T-shirts:

*   The price of a T-shirt in the United States rises by $2.
*   The quantity of T-shirts bought in the United States decreases.
*   The quantity of T-shirts produced in the United States increases.
*   The quantity of T-shirts imported into the United States decreases.
*   The U.S. government collects a tariff revenue.

**FIGURE 18.3**

The Effects of a Tariff

MyEconLab Animation

**(a) Free trade**

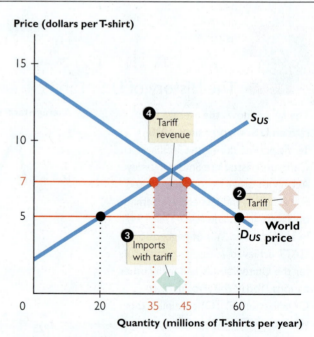

**(b) Market with tariff**

The world price of a T-shirt is $5. With free trade, in part (a), Americans buy 60 million T-shirts. The United States produces 20 million T-shirts and ❶ imports 40 million T-shirts. ❷ With a tariff of $2 per T-shirt in part (b), the domestic price rises

to $7 a T-shirt (the world price plus the tariff). Domestic production increases, purchases decrease, and ❸ the quantity imported decreases. ❹ The U.S. government collects tariff revenue of $2 on each T-shirt imported, which is shown by the purple rectangle.

*Rise in Price of a T-Shirt*   To buy a T-shirt, Americans must pay the world price plus the tariff, so the price of a T-shirt rises by $2 to $7. Figure 18.3(b) shows the new domestic price line, which lies $2 above the world price line.

*Decrease in Purchases*   The higher price of a T-shirt brings a decrease in the quantity demanded, which Figure 18.3(b) shows as a movement along the demand curve from 60 million T-shirts at $5 a T-shirt to 45 million T-shirts at $7 a T-shirt.

*Increase in Domestic Production*   The higher price of a T-shirt stimulates domestic production, which Figure 18.3(b) shows as a movement along the supply curve from 20 million T-shirts at $5 a T-shirt to 35 million T-shirts at $7 a T-shirt.

*Decrease in Imports*   T-shirt imports decrease by 30 million from 40 million to 10 million a year. Both the decrease in purchases and the increase in domestic production contribute to this decrease in imports.

*Tariff Revenue*   The government's tariff revenue is $20 million—$2 per T-shirt on 10 million imported T-shirts—shown by the purple rectangle.

## Winners, Losers, and the Social Loss from a Tariff

A tariff on an imported good creates winners and losers. When the U.S. government imposes a tariff on an imported good,

- U.S. consumers of the good lose.
- U.S. producers of the good gain.
- U.S. consumers lose more than U.S. producers gain.

*U.S. Consumers of the Good Lose*   Because the price of a T-shirt in the United States rises, the quantity of T-shirts demanded decreases. The combination of a higher price and smaller quantity bought makes U.S. consumers of T-shirts worse off.

*U.S. Producers of the Good Gain*   Because the price of an imported T-shirt rises by the tariff, U.S. T-shirt producers are now able to sell their T-shirts for a higher price—the world price plus the tariff. As the price of a T-shirt rises, U.S. producers increase the quantity supplied. The combination of a higher price and a larger quantity produced increases producers' profits, so U.S. producers of T-shirts gain.

*U.S. Consumers Lose More Than U.S. Producers Gain*   Consumers lose from the tariff for three reasons:

- They pay a higher price to domestic producers.
- They purchase a smaller quantity of the good.
- They pay tariff revenue to the government.

The tariff revenue is a loss to consumers of T-shirts but a gain to consumers of public services paid for by the tariff. The higher price paid to domestic producers pays for the higher cost of domestic production. The increased domestic production could have been obtained at lower cost as an import. Consumers lose and no one gains from the decreased quantity of T-shirts.

Let's now look at the second tool for restricting trade: quotas.

**Import quota**

A quantitative restriction on the import of a good that limits the maximum quantity of a good that may be imported in a given period.

## ■ Import Quotas

An **import quota** is a quantitative restriction on the import of a good that limits the maximum quantity of a good that may be imported in a given period. The United States imposes import quotas on many items, including sugar and steel. Quotas enable the government to satisfy the self-interest of people who earn their incomes in import-competing industries. You will see that like a tariff, a quota on imports decreases the gains from trade and is not in the social interest.

### The Effects of an Import Quota

Figure 18.4 illustrates the effects. Figure 18.4(a) shows the situation with free international trade. Figure 18.4(b) shows what happens with a quota that limits imports to 10 million T-shirts a year. The U.S. supply curve of T-shirts becomes the domestic supply curve, $S_{US}$, plus the quantity that the quota permits to be imported. So the U.S. supply curve becomes the curve labeled $S_{US}$ + *quota*.

The price of a T-shirt rises to $7, the quantity of T-shirts bought in the United States decreases to 45 million a year, the quantity of T-shirts produced in the United States increases to 35 million a year, and the quantity of T-shirts imported into the United States decreases to the quota quantity of 10 million a year. All these effects of a quota are identical to the effects of a tariff set at $2 per T-shirt, as you can check in Figure 18.3(b).

### FIGURE 18.4

The Effects of an Import Quota

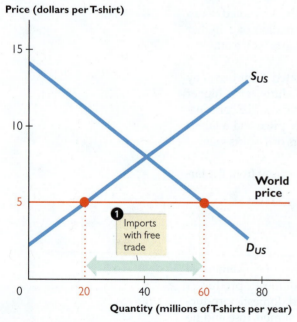

**(a) Free trade**

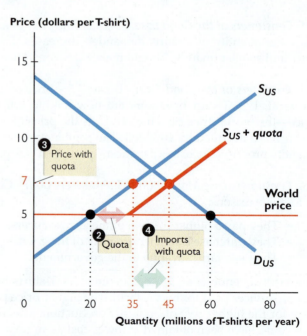

**(b) Market with quota**

With free trade, in part (a), Americans buy 60 million T-shirts at the world price. The United States produces 20 million T-shirts and ❶ imports 40 million T-shirts. ❷ With an import quota of 10 million

T-shirts, in part (b), the U.S. supply curve becomes $S_{US}$ + *quota*. ❸ The price rises to $7 a T-shirt. Domestic production increases, purchases decrease, and ❹ the quantity imported decreases.

### Winners, Losers, and the Social Loss from an Import Quota

An import quota creates winners and losers that are similar to those of a tariff but with an interesting difference. When the government imposes an import quota,

- U.S. consumers of the good lose.
- U.S. producers of the good gain.
- Importers of the good gain.
- Society loses.

*U.S. Consumers of the Good Lose*   Because the price of a T-shirt in the United States rises, the quantity of T-shirts demanded decreases. The combination of a higher price and smaller quantity bought makes the consumer worse off. So the U.S. consumers lose when a quota is imposed.

*U.S. Producers of the Good Gain*   Because the price of a T-shirt rises, U.S. T-shirt producers increase production. The combination of a higher price and larger quantity produced increases producers' profits. So the U.S. producers gain from the quota.

*Importers of the Good Gain*   The importer is able to buy T-shirts on the world market at the world price, and sell them in the domestic market at the domestic price. Because the domestic price exceeds the world price, the importer gains.

*Society Loses*   Society loses because the loss to consumers exceeds the gains of domestic producers and importers. Just like the social losses from a tariff, there is a social loss because part of the higher price paid to domestic producers pays the higher cost of domestic production. There is a social loss from the decreased quantity of the good bought at the higher price.

## ■ Other Import Barriers

Two sets of policies that influence imports are

- Health, safety, and regulation barriers
- Voluntary export restraints

### Health, Safety, and Regulation Barriers

Thousands of detailed health, safety, and other regulations restrict international trade. For example, U.S. food imports are examined by the Food and Drug Administration to determine whether the food is "pure, wholesome, safe to eat, and produced under sanitary conditions." The discovery of BSE (mad cow disease) in just one U.S. cow in 2003 was enough to close down international trade in U.S. beef. The European Union bans imports of most genetically modified foods, such as U.S.-produced soybeans. Although regulations of the type we've just described are not designed to limit international trade, they have that effect.

### Voluntary Export Restraints

A *voluntary export restraint* is like a quota allocated to a foreign exporter of the good. A voluntary export restraint decreases imports just like an import quota does, but the foreign exporter gets the profit from the gap between the domestic price and the world price.

MyEconLab Study Plan 18.2
Key Terms Quiz
Solutions Video

 CHECKPOINT 18.2

**Explain the effects of international trade barriers.**

## Practice Problems

Before 1995, the United States imposed tariffs on goods imported from Mexico and Mexico imposed tariffs on goods imported from the United States. In 1995, Mexico joined NAFTA. U.S. tariffs on imports from Mexico and Mexican tariffs on imports from the United States are gradually being removed.

1. Explain how the price that U.S. consumers pay for goods imported from Mexico and the quantity of U.S. imports from Mexico have changed. Who, in the United States, are the winners and losers from this free trade?

2. Explain how the quantity of U.S. exports to Mexico and the U.S. government's tariff revenue from trade with Mexico have changed.

3. Suppose that this year, tomato growers in Florida lobby the U.S. government to impose an import quota on Mexican tomatoes. Explain who, in the United States, would gain and who would lose from such a quota.

## In the News

### The Trans-Pacific Partnership (TPP)
If the TPP comes into effect, Canada will remove import quotas on American milk, Japan will free imports of American beef, and the United States will remove import tariffs on items such as steel, auto-parts, garments, and solar panels.

Source: *The New York Times*, October 6, 2015

Explain how the changes described in the news clip will change U.S. exports and imports and who in the United States will gain and lose from the TPP.

## Solutions to Practice Problems

1. The price that U.S. consumers pay for goods imported from Mexico has fallen and the quantity of U.S. imports from Mexico has increased. The winners are U.S. consumers of goods imported from Mexico and the losers are U.S. producers of goods imported from Mexico.

2. The quantity of U.S. exports to Mexico has increased and the U.S. government's tariff revenue from trade with Mexico has fallen.

3. With an import quota, the price of tomatoes in the United States would rise and the quantity bought would decrease, so consumers would lose. Growers would receive a higher price and produce a larger quantity, so they would gain. Consumers would lose more than tomato growers would gain, so the U.S. society would have a net loss.

## Solution to In the News

Removing trade barriers on milk and beef will raise the price at which U.S. farmers can sell each item and exports will increase. U.S. farmers will gain and U.S. consumers will lose. Removing U.S. tariffs on steel and other manufactures will lower their prices in the United States and increase U.S. imports. With the lower prices, U.S. consumer surplus increases—consumers gain. U.S. producer surplus decreases—producers lose. For both exports and imports, total surplus increases.

## 18.3    THE CASE AGAINST PROTECTION

MyEconLab Concept Video

For as long as nations and international trade have existed, people have debated whether free international trade or protection from foreign competition is better for a country. The debate continues, but most economists believe that free trade promotes prosperity for all countries while protection reduces the potential gains from trade. We've seen the most powerful case for free trade: All countries benefit from their comparative advantage. But there is a broader range of issues in the free trade versus protection debate. Let's review these issues.

### ■ Three Traditional Arguments for Protection

Three traditional arguments for protection and restricting international trade are

- The national security argument
- The infant-industry argument
- The dumping argument

Let's look at each in turn.

### The National Security Argument

The national security argument is that a country must protect industries that produce defense equipment and armaments and those on which the defense industries rely for their raw materials and other intermediate inputs. This argument for protection can be taken too far.

First, it is an argument for international isolation, for in a time of war, there is no industry that does not contribute to national defense. Second, if the case is made for boosting the output of a strategic industry—say aerospace—it is more efficient to achieve this outcome with a subsidy financed out of taxes than with a tariff or import quota. A subsidy would keep the industry operating at the scale that is judged appropriate, and free international trade would keep the prices faced by consumers at their world market levels.

*Should producers of national security equipment be protected from international competition?*

### The Infant-Industry Argument

The **infant-industry argument** is that it is necessary to protect a new industry to enable it to grow into a mature industry that can compete in world markets. The argument is based on an idea called *learning-by-doing*. By working repeatedly at a task, workers become better at that task and can increase the amount they produce in a given period.

There is nothing wrong with the idea of learning-by-doing. It is a powerful engine of human capital accumulation and economic growth. Learning-by-doing can change comparative advantage. If on-the-job experience lowers the opportunity cost of producing a good, a country might develop a comparative advantage in producing that good.

But learning-by-doing does not justify protection. It is in the self-interest of firms and workers who benefit from learning-by-doing to produce the efficient quantities. If the government protected these firms to boost their production, there would be an inefficient overproduction.

The historical evidence is against the protection of infant industries. Countries in East Asia that have not given such protection have performed well. Countries that have protected infant industries, as India once did, have performed poorly.

**Infant-industry argument**
The argument that it is necessary to protect a new industry to enable it to grow into a mature industry that can compete in world markets.

*India's protection of manufacturing industries from international competition is generally regarded as a failure.*

## The Dumping Argument

**Dumping**

When a foreign firm sells its exports at a lower price than its cost of production.

**Dumping** occurs when a foreign firm sells its exports at a lower price than its cost of production. You might be wondering why a firm would ever want to sell any of its output at a price below the cost of production. Wouldn't such a firm be better off either selling nothing, or, if it could do so, raising its price to at least cover its costs? Two possible reasons why a firm might sell at a price below cost and therefore engage in dumping are

- Predatory pricing
- Subsidy

*China, a major producer of solar panels, is accused of dumping them on the U.S. and European markets.*

*Predatory Pricing*   A firm that engages in *predatory pricing* sets its price below cost in the hope that it can drive its competitors out of the market. If a firm in one country tries to drive out competitors in another country, it will be *dumping* its product in the foreign market. The foreign firm sells its output at a price below its cost to drive domestic firms out of business. When the domestic firms have gone, the foreign firm takes advantage of its monopoly position and charges a higher price for its product. The higher price will attract new competitors, which makes it unlikely that this strategy will be profitable. For this reason, economists are skeptical that this type of dumping occurs.

*Subsidy*   A *subsidy* is a payment by the government to a producer. A firm that receives a subsidy is able to sell profitably for a price below cost. Subsidies are very common in almost all countries. The United States and the European Union subsidize the production of many agricultural products and dump their surpluses on the world market. This action lowers the prices that farmers in developing nations receive and weakens the incentive to expand farming in poor countries. India and Europe have been suspected of dumping steel in the United States.

Whatever its source, dumping is illegal under the rules of the WTO, NAFTA, and CAFTA and is regarded as a justification for temporary tariffs. Consequently, anti-dumping tariffs have become important in today's world.

But there are powerful reasons to resist the dumping argument for protection. First, it is virtually impossible to detect dumping because it is hard to determine a firm's costs. As a result, the test for dumping is whether a firm's export price is below its domestic price. This test is a weak one because it can be rational for a firm to charge a lower price in markets in which the quantity demanded is highly sensitive to price and a higher price in a market in which demand is less price-sensitive.

Second, it is hard to think of a good that is produced by a single firm. Even if all the domestic firms were driven out of business in some industry, it would always be possible to find several and usually many alternative foreign sources of supply and to buy at prices determined in competitive markets.

Third, if a good or service were a truly global natural monopoly, the best way to deal with it would be by regulation—just as in the case of domestic monopolies. Such regulation would require international cooperation.

The three arguments for protection that we've just examined have an element of credibility. The counterarguments are in general stronger, so these arguments do not make the case for protection. They are not the only arguments that you might encounter. There are many others, four of which we'll now examine.

# ■ Four Newer Arguments for Protection

Four newer and commonly made arguments for restricting international trade are that protection

- Saves jobs
- Allows us to compete with cheap foreign labor
- Brings diversity and stability
- Penalizes lax environmental standards

## Saves Jobs

When Americans buy imported goods such as shoes from Brazil, U.S. workers who produce shoes lose their jobs. With no earnings and poor prospects, these workers become a drain on welfare and spend less, which creates a ripple effect of further job losses. The proposed solution is to protect U.S. jobs by banning imports of cheap foreign goods. The proposal is flawed for the following reasons.

First, free trade does cost some jobs, but it also creates other jobs. It brings about a global rationalization of labor and allocates labor resources to their highest-valued activities. Because of international trade in textiles, tens of thousands of workers in the United States have lost jobs because shoe factories and textile mills have closed. Tens of thousands of workers in other countries now have jobs because shoe factories and textile mills have opened there. And tens of thousands of U.S. workers now have better-paying jobs than as shoe makers or textile workers because other export industries have expanded and created more jobs than have been destroyed.

Second, imports create jobs. They create jobs for retailers that sell imported goods and for firms that service those goods. They also create jobs by creating incomes in the rest of the world, some of which are spent on imports of U.S.-made goods and services.

Protection saves some particular jobs, but it does so at a high cost. For example, until 2005, textile jobs in the United States were protected by import quotas imposed under an international agreement called the Multifiber Arrangement (or MFA). The U.S. International Trade Commission (ITC) estimated that because of import quotas, 72,000 jobs existed in textiles that would otherwise disappear and annual clothing expenditure in the United States was $15.9 billion ($160 per family) higher than it would be with free trade. An implication of the ITC estimate is that each textile job saved cost consumers $221,000 a year. The end of the MFA led to the destruction of a large number of textile jobs in the United States and Europe in 2005.

*Few shoe factories remain in the United States and manufacturing jobs have been lost …*

*… but well-paid professional and service jobs have been created to replace the lost manufacturing jobs.*

## Allows Us to Compete with Cheap Foreign Labor

With the removal of protective tariffs in U.S. trade with Mexico, some people said that jobs would be sucked into Mexico and that the United States would not be able to compete with its southern neighbor. Let's see what's wrong with this view.

Labor costs depend on the wage rate and the quantity a worker produces. For example, if a U.S. auto worker earns $30 an hour and produces 15 units of output an hour, the average labor cost of a unit of output is $2. If a Mexican auto worker earns $3 an hour and produces 1 unit of output an hour, the average labor cost of a unit of output is $3. Other things remaining the same, the greater the output a worker produces, the higher is the worker's wage rate. High-wage workers produce a large output. Low-wage workers produce a small output.

Although high-wage U.S. workers are more productive, on the average, than lower-wage Mexican workers, there are differences across industries. U.S. labor is relatively more productive in some activities than in others. For example, the productivity of U.S. workers in producing movies, financial services, and customized computer chips is relatively higher than their productivity in the production of metals and some standardized machine parts. The activities in which U.S. workers are relatively more productive than their Mexican counterparts are those in which the United States has a comparative advantage. By engaging in free trade, increasing our production and exports of the goods and services in which we have a comparative advantage, and decreasing our production and increasing our imports of the goods and services in which our trading partners have a comparative advantage, we can make ourselves and the citizens of other countries better off.

### Brings Diversity and Stability

A diversified investment portfolio is less risky than one that has all of its eggs in one basket. The same is true for an economy's production. A diversified economy fluctuates less than an economy that produces only one or two goods.

Most economies, whether the rich, advanced United States, Japan, and Europe or the developing China and Brazil, have diversified production and do not have this type of stability problem. A few economies, such as Saudi Arabia, have a comparative advantage that leads to the specialized production of only one good. But even these economies can stabilize their income and consumption by investing in a wide range of production activities in other countries.

### Penalizes Lax Environmental Standards

A new argument for protection is that many poorer countries, such as Mexico, do not have the same environmental standards that we have, and because they are willing to pollute and we are not, we cannot compete with them without tariffs. If these countries want free trade with the richer and "greener" countries, then they must raise their environmental standards.

This argument for trade restrictions is not entirely convincing. A poor country is less able than a rich one to devote resources to achieving high environmental standards. If free trade helps a poor country to become richer, then it will also help that country to develop the means to improve its environment. But there probably is a case for using the negotiation of free trade agreements such as NAFTA and CAFTA to hold member countries to higher environmental standards. There is an especially large payoff from using such bargaining to try to avoid irreversible damage to resources such as tropical rainforests.

So the four common arguments that we've just considered do not provide overwhelming support for protection. They all have flaws and leave the case for free international trade a strong one.

### ■ Why Is International Trade Restricted?

Why, despite all the arguments against protection, is international trade restricted? One reason that applies to developing nations is that the tariff is a convenient source of government revenue, but this reason does not apply to the United States where the government has access to income taxes and sales taxes.

Political support for international trade restrictions in the United States and most other developed countries arises from rent seeking. **Rent seeking** is lobbying and other political activity that seeks to capture the gains from trade. You've seen that free trade benefits consumers but shrinks the producer surplus of firms that compete in markets with imports.

The winners from free trade are the millions of consumers of low-cost imports, but the benefit per individual consumer is small. The losers from free trade are the producers of import-competing items. Compared to the millions of consumers, there are only a few thousand producers.

Now think about imposing a tariff on clothing. Millions of consumers will bear the cost in the form of a higher price and a smaller quantity and a few thousand garment makers and their employees will share the gain arising from the higher price and larger quantity.

Because the gain from a tariff is large, producers have a strong incentive to incur the expense of lobbying *for* a tariff and *against* free trade. On the other hand, because each consumer's loss is small, consumers have little incentive to organize and incur the expense of lobbying *for* free trade. The gain from free trade for any one person is too small for that person to spend much time or money on a political organization to lobby for free trade. The loss from free trade will be seen as being so great by those bearing that loss that they will find it profitable to join a political organization to prevent free trade. Each group weighs benefits against costs and chooses the best action for themselves, but the anti-free-trade group will undertake more political lobbying than will the pro-free-trade group.

**Rent seeking**
Lobbying and other political activity that aims to capture the gains from trade.

# EYE on YOUR LIFE
## International Trade

MyEconLab Critical Thinking Exercise

International trade plays an extraordinarily large role in your life in three broad ways. It affects you as a

- Consumer
- Producer
- Voter

As a *consumer*, you benefit from the availability of a wide range of low-cost, high-quality goods and services that are produced in other countries.

Look closely at the labels on the items you buy. Where was your computer made? Where were your shirt and your shoes made? Where are the fruits and vegetables that you buy, especially during winter, grown?

The answers to all these questions are most likely Asia, Mexico, or South America. A few items were produced in Europe, Canada, and the United States.

As a *producer* (or as a potential producer if you don't yet have a job), you benefit from huge global markets for U.S. products. Your job prospects would be much dimmer if the firm for which you work didn't have global markets in which to sell its products.

People who work in the aircraft industry, for example, benefit from the huge global market for large passenger jets. Airlines from Canada to China are buying Boeing 737 and 787 aircraft as fast as they can be pushed out of the production line.

Even if you were to become a college professor, you would benefit from international trade in education services when your school admits foreign students.

As a *voter*, you have a big stake in the politics of free trade versus protection. As a buyer, your self-interest is hurt by tariffs and quotas on imported goods. Each time you buy a $20 sweater, you contribute $5 to the government in tariff revenue. But as a worker, your self-interest might be hurt by freer access to U.S. markets for foreign producers.

So as you decide how to vote, you must figure out what trade policy serves your self-interest and what best serves the social interest.

MyEconLab Study Plan 18.3
Key Terms Quiz
Solutions Video

 ## CHECKPOINT 18.3

**Explain and evaluate arguments used to justify restricting international trade.**

## Practice Problems

1. Japan grows rice and sets an import quota on rice. California rice growers would like to export more rice to Japan. What are Japan's arguments for restricting imports of Californian rice? Are these arguments correct? Who loses from this restriction in trade?

2. The United States produces steel and, from time to time, has limited imports of steel from Europe. What argument has the United States used to justify this quota? Who wins from this restriction? Who loses?

3. The United States maintains an import quota on sugar. What is the argument for this import quota? Is this argument flawed? If so, explain why.

## In the News

**India looks at raising duty on steel imports to 20%**
India's steel imports are 58 percent higher than a year ago and the country's steel producers have complained that cheap imports have driven market prices below their production costs.

Source: *The Financial Times*, September 10, 2015

What is the argument that Indian steel producers are using to support an increase in the tariff on steel imports? What is wrong with their argument?

## Solutions to Practice Problems

1. The main arguments are that Japanese rice is a better quality rice and that the quota limits competition faced by Japanese farmers. The arguments are not correct. If Japanese consumers do not like the quality of Californian rice, they will not buy it. The quota limits competition and allows Japanese farmers to use their land less efficiently. The big losers are the Japanese consumers who pay about three times the U.S. price for rice.

2. The U.S. argument is that European producers dump steel on the U.S. market. With an import quota, U.S. steel producers will face less competition and U.S. jobs will be saved. Workers in the steel industry and owners of steel companies will win at the expense of U.S. buyers of steel.

3. The argument is that the import quota protects the jobs of U.S. workers. The argument is flawed because the United States does not have a comparative advantage in producing sugar and so an import quota allows the U.S. sugar industry to be inefficient. With free international trade in sugar, the U.S. sugar industry would exist but it would be much smaller and more efficient.

## Solution to In the News

Indian steel producers are using the dumping argument: Protection is needed because foreign producers are selling steel in India at prices below the cost of production. What's wrong with this argument is that it is difficult to determine whether foreign producers are selling at prices below their costs and unlikely that they would want to do so. So foreign producers might have a comparative advantage in producing steel.

# CHAPTER SUMMARY

## Key Points

**1.** **Explain how markets work with international trade and identify the gains from international trade and its winners and losers.**

- Comparative advantage drives international trade.
- When the world price of a good is lower than the price that balances domestic demand and supply, a country gains by decreasing production and importing the good.
- When the world price of a good is higher than the price that balances domestic demand and supply, a country gains by increasing production and exporting the good.
- Compared to a no-trade situation, in a market with imports, consumers gain and producers lose, but the gains exceed the losses.
- Compared to a no-trade situation, in a market with exports, producers gain and consumers lose, but the gains exceed the losses.

**2.** **Explain the effects of international trade barriers.**

- Countries restrict international trade by imposing tariffs, import quotas, and other import barriers.
- Trade restrictions raise the domestic price of imported goods, lower the quantity imported, decrease consumer surplus, increase producer surplus, and create a deadweight loss.

**3.** **Explain and evaluate arguments used to justify restricting international trade.**

- The arguments that protection is necessary for national security, for infant industries, and to prevent dumping are weak.
- Arguments that protection saves jobs, allows us to compete with cheap foreign labor, makes the economy diversified and stable, and is needed to penalize lax environmental standards are flawed.
- Trade is restricted because protection brings small losses to a large number of people and large gains to a small number of people.

## Key Terms

MyEconLab Key Terms Quiz

Dumping, 470
Exports, 456
Import quota, 466
Imports, 456

Infant-industry argument, 469
Rent seeking, 473
Tariff, 463

# CHAPTER CHECKPOINT

## Study Plan Problems and Applications

Use Figures 1 and 2 to work Problems **1** to **4**. Figure 1 and Figure 2 show the markets for shoes if there is no trade between the United States and Brazil.

**FIGURE 1   U.S. SHOE MARKET**

**1.** Which country has a comparative advantage in producing shoes? With international trade, explain which country would export shoes and how the price of shoes in the importing country and the quantity produced by the importing country would change. Explain which country gains from this trade.

**2.** The world price of a pair of shoes is $20. Explain how consumers and producers in the United States gain or lose as a result of international trade. On the graph, show the change in U.S. purchases, production, and the price of a pair of shoes.

**3.** The world price of a pair of shoes is $20. Explain how consumers and producers in Brazil gain or lose as a result of international trade. Show the change in Brazil's purchases, production, and the price of a pair of shoes.

**4.** Who in the United States loses from free trade in shoes with Brazil? Explain.

**FIGURE 2   BRAZIL'S SHOE MARKET**

Use the following information to work Problems **5** to **7**.

**5.** The supply of roses in the United States is made up of U.S.-grown roses and imported roses. Draw a graph to illustrate the U.S. rose market with free international trade. On your graph, mark the price of roses and the quantities of roses bought, produced, and imported into the United States.

**6.** Who in the United States loses from this trade in roses and would lobby for a restriction on the quantity of imported roses? Suppose that the U.S. government put a tariff on rose imports. Show on your graph the effect of the tariff on U.S. consumers and U.S. producers. Show the government's tariff revenue.

**7.** Suppose that the U.S. government puts an import quota on roses. Show on your graph the effect on the quantity bought by U.S. consumers, the quantity produced by U.S. rose growers, and the quantity imported.

Use the following information to work Problems **8** to **10**.

### U.S. steelmakers seek antidumping action

Steelmakers want the United States to put restrictions on imports from five nations, alleging unfair pricing of steel for the automobile and construction industries.

Source: *Wall Street Journal*, June 3, 2015

**8.** Explain who in the United States gains and who loses from restrictions on steel imports. How do you expect the prices of automobiles and office towers to be affected?

**9.** What is dumping? Who in the United States loses from foreign firms' dumping of steel?

**10.** Explain what an antidumping tariff is. What argument might U.S. steelmakers use to get the government to raise the tariff on steel imports?

 **11.** Read *Eye on Globalization* on p. 461 and draw two graphs to show how U.S. consumers gain from iPads manufactured in China and why Chinese workers also gain.

## Instructor Assignable Problems and Applications

MyEconLab Homework, Quiz, or Test if assigned by instructor

Use the following information to work Problems **1** and **2**.

**The future of U.S.–India relations**
In May 2009, Secretary of State Hillary Clinton gave a major speech covering all the issues in U.S.–India relations. On economic and trade relations she noted that India maintains significant barriers to U.S. trade. The United States also maintains barriers against Indian imports such as textiles. Mrs. Clinton, President Obama, and Anand Sharma, the Indian Minister of Commerce and Industry, say they want to dismantle these trade barriers.

Source: www.state.gov

1. Explain who in the United States would gain and who might lose from dismantling trade barriers between the United States and India.

2. Draw a graph of the U.S. market for textiles and show how removing a tariff would change the quantities produced, bought, and imported. Explain why the gains exceed the losses.

3. The United States exports wheat. Draw a graph to illustrate the U.S. wheat market if there is free international trade in wheat. On your graph, mark the price of wheat and the quantities bought, produced, and exported by the United States.

4. Suppose that the world price of sugar is 20 cents a pound, Brazil does not trade internationally, and the equilibrium price of sugar in Brazil is 10 cents a pound. Brazil then begins to trade internationally.

   • How does the price of sugar in Brazil change? Do Brazilians buy more or less sugar? Do Brazilian sugar growers produce more or less sugar?
   • Does Brazil export or import sugar and why?

5. The United States exports services and imports coffee. Why does the United States gain from exporting services and importing coffee? How do economists measure the net gain from this international trade?

6. In the 1950s, Ford and General Motors established a small car-producing industry in Australia and argued for a high tariff on car imports. The tariff has remained through the years. Until 2000, the tariff was 22.5 percent. What might have been Ford's and General Motors' argument for the high tariff? Is the tariff the best way to achieve the goals of the argument?

Use Figure 1 and the following information to work Problems **7** to **9**.

Figure 1 shows the car market in Mexico when Mexico places no restriction on the quantity of cars imported. The world price of a car is $10,000.

7. If the government of Mexico introduces a $2,000 tariff on car imports, what will be the price of a car in Mexico, the quantity of cars produced in Mexico, the quantity imported into Mexico, and the government's tariff revenue?

8. If the government of Mexico introduces an import quota of 4 million cars a year, what will be the price of a car in Mexico, the quantity of cars produced in Mexico, and the quantity imported?

9. What argument might be used to encourage the government of Mexico to introduce a $2,000 tariff on car imports from the United States? Who will gain and who will lose as a result of Mexico's tariff?

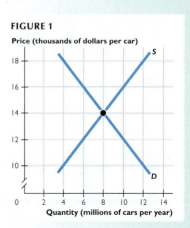

**FIGURE 1**

Price (thousands of dollars per car)

MyEconLab Chapter 18 Study Plan

# Multiple Choice Quiz

1. The fundamental force driving international trade is comparative _____.
    A. advantage: a country exports those goods that have high prices
    B. abundance: the country that produces more than it needs exports the good
    C. advantage: the country with the lower opportunity cost of production exports the good
    D. cost: a country trades with other countries that produce cheaper goods

2. A country will export wheat if, with no international trade, _____.
    A. it produces a surplus of wheat
    B. its opportunity cost of producing wheat is below the world price
    C. its domestic price of wheat exceeds the world price
    D. other countries have a shortage of wheat

3. With free trade between the United States and Canada, the United States exports tomatoes and Canada exports maple syrup. U.S. consumers _____.
    A. of tomatoes gain and Canadian consumers of maple syrup lose
    B. of both tomatoes and maple syrup gain more than either producer
    C. of maple syrup gain more than U.S. producers of maple syrup lose
    D. of tomatoes gain more than U.S. producers of tomatoes lose

4. With free trade between China and the United States, the winners are _____ and the losers are _____.
    A. U.S. consumers of U.S. imports; U.S. producers of the U.S. imported good
    B. China's consumers of China's imports; China's producers of its export good
    C. U.S. producers of the U.S. export good; U.S. consumers of U.S. imports
    D. China's consumers of China's export good; China's producers of its imported good

5. The U.S. tariff on paper _____ the U.S. price of paper, _____ U.S. production of paper, and _____the U.S. gains from trade.
    A. raises; increases; increases
    B. doesn't change; increases; increases
    C. doesn't change; doesn't change; decreases
    D. raises; increases; decreases

6. If Korea imposes an import quota on U.S. oranges, losers include Korean _____ of oranges and U.S. _____ of oranges.
    A. consumers; consumers
    B. consumers; producers
    C. producers; consumers
    D. producers; producers

7. The people who support restricted international trade say that _____.
    A. protection saves jobs, in both the U.S. and foreign economies
    B. U.S. firms won't be able to compete with low-wage foreign labor if trade is free
    C. outsourcing sends jobs abroad, which brings diversification and makes our economy more stable
    D. protection is needed to enable U.S. firms to produce the things at which they have a comparative advantage.

Why does our dollar fluctuate?

# International Finance

**When you have completed your study of this chapter, you will be able to**

**1** Describe a country's balance of payments accounts and explain what determines the amount of international borrowing and lending.

**2** Explain how the exchange rate is determined and why it fluctuates.

MyEconLab Big Picture Video

## 19.1 FINANCING INTERNATIONAL TRADE

When Apple, Inc. imports iPods manufactured in Taiwan, it pays for them using Taiwanese dollars. When a French construction company buys an earthmover from Caterpillar, Inc., it uses U.S. dollars. Whenever we buy things from another country, we pay in the currency of that country. It doesn't make any difference what the item being traded is; it might be a consumption good or a service or a capital good, a building, or even a firm.

We're going to study the markets in which different types of currency are bought and sold. But first we're going to look at the scale of international trading and borrowing and lending and at the way in which we keep our records of these transactions. These records are called the balance of payments accounts.

### ■ Balance of Payments Accounts

**Balance of payments accounts**
The accounts in which a nation records its international trading, borrowing, and lending.

A country's **balance of payments accounts** record its international trading, borrowing, and lending. There are in fact three balance of payments accounts:

- Current account
- Capital and financial account
- Official settlements account

**Current account**
Record of receipts from the sale of goods and services to other countries (exports), minus payments for goods and services bought from other countries (imports), plus the net amount of interest and transfers received from and paid to other countries.

The **current account** records receipts from the sale of goods and services to other countries (exports), minus payments for goods and services bought from other countries (imports), plus the net amount of interest and transfers (such as foreign aid payments) received from and paid to other countries. The **capital and financial account** records foreign investment in the United States minus U.S. investment abroad. The **official settlements account** records the change in U.S. official reserves. **U.S. official reserves** are the government's holdings of foreign currency. If U.S. official reserves increase, the official settlements account balance is negative. The reason is that holding foreign money is like investing abroad and U.S. investment abroad is a minus item in the capital and financial account. (And if official reserves decrease, the official settlements account balance is positive.)

**Capital and financial account**
Record of foreign investment in the United States minus U.S. investment abroad.

**Official settlements account**
Record of the change in U.S. official reserves.

**U.S. official reserves**
The government's holdings of foreign currency.

The sum of the balances on the three accounts always equals zero. That is, to pay for our current account deficit, we must either borrow more from abroad than we lend abroad or use our official reserves to cover the shortfall.

Table 19.1 shows the U.S. balance of payments accounts in 2015. Items in the current account and capital and financial account that provide foreign currency to the United States have a plus sign; items that cost the United States foreign currency have a minus sign. The table shows that in 2015, U.S. imports exceeded U.S. exports and the current account deficit was $463 billion. To pay for imports that exceeded the value of our exports we borrowed from the rest of the world. The capital and financial account tells us by how much. We borrowed $402 billion (foreign investment in the United States) and made $200 billion of loans to the rest of the world (U.S. investment abroad). With other net foreign borrowing of −$1 billion, the capital and financial account balance would be $201 billion. Omitted items and measurement error create an unusually large statistical discrepancy of $268 billion. Official reserves increased by $6 billion and are shown in Table 19.1 as a negative $6 billion, a convention that makes the three accounts sum to zero.

You might better understand the balance of payments accounts and the way in which they are linked if you think about the income and expenditure, borrowing and lending, and bank account of an individual.

# EYE on the U.S. ECONOMY
## The U.S. Balance of Payments

The numbers in Table 19.1 provide a snapshot of the U.S. balance of payments in 2015. This figure puts this snapshot into perspective by showing how the balance of payments evolved from 1980 to 2015.

A current account deficit emerged during the 1980s but briefly disappeared with a near-zero balance in the recession of the early 1990s. As the economy resumed its expansion during the 1990s, the current account deficit increased and kept on increasing until 2006.

As economic growth slowed and the economy went into recession, imports shrank and so did the current account deficit.

The capital and financial account balance is almost a mirror image of the current account balance and the reason is that the official settlements

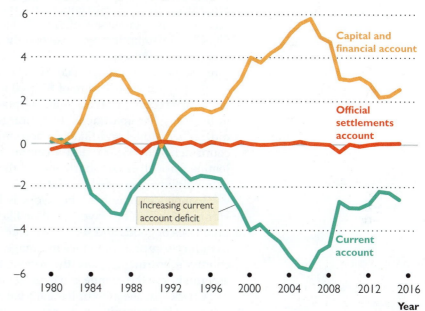

Balance of payments (percentage of GDP)

SOURCE OF DATA: Bureau of Economic Analysis.

balance—the change in foreign exchange reserves—is very small in comparison with the balances on the other two accounts.

---

■ **TABLE 19.1**

### The U.S. Balance of Payments Accounts in 2015

| | (billions of dollars) |
|---|---|
| **Current account** | |
| Exports of goods and services | +2,261 |
| Imports of goods and services | −2,761 |
| Net interest | +193 |
| Net transfers | −156 |
| **Current account balance** | **−463** |
| | |
| **Capital and financial account** | |
| Foreign investment in the United States | +402 |
| U.S. investment abroad | −200 |
| Other net foreign investment in the United States | −1 |
| Statistical discrepancy | +268 |
| **Capital and financial account balance** | **+469** |
| | |
| **Official settlements account** | |
| **Official settlements account balance** | **−6** |

The three balance of payments accounts are the current account, the capital and financial account, and the official settlements account.

The sum of the balances on the three accounts is always zero. That is, the official settlements account balance always equals the negative of the sum of the current account balance and the capital and financial account balance.

In 2015, the statistical discrepancy was unusually large.

SOURCE OF DATA: Bureau of Economic Analysis.

### Personal Analogy

You have a set of personal balance of payments accounts that parallel those of a nation. You have a current account, a capital account, and a settlements account.

Your current account records your income from supplying the services of factors of production and your expenditure on goods and services. Consider, for example, Joanne. She worked in 2015 and earned an income of $25,000. Joanne has $10,000 worth of investments that earned her interest of $1,000. Joanne's current account shows an income of $26,000. Joanne spent $18,000 buying goods and services for consumption. She also bought a new apartment, which cost her $60,000. So Joanne's total expenditure was $78,000. The difference between her expenditure and her income is $52,000 ($78,000 minus $26,000).

To pay for expenditure of $52,000 in excess of her income, Joanne has to use her bank account or take a loan. Suppose that Joanne took a mortgage of $50,000 to help buy her apartment. This mortgage was the only borrowing that Joanne did, so her capital and financial account surplus was $50,000. With a current account deficit of $52,000 and a capital and financial account surplus of $50,000, Joanne was still $2,000 short. She got that $2,000 from her own bank account. Her cash holdings decreased by $2,000. Joanne's settlements balance was $2,000.

Joanne's income from her work is like a country's income from its exports. Her income from her investments is like a country's interest from foreigners. Her purchases of goods and services, including her purchase of an apartment, are like a country's imports. Joanne's mortgage—borrowing from someone else—is like a country's borrowing from the rest of the world. The change in Joanne's bank account is like the change in a country's official reserves.

Check that the sum of Joanne's balances is zero. Her current account balance is −$52,000, her capital and financial account balance is +$50,000, and her settlements account balance is +$2,000, so the sum of the three balances is zero.

## ■ Borrowers and Lenders, Debtors and Creditors

**Net borrower**

A country that is borrowing more from the rest of the world than it is lending to the rest of the world.

A country that is borrowing more from the rest of the world than it is lending to the rest of the world is called a **net borrower**. Similarly, a **net lender** is a country that is lending more to the rest of the world than it is borrowing from it.

**Net lender**

A country that is lending more to the rest of the world than it is borrowing from the rest of the world.

The United States is a net borrower, but it is a relative newcomer to the ranks of net borrower nations. Throughout the 1960s and most of the 1970s, the United States was a net lender. It had a surplus on its current account and a deficit on its capital and financial account. It was not until 1983 that the United States became a significant net borrower. Between 1983 and 1987, U.S. borrowing increased each year. Then it decreased and was briefly zero in 1991. From 1991 through 2006, U.S. borrowing increased, but after 2006 it decreased. The average net foreign borrowing by the United States between 1983 and 2015 was $313 billion a year.

Most countries are net borrowers like the United States. But a small number of countries, including China and oil-rich Saudi Arabia, are net lenders.

**Debtor nation**

A country that during its entire history has borrowed more from the rest of the world than it has lent to the rest of the world.

A net borrower might be reducing its net assets held in the rest of the world, or it might be going deeper into debt. A nation's total stock of foreign investment determines whether the nation is a debtor or creditor. A **debtor nation** is a country that during its entire history has borrowed more from the rest of the world than it has lent to the rest of the world. A debtor nation has a stock of outstanding debt to the rest of the world that exceeds the stock of its own claims on the rest of the world. A **creditor nation** is a country that during its entire history has invested more in the rest of the world than other countries have invested in it.

**Creditor nation**

A country that during its entire history has invested more in the rest of the world than other countries have invested in it.

# ■ Current Account Balance

What determines a country's current account balance and net foreign borrowing? Why has the United States had a deficit every year since 1980 but one?

In popular political commentary, the blame for a long string of deficits is placed on an unfair, unlevel playing field. The suggestion is that successive U.S. governments have negotiated trade deals that have disadvantaged the United States, lost export markets, encouraged imports, and cost American jobs. The implication of this view is that the current account deficit can be turned around by a return to tariffs and other trade restrictions that enable high-cost U.S. producers to compete with low-cost foreign producers.

This line of reasoning is wrong for three reasons: First, it doesn't fit the timing of trade deals. Second, trade deals influence what and how much we trade with other countries, not the balance of that trade. And third, the government budget deficit and private saving deficit is the source of the current account deficit.

Let's explore these three reasons for rejecting the politically popular story.

## Timing

The U.S. current account deficit started in 1982, peaked in 1987, shrank to zero in 1991, increased to a new and higher peak in 2006, and then shrank again. (The figure in *Eye on the U.S. Economy* on p. 481 shows the details.) This timing and direction of change in the current account deficit does not align with the timing of U.S. trade agreements shown in Table 19.2. The current account was already in deficit when the first trade deals were signed. Following the start of NAFTA in 1994, the deficit did increase but after 2006, with NAFTA still in place, the deficit decreased. By 2007, with nine major trade deals operating, the deficit started to fall. This lack of alignment of trade deals and current account deficit makes clear that we need to look elsewhere for the cause of the deficit.

## Free Trade Agreements and the Quantity of Trade

When trade barriers are removed in a free trade agreement, the quantity of both exports and imports increases. Exports increase because buyers in the other country face lower prices for U.S.-produced goods and services. And U.S. imports increase because Americans get foreign-produced items at lower prices. The data confirm these trade-creating effects. In 1980, before the trade deals in place today, U.S. international trade (the sum of exports and imports) was 12 percent of GDP. Today, as a consequence of the deals in place, U.S. international trade has grown to 29 percent of GDP.

## Current Account Deficit, Budget Deficit, and Private Saving Deficit

You are now going to see why the government budget deficit and the gap between private sector saving and investment—the private sector deficit—is the source of the current account deficit.

Begin by recalling that exports of goods and services ($X$) and imports of goods and services ($M$) are the largest items in the current account (see Table 19.1). Exports minus imports are net exports ($NX$) and fluctuations in net exports are the main source of fluctuations in the current account balance.

To see how the government budget along with private saving and investment determine net exports, we need to recall some of the things that we learned about the national income accounts in Chapter 5. Table 19.3 will refresh your memory and summarize some calculations.

**TABLE 19.2**
**U.S. TRADE AGREEMENTS**

| Start year | Countries |
| --- | --- |
| 1985 | Israel |
| 1988 | Canada |
| 1994 | NAFTA (Canada and Mexico) |
| 2001 | Jordan |
| 2004 | Australia, Chile, Singapore |
| 2005 | CAFTA (6 Central American countries) |
| 2006 | Morroco, Oman |
| 2007 | Peru |
| 2012 | Panama, Columbia, South Korea |

Part (a) of Table 19.3 lists the national income variables with their symbols. Part (b) defines three balances. *Net exports* are exports of goods and services minus imports of goods and services.

**Private sector balance**
Saving minus investment.

The **private sector balance** is saving minus investment. If saving exceeds investment, a private sector surplus is lent to other sectors. If investment exceeds saving, borrowing from other sectors finances a private sector deficit.

**Government sector balance**
The sum of the budget balances of the federal, state, and local governments—net taxes minus government expenditure on goods and services.

The **government sector balance** is the sum of the budget balances of the federal, state, and local governments. It is equal to net taxes minus government expenditure on goods and services. If that number is positive, a government sector surplus is lent to other sectors; if that number is negative, borrowing from other sectors must finance a government sector budget deficit.

Part (b) of Table 19.3 shows the values of these balances for the United States in 2015. As you can see, net exports were −$522 billion, a deficit. The private sector saved $3,317 billion and invested $3,057 billion, so it had a surplus of $260 billion. The government sector's revenue from net taxes was $2,436 billion and its expenditure was $3,218 billion, so the government sector balance was −$782 billion, a deficit.

Part (c) of Table 19.3 shows the relationship among the three balances.

■ **TABLE 19.3**

Net Exports, the Government Budget, Saving, and Investment

|  | Symbols and equations | United States in 2015 (billions of dollars) |
|---|---|---|
| Net exports equals exports minus imports. | **(a) Variables** |  |
|  | Exports    $X$ | 2,264 |
|  | Imports    $M$ | 2,786 |
| The private sector balance equals saving minus investment. | Investment    $I$ | 3,057 |
|  | Saving    $S$ | 3,317 |
|  | Government expenditure    $G$ | 3,218 |
| The government sector balance equals net taxes minus government expenditure on goods and services. | Net taxes    $NT$ | 2,436 |
|  | **(b) Balances** |  |
| These three balances are related: Net exports equals the sum of the private sector and government sector balances. | Net exports    $X - M$ | $2{,}264 - 2{,}786 = -522$ |
|  | Private sector balance    $S - I$ | $3{,}317 - 3{,}057 = 260$ |
|  | Government sector balance    $NT - G$ | $2{,}436 - 3{,}218 = -782$ |
|  | **(c) Relation among balances** |  |
|  | National accounts   $Y = C + I + G + X - M = C + S + NT$ |  |
|  | Rearranging:   $(X - M) = (S - I) + (NT - G)$ |  |
|  | Net exports    $X - M$ | −522 |
|  | Equals: |  |
|  | Private sector balance    $S - I$ | 260 |
|  | Plus: |  |
|  | Government sector balance    $NT - G$ | −782 |

SOURCE OF DATA: Bureau of Economic Analysis, 2016. (The *National Income and Product Accounts* measures of exports and imports are slightly different from the Balance of Payments Accounts measures in Table 19.1 on p. 481. The government sector includes state and local governments.)

From the national income accounts, we know that real GDP, $Y$, is the sum of consumption expenditure, $C$; investment, $I$; government expenditure on goods and services, $G$; and net exports, $(X - M)$. Real GDP also equals the sum of consumption expenditure, $C$, saving, $S$, and net taxes, $NT$. Rearranging these equations tells us that net exports equals $(S - I)$, the private sector balance, plus $(NT - G)$, the government sector balance. That is,

$$\text{Net exports} = (S - I) + (NT - G)$$

Should we be concerned that the United States is a net borrower? The answer is probably not. Our international borrowing finances the purchase of new capital goods. In 2015, businesses spent $3,057 billion on new buildings, plant, and equipment. Governments spent $613 billion on defense equipment and public structures. All these purchases added to the nation's capital, and much of it increased labor productivity. Governments also purchased education and healthcare services, which increased human capital.

Our international borrowing is financing private and public investment, not consumption.

# EYE on the GLOBAL ECONOMY
## Current Account Balances Around the World

The figure shows a sample of current account balances around the world in 2015. No country or region has a balanced current account with the value of exports and other receipts equal to the value of imports and other payments.

The United States has the largest current account deficit, and other advanced economies, the Euro area, China, and developing Asian economies have large surpluses.

Countries with deficits have government budget deficits and a shortage of saving to finance investment. Surplus countries also mostly have government budget deficits but have high levels of saving that more than covers the cost of business investment.

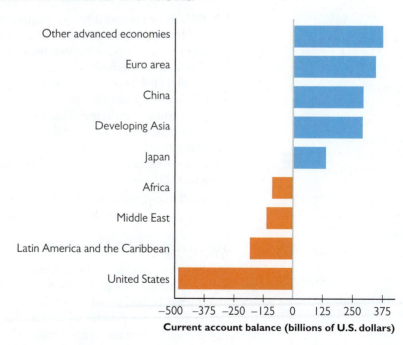

SOURCE OF DATA: International Monetary Fund, *World Economic Outlook*, April 2016

MyEconLab Study Plan 19.1
Key Terms Quiz
Solutions Video

 CHECKPOINT 19.1

**Describe a country's balance of payments accounts and explain what determines the amount of international borrowing and lending.**

## Practice Problems

Use the following information about the United States to work Problems **1** and **2**.

Imports of goods and services: $2,000 billion; interest paid to the rest of the world: $500 billion; interest received from the rest of the world: $400 billion; decrease in U.S. official reserves: $10 billion; government sector balance: $200 billion; saving: $1,800 billion; investment: $2,000 billion; net transfers: zero.

1. Calculate the current account balance, the capital and financial account balance, the official settlements account balance, and exports of goods and services.

2. Is the United States a debtor or a creditor nation?

## In the News

**U.S. current account deficit highest in 7 years**
The U.S. current account deficit in 2015 was $484 billion, up from $390 billion in 2014, and the highest since 2008. Some politicians say the deficit is the result of bad trade deals with nations engaged in unfair trading practices.
Source: *U.S. News & World Report*, March 17, 2016

Explain how the sum of the government budget balance and the personal sector balance changed in 2015; and explain why the politicians are wrong.

## Solutions to Practice Problems

1. The current account balance equals net exports plus net interest from abroad (−$100 billion) plus net transfers (zero). Net exports equal the government sector balance ($200 billion) plus the private sector balance. The private sector balance equals saving ($1,800 billion) minus investment ($2,000 billion), which is −$200 billion So net exports are zero, and the current account balance is −$100 billion.
   The capital and financial account balance is the negative of the sum of the current account and official settlements account balances, which is $90 billion.
   The official settlements account balance is a *surplus* of $10 billion.
   Exports equal net exports (zero) plus imports ($2,000 billion), which equals $2,000 billion.

2. The United States is a debtor nation because it pays more in interest to the rest of the world than it receives in interest from the rest of the world.

## Solution to In the News

The link between the sector balances is: $(X - M) = (S - I) + (NT - G)$. The current account balance is mainly net exports, which decreased (became more negative) by $94 billion ($484 − $390). The sum of the government budget balance $(NT - G)$ and the private sector balance $(S - I)$ also decreased by $94 billion. The politicians are incorrect because the U.S. current account has been in deficit since long before most of the trade deals were negotiated and the budget deficit financed by foreign borrowing is the main source of the current account deficit.

## 19.2   THE EXCHANGE RATE

MyEconLab Concept Video

When we buy foreign goods or invest in another country, we pay using that country's currency. When foreigners buy U.S.-made goods or invest in the United States, they pay in U.S. dollars. We get foreign currency and foreigners get U.S. dollars in the foreign exchange market. The **foreign exchange market** is the market in which the currency of one country is exchanged for the currency of another. The foreign exchange market is not a place like a downtown flea market or produce market. It is made up of thousands of people: importers and exporters, banks, and specialist traders of foreign exchange, called foreign exchange brokers. The foreign exchange market opens on Monday morning in Hong Kong, which is still Sunday evening in New York. As the day advances, markets open in Singapore, Tokyo, Bahrain, Frankfurt, London, New York, Chicago, and San Francisco. As the U.S. West Coast markets close, Hong Kong is only an hour away from opening for the next business day. Dealers around the world are in continual contact, and on a typical day in 2016, around $5 trillion is traded.

The price at which one currency exchanges for another is called a **foreign exchange rate**. For example, in August 2016, one U.S. dollar bought 90 euro cents. The exchange rate was 0.90 euros per dollar. We can also express the exchange rate in terms of dollars per euro, which in August 2016 was $1.11 per euro. Figure 19.1 shows the history of the U.S. dollar exchange rate against the euro since 2000 in terms of euros per dollar.

**Currency appreciation** is the rise in the value of one currency in terms of another currency. For example, when the dollar rose from just over 1.00 euros to 1.17 euros in 2000, the dollar appreciated by 17 percent.

**Foreign exchange market**
The market in which the currency of one country is exchanged for the currency of another.

**Foreign exchange rate**
The price at which one currency exchanges for another.

**Currency appreciation**
The rise in the value of one currency in terms of another currency.

**FIGURE 19.1**

The U.S. Dollar Exchange Rate Against the Euro

MyEconLab Real-time data

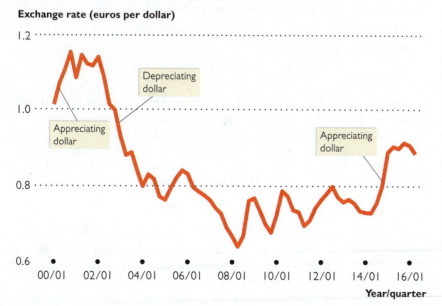

In 2000, and again in 2015, the value of the dollar rose against the euro—the dollar *appreciated*. From 2002 to 2008, the value of the dollar fell against the euro—the dollar *depreciated*. The overall fall was from a high of 1.17 euros per dollar in 2001 to a low of 0.64 euros per dollar in 2008.

From 2008 to 2014, through the turmoil of global financial crisis and repeated financial and political crises in Europe, the value of the dollar against the euro fluctuated between around 0.70 and 0.80 euros per dollar.

SOURCE OF DATA: Board of Governors of the Federal Reserve System.

**Currency depreciation**
The fall in the value of one currency in terms of another currency.

**Currency depreciation** is the fall in the value of one currency in terms of another currency. For example, when the dollar fell from 1.17 euros in 2000 to 0.63 euros in 2008, the dollar depreciated by 46 percent. Why does the U.S. dollar fluctuate in value? Why does it sometimes depreciate and sometimes appreciate?

The exchange rate is a price. And like all prices, demand and supply determine the exchange rate. So to understand the forces that determine the exchange rate, we need to study demand and supply in the foreign exchange market. We'll begin by looking at the demand side of the market.

## ■ Demand in the Foreign Exchange Market

The quantity of U.S. dollars that traders plan to buy in the foreign exchange market in a given period of time depends on many factors, but the main ones are

- The exchange rate
- Interest rates in the United States and other countries
- The expected future exchange rate

Let's look first at the relationship between the quantity of dollars demanded in the foreign exchange market and the exchange rate.

## ■ The Law of Demand for Foreign Exchange

People do not buy dollars because they enjoy them. The demand for dollars is a *derived demand*. People demand dollars so that they can buy U.S.-made goods and services (U.S. exports). They also demand dollars so that they can buy U.S. assets such as bank accounts, bonds, stocks, businesses, and real estate. Nevertheless, the law of demand applies to dollars just as it does to anything else that people value.

Other things remaining the same, the higher the exchange rate, the smaller is the quantity of dollars demanded. For example, if the price of the U.S. dollar rises from 0.70 euros to 0.80 euros but nothing else changes, the quantity of U.S. dollars that people plan to buy decreases. Why does the exchange rate influence the quantity of dollars demanded? There are two separate reasons, and they are related to the two sources of the derived demand for dollars. They are

- Exports effect
- Expected profit effect

### Exports Effect

The larger the value of U.S. exports, the larger is the quantity of dollars demanded. But the value of U.S. exports depends on the exchange rate. For example, if the exchange rate falls from 0.70 euros to 0.60 euros per U.S. dollar, other things remaining the same, the cheaper are U.S.-made goods and services to people in Europe, the more the United States exports, and the greater is the quantity of U.S. dollars demanded to pay for those exports.

### Expected Profit Effect

The larger the expected profit from holding dollars, the greater is the quantity of dollars demanded in the foreign exchange market. But expected profit depends on today's exchange rate and the expected future exchange rate. For a given expected future exchange rate, the lower the exchange rate today, the larger is the expected profit from holding dollars and the greater is the quantity of dollars demanded in the foreign exchange market.

**FIGURE 19.2**

The Demand for Dollars

MyEconLab Animation

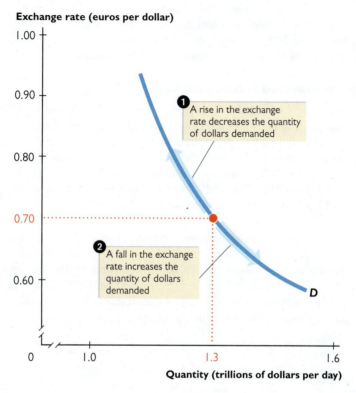

Exchange rate (euros per dollar)

① A rise in the exchange rate decreases the quantity of dollars demanded

② A fall in the exchange rate increases the quantity of dollars demanded

*D*

Quantity (trillions of dollars per day)

Other things remaining the same, the quantity of dollars that people plan to buy in the foreign exchange market depends on the exchange rate.

① If the exchange rate rises, the quantity of dollars demanded decreases and there is a movement up along the demand curve for dollars.

② If the exchange rate falls, the quantity of dollars demanded increases and there is a movement down along the demand curve for dollars.

To understand this effect, suppose that you think the dollar will be worth 0.80 euros by the end of the month. If a dollar costs 0.75 euros today, you buy dollars. But a person who thinks that the dollar will be worth 0.75 euros at the end of the month does not buy dollars. Now suppose that today's exchange rate falls to 0.65 euros per dollar. More people think that they can profit from buying dollars, so the quantity of dollars demanded today increases.

Figure 19.2 shows the demand curve for U.S. dollars in the foreign exchange market. For the two reasons we've just reviewed, when the foreign exchange rate rises, other things remaining the same, the quantity of dollars demanded decreases and there is a movement up along the demand curve, as shown by the arrow. When the exchange rate falls, other things remaining the same, the quantity of dollars demanded increases and there is a movement down along the demand curve, as shown by the arrow.

## ■ Changes in the Demand for Dollars

A change in any other influence on the quantity of U.S. dollars that people plan to buy in the foreign exchange market brings a change in the demand for dollars. These other influences are

- Interest rates in the United States and other countries
- The expected future exchange rate

## Interest Rates in the United States and Other Countries

**U.S. interest rate differential**
The U.S. interest rate minus the foreign interest rate.

If you can borrow in another country and lend in the United States at a higher interest rate, you will make a profit. What matters is not the values of the foreign and U.S. interest rates, but the gap between them. This gap, the U.S. interest rate minus the foreign interest rate, is called the **U.S. interest rate differential**. The larger the U.S. interest rate differential, the greater is the demand for U.S.-dollar assets and the greater is the demand for dollars.

## The Expected Future Exchange Rate

Suppose you are the finance manager of the German automaker BMW. The exchange rate is 0.70 euros per dollar, and you expect that by the end of the month, it will be 0.80 euros per dollar. You spend 700,000 euros today and buy $1,000,000. At the end of the month, the dollar equals 0.80 euros, as you predicted, and you sell the $1,000,000. You get 800,000 euros. You've made a profit of 100,000 euros. The higher the expected future exchange rate, the greater is the expected profit and the greater is the demand for dollars today.

Figure 19.3 summarizes the influences on the demand for dollars. A rise in the U.S. interest rate differential or a rise in the expected future exchange rate increases the demand for dollars today and shifts the demand curve rightward from $D_0$ to $D_1$. A fall in the U.S. interest rate differential or a fall in the expected future exchange rate decreases the demand for dollars today and shifts the demand curve leftward from $D_0$ to $D_2$.

**FIGURE 19.3**

Changes in the Demand for Dollars

MyEconLab Animation

① The demand for dollars increases if:

■ The U.S. interest rate differential increases.
■ The expected future exchange rate rises.

② The demand for dollars decreases if:

■ The U.S. interest rate differential decreases.
■ The expected future exchange rate falls.

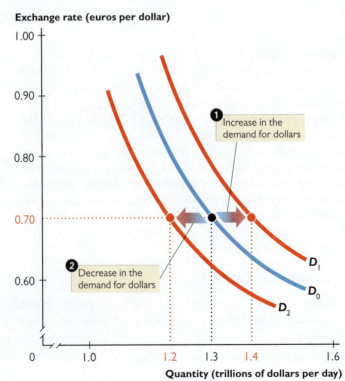

# ■ Supply in the Foreign Exchange Market

The quantity of U.S. dollars that traders plan to sell in the foreign exchange market in a given period of time depends on many factors, but the main ones are

- The exchange rate
- Interest rates in the United States and other countries
- The expected future exchange rate

Does this list of factors seem familiar? It should: It is the same list as that for demand. The demand side and the supply side of the foreign exchange market are influenced by all the same factors. But the ways in which these three factors influence supply are the opposite of the ways in which they influence demand.

Let's look first at the relationship between the quantity of dollars supplied in the foreign exchange market and the exchange rate.

# ■ The Law of Supply of Foreign Exchange

Traders supply U.S. dollars in the foreign exchange market when people and businesses buy other currencies. They buy other currencies so that they can buy foreign-made goods and services (U.S. imports). Traders also supply dollars and buy foreign currencies so that people and businesses can buy foreign assets such as bank accounts, bonds, stocks, businesses, and real estate. The law of supply applies to dollars just as it does to anything else that people plan to sell.

Other things remaining the same, the higher the exchange rate, the greater is the quantity of dollars supplied in the foreign exchange market. For example, if the price of the U.S. dollar rises from 0.70 euros to 0.80 euros but nothing else changes, the quantity of U.S. dollars that people plan to sell in the foreign exchange market increases. Why does the exchange rate influence the quantity of dollars supplied?

There are two reasons, and they parallel the two reasons on the demand side of the market. They are

- Imports effect
- Expected profit effect

## Imports Effect

The larger the value of U.S. imports, the larger is the quantity of foreign currency demanded to pay for these imports. And when people buy foreign currency, they supply dollars. So the larger the value of U.S. imports, the greater is the quantity of dollars supplied in the foreign exchange market. But the value of U.S. imports depends on the exchange rate. The higher the exchange rate, other things remaining the same, the cheaper are foreign-made goods and services to Americans. So the more the United States imports, the greater is the quantity of U.S. dollars supplied in the foreign exchange market to pay for these imports.

## Expected Profit Effect

The larger the expected profit from holding a foreign currency, the greater is the quantity of that currency demanded and the greater is the quantity of dollars supplied in the foreign exchange market. But the expected profit depends on today's exchange rate and the expected future exchange rate. For a given expected future exchange rate, the higher the exchange rate today, the larger is the expected profit from selling dollars and the greater is the quantity of dollars supplied in the foreign exchange market.

### FIGURE 19.4

### The Supply of Dollars

Other things remaining the same, the quantity of dollars that people plan to sell in the foreign exchange market depends on the exchange rate.

**❶** If the exchange rate rises, the quantity of dollars supplied increases and there is a movement up along the supply curve of dollars.

**❷** If the exchange rate falls, the quantity of dollars supplied decreases and there is a movement down along the supply curve of dollars.

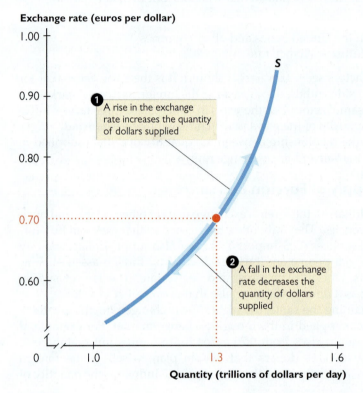

For the two reasons we've just reviewed, other things remaining the same, when the exchange rate rises, the quantity of dollars supplied increases, and when the exchange rate falls, the quantity of dollars supplied decreases. Figure 19.4 shows the supply curve of U.S. dollars in the foreign exchange market. In this figure, when the exchange rate rises, other things remaining the same, there is an increase in the quantity of dollars supplied and a movement up along the supply curve, as shown by the arrow. When the exchange rate falls, other things remaining the same, there is a decrease in the quantity of dollars supplied and a movement down along the supply curve, as shown by the arrow.

### ■ Changes in the Supply of Dollars

A change in any other influence on the quantity of U.S. dollars that people plan to sell in the foreign exchange market brings a change in the supply of dollars, and the supply curve of dollars shifts. Supply either increases or decreases. These other influences on supply parallel the other influences on demand but have exactly the opposite effects. These influences are

- Interest rates in the United States and other countries
- The expected future exchange rate

## Interest Rates in the United States and Other Countries

The larger the U.S. interest rate differential, the smaller is the demand for foreign assets and the smaller is the supply of dollars in the foreign exchange market.

## The Expected Future Exchange Rate

Other things remaining the same, the higher the expected future exchange rate, the smaller is the supply of dollars. To see why, suppose that the dollar is trading at 0.70 euros per dollar today and you think that by the end of the month, the dollar will trade at 0.80 euros per dollar. You were planning on selling dollars today, but you decide to hold off and wait until the end of the month. If you supply dollars today, you get only 0.70 euros per dollar. But at the end of the month, if the dollar is worth 0.80 euros as you predict, you'll get 0.80 euros for each dollar you supply. You'll make a profit of 0.10 euros per dollar. So the higher the expected future exchange rate, other things remaining the same, the smaller is the expected profit from selling U.S. dollars and the smaller is the supply of dollars today.

Figure 19.5 summarizes the influences on the supply of dollars. A rise in the U.S. interest rate differential or the expected future exchange rate decreases the supply of dollars today and shifts the supply curve leftward from $S_0$ to $S_1$. A fall in the U.S. interest rate differential or the expected future exchange rate increases the supply of dollars today and shifts the supply curve rightward from $S_0$ to $S_2$.

### FIGURE 19.5

Changes in the Supply of Dollars                    MyEconLab Animation

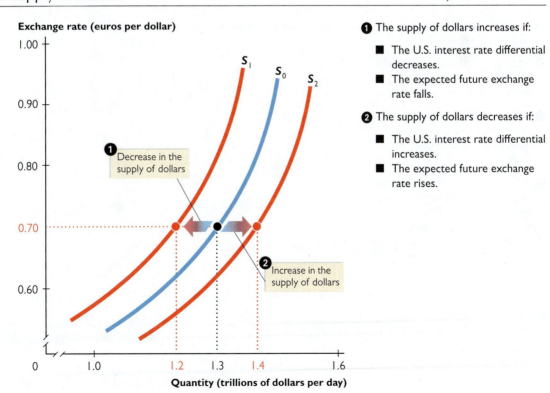

❶ The supply of dollars increases if:
- The U.S. interest rate differential decreases.
- The expected future exchange rate falls.

❷ The supply of dollars decreases if:
- The U.S. interest rate differential increases.
- The expected future exchange rate rises.

### ■ Market Equilibrium

Demand and supply in the foreign exchange market determine the exchange rate. Just as in all the other markets you've studied, the price (the exchange rate) acts as a regulator. If the exchange rate is too high, there is a surplus—the quantity supplied exceeds the quantity demanded. If the exchange rate is too low, there is a shortage—the quantity supplied is less than the quantity demanded. At the equilibrium exchange rate, there is neither a shortage nor a surplus. The quantity supplied equals the quantity demanded.

Figure 19.6 illustrates market equilibrium. The demand for dollars is *D*, and the supply of dollars is *S*. The equilibrium exchange rate is 0.70 euros per dollar. At this exchange rate, the quantity demanded equals the quantity supplied and is $1.3 trillion a day. If the exchange rate is above 0.70 euros, for example, 0.80 euros per dollar, there is a surplus of dollars and the exchange rate falls. If the exchange rate is below 0.70 euros, for example, 0.60 euros per dollar, there is a shortage of dollars and the exchange rate rises.

The foreign exchange market is constantly pulled to its equilibrium by the forces of supply and demand. Foreign exchange dealers are constantly looking for the best price they can get. If they are selling, they want the highest price available. If they are buying, they want the lowest price available. Information flows from dealer to dealer through the worldwide computer network, and the price adjusts second by second to keep buying plans and selling plans in balance. That is, price adjusts second by second to keep the market at its equilibrium.

**FIGURE 19.6**

Equilibrium Exchange Rate

MyEconLab Animation

The demand curve for dollars is *D*, and the supply curve is *S*.

**❶** If the exchange rate is 0.80 euros per dollar, there is a surplus of dollars and the exchange rate falls.

**❷** If the exchange rate is 0.60 euros per dollar, there is a shortage of dollars and the exchange rate rises.

**❸** If the exchange rate is 0.70 euros per dollar, there is neither a shortage nor a surplus of dollars and the exchange rate remains constant. The market is in equilibrium.

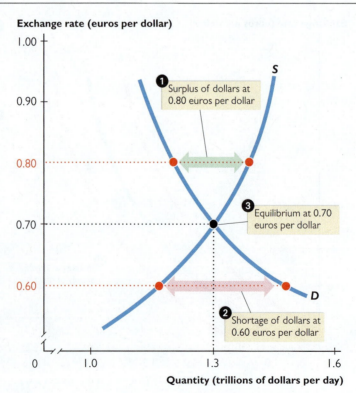

# EYE on the DOLLAR

MyEconLab Critical Thinking Exercise

## Why Does Our Dollar Fluctuate?

Our dollar fluctuates: Sometimes its value rises and sometimes it falls. Let's see what makes our dollar fluctuate by looking at two episodes in its bouncing life.

### A Falling Dollar: 2001–2008

Between 2001 and 2008, the dollar fell from 1.15 euros to 0.64 euros per dollar. Figure 1 explains this fall.

In 2001, the demand and supply curves were those labeled $D_{01}$ and $S_{01}$. The exchange rate was 1.15 euros per dollar. During the next few years, U.S. economic growth slipped below the European growth rate, European inflation fell, interest rates in Europe exceeded those in the United States, and the U.S. current account deficit continued to increase.

Under these conditions, currency traders expected the exchange rate to fall. The demand for dollars decreased and the supply of dollars increased. The demand curve shifted leftward to $D_{08}$ and the supply curve shifted rightward to $S_{08}$. The exchange rate fell to 0.64 euros per dollar.

From 2008 to 2014, the dollar fluctuated around a slightly rising trend. Then, in 2015, the dollar appreciated very quickly.

### A Rising Dollar: 2014–2015

The dollar appreciated against the euro when it rose from 0.73 euros per dollar in 2014 to 0.90 euros per dollar in 2015. Figure 2 explains why this happened.

In 2014, the demand and supply curves were those labeled $D_{14}$ and $S_{14}$. The equilibrium exchange rate was 0.73 euros per dollar—where the quantity of dollars supplied equaled the quantity of dollars demanded.

During 2015, the U.S. economy expanded faster than the European economy. In Europe, interest rates were expected to fall as the central bank tried to stimulate a stagnant economy. U.S. interest rates were low, but the Fed's next move was expected to be upward. In this environment, the dollar was expected to appreciate against the euro.

With an expected dollar appreciation, the demand for dollars increased and the supply of dollars decreased. The demand curve shifted from $D_{14}$ to $D_{15}$ and the supply curve shifted from $S_{14}$ to $S_{15}$. These two reinforcing shifts made the exchange rate rise to 0.90 euros per dollar.

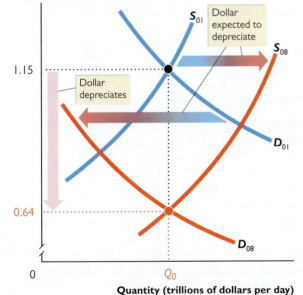

**Figure 1 2001 to 2008**

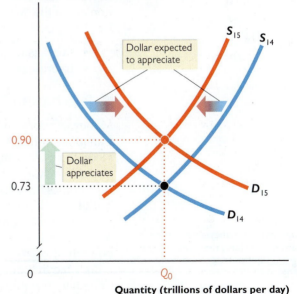

**Figure 2 2014 to 2015**

### Why Exchange Rates Are Volatile

You've seen that sometimes the dollar depreciates and at other times it appreciates. The exchange rates of other currencies are similarly volatile. The Japanese yen, Canadian dollar, and Mexican peso along with most currencies swing between appreciation and depreciation. Yet the quantity of dollars (and other currencies) traded in the foreign exchange market each day barely changes. Why?

A large part of the answer is that everyone in the foreign exchange market is potentially either a buyer or a seller—a demander or a supplier. Each trader has a price above which he or she will sell and below which he or she will buy.

This fact about the participants in the foreign exchange market means that supply and demand are not independent. The same shocks to the foreign exchange market that change the demand for a currency also change its supply. Demand and supply change in *opposite directions*, and the result is large price changes and small quantity changes.

The two key influences that change both demand and supply in the foreign exchange market are the interest rate differential and the expected future exchange rate.

A rise in the U.S. interest rate differential *increases* the *demand* for U.S. dollars in the foreign exchange market and *decreases* the *supply*. A rise in the expected future exchange rate also increases the demand for U.S. dollars and decreases the supply.

These common influences that change demand and supply in *opposite directions* bring changes in the exchange rate and little change in the quantities of currencies traded. They can bring cumulative movements in the exchange rate or frequent changes of direction—volatility.

MyEconLab Concept Video

### ■ Exchange Rate Expectations

The changes in the exchange rate that we've just considered occur in part because the exchange rate is expected to change. This explanation sounds a bit like a self-fulfilling forecast. What makes expectations change? The answer is new information about the deeper forces that influence the value of money. There are two such forces:

- Purchasing power parity
- Interest rate parity

### ■ Purchasing Power Parity

Money is worth what it will buy. But two kinds of money, U.S. dollars and Canadian dollars, for example, might buy different amounts of goods and services. Suppose a Big Mac costs $4 (Canadian) in Toronto and $3 (U.S.) in New York. If the Canadian dollar exchange rate is $1.33 Canadian per U.S. dollar, the two monies have the same value. You can buy a Big Mac in either Toronto or New York for either $4 Canadian or $3 U.S.

The situation we've just described is called **purchasing power parity**, which means equal value of money. If purchasing power parity does not prevail, some powerful forces go to work. To understand these forces, suppose that the price of a Big Mac in New York rises to $4 U.S., but in Toronto the price remains at $4 Canadian. Suppose the exchange rate remains at $1.33 Canadian per U.S. dollar. In this case, a Big Mac in Toronto still costs $4 Canadian or $3 U.S. But in

**Purchasing power parity**
Equal value of money—a situation in which money buys the same amount of goods and services in different currencies.

# EYE on the GLOBAL ECONOMY
## Purchasing Power Parity

Purchasing power parity (PPP) is a long-run phenomenon. In the short run, deviations from PPP can be large.

The figure shows the large range of deviations from PPP in August 2016, which stretches from 30 percent overvalued to 65 percent undervalued.

The Swiss franc and the Icelandic krona were the most overvalued currencies and according to PPP, they will depreciate at some point in the future.

The most undervalued currencies in August 2016 were the Russian ruble and South African rand. PPP predicts that these currencies will appreciate at some time in the future.

PPP theory predicts that a currency might depreciate or appreciate but the theory does not help to predict *when* it will depreciate or appreciate.

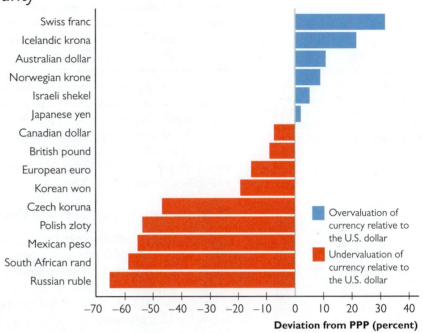

SOURCE OF DATA: PACIFIC FX Service, University of British Columbia.

New York, it costs $4 U.S. or $5.32 Canadian. Money buys more in Canada than in the United States. Money is not of equal value in both countries.

If all (or most) prices have increased in the United States and not increased in Canada, then people will generally expect that the U.S. dollar exchange rate is going to fall. The demand for U.S. dollars decreases, and the supply of U.S. dollars increases. The U.S. dollar exchange rate falls, as expected. If the U.S. dollar falls to $1.00 Canadian and there are no further price changes, purchasing power parity is restored. A Big Mac now costs $4 in either U.S. dollars or Canadian dollars in both New York and Toronto.

If prices increase in Canada and other countries but remain constant in the United States, then people will generally expect that the value of the U.S. dollar in the foreign exchange market is too low and that the U.S. dollar exchange rate will rise. The demand for U.S. dollars increases, and the supply of U.S. dollars decreases. The U.S. dollar exchange rate rises, as expected.

Ultimately, the value of money is determined by prices. So the deeper forces that influence the exchange rate have tentacles that spread throughout the economy. If prices in the United States rise faster than those in other countries, the exchange rate falls. And if prices in the United States rise more slowly than those in other countries, the exchange rate rises.

### Interest Rate Parity

Suppose a Canadian dollar bank deposit in a Toronto bank earns 5 percent a year and a U.S. dollar bank deposit in a New York bank earns 3 percent a year. Why does anyone deposit money in New York? Why doesn't all the money flow to Toronto? The answer is: Because of exchange rate expectations. Suppose people expect the Canadian dollar to depreciate by 2 percent a year. This 2 percent depreciation must be subtracted from the 5 percent interest to obtain the net return of 3 percent a year that an American can earn by depositing funds in a Toronto bank. The two returns are equal. This situation is one of **interest rate parity**—equal interest rates when exchange rate changes are taken into account.

Interest rate parity always prevails. Funds move to get the highest return available. If interest rate parity did not hold because the Canadian dollar had too high a value in the foreign exchange market, the expected return in Toronto would be lower than in New York. In seconds, traders would sell the Canadian dollar, its exchange rate would fall, and the expected return from lending in Toronto would rise to equal that in New York.

### ■ Monetary Policy and the Exchange Rate

Monetary policy influences the interest rate (see Chapter 12, pp. 304–307), so monetary policy also influences the interest rate differential and the exchange rate. If the Fed increases the U.S. interest rate and other central banks keep interest rates in other countries unchanged, the value of the U.S. dollar rises in the foreign exchange market. If other central banks increase their interest rates and the Fed keeps the U.S. interest rate unchanged, the value of the U.S. dollar falls in the foreign exchange market. So exchange rates fluctuate in response to changes and expected changes in monetary policy in the United States and around the world.

### ■ Pegging the Exchange Rate

Some central banks try to avoid exchange rate fluctuations by pegging the value of their currency against another currency. Suppose the Fed wanted to keep the dollar at 0.70 euros per dollar. If the exchange rate rose above 0.70 euros, the Fed would sell dollars and if it fell below 0.70 euros, the Fed would buy dollars.

Figure 19.7 illustrates foreign exchange market intervention. The supply of dollars is $S$, and initially, the demand for dollars is $D_0$. The equilibrium exchange rate is 0.70 euros per dollar, which is also the Fed's target—the horizontal red line.

If the demand for dollars increases to $D_1$, the Fed increases the supply of dollars—sells dollars—and prevents the exchange rate from rising. If the demand for dollars decreases to $D_2$, the Fed decreases the supply of dollars—buys dollars—and prevents the exchange rate from falling.

When the Fed buys dollars, it uses its reserves of euros; when the Fed sells dollars, it takes euros in exchange and its reserves of euros increase. As long as the demand for dollars fluctuates around and on average remains at $D_0$, the Fed's reserves of euros fluctuate but neither run dry nor persistently increase.

But if the demand for dollars decreased permanently to $D_2$, the Fed would have to buy dollars and sell euros every day to maintain the exchange rate at 0.70 euros per dollar. The Fed would soon run out of euros, and when it did, the dollar would sink. If the demand for dollars increased permanently to $D_1$, the Fed would have to sell dollars and buy euros every day. The Fed would be piling up unwanted euros and at some point would let the dollar rise.

**FIGURE 19.7**

Foreign Exchange Market Intervention

MyEconLab Animation

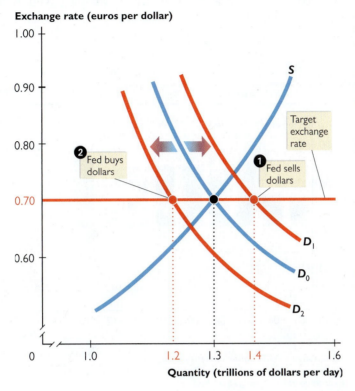

Exchange rate (euros per dollar)

Quantity (trillions of dollars per day)

Initially, the demand for dollars is $D_0$, the supply of dollars is $S$, and the exchange rate is 0.70 euros per dollar. The Fed can intervene in the foreign exchange market to keep the exchange rate close to its target rate (0.70 euros per dollar in this example).

❶ If demand increases from $D_0$ to $D_1$, the Fed sells dollars to increase the supply of dollars and maintain the exchange rate.

❷ If demand decreases from $D_0$ to $D_2$, the Fed buys dollars to decrease the supply of dollars and maintain the exchange rate.

Persistent intervention on one side of the market cannot be sustained.

## ◼ The People's Bank of China in the Foreign Exchange Market

Although the Fed could peg the value of the dollar, it chooses not to do so. But China's central bank, the People's Bank of China, does intervene to peg the value of its currency—the yuan. *Eye on the Global Economy* on p. 501 shows the result of this intervention.

During much of the period that the yuan was pegged to the U.S. dollar, China piled up U.S. dollar reserves. Figure 19.8(a) shows the numbers. During 2007 to 2009, China's reserves increased by more than $1 trillion.

Figure 19.8(b), which shows the market for U.S. dollars priced in terms of the yuan, explains why China's reserves increased. The demand curve $D$ and supply curve $S$ intersect at 5 yuan per dollar. If the People's Bank of China took no actions in the foreign exchange market, this exchange rate would be the equilibrium rate. (This particular value is only an example. No one knows what the yuan-dollar exchange rate would be with no intervention.)

By intervening in the market and buying U.S. dollars, the People's Bank can peg the yuan at 6.10 yuan per dollar. But to do so, it must keep holding the dollars that it buys. In Figure 19.8(b), the People's Bank buys $76 billion (the actual quantity that the People's Bank bought in 2012).

Only by allowing the yuan to appreciate can China stop accumulating dollars. Since July 2005, the People's Bank has permitted the yuan to rise in value.

But China continues to intervene in the foreign exchange market to manage the rate of appreciation of the yuan. The scale of intervention fell sharply in 2012. Eventually, when China's foreign exchange market becomes more accustomed to a floating yuan, it is possible that the People's Bank will end its intervention and the value of the yuan will be determined by market forces.

### FIGURE 19.8

## China's Foreign Exchange Market Intervention

MyEconLab Real-time data

China was piling up reserves of U.S. dollars during 2005 through 2013. The build-up of reserves was very large. Part (a) shows the numbers.

Part (b) shows the market for the U.S. dollar in terms of the Chinese yuan. Note that a higher exchange rate (yuan per dollar) means a lower value of the yuan and a higher value of the dollar. The yuan appreciates when the number of yuan per dollar decreases.

❶ With demand curve D and supply curve S, the equilibrium exchange rate is 5 yuan per dollar. (The actual equilibrium value is not known, and the value assumed is only an example.)

❷ In 2012, the People's Bank of China had a target exchange rate of 6.10 yuan per dollar. At this exchange rate, the yuan is *undervalued*.

❸ To keep the exchange rate pegged at its target level, the People's Bank of China must buy U.S. dollars in exchange for yuan, and China's reserves of U.S. dollars pile up.

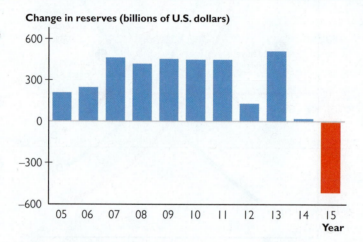

**(a) Change in U.S. dollar reserves**

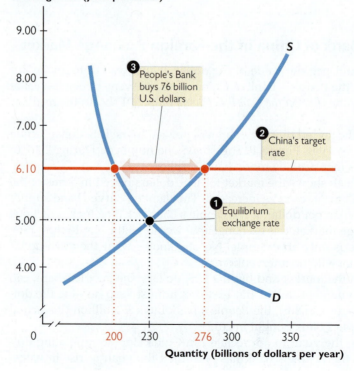

**(b) Managing the yuan**

SOURCE OF DATA: The People's Bank of China.

# EYE on the GLOBAL ECONOMY
## The Managed Yuan

The Chinese central bank, the People's Bank of China, pegged the value of the yuan in terms of the U.S. dollar for more than 10 years. The figure shows the value of the yuan (yuan per U.S. dollar) from the early 1990s to 2016.

The yuan was devalued in January 1994. It appreciated a bit during 1994 and 1995. But it was then pegged at 8.28 yuan per U.S. dollar, a value that the People's Bank of China maintained for more than 10 years. In July 2005, the yuan began a managed float—a managed appreciation of the yuan. Then, in July 2008, the exchange rate was again pegged, this time at 6.8 yuan per dollar. Since early 2010, the yuan has again been on a managed float.

SOURCE OF DATA: PACIFIC FX Service, University of British Columbia.

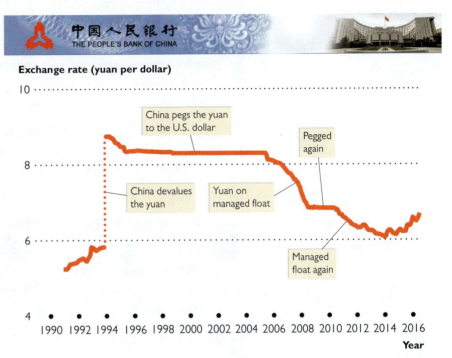

# EYE on YOUR LIFE

MyEconLab Critical Thinking Exercise

## Your Foreign Exchange Transactions

If you plan to go to Europe for a vacation next summer, you will need some euros. What is the best way to get euros?

You could just take your ATM/debit card or credit card and use an ATM in Europe. You'll get euros from the cash machine, and your bank account in the United States will get charged for the cash you obtain.

When you get euros, the number of euros you request is multiplied by the exchange rate to determine how many dollars to take from your bank account.

You have just made a transaction in the foreign exchange market. You have exchanged dollars for euros.

The exchange rate that you paid was probably costly. Your bank took a commission for helping you get euros. Some banks charge as much as 5 percent. Check in advance. It might be better to buy euros from your bank before you leave on your trip.

Another question has possibly occurred to you: How many euros will your budget buy next summer? Should

you get the euros now at a price that is certain or would it be better to wait until closer to your travel date and take a chance on the value of the dollar then?

No one can answer this question. But you can buy euros today at a fixed price for delivery at a later date. (This transaction is made in a market called the forward exchange market.) Again, though, you'll end up paying a big commission for the service.

MyEconLab Study Plan 19.2
Key Terms Quiz
Solutions Video

 CHECKPOINT 19.2

**Explain how the exchange rate is determined and why it fluctuates.**

## Practice Problems

Suppose that yesterday, the U.S. dollar was trading in the foreign exchange market at 100 yen per dollar. Today, the U.S. dollar is trading at 105 yen per dollar.

1. Which currency appreciated and which depreciated today?

2. List the events that could have caused today's change in the value of the U.S. dollar in the foreign exchange market. Did the events on your list change the demand for U.S. dollars, the supply of U.S. dollars, or both the demand for and supply of U.S. dollars?

3. If the Fed had tried to stabilize the exchange rate at 100 yen per dollar, what action would it have taken? How would U.S. official reserves have changed?

## In the News

**U.S. dollar strengthens against most main rivals**
One U.S. dollar bought ¥113.885 on Tuesday and ¥114.600 on Monday. One euro bought $1.1143 on Tuesday and $1.1155 on Monday. The Fed has raised interest rates and the European Central Bank is likely to lower interest rates.
*Source: Wall Street Journal, February 16, 2016*

1. Did the dollar appreciate or depreciate against the euro and the Japanese yen on Tuesday? Did the euro and the yen appreciate or depreciate against the dollar on Tuesday?

2. What events changed the exchange rate between the euro and the dollar?

## Solutions to Practice Problems

1. Because the price of the U.S. dollar is a larger number of yen, the U.S. dollar has appreciated. The yen has depreciated because it buys fewer dollars.

2. The main events might be an increase in the U.S. interest rate, a decrease in the Japanese interest rate, or a rise in the expected future exchange rate of the U.S. dollar.
   The events listed change both the demand for and supply of U.S. dollars. The events increase the demand for and decrease the supply of U.S. dollars.

3. To stabilize the exchange rate, the Fed would have sold U.S. dollars to increase the supply of dollars in the foreign exchange market. When the Fed sells U.S. dollars, it buys foreign currency, so U.S. official reserves would have increased.

## Solutions to In the News

1. Because one dollar bought fewer yen on Tuesday, the dollar depreciated against the yen and the yen appreciated against the dollar. Because one euro bought fewer dollars on Tuesday, the euro depreciated against the dollar and the dollar appreciated against the euro.

2. A change and expected future change in the U.S.- Europe interest rate differential increased demand and decreased supply in the market for U.S. dollars and decreased demand and increased supply in the market for euros. These changes depreciated the euro and appreciated the U.S. dollar.

# CHAPTER SUMMARY

## Key Points

**1. Describe a country's balance of payments accounts and explain what determines the amount of international borrowing and lending.**

- Foreign currency is used to finance international trade and the purchase of foreign assets.
- A country's balance of payments accounts record its international transactions.
- Historically, the United States has been a net lender to the rest of the world, but in 1983 that situation changed and the United States became a net borrower. In 1989 the United States became a debtor nation.
- Net exports are equal to the private sector balance plus the government sector balance.

**2. Explain how the exchange rate is determined and why it fluctuates.**

- Foreign currency is obtained in exchange for domestic currency in the foreign exchange market.
- The exchange rate is determined by demand and supply in the foreign exchange market.
- The lower the exchange rate, the greater is the quantity of dollars demanded. A change in the exchange rate brings a movement along the demand curve for dollars.
- Changes in the expected future exchange rate and the U.S. interest rate differential change the demand for dollars and shift the demand curve.
- The lower the exchange rate, the smaller is the quantity of dollars supplied. A change in the exchange rate brings a movement along the supply curve of dollars.
- Changes in the expected future exchange rate and the U.S. interest rate differential change the supply of dollars and shift the supply curve.
- Fluctuations in the exchange rate occur because fluctuations in the demand for and supply of dollars are not independent.
- A central bank can intervene in the foreign exchange market to smooth fluctuations in the exchange rate.

## Key Terms

MyEconLab Key Terms Quiz

Balance of payments accounts, 480
Capital and financial account, 480
Creditor nation, 482
Currency appreciation, 487
Currency depreciation, 488
Current account, 480

Debtor nation, 482
Foreign exchange market, 487
Foreign exchange rate, 487
Government sector balance, 484
Interest rate parity, 498
Net borrower, 482

Net lender, 482
Official settlements account, 480
Private sector balance, 484
Purchasing power parity, 496
U.S. interest rate differential, 490
U.S. official reserves, 480

MyEconLab Chapter 19 Study Plan

## CHAPTER CHECKPOINT

### Study Plan Problems and Applications

**TABLE 1**

| Item | (billions of dollars) |
|---|---|
| Imports | 150 |
| Exports of goods and services | 50 |
| Net interest | −10 |
| Net transfers | 35 |
| Foreign investment in Antarctica | 125 |
| Antarctica's investment abroad | 55 |

Table 1 gives some data that describe the economy of Antarctica in 2050. Use Table 1 to answer Problems **1** and **2**.

1. Calculate Antarctica's current account balance, capital and financial account balance, and the increase in Antarctica's official reserves.

2. Is Antarctica a debtor nation or a creditor nation? Are its international assets increasing or decreasing? Is Antarctica borrowing to finance investment or consumption? Explain.

3. **U.S. trade gap widened in June due to import surge**
   The U.S. trade deficit soared in June to $44.5 billion. Higher oil prices and increased purchases of pharmaceuticals and smartphones swelled imports.
   Source: *Wall Street Journal*, August 5, 2016

   Explain how the United States pays for its international trade deficit.

4. The U.S. dollar depreciates. Explain which of the following events could have caused the depreciation and why.

   - The Fed intervened in the foreign exchange market. Did the Fed buy or sell U.S. dollars?
   - People began to expect that the U.S. dollar would depreciate.
   - The U.S. interest rate differential increased.
   - Foreign investment in the United States increased.

Suppose that the inflation rate is lower in Japan than it is in the United States, and that the difference in the inflation rates persists for some years. Use this information to answer Problems **5** to **7**.

5. Will the U.S. dollar appreciate or depreciate against the yen and will purchasing power parity be violated? Why or why not?

6. Will U.S. interest rates be higher or lower than Japanese interest rates and will interest rate parity hold? Why or why not?

7. Explain how the expected future exchange rate will change.

8. Suppose that the U.K. pound is trading at 1.82 U.S. dollars per U.K. pound and at this exchange rate purchasing power parity holds. The U.S. interest rate is 2 percent a year and the U.K. interest rate is 4 percent a year. Calculate the U.S. interest rate differential. What is the U.K. pound expected to be worth in terms of U.S. dollars one year from now?

9. **Pound plunges on U.K. vote to leave the European Union**
   Britain's vote to leave the European Union lowered the pound from $1.50 to $1.32 in tumultuous hours of foreign exchange trading.
   Source: *Wall Street Journal*, June 24, 2016

   Did the vote to leave the European Union make the British pound appreciate of depreciate against the U.S. dollar? Which of the influences on demand and supply in the foreign exchange market most likey changed to bring this rapid and large change in the dollar-pound exchange rate?

10. Read *Eye on the Dollar* on p. 495. When and why did the dollar rise against the euro and when and why did it fall?

# Instructor Assignable Problems and Applications

1. If the European Central Bank starts to raise its policy interest rate before the Fed starts to raise the federal funds rate target, what do you predict will happen to the dollar-euro exchange rate? Illustrate your answer with an appropriate graphical analysis.

2. Table 1 gives some data that describe the economy of Atlantis in 2020. Calculate the current account balance, the capital and financial account balance, the government sector balance, and the private sector balance.

3. The U.S. dollar appreciates, and U.S. official reserves increase. Explain which of the following events might have caused these changes to occur and why.

   - The Fed intervened in the foreign exchange market and sold U.S. dollars.
   - The Fed conducted an open market operation and sold U.S. bonds.
   - People began to expect that the U.S. dollar would appreciate.
   - The U.S. interest rate differential narrowed.

4. Which of the following events might have caused the euro to appreciate and why?

   - The European Central Bank sold euros in the foreign exchange market.
   - The Fed intervened in the foreign exchange market and bought U.S. dollars.
   - The EU interest rate differential increased.
   - Profits increased in Europe, and U.S. investment in Europe surged.

**TABLE 1**

| Item | (billions of dollars) |
|---|---|
| Government expenditure | 200 |
| Saving | 100 |
| Increase in official reserves of Atlantis | 5 |
| Net foreign investment in Atlantis | 50 |
| Net taxes | 150 |
| Investment | 125 |

Use the following information to work Problems **5** and **6**.

Suppose that the euro keeps appreciating against the U.S. dollar. The Fed decides to stop the euro from appreciating (stop the U.S. dollar from depreciating) and intervenes in the foreign exchange market.

5. What actions might the Fed take in the foreign exchange market? Could these actions persist in the long run? Would the Fed's actions prevent interest rate parity from being achieved? Why or why not?

6. Are there any other actions that the Fed could take to raise the foreign exchange value of the dollar? Explain your answer.

Use the following information to work Problems **7** and **8**.

In August 2013, the exchange rate between the U.S. dollar and the Brazilian real was 3.125 real per dollar. In the same month, the price of a Big Mac was 23 real in Sao Paulo and $3.99 in New York. Brazil's interest rate was 14.25 percent per year and the U.S. interest rate was 1 percent per year.
                    Sources: Pacific Exchange Rate Service and *The Economist*

7. Does purchasing power parity (PPP) hold between Brazil and the United States? If not, does PPP predict that the Brazilian real will appreciate or depreciate against the U.S. dollar?

8. Does interest rate parity hold between Brazil and the United States? If interest rate parity does hold, what is the expected rate of appreciation or depreciation of the Brazilian real against the U.S. dollar? If the Fed raised the interest rate while the Brazilian interest rate remained at 14.25 percent a year, how would the expected appreciation or depreciation of the real change?

MyEconLab Chapter 19 Study Plan

## Multiple Choice Quiz

**1.** The current account balance equals _____.

    A. exports minus imports plus net interest and net transfers

    B. net exports plus net foreign investment in the United States

    C. the capital and financial account balance minus the official settlements account balance

    D. net exports plus the official settlements balance

**2.** China's official reserves have ballooned, fueled by strong foreign investment and large trade surpluses. China is a net _____ and a _____ nation.

    A. lender; debtor

    B. borrower; debtor

    C. lender; creditor

    D. borrower; creditor

**3.** Net exports equal the _____.

    A. private sector balance plus the government sector balance

    B. private sector balance minus the government sector balance

    C. government sector balance minus the private sector balance

    D. private sector balance plus the government's budget deficit

**4.** A net exports deficit will become a surplus if _____.

    A. the government budget deficit is turned into a surplus and the private sector has a surplus

    B. the private sector surplus adjusts to equal the government sector deficit

    C. private saving and government saving exceed private investment

    D. the country appreciates its currency

**5.** The quantity of U.S. dollars demanded in the foreign exchange market increases if _____.

    A. the value of U.S. imports increases

    B. traders expect the future exchange rate to rise

    C. the U.S. interest rate rises relative to those in other countries

    D. the U.S. dollar depreciates against other currencies

**6.** The supply of U.S. dollars in the foreign exchange market increases if _____.

    A. the value of U.S. imports increases

    B. the U.S. interest rate differential decreases

    C. the U.S. dollar depreciates against other currencies

    D. the U.S. dollar is expected to appreciate against other currencies in the future

**7.** Purchasing power parity _____.

    A. holds if the price of a good is the same number of euros, pounds, or dollars

    B. means that the value of the euro, the pound, and the dollar are equal

    C. always holds because exchange rates adjust automatically

    D. implies that international trade is competitive

**8.** To keep the yuan-U.S. dollar exchange rate constant, _____.

    A. the Fed agrees not to sell U.S. dollars in the foreign exchange market

    B. the People's Bank of China buys U.S. dollars

    C. the Fed and the People's Bank agree on the value of the exchange rate

    D. the Fed does not buy yuan in the foreign exchange market

# Glossary

**Absolute advantage** When one person (or nation) is more productive than another—needs fewer inputs or takes less time to produce a good or perform a production task. (p. 73)

**Aggregate demand** The relationship between the quantity of real GDP demanded and the price level when all other influences on expenditure plans remain the same. (p. 334)

**Aggregate planned expenditure** Planned consumption expenditure plus planned investment plus planned government expenditure plus planned exports minus planned imports. (p. 354)

**Aggregate supply** The relationship between the quantity of real GDP supplied and the price level when all other influences on production plans remain the same. (p. 328)

**Automatic fiscal policy** A fiscal policy action that is triggered by the state of the economy. (p. 409)

**Automatic stabilizers** Features of fiscal policy that stabilize real GDP without explicit action by the government. (p. 409)

**Balance of payments accounts** The accounts in which a nation records its international trading, borrowing, and lending. (p. 480)

**Balanced budget multiplier** The effect on aggregate demand of a *simultaneous* change in government expenditure and taxes that leaves the budget balance unchanged. (p. 411)

**Barter** The direct exchange of goods and services for other goods and services, which requires a double coincidence of wants. (p. 271)

**Benefit** The benefit of something is the gain or pleasure that it brings, measured by what you are willing to give up to get it. (p. 9)

**Black market** An illegal market that operates alongside a government-regulated market. (p. 171)

**Bond** A promise to pay specified sums of money on specified dates. (p. 245)

**Budget balance** Tax revenues minus outlays. (p. 402)

**Business cycle** A periodic but irregular up-and-down movement of total production and other measures of economic activity. (p. 130)

**Capital** Tools, instruments, machines, buildings, and other items that have been produced in the past and that businesses now use to produce goods and services. (pp. 37, 244)

**Capital and financial account** Record of foreign investment in the United States minus U.S. investment abroad. (p. 480)

**Capital goods** Goods bought by businesses and governments to increase productive resources to use over future periods to produce other goods. (p. 34)

**Chained Consumer Price Index** A measure of the price level calculated using current month and previous month prices and expenditures. (p. 176)

**Chained-dollar real GDP** The measure of real GDP calculated by the Bureau of Economic Analysis. (p. 141)

**Change in demand** A change in the quantity that people plan to buy when any influence on buying plans other than the price of the good changes. (p. 87)

**Change in the quantity demanded** A change in the quantity of a good that people plan to buy that results from a change in the price of the good with all other influences on buying plans remaining the same. (p. 87)

**Change in the quantity supplied** A change in the quantity of a good that suppliers plan to sell that results from a change in the price of the good with all other influences on selling plans remaining the same. (p. 92)

**Change in supply** A change in the quantity that suppliers plan to sell when any influence on selling plans other than the price of the good changes. (p. 92)

**Circular flow model** A model of the economy that shows the circular flow of expenditures and incomes that result from decision makers' choices and the way those choices interact to determine what, how, and for whom goods and services are produced. (p. 48)

**Classical growth theory** The theory that the clash between an exploding population and limited resources will eventually bring economic growth to an end. (p. 228)

**Classical macroeconomics** The view that the market economy works well, that aggregate fluctuations are a natural consequence of an expanding economy, and that government intervention cannot improve the efficiency of the market economy. (p. 192)

**Comparative advantage** The ability of a person to perform an activity or produce a good or service at a lower opportunity cost than anyone else. (p. 73)

**Complement** A good that is consumed with another good. (p. 87)

**Complement in production** A good that is produced along with another good. (p. 92)

**Consumer Price Index** A measure of the average of the prices paid by urban consumers for a fixed market basket of consumption goods and services. (p. 168)

**Consumption expenditure** The expenditure by households on consumption goods and services. (p. 117)

**Consumption function** The relationship between consumption expenditure and disposable income, other things remaining the same. (p. 354)

**Consumption goods and services** Goods and services that individuals and governments buy and use in the current period. (p. 34)

**Core inflation rate** The annual percentage change in the PCEPI excluding the prices of food and energy. (p. 177)

**Cost of living index** A measure of the change in the amount of money that people need to spend to achieve a given standard of living. (p. 174)

**Cost-push inflation** An inflation that begins with an increase in costs. (p. 345)

**Creditor nation** A country that during its entire history has

invested more in the rest of the world than other countries have invested in it. (p. 482)

**Cross-section graph** A graph that shows the values of an economic variable for different groups in a population at a point in time. (p. 24)

**Crowding-out effect** The tendency for a government budget deficit to raise the real interest rate and decrease investment. (p. 262)

**Currency** Notes (dollar bills) and coins. (p. 272)

**Currency appreciation** The rise in the value of one currency in terms of another currency. (p. 487)

**Currency depreciation** The fall in the value of one currency in terms of another currency. (p. 488)

**Current account** Record of receipts from the sale of goods and services to other countries (exports), minus payments for goods and services bought from other countries (imports), plus the net amount of interest and transfers received from and paid to other countries. (p. 480)

**Cyclical surplus or deficit** The budget balance that arises because tax revenues and outlays are not at their full-employment levels. (p. 410)

**Cyclical unemployment** The fluctuating unemployment over the business cycle that increases during a recession and decreases during an expansion. (p. 157)

**Debtor nation** A country that during its entire history has borrowed more from the rest of the world than it has lent to the rest of the world. (p. 482)

**Deflation** A situation in which the price level is *falling* and the inflation rate is *negative*. (p. 171)

**Demand** The relationship between the quantity demanded and the price of a good when all other influences on buying plans remain the same. (p. 85)

**Demand curve** A graph of the relationship between the quantity demanded of a good and its price when all the other influences on buying plans remain the same. (p. 86)

**Demand for labor** The relationship between the quantity of labor demanded and the real wage rate when all other influences on firms' hiring plans remain the same. (p. 197)

**Demand for loanable funds** The relationship between the quantity of loanable funds demanded and the real interest rate when all other influences on borrowing plans remain the same. (p. 251)

**Demand for money** The relationship between the quantity of money demanded and the nominal interest rate, when all other influences on the amount of money that people wish to hold remain the same. (p. 302)

**Demand-pull inflation** An inflation that starts because aggregate demand increases. (p. 344)

**Demand schedule** A list of the quantities demanded at each different price when all the other influences on buying plans remain the same. (p. 86)

**Depreciation** The decrease in the value of capital that results from its use and from obsolescence. (p. 124)

**Diminishing returns** The tendency for each additional hour of labor employed to produce a successively smaller additional amount of real GDP. (p. 196)

**Direct relationship** A relationship between two variables that move in the same direction. (p. 26)

**Discouraged worker** A marginally attached worker who has not made specific efforts to find a job within the past four weeks because previous unsuccessful attempts to find a job were discouraging. (p. 148)

**Discretionary fiscal policy** A fiscal policy action that is initiated by an act of Congress. (p. 409)

**Discretionary monetary policy** Monetary policy that is based on expert assessment of the current economic situation. (p. 446)

**Dumping** When a foreign firm sells its exports at a lower price than its cost of production. (p. 470)

**Economic freedom** A condition in which people are able to make personal choices, their private property is protected by the rule of law, and they are free to buy and sell in markets. (p. 234)

**Economic growth** The sustained expansion of production possibilities. (pp. 70, 216)

**Economic growth rate** The annual percentage change of real GDP. (p. 216)

**Economic model** A description of the economy or part of the economy that includes only those features assumed necessary to explain the observed facts. (p. 15)

**Economics** The social science that studies the choices that individuals, businesses, government, and entire societies make

as they cope with *scarcity*, the influences on those choices, and the arrangements that coordinate them. (p. 2)

**Efficiency wage** A real wage rate that is set above the full-employment equilibrium wage rate to induce greater work effort. (p. 207)

**Employment–population ratio** The percentage of the people of working age who are employed. (p. 147)

**Entrepreneurship** The human resource that organizes labor, land, and capital to produce goods and services. (p. 38)

**Equation of exchange** An equation that states that the quantity of money multiplied by the velocity of circulation equals the price level multiplied by real GDP. (p. 313)

**Equilibrium expenditure** The level of aggregate expenditure that occurs when aggregate *planned* expenditure equals real GDP. (p. 362)

**Equilibrium price** The price at which the quantity demanded equals the quantity supplied. (p. 96)

**Equilibrium quantity** The quantity bought and sold at the equilibrium price. (p. 96)

**Excess reserves** A bank's actual reserves minus its desired reserves. (p. 286)

**Expected inflation rate** The inflation rate that people forecast and use to set the money wage rate and other money prices. (p. 387)

**Exports** The goods and services that firms in one country sell to people and firms in other countries. (p. 456)

**Exports of goods and services** Items that firms in the United States produce and sell to the rest of the world. (p. 118)

**Factor markets** Markets in which the services of factors of production are bought and sold. (p. 48)

**Factors of production** The productive resources that are used to produce goods and services— land, labor, capital, and entrepreneurship. (p. 36)

**Federal funds rate** The interest rate at which banks can borrow and lend reserves (interbank loans) in the federal funds market. (pp. 287, 430)

**Federal Open Market Committee** The Fed's main policy-making committee. (p. 282)

**Federal Reserve System (the Fed)** The central bank of the United States. (p. 281)

**Fiat money** Objects that are money because the law decrees or orders them to be money. (p. 272)

**Final good or service** A good or service that is produced for its final user and not as a component of another good or service. (p. 116)

**Financial institution** A firm that operates on both sides of the market for financial capital: It borrows in one market and lends in another. (p. 247)

**Financial stability** A situation in which financial markets and institutions function normally to allocate capital resources and risk. (p. 429)

**Firms** The institutions that organize the production of goods and services. (p. 48)

**Fiscal imbalance** The present value of the government's commitments to pay future benefits minus the present value of its tax revenues. (p. 406)

**Fiscal policy** Changing taxes, transfer payments, and government expenditure on goods and services. (p. 337) The use of the federal budget to achieve the macroeconomic objectives of high and sustained economic growth and full employment. (p. 402)

**Foreign exchange market** The market in which the currency of one country is exchanged for the currency of another. (p. 487)

**Foreign exchange rate** The price at which one currency exchanges for another. (p. 487)

**Frictional unemployment** The unemployment that arises from people entering and leaving the labor force, from quitting jobs to find better ones, and from the ongoing creation and destruction of jobs—from normal labor turnover. (p. 156)

**Full employment** When the unemployment rate equals the natural unemployment rate. (p. 157)

**Full-employment equilibrium** When equilibrium real GDP equals potential GDP. (p. 341)

**Full-time workers** People who usually work 35 hours or more a week. (p. 149)

**GDP price index** An average of the current prices of all the goods and services included in GDP expressed as a percentage of base-year prices. (p. 181)

**Generational imbalance** The division of the fiscal imbalance between the current and future generations. (p. 407)

**Goods and services** The objects (goods) and the actions (services) that people value and produce to satisfy human wants. (p. 3)

**Goods markets** Markets in which goods and services are bought and sold. (p. 48)

**Government expenditure multiplier** The effect of a change in government expenditure on goods and services on aggregate demand. (p. 411)

**Government expenditure on goods and services** The expenditure by all levels of government on goods and services. (p. 118)

**Government sector balance** The sum of the budget balances of the federal, state, and local governments— net taxes minus government expenditure on goods and services. (p. 484)

**Great Depression** A period of high unemployment, low incomes, and extreme economic hardship that lasted from 1929 to 1939. (p. 151)

**Gross domestic product (GDP)** The market value of all the final goods and services produced within a country in a given time period. (p. 116)

**Gross investment** The total amount spent on new capital goods. (p. 244)

**Households** Individuals or groups of people living together. (p. 48)

**Human capital** The knowledge and skill that people obtain from education, on-the-job training, and work experience. (p. 37)

**Hyperinflation** Inflation at a rate that exceeds 50 percent a *month*

(which translate to 12,875 percent a year). (p. 317)

**Import quota** A quantitative restriction on the import of a good that limits the maximum quantity of a good that may be imported in a given period. (p. 466)

**Imports** The goods and services that people and firms in one country buy from firms in other countries. (p. 456)

**Imports of goods and services** Items that households, firms, and governments in the United States buy from the rest of the world. (p. 118)

**Incentive** A reward or a penalty— a "carrot" or a "stick"—that encourages or discourages an action. (p. 11)

**Induced taxes** Taxes that vary with real GDP. (p. 409)

**Infant-industry argument** The argument that it is necessary to protect a new industry to enable it to grow into a mature industry that can compete in world markets. (p. 469)

**Inferior good** A good for which demand decreases when income increases and demand increases when income decreases. (p. 87)

**Inflation rate** The percentage change in the price level from one year to the next. (p. 171)

**Inflation targeting** A monetary policy strategy in which the central bank makes a public commitment to achieving an explicit inflation target and to explaining how its policy actions will achieve that target. (p. 447)

**Inflationary gap** A gap that exists when real GDP exceeds potential GDP and that brings a rising price level. (p. 341)

**Interest** Income paid for the use of capital. (p. 39)

**Interest rate parity** Equal interest rates—a situation in which the interest rate in one currency equals the interest rate in another currency when exchange rate changes are taken into account. (p. 498)

**Intermediate good or service** A good or service that is used as a component of a final good or service. (p. 116)

**Inverse relationship** A relationship between two variables that move in opposite directions. (p. 27)

**Investment** The purchase of new *capital goods*—tools, instruments, machines, buildings, and additions to inventories. (p. 117)

**Job rationing** A situation that arises when the real wage rate is above the full-employment equilibrium level. (p. 206)

**Job search** The activity of looking for an acceptable vacant job. (p. 205)

**Keynesian macroeconomics** The view that the market economy is inherently unstable and needs active government intervention to achieve full employment and sustained economic growth. (p. 192)

*k*-**percent rule** A monetary policy rule that makes the quantity of money grow at *k* percent per year, where *k* equals the growth rate of potential GDP. (p. 449)

**Labor** The work time and work effort that people devote to producing goods and services. (p. 37)

**Labor force** The number of people employed plus the number unemployed. (p. 146)

**Labor force participation rate** The percentage of the working-age population who are members of the labor force. (p. 148)

**Labor productivity** The quantity of real GDP produced by one hour of labor. (p. 220)

**Land** The "gifts of nature," or *natural resources*, that we use to produce goods and services. (p. 36)

**Law of demand** Other things remaining the same, if the price of a good rises, the quantity demanded of that good decreases; and if the price of a good falls, the quantity demanded of that good increases. (p. 85)

**Law of diminishing marginal returns** If the quantity of capital is small, an increase in capital brings a large increase in production; and if the quantity of capital is large, an increase in capital brings a small increase in production. (p. 221)

**Law of market forces** When there is a surplus, the price falls; when there is a shortage, the price rises. (p. 96)

**Law of supply** Other things remaining the same, if the price of a good rises, the quantity supplied of that good increases; and if the price of a good falls, the quantity supplied of that good decreases. (p. 90)

**Linear relationship** A relationship that graphs as a straight line. (p. 26)

**Loanable funds market** The aggregate of all the individual financial markets. (p. 250)

**Long-run Phillips curve** The vertical line that shows the relationship between inflation and unemployment when the economy is at full employment. (p. 386)

**Loss** Income earned by an entrepreneur for running a business when that income is negative. (p. 39)

**M1** Currency held by individuals and firms, traveler's checks, and checkable deposits owned by individuals and businesses. (p. 272)

**M2** M1 plus savings deposits and small time deposits, money market funds, and other deposits. (p. 272)

**Macroeconomic equilibrium** When the quantity of real GDP demanded equals the quantity of real GDP supplied at the point of intersection of the *AD* curve and the *AS* curve. (p. 340)

**Macroeconomics** The study of the aggregate (or total) effects on the national economy and the global economy of the choices that individuals, businesses, and governments make. (p. 3)

**Margin** A choice on the margin is a choice that is made by comparing *all* the relevant alternatives systematically and incrementally. (p. 10)

**Marginal benefit** The benefit that arises from a one-unit increase in an activity. The marginal benefit of something is measured by what you *are willing to* give up to get *one additional* unit of it. (p. 10)

**Marginal cost** The opportunity cost that arises from a one-unit increase in an activity. The marginal cost of something is what you *must* give up to get one additional unit of it. (p. 10)

**Marginal propensity to consume** The fraction of a change in disposable income that is spent on consumption—the change in consumption expenditure divided by the change in disposable income that brought it about. (p. 356)

**Marginal propensity to import** The fraction of an increase in real GDP that is spent on imports— the change in imports divided by the change in real GDP. (p. 358)

**Marginal tax rate** The fraction of a change in real GDP that is paid in income taxes—the change in tax payments divided by the change in real GDP. (p. 368)

**Marginally attached worker** A person who does not have a job, is available and willing to work, has not made specific efforts to find a job within the previous four weeks, but has looked for work sometime in the recent past. (p. 148)

**Market** Any arrangement that brings buyers and sellers together and enables them to get information and do business with each other. (p. 48)

**Market equilibrium** When the quantity demanded equals the quantity supplied—buyers' and sellers' plans are in balance. (p. 96)

**Means of payment** A method of settling a debt. (p. 270)

**Medium of exchange** An object that is generally accepted in return for goods and services. (p. 271)

**Microeconomics** The study of the choices that individuals and businesses make and the way these choices interact and are influenced by governments. (p. 2)

**Minimum wage law** A government regulation that makes hiring labor services for less than a specified wage illegal. (pp. 105, 207)

**Monetarist macroeconomics** The view that the market economy works well, that aggregate fluctuations are the natural consequence of an expanding economy, but that fluctuations in the quantity of money generate the business cycle. (p. 193)

**Monetary base** The sum of coins, Federal Reserve notes, and banks' reserves at the Fed. (p. 283)

**Monetary policy** Changing the quantity of money and the interest rate. (p. 337)

**Monetary policy instrument** A variable that the Fed can directly control or closely target and that influences the economy in desirable ways. (p. 430)

**Money** Any commodity or token that is generally accepted as a means of payment. (p. 270)

**Money multiplier** The number by which a change in the monetary base is multiplied to find the resulting change in the quantity of money. (p. 291)

**Multiplier** The amount by which a change in any component of autonomous expenditure is magnified or multiplied to determine the change that it generates in equilibrium expenditure and real GDP. (p. 366)

**National debt** The amount of government debt outstanding— the debt that has arisen from past budget deficits. (p. 403)

**Natural rate hypothesis** The proposition that when the inflation rate changes, the unemployment rate changes *temporarily* and eventually returns to the natural unemployment rate. (p. 388)

**Natural unemployment rate** The unemployment rate when all the unemployment is frictional and structural and there is no cyclical unemployment. (p. 157)

**Negative relationship** A relationship between two variables that move in opposite directions. (p. 27)

**Net borrower** A country that is borrowing more from the rest of the world than it is lending to the rest of the world. (p. 482)

**Net exports of goods and services** The value of exports of goods and services minus the value of imports of goods and services. (p. 118)

**Net investment** The change in the quantity of capital— equals gross investment minus depreciation. (p. 244)

**Net lender** A country that is lending more to the rest of the world than it is borrowing from the rest of the world. (p. 482)

**Net taxes** Taxes paid minus cash benefits received from governments. (p. 118)

**Net worth** The total market value of what a financial institution has lent minus the market value of what it has borrowed. (p. 248)

**New growth theory** The theory that our unlimited wants will lead us to ever greater productivity and perpetual economic growth. (p. 228)

**Nominal GDP** The value of the final goods and services produced in a given year expressed in terms of the prices of that same year. (p. 126)

**Nominal interest rate** The dollar amount of interest expressed as a percentage of the amount loaned. (p. 184)

**Nominal wage rate** The average hourly wage rate measured in *current* dollars. (p. 182)

**Normal good** A good for which demand increases when income increases and demand decreases when income decreases. (p. 87)

**Official settlements account** Record of the change in U.S. official reserves. (p. 480)

**Okun's Law** For each percentage point that the unemployment rate is above the natural unemployment rate, real GDP is 2 percent below potential GDP. (p. 381)

**Open market operation** The purchase or sale of government securities—U.S. Treasury bills and bonds—by the New York Fed in the open market. (p. 283)

**Opportunity cost** The opportunity cost of something is the best thing you *must* give up to get it. (p. 8)

**Output gap** Real GDP minus potential GDP expressed as a percentage of potential GDP. (p. 161)

**Part time for economic reasons** People who work 1 to 34 hours per week but are looking for full-time work and cannot find it because of unfavorable business conditions. (p. 149)

**Part-time workers** People who usually work less than 35 hours a week. (p. 149)

**PCEPI** An average of the current prices of the goods and services included in the consumption expenditure component of GDP expressed as a percentage of base-year prices. (p. 177)

**Physical capital** The tools, instruments, machines, buildings, and other items that have been produced in the past and that are used to produce goods and services. (p. 244)

**Positive relationship** A relationship between two variables that move in the same direction. (p. 26)

**Potential GDP** The value of real GDP when all the economy's factors of production—labor, capital, land, and entrepreneurial ability—are fully employed. (pp. 129, 161, 195)

**Price cap** A government regulation that places an upper limit on the price at which a particular good, service, or factor of production may be traded. (p. 107)

**Price ceiling** A government regulation that places an *upper* limit on the price at which a particular good, service, or factor of production may be traded. (p. 107)

**Price floor** A government regulation that places a *lower* limit on the price at which a particular good, service, or factor of production may be traded. (p. 105)

**Price level** An average of the level of prices during a given period. (p. 171)

**Private sector balance** Saving minus investment. (p. 484)

**Production efficiency** A situation in which the economy is getting all that it can from its resources and cannot produce more of one good or service without producing less of something else. (p. 62)

**Production function** A relationship that shows the maximum quantity of real GDP that can be produced as the quantity of labor employed changes and all other influences on production remain the same. (p. 196)

**Production possibilities frontier** The boundary between the combinations of goods and services that can be produced and the combinations that cannot be produced, given the available factors of production and the state of technology. (p. 60)

**Productivity curve** The relationship that shows how real GDP per hour of labor changes as the quantity of capital per hour of labor changes. (p. 222)

**Profit** Income earned by an entrepreneur for running a business. (p. 39)

**Property rights** Social arrangements that govern the protection of private property—legally established titles to the ownership, use, and disposal of factors of production and goods and services that are enforceable in the courts. (p. 234)

**Purchasing power parity** Equal value of money—a situation in which money buys the same amount of goods and services in different currencies. (p. 496)

**Quantity demanded** The amount of any good, service, or resource that people are willing and able to buy during a specified period at a specified price. (p. 85)

**Quantity of labor demanded** The total labor hours that all the firms in the economy plan to hire during a given time period at a given real wage rate. (p. 197)

**Quantity of labor supplied** The number of labor hours that all the households in the economy plan to work during a given time period at a given real wage rate. (p. 199)

**Quantity of money demanded** The amount of money that households and firms choose to hold. (p. 301)

**Quantity supplied** The amount of any good, service, or resource that people are willing and able to sell during a specified period at a specified price. (p. 90)

**Quantity theory of money** The proposition that when real GDP equals potential GDP, an increase in the quantity of money brings an equal percentage increase in the price level. (p. 312)

**Rational choice** A choice that uses the available resources to best achieve the objective of the person making the choice. (p. 9)

**Rational expectation** The forecast resulting from use of all the relevant data and economic science. (p. 393)

**Real business cycle** A cycle that results from fluctuations in the pace of growth of labor productivity and potential GDP. (p. 343)

**Real GDP** The value of the final goods and services produced in a given year expressed in terms of the prices in a *base year*. (p. 126)

**Real interest rate** The goods and services forgone in interest expressed as a percentage of the amount loaned and calculated as the nominal interest rate minus the inflation rate. (p. 184)

**Real wage rate** The average hourly wage rate measured in the dollars of a given reference base year. (p. 182)

**Recession** A period during which real GDP decreases for at least two successive quarters; or defined by the NBER as "a period of significant decline in total output, income, employment, and trade, usually lasting from six months to a year, and marked by contractions in many sectors of the economy." (p. 130)

**Recessionary gap** A gap that exists when potential GDP exceeds real GDP and that brings a falling price level. (p. 341)

**Reference base period** A period for which the CPI is defined to equal 96. Currently, the reference base period is 1982–1984. (p. 168)

**Rent** Income paid for the use of land (p. 39)

**Rent ceiling** A regulation that makes it illegal to charge more than a specified rent for housing. (p. 170)

**Rent seeking** Lobbying and other political activity that aims to capture the gains from trade. (p. 473)

**Reserves** The currency in the bank's vaults plus the balance on its reserve account at a Federal Reserve Bank. (p. 277)

**Rule-based monetary policy** A monetary policy that is based on a rule for setting the policy instrument. (p. 446)

**Rule of 70** The number of years it takes for the level of any variable to double is approximately 70 divided by the annual percentage growth rate of the variable. (p. 218)

**Saving** The amount of income that is not paid in net taxes or spent on consumption goods and services. (p. 118)

**Scarcity** The condition that arises because wants exceed the ability of resources to satisfy them. (p. 2)

**Scatter diagram** A graph of the value of one variable against the value of another variable. (p. 24)

**Self-interest** The choices that are best for the individual who makes them. (p. 4)

**Short-run Phillips curve** The relationship between the inflation rate and the unemployment rate when the natural unemployment rate and the expected inflation rate remain constant. (p. 380)

**Slope** The change in the value of the variable measured on the $y$-axis divided by the change in the value of the variable measured on the $x$-axis. (p. 29)

**Social interest** The choices that are best for society as a whole. (p. 4)

**Stagflation** A combination of recession (falling real GDP) and inflation (rising price level). (p. 345)

**Stock** A certificate of ownership and claim to the profits that a firm makes. (p. 246)

**Structural surplus or deficit** The budget balance that would occur if the economy were at full employment. (p. 410)

**Structural unemployment** The unemployment that arises when changes in technology or international competition change the skills needed to perform jobs or change the locations of jobs. (p. 156)

**Substitute** A good that can be consumed in place of another good. (p. 87)

**Substitute in production** A good that can be produced in place of another good. (p. 92)

**Supply** The relationship between the quantity supplied and the price of a good when all other influences on selling plans remain the same. (p. 90)

**Supply curve** A graph of the relationship between the quantity supplied of a good and its price when all the other influences on selling plans remain the same. (p. 91)

**Supply of labor** The relationship between the quantity of labor supplied and the real wage rate when all other influences on work plans remain the same. (p. 199)

**Supply of loanable funds** The relationship between the quantity of loanable funds supplied and the real interest rate when all other influences on lending plans remain the same. (p. 253)

**Supply of money** The relationship between the quantity of money supplied and the nominal interest rate. (p. 304)

**Supply schedule** A list of the quantities supplied at each different price when all the other influences on selling plans remain the same. (p. 91)

**Supply-side effects** The effects of fiscal policy on potential GDP and the economic growth rate. (p. 416)

**Tariff** A tax imposed on a good when it is imported. (p. 463)

**Tax multiplier** The effect of a change in taxes on aggregate demand. (p. 411)

**Tax wedge** The gap created by a tax between what a buyer pays and what a seller receives. In the labor market, it is the gap between the before-tax wage rate and the after-tax wage rate. (p. 417)

**Time-series graph** A graph that measures time on the $x$-axis and the variable or variables in which we are interested on the $y$-axis. (p. 24)

**Tradeoff** An exchange—giving up one thing to get something else. (pp. 8, 63)

**Transfer payments** Social Security benefits, Medicare and Medicaid benefits, unemployment benefits, and other cash benefits. (p. 403)

**Transfer payments multiplier** The effect of a change in transfer payments on aggregate demand. (p. 411)

**Trend** A general tendency for the value of a variable to rise or fall over time. (p. 24)

**Unemployment rate** The percentage of the people in the labor force who are unemployed. (p. 147)

**Union wage** A wage rate that results from collective bargaining between a labor union and a firm. (p. 207)

**U.S. interest rate differential** The U.S. interest rate minus the foreign interest rate. (p. 490)

**U.S. official reserves** The government's holdings of foreign currency. (p. 480)

**Velocity of circulation** The average number of times that each dollar of money is used during a year to buy final goods and services. (p. 312)

**Wages** Income paid for the services of labor. (p. 39)

**Wealth** The value of all the things that people own. (p. 245)

**Working-age population** The total number of people aged 16 years and over who are not in jail, hospital, or some other form of institutional care or in the U.S. Armed Forces. (p. 146)

# Index

# Photo Credits

# The Pearson Series in Economics

**Abel/Bernanke/Croushore**
*Macroeconomics\**

**Bade/Parkin**
*Foundations of Economics\**

**Berck/Helfand**
*The Economics of the Environment*

**Bierman/Fernandez**
*Game Theory with Economic Applications*

**Blanchard**
*Macroeconomics\**

**Boyer**
*Principles of Transportation Economics*

**Branson**
*Macroeconomic Theory and Policy*

**Bruce**
*Public Finance and the American Economy*

**Carlton/Perloff**
*Modern Industrial Organization*

**Case/Fair/Oster**
*Principles of Economics\**

**Chapman**
*Environmental Economics: Theory, Application, and Policy*

**Daniels/VanHoose**
*International Monetary & Financial Economics*

**Downs**
*An Economic Theory of Democracy*

**Farnham**
*Economics for Managers*

**Fort**
*Sports Economics*

**Froyen**
*Macroeconomics*

**Fusfeld**
*The Age of the Economist*

**Gerber**
*International Economics\**

**Gordon**
*Macroeconomics\**

**Greene**
*Econometric Analysis*

**Gregory/Stuart**
*Russian and Soviet Economic Performance and Structure*

**Hartwick/Olewiler**
*The Economics of Natural Resource Use*

**Heilbroner/Milberg**
*The Making of the Economic Society*

**Heyne/Boettke/Prychitko**
*The Economic Way of Thinking*

**Hubbard/O'Brien**
*Economics\**

*InEcon Money, Banking, and the Financial System\**

**Hubbard/O'Brien/Rafferty**
*Macroeconomics\**

**Hughes/Cain**
*American Economic History*

**Husted/Melvin**
*International Economics*

**Jehle/Reny**
*Advanced Microeconomic Theory*

**Keat/Young/Erfle**
*Managerial Economics*

**Klein**
*Mathematical Methods for Economics*

**Krugman/Obstfeld/Melitz**
*International Economics: Theory & Policy\**

**Laidler**
*The Demand for Money*

**Lynn**
*Economic Development: Theory and Practice for a Divided World*

**Miller**
*Economics Today\**

*Understanding Modern Economics*

**Miller/Benjamin**
*The Economics of Macro Issues*

**Miller/Benjamin/North**
*The Economics of Public Issues*

**Mishkin**
*The Economics of Money, Banking, and Financial Markets\**

*The Economics of Money, Banking, and Financial Markets, Business School Edition\**

*Macroeconomics: Policy and Practice\**

**Murray**
*Econometrics: A Modern Introduction*

**O'Sullivan/Sheffrin/Perez**
*Economics: Principles, Applications and Tools\**

**Parkin**
*Economics\**

**Perloff**
*Microeconomics\**

*Microeconomics: Theory and Applications with Calculus\**

**Perloff/Brander**
*Managerial Economics and Strategy\**

**Pindyck/Rubinfeld**
*Microeconomics\**

**Riddell/Shackelford/Stamos/Schneider**
*Economics: A Tool for Critically Understanding Society*

**Roberts**
*The Choice: A Fable of Free Trade and Protection*

**Scherer**
*Industry Structure, Strategy, and Public Policy*

**Schiller**
*The Economics of Poverty and Discrimination*

**Sherman**
*Market Regulation*

**Stock/Watson**
*Introduction to Econometrics*

**Studenmund**
*Using Econometrics: A Practical Guide*

**Todaro/Smith**
*Economic Development*

**Walters/Walters/Appel/Callahan/Centanni/Maex/O'Neill**
*Econversations: Today's Students Discuss Today's Issues*

**Williamson**
*Macroeconomics*

\*denotes MyEconLab titles

Visit www.myeconlab.com to learn more.